Federalism and Internal Conflicts

Series Editor

Soeren Keil, University of Fribourg, Fribourg, Switzerland
Eva Maria Belser, University of Fribourg, Fribourg, Switzerland

This series engages in the discussions on federalism as a tool of internal conflict resolution. Building on a growing body of literature on the use of federalism and territorial autonomy to solve ethnic, cultural, linguistic and identity conflicts, both in the West and in non-Western countries, this global series assesses to what extent different forms of federalism and territorial autonomy are being used as tools of conflict resolution and how successful these approaches are.

We welcome proposals on theoretical debates, single case studies and short comparative pieces covering topics such as

- Federalism and peace-making in contemporary intra-state conflicts
- The link between federalism and democratization in countries facing intra-state conflict
- Secessionism, separatism, self-determination and power-sharing
- Inter-group violence and the potential of federalism to transform conflicts
- Successes and failures of federalism and other forms of territorial autonomy in post-conflict countries
- Federalism, decentralisation and resource conflicts
- Peace treaties, interim constitutions and permanent power sharing arrangements
- The role of international actors in the promotion of federalism (and other forms of territorial autonomy) as tools of internal conflict resolution
- Federalism and state-building
- Federalism, democracy and minority protection

For further information on the series and to submit a proposal for consideration, please get in touch with Ambra Finotello ambra.finotello@palgrave.com, or series editors Soeren Keil soeren.keil@unifr.ch and Eva Maria Belser evamaria.belser@unifr.ch.

Martin Belov
Editor

Constitutional Polycrisis and Emergency Constitutionalism

palgrave
macmillan

Editor
Martin Belov
Faculty of Law
Sofia University St. Kliment Ohridski
Sofia, Bulgaria

ISSN 2946-5370 ISSN 2946-5389 (electronic)
Federalism and Internal Conflicts
ISBN 978-3-032-06515-5 ISBN 978-3-032-06516-2 (eBook)
https://doi.org/10.1007/978-3-032-06516-2

This work was supported by European Union-NextGenerationEU, through the National Recovery and Resilience Plan of the Republic of Bulgaria (bg-rrp-2.004-0008).

This Palgrave Macmillan imprint is published by the registered company Springer Nature Switzerland AG.
The registered company address is: Gewerbestrasse 11, 6330 Cham, Switzerland.

Acknowledgments

This book and all of its chapters are financed by the European Union-Next-GenerationEU, through the National Recovery and Resilience Plan of the Republic of Bulgaria, project No BG-RRP-2.004-0008.

Contents

Editors and Contributors

About the Editor

Martin Belov is Professor in Constitutional and Comparative Constitutional Law at the University of Sofia 'St. Kliment Ohridski'. He is the Vice Dean of the University of Sofia. Kliment Ohridski, Faculty of Law, is responsible for the international relations and digitalization. Martin Belov is an adjunct professor at the University Roma Tre, Rome, Italy (since 2019). Martin Belov has been a Sutherland Fellow at UCD (Dublin, Ireland) (2024). He has been visiting professor at University of Teramo (2025), University of Milano (Italy) (2024), University of Trento (Italy), (2024), University of Catania (Italy) (2024), EURAC (Bolzano, Italy) (2024), Reichman University, Harry Radzyner Law School (Herzliya, Israel) (2021–2023), University of Zagreb, Croatia (2023), Jagiellonian University of Cracow, Poland, (2024 and 2022), 'Aristoteles' University of Thessaloniki, Greece, (2022), University Paris II Pantheon-Assas (2019), Goethe-University Frankfurt am Main, Germany (2019), University of Girona, Spain (2019), University 'Pompeu Fabra', Barcelona, Spain (2019), Europa-University Viadrina, Frankfurt/Oder, Germany (2017 and 2018), University of Bari, Italy (2018), European Law and Governance School, Athens (2017–2018 and 2020–2021), University of Södertorn, Stockholm, Sweden (2017), Scuolla Superiore Sant'Anna,

Pisa, Italy (2016), University of Warsaw, Poland (2015), University of Lisbon, Portugal (2012), State University of Milan, Italy (2011), University of Cologne, Germany (2007–2009) etc. Martin Belov has been a project researcher at the Max-Planck Institute for European Legal History, Frankfurt am Main, Germany (2010–2012) and a visiting researcher at the Institute for Federalism, Fribourg, Switzerland (2014). He has specialized at the University of Oxford (UK) (2017), Max-Planck Institute for Comparative Public Law and International Law, Heidelberg, Germany (2009) and many other academic institutions. Martin Belov is a member of the European Group of Public Law, the International Association of Legislation, the Advisory Board of the Central and Eastern European Forum of Young Legal, Political and Social Theorists, and other scientific and academic organizations. Martin Belov is a member of the scientific boards of many academic journals. He has participated in numerous international research projects (including Horizon 2020 and Recovery Fund projects, the German Cluster of Excellence projects, etc.). He has published 25 books (some of which are edited volumes) and 111 scientific papers and book chapters.

Notes on Contributors

Laurianne Allezard is a postdoctoral researcher in public law at the Faculty of Law at Lund University and a visiting fellow at the European University Institute. Her research explores mainly the role of science in contemporary constitutionalism, particularly in relation to climate and environmental emergencies, as well as the use of constitutional identity in times of crisis. She completed her PhD in 2021 in France, on identities within Constitutions. She has previously held academic positions in France and Hungary, and has taught extensively in comparative constitutional law, European Union law, and international human rights. She is currently part of the project "Understanding Constitutional Safeguards for State of Emergency: The Case of Covid-19 and Prospects for Climate Action" led by Pr Xavier Groussot (Lund University) and Sanja Bogojevic (Oxford University), funded by Marianne och Marcus Wallenbergs Stiftelse.

Antonia Baraggia is Professor in Constitutional Law at the University of Milan.

Gavin Barrett is Professor of EU Constitutional and Economic Law in the Sutherland Law School, University College Dublin, and the holder of the Jean Monnet Chair in European Economic and Constitutional Law there. He is also the Head of Widening Participation in the School. He is the author or editor of several books on EU and constitutional law, most recently editing a special edition of the Irish Jurist on the topic of Law in a Time of Crises (2024) and co-editing European Sovereignty: The Legal Dimension (Springer, 2025). He has written extensively on various current themes of EU law and has published articles in EU Law Live, the Common Market Law Review, the European Law Review, the European Constitutional Law Review, the Yearbook of European Law, the Cambridge Yearbook of European Legal Studies, the European Law Journal, the Journal of European Integration, the Journal of Legislative Studies, the Maastricht Journal of European and Comparative Law, the Industrial Law Journal, Verfassungsblog, Europarecht, the Jahrbuch für direkte Demokratie, the Irish Jurist and the Dublin University Law Journal as well as writing numerous book chapters.

Cosmin Cercel is Professor of Comparative Legal History at the University of Ghent, where he leads the ERC CoG—funded project EMERGE Rethinking emergency from a legal historical perspective. His research focuses on genealogies of law and politics with specific reference to twentieth-century continental legal history. He is the author of Towards a Jurisprudence of State-Communism (Routledge, 2018). He has co-edited States of Exception: Law, Theory, History (Routledge 2020), Law, Culture and Identity in Central and Eastern Europe (Routledge 2023) and Legal Form: Pashukanis and the Marxist Critique of Law (Routledge 2024). Recent publications include: "Darker Legacies of Anti-corruption: Fascist Criticisms of the Law in Interwar Romania", International Journal of Law in Context (2024) Issue 3, 1–15 and 'Fascist Claims to Sovereign Power: Law, Politics and the Romanian Legionary Movement' (2023) 32 (2) Contemporary European History 1.

Djordje Gardasevic is a Professor of Constitutional Law at the University of Zagreb Faculty of Law (Croatia). He earned his L.L.M. degree at the Central European University in Budapest (thesis title: 'Independence and Impartiality of Courts—Article 6 of the ECHR') and his PhD at the University of Zagreb Faculty of Law (thesis title: 'Restrictions of Human Rights and Fundamental Freedoms in States of Emergency'). He participated, among other events, at the 7th and 9th World Congresses of the International Association for Constitutional Law (Athens, 2007; Oslo, 2014), the 22nd and 23rd Congresses of the International Political Science Association—IPSA (Madrid, 2012; Montreal, 2014), the APSA Annual Meeting (San Francisco, 2015), the Annual Conferences of the International Society of Public Law (ICON-S, Wroclaw, 2022, Madrid 2024) and the ASN World Conventions (New York, 2017, 2018 and 2019). His research interests include: states of emergency, fundamental rights and freedoms, constitutional theory and comparative constitutional law. Since 2021, he has served as an external member of the Committee for Constitution, Standing Orders and Political System of the Croatian Parliament

Michael S. Green is the Woodbridge Professor of Law at William & Mary Law School in Williamsburg, Virginia, USA. He holds a Ph.D. in Philosophy from Yale University and a J.D. from Yale Law School. Green has written on a wide variety of topics: how provisions in the United States Constitution can be understood in the light of Lockean political theory; Hans Kelsen's legal monism; the relationship between the philosophy of language and theories of law; American legal realism; Neo-Kantian influences on Friedrich Nietzsche; and the many aspects of the so-called Erie doctrine — a foundation of the legal system of the United States. Green's current work is primarily on the intersections between private international law and the philosophy of law.

Alan Greene is a Reader in Constitutional Law and Human Rights at Birmingham Law School. His research focuses on emergency powers, constituent power, and the limits of constitutionalism. He is the author of Emergency Powers in a Time of Pandemic (Bristol University Press, 2020) and Permanent States of Emergency and the Rule of Law: Constitutions in an Age of Crisis (Hart Publishing, 2018), which was shortlisted for the Society of Legal Scholars' Birks Prize for Outstanding Legal Scholarship

Soeren Keil is a Senior Teaching and Research Fellow at the University of Passau in Germany. He works in the field of International Politics with a special focus on institution-building in post-conflict societies, decentralization, federalism and power-sharing. He has published widely on federalism, conflict resolution and EU integration with a regional specialization on the Western Balkans. He has worked as an adviser to several international organizations and governments. Before joining the University of Passau in October 2024, he was the Academic Head of the International Research and Consulting Centre at the Institute of Federalism, University of Fribourg in Switzerland. He is the Scientific Coordinator of the EU Horizon Europe project "LEGITIMULT—Legitimate Crisis Governance in Multilevel Systems".

Allison McCulloch is Professor of Political Science at Brandon University, Canada. She is the author of Power-Sharing and Political Stability in Deeply Divided Societies, and the editor of several volumes on power-sharing arrangements, including Power-Sharing: Empirical and Normative Challenges and Power-Sharing Pacts and the Women, Peace and Security Agenda. Her research considers the interplay between adoptability, functionality, and adaptability in the life cycle of power-sharing agreements. This includes investigating the dynamics of inclusion and exclusion intrinsic to power-sharing practice and exploring how such arrangements can be made more inclusive of identities beyond the ethnonational divide.

Francesco Palermo , PhD, is a professor of Comparative Public Law at the University of Verona and Director of the Institute for Comparative Federalism at Eurac Research in Bolzano/Bozen. He has been senior legal adviser to the OSCE High Commissioner on National Minorities, president of the Advisory Committee under the Council of Europe's Framework Convention for the Protection of National Minorities, president of the International Association of Centers for Federal Studies (IACFS), a non-party member of the Italian Senate, Constitutional Adviser to the Congress of Local and Regional Authorities of the Council of Europe, and member of the Scientific Committee of the European Union Agency for Fundamental Rights. Full CV at: http://www.eurac.edu/fpalermo

Dora Pavković is a research assistant at the Department of Constitutional Law at the University of Zagreb Faculty of Law. The topic of her doctoral thesis is: "Constitutional Identity in the Member States of the European Union". Her main research interests include, apart from constitutional identity, the crisis of liberal democracy in Central Europe, the independence of the judiciary, and the COVID-19 crisis. She is a member of the board of directors of the Croatian Association for Constitutional Law.

Yaniv Roznai is an Associate Professor and Vice-Dean at the Harry Radzyner Law School, and Co-director at the Rubinstein Center for Constitutional Challenges, Reichman University. He is a Co-Chair of the Israeli Section of the International Society of Public Law (ICON-S). Prof. Roznai's scholarship focuses on comparative constitutional law and constitutional theory. In 2015, Prof. Roznai was awarded the 2014 Thesis Prize of the European Group of Public Law for his PhD dissertation. His book, "Unconstitutional Constitutional Amendments—The Limits of Amendment Powers" (OUP 2017), was awarded the Inaugural ICONS Book

Prize. His book "Constitutional Revolution", co-authored with Prof. Gary Jacobsohn, was published with Yale University Press in 2020. Prof. Roznai was awarded the 2018 Israeli Association of Public Law Gorni Prize for Young Researchers, the 2019 Justice Cheshin Prize for Excellence in Legal Research for Young Researchers, the "Knight of Government Quality 2020" award, and the Fattal Prize for Excellence in Legal Research for 2025.

Catarina Santos Botelho (ORCID ID 0000-0002-6076-1835) holds a LLB (2004), a Master's (2009), and a PhD (2015) degrees in Law. She is a Professor of Law and Chair of Constitutional Law at Porto Faculty of Law, Universidade Católica Portuguesa (Portugal) and a researcher at the Católica Research Centre for the Future of Law. Coordinator of master's programmes. Series Co-Editor of Constitutionalism in Latin America and the Caribbean (Hart Publishing). Council Coordination member of the Academic Network on the European Social Charter and Social Rights (ANESC). Coordinator of the Observatory for the Protection of Social Rights in the European Context. Co-coordinates the pioneer Interdisciplinary Postgraduate Course on Human Rights (Law, Psychology, and Socioeconomics). Member of the International Society of Public Law (ICON). Founding member of ICON.S Portugal. Member of the International Association of Electoral Law. Her research interests include, but are not limited to, constitutional theory and legal philosophy, global constitutional law, comparative constitutional studies, political parties, human rights, social rights, and intergenerational justice. Output available at https://papers.ssrn.com/sol3/cf_dev/AbsByAuth.cfm?per_id=2648471

Guillaume Tusseau was trained both in political science and law. After holding positions in the Universities of Paris II (Panthéon-Assas) and Rouen, he is currently Professor of Public Law at Sciences Po Law School, in Paris, where he is head of the Law School's research center, and a member of the Institut universitaire de France. He has been a member of the Conseil supérieur de la magistrature (French High Council for the Judiciary) from 2015 to 2019. His main areas of interest are comparative constitutional law and legal theory, both fields in which he has extensively taught and published. Among his latest publications are: 'Debating Legal Pluralism and Constitutionalism: New Trajectories for Legal Theory in the Global Age', ed. (Springer, 2020), 'Contentieux constitutionnel comparé. Une introduction critique au droit processuel constitutionnel' (Lextenso, 2021), 'Droit constitutionnel et institutions politiques'

(Le Seuil, 2024), 'Research Handbook on Law and Utilitarianism', ed. (Edward Elgar, 2024).

Marta Vicente (ORCID ID 0000-0001-7454-2732) has a Law degree from the Coimbra Faculty of Law (2009), a master's degree in Administrative law (2011) and a Ph.D in Public law from the same institution (2021). Between 2012 and 2015, she worked as an advisor to the Portuguese Constitutional Court Judge's Office. Between 2020 and 2022, she was a member of the Disciplinary Board of the Portuguese Football Federation. She is currently a Professor of Law at Porto Law School of Universidade Católica Portuguesa, where she lectures on Constitutional law, Tax Law and International Investment Law. She has been, since 2022, the CELIS (Common European Law on Investment Screening) Institute Assistant Country Reporter for Portugal. She is the author and co-author of several scientific works in the fields of constitutional law, international investment law and international arbitration. Output available at https://ssrn.com/author=522107

CHAPTER 1

Crisis as Opportunity and Emergency as Normalcy in the Transformative Age

Martin Belov

We live in turbulent and transformative times when crisis seems to be the "new normal" and transition is a phase of history instead of a short-lived period marked by deep but temporary socio-legal shifts and ruptures. Authority, to an extent, paradoxically, is both shrinking and being reaffirmed in authoritarian, populist, or technocratic ways and manners. Institutional trust is shrinking, and constitutional orders are deconstructed, eroded, and on the edge of axiological, institutional, and performative implosion. Imaginaries of crisis and fear are on the rise, triggering tendencies towards constitutional twilight[1] and constitutional darkness. The constitutional orders are struggling with securing both input legitimacy[2] based on democratic participation and inclusion, and output legitimacy[3]

This chapter is produced as part and funded by the European Union-NextGenerationEU, through the National Recovery and Resilience Plan of the Republic of Bulgaria, project No bg-rrp-2.004-0008.

[1] See also Petra Dobner and Martin Loughlin (eds) *The Twilight of Constitutionalism?* (OUP 2010), 1–370.

[2] For the input legitimacy see Philip Kiiver, *The National Parliaments in the European Union: A Critical View on EU Constitution-Building* (Kluwer Law International, 2006) 95.

[3] For the output legitimacy see e.g., Simona Piattoni, *The Theory of Multi-level Governance: Conceptual, Empirical, and Normative Challenges* (Oxford University Press, 2010), 210–227.

M. Belov (ed.), *Constitutional Polycrisis and Emergency Constitutionalism*, Federalism and Internal Conflicts,
https://doi.org/10.1007/978-3-032-06516-2_1

grounded in efficiency. In other words, democratic alienation and disempowerment are paralleled by substantial malfunctioning and inefficiency. The result is the rule of law in crisis[4] and representative democracy in flux,[5] with a visible trend towards post-democracy.[6] Constitutional orders are stretched between tendencies of populism, illiberalism, and majoritarian–identitarian rule and technocracy, oligarchy, and technofeudalism.[7]

This period can be defined as a quantum age due to its transformative potential that is mixed with a huge degree of certainty about the uncertainty of the final form in which constitutional polytransition shall end. Focusing on a particular crisis, its manifestations and elements prevents the proper understanding of the general picture. The ongoing transition is stretched between constitutional energy (the principal potential and essence of the various elements that are part of crisis, emergency, and shifts) and the constitutional matter—the ways in which constitutional phenomena manifest and unfold in the socio-legal context and on the plane of constitutional imaginaries.

Hence, a crisis is both peril and opportunity in the context of emergency as normalcy. A multitude of transformative tendencies are producing a melting pot of creative destruction of the established axiological, institutional, geopolitical, and attitudinal orders. They are challenging the conceptual stability of the intellectual matrixes we use for ordering the world, the constitutional models for ordering constitutional orders,[8] the core normative ideologies of global Modernity, and the value

[4] See Martin Belov (ed) *Rule of Law in Crisis: Constitutionalism in a State of Flux* (Routledge, 2023), 1–292 and more precisely Martin Belov, 'Rule of Law and Democracy in Times of Transitory Constitutionalism, Constitutional Polycrisis and Emergency Constitutionalism: Towards a Global Algorithmic Technocracy?' in Martin Belov (ed) *Rule of Law in Crisis: Constitutionalism in a State of Flux* (Routledge, 2023), 21–47.

[5] See Martin Belov (ed) *Representative Democracy in Flux. Deconstructive Narratives from a Legal and Constitutional Perspective*, Routledge, 2025, 1–312.

[6] For the concept of post-democracy see Colin Crouch, *Post-Democracy* (Polity, 2004), 1–144.

[7] For the concept of technofeudalism see Yannis Varoufakis, *Technofeudalism: What Killed Capitalism* (Melville House, 2024), 1–304.

[8] See Martin Belov, Three Models for Ordering Constitutional Orders, in Pravni Zapisi, Year XIII, Nr. 2 (2022), 361–387.

consensus of the increasingly fragile constitutionally framed socio-political communities.

Thus, we are facing the risk of approaching a period in history marked not just by post-democracy, but also by constitutional sclerosis, erosion, and deconstitutionalization. These tendencies may produce dark constitutionalism based on negative emotional politics and constitutional anthropology of obedience, oppression, and fear. Consequently, post-democracy can shift into post-constitutionalism as a regime of constitutionally eroded non-liberty.

Conversely, the deep and structural crisis of the constitutional orders may allow for a transition to an upgraded form of constitutionalism. Thus, constitutional polytransition, that is currently marked by the rule of law and representative democracy in flux, can also be an opportunity for reform of constitutionalism in multiple aspects. Nevertheless, a crisis as an opportunity should not be mistaken for an emergency as normalcy. Regretfully, there is a tendency for the normalization of crisis and emergency, both in theory and in practice. The blurring of the demarcation line between crisis, emergency, and normalcy is a dangerous phenomenon that is addressed by many chapters in this book. Hence, one of the aims of this edited volume is to provide a conceptual response to the meltdown of authority in the context of constitutional polycrisis and constitutional polytransition.

The irreversibility and structural character of the civilizational shift in which we live is triggered by the overlap of constitutional polycrisis[9] and constitutional polytransition.[10] Constitutional polycrisis consists of the multitude of crises that overlap and jointly produce structural transformation of the legal, political, and constitutional orders with regard to their

[9] See Martin Belov, 'The Conceptual Shapes of Constitutional Polycrisis: Deconstruction, Asymmetries and Post-Modern Anxieties of Constitutional Normalcy' (2023) 70 Irish Jurist, special issue Law in a Time of Crisis' 393–410, Martin Belov, 'Rule of Law in Europe in Times of Constitutional Polycrisis, Constitutional Polytransition and Democratic Discontent' (2023) 3 Diritto pubblico comparato ed europeo 875–884, and Martin Belov, 'Rule of Law and Democracy in Times of Transitory Constitutionalism, Constitutional Polycrisis and Emergency Constitutionalism: Towards a Global Algorithmic Technocracy?' in Martin Belov (ed) *Rule of Law in Crisis: Constitutionalism in a State of Flux* (Routledge, 2023) 21–47.

[10] See Martin Belov, 'Rule of Law in Europe in Times of Constitutional Polycrisis, Constitutional Polytransition and Democratic Discontent', 2023, 3, Diritto pubblico comparato ed europeo, Rivista trimestrale 875–884.

axiology, institutional balance, constitutional imaginaries, and practical performance. Constitutional polytransition is the multitude of transitions that cumulate and result in a trajectorial shift of constitutional order and constitutional civilization.

The multitude of vectors of crisis, change, and transition are among the reasons for the quantum features of the current crossroad of times. Other factors for quantum shifts are the principal stretching of constitutional phenomena between their abstract potential, which can be defined as constitutional energy, and the patterns in which this energy manifests itself and transforms into constitutional matter on the surface of the socio-legal relations and the shared constitutional imaginaries.[11]

The moment of space-time when constitutional polycrisis overlaps with constitutional polytransition is a situation of meltdown of authorities, legitimacy schemes, and shared durable collective beliefs entrenched in the constitutional anthropology of Modernity. The implosion of authority, the demise of constitutional trust, the shaking of the pillars of constitutional obedience, and the spill over of factors of deconstruction produce shifts between the realms of normalcy, emergency, and crisis. One of the visible results of this complex vortex of creative deconstruction is emergency constitutionalism.

This book offers a range of critical narratives on the interplay between constitutional polycrisis and emergency constitutionalism. They are integrated by the desire to both expose cracks in the current schemes for taming conflict, crisis, and non-normalcy and to demonstrate the constitutional shapes of the emerging post-crisis and post-transition world order. The book shows that a constitutional crisis is a multidimensional phenomenon. It outlines the legal (normative-institutional), socio-legal (empirical,

[11] For the concept, types and features of constitutional imaginaries see Martin Belov, Imaginaries of Representation: There and Back Again, in Belov, M. (ed) Representative Democracy in Flux. Deconstructive Narratives from a Legal and Constitutional Perspective, Routledge, 2025, Martin Belov, 'Constitutional Transitions and Transitional Imaginaries: Bridging Legacies of the Constitutional Past and Aspirations for the Constitutional Future' in Martin Belov and Florczak-Wątor (eds) *Constitutional Traditions and Constitutional Transitions. Legal and Socio-Legal Perspectives* (Edward Elgar, 2024), Martin Belov, Transitory Imaginaries in Central and Eastern Europe: Reconsidering Constitutional Tradition and Constitutional Transition from Symbolic-Imaginary Perspective, in Review of Central and East European Law, Special issue, Volume 49, No. 2–4, 2024, and Martin Belov, Constitutional Imaginaries in Central and Eastern Europe—Layered Narratives on Symbolic-Imaginary Constitutionalism in a Region Marked by Semi-Permanent Transformation and Transition, in Review of Central and East European Law, Special issue, Volume 49, No. 2–4, 2024.

performative, and socio-institutional), theoretical (conceptual and phenomenological), and imaginary dimensions of crisis. Constitutional crisis is used as a juncture of deconstructive and reconstructive narratives on constitutional change allocated on the edge of epochs. It is conceptualized as a formative phenomenon that durably shapes constitutionalism as a legal, socio-legal, theoretical, and imaginary phenomenon.

In this context, emergency constitutionalism is conceived as a response of the constitutional order to the challenges of constitutional polycrisis. It is the legal shape and socio-legal matrix for reordering the constitutional disorder. The book critically exposes the fallacy of emergency constitutionalism, which consists of the claim that an emergency is a temporal and efficient response to a crisis. It shows that emergency constitutionalism may be the formative tool of a new crisis-borne and emergency-related normalcy. Emergency constitutionalism may be the institutional tool-kit and conceptual framework for transforming crisis into "the new normal" and for justifying emergency governance within the institutional patchwork of quasi-constitutionality. Thus, emergency constitutionalism may be a form of governance preconditioned upon the quasi-permanency of crisis. It can serve as an instrument of governance in parallel to or even beyond constitutionalism as a framework for maximization of the benefits of the human condition based on freedom, autonomy, and self-determination.

The mission of this book is to raise awareness of the tendencies towards paternalism, technocracy, emergency governance, government, and populism through dark emotions and especially fear. These tendencies are gaining momentum, fertilized by constitutional polycrisis in the context of constitutional polytransition. They may eventually lead to dark constitutionalism as a new model of anti-constitutionalism masquerading as formal constitutionalism. It will result in constitutional order sustaining a status quo of fear, anger, hate, and despair, thus justifying the existence of a technocratic emergency Leviathan. In the context of constitutional polycrisis, this Leviathan can be multifaced and multiheaded like an (un)constitutional hydra. The heads of such (un)constitutional hydra can be the national security Leviathan, the pandemic Leviathan, the digital Leviathan, etc.[12]

[12] See Martin Belov, 'The Role of Fear Politics in Global Constitutional 'Ernstfall': Images of Fear under COVID-19 Health Paternalism' in Martin Belov (ed) *Populist Constitutionalism and Illiberal Democracies. Between Constitutional Imagination, Normative Entrenchment and Political Reality* (Intersentia, 2021), 187–221.

This general task of the book is accomplished in several analytical steps, and the structure of the monograph reflects that logic. The book aims at exploring constitutional polycrisis and emergency constitutionalism as interrelated phenomena in the context of constitutional polytransition, deconstitutionalization, and constitutional twilight. Hence, it starts with a conceptual analysis of crisis, normalcy, and emergency. The key concepts of authority, legitimacy, order, and efficiency are tapped into the network of socio-legal deconstruction produced by crisis and emergency. Crisis and emergency are explored in their various, contradictory, and even antipodal manifestations as holistic and substantial or as argumentative and narrative-based concepts. They are exposed as narrative strategies but also as constitutional imaginaries that are capable of producing a web of quantum entanglement in dark constitutional politics.

The interpretative approach to emergency and crisis is also demonstrated against the background of important theories and the case-law of key apex courts. The contributors to this volume stipulate that constitutional interpretation of emergencies proves a degree of sustainability of typical arguments over time. They outline and critically explore the theoretical, normative, and jurisprudential argumentative shapes of crisis, emergency, and normalcy. Moreover, the use of different strategies for coping with emergencies is exposed. One of the most original strategies among them is the use of the topical concept of constitutional identity as a source of legal argumentation in the constitutional crisis and emergency discourse. Hence, the book can be regarded as a contribution to the argumentative approach to constitutional conflict in times of democratic instability, constitutional dissensus, and discontent.

Special emphasis is put on the performance of multilevel constitutional orders—national, multicultural, and supranational forms of multilevel constitutionalism within and beyond the statehood—in the context of constitutional polycrisis and emergency constitutionalism. The book explores how federations, but also quasi-federal constitutional orders such as the regionalized states with elements of subnational constitutionalism and the EU, cope with crisis and emergency. The book suggests comparative insights from emergency provisions in European democracies during the COVID-19 pandemic. This is done through comparative analysis and case studies. Moreover, the book explores the impact of emergency constitutionalism on pluralist and consociational constitutional orders. It assesses the crisis management experience of multicultural societies within and beyond statehood. Hence, the book is an attempt at conceptualizing emergency constitutionalism and constitutional polycrisis in the context of multilayered, pluralist, and complex constitutional orders. It explores its conflictual and deconstructive potential.

Last but not least, the book analyses the rise of populism in times of constitutional polycrisis, constitutional polytransition, and emergency constitutionalism. It exposes populism both as a result of crisis, emergency, and transition and as a factor for crisis. The book explores the impact of populism on the ongoing transformations of the global economic constitution, which is very much an object of deconstruction and in the course of transition. Thus, it outlines the shapes of economic populism and its constitutional dimensions and contributions to crisis, dissensus, and discontent. It demonstrates the historic patterns of stabilization of emergency as normalcy and the misuse of crisis management measures as tools for the establishment of authoritarian and totalitarian regimes justified through recourse to crisis. It explores the role of militant democracy, militant constitutionalism, and militant constitutional identity for coping with crisis and emergency.

To sum up, crises and emergencies are complex and multilayered phenomena. Thus, they require multidiscursive analysis. Such analysis must take into account their legal, socio-legal, and imaginary aspects and perspectives. It must explore crisis as fact and imaginary, and emergency as a legal matrix created in response to it. Moreover, crises and emergencies are not confined to a certain jurisdiction. They have subnational, national, regional, supranational, international, transnational, and global dimensions. Moreover, since the beginning of the twenty-first century, it is hardly possible to speak of "crisis" in the singular. Instead, constitutional polycrisis unfolds as the "new normal".

This book is a collective attempt at analytical epistemology of crisis and emergency from these multilayered perspectives. It is critical to deconstruct intuitive assumptions and established truths regarding crisis, emergency, and normalcy. It is a creative reconstruction of new analytical paradigms, such as constitutional polycrisis and emergency constitutionalism, that should be capable of mastering the constitutional disorder and constitutionalism in flux that is currently unfolding.

Part I of the book outlines some of the key elements of the theoretical foundations of constitutional emergencies. It explores the conceptual shapes of constitutional crisis and emergency. It analyses the concept of emergency from the perspectives of authority, narration, and entanglement in transpersonal webs of meaning. The first part addresses conceptual issues of legitimacy, obedience, authority, ontology, and teleology of crisis and emergency.

Why do we obey authority in emergencies? To what extent do we do so, and is there measurability of the extent to which we are allowed to disobey and deviate from authoritative patterns of behavior? Are there any reasons why we can or should relinquish obedience? Are they valid only in an emergency, or can they also be activated in times of normalcy? Can an emergency count as an excuse for deviation from normatively prescribed rules grounded in authority? If yes, which kinds of emergency situations are permissible for such deviation behavior? Are authorities themselves allowed to deviate from normative structures of authority in times of crisis and emergency due to higher reasons and shifting contexts? These are some of the key questions that concern the relationship between authority, normalcy, emergency, and crisis. They are even more important in times of the current constitutional polycrisis and constitutional polytransition.

Authority, together with legitimacy, is a structural asset of each political and constitutional order. Disobedience to authority—by the people or the office holders—may produce delegitimation of the public power and its cohesive imaginary glue. Exceptional deviation from authoritative rules and orders might be possible, but its reasons, conditions, and justification must be properly explored and assessed. Especially in the context of constitutional polycrisis, when emergency is gradually normalized, and the boundaries of crisis, emergency, and normalcy are increasingly volatile, the reconsideration of the grounds of obedience to authority is not only theoretically interesting but also pragmatically valuable.

In Chapter 2, Michael Green offers a critical analysis of the perplexed and varied relationship between authority and emergency. He is using Joseph Raz's service conception of authority as a paradigmatic framework in order to expose the tensions between authority and obedience in times of normalcy and emergency. He is also engaging with arguments stemming from other theoretical paradigms relevant to the issues of the legitimacy of obedience: Lockean, Hobbesian, and others.

Green distinguishes between authority, meta-authority, and higher authority. He defines meta-authority as "authority about the existence of authority and its scope." In his account, "submission to authority is a matter of probabilities. Like reliance on one's own judgment, such submission has dangers, and sometimes they materialize." Green stipulates that:

> The existence and scope of the constitution's higher-order authority over [...] officials is a contingent matter. The fact that the constitution enabled the officials to have whatever authority over the citizenry they possess does

> not mean that the constitution (or its drafters and ratifiers) necessarily possess the higher-order authority that they claim. Whether there is such authority depends upon whether the [Raz's normal justification thesis] is satisfied.

The probabilistic approach is in line with the concept of quantum constitutionalism that I am developing in many publications, but also in Chapter 4 of this edited volume. From a quantum perspective, the quantum concept of authority can mean a phenomenon that is in a permanent process of making and unmaking. It is stretched between its principal potential and its concrete manifestations in the legal order, the socio-legal reality, and the constitutional consciousness.

According to Michael Green, "the service conception can generate a coherent account of the authority of a constitution over officials in emergencies." His aim is to show "how officials may identify emergency exceptions to constitutional restrictions in a manner that preserves the constitution's authority—that does not turn the constitution into mere advice about how to act." One of the important statements that the author makes is that "authority exists when coercion is morally permissible." Moral permissibility is rather vague and prone to interpretation. Moreover, Green suggests that "submission to both authority and meta-authority is not absolute." This is why he is also interested in the interpretation of authoritative directives.

In Chapter 3, Guillaume Tusseau offers an enlightening plurality of approaches to the concept of constitutional emergency. More precisely, the chapter suggests that there are two main approaches. They are defined by the author as platonic and argumentative approaches. Tusseau is skeptical about the essentialist understanding of emergency. He believes that a self-sufficient, holistic or generally convincing conceptual approach to emergency is non-feasible. Instead, he proposes a fuzzy, argumentative, and variable understanding of emergency as a contextual phenomenon dependent on the socio-legal context of its argumentative (mis)use by office holders, power players, and other narrators.

This approach is very much in line with the concepts of narrative sovereignty and quantum constitutionalism that I am developing in several recent publications,[13] but especially in the next chapter, Chapter 4 of this edited volume. Quantum phenomenology of constitutional concepts

[13] See e.g., Martin Belov, *Constitutional semiotics. The Conceptual Foundations of a Constitutional Theory and Meta-Theory* (Hart publishing, 2022), 1–349.

means that while they have some principal features ("constitutional energy"), they are projected in time-space and unfold in certain constitutional matter due to the specifics of the context and their deliberate shaping by the intent of the authoritative players. The process of this explication of the "constitutional energy" into "constitutional matter" is modulated and entangled by the narrative impact of the authoritative and semi-authoritative constitutional narrators.

Tusseau's chapter is a convincing contribution to a narrative theory of constitutionalism. This is because it demonstrates the non-essentialist, narrative character of constitutional phenomena and more precisely of the concept of (constitutional) emergency. The author suggests that "constitutional emergency [...] testifies to the fact that legal discourse is not necessarily a language that denotes things. It largely belongs to the persuasive, justificatory, and even emotional discourse." In his account, "the main pillars of the grammar of contemporary constitutionalism are thus affected by emergency situations."

Tusseau shows the main aspects of what he defines as a traditional or Platonist perspective, looking for a unique and true definition of emergency. He suggests that "either 'real' emergency does not exist, or there is no way of knowing it with certainty."

According to Tusseau, the Platonist approach to constitutional emergency comprises four versions that are based on ontological realism. He critically outlines and explores them. Tusseau suggests that the "various definitions of emergency lead to one of two conclusions. Either there is no real emergency, or there is no way of knowing with certainty. It is therefore impossible to verify the truth of a claim invoking emergency." Thus, he believes that emergency is an argument, not a reality.

This is the reason why he proposes an argumentative approach to constitutional emergency. Tusseau explores the structure of the various narrative-based concepts of constitutional emergency used by legal actors and the argumentative use of emergency by legal actors. He analyzes the modalities of denotation and connotation of the concept of emergency. Tusseau suggests that "the concept of emergency, as it is present in legal discourses, may have no denotation at all, or a denotation that is ultimately not so important. In such a case, the word is used without the intention of referring to any particular empirical fact. All that matters is how the word 'sounds' to (the ears of) legal actors." Hence, according to him, "emergency can therefore be seen as nothing more than a label or a slogan. Since this word does not denote anything in particular, what is essential may be that it connotes a kind of sufficient reason that justifies the action of some authority. By not looking for what it refers to, but by considering it as an argument, it is possible to understand how the invocation of an emergency is used in the strategies of constitutional actors."

The main claim of Chapter 4, written by me, is that constitutional imaginaries are elements of a quasi-neural meta-personal network of consciousness through which the people understand the constitutional order. This network is based on textual, visual, and performative narratives that inspire, engage with, and organize the collective constitutional conscious, subconscious, and unconscious. It produces meaning on the basis of imaginary constitutional enchantment through affectual and emotional nudging and symbolic engagement with constitutional archetypes and other anthropological structures of collective constitutional "make-believe." The chapter shows that the constitutional imaginaries of crisis and emergency are a result of competing narratives, which may amount to battles for control of the narrative. They are ensuing from narrative sovereignty as the ultimate source of narrative quantum entanglement of meaning. The narratives are producing—alternatively or cumulatively—constitutional imaginaries which are shaping the collective constitutional conscious, subconscious, and unconscious. The analysis of the narrative-based character of constitutional imaginaries of crisis and emergency is then followed by an outlining of the fundamental concepts of quantum constitutionalism, cloud constitutionalism, and quantum entanglement of the constitutional order via constitutional imaginaries. This allows for the proper embedding of crisis and emergency in the context of quantum constitutionalism.

Part II of the book is devoted to the role of interpretation in shaping emergencies. This problem is also explored in other chapters of this volume, for example, in Chapters 4 and 7, addressing the narrative character of crisis and emergency and the role of constitutional courts in shaping emergency constitutionalism. Nevertheless, Part II is focused on the interplay between emergency, identity, and interpretation. Special emphasis is put on the role of constitutional identity and sovereignty for making and unmaking emergency (mis)use. Moreover, the contributions to this part of the book provide an outline of some of the main theoretical approaches to emergency and crisis and demonstrate the logic behind them.

In Chapter 5, Djordje Gardasevic and Dora Pavković provide a critical outline and systematization of some of the main viewpoints on emergency that have been developed in constitutional theory and the case-law of apex courts. They strive to present the degree of continuity between the arguments, the most important differences, and the key departures from them in the course of time. Hence, they provide an overview of the constitutional interpretation of emergencies and explore the sustainability of typical arguments launched by theorists and courts over time.

Djordje Gardasevic and Dora Pavković, similarly to Guillaume Tusseau, believe that there is no single, holistic, and essential definition of emergency. According to them, "despite the generally accepted definitions in constitutional documents [...] the perception is that real emergencies can never truly be foreseen. As such, real emergencies are often perceived as sui generis situations with no real historical precedent."

Gardasevic and Pavković differentiate several key analytical approaches to emergencies. They also constitute politically constitutionally based and constitutionally relevant choices regarding the institution that should be in charge of mastering the emergency. Hence, the authors distinguish between executive unilateralists, civil libertarians, democratic formalists, and proponents of the process-based approach. Gardasevic and Pavković make an overview and critical comparison of these main theoretical choices, which are appropriately followed by an exploration of the judicial understanding of the concept of emergency. To sum up, Chapter 5 constitutes a valuable outline of the emergency as a key constitutional concept shaped through both constitutional theory and apex courts.

Alan Greene's Chapter 6 offers a comparison between constitutional identity and states of exception. In fact, both concepts are deeply related to sovereignty, and the author is engaging in argumentation against Schmittian understanding of the Constitution as a blank check for political will imposition games in times of crisis. Greene makes an original attempt at proving that "instances where constitutional identity and emergency powers have collided demonstrate that constitutional identity has the potential to tame and control emergencies." Moreover, Greene argues that "by understanding constitutional identity through this lens of exception, the utility of constitutional identity can be revealed but also, importantly, its fundamental dangers."

Greene raises several important questions that are traditionally at the center of the analysis of emergency constitutionalism. The most important of them are: "what constitutes an emergency; who gets to decide that an emergency exists; when, if ever, does an emergency end; what actions are permissible or impermissible; and what safeguards, if any, are necessary on emergency powers." Greene defines emergency as a "crisis identified and labelled by a state to be of such magnitude that it is deemed to cross a threat severity threshold, necessitating urgent, exceptional, and, consequently, temporary actions by the state not permissible when normal conditions exist."

Greene's chapter is an important contribution to the exploration of emergency constitutionalism and constitutional polycrisis in multifold ways. It defines the main elements of states of emergency and states of exception. It compares the constitutional identity with the state of exception due to their implicit dependence on discretion, interpretation, and imposition in case of emergency, conflict, and anomy. It also tries to depart from "business as usual models of emergency accommodation."

There is an important parallel between Guillaume Tusseau's and Alan Greene's chapters. Both of the authors suggest that emergency is not an eternal, holistic, and essentialist concept. Instead, it is narratively based and produced through power transformed into legal and political arguments. For example, Greene suggests that we should possibly have to "shift focus away from what has been labelled as 'an emergency' or 'constitutional identity' and instead focus on who is doing the labelling and invoking the concept of emergency or constitutional identity."

An important claim that Greene makes is that "emergency powers must be conceptualized as temporary in order to avoid this proxy-constitutional amendment scenario. Failure to do so results in the constitution being amended in a manner not envisaged and so, to all intents and purposes, a permanent state of emergency operates similar to an exercise of constituent power by destroying the suspended constitutional norms."

This suggestion is, in fact, a critical warning against the semi-permanency of emergencies that have unfolded in recent decades. Such a chronic emergency, in my account, amounts to a constitutional polycrisis where the emergency is becoming normalcy or "the new normal." Thus, I believe that it produces a semi-permanent state of exception that allows for the rise of multifaced Leviathan, as mentioned above. This is actually the Schmittian world of a non-controlled quasi-existential state of exception (*Ernstfall*) that Greene wants to argue against in his chapter.

Laurianne Allezard's Chapter 7 explores the French approach to legislative justification in the context of environmental and climate crises. It polemically assesses the mismatch between the principle obligation to rationalize legislation and its weak and formal implementation. The author criticizes the reliance mostly on "vague or opportunistically invoked notions such as 'general interest' or 'urgency,' with minimal scrutiny from the Constitutional Council," while neglecting scientific evidence in case of crisis and proclamation of emergency. Thus, the author demonstrates how the justification requirement is much more of a rhetorical device instead of being a binding legal constraint.

The central claim of Allezard is that "scientific knowledge is instrumentalized selectively, and frequently delegated to administrative or regulatory authorities with unclear accountability." She points out the inadequacy of such an approach in times of crisis and transition. Moreover, according to her, in the context of constitutional polycrisis, "the inadequacy of this framework raises concerns about the current and future legitimacy of law." The author suggests that "the French case illustrates a classical constitutional posture, in which formalist habits and institutional inertia create obstacles to the development of more rational and sustainable responses to long-term crises." One of the main claims of the chapter is that constitutional crisis management and legal institutionalization and praxis of emergency constitutionalism must go "beyond positivist formalism towards a constitutional culture grounded in empirical justification and transparent public reasoning."

Part III of the book is devoted to federalism as an institutional framework of crisis and emergency. It explores the ways a crisis impacts multilevel constitutional orders. It also analyses the ways federalism and multilevel orders can restrain crises and produce meaningfully designed emergencies. In addition, Part III deals with the performance of pluralist and consociational orders in times of constitutional polycrisis and in the context of emergency constitutionalism.

Chapter 8, written by Francesco Palermo, discusses the tense interplay between emergency constitutionalism, federalism, and pluralism. Palermo emphasizes the fact that constitutions are ill-equipped to cope with constitutional polycrisis due to several reasons. They mostly address military threats, for example, wars. Moreover, they do not allow participatory processing of the crisis. According to Palermo, federalism may give an answer to both issues. He suggests that federalism provides for a non-emergency-driven approach to crises. In his account, "federalism is a tool that significantly helps make emergency decisions more coordinated and more pluralistic, thus more legitimate."

The author defines an emergency as the Constitution's worst enemy. He demonstrates why federalism may be a solution for minimizing threats to constitutionalism in times of crisis and emergency. Palermo suggests that one of the main missions of contemporary constitutionalism is to promote pluralism. He suggests that federalism is capable of minimizing the detrimental effects of crisis and emergency, for example, concentration of power, limitation of human rights, the rise of an autocratic executive, etc., on constitutionalism. Against the backdrop of the experiences with the COVID-19 pandemic regimes, Palermo suggests that federal systems' recourse to the state of emergency is much rarer than in unitary systems or in those with non-federal decentralization.

The author explores the role of federalism in the current age of transition from government to governance. He claims that "federalism—with its institutions, procedures, structured relations, and mechanisms for the prevention and resolution of conflicts—can provide inspiration for the development of a theory and (more importantly) procedural solutions for the growing demands for pluralist (participatory, inclusive, multilevel) democracy." The chapter concludes with the extremely important statement that in the age of constitutional polycrisis and constitutional polytransition, "the challenge will be to deal with problems in an ordinary, not extraordinary way, and to come up with solutions that are as democratically legitimate as possible, thus inclusive and participatory, so as to limit disaffection, alienation, and opposition to the extent possible." Hence, he believes that federalism can be a solution for coping with crises and emergencies in an increasingly polycentric world.

In Chapter 9, Soeren Keil explores the role of multilevel constitutionalism and multilevel governance on pandemic management. The chapter has specific added value since it is grounded on data collected from various countries in Europe during the COVID-19 pandemic. These data allow for both conceptual and empirical analysis of the responses to the pandemic in unitary, decentralized, regional, and federal countries. Hence, the chapter explores the relationship between emergency constitutionalism and multilevel constitutionalism.

Keil polemically assesses the intuitive suggestion that centralization fosters efficiency. He demonstrates that the authority, efficiency, and legitimacy of the emergency responses during the COVID-19 pandemic do not automatically stem from centralization or decentralization of power. Rather, they are dependent on a range of factors that vary in the constitutional orders and the specific socio-political contexts of their functioning.

Hence, Soeren Keil explores the variety of institutional and political responses to COVID-19, offering a comparative analysis of the EU Member States, Switzerland, and Norway. He shows the impact of COVID-19 measures on the "already fragile democratic institutions through the increased centralization of powers" and the tendency to "an overall democratic recession, during the pandemic management period" that "posed a challenge to existing competence distributions and intergovernmental relations." The chapter demonstrates the weaknesses of the intuitive centralization hypothesis and shows the divergence in crisis responses. It presents the role of COVID-19 on centralization, decentralization, and institutional realignment of power in the context of emergency constitutionalism.

Gavin Barrett's Chapter 10 is devoted to the EU responses to crisis and emergency. It is an important contribution to the overall topic of Part III of this book related to the impact of crisis and emergency on multilevel constitutional orders. The rest of the chapters of this part address this topic from a federalist perspective. They explore the performance of federations and quasi-federal national and multicultural state constitutional orders in the face of the challenges produced by crisis and emergency. At the same time, Barrett's chapter offers an important contribution to this federalist polycrisis discourse, adding the EU perspective.

The author explores crises and emergencies in the EU multilevel constitutional order from a range of perspectives. The most important layers of analysis are the normative-institutional, historic, and socio-legal. The analysis is both problem-oriented and institution-oriented, giving conceptual, historic, and pragmatic perspectives on the way the EU copes with constitutional polycrisis.

Barrett suggests that crisis is a permanent companion of the EU integration and the EU as its institutional focus and climax. He proves that thesis by reminding us of its foundational crisis-based and crisis-solving logic, but also the history of the semi-permanent crisis, especially in the current age of constitutional polycrisis. The author outlines several important conceptualizations of crisis—structural and functional, axiological, institutional and policy-related. He stipulates that "drawing neat lines between crises and emergencies is no easy task" since "both the Treaties and implementing legislation cloud the distinction and use the words interchangeably." According to him, "the traditional concept of a state of emergency appears in any case to have no application to the European Union."

Furthermore, Barrett explores the role of emergency constitutionalism in EU Law and in the EU integration. He suggests that there are two main reasons for the inapplicability of more traditional concepts of state of emergency to the European Union: the boundedness of the EU by the doctrine of limited powers and its lack of an express general emergency clause and general emergency regime. Nevertheless, according to the author, this does not prevent the use of the rhetoric of emergency by the EU and its Member States, which may be new while "oscillating on the very edge of legality." This argumentative, interpretative, and narrative recourse to emergency as a strategy for coping with crisis has been emphasized by many contributions to this volume. It is particularly visible in Chapter 3 (Tusseau), Chapter 4 (Belov), and Chapter 5 (Gardasevic). Gavin Barrett also identifies three types of emergency-related provisions in the EU law. These are Treaty provisions that essentially clear the way for Member States to act in an emergency, Treaty provisions that require Member States to act in solidarity with one another in times of crisis or emergency and provisions that provide for action on the part of the European Union.

Barrett admits that "responses to crises can vary from one crisis to another." He outlines the main institutional responses to the various crises that have hit the EU and Member States' orders in recent years. Barrett suggests that "the EU does seem to be integrating further because of crises, 'resilience' has now become a key concept in European Union policy discourse," and "the institutional impact of crises has been considerable." Nevertheless, in his account, "the benefits derived from crisis-driven actions sometimes may not be as directly related to the crisis itself as one might have expected." He proposes a more holistic and consistent approach to dealing with constitutional polycrisis.

Very important conclusions are drawn with regard to the tendencies to post-democracy, expertocracy, emergency and crisis-driven technocratic governance, and executive federalism. Barrett detects "a shift from a rules-based approach to crises [...] to a more politicized events-based approach, involving political choices." These tendencies are detrimental to the legitimacy and democratic authority of the EU and its Member States.

In Chapter 11, Allison McCulloch explores the interrelation between consociational constitutionalism, power-sharing, crisis, and emergency. She is exposing the entrenchment of crisis in consociationalism and power-sharing rules, schemes, and paradigms as a side effect of their capacity to tame conflict, crisis, and emergency. Hence, while power-sharing agreements are supposed to be a way out of crisis, they are, in many cases, a form of perpetuated crisis or constitutionalism amid a durable, prolonged and even constitutionally entrenched crisis.

McCulloch points out that consociational power-sharing between rival ethnic groups or between former combatants is typically perceived and conceptualized as a means of ending wars and supporting democratization.

They are tools for transitions from war to peace or from autocracy to democracy that are based upon executive power-sharing, group autonomy, proportionality and veto powers. In that regard, McCulloch aims to explore "three adoption-to-adaptation problems: ambiguous provisions can give way to serious disagreements about their meaning; some clauses of an agreement needed to elicit agreement are ignored thereafter; and some provisions become seemingly 'unreformable,' leaving divided societies 'stuck' with anachronistic rules and institutions." McCulloch demonstrates how power-sharing and political crisis are ineluctably related. Moreover, she shows that "power-sharing is, above all, a response to crisis," but "also risks becoming the crisis."

McCulloch's key assumption is that "power-sharing agreements are often negotiated within a context of crisis and urgency: the kinds of emergency conditions that exist at war's end, after authoritarian collapse, or in the context of deep ethnic divisions." As a result, this produces constructive ambiguity and "stickiness" or rigidity of power-sharing provisions—two phenomena which are explored in conceptual and comparative perspective by the author. In fact, the concept of constructive ambiguity is related to narrative sovereignty—a problem that is explored in several chapters of this volume, but especially in Chapter 4. Another link between the concept of constitutional imaginaries of crisis and emergency, explored in Chapter 4, and the imaginaries in times of transition from conflict and disruption to consociational forms of government is the "symbolic weight" of the institutions analyzed by McCulloch in Chapter 11.

Part IV explores the interplay between populism, emergency, and crisis. It focuses on three key phenomena. These are populism, emergency power misuse in the context of crisis, and militant constitutionalism. They are bound together by the interest in the enabling role of crisis and emergency for the misuse of power to reshape the constitutional forms of normalcy. Thus, they contribute to the debate on internal conflict and constitutional discontent and the possible responses to it by the citizens, leaders, and public power institutions.

Chapter 12 is written by Marta Vicente and Catarina Santos Botelho. It explores the impact of populism on the current economic transformations in the global economic constitution. Populism is widely discussed in the scientific literature, especially during the last decade. Thus, the authors only summarize its main features and critically assess its use as an instrument for labelling a range of loosely related phenomena, frequently with a focus on right-wing extremism. In contrast, Marta Vicente and Catarina Santos Botelho adopt a nuanced approach addressing the concept of populism in an economic sense. Their aim is to explore how economic populism affects the global economic constitution. They assess populism from the viewpoint of the global economy and the global economic constitution.

Vicente and Santos Botelho suggest a concise overview of the literature on the concept of populism and the principal debates around its meaning. They demonstrate the main features and aspects of the global economic constitution and the key points of criticism towards it by populism, while also exploring the main tendencies in the ongoing deconstruction of the global economic constitution associated with populist movements.

The authors analyze three significant tendencies in the global economic constitution that are intertwined with populist strategies and claims. According to Vicente and Santos Botelho, these are the weaponization of the world economy, the demise of the rule of law as neoliberal legality, and the withdrawal from the international economic system. They demonstrate the emergence and development of the "geoeconomic narrative" and "strategic sovereignty" in the context of the "weaponization of the world economy" and the demise of the rule of law as neoliberal legality.

Hence, Vicente and Santos Botelho's chapter is an important contribution not just for the scientific analysis of populism per se. It offers valuable insights with regard to the role of economic and financial fractures of the global economic constitution in times of crisis and transition. Thus, it is logically interrelated with both the chapters belonging to Part IV that address populism, crisis and emergency and some of the previous chapters, for example, Gavin Barrett's chapter, addressing the economic and financial aspects of the constitutional polycrisis.

In Chapter 13 entitled "Contexts of Crisis: Sovereign Power, Constitutional Change and Dictatorship in Interwar Romania," Cosmin Cercel accomplishes a historical, conceptual, and socio-legal analysis of the transformative potential of emergency. He offers an overview of the history of crisis and emergency in Interwar Romania that demonstrates the huge transformative potential of emergency to serve as a trigger and loophole of parallel legality and normalization of emergency through recourse to semi-permanent real or invented crisis. Although the chapter is mostly a historic case-study, its great value for this edited volume consists in the conceptualization of emergency constitutionalism as "authoritarianism in the making."

Cercel emphasizes the essentially conservative nature of emergency measures and reflects on the conceptual and material continuity between emergency regimes and authoritarian legality. He suggests that "rather than being a temporary measure meant to protect and secure the constitutional order, an emergency has the potential to change constitutional arrangements by developing a level of autonomy that materializes itself in a parallel legality." He demonstrates, against the background of the Romanian history of the late nineteenth and the first half of the twentieth century, that emergency was not necessarily always paralleled by a real and massive crisis. Moreover, emergencies were neither temporarily limited nor restrained from interfering in the realm of the constitution. Hence, an emergency constitutionalism has been gradually established. At times, it was a coherent and consistent project, while in other periods it was more a patchwork of legal forms covering political will for authoritarian concentration of power.

Cercel's chapter is an important study of the transformation of the commissarial into constitutional and then sovereign dictatorship that usually disregards or even deconstructs the inner limitations of emergency. It shows the transformative potential of emergency, consisting in its capacity to alter and transform constitutional arrangements. It shows how the prerogative state (in this case, the modern Romanian state) is taking over legal structures and forms by not just dismantling them, but also by integrating them into a new form of emergency constitutionalism and emergency legality. In the words of the author, "this is not only the specific inertia that emergency measures have, and their possibility of being embedded within the constitutional order, but the very possibility that an accumulation of emergency-based legislation, and a specific type of emergency-based legal interpretation does affect the existing constitutional arrangements, actually giving rise to a silent or explicit constitutional change."

Antonia Baraggia's Chapter 14 explores militant constitutionalism in times of polycrisis from an EU perspective. The chapter revolves around three key concepts. These are militant democracy, militant constitutionalism, and militant constitutional identity. The author analyses their main elements and the process of their interplay in the case of the EU. This is done mostly through the prism of the case-law of the CJEU.

The analysis is done in several steps. Baraggia commences with an introduction of the concept of militant democracy. She outlines several models of militant democracy—historic and contemporary, holistic or problem-focused. These models are all national and have unfolded in the context of constitutionalism within statehood. Thus, Baraggia's task is to extrapolate their *raison d'être* in the sphere of supranational constitutionalism of the EU. More precisely, the overall logic of the chapter is to explore the conflictual interplay between the constitutional order of the EU and the constitutional orders of its Member States from the point of view of (in)compatibilities with a potential for constitutional implosion. Antonia Baraggia suggests that while "militant democracy is anchored in a classic understanding of the rise of authoritarian regimes rooted in extremism and violence," it is "not well suited to represent the defense against new forms of authoritarian regimes."

The next analytical step is exploring EU militant constitutionalism. After broadly introducing the concept, Baraggia poses the question of whether the EU is moving towards a militant constitutional model. She presents the new role of the concept of European identity in the legal reasoning of the CJEU with regard to the novel concept of militant identity. Baraggia suggests that the use of conditionality may be considered a tool of militant constitutionalism. She concludes with an analysis of the strategic case-law of the CJEU shaping what she defines as a "militant conception of the EU values."

The last chapter, Chapter 15, of this edited volume is devoted to the rather problematic judicial reform in Israel in the period before and after the critical events on 7 October 2023. It explores the ways the constitutional crisis stemming from these reforms and the post-7 October security crisis are becoming intertwined and mutually reinforcing phenomena. Yaniv Roznai demonstrates the detrimental effects of security-related emergencies on constitutional normalcy and particularly on the rule of law. He shows how the overlap of multiple crises can produce the demise of authority and implosion of democratic order based on the rule of law. The analysis is embedded within concerns stemming from the broader theoretical framework of populist constitutionalism and security-driven populism. Roznai demonstrates "how wartime dynamics are fostering the persistence and deepening of the constitutional crisis, how the security crisis can enable and facilitate a populist constitutional project, and how and why the judicial overhaul has deepened under the fog of war." The author suggests that "this phenomenon illustrates how security crises can serve to entrench executive authority rather than curtail it, especially in hybrid regimes with weak constitutional safeguards" and how "crises have often served as catalysts for the expansion of executive power and even for constitutional revolutions." According to Roznai, "in Israel, which is anyway in a constant and continuing state of emergency, the ongoing war created a continuous state of exception—blurring the lines between emergency governance and regular policymaking."

The chapter is a valuable research of several important elements of polycrisis and emergency constitutionalism in times when emergency is becoming the "new normal." It explores the phenomena of "abusive constitutionalism" and "stealth authoritarianism."

Roznai devotes special attention to the socio-legal aspects of the problem of security in an emergency. He demonstrates the role of national trauma, political identity, and collective fears and taboos for reshaping the democratic architecture, producing unconstitutional constitutional reforms, and promoting emergency regimes and security-based populist regimes. Thus, the chapter is an important contribution to the research of constitutional polycrisis and emergency constitutionalism and thus to the overall mission of this book.

References

Belov, M. (ed.) *Rule of Law in Crisis: Constitutionalism in a State of Flux*. Routledge, 2023, pp. 1–292

Belov, M. Rule of Law and Democracy in Times of Transitory Constitutionalism, Constitutional Polycrisis and Emergency Constitutionalism: Towards a Global Algorithmic Technocracy? In: Belov, M. (ed.) *Rule of Law in Crisis: Constitutionalism in a State of Flux*. Routledge, 2023, pp. 21–47

Belov, M. (ed.) *Representative Democracy in Flux: Deconstructive Narratives from a Legal and Constitutional Perspective*. Routledge, 2025, pp. 1–312

Belov, M. The Conceptual Shapes of Constitutional Polycrisis: Deconstruction, Asymmetries and PostModern Anxieties of Constitutional Normalcy. *Irish Jurist*, 70, Special Issue 'Law in a Time of Crisis', 2023, pp. 393–410

Belov, M. Rule of Law in Europe in Times of Constitutional Polycrisis, Constitutional Polytransition and Democratic Discontent. *Diritto pubblico comparato ed europeo*, 3, 2023, pp. 875–884

Belov, M. The Role of Fear Politics in Global Constitutional 'Ernstfall': Images of Fear under COVID-19 Health Paternalism. In: Belov, M. (ed.) *Populist Constitutionalism and Illiberal Democracies: Between Constitutional Imagination, Normative Entrenchment and Political Reality*. Intersentia, 2021, pp. 187–221

Belov, M. Imaginaries of Representation: There and Back Again. In: Belov, M. (ed.) *Representative Democracy in Flux: Deconstructive Narratives from a Legal and Constitutional Perspective*. Routledge, 2025

Belov, M., & Florczak-Wątor, M. Constitutional Transitions and Transitional Imaginaries: Bridging Legacies of the Constitutional Past and Aspirations for the Constitutional Future. In: Belov, M., & Florczak-Wątor, M. (eds.) *Constitutional Traditions and Constitutional Transitions: Legal and Socio-Legal Perspectives*. Edward Elgar, 2024

Belov, M. Transitory Imaginaries in Central and Eastern Europe: Reconsidering Constitutional Tradition and Constitutional Transition from Symbolic-Imaginary Perspective. *Review of Central and East European Law*, Special Issue, 49(2–4), 2024

Belov, M. Constitutional Imaginaries in Central and Eastern Europe—Layered Narratives on Symbolic-Imaginary Constitutionalism in a Region Marked by Semi-Permanent Transformation and Transition. *Review of Central and East European Law*, Special Issue, 49(2–4), 2024

Belov, M. Three Models for Ordering Constitutional Orders. *Pravni Zapisi*, Year XIII, Nr. 2, 2022, pp. 361–387

Belov, M. *Constitutional Semiotics: The Conceptual Foundations of a Constitutional Theory and Meta-Theory*. Hart Publishing, 2022, pp. 1–349

Crouch, C. *Post-Democracy*. Polity, 2004, pp. 1–144

Dobner, P., & Loughlin, M. (eds.) *The Twilight of Constitutionalism?* Oxford University Press, 2010, pp. 1–370

Kiiver, P. *The National Parliaments in the European Union: A Critical View on EU Constitution-Building*. Kluwer Law International, 2006, p. 95

Piattoni, S. *The Theory of Multi-level Governance: Conceptual, Empirical, and Normative Challenges*. Oxford University Press, 2010, pp. 210–227

Varoufakis, Y. *Technofeudalism: What Killed Capitalism*. Melville House, 2024, pp. 1–304

PART 1

The Conceptual Shapes of Constitutional Crisis and Emergency

CHAPTER 2

Authority, Meta-Authority, and Emergency

Michael S. Green

2.1 Introduction

Submission to authority can seem irrational. Reason demands acting on the balance of reasons for action of which one is aware, but those who submit to authority act on the authority's directive even if it is contrary to that balance. Conceptions of authority, therefore, tend to vacillate between two unacceptable alternatives. The first preserves authority at the cost of rationality. Subjects must obey the authority blindly, come what may. The second preserves rationality at the cost of authority. The authority's directive turns into defeasible advice about how to act.

This dichotomy is evident in views about how governmental officials should treat constitutional restrictions in emergencies. Those who emphasize authority conclude that officials are obligated to follow the constitution even—indeed, especially—in an emergency, no matter

This chapter is produced as part and funded by the European Union-NextGenerationEU, through the National Recovery and Resilience Plan of the Republic of Bulgaria, project No bg-rrp-2.004-0008.

M. Belov (ed.), *Constitutional Polycrisis and Emergency Constitutionalism*, Federalism and Internal Conflicts,
https://doi.org/10.1007/978-3-032-06516-2_2

how strongly the officials think that another course of action will be in the public interest.[1] Conversely, those who accept that officials, relying on their own reasoning, can identify emergency exceptions to constitutions, conclude that officials are always engaged in unrestricted all-things-considered reasoning about how to act in the public interest—emergency or not.[2]

Joseph Raz's service conception of authority has been a great advance in avoiding such dichotomies. The heart of the service conception is the normal justification thesis (NJT), under which authority exists when subjects are more likely to abide by relevant preexisting reasons for action by following the authority's directive than by acting on their own judgment about what those reasons recommend.[3] Notice that the subject is *more likely* to conform to the relevant reasons for action by following the authority. The fact that, in a particular case, the subject is objectively right and the authority wrong does not make authority evaporate. Submission to authority is a matter of probabilities. Like reliance on one's own judgment, such submission has dangers, and sometimes they materialize.

Raz's theory can explain the suspension of judgment in submission to authority, because an authority's directive preempts the relevant preexisting reasons for action in the subject's motivation. The authority's directive replaces those reasons, rather than functioning as a new reason for action that is added to them. In that sense, the subject follows the authority's directive blindly. But it can also explain how authority is compatible with

[1] E.g., *Ex parte Milligan*, 71 US 2, 120-21 (1866) ("The Constitution of the United States is a law for rulers and people, equally in war and in peace, and covers with the shield of its protection all classes of men, at all times and under all circumstances. No doctrine involving more pernicious consequences was ever invented by the wit of man than that any of its provisions can be suspended during any of the great exigencies of government.")

[2] An arguable example is Carl Schmitt, charitably interpreted. Carl Schmitt, *Political Theology: Four Chapters on the Concept of Sovereignty* (University of Chicago Press 2005).

[3] Raz understands there to be several other requirements for authority. One is the dependence thesis—that the would-be authority, in issuing its directive, attempted to weigh the relevant preexisting reasons that applied to the subject. Joseph Raz, *Ethics in the Public Domain* (OUP 1994) 214. Another is the independence condition: that it is better for the subject to conform to the dependent reasons than for it to decide for itself. Joseph Raz, "The Problem of Authority: Revisiting the Service Conception" (2006) 90 Minnesota L R 1003, 1014–1016. When I say the NJT is satisfied, I mean these other requirements are too.

rationality, for the fact that the NJT is satisfied is, in principle, something that subjects of an authority can themselves recognize.[4]

I will try to show how the service conception can generate a coherent account of the authority of a constitution over officials in emergencies. My goal is to explain how officials may identify emergency exceptions to constitutional restrictions in a manner that preserves the constitution's authority—that does not turn the constitution into mere advice about how to act. But I also hope to explain why emergency exceptions should, in general, be rare. One important part of my account is the role of *meta-authority*: authority about the existence of authority and its scope.

2.2 The Service Conception of Authority

To get a feel for the service conception, consider a simple example of authority. You are twelve years old, and your mother tells you to stay in the house while she goes to the store.[5] Some relevant reasons for and against going outside might be: (1) that it is fun and (2) that traffic makes it dangerous. Your mother, taking the relevant reasons into account, determined that you should stay inside. If she is an authority, it is because the NJT is satisfied: you are more likely to act on the balance of the relevant reasons for action by abiding by her directive than by acting on your own judgment. That makes her directive, as Raz puts it, a *protected reason*: it is a reason not to go outside and an *exclusionary reason* not to act on the relevant preexisting reasons to go outside (such as fun).[6] Her directive should preempt those preexisting reasons in your practical reasoning. In this sense, submission to her authority means suspending your judgment about what to do.

Of course, if you go outside and your mother finds out, she is likely to punish you—and, we can assume, would be justified in doing so. The probability of punishment is another reason for you to conform to your

[4] Raz (2006) (n 3) 1018 ("[I]n following authority, just as in following advice, . . . one's ultimate self-reliance is preserved, for it is one's own judgment which directs one to recognize the authority of another...").

[5] Timothy Endicott, "Interpretation, Jurisdiction, and the Authority of Law" (2007) 6 Am Phil Ass'n Newsletter 14. This chapter relies heavily on Endicott's argument.

[6] Joseph Raz, *The Authority of Law* (OUP 1979) 18.

mother's directive. There is no suspension of judgment if you stay in the house because the dangers of traffic *plus the probability of punishment* outweigh the fun. So why not understand authority in terms of the justifiability of punishing violations of one's directives (or otherwise coercing conformity with them)?[7] That does not mean that the bare capacity to coerce makes one an authority. A gunman does not have authority. But authority exists when coercion is morally permissible.

One deficiency of this "Hobbesian" approach is that authority can exist without any capacity to coerce. Your mother would retain her authority even if she was not able to punish you for disobedience. (This is crucial for making sense of a constitution's authority over officials, for neither a constitution nor its drafters and ratifiers has the capacity to coerce official conformity with their directives.) What is more, even when authorities can coerce, they generally claim more than the fact that such coercion is justified. They claim the normative power to create duties, independent of the possibility of punishment, through their directives: the power to give the subject a duty to φ, by telling the subject to φ, even if, in fact, the balance of preexisting reasons for action recommends not φ-ing (because in the particular situation, the subject is objectively right and the authority wrong).

Consider a government that puts a stop sign at an intersection. In so doing, it claims to have given drivers a duty to stop, even if there is no possibility of punishment (there is a police strike), and even if, according to the balance of preexisting reasons for action, going through the intersection without stopping is permissible (it is four in the morning and there is little chance of an accident). Raz's service conception is an account of how this is possible.

But there is a fundamental problem with the service conception. Why don't subjects, recognizing that the NJT is satisfied, just change their beliefs about relevant reasons for action accordingly, and act on the reformed balance of reasons for action?[8] This worry does not merely arise when authority exists due to greater expertise or less bias.[9] It also arises when the authority is able to solve coordination problems and prisoner's dilemmas.

[7] Robert Ladenson, "In Defense of a Hobbesian Conception of Law" (1980) 9 Philosophy & Public Affairs 134.

[8] Heidi M Hurd, "Challenging Authority" (1991) 100 Yale L J 1611; Scott J. Shapiro, "Authority" in Jules Coleman and Scott Shapiro (eds.), *The Oxford Handbook of Jurisprudence and Philosophy of Law* (OUP 2002).

[9] Here the worry is the difference between theoretical and practical authority.

If an authority, by announcing "Drive on the right!" makes driving on the right the salient option—and so solves the coordination problem of what side to drive on—why can't subjects just recognize that salience and then act on the new reasons for action of which they are aware?

Submission to authority is needed because subjects might still better satisfy the relevant reasons for action by acting on the authority's directive than by acting on a reformed balance of reasons for action. As Scott Shapiro has argued, an authority's service might require subjects' self-constraint, in which they bind themselves to following the authority's directive.[10] The fact that subjects have committed to conformity shows its riskiness, but (if the NJT is satisfied) it is less risky than reliance on their own judgment.

In understanding this self-constraint in submission to authority, it is helpful to compare it to a subject's own resolutions.[11] Assume I resolve to exercise for half an hour in the morning every day. To be effective, I must bind myself to following the resolution—constraining my future self. If each morning I instead act on the balance of reasons as I see them, I will likely give too much weight to the inconvenience of exercising compared to its benefits. Sometimes this attempt at self-constraint will fail. Despite my resolution, I might find myself choosing not to exercise, because at the time, I take the inconvenience of doing so to be greater than its benefits. Here I am irrational, for I fail to take advantage of the service that my resolution provides. But if my self-constraint succeeds, I will act on my resolution, not on the reasons for action of which I am aware. That does not mean that I cannot *think* about those reasons. But my action will not follow from them.

To say that there is self-constraint in making a resolution does not mean that this constraint is absolute, however. Imagine that one morning, a friend calls and says she needs to be taken to the hospital. I decide that I don't have to act on my resolution to exercise that day. In doing so, I am surely rational. But it creates a puzzle. In deciding not to act on my resolution, I must have been open to releasing myself from my resolution's self-constraint if an exception should be made. And such openness seems to be precisely what I have bound myself to resist.

[10] Shapiro (n 8). See also Scott J Shapiro, *Legality* (Harvard Univ Press 2011), which relies on the work of Michael Bratman, eg Michael Bratman, *Intention, Plans and Practical Reason* (Univ of Chicago Press 1987).

[11] This is a similarity Raz himself has acknowledged. Joseph Raz, "Reasons for Actions, Decisions, and Norms" (1975) 85 Mind 481.

I confess that I have no developed account of how such release occurs, but it seems to rely on certain easily identifiable events that can trigger release without excessively undermining the self-constraint the resolution was meant to create.[12] In the triggers' absence, we act on our resolutions, not our reasons for action as we perceive them. We do not interpret our resolutions to see whether an exception should be made, for if we engage in such interpretation, we risk undermining the service that our resolutions provide. But if a trigger comes into play, we are released from our self-constraint and can determine whether acting on the resolution is appropriate.

The matter would be different if my resolution had been "exercise every day, except when a friend needs to go to the hospital." But because I did not think about such exceptions, my resolution needs to be interpreted. The worry, however, is that such an interpretation will undermine the resolution's benefits. To keep this from happening, I need to interpret the resolution in a manner that fosters its service to me. Such an interpretation might go something like this: The problem that my resolution was meant to solve was my giving excessive weight to the everyday inconvenience of exercising. That reason not to exercise should still be preempted by my resolution. But emergency hospital trips should not.

But what if I am wrong and emergency hospital trips *were* within my resolution's scope? That does not matter, for if they were, I was not a proper self-authority. The resolution was irrational and should be ignored. To repeat, I should interpret my resolution in a manner that fosters its service to me. Since an interpretation of my resolution as preempting the need to take friends to the hospital does not foster such service, it should be rejected. Notice that in interpreting my resolution in this way, it still preempts some reasons for action. It is still the case that I should not act on the everyday inconvenience of exercising in my decision to take my friend to the hospital.

With these lessons concerning the self-authority of a resolution in mind, let us turn to cases where the authority and the subject are different. Consider, once again, your mother's directive to stay inside while she goes to the store. Assume she satisfies the NJT, but you ignore her directive and go outside to play. Here, you acted irrationally by failing to take advantage of the service that her directive provided. Conversely, if you successfully bind your will to her directive and so are able to stay in the house, even

[12] For an attempted account of these "reconsideration triggers," see Cheshire Calhoun, "What Good is Commitment?" (2009) 119 Ethics 613.

though the balance of reasons that you are aware of recommends playing outside, you act rationally by taking advantage of the directive's service.

Now, assume that while your mother is gone, the house catches on fire.[13] The fire triggers an interpretation of her directive, which should be guided by the goal of fostering its service for you.[14] Suitably elaborated, your interpretation might look like this: The problem that her directive was meant to solve was that I give excessive weight to certain reasons for going outside, like fun. I should interpret her directive as preempting those reasons. But I should not interpret fires as preempted. In leaving the house, I am not denying that she is an authority, for I still should not take reasons for action that were within her directive's scope into account in my decision to go outside.

And what if I am wrong and fires were within her directive's scope? That does not matter, for if they were, she was not an authority in issuing her directive. I would be *less* likely to abide by the relevant reasons for action by following her directive than by using my own judgment. Since an interpretation of her directive as including fires within its scope is incompatible with her service as an authority, it should be rejected.

One might think that this account of the interpretation of authoritative directives overemphasizes the subject's reasoning. The real reason you should not take fire to be within the scope of your mother's directive is that she would have said it was not if asked. But it is unclear how appealing to this counterfactual limits your reliance on your own judgment in interpreting her directive, since if she *had* said that fire was within its scope, you should conclude that she is not an authority and thus that the directive should be ignored.

I have described you as interpreting your mother's directive in a manner that enhances her service as an authority for you. But one might wonder how, if your judgment is sufficiently defective to generate your mother's authority, you can engage in such interpretation. Assume that instead of a fire occurring while your mother is gone, a friend visits you. Since you give fun an improper weight (thereby creating your mother's authority), won't you simply conclude that your mother's directive should not be interpreted as preempting the *special* fun of your friend's visit?

When an authority exists because it is better at determining the proper balance of reasons for action—whether due to greater expertise or less bias—there is indeed a worry that the subject will misjudge when authority

[13] I borrow this example from Endicott (n 5).

[14] Ibid 15–16.

exists and so misinterpret the scope of the authority's directive. But even when authority exists due to such cognitive superiority, it is still *possible* for subjects to reliably recognize its existence. I don't have to be a doctor to recognize an authoritative medical directive. This is true even when I determine authoritative directives, in part, based on the *content* of the directive issued. Despite my meager knowledge of medicine, I know that someone with an M.D. from Harvard Medical School who tells me to eat a pound of lard a day to lower my cholesterol is not an authority, whereas someone with such an M.D. who recommends a well-known drug like Lipitor likely is.[15]

Reliably recognizing authority is easier when authority exists simply because of the authority's situation, not its greater ability to determine the proper balance of relevant reasons for action. Some examples are when authority exists due to its ability to solve coordination problems and prisoner's dilemmas. Consider the fact that we all have a moral obligation to preserve the environment by not polluting in a manner that is fairly distributed among us. Acting on our own judgment, we will have a hard time abiding by our obligation. The proper level of effort in avoiding pollution is hard to determine. Left to our own devices, we would come up with different standards, which is unfair to those who do more than others. What is more, how much effort we should put into not polluting depends upon the extent of others' efforts. If everyone else is polluting indiscriminately, our efforts are probably better devoted elsewhere.

The government can solve these problems by creating an environmental regulation and enforcing it uniformly. Notice that the government's ability to aid people in fulfilling their moral obligation is different from the fact that it may justifiably coerce those who refuse to recognize their obligation. The attitude of those who recognize the government's authority is not one of grudging obedience, but of thanks. Notice as well that the government can possess this authority even if the regulation it comes up with is no better—or even worse—than the one that a subject could have come up with on its own. Because the government's authority is not due to any cognitive failure on our part, it is easy to see how we can reliably recognize its existence and scope—and so reliably interpret governmental directives in a manner that fosters their authority.[16]

[15] Joseph Raz, *Morality of Freedom* (OUP 1986) 62.

[16] Another situation is when someone is an authority, not due to cognitive superiority, but simply because it has already made a judgment about the balance of considerations, such that it would be wasteful for the subject to go over the same ground.

Let us recap where we stand. Just as we have the capacity to bind ourselves to our own decisions, so we have the capacity to bind ourselves to others' decisions, in the form of directives. If the person issuing the directive satisfies the NJT, this act of binding will provide a service for us. But circumstances can arise in which we must interpret the directive. If so, we should interpret it in a manner that fosters its authority for us. Even when we conclude that an exception to the directive exists, it can still function as an authority, for it can still preempt reasons for action that we interpret to be within its scope.

2.3 Citizenry in an Emergency

With the service conception in mind, let us consider an example of the law's authority over the citizenry in an emergency. Imagine that, due to a recent riot, a curfew has been established, which requires people not to go outside after 10 p.m. Neither the language of the curfew nor any other law makes an exception to the curfew for house fires. You know that the government will not punish you for violating the curfew, because police enforcement has been directed to areas closer to the riot.

Assume that the curfew satisfies the NJT. In binding yourself to act on the curfew, rather than the reasons for action of which you are aware, the curfew performs a service for you—allowing you to better satisfy your reasons for action than you would be able to otherwise. But assume that soon after 10 p.m., your house catches on fire. This triggers a reconsideration of your commitment to abide by the directive. You must now interpret the directive to determine its exclusionary scope. Suitably elaborated, your interpretation might look like the following: The problem that the curfew was meant to solve is that people will give excessive weight to certain everyday reasons to go outside, like the pleasantness of taking a walk, and not enough weight to the dangers of the riot and the needs of the police to easily identify rioters. But fire should not be interpreted as falling within the curfew's scope. In going outside, I am not denying that the government is an authority, for I still should not take the pleasantness of going for a walk into account in my decision to go outside. And what if the curfew *did* take fire within its scope? That does not matter, for if it did, the curfew would not satisfy the NJT. My interpretation of the curfew should be guided by the goal of fostering its service as an authority.[17] Since an interpretation that includes fire within its scope is incompatible with that service, it should be rejected.

To repeat, if the curfew takes fire within its exclusionary scope, it should be ignored, for in that area, it is not authoritative. But does the curfew take fire within its scope? It seems clear that the law claims authority over you, independently of the capacity to justifiably coerce and punish.[18] And, we can assume, the authority that the law claims is that the NJT is satisfied with its directives. In other words, the law claims that you are more likely to abide by relevant reasons for action by following the curfew than by acting on your own judgment about what the balance of reasons recommends. Furthermore, it seems that the law claims the capacity for *absolute* authority, in the sense that it can, through its directives, preempt all reasons for action, including those in an emergency.[19] It is true that there might be *legal* limits on the reasons for action that the law can preempt. But these limits are self-imposed, in the sense that they can be legally changed. A constitutional limit, for example, can be changed through a constitutional amendment.

But does the law, in enacting the curfew without an exception for fires, *actually* claim to have preempted all reasons not subject to legal exceptions? Raz apparently thinks so.[20] For Raz, therefore, the fact that you may go outside means that the curfew does not have the authority it claims. To be sure, the curfew has some authority, because it still preempts certain reasons for action (such as the pleasantness of going for a walk). But because it also claims to have preempted your reasons to go outside due to fire, its claim is false.

Another possibility, emphasized by Timothy Endicott, is that the law—although claiming the capacity for unlimited authority—does not actually assert such authority in connection with every directive. It might instead claim that its directive has an unspecified exclusionary scope.[21] In entertaining this possibility, the goal is not to explain how the law's claim of authority is always true. Even the claim of unspecified exclusionary scope

[17] Endicott (n 5) 15-16.

[18] To say that law claims anything may sound odd. But the idea is that legal officials, when speaking and acting in their official capacity, suggest a claim of authority. ibid 17.

[19] Raz (n 6) 116; Raz (n 15) 77.

[20] Raz (n 6) 33.

[21] Endicott (n 5) 17-18.

can be false. The idea is that it is a more reasonable view of what the law actually, if sometimes falsely, claims.

One reason to treat the law as claiming only an unspecified exclusionary scope is the fact that when legal officials subsequently create an exception that accommodates a compelling reason for action—for example, when a court recognizes an exception to the curfew for fires—they take themselves to be only clarifying what the law previously demanded. Another reason is that if the law claimed that its directives preempted all reasons for action except for those that have been legally recognized through exceptions, its claim would not merely be possibly false, but manifestly false, making it hard to see how the law could even plausibly make such a claim.

That is not to say that a law's claim to preempt reasons for action that arise in emergencies is always false. It is often the case that people in emergencies would be more likely to abide by their reasons for action by acting on a directive than by acting on the balance of reasons as they perceive them. An example would be a law forbidding people from using their garden hoses to protect their homes during a wildfire, because that will lower water pressure, thereby impeding firefighters' efforts.

2.4 Meta-Authority

We seem to have the middle path that we wanted. In submitting to authority, subjects suspend their judgment (about preempted reasons for action), binding themselves to follow the authority's directive. But when the interpretation of the directive is triggered, they rely on their own judgment about the law's authority and its scope. The interpreted directive still has authority, for it preempts reasons for action that the subject judges are within the directive's scope.

But there is arguably more surrender of judgment to law's authority than this model suggests. We have understood the subject, in interpreting an authority's directive, as engaging in unrestricted reasoning about the authority's existence and scope. But it is possible that the law might have authority *over its own authority*. Assume that there is no fire, but the fact that you are so far from the riot triggers an interpretation of the curfew. Because you think that the NJT is satisfied only in the area closer to the riot, but not in your neighborhood, you go outside to take a walk. In setting up your judgment about whether the NJT was satisfied against the government's, you have arguably acted contrary to the government's meta-authority to settle whether it has authority. The law does not merely implicitly assert meta-authority when issuing directives—sometimes legal directives are explicitly meta-authoritative, for example, when a court asserts jurisdiction to determine its own jurisdiction.[22]

There is nothing in Raz's service conception of authority that excludes the possibility of meta-authority: subjects can be more likely to act on actual authority by following a meta-authority's directive than by acting on their own judgment about whether authority exists. The possibility of meta-authority is easiest to see when the meta-authority and the identified authority are different. Subject S may rationally act on A2's directive about whether A1 is an authority for S. I can go to an internist to find a good allergist. But there is no reason that S cannot rationally act on A1's directives concerning A1's authority for S.

Indeed, such meta-authority can be crucial for authority, because the existence and scope of authority can itself be a matter of intense disagreement. If people act on their own judgment about when authority exists, their disagreement will mean that they are less likely to benefit from the service that an authority could provide. This is particularly true when identifying an authority that solves coordination and prisoner's dilemma problems.

To see the importance of meta-authority, consider the problems faced by a theory of authority that arguably does not allow for it. An example is voluntarist (Lockean) theories, in which governmental authority is based on the consent of the governed and is limited by the scope of that consent.

Locke's theory is like Raz's in the sense that authority allows people to better abide by their preexisting reasons for action than they would by acting on their own judgment. To be sure, Locke has a narrower understanding of the reasons for action that authority serves, limiting them to natural rights. And he has a narrower understanding of the way that authority allows people to better satisfy those reasons for action. For Locke, the primary worry about reliance on one's own judgment is improper punishment of perceived violations of natural rights.[23] Raz understands authority to allow subjects to better abide by their preexisting reasons for action in a wider variety of ways. Most importantly, Raz sees us as having a reason to

[22] Eg Durfee v Duke, 375 US 106 (1963) (judgment of Nebraska state court that bottom land in the Missouri River was in Nebraska, giving it jurisdiction, was binding on other courts even if in error).

[23] John Locke, *The Second Treatise of Government* in *Political Writings of John Locke* (Penguin Pub 1993) § 7.

submit to authority independently of consent. For Locke, one can permissibly choose to reject the service that authority provides.

But an important similarity between Raz and Locke is that the existence of authority is an objective normative fact, about which people may disagree. This is so, even though the function of authority is, at least in part, to bring about agreement. The possibility of disagreement about authority, thereby undermining its beneficial effects, makes meta-authority useful. And yet, in Locke's theory, no meta-authority seems available.

Assume everyone in fact consented to governmental authority, and the government's actions are within the scope of their consent. It remains possible that some people will think that they did not consent or think that the government's action is not within the scope of their consent. If so, universal consent to governmental authority will leave people no better off than they were before. Instead of being faced with violent disagreement about natural rights, they are faced with violent disagreement about consent and its scope. Consent theories work only on the assumption that significant disagreement about consent does not materialize. One benefit of Raz's approach is that, unlike Locke's, the very problem described above can justify meta-authority—submission to a directive about the existence of authority and its scope. When faced with a candidate authority, the candidate's meta-authority can settle its status as an authority.

I have emphasized the role of the government's meta-authority in helping to solve problems of disagreement concerning authority. But there are many other reasons that meta-authority might exist. For example, the government may have greater expertise about whether the situation is one creating authority, such as whether the community faces a coordination or prisoner's dilemma problem. Or even if the government has no expertise on the matter, the fact that it has already expended time and effort making such a determination can render subjects' deliberation about the matter wasteful.

Meta-authority generates an even stronger pull toward acting on a candidate authority's directive. Let us return to the scenario where the fact that you are so far from the riot triggers your interpretation of the curfew. If the law has meta-authority, you will be more likely to correctly determine the law's authority by binding yourself to following the law's claim of authority than by relying on your own judgment concerning the matter. If you take advantage of this service, you will interpret the distance from the riot to be a consideration that is within the law's preemptive scope, even if you would not have so concluded if you had relied on your own judgment. Meta-authority can lead to an expansive reading of a directive's exclusionary scope. Or, when multiple candidate authorities exist, it can justify submission to the first that asserted meta-authority.

But the fact remains that, like submission to authority, submission to meta-authority is not absolute. Assume that you have submitted to the law's authority and its meta-authority. Despite your submission to the law's authority, the fire triggers your interpretation of the curfew. Unlike in the distance-from-the-riot example, fire might also trigger an interpretation of the scope of the law's meta-authority. And, in interpreting this scope, you should conclude that the law's meta-authority to settle its authority does not extend to fires.

2.5 Higher-Order Authority

So far, I have spoken of the law, in the abstract, as claiming authority over the citizenry when issuing directives. These claims, I have argued, can be false or partially false. Because of this possibility, the citizenry sometimes must interpret the preemptive scope of the law's directives in a manner that supports, as much as possible, the law's status as an authority.

But the law consists of directives issued by officials who are themselves in claimed authority relationships to one another. Assume a legislature passes a statute establishing an environmental agency, which will then create environmental regulations. The legislature claims authority over the agency's employment of its authority (and coercive force) over the citizenry.

The service conception can help us understand the nature of the legislature's claimed authority. Assume the officials in the agency have authority over the citizenry—they can enhance the citizenry's ability to abide by their reasons for action concerning the environment by issuing directives. They therefore have reasons to provide this service. But, in many areas, they can better satisfy these reasons by following an authority's directive than by acting on their own judgment. One important reason is that they need to coordinate their exercise of authority with one another and with other governmental officials seeking to assert authority.

The legislature can function as this authority about the exercise of authority, which we can call *higher-order authority*. Notice that higher-order authority is not meta-authority. Although the legislature, in claiming higher-order authority over the agency, likely also claims meta-authority concerning its higher-order authority, the two are different. It is possible that no one claims meta-authority concerning the legislature's higher-order authority, or the meta-authority might be claimed by a third entity.

I have described the legislature as *claiming* higher-order authority over the agency—allowing for the possibility that its claim is false, or partially false. Given that the legislature was responsible for the agency's creation and "delegated" its authority to the agency, one might argue that the legislature must have complete authority over the agency's exercise of authority, even if it remains a contingent matter whether the agency in fact has authority over the citizenry.

But one valuable consequence of the service conception is that it recommends abandoning this rigid notion of "delegation" of authority. It is true that the legislature is responsible for the agency's being in a position to have whatever authority it possesses concerning the citizenry. And it is highly likely that, in most cases, the legislature has higher-order authority: the agency's officials would better provide their service for the citizenry by following the legislature's directives than by coming to their own conclusion about how to exercise their authority. Furthermore, because of how important it is to the agency's authority that its officials avoid disagreement with one another (and with other governmental officials) concerning higher-order authority and its scope, it is also likely that the legislature possesses meta-authority concerning its higher-order authority. But this higher-order authority and meta-authority remain contingent facts that must, in principle, be justifiable to the agency's officials. The legislature's claims of authority concerning the agency are no more necessarily true than the agency's claims of authority concerning the citizenry. That means that sometimes the agency's officials should use their own judgment to interpret the preemptive scope of the legislature's directives, in a manner that fosters, as much as possible, its authority.

Granted, there are other reasons that the officials in the agency should follow the legislature's directives, independently of the legislature's higher-order authority and meta-authority. One is that these officials, unlike most citizens,[24] implicitly promised to act in conformity with the law (including the legislature's directives) and may have done so explicitly.[25] Also relevant are so-called rule-of-law values: that deviation from the legislature's directives can frustrate citizens' reliance interests, can undermine

[24] A John Simmons, *Moral Principles and Political Obligations* (Princeton Univ Press 1979).

[25] Raz (n 6) 239; Michael S. Moore, "Authority, Law, and Razian Reasons" (1989) 62 S Cal L Rev 827, 835-36.

citizens' tendency to conform to the law (and thus the effectiveness of legal institutions), and—insofar as different citizens would be treated differently by different agency officials—can treat citizens unfairly.[26]

Raz himself recognizes these extra considerations in favor of official conformity with law. But he appears to treat them as pro tanto reasons only,[27] which can be outweighed by other reasons for action. Thus, I understand Raz as allowing that officials may sometimes act contrary to the law. And I think he is right to do so.

2.6 The Constitution's Authority over Officials in an Emergency

The same points that I have made concerning the relationship between an agency's officials and a legislature apply to all the officials in a legal system, including the legislature and courts, in their relationship to a constitution. The existence and scope of the constitution's higher-order authority over those officials is a contingent matter. The fact that the constitution enabled the officials to have whatever authority over the citizenry they possess does not mean that the constitution (or its drafters and ratifiers) necessarily possess the higher-order authority that they claim. Whether there is such authority depends upon whether the NJT is satisfied—that is, whether officials are more likely to act according to their reasons for action (especially their reasons to provide the service of authority to the citizenry) by following the constitution's directives than by acting on those reasons directly. Officials might rightly conclude that the constitution's claim is false—even when one takes into account the constitution's meta-authority. And refusal to conform to the constitution can be appropriate even when one adds officials' other reasons for such conformity, such as consent and rule-of-law values. All these considerations simply make the appropriateness of such refusal rarer. In short, officials may legitimately find exceptions to a constitution in cases of emergency.

[26] Raz (n 6) 21-29; Moore (n 25) 835-36.

[27] Joseph Raz, "The Obligation to Obey: Revision and Tradition" (1985) 1 Notre Dame J L Ethics & Pub Pol'y 139. Indeed, he is skeptical about how much is added by consent over and above the NJT being satisfied. Joseph Raz, "Government by Consent" (1987) 29 Nomos 76.

For a possible example, consider the United States Supreme Court's recognition, in *New York v. Quarles*,[28] of a "public safety" exception to the requirement under the Fifth Amendment privilege against self-incrimination (first articulated in *Miranda v. Arizona*[29]) to inform suspects of their right to remain silent and their right to an attorney before custodial interrogation. In *Quarles*, an officer found a suspect in a supermarket who he believed had discarded a gun. Concerned about the danger of the discarded gun to bystanders, the officer asked the suspect where the gun was without reading him his rights.

The officer's argument for not acting on the Fifth Amendment and *Miranda* would go something like this: The Fifth Amendment and *Miranda* should be interpreted in a manner that fosters their authority. They have authority because I would be more likely to act on the proper balance between the goals of efficient criminal law enforcement and respect for suspects' autonomy by acting on these legal directives than by coming to my own conclusion about what the balance recommends. I am unreliable because I am likely to give excessive weight to efficient law enforcement. But, properly interpreted, the danger to bystanders of a discarded gun is not within the directives' preemptive scope. Furthermore, if the law claimed that such danger was within their scope, it would not be an authority in so doing. That does not mean that the directives do not have authority at all. They still preempt many reasons for action concerning whether I should inform suspects of their rights, such as whether refusing to inform them might reduce the incidence of crime. But they should not be interpreted to preempt immediate dangers to bystanders.

In coming to this conclusion, the officer also overrode any meta-authority that the Fifth Amendment and the Supreme Court possess. There are strong reasons for the officer, in determining how to act, not to disagree with other officials about the existence and scope of the Fifth Amendment and the Supreme Court's authority. But their meta-authority is also contingent and, in this case, insufficient. It is also true that, in coming to his conclusion, the officer overrode his implied (and maybe explicit) promise to obey the law, as well as rule-of-law values that recommend conformity with law. But these too are pro tanto reasons for action that can, and in this case should, be overcome.

[28] 467 US 649 (1984).

[29] Miranda v Arizona, 384 US 436 (1966).

The Supreme Court agreed with the officer's choice, ruling that protecting the public from an immediate threat outweighs the usual requirement of issuing *Miranda* warnings. In describing the officer as "justified in failing to make available to respondent the procedural safeguards associated with the privilege against compulsory self-incrimination since *Miranda*,"[30] the Court didn't make clear whether the officer was justified in refusing to conform to the law, because the law lacked authority in this area, or whether the law—claiming only an unspecified preemptive scope—did not purport to apply to the officer's scenario. Thus, they do not make it clear whether they were recognizing a preexisting exception to *Miranda* or creating an exception.

Either way, the Court was arguably engaging in much the same reasoning concerning the Fifth Amendment and their prior decision in *Miranda* that the officer was. The Court recognized that the higher-order authority and meta-authority of the Fifth Amendment and *Miranda* are contingent, and thus that they must be interpreted in a manner that fosters whatever service they can provide. There is no absolute reason for the Court to follow them, even when one adds the Justices' consent to obey the law and rule-of-law values. That does not mean that the Amendment and *Miranda* do not have authority, for they still preempt other reasons for action that the Justices would otherwise take into account in coming up with rules for custodial interrogation, such as the proper balance between the goals of efficient criminal law enforcement and respect for the suspects' autonomy. But, using their own judgment about the directives' preemptive scope, they concluded that the directives do not preempt the concerns about immediate public safety implicated in *Quarles*.

References

Bratman, M. *Intention, Plans and Practical Reason*. Univ of Chicago Press, 1987

Calhoun, C. "What Good is Commitment?" 119 *Ethics*, 2009, 613

Endicott, T. "Interpretation, Jurisdiction, and the Authority of Law" 6 *American Philosophical Association Newsletter*, 2007, 14

Hurd, H.M. "Challenging Authority" 100 *Yale Law Journal*, 1991, 1611

Ladenson, R. "In Defense of a Hobbesian Conception of Law" 9 *Philosophy & Public Affairs*, 1980, 134

Locke, J. *The Second Treatise of Government in Political Writings of John Locke*. Penguin Pub, 1993

[30] 467 US 655.

Moore, M.S. "Authority, Law, and Razian Reasons" 62 *Southern California Law Review*, 1989, 827
Raz, J. "Government by Consent" 29 *Nomos*, 1987, 76
Raz, J. "Reasons for Actions, Decisions, and Norms" 85 *Mind*, 1975, 481
Raz, J. "The Obligation to Obey: Revision and Tradition" 1 *Notre Dame Journal of Law, Ethics & Public Policy*, 1985, 139
Raz, J. "The Problem of Authority: Revisiting the Service Conception" 90 *Minnesota Law Review*, 2006, 1003
Raz, J. *Ethics in the Public Domain*. OUP, 1994
Raz, J. *Morality of Freedom*. OUP, 1986
Raz, J. *The Authority of Law*. OUP, 1979
Schmitt, C. *Political Theology: Four Chapters on the Concept of Sovereignty* (G Schwab tr). University of Chicago Press, 2005
Shapiro, S.J. "Authority" in Coleman, J., & Shapiro, S. (eds.) *The Oxford Handbook of Jurisprudence and Philosophy of Law*. OUP, 2002, 382–439
Shapiro, S.J. *Legality*. Harvard Univ Press, 2011
Simmons, A.J. *Moral Principles and Political Obligations*. Princeton Univ Press, 1979

U.S. Cases

Durfee v. Duke, 375 US 106 (1963)
Ex parte Milligan 71 US 2 (1866)
Miranda v. Arizona, 384 US 436 (1966)
New York v. Quarles, 467 US 649 (1984)

CHAPTER 3

The Concept of Constitutional Emergency: Towards an Argumentative Approach

Guillaume Tusseau

3.1 Presence of a Constitutional Emergency

"States of emergency," "states of necessity," "states of exception," "states of alarm," "states of siege," "states of prevention," "states of defense," "states of public calamity," whatever they are officially called in the respective legal system, whether they relate to public security, terrorism, war, disaster, aggression, public health, climate, economic collapse, political deadlock, or other factors, have become commonplace. Not only are they increasingly present in constitutional documents, but they are also increasingly used in practice.[1] While some

This chapter is produced as part and funded by the European Union-NextGenerationEU, through the National Recovery and Resilience Plan of the Republic of Bulgaria, project No bg-rrp-2.004-0008.

[1] David Dyzenhaus, *The Constitution of Law. Legality in a Time of Emergency* (Cambridge University Press, 2006); David Dyzenhaus, "States of Emergency", in Michel Rosenfeld, András Sajó (eds), *The Oxford Handbook of Comparative Constitutional Law*

M. Belov (ed.), *Constitutional Polycrisis and Emergency Constitutionalism*, Federalism and Internal Conflicts,
https://doi.org/10.1007/978-3-032-06516-2_3

states have recourse to pre-existing regimes in such situations, others have to devise new ones once the problem has arisen. For example, in 2015, France activated in the face of terrorism a pre-existing "état d'urgence" , which stemmed from a statute dating back to the Algerian war.[2] Conversely, in the face of the COVID-19 pandemic, France had to create a fully-fledged new "state of public health emergency".[3] The political debates triggered by the activation of these two regimes gave rise to complex and heated discussions reminiscent of very classical analyses.[4] Indeed, from an institutional design point of view, most of what needs to be said was said long ago by Machiavelli. In his 1531 *Discourses on Livy*, he wrote:

> [A]mong the other Roman orders, [dictatorship] deserves to be considered and numbered among those that were the cause of the greatness of so great an empire, for without such an order, cities escape from extraordinary accidents with difficulty. [...] For when a like mode is lacking in a republic, it is necessary either that it be ruined by observing the orders or that it break them so as not to be ruined. In a republic, one would not wish anything ever to happen that has to be governed with extraordinary modes. For although the extraordinary mode may do good then, nonetheless the example does ill; for if one sets up a habit of breaking the orders

(Oxford University Press, 2012), 442–462; Christian Bjørnskov, Stefan Voigt, "The Architecture of Emergency Constitutions" (2018) 16 *International Journal of Constitutional Law* 101–127, 101; Oren Gross, "Constitutions and Emergency Regimes", in Tom Ginsburg, Rosalind Dixon (eds), *Comparative Constitutional Law* (Edward Elgar, 2011) 334–355; Mary Luz Tobón, David Mendieta, Antonio Gasparetto, "Los modelos constitucionales de los estados de excepción en época de crisis global", (2021) 3 *Revista jurídica Unicuritiba*, 1–35.

[2] Loi n° 55-385 du 3 avril 1955 relative à l'état d'urgence.

[3] Loi n° 2020-290 du 23 mars 2020 d'urgence pour faire face à l'épidémie de COVID-19.

[4] See e.g. Stéphanie Hennette-Vauchez (dir.), *Ce qui reste(ra) toujours de l'urgence* (Institut universitaire Varenne, 2018); AA. VV., "L'état d'exception, nouveau régime de droit commun des droits et libertés? Du terrorisme à l'urgence sanitaire. XXXVIe Table ronde internationale du 11 septembre 2020", *Annuaire international de justice constitutionnelle*, n° 36, 2020; Stéphanie Hennette Vauchez, *La démocratie en état d'urgence. Quand l'exception devient permanente* (Le Seuil, 2022); Olivier Beaud, Cécile Guérin-Bargues, Samy Benzina, *L'état d'urgence sécuritaire et sanitaire. Une étude constitutionnelle, historique et critique*, (3rd ed, Dalloz, 2023).

for the sake of good, then later, under that coloring, they are broken for ill.[5]

Emergencies do indeed challenge the normal constitutional order. If nothing is provided for, the public authorities will almost certainly remain trapped in legal constraints that prevent them from facing the situation, or they will take it upon themselves to ignore all constitutional rules in order to meet the circumstances. In either case, constitutional law and the fundamental values it represents are threatened. The establishment of constitutional norms to govern such situations may therefore appear to be a prudent course of action. But is it possible to satisfactorily regulate what is sudden, confusing and unpredictable? The conditions attached to the exercise of special powers, and the scope of those powers, may seem counterproductive in an emergency, preventing an appropriate response. From another point of view, will the creation of such devices not encourage the misuse of the state of emergency as a pretext to wage an illegal political battle or to introduce permanent changes in the law without respecting legal forms?[6] As Guy Debord put it: "The instrument that has been developed must be used, and its use will reinforce the very conditions that favored its use. In this way, emergency procedures become permanent procedures".[7] Once again, the values of the legal order could be threatened.[8]

There is thus a dilemma, symptomatic of "risk constitutionalism",[9] between the risk of the government having too much power and the risk of it having too little.[10] It is rooted in the curious self-reflexive paradox

[5] Niccolo Machiavelli, *Discourses on Livy* (Harvey C. Mansfield, Nathan Tarcov tr, The University of Chicago Press, 1998), p. 139 (I, 34).

[6] Guy Braibant, "L'Etat face aux crises" (1979) 10 *Pouvoirs*, 5–9; François Burdeau, Maurice Quesnet, "De l'inefficacité des pouvoirs de crise en France de la Révolution à Vichy" (1979) 10 *Pouvoirs*, 11–20; Linda Camp Keith, Steven C. Poe, "Are Constitutional State of Emergency Clauses Effective? An Empirical Exploration" (2004) 26 *Human Rights Quarterly* 1071–1097; Michael Freeman, *Freedom or Security. The Consequences for Democracies Using Emergency Powers to Fight Terror* (Praeger, 2003).

[7] Guy Debord, *Commentaires sur la société du spectacle* (Gallimard, 1992) 107.

[8] Giuseppe Marazzita, *L'emergenza costituzionale* (A. Giuffrè, 2003) 41.

[9] See Adrian Vermeule, *The Constitution of Risk* (Cambridge University Press, 2013).

[10] Frederick Schauer, "The Constitution of Fear", (1995) 12 *Constitutional Commentary* 203–206, 205; Oren Gross, "Emergency's Challenges", in Richard Albert, Yaniv Roznai (eds), *Constitutionalism under Extreme Conditions: Law, Emergency, Exception* (Springer, 2020) 428–430.

that, in order to deal with an emergency that threatens the fundamental values of the legal order, it may be necessary to accept that these values are temporarily mistreated precisely so that they can be restored in the longer term.[11]

Emergencies have multiple disruptive effects on the most profound aspects of constitutional law. According to Article 16 of the Declaration of the Rights of Man and of the Citizen, which provides a canonical definition of a constitution, "any society which does not provide for the guarantee of rights or defines the separation of powers has no constitution". Both the separation of powers and fundamental rights are affected by emergency situations.[12] In terms of horizontal separation of powers, the army may be entitled to make decisions that are normally made by civilian authorities. The executive is often given more power than usual and can intervene in areas that are traditionally the province of the legislature, while not being subject to the usual checks and balances of the judiciary.[13] Similarly, national governments are allowed to ignore the traditional vertical separation of powers and take decisions that affect the normally reserved powers of local governments.[14] With regard to fundamental rights, normally prohibited restrictions or suspensions become acceptable in emergency situations due to a revised application of the proportionality test.[15] The main

[11] On that issue, see Clinton L. Rossiter, *Constitutional Dictatorship. Crisis Government in the Modern Democracies* (Princeton University Press, 1948); Naomi Claire Lazar, *States of Emergency in Liberal Democracies* (Cambridge University Press, 2009), esp. 136–162; Christian Bjørnskov, Stefan Voigt, "The Architecture of Emergency Constitutions" (2018) 16 *International Journal of Constitutional Law* 101–127, 103. On the tensions between relaxing constitutional values and strict enforcement of the constitution in times of emergency, see Eric A. Posner, Adrian Vermeule, "Accommodating Emergencies" (2003) 56 *Stanford Law Review* 605–644. On the distinction of emergencies in contexts in which legality is to be preserved and those in which is has to be established, see Victor V. Ramraj, "The Emergency Powers Paradox", in Victor V. Ramraj, Arun K. Thiruvengadam (eds) *Emergency Powers in Asia. Exploring the Limits of Legality* (Cambridge University Press, 2010) 21–55.

[12] See e.g. Elliot Bulmer, *Emergency Powers. International IDEA Constitution-Building Primer 18* (International IDEA, 2018) 20–26.

[13] See e.g. Elena Griglio, "Parliamentary Oversight Under the COVID-19 Emergency: Striving Against Executive Dominance" (2020) 8 *The Theory and Practice of Legislation* 49–70; Jan Petrov, "The COVID-19 Emergency in the Age of Executive Aggrandizement: What Role for Legislative and Judicial Checks?" (2020) 8 *The Theory and Practice of Legislation* 71–92.

[14] Guillaume Tusseau, *Les normes d'habilitation* (Dalloz, 2006) 584–591.

[15] See e.g. Ladislav Vyhnánek, Anna Blechová, Michael Bátrla, Jakub Míšek, Tereza Novotná, Amnon Reichman and Jakub Harašta, "The Dynamics of Proportionality:

pillars of the grammar of contemporary constitutionalism are thus affected by emergency situations. For this reason, some authors suggest identifying full-fledged "emergency constitutions" within constitutions, which make room for an *ad hoc* order of powers and regime for fundamental rights in extraordinary circumstances.[16]

One of the issues that precedes the choices that actors make[17] and the normative theses that theorists[18] develop regarding (a) the establishment of an emergency regime and (b) the precise content of that regime is conceptual, not technical or political. Before these two issues can be

Constitutional Courts and the Review of COVID-19 Regulations" (2024) 25 *German Law Journal* 386–406; Ioannis Michalis, "Le contrôle de proportionnalité pendant les crises dans les jurisprudences française et allemande", in Xavier Dupré de Boulois, Xavier Philippe (dir.), *Gouverner et juger en période de crise* (Mare & Martin, 2023) 321–333.

[16] Bruce Ackerman, "The Emergency Constitution", (2004) 113 *The Yale Law Journal* 1029–1091; Oren Gross, "Providing for the Unexpected: Constitutional Emergency Provisions" (2003) 33 *Israel Yearbook on Human Rights* 13–43; Christian Bjørnskov, Stefan Voigt, "The Architecture of Emergency Constitutions" (2018) 16 *International Journal of Constitutional Law* 101–127; Christian Bjørnskov, Stefan Voigt, "Why do Governments Call a State of Emergency? On the Determinants of Using Emergency Constitutions" (2018) 54 *European Journal of Political Economy* 110–123; Andrés Cervantes, Mario Matarrita, Sofía Reca, "Los estados de excepción en tiempos de pandemia: un studio comparado en América Latina" (2020) 20 *Cuadernos Manuel Giménez Abad* 179–206.

[17] For an overview of the dilemmas of constitutional designers, see e.g. Elliot Bulmer, *Emergency Powers. International IDEA Constitution-Building Primer 18* (International IDEA, 2018); Anna Jonsson Cornell, Janne Salminen, "Emergency Laws in Comparative Constitutional Law—The Case of Sweden and Finland" (2018) 19 *German Law Journal* 219–250.

[18] For an overview, see e.g. Oren Gross, Fionnuala Ni Aolain, *Law in Times of Crisis: Emergency Powers in Theory and Practice* (Cambridge University Press, 2006); John Ferejohn, Pasquale Pasquino, "Emergency Powers", in John S. Dryzek, Bonnie Honig Anne Phillips (eds), *Oxford Handbook of Political Theory* (Oxford University Press, 2009) 333–348; Naomi Claire Lazar, *States of Emergency in Liberal Democracies* (Cambridge University Press, 2009); Victor V. Ramraj, Arun K. Thiruvengadam (eds) *Emergency Powers in Asia. Exploring the Limits of Legality* (Cambridge University Press, 2010); David Dyzenhaus, "The State of Emergency in Legal Theory", in Victor V. Ramraj, M. Hor, Kent Roach (eds), *Global Anti-Terrorism Law and Policy* (Cambridge University Press, 2005) 65–89; Victor V. Ramraj, "Emergency Powers and Constitutional Theory" (2011) 41 *Hong Kong Law Journal* 481–515; Sébastien Lafrance, Shruti Bedi, Hanna de Gregorio Leão, "Constitutional Theories of Emergency Powers and Their Limits: Perspectives From Vietnam, India and Canada" (2021) 4 *Vietnamese Journal of Legal Sciences* 1–33; Victor V. Ramraj, "The Constitutional Politics of Emergency Powers", in Mark Tushnet, Dimitry Kochenov (eds) *Research Handbook on the Politics of Constitutional Law* (Routledge, 2023) 163–175; A leading reference in the current debate is Giorgio Agamben, *State of Exception* (tr Kevin Attell, The University of Chicago Press, 2005).

discussed, the preliminary question of isolating a proper concept of constitutional emergency must be addressed. According to Pierre-Laurent Frier, for example, research on the subject is unsatisfactory: "The problem is linked to the concept itself. It is necessary to reflect on its content, on its definition, on the elements of which it is composed, in order to define it as well as possible, to make it clearer by comparing it and, if necessary, contrasting it with other related concepts. Such research seeks to provide the necessary clarification by rejecting some escape routes in order to avoid hiding behind the vague and indefinable character of 'emergency.'"[19]

This chapter will examine, in turn, two main ways of approaching this issue. A traditional approach in legal practice and scholarship takes a Platonist orientation. It seeks to identify the unique and true definition of an emergency. This strategy is based on questionable assumptions and leads to an impasse. As a close examination of this legal discourse on constitutional powers reveals, either there is no such thing as "real" emergency, or there is no way of knowing it with certainty. This chapter offers an alternative, argumentative strategy. Based on Gottlob Frege's distinction between sense and reference, it argues that while what the term "emergency" precisely designates is relatively indifferent, in practice, only the sense of the term, that is, its connotation as a kind of "green light" for certain actions and decisions, is relevant. Consequently, a pragmatic examination of what legal actors "make" of emergency must highlight the respective strengths and weaknesses of the constitutional emergency argument.

3.2 A Platonist Approach to Constitutional Emergency

Writers who have taken an interest in constitutional emergency in law have tended to search for its unique and true definition. This gives this approach an undeniable tendency towards Platonism.

3.2.1 Four Versions of a Similar Paradigm

In an article on emergency in French administrative law, one author asked what seemed to be a rather commonsense question: "How can [legal actors] claim an emergency if it does not exist?"[20] Ontological realism

[19] Pierre-Laurent Frier, *L'urgence* (LGDJ, 1987) 6.

[20] See e.g. Guillaume Pambou-Tchivounda, "Recherche sur l'urgence en droit administratif français" (1983) *Revue du droit public* 81–135, 84.

assumes that there is an objectively knowable reality somewhere, which would be the thing "emergency" to which the word "emergency" would refer. Such a perspective manifests itself in a number of ways.

First, some authors admit from the outset that they are looking for the essence or nature of the emergency. Guillaume Pambou-Tchivounda, for example, sought to "give a faithful account of the nature of emergency,"[21] of the "true measure of the legal nature of emergency,"[22] of the "essence"[23] of emergency. After him, Frier wanted to "discover the real reason, the real end of the law of exception,"[24] which should be "clearly defined and distinguished from other concepts with which it has often been confused."[25] Giuseppe Marazzita also wanted to discover a single concept of emergency, drawing on examples from the constitutional history of Western Europe.[26]

Secondly, other authors try to identify the elements of an emergency in the same way as one would try to isolate the constituent elements of a complex chemical substance. According to Christian Gabolde,

> There is no pure notion of emergency in the decisions of administrative jurisprudence. [...] Although it is true that the notion of emergency is often combined with a similar or close notion (such as that of necessity and that of legality in wartime), it has its own life, its own causes, its own modalities and even its own distortions. To use a metaphor, the concept of emergency is like a metal that would only exist in a pure state in combination with another body. As a metal, it would still have its own qualities and characteristics, which would only be revealed through analysis.[27]

Such ideas are based on the belief in the existence of a definite object whose properties can be detected. To illustrate this belief, Anne Vander

[21] Guillaume Pambou-Tchivounda, "Recherche sur l'urgence en droit administratif français" (1983) *Revue du droit public* 81–135, 82.

[22] Guillaume Pambou-Tchivounda, "Recherche sur l'urgence en droit administratif français" (1983) *Revue du droit public* 81–135, 93.

[23] Guillaume Pambou-Tchivounda, "Recherche sur l'urgence en droit administratif français" (1983) *Revue du droit public* 81–135, 84, 132

[24] Pierre-Laurent Frier, *L'urgence* (LGDJ, 1987) 503.

[25] Pierre-Laurent Frier, *L'urgence* (LGDJ, 1987) 176.

[26] Giuseppe Marazzita, *L'emergenza costituzionale* (A. Giuffrè, 2003) 11.

[27] Christian Gabolde, *Essai sur la notion d'urgence en droit administrative* (University of Paris, 1951) 63.

Stichele isolated two components of emergency in the Belgian context. One is the threat of danger or serious harm.[28] The other is the need to challenge an existing legal rule in order to confront such a problem. Referring to the work of Philippe Jestaz,[29] Pambou-Tchivounda agreed with this analysis. Emergency is first of all a

> serious threat to an interest which must be safeguarded by appropriate intervention [...]. The second element of emergency is the nature of the means that must be used to put an end not only to the imminence of the danger but also to the danger itself. The essential quality of these means is, first of all, speed and efficiency. It must be proportionate to the end which justifies it.[30]

Thirdly, another category of authors attempts to give a definition *per genus proximum et differentiam specificam* of emergency. They draw subtle distinctions between the emergency and other phenomena, such as exceptional circumstances, constitutional crises, the state of necessity, the state of war, *force majeure*, etc., and study the shifts that blur their respective places.[31]

Fourthly, a final set of assertions, emanating from scholars or from the legal actors themselves, consists in declaring that "an emergency is such and such a thing," that "there is indeed an emergency here," but that, on the contrary, "there is no emergency in such and such situations." For example, Article 18(1) of the Constitution of Belize provides that

> In this Part, 'period of public emergency' means any period during which-
> a. Belize is engaged in any war; or
> b. There is in force a proclamation by the Governor-General declaring that a state of public emergency exists; or
> c. there is in force a resolution of the National Assembly declaring that democratic institutions in Belize are threatened by subversion.

[28] Anne Vander Stichele, *La notion d'urgence en droit public* (Bruylant, 1986) 124.

[29] Philippe Jestaz, *L'urgence et les principes classiques du droit civil* (LGDJ, 1968).

[30] Guillaume Pambou-Tchivounda, "Recherche sur l'urgence en droit administratif français" (1983) *Revue du droit public* 81–135, 94–95

[31] See Michel Vasseur, "Urgence et droit civil" (1954) *Revue trimestrielle de droit civil* 403–437, 407; Pierre-Laurent Frier, *L'urgence* (LGDJ, 1987) 123–177; Giuseppe Marazzita, *L'emergenza costituzionale* (A. Giuffrè, 2003).

Similarly, to justify his declaration of a "public emergency in economic, financial, fiscal, administrative, social security, tariff, health and social matters until 31 December 2025,"[32] the Argentine President's Decree 70/2023 reads:

> No federal government has received a worse institutional, economic and social inheritance than that received by the current administration, making it essential to adopt measures to overcome the emergency situation created by the exceptional economic and social conditions that the Nation is suffering, especially as a result of a series of interventionist decisions. [...] That due to the irresponsible actions of the outgoing government, the ARGENTINE REPUBLIC is facing an emergency never before seen in the country's history with the distinct possibility of inflation accelerating to 15,000% per year. [...] That for all the above reasons, there is no doubt that the situation in Argentina is extremely critical and unprecedented in our history.

These statements, which amount to ostensive definitions,[33] implicitly claim that it is possible to identify the presence or absence of an emergency precisely and indisputably. As in the previous three strategies, it is assumed that the thing "emergency" is objectively identifiable. A definition that captures its profound nature, without ambiguity or uncertainty, makes it possible to know it and to prohibit abusive invocations. Such an approach, based on a form of ontological realism, is open to a number of criticisms.

3.2.2 *Critical Assessment*

When adopted by legal scholars, ontological realism is based on an illusion that leads to a methodological error. The illusion is that the words contained in legal discourses necessarily refer to things that exist outside those discourses. The fact that the word "emergency" appears in legal discourses implicitly suggests that this word refers to a tangible phenomenon

[32] Decreto 70/2023, Bases para la reconstrucción de la economía argentina, DNU-2023-70-APN-PTE, Article 1. See generally Ricardo Haro, "Los decretos de necesidad y urgencia en la doctrina judicial de la Corte suprema de justicia de Argentina" (2001) 7 *Ius & Praxis* 61-72; Darío Germán Spada, "Decretos de necesidad y urgencia: naturaleza—reseña de su utilización—evolución jurisprudencial" (2010) 2 *Administración y derecho. Revista de doctrina y jurisprudencia* 2-22.

[33] Ludwig Wittgenstein, *Philosophische Untersuchungen / Philosophical Investigations* (tr G.E.M. Anscombe, P.M.S. Hacker, Joachim Schulte, 4th ed., Wiley-Blackwell, 2009).

or reality.[34] The resulting methodological error is to understand these objects by means of instruments that are not relevant. It is therefore radically impossible to construct a real definition of constitutional emergency. It is not an empirical object like stones and water. It is not empirically perceptible or comprehensible, so the Aristotelian method of definition is not appropriate. It can, of course, be conceived as a purely "ideal reality". But such spheres of ideality, if they exist, can hardly be known with certainty by objective methods. Finally, despite the variety of definitions presented by scholars as the only correct one, each is as valuable as any other. This follows from the fact that no one has an objective and neutral criterion of validation. Such a criterion would itself result from a definition, which would be the only true one if we had an objective criterion to assess it, determined by a real definition, which would only be true if we had an objective criterion, and so on. Such an infinite regression cannot be accepted. It is therefore advisable to reject the Platonist orientation and to admit that there is no essence of emergency and, consequently, no definition that is true, authentic, unique or valid everywhere.

Legal scholars hardly ignore these difficulties. The predominance of a realistic approach to the definition of emergency is less the result of a methodological error than of a political choice. What is at stake for jurists is the claim to be able to identify emergency situations *hic et nunc* and to distinguish them rigorously and objectively from other situations, in line with what legal actors say. In a text written by Frier, it is noted that "the jurisprudence has often recognized, under the pretext of force majeure, the legality of an action that was *in reality* based on an emergency."[35] Later, he wrote that "the issue is more delicate when, under the pretext of other concepts or by using other words, regulations and/or judges *in reality* make the emergency the motive for resorting to exceptional rules".[36] Thus, some authors denounce "mistakes" or "emergency frauds"[37] when an authority abuses its power. But since the reality of the emergency does

[34] On such a tendency, see Jeremy Bentham, *De l'ontologie et autres textes sur les fictions* (ed Philip Schofield, tr Jean-Pierre Cléro, Christian Laval, Seuil, 1997) 87; Ludwig Wittgenstein, *Dictées : à Friedrich Waismann et pour Moritz Schlick, années 1930* (tr and ed. Antonia Soulez, pres. Gordon Baker, postf. Brian McGuinness, Librairie philosophique J. Vrin, 2015) 304, 307-308.

[35] Pierre-Laurent Frier, *L'urgence* (LGDJ, 1987) 123, italics supplied.

[36] Ibid. 182, italics supplied.

[37] Giuseppe Marazzita, *L'emergenza costituzionale* (A. Giuffrè, 2003) 83; Achille Mestre, *Le Conseil d'Etat, protecteur des prérogatives de l'administration* (LGDJ, 1974) 224.

not exist (or at least cannot be known with certainty), what lawyers are doing is not questioning a cognitive error, but criticizing a decision or a choice made by an authority in the name of other decisions, other choices, in other words, in the name of other preferences. From a methodological point of view, it is an illegitimate attempt to influence the production of law in the name of science.

When lawmakers, as opposed to legal scholars, resort to conceptual realism, their aim is to make other actors understand that there is a certain notion of emergency and that, according to this notion, they are objectively entitled to produce certain norms or to control the validity of these norms. Such a justification tends to hide the exercise of the power inherent in qualifying a situation or event as an emergency. In parliament, for example, it is in the interest of the representatives to believe, or at least to pretend to believe, that there is a reality of emergency, in order to criticize the government and pretend that it is wrong and maneuvering when it invokes an emergency to facilitate the passage of a law. What is at stake here is the assertion that there is objectively no emergency in the light of the information resulting from an honest assessment. It is also not in the government's interest to admit that the reference to an emergency is of an indeterminate nature. On the one hand, they could be in opposition later and use the same arguments. On the other hand, they can turn the argument around and claim that, contrary to what the opposition is saying, there is an objective emergency if the situation is looked at without partisan blinkers. Although it may be in the strategic interest of legal actors to demonstrate conceptual realism, this is not always the case for legal scholars. Either their ontological realism is genuine, in which case they may appear naive and take the discourse of legal actors at face value, thus revealing themselves to be dupes of the ideologies and the power of which they are an expression; or their ontological realism is also strategic, in which case legal scholars abandon the idea of conforming to a positivist meta-science, that is, of being content to describe their object rather than trying to influence it.

The various definitions of emergency that appear in legal practice and in legal scholarship lead to one of two conclusions. Either there is no real emergency, or there is no way of knowing with certainty. It is therefore impossible to verify the truth of a claim invoking an emergency. Consequently, it must be banned from scientific discourse or, more simply, from any clear statement that implies the possibility of being objectively tested by one's interlocutor.

For Naomi Lazar, “Emergency is among those words that Wittgenstein has taught us to think of as naming not one but a family of concepts, which resemble each other in much the manner that families do.”[38] Similarly, Oren Gross argues that “bright-line distinctions between normalcy and emergency are frequently untenable”[39] and that “[t]he very concept of ‘emergency’ is an elastic one.”[40] Given the difficulty of producing a true definition that, by means of conditions that are at once individually necessary and collectively sufficient, would establish the characteristics likely to condense the essence of constitutional emergency, alternative strategies must be imagined. One of them, based on an agnostic approach to the existence of a single true concept of emergency, is based on the assertion that “emergency is an argument, not a reality”.[41]

3.3 An Argumentative Approach to Constitutional Emergency

Against the kind of difficulty one faces in trying to define a legal concept, the Danish legal realist Alf Ross asserted that

> Questions of the type ‘what is ...?’ should be avoided in logical analysis because they smell of essentialism. You may ask what a certain substance, for instance ‘water’, or ‘powder’, is when it is manifest what you mean (designate) by the term ‘water’ or ‘powder’. The question is inappropriate when the principal problem is to determine the meaning with which the word is

[38] Naomi Claire Lazar, *States of Emergency in Liberal Democracies* (Cambridge University Press, 2009) 7.

[39] Oren Gross, “Emergency’s Challenges”, in Richard Albert, Yaniv Roznai (eds), *Constitutionalism under Extreme Conditions: Law, Emergency, Exception* (Springer, 2020) 428-430, 428; Oren Gross, “Constitutions and Emergency Regimes”, in Tom Ginsburg, Rosalind Dixon (eds), *Comparative Constitutional Law* (Edward Elgar, 2011) 334-355, 349.

[40] Oren Gross, “Emergency’s Challenges”, in Richard Albert, Yaniv Roznai (eds), *Constitutionalism under Extreme Conditions: Law, Emergency, Exception* (Springer, 2020) 428-430, 429. See also Karin Loevy, *Emergencies in Public Law: The Legal Politics of Containment* (Cambridge University Press, 2016) 8–9, 57–121.

[41] Eleonora Bottini, “Comparer les états d’urgence en Europe”, in Stéphanie Hennette-Vauchez (dir.), *Ce qui reste(ra) toujours de l’urgence* (Institut universitaire Varenne, 2018), 51–70, 53.

actually used, or the meaning which logically could be ascribed to it but only diffusesly appears in common use.[42]

While thinking in this way, there is no point in trying to reveal the hidden essence of the emergency. Therefore, it is possible to focus on a linguistic analysis of the issue by means of a two-step approach. The first step is to examine the structure of the "concept(s)" of constitutional emergency used by legal actors. The second step is based on the idea, inherited in particular from Ludwig Wittgenstein, that the meaning of words depends essentially on the way in which they are used.[43] This leads to an examination of the argumentative use of emergency by legal actors.

3.3.1 *The Concept of Emergency*

A relatively unsophisticated use of Gottlob Frege's distinction between sense and reference[44] will help to clarify the concept of emergency. The "extension," "denotation," or "reference" of a word is the group of objects which it designates. The "intension", "connotation," or "sense" of that word determines the principle by which those objects are selected. Two words can have the same denotation, that is, they can refer to the same object. The expression "the most beautiful person in the world" and the expression "the smartest person in the world" may refer to the same individual. But the criteria for selecting this unique object are not the same: the two expressions do not have the same connotation. Denotation is the most objective and neutral meaning of a word. Connotation refers to the more numerous and subjective meanings. Denotation corresponds to the question "What do you see in this picture?" and connotation to the question "What does this picture make you think of?" For example, the word "hospital" denotes an institution where patients are treated for a period of time. For some people, it has a positive connotation (caring staff, good quality treatment, etc.), whereas for others, it has a negative connotation (endless waiting, hospital-acquired disease, etc.). It implies a cultural or social value, a context, an emotional or ideological charge. It is possible to apply this distinction to the concept of emergency in order to successively study its denotation and connotation.

[42] Alf Ross, "Book Review: Kelsen, Hans, *What is Justice? Justice, Law and Politics in the Mirror of Science. Collected Essays*", (1957) 45 *California Law Review* 564-570, 565.

[43] Ludwig Wittgenstein, *Philosophische Untersuchungen / Philosophical Investigations* (tr G.E.M. Anscombe, P.M.S. Hacker, Joachim Schulte, 4th ed., Wiley-Blackwell, 2009).

[44] Gottlob Frege, "Sense and Reference" (1948) 57 *The Philosophical Review* 209-230.

3.3.1.1 Denotation of the Concept of Emergency

The study of the denotation of the word "emergency," i.e., the situations it is used to designate, makes it possible to perceive the variety of situations described as "urgent" by legal actors.[45] These situations include natural events (earthquakes, volcanic eruptions, fires, floods, epidemics, environmental disasters, etc.),[46] political events (changes in the institutional order, federal intervention, state of siege, civil war, terrorism, etc.) or economic events (inflation, recession, etc.).[47] As stated in a case concerning Malaysia, "the natural meaning of the word [emergency] itself is capable of covering a very wide range of situations and occurrences, including events as diverse as wars, famines, earthquakes, floods, epidemics and the collapse of civil government."[48] It is almost impossible to know beforehand which situations can be called urgent *hic et nunc*. There is a great deal of disorder, and no clear link can be established between a particular type of event and the fact that it is called an emergency.

At a deeper level, the fact that it is impossible to anticipate the designation of an emergency may be one of the fundamental legal functions of this word. When reference is made to an emergency in a legal text, the intention is to give the authorities the means to deal with the situation. Constituents often insist that it is better not to constrain the constituted

[45] Clinton L. Rossiter, *Constitutional Dictatorship. Crisis Government in the Modern Democracies* (Princeton University Press, 1948) 6; Giuseppe Marazzita, *L'emergenza costituzionale* (A. Giuffrè, 2003) 162-163, 343; Oren Gross, "Providing for the Unexpected: Constitutional Emergency Provisions" (2003) 33 *Israel Yearbook on Human Rights* 13–43, 24; David Bonner, *Emergency Powers in Peacetime* (Sweet & Maxwell, 1985) 3–5; Naomi Claire Lazar, *States of Emergency in Liberal Democracies* (Cambridge University Press, 2009) 8; Kent Roach, "Ordinary Law for Emergencies and Democratic Derogations From Rights", in Victor V. Ramraj (ed), *Emergencies and the Limits of Legality* (Cambridge University Press, 2008) 229–257.

[46] See e.g. Alan Greene, *Emergency Powers in a Time of Pandemic* (Bristol University Press, 2020); Andrés Cervantes, Mario Matarrita, Sofía Reca, "Los estados de excepción en tiempos de pandemia: un studio comparado en América Latina" (2020) 20 *Cuadernos Manuel Giménez Abad* 179-206; Tom Ginsburg, Mila Versteeg, "The Bound Executive: Emergency Powers During the Pandemic" (2021) 19 *International Journal of Constitutional Law* 1498-1535; Nuria González Martín (ed), *COVID-19 y su circunstancia. Una visión jurídica plural de la pandemia*, 5 Vol. (Instituto de estudios constitucionales del Estado de Querétaro, 2021); Pablo Riberi (ed), *Pandemocracy in Latin America. Revisiting the Political and Constitutional Dimension of the Pandemic* (Hart, 2024).

[47] See e.g. Tom Ginsburg, Mark D. Rosen, Georg Vanberg (eds), *Constitutions in Times of Financial Crisis* (Cambridge University Press, 2019).

[48] *Ningkan v. Government of Malaysia* [1970] AC 379, 390.

authorities too much, because it is difficult to anticipate the circumstances that may make it necessary to depart from the normal rules. For this reason, some members of constituent assemblies even believe that no text should be written on the subject, since any statement could render the authorities powerless. According to Alexander Hamilton, for example,

> It is impossible to foresee or to define the extent and variety of national exigencies, and the correspondent extent and variety of the means which may be necessary to satisfy them. The circumstances that endanger the safety of nations are infinite, and for this reason, no constitutional shackles can wisely be imposed on the power to which the care of it is committed.[49]

Thus, when an emergency is provided for in a text, it is defined vaguely and sometimes not at all. The constitutional provisions that attempt to anticipate such situations are often limited to defining a procedure for counterattack, but not the counterattack itself.[50] Consequently, the vaguer the term "emergency" is left, the more it plays the role it is given in legal discourses.

This allows us to propose a rather radical thesis. The concept of emergency, as it is present in legal discourses, may have no denotation at all, or a denotation that is ultimately not so important. In such a case, the word is used without the intention of referring to any particular empirical fact. All that matters is how the word "sounds" to (the ears of) legal actors. For example, when the government declares an emergency under Article 61 of the French Constitution in order to speed up the examination of a bill by the Constitutional Council, the content of the emergency in question is irrelevant. The mere use of the word is enough to modify the applicable constitutional norms. The word "emergency" can fulfil the functions it is expected to fulfil, irrespective of its ability to refer to something specific. As the Judicial Committee of the Privy Council has said in a particularly lucid way in a case regarding India, "a state of emergency is something that does not permit of any exact definition. It connotes a state of matters calling for drastic action."[51]

[49] *The Federalist*, n° 23.

[50] Pierre-Laurent Frier, *L'urgence* (LGDJ, 1987) 280; Giuseppe Marazzita, *L'emergenza costituzionale* (A. Giuffrè, 2003) 207–208.

[51] *Bhagat Singh & Others v. The King Emperor* AIR [1931] PC 111. See also Oren Gross, "Emergency's Challenges", in Richard Albert, Yaniv Roznai (eds), *Constitutionalism under Extreme Conditions: Law, Emergency, Exception* (Springer, 2020) 428-430, 428; Oren Gross, "Constitutions and Emergency Regimes", in Tom Ginsburg, Rosalind Dixon (eds), *Comparative Constitutional Law* (Edward Elgar, 2011) 334-355, 349.

3.3.1.2 Connotation of the Concept of Emergency

Karin Loevy proposed a fourfold understanding of what she calls the "emergency paradigm": "particularly defined conditions (feature number 1), allow for authorized deviations from norms (feature number 2); of a given jurisdiction (feature number 3) for a limited period of time (feature number 4)."[52] Giuseppe Marazzita analysed the constitutional emergency as follows: "Legal emergency is a complex situation that can be logically and chronologically divided into two moments: *the urgent fact* (or extraordinary fact) and *the state of exception* (or emergency regime) [...]. Their relationship is not direct, but is established by a *judgment of necessity.*"[53] The granting of the *nomen juris* "emergency" is not automatic. It is the result of a decision and a value judgement that are relative and contingent. It is interesting to examine how legal actors invoke necessity.

There is a peculiarity in the legal situations in which an emergency is invoked. As Vander Stichele notes,

> Behind these various assumptions, there seems to be an obvious basic idea. [...] In an emergency, the authorities [...] can, without it being illegal, on the one hand go beyond the normal limits of their own competence, and on the other hand make use of their powers without respecting the formalities [...] that could hinder their necessary action. In other words, because of the emergency, the rules of procedure and competence that normally govern the action of the authorities are temporarily rejected. In this case, the state of emergency fulfils a derogatory function.[54]

Invoking an emergency is a way of ignoring existing laws. This does not mean that it is illegal or unconstitutional, but that new norms are created that are different from those that apply in times that are considered normal. Such power-conferring norms may even be produced *a posteriori*, especially by a judge, or by means of self-conferring power.[55] But they are

[52] Karin Loevy, *Emergencies in Public Law: The Legal Politics of Containment* (Cambridge University Press, 2016) 7. See also *ibid.*, 55–251.

[53] Giuseppe Marazzita, *L'emergenza costituzionale* (A. Giuffrè, 2003) 161.

[54] Anne Vander Stichele, *La notion d'urgence en droit public* (Bruylant, 1986) 7.

[55] See Guillaume Tusseau, *Les normes d'habilitation* (Dalloz, 2006) 482–502.

still legal norms, justified and expressed in legal terms, and their application leads to the production of legal norms.[56]

The approximate denotation of the concept of emergency does not seem to be an obstacle to the function of emergency in legal discourses. As Karl Olivecrona's analysis suggests, it is enough for the term "emergency" itself to have an impact on the various actors who are part of the legal machine, and for it to act as a green or red light for the action of the other authorities of the system and of individuals.[57] It can be argued that, to a certain extent, what is meant by the term "emergency" is not important. What makes a situation an emergency is strictly circumstantial and unpredictable. In this case, the sole expression or qualification could play a role in legal discourses, not so much as a precise designation of some kind of legal entity, but as an instrument within the framework of rhetorical or argumentative strategies aimed at conquering or maintaining positions of power.

An emergency can therefore be seen as nothing more than a label or a slogan. Since this word does not denote anything in particular, what is essential may be that it connotes a kind of sufficient reason that justifies the action of some authority. By not looking for what it refers to, but by considering it as an argument, it is possible to understand how the invocation of an emergency is used in the strategies of constitutional actors.

3.3.2 The Argumentative Uses of Emergency

Understood as one argument among others in the battery of arguments available to legal actors, constitutional emergency is nothing more than a means to an end. As such, what legal actors make of emergencies in particular contexts is simultaneously determined by the strengths and weaknesses of such an argument. I intend to substantiate this claim by focusing on the impact of constitutional emergencies on the normative powers of legal actors.

[56] In that sense, see Michel Troper, "L'état d'exception n'a rien d'exceptionnel", in *L'Etat d'exception dans tous ses états* (Parenthèses, 2007) 163-175.

[57] Karl Olivecrona, *Law as Fact* (Humprey Milford, Oxford University Press, 1939); Karl Olivecrona, *Law as Fact* (2nd ed Stevens and sons, 1971). In the same sense, see Alf Ross, *On Law and Justice* (tr Margaret Dutton, Stevens & Sons Limited, 1958) 158–160.

3.3.2.1 The Strengths of the Argument

I propose to identify four characteristics of the emergency argument. It is at once extensive, intense, discriminating, and restrictive.

First, the scope of the emergency argument is quite broad. It can, for example, justify any modification of power-conferring norms. An emergency may affect each of the four elements that can be distinguished in a power-conferring norm indifferently, both separately and simultaneously.[58] It can justify (1) the empowerment of new legal actors, even *de facto* authorities; (2) the modification of the decision-making process, especially in order to speed it up; (3) the extension of the scope of application of normative power; and finally (4) the extension of the variety of norms that can be produced with regard to this scope of regulation and, in particular, the extension of the restrictions on fundamental rights. Moreover, the argument of necessity can operate independently of any text[59] and can contribute to justifying the emergence of completely new power-conferring norms based, for example, on a doctrine of *force majeure* or *de facto* authorities.[60]

Encapsulated in the maxim *Salus populi suprema lex*, the argument of emergency is thus the basis for a modification of the norms conferring power, justified by the will to give the means of action to the "organ considered most capable of finding a solution to the crisis."[61] The legitimate holder of the competence is the one whose intervention is necessary *hic et nunc* on a practical level, the practical necessity also determining the extent of such a competence.

[58] Guillaume Tusseau, *Les normes d'habilitation* (Dalloz, 2006); Guillaume Tusseau, "Theoretical Deflation: The EU Order of Competences and Power-conferring Norms Theory", in Loïc Azoulai (ed.), *The Question of Competence in the European Union* (Oxford University Press, 2014) 39-62; Guillaume Tusseau, "Testing the Utility of a Concept of Power-conferring Norm: a Proposal", in Gonzalo Villa-Rosas, Torben Spaak (eds), *Legal Power and Legal Competence. Meaning, Normativity, Officials and Theories* (Springer, 2023) 89–109.

[59] Guillaume Tusseau, *Les normes d'habilitation* (Dalloz, 2006) 591–602.

[60] See e.g. Albert Constantineau, *A Treatise on the De Facto Doctrine in its Relation to Public Officers and Public Corporations Based upon the English, American, and Canadian Cases Including Comments Upon Extraordinary Legal Remedies in Reference to the Trial of Title to Office, and Corporate Existence* (The Canada Law Book Co., The Lawyers Co-operative Publishing Co., 1910).

[61] Philippe Terneyre, "Les adaptations aux circonstances du principe de constitutionnalité. Contribution du Conseil constitutionnel à un droit constitutionnel de la nécessité" (1987) *Revue du droit public* 1489–1515.

Secondly, this is why this argument is particularly powerful. It is used to justify numerous derogations from the normal separation of powers or the normal regime of fundamental rights. According to Marazzita, the first characteristic of an emergency is that it legitimizes behavior that would otherwise be illegal.[62] It suspends ordinary norms, at least temporarily, and replaces them with a different, exceptional organization that may lead to a different regulation of individual behavior. The argument is particularly radical because it justifies, in certain circumstances, the granting of nothing less than unlimited powers to a self-appointed authority. Moreover, no explicit textual formulation seems able to resist it. As James Madison wrote to Thomas Jefferson,

> I am inclined to think that *absolute* restrictions in cases that are doubtful, or where emergencies may overrule them, ought to be avoided. The restrictions however strongly marked on paper will never be regarded when opposed to the decided sense of the public; and after repeated violations in extraordinary cases, they will lose even their ordinary efficacy. Should a Rebellion or insurrection alarm the people as well as the Government, and a suspension of the Hab. Corp. be dictated by the alarm, no written prohibitions on earth would prevent the measure.[63]

Article 150 (4) of the Malaysian Constitution provides a telling illustration of this emergency outcome: "While a Proclamation of Emergency is in force the executive authority of the Federation shall, notwithstanding anything in this Constitution, extent to any matter within the legislative authority of a State and to the giving of directions to the Government of a State or to any officer or authority thereof."[64] It would be hard to imagine a broader conferral of powers, and Article 150 (8) excludes any significant judicial review.

Thirdly, because of its scope, the emergency argument justifies the exact modification of the ordinary constitutional order that is necessary for the desired action, and does so in a discriminating manner. It allows for the precise proportionality of the appropriate extension. For this reason, the adequacy, proportionality or "graduality"[65] between the emergency

[62] Giuseppe Marazzita, *L'emergenza costituzionale* (A. Giuffrè, 2003) 44, 216–223.

[63] Letter of Octobre 17, 1788, in Robert A. Rutland, Charles F. Hobson, William M.E. Rachal, Jeanne K. Sisson (eds), *The Papers of James Madison* (University Press of Virginia, 1977) Vol. 11, 299.

[64] Italics supplied.

[65] See e.g. Constitutional Chamber of the Supreme Court of Salvador, n° 21-2020AC.

in question and the measures to be taken is often mentioned, especially in relation to the interests that the situation jeopardizes.[66] For example, the Spanish Organic Law 1/1981 requires that the time and geographical scope of the implementation of the measures taken, as well as the fundamental rights affected by them, must be minimal. Article 1.2 states that "the measures to be taken in cases of alarm, exception and siege, as well as their duration, shall in any case be those strictly necessary to ensure a return to normality. They shall be applied proportionately to the circumstances." Similarly, in the Czech Republic, Article 2(1) of the Constitutional Act of 22 April 1998, No. 110/1998 SB, on the security of the Czech Republic, provides that a state of emergency, a state of threat to the State or a state of war may be declared "in accordance with the intensity, territorial extent and character of the situation."

Emergency does not seem to be an absolute concept, but rather one that is relative to the realization of a goal that may be more or less urgent. The argument of emergency, which is in itself brutal and indeterminate, is the basis for an allocation of power that is precisely tailored to the objectives pursued by those who use it.[67]

Fourthly, an emergency may appear to be a particularly strong and hardly contestable justification. The measures taken on the basis of the emergency may be considered both necessary and compelling. In this way, emergency powers appear less as pure faculties than as powers that the authorities are constitutionally obliged to use.[68] "While all the State's emergency powers must indeed derive from the positive constitution, these powers can also include *implied powers*, since the constitution inherently contains a general obligation to sustain it."[69]

[66] Michel Vasseur, "Urgence et droit civil" (1954) *Revue trimestrielle de droit civil* 407, 430; Guillaume Pambou-Tchivounda, "Recherche sur l'urgence en droit administratif français" (1983) *Revue du droit public* 81–135, 94–95; Pierre-Laurent Frier, *L'urgence* (LGDJ, 1987) 18, 32, 87, 113–114; Imtiaz Omar, *Emergency Powers and the Courts in India and Pakistan* (Kluwer Law International, 2002) 131.

[67] In that sense, see Giuseppe Marazzita, *L'emergenza costituzionale* (A. Giuffrè, 2003) 73–76; Anne Vander Stichele, *La notion d'urgence en droit public* (Bruylant, 1986) 129–137.

[68] In that sense see Clinton L. Rossiter, *Constitutional Dictatorship. Crisis Government in the Modern Democracies* (Princeton University Press, 1948) 142–143, 146; Pierre-Laurent Frier, *L'urgence* (LGDJ, 1987) 17–56, 124; Giuseppe Marazzita, *L'emergenza costituzionale* (A. Giuffrè, 2003) 191–194, 244, 248; Oren Gross, "Chaos and Rules: Should Responses to Violent Crises Always Be Constitutional?" (2003) 112 *The Yale Law Journal* 1011–1134, 1106–1107.

[69] András Jakab, "German Constitutional Law and Doctrine on State of Emergency—Paradigms an Dilemmas of a Traditional (Continental) Discourse" (2005) 7 *German Law Review* 453–477, 473

The authorities that begin to act against ordinary norms can claim that they have a real legal obligation to act in this way. Given the circumstances, they cannot avoid it, nor hide behind respect for the law and fail to respond. They must fulfil their duty, which is to protect, in spite of the circumstances, the values which, in normal circumstances, are those of the legal order.

Jefferson, for example, believed that "the laws of necessity, of self-preservation, of saving our country when in danger, are of higher obligation. To lose our country by a scrupulous adherence to written law would be to lose the law itself."[70] Lincoln echoed this sentiment when he asked Congress in a special session, "Are all the laws, but one, to go unexecuted, and the government itself go to pieces, lest that one be violated?"[71] He justified his suspension of *habeas corpus* by the need to prevent the government from being destroyed by the secession of the southern States. According to his Attorney General, Edward Bates, who tried to base his action on the law, the President had the power to do so, and it was even his duty.[72]

The principle of the survival of the State was also used by the Argentinean Supreme Court in its decision *Peralta, Luis Arcenio y otro c/ Estado Nacional s/ amparo* to recognize that, given the situation, the State had to do something to preserve the vital interests of the community.[73] The Greek Court of Cassation also ruled that "for the security of the State itself or of the people [...]—which is the supreme law—the executive has

[70] Letter to J.B. Colvin of September 20, 1810, http://press-pubs.uchicago.edu/founders/documents/a2_3s8.html, last accessed 10/04/2025. See Clinton L. Rossiter, *Constitutional Dictatorship. Crisis Government in the Modern Democracies* (Princeton University Press, 1948) 61-62, 67, 293; Kevin Jon Heller, "The Rhetoric of Necessity (or, Sanford Levinson's Pinteresque Conversation)" (2006) 40 *Georgia Law Review* 784–787.

[71] Message to Congress assembled in extraordinary session of July 4, 1861, in Roy Prentice Balser (ed.), *The Collected Works of Abraham Lincoln* (Rutgers University Press, 1953) Vol. 4, 430.

[72] July 5, 1861, X *Op. Atty. Gen.* 74, quoted by Clinton L. Rossiter, *Constitutional Dictatorship. Crisis Government in the Modern Democracies* (Princeton University Press, 1948) 227

[73] Fallos 313:1513 (1990). See Alberto Ricardo Dalla Via, "La emergencia constitucional en Argentina y America Latina", in Giuseppe de Vergottini (a cura di), *Costituzione ed emergenza in America latina. Argentina, Chile, Ecuador, Perù, Venezuela, Convenzione interamericana* (G. Giappichelli, 1997) 1–64; Alberto Ricardo Dalla Via, "La emergencia y el Estado constitucional de derecho", http://www.derecho.uba.ar/publicaciones/pensar-en-derecho/revistas/16/la-emergencia-y-el-estado-constitucional-de-derecho.pdf, last accessed 10/04/2025.

not only the right but the duty to issue decrees that have the content of a law."[74] Similarly, the French Constitutional Council has stated that "the State has the *duty* to ensure that the institutions of the Republic, the continuity of the life of the nation and the guarantee of the rights and freedoms of citizens are respected."[75]

The emergency argument has so much going for it in terms of the strategies of legal actors that it may seem strange that it is so rarely used. This may be explained by the weaknesses that counterbalance the aforementioned advantages.

3.3.2.2 The Weaknesses of the Argument

According to Elliot Bulmer, "A state of emergency is supposed to be a temporary response to a particular urgent need. The intention should be to use the powers conferred by a state of emergency only to address that urgent need and then restore constitutional normality as soon as possible."[76] With this in mind, I propose to identify four additional characteristics of the emergency argument. It is limited in that it is a temporary, exceptional and self-defeating argument with a specific purpose.

First, the invocation of an emergency to exercise exceptional powers can only be temporary. As Gross has noted, "the principle of a temporary period of time, which is so inherent to the fundamental understanding of the concept of emergency, demands that the state of emergency be short-lived."[77] Emergencies are not meant to last indefinitely: "Emergency situations may have different traits. [...] Whatever the case, they are by

[74] Ruling n° 43/1919.

[75] Décision n° 85-188 DC, italics added.

[76] Elliot Bulmer, *Emergency Powers. International IDEA Constitution-Building Primer 18* (International IDEA, 2018) 18.

[77] Oren Gross, "Providing for the Unexpected: Constitutional Emergency Provisions" (2003) 33 *Israel Yearbook on Human Rights* 13–43, 32. Also see Oren Gross, "Chaos and Rules: Should Responses to Violent Crises Always Be Constitutional?" (2003) 112 *The Yale Law Journal* 1011–1134, 1036, 1070–1075, 1089-1090; Oren Gross, "Emergency's Challenges", in Richard Albert, Yaniv Roznai (eds), *Constitutionalism under Extreme Conditions: Law, Emergency, Exception* (Springer, 2020) 428-430, 428; Clinton L. Rossiter, *Constitutional Dictatorship. Crisis Government in the Modern Democracies* (Princeton University Press, 1948) 8, 24, 67–68, 306; Giuseppe Marazzita, *L'emergenza costituzionale* (A. Giuffrè, 2003) 76–80; Pierre-Laurent Frier, *L'urgence* (LGDJ, 1987) 137; Giuseppe Marazzita, *L'emergenza costituzionale* (A. Giuffrè, 2003) 223–227; Imtiaz Omar, *Emergency Powers and the Courts in India and Pakistan* (Kluwer Law International, 2002) 15.

definition extraordinary and impermanent."[78] Therefore, while it justifies much, it can only do so for a limited period of time.

This is often reflected in the time limits imposed on the proclamation of a state of emergency and the strict conditions for its renewal. For example, Article 230 of the Polish Constitution limits the President's declaration of a state of emergency to 90 days and allows it to be extended only with the consent of the Sejm and for no more than 60 days. Similarly, Article 144 of the Constitution of the Republic of Lithuania provides for a state of emergency for a maximum of six months. In Canada, the Emergencies Act[79] allows the government to declare four types of emergencies: (1) "public welfare emergency" in the event of a natural disaster; (2) "public order emergency" in the event of a serious threat to the security of the State; (3) "international emergency" in the event of acts of intimidation against Canada or other countries; and (4) "war emergency" in the event of an actual or imminent armed conflict involving Canada or its allies. The duration of the declaration of the state of emergency varies, from 30 days for the first to 120 days for the last, as do the powers granted. Moreover, in some jurisdictions, measures adopted under a state of emergency may only be valid for a limited period of time. This is the case in Greece, where Article 48 of the Constitution limits the application of such norms to 15 days, renewable for two weeks at a time. Similarly, in Israel, on the basis of Article 39 of the Basic Law: Government, in Singapore, Article 150.6 of the Constitution reads:

> At the expiration of a period of 6 months beginning with the date on which a Proclamation of Emergency ceases to be in force, any ordinance promulgated in pursuance of the Proclamation and, to the extent that it could not have been validly made but for this Article, any law made while the Proclamation was in force, shall cease to have effect, except as to things done or omitted to be done before the expiration of that period.

Significantly, Article 25(6) of the Constitution of East Timor states that "the authorities shall restore constitutional normality as soon as possible." Emergency is thus an argument that actors can hardly overuse

[78] Anna Jonsson Cornell, Janne Salminen, "Emergency Laws in Comparative Constitutional Law—The Case of Sweden and Finland" (2018) 19 *German Law Journal* 219–250, 220; Alan Greene, *Permanent States of Emergency and the Rule of Law. Constitutions in an Age of Crisis* (Hart, 2020).

[79] Emergencies Act (1985, c. 22).

convincingly. It is difficult to use repeatedly. As Gross points out, an emergency can only be meaningful if it is contrasted with a notion of normality.[80] The fact that it is necessarily temporary explains the criticism that the long duration of the state of emergency, or the repetition of emergency measures, provokes.

Writing about Argentina's constitutional law, Alberto Ricardo Dalla Via observed that "the state of emergency has been mentioned so often that the very concept of the state of emergency is undergoing a crisis, because the periods of abnormality are really numerous and follow one another rather quickly for nothing."[81] In fact, this State is used to the state of emergency being proclaimed *sine die*, as well as to the disproportionate use of emergency decrees.[82] In Peru, too, Article 137.1 of the 1993 Constitution, like previous constitutions, stipulates that the state of emergency cannot last longer than 60 days. In the 1980s, however, it was almost permanent, having been renewed more than thirty times between 1983 and 1987.[83] Similarly, the repeated renewals of emergency powers in Paraguay or Egypt have appeared puzzling and illegitimate.[84]

Israel has been under a state of emergency since 1948. Initially limited to the War of Independence, it became permanent and is still in force more than 70 years later. India and Pakistan, as well as Egypt,[85] are

[80] Oren Gross, "Emergency's Challenges", in Richard Albert, Yaniv Roznai (eds), *Constitutionalism under Extreme Conditions: Law, Emergency, Exception* (Springer, 2020) 428-430; Oren Gross, "Constitutions and Emergency Regimes", in Tom Ginsburg, Rosalind Dixon (eds), *Comparative Constitutional Law* (Edward Elgar, 2011) 334–355, 349.

[81] Alberto Ricardo Dalla Via, "La emergencia constitucional en Argentina y America Latina", in Giuseppe de Vergottini (a cura di), *Costituzione ed emergenza in America latina. Argentina, Chile, Ecuador, Perù, Venezuela, Convenzione interamericana* (G. Giappichelli, 1997) 1–64. See also Juan Santiago Ylarri, "Permanent Economic Emergency in Argentina and its Constitutional Implications" (2020) 13 *Mexican Law Review* 87–114.

[82] See Article 99.3 of the Constitution

[83] Linda Camp Keith, Steven C. Poe, "Are Constitutional State of Emergency Clauses Effective? An Empirical Exploration" (2004) 26 *Human Rights Quarterly* 1071–1097, 1078. More generally see Diego Valadés, *La dictadura constitucional en America Latina* (UNAM, Instituto de investigaciones jurídicas, 1974); Brian Loveman, *The Constitution of Tyranny. Regimes of Exception in Spanish America* (Pittsburgh University Press, 1993); Giuseppe de Vergottini (a cura di), *Costituzione ed emergenza in America latina. Argentina, Chile, Ecuador, Perù, Venezuela, Convenzione interamericana* (G. Giappichelli, 1997).

[84] Elliot Bulmer, *Emergency Powers. International IDEA Constitution-Building Primer 18* (International IDEA, 2018) 7.

[85] For example see Sadiq Reza, "Endless Emergency: The Case of Egypt" (2007) 10 *New Criminal Law Review* 532–553.

accustomed to perpetual states of emergency.[86] "While the initial validity of most of the proclamations of emergency in Pakistan and India cannot be seriously questioned, the protracted continuation of the states of emergency, long after the crises that originally justified their issue have ceased to exist, indicates that the notional political controls envisaged by the respective Constitutions have failed."[87] The new extension of the state of emergency by the military regime in Myanmar in January 2025 has also drawn criticism.

An emergency, as it is usually understood in legal arguments, can only be temporary, even if it is not possible to give a precise date due to the indeterminate nature of what it denotes. So, too, is the modification of the norms that confer power, which this argument helps to justify. Sooner or later, the state of emergency and the alteration of the power-conferring norms must come to an end.

Secondly, this is mainly due to the fact that the emergency appears as an exceptional situation.[88] It justifies modified constitutional regimes all the more because it is neither constant nor daily, but rare.

This is why the repeated declarations of emergencies in the French legislative process are so controversial today. During the session of 5 October 2005, for example, the President of the Senate declared: "May the government give us the time we need to think so that we can make good laws." A few days later, when the government declared the bill on transport safety and development to be an emergency, he added: "Mr. Minister of State, please inform the Prime Minister that we senators do not like these repeated declarations of emergency. Although it is true that some bills must be discussed as a matter of urgency, we understand less well why

[86] See Imtiaz Omar, *Emergency Powers and the Courts in India and Pakistan* (Kluwer Law International, 2002) 7, 29–31, 129; Paula R. Newberg, *Judging the State. Courts and Constitutional Politics in Pakistan* (Cambridge University Press, 1995); Prithvi Nath Dhar, *Indira Gandhi, The "Emergency", and Indian Democracy* (Oxford University Press, 2000). For other examples, see John Hatchard, "States of Siege/Emergency in Africa" (1993) 37 *Journal of African Law* 104–108; Victor V. Ramraj, Arun K. Thiruvengadam (eds) *Emergency Powers in Asia. Exploring the Limits of Legality* (Cambridge University Press, 2010).

[87] Imtiaz Omar, *Emergency Powers and the Courts in India and Pakistan* (Kluwer Law International, 2002) xi.

[88] For example see Clinton L. Rossiter, *Constitutional Dictatorship. Crisis Government in the Modern Democracies* (Princeton University Press, 1948) 301, 303; Oren Gross, "What Emergency Regime?" (2006) 13 *Constellations* 74–88, e.g. at 74: "Temporal duration and exceptional nature of the threat are common starting points for the many competing definitions of 'emergency'."

this is the case for other bills".[89] In the absence of some measured use, the argument of emergency will hardly be effective in convincing that the ordinary constitutional norms should be modified.

Third, a similar process of argumentation limits the strength of the emergency argument. Gross argued that "a constitutional dictature must be temporary and self-destroying."[90] Similarly, Schmitt wrote that "a dictature which does not depend on a result which corresponds to a normative idea and which must be achieved, and which does not aim at making itself superfluous, is nothing other than a kind of despotism".[91] Adam Przeworski also noted that "Dictatorships were seen as something abnormal and something to self-dissolve when the situation is restored to normal."[92]

This last characteristic imposes a kind of constraint on the use of the emergency argument. The latter is the basis for a massive grant of powers. But such a grant is only justified insofar as it makes it possible to deal with the situation effectively. That is why, when an emergency is invoked, it is limited in time. The state of emergency is created precisely in order to lead to its own suppression. According to this logic, the argument of emergency is all the more efficient because it is not often used. In this respect, one can quote what Jacques Mourgeon wrote about crisis: "Regardless of its actual occurrence, the crisis [is] conceived as abnormal, unusual and therefore temporary. The very idea of crisis limits the crisis."[93]

Fourthly, an emergency appears as a teleological concept. Doing something is not urgent in itself, but linked to a purpose. In constitutional law, such a purpose is often presented as the preservation and restoration of the form of the State, the form of government or the fundamental values of the constitutional order. Emergency powers are thus

[89] Quoted in Conseil d'Etat, *Rapport public 2006. Sécurité juridique et complexité du droit* (La documentation française, 2006) 367

[90] Oren Gross, "Providing for the Unexpected: Constitutional Emergency Provisions" (2003) 33 *Israel Yearbook on Human Rights* 13–43, 29. See Clinton L. Rossiter, *Constitutional Dictatorship. Crisis Government in the Modern Democracies* (Princeton University Press, 1948) 8, 24, 67–68.

[91] Carl Schmitt, *La dictature* (tr Mira Köller, Dominique Séglard, Le Seuil, 2000) 18.

[92] Adam Przeworski, "A Conceptual History of Political Regimes: Democracy, Dictatorship, and Authoritarianism", in Jerzy J. Wiatr (ed), *New Authoritarianism. Challenges to Democracy in the 21st Century* (Verlag Barbara Budrich, 2019) 17-36, 23.

[93] Jacques Mourgeon, "Les crises et les libertés publiques", (1979) 10 *Pouvoirs* 41–51, 45.

subordinated to an objective. Article 58(2) of the Constitution of Kenya and Article 37(1)(b) of the Constitution of South Africa, for example, stipulate that the declaration of a state of emergency must be "necessary" to deal with the circumstances for which this exceptional regime is activated. In concrete terms, its aim is nothing less than to restore the conditions in which the state of emergency is no longer necessary, that is, to abolish itself. Once a state of emergency has been declared, the resulting measures must be strictly adapted to the circumstances. For example, Article 5 of the Slovak Constitutional Act 227/2002 on State Security in Times of War, Hostilities, Extraordinary Circumstances and Emergencies reads as follows:

(1) The Government may declare a state of emergency only if there is a threat or imminent danger of threat to life and health of people due to a pandemic, to the environment, or considerable threat to property as a result of a natural disaster, industrial or other operational accident, or a traffic accident; a state of emergency may only be declared in the affected or imminently threatened area.
(2) A state of emergency may only be declared to the necessary extent, for the necessary time and for no longer than 90 days.
(3) If a state of emergency is declared, fundamental rights and freedoms may be restricted and duties imposed to the necessary extent and for the necessary time in relation to the severity of the threat and in the affected or imminently threatened area.

In the meantime, decisions must be taken to restore the normal order of things. The measures taken must be strictly appropriate and proportionate to that end, and although they may be outside existing norms, they must never aim to promote values that are alien to the normal legal order. For example, Article 19(8) of the Portuguese Constitution states that "the declaration of a state of siege or a state of emergency confers on the authorities the power to take the measures necessary and appropriate for the rapid restoration of constitutional normality." Similarly, in Chad, Article 97 of the Constitution states that "the measures taken pursuant to the preceding article must be motivated by the desire to ensure that the constitutional public authorities have the means to fulfil their mission in the shortest possible time." This is why, in times of crisis, it is often impossible to amend the Constitution. It is precisely the fundamental values enshrined in the Constitution that are to be protected by recourse to exceptional powers. For example, Article 152(3) of the Romanian

Constitution stipulates that "the Constitution may not be amended during a state of siege, a state of emergency or a time of war."[94]

As Schmitt insisted when he mentioned the idea of a commissarial dictatorship,[95] the use of renewed powers can have no other purpose than to restore the status *quo ante*.[96] It seems fundamentally conservative,[97] since "[w]hat an emergency may bring is rule-change, not rule-abandonment."[98]

3.4 Concluding Remarks

This elementary mapping of what legal actors make of emergency in their argumentative practice is by no means definitive or rigid. In particular, it should be noted that the argumentative limits of the invocation of an emergency, for those who seek to act on this basis, are resources for the actor who has been given the power to control it, be it a judge—whose intervention is sometimes explicitly guaranteed by constitutions,[99] a political institution, and in particular the legislative assemblies,[100] an NGO or

[94] Also see Article 54.8.b of the 1920 Constitution of Tchecoslovaquia; Article 169 of the Spanish Constitution; Article 60.III.1 of the Brazialian Constitution, Article 289 of the Portuguese Constitution; Article 115e of the German Basic Law; Article 228.of the Polish Constitution; Article 140.III of the Bolivian Constitution.

[95] Carl Schmitt, *La dictature* (tr Mira Köller, Dominique Séglard, Le Seuil, 2000) esp. 14, 48–49, 130, 141–142.

[96] Clinton L. Rossiter, *Constitutional Dictatorship. Crisis Government in the Modern Democracies* (Princeton University Press, 1948) 7; Pasquale Pasquino, "Urgence et État de droit. Le gouvernement d'exception dans la théorie constitutionnelle" (2003) 51 *Les cahiers de la sécurité intérieure. Revue trimestrielle de sciences sociales* 9-29, 19.

[97] John Ferejohn, Pasquale Pasquino, "The Law of Exception: A Typology of Emergency Powers" (2004) 2 *International Journal of Constitutional Law* 210-239.

[98] Tom Campbell, "Emergency Strategies for Prescriptive Legal Positivists: Anti-Terrorist Law and Legal Theory", in Victor V. Ramraj (ed), *Emergencies and the Limits of Legality* (Cambridge University Press, 2008) 201-228, 209-210. Also see Giuseppe Marazzita, *L'emergenza costituzionale* (A. Giuffrè, 2003) 237-239; Clinton L. Rossiter, *Constitutional Dictatorship. Crisis Government in the Modern Democracies* (Princeton University Press, 1948) 7, 67, 287, 298, 302, 303; David Bonner, *Emergency Powers in Peacetime* (Sweet & Maxwell, 1985) 21.

[99] Guillaume Tusseau, *Contentieux constitutionnel comparé. Une introduction critique au droit processual constitutionnel* (Lextenso, 2021) 909-910. See e.g. art. 58 C Kenya; art. 129 C Slovakia; art. 37 C South Africa; art. 436 C Ecuador; art. VII.18 C Philippines.

[100] See e.g. Mark Tushnet, "The Political Constitution of Emergency Powers: Parliamentary and Separation-of-Powers Regulation" (2008) 3 *International Journal of Law in Context* 275–288.

the citizens in general. For the latter, the very weaknesses of the emergency argument are the resources that justify their own normative productions. This testifies to the existence of a specific constitutional linguistic game.

In Argentina, for example, the declaration of a state of emergency must meet certain constitutional conditions. The Supreme Court, according to a large body of case law, requires that there be an emergency that obliges the State to protect the vital interests of the community, that the norms that are produced aim to preserve the general interests of society, that the duration of the exceptional regulation of individual and social rights be temporary and limited to what is indispensable to remedy the causes that have made it necessary, and that the means chosen by the authorities be reasonable.[101] In a case decided in 1925, for example, the court ruled that

> This emergency regime, which fundamentally affects the right to use and dispose of property, has been tolerated by judicial decisions only in consideration of the moment of extreme economic oppression of the tenants due to the absence of one of the factors that regulate prices in the real estate rental business, that is to say, the lack of supply of rooms, and above all as a transitory and short-term measure [...]. But this abnormal regime cannot be sufficiently justified when it becomes, in fact, a habitual norm in the relations between landlords and tenants, as is the case with the repeated extensions granted to tenants, and much less when it is intended to act in an environment very different from that which gave rise to the original enactment of these laws.[102]

This was also the attitude of Egypt's Supreme Constitutional Court, which once banned an emergency law because

> from the statement of the motives [justifying it] there seemed to appear only the simple desire to amend laws relative to personal status [...]. Though it is true that it may be considered as a stimulant and an objective proper to incite legislative power to elaborate new laws or to remedy shortcomings of the current legislation, it still is not enough to meet the conditions laid out by Article 147 subsection 1 of the Constitution. For the invoked motives show quite well that, the People's Assembly being in recess, there was no

[101] For example see *Ercolano de Lanteri* (Fallos, 136:161); *Avico c/ De la Pesa/ mora hipotecaria* (Fallos, 172:371); *Cine Callao S.A. s/escasez de trabajo* (Fallos, 247:121); *Peralta, Luis Arcenio y otro c/ Estado Nacional* (Fallos, 313:1513); *Mate de Larangeira Mendez S.A.* (Fallos, 369:399).

[102] *Mango, Leonardo c/ Traba, Ernesto* (Fallos, 144:219).

circumstance proper to create that situation that calls for the granting to the President of the Republic of an exceptional authorization to legislate.[103]

The emergency that is the condition for the validity of these exceptional norms is simultaneously controlled by different parties. The concept(s) of constitutional emergency can only coalesce in specific contexts, as the result(s) of the iterated strategic interactions of a plurality of competing legal actors.

Having examined various manifestations of emergency, the question "what is a constitutional emergency?" can be answered as follows. If the word "emergency" denotes something, it does not denote a specific reality with any unity. Moreover, the word may not denote anything precise, or even anything at all. But this does not prevent it from being used in legal discourses. For these are less the result of reason and knowledge than of power and its justifications. Legal language is not necessarily a language that denotes things. It belongs largely to persuasive, justificatory and even emotional discourse, which is another way of saying, with Thomas Hobbes, that "*auctoritas non veritas facit legem.*"[104]

References

AA. VV. "L'état d'exception, nouveau régime de droit commun des droits et libertés? Du terrorisme à l'urgence sanitaire. XXXVIe Table ronde internationale du 11 septembre 2020" 36 Annuaire international de justice constitutionnelle, 2020, 85–646

Ackerman, B. "The Emergency Constitution" 113 Yale Law Journal, 2004, 1029

Agamben, G. *State of Exception* (tr K. Attell). Univ of Chicago Press, 2005

Beaud, O., Guérin-Bargues, C., Benzina, S. *L'état d'urgence sécuritaire et sanitaire. Une étude constitutionnelle, historique et critique* (3rd ed). Dalloz, 2023

Bentham, J. *De l'ontologie et autres textes sur les fictions* (ed P. Schofield, tr J.-P. Cléro, C. Laval). Seuil, 1997

Bernard-Maugiron, N. *Le politique à l'épreuve du judiciaire: la justice constitutionnelle en Egypte.* Bruylant, 2003

Bjørnskov, C., Voigt, S. "The Architecture of Emergency Constitutions" 16 International Journal of Constitutional Law, 2018, 101

[103] Constitutional Court of Egypt, 4 May 1985, n° 28/2[c], *Recueil* Vol. 3, 195, 206, quoted by Nathalie Bernard-Maugiron, *Le politique à l'épreuve du judiciaire : la justice constitutionnelle en Egypte* (Bruylant, 2003) 489.

[104] Thomas Hobbes, *Leviathan, sive, De materia, forma, & potestate civitatis ecclesiasticae et civilis* (Joan Blaeu, 1668) Ch. XXVI.

Bjørnskov, C., Voigt, S. "Why do Governments Call a State of Emergency? On the Determinants of Using Emergency Constitutions" 54 European Journal of Political Economy, 2018, 110

Bonner, D. *Emergency Powers in Peacetime*. Sweet & Maxwell, 1985

Bottini, E. "Comparer les états d'urgence en Europe" in Hennette-Vauchez, S. (dir.) *Ce qui reste(ra) toujours de l'urgence*. Institut universitaire Varenne, 2018, 51

Braibant, G. "L'Etat face aux crises" 10 Pouvoirs, 1979, 5

Bulmer, E. *Emergency Powers. International IDEA Constitution-Building Primer 18*. International IDEA, 2018

Burdeau, F., Quesnet, M. "De l'inefficacité des pouvoirs de crise en France de la Révolution à Vichy" 10 Pouvoirs, 1979, 11

Camp Keith, L., Poe, S.C. "Are Constitutional State of Emergency Clauses Effective? An Empirical Exploration" 26 Human Rights Quarterly, 2004, 1071

Campbell, T. "Emergency Strategies for Prescriptive Legal Positivists: Anti-Terrorist Law and Legal Theory" in Ramraj, V.V. (ed.) *Emergencies and the Limits of Legality*. CUP, 2008, 201

Cervantes, A., Matarrita, M., Reca, S. "Los estados de excepción en tiempos de pandemia: un studio comparado en América Latina" 20 Cuadernos Manuel Giménez Abad, 2020, 179

Conseil d'Etat. *Rapport public 2006. Sécurité juridique et complexité du droit*. La documentation française, 2006

Constantineau, A. *A Treatise on the De Facto Doctrine in its Relation to Public Officers and Public Corporations*. The Canada Law Book Co./The Lawyers Co-operative Publishing Co., 1910

Dalla Via, A.R. "La emergencia constitucional en Argentina y America Latina" in de Vergottini, G. (a cura di) *Costituzione ed emergenza in America latina*. G. Giappichelli, 1997, 1

Dalla Via, A.R. "La emergencia y el Estado constitucional de derecho" http://www.derecho.uba.ar/publicaciones/pensar-en-derecho/revistas/16/la-emergencia-y-el-estado-constitucional-de-derecho.pdf, last accessed 10/04/2025

de Vergottini, G. (a cura di) *Costituzione ed emergenza in America latina. Argentina, Chile, Ecuador, Perù, Venezuela, Convenzione interamericana*. G. Giappichelli, 1997

Debord, G. *Commentaires sur la société du spectacle*. Gallimard, 1992

Dyzenhaus, D. "States of Emergency" in Rosenfeld, M., Sajó, A. (eds.) *The Oxford Handbook of Comparative Constitutional Law*. OUP, 2012, 442

Dyzenhaus, D. "The State of Emergency in Legal Theory" in Ramraj, V.V., Hor, M., Roach, K. (eds.) *Global Anti-Terrorism Law and Policy*. CUP, 2005, 65

Dyzenhaus, D. *The Constitution of Law. Legality in a Time of Emergency*. CUP, 2006

Ferejohn, J., Pasquino, P. "Emergency Powers" in Dryzek, J.S., Honig, B., Phillips, A. (eds.) *Oxford Handbook of Political Theory*. OUP, 2009, 333

Ferejohn, J., Pasquino, P. "The Law of Exception: A Typology of Emergency Powers" 2 International Journal of Constitutional Law, 2004, 210

Freeman, M. *Freedom or Security. The Consequences for Democracies Using Emergency Powers to Fight Terror*. Praeger, 2003

Frege, G. "Sense and Reference" 57 Philosophical Review, 1948, 209

Frier, P.-L. *L'urgence*. LGDJ, 1987

Gabolde, C. *Essai sur la notion d'urgence en droit administrative*. Univ of Paris, 1951

Germán Spada, D. "Decretos de necesidad y urgencia: naturaleza—reseña de su utilización—evolución jurisprudencial" 2 Administración y derecho. Revista de doctrina y jurisprudencia, 2010, 2

Ginsburg, T., Rosen, M.D., Vanberg, G. (eds.) *Constitutions in Times of Financial Crisis*. CUP, 2019

Ginsburg, T., Versteeg, M. "The Bound Executive: Emergency Powers During the Pandemic" 19 International Journal of Constitutional Law, 2021, 1498

González Martín, N. (ed.) *Covid-19 y su circunstancia. Una visión jurídica plural de la pandemia*, 5 vols. Instituto de estudios constitucionales del Estado de Querétaro, 2021

Greene, A. *Emergency Powers in a Time of Pandemic*. Bristol Univ Press, 2020

Greene, A. *Permanent States of Emergency and the Rule of Law. Constitutions in an Age of Crisis*. Hart, 2020

Griglio, E. "Parliamentary Oversight Under the Covid-19 Emergency: Striving Against Executive Dominance" 8 Theory and Practice of Legislation, 2020, 49

Gross, O. "Chaos and Rules: Should Responses to Violent Crises Always Be Constitutional?" 112 Yale Law Journal, 2003, 1011

Gross, O. "Constitutions and Emergency Regimes" in Ginsburg, T., Dixon, R. (eds.) *Comparative Constitutional Law*. Edward Elgar, 2011, 334

Gross, O. "Emergency's Challenges" in Albert, R., Roznai, Y. (eds.) *Constitutionalism under Extreme Conditions: Law, Emergency, Exception*. Springer, 2020, 428

Gross, O. "Providing for the Unexpected: Constitutional Emergency Provisions" 33 Israel Yearbook on Human Rights, 2003, 13

Gross, O. "What Emergency Regime?" 13 Constellations, 2006, 74

Gross, O., Ni Aolain, F. *Law in Times of Crisis: Emergency Powers in Theory and Practice*. CUP, 2006

Haro, R. "Los decretos de necesidad y urgencia en la doctrina judicial de la Corte suprema de justicia de Argentina" 7 *Ius & Praxis*, 2001, 61–72

Hatchard, J. "States of Siege/Emergency in Africa" 37 *Journal of African Law*, 1993, 104–108

Heller, K.J. "The Rhetoric of Necessity (or, Sanford Levinson's Pinteresque Conversation)" 40 *Georgia Law Review*, 2006, 784–787

Hennette Vauchez, S. *La démocratie en état d'urgence. Quand l'exception devient permanente*. Le Seuil, 2022

Hennette-Vauchez, S. (dir.) *Ce qui reste(ra) toujours de l'urgence*. Institut universitaire Varenne, 2018

Hobbes, T. *Leviathan, sive, De materia, forma, & potestate civitatis ecclesiasticae et civilis*. Joan Blaeu, 1668

Jakab, A. "German Constitutional Law and Doctrine on State of Emergency—Paradigms and Dilemmas of a Traditional (Continental) Discourse" 7 *German Law Review*, 2005, 453–477

Jestaz, P. *L'urgence et les principes classiques du droit civil*. LGDJ, 1968

Jonsson Cornell, A., & Salminen, J. "Emergency Laws in Comparative Constitutional Law—The Case of Sweden and Finland" 19 *German Law Journal*, 2018, 219–250

Lafrance, S., Bedi, S., & De Gregorio, L.H. "Constitutional Theories of Emergency Powers and Their Limits: Perspectives From Vietnam, India and Canada" 4 *Vietnamese Journal of Legal Sciences*, 2021, 1–33

Lazar, N.C. *States of Emergency in Liberal Democracies*. Cambridge University Press, 2009

Loevy, K. *Emergencies in Public Law: The Legal Politics of Containment*. Cambridge University Press, 2016

Loveman, B. *The Constitution of Tyranny. Regimes of Exception in Spanish America*. Pittsburgh University Press, 1993

Machiavelli, N. *Discourses on Livy* (H.C. Mansfield & N. Tarcov tr). University of Chicago Press, 1998

Marazzita, G. *L'emergenza costituzionale*. A. Giuffrè, 2003

Mestre, A. *Le Conseil d'Etat, protecteur des prérogatives de l'administration*. LGDJ, 1974

Michalis, I. "Le contrôle de proportionnalité pendant les crises dans les jurisprudences française et allemande" in Dupré de Boulois, X., & Philippe, X. (dir.) *Gouverner et juger en période de crise*. Mare & Martin, 2023, 321–333

Mourgeon, J. "Les crises et les libertés publiques" 10 *Pouvoirs*, 1979, 41–51

Nath Dhar, P. *Indira Gandhi, The "Emergency", and Indian Democracy*. Oxford University Press, 2000

Newberg, P.R. *Judging the State. Courts and Constitutional Politics in Pakistan*. Cambridge University Press, 1995

Olivecrona, K. *Law as Fact*. 2nd ed, Stevens and Sons, 1971

Olivecrona, K. *Law as Fact*. Humphrey Milford, Oxford University Press, 1939

Omar, I. *Emergency Powers and the Courts in India and Pakistan*. Kluwer Law International, 2002

Pambou-Tchivounda, G. "Recherche sur l'urgence en droit administratif français" *Revue du droit public*, 1983, 81–135

Pasquino, P. "Urgence et État de droit. Le gouvernement d'exception dans la théorie constitutionnelle" 51 *Les cahiers de la sécurité intérieure. Revue trimestrielle de sciences sociales*, 2003, 9–29

Petrov, J. "The Covid-19 Emergency in the Age of Executive Aggrandizement: What Role for Legislative and Judicial Checks?" 8 *The Theory and Practice of Legislation*, 2020, 71–92

Posner, E.A., & Vermeule, A. "Accommodating Emergencies" 56 *Stanford Law Review*, 2003, 605–644

Prentice Balser, R. (ed.) *The Collected Works of Abraham Lincoln*. Rutgers University Press, 1953

Przeworski, A. "A Conceptual History of Political Regimes: Democracy, Dictatorship, and Authoritarianism" in Wiatr, J.J. (ed.) *New Authoritarianism. Challenges to Democracy in the 21st Century*. Verlag Barbara Budrich, 2019, 17–36

Ramraj, V.V. "Emergency Powers and Constitutional Theory" 41 *Hong Kong Law Journal*, 2011, 481–515

Ramraj, V.V. "The Constitutional Politics of Emergency Powers" in Tushnet, M., & Kochenov, D. (eds.) *Research Handbook on the Politics of Constitutional Law*. Routledge, 2023, 163–175

Ramraj, V.V. "The Emergency Powers Paradox" in Ramraj, V.V., & Thiruvengadam, A.K. (eds.) *Emergency Powers in Asia. Exploring the Limits of Legality*. Cambridge University Press, 2010, 21–55

Ramraj, V.V., & Thiruvengadam, A.K. (eds.) *Emergency Powers in Asia. Exploring the Limits of Legality*. Cambridge University Press, 2010

Reza, S. "Endless Emergency: The Case of Egypt" 10 *New Criminal Law Review*, 2007, 532–553

Riberi, P. (ed.) *Pandemocracy in Latin America. Revisiting the Political and Constitutional Dimension of the Pandemic*. Hart, 2024

Roach, K. "Ordinary Law for Emergencies and Democratic Derogations From Rights" in Ramraj, V.V. (ed.) *Emergencies and the Limits of Legality*. Cambridge University Press, 2008, 229–257

Ross, A. "Book Review: Kelsen, Hans, What is Justice? Justice, Law and Politics in the Mirror of Science. Collected Essays" 45 *California Law Review*, 1957, 564–570

Ross, A. *On Law and Justice* (M. Dutton tr). Stevens & Sons, 1958

Rossiter, C.L. *Constitutional Dictatorship. Crisis Government in the Modern Democracies*. Princeton University Press, 1948

Rutland, R.A., Hobson, C.F., Rachal, W.M.E., & Sisson, J.K. (eds.) *The Papers of James Madison*. Vol. 11. University Press of Virginia, 1977, 299

Schauer, F. "The Constitution of Fear" 12 *Constitutional Commentary*, 1995, 203–206

Schmitt, C. *La dictature* (M. Köller & D. Séglard tr). Le Seuil, 2000
Terneyre, P. "Les adaptations aux circonstances du principe de constitutionnalité. Contribution du Conseil constitutionnel à un droit constitutionnel de la nécessité" *Revue du droit public*, 1987, 1489–1515
Tobón, M.L., Mendieta, D., & Gasparetto, A. "Los modelos constitucionales de los estados de excepción en época de crisis global" 3 *Revista jurídica Unicuritiba*, 2021, 1–35
Troper, M. "L'état d'exception n'a rien d'exceptionnel" in Théodorou, S. (ed.), *L'exception dans tous ses états*. Parenthèses, 2007, 163–175
Tushnet, M. "The Political Constitution of Emergency Powers: Parliamentary and Separation-of-Powers Regulation" 3 *International Journal of Law in Context*, 2008, 275–288
Tusseau, G. "Testing the Utility of a Concept of Power-conferring Norm: a Proposal" in Villa-Rosas, G., & Spaak, T. (eds.) *Legal Power and Legal Competence. Meaning, Normativity, Officials and Theories*. Springer, 2023, 89–109
Tusseau, G. "Theoretical Deflation: The EU Order of Competences and Power-conferring Norms Theory" in Azoulai, L. (ed.) *The Question of Competence in the European Union*. Oxford University Press, 2014, 39–62
Tusseau, G. *Contentieux constitutionnel comparé. Une introduction critique au droit processual constitutionnel*. Lextenso, 2021
Tusseau, G. *Les normes d'habilitation*. Dalloz, 2006
Valadés, D. *La dictadura constitucional en America Latina*. UNAM, Instituto de investigaciones jurídicas, 1974
Vander Stichele, A. *La notion d'urgence en droit public*. Bruylant, 1986
Vasseur, M. "Urgence et droit civil" 52 *Revue trimestrielle de droit civil*, 1954, 403–437
Vermeule, A. *The Constitution of Risk*. Cambridge University Press, 2013
Vyhnánek, L., Blechová, A., Bátrla, M., Míšek, J., Novotná, T., Reichman, A., & Harašta, J. "The Dynamics of Proportionality: Constitutional Courts and the Review of COVID-19 Regulations" 25 *German Law Journal*, 2024, 386–406
Wittgenstein, L. *Dictées: à Friedrich Waismann et pour Moritz Schlick, années 1930* (A. Soulez tr & ed., G. Baker pres., B. McGuinness postf.). Librairie philosophique J. Vrin, 2015
Wittgenstein, L. *Philosophische Untersuchungen / Philosophical Investigations*. 4th ed. (G.E.M. Anscombe, P.M.S. Hacker, & J. Schulte trs). Wiley-Blackwell, 2009
Ylarri, J.S. "Permanent Economic Emergency in Argentina and its Constitutional Implications" 13 *Mexican Law Review*, 2020, 87–114

CHAPTER 4

The Constitutional Imaginaries of Crisis and Emergency: Between Battle of Narratives and Entanglement in Quantum Constitutionalism

Martin Belov

4.1 Introduction

Emergency has been widely explored in legal and political theory. The conceptual issues of emergency, its history, types, and constitutional regimes have been analyzed in legal and political theory in much detail.[1] Crisis has been an analytical object of social sciences and humanities, but less of legal scholarship. The reason is that an emergency is a constitutional phenomenon that is traditionally institutionalized in the constitutions and

This chapter is produced as part and funded by the European Union-NextGenerationEU, through the National Recovery and Resilience Plan of the Republic of Bulgaria, project No bg-rrp-2.004-0008.

[1] See e.g., Richard Albert and Yaniv Roznai (eds.) *Constitutionalism Under Extreme Conditions: Law, Emergency, Exception* (Springer, 2020), 1–466, Alan Greene, *Permanent States of Emergency and the Rule of Law. Constitutions in an Age of Crisis* (Hart, 2018) 1–223, Martin Belov (ed), *Rule of Law in Crisis: Constitutionalism in a State of Flux* (Routledge, 2023) and Martin Belov, *Courts and Judicial Activism under Crisis Conditions: Policy Making in a Time of Illiberalism and Emergency Constitutionalism* (Routledge, 2021).

M. Belov (ed.), *Constitutional Polycrisis and Emergency Constitutionalism*, Federalism and Internal Conflicts,
https://doi.org/10.1007/978-3-032-06516-2_4

the constitutional law. At the same time, a crisis is usually considered a factual phenomenon that is only indirectly regulated by law, and when it happens, it mostly does so through the lens of emergency. Thus, the traditional positivist and institutionalist approaches tackle crisis indirectly by subsuming it under the concept and regimes of emergency. Hence, emergencies and their constitutional and administrative regimes provide the legal instruments for coping with crises. Nevertheless, both crisis and emergency gained huge attention since the beginning of the twenty-first century. The literature on crisis and emergency has mushroomed in the current age of constitutional polycrisis and constitutional polytransition.[2]

This chapter is not devoted to the constitutional regimes of emergency and the legal framing of crisis-as-emergency. It will not explore the types, procedures, and preconditions of an emergency. It is not a historical overview of the crisis and emergency. It does not provide a typology of crisis and emergency or an analysis of their normative-institutional or empirical manifestations.

Instead, the chapter explores the epistemology of emergency from a symbolic-imaginary perspective. Hence, it rests upon several fundamental concepts that organize the analysis and the argumentative logic. These are the concepts of constitutional imaginary, quantum constitutionalism, cloud constitutionalism, quantum entanglement, narrative sovereignty, and layered narrative.

The analysis starts with an explanation of why crises and emergencies are signified and represented in the form of layered narratives. It shows that the constitutional imaginaries of crisis and emergency are a result of competing narratives, which may amount to battles for control of the narrative. They are ensuing from narrative sovereignty as the ultimate source of narrative quantum entanglement of meaning. The narratives are producing—alternatively or cumulatively—constitutional imaginaries which are shaping the collective constitutional consciousness, subconscious, and unconscious.

The analysis of the narrative-based character of constitutional imaginaries of crisis and emergency is then followed by an outlining of the fundamental concepts of quantum constitutionalism, cloud constitutionalism,

[2] See Martin Belov, 'The Conceptual Shapes of Constitutional Polycrisis: Deconstruction, Asymmetries and Post-Modern Anxieties of Constitutional Normalcy' (2023) 70 Irish Jurist, special issue Law in a Time of Crisis' 393–410, Martin Belov, 'Rule of Law in Europe in Times of Constitutional Polycrisis, Constitutional Polytransition and Democratic Discontent' (2023) 3 Diritto pubblico comparato ed europeo 875–884, and Martin Belov, 'Rule of Law and Democracy in Times of Transitory Constitutionalism, Constitutional Polycrisis and Emergency Constitutionalism: Towards a Global Algorithmic Technocracy?' in Martin Belov (ed) *Rule of Law in Crisis: Constitutionalism in a State of Flux* (Routledge, 2023) 21–47.

and quantum entanglement of the constitutional order via constitutional imaginaries. This allows for the proper embedding of crisis and emergency in the context of quantum constitutionalism.

Furthermore, a symbolic-imaginary conceptual epistemology of crisis and emergency is provided. It allows for a proper understanding of the nature of crisis and emergency as concepts of symbolic-imaginary constitutionalism. The chapter continues with a typology of the constitutional imaginaries of crisis and emergency. Several important types of such imaginaries are outlined and explored. These are the temporal imaginaries of crisis and emergency, the spatial imaginaries of crisis and emergency, the imaginaries of crisis related to the implosion of the constitutional order, and the imaginaries for signification of crisis and emergency as symbolic-imaginary dissociation, alienation, and disgrace.

The chapter concludes with an analysis of the crisis as an opportunity, salvation or element of the constitutional fabric of quantum constitutionalism. It discusses the imaginaries of crisis beyond emergency regimes and fear constitutionalism.

The main claim of this chapter is that constitutional imaginaries are elements of a quasi-neural meta-personal network of consciousness through which the people understand the constitutional order. This network is based on textual, visual, and performative narratives that inspire, engage with, and organize the collective constitutional conscious, subconscious, and unconscious. It produces meaning on the basis of imaginary constitutional enchantment through affectual and emotional nudging and symbolic engagement with constitutional archetypes and other anthropological structures of collective constitutional 'make-believe'.[3]

In contrast to the traditional and predominant understanding that constitutional knowledge and meaning are derived from constitutional texts via reason, the chapter claims that the people get to know the constitutional order through imaginary phenomenology via intellect, intuition, and emotional engagement and experience. Thus, constitutional ideas are manifested, shared, negotiated, and projected in the collective constitutional conscious, subconscious, and unconscious. This happens through ideas signified on various textual, but also visual and performative, planes.

Constitutional imaginaries are elements of the communicative network through which the process of construction, deconstruction, and

[3] See Kendall Walton, *Mimesis as Make-Believe, On the Foundations of Representational Arts* (Harvard University Press, 1993) 1–480 and Cornelius Castoriadis, *The Imaginary Institution of Society* (Polity Press, 1987) 160–165.

reconstruction of constitutional meaning unfolds. Constitutionalism as a networked imaginary-sharing experience is based on reason and text, but also on intuition, emotions, and higher consciousness. It is powering quantum constitutionalism. It is contained in cloud constitutionalism. It is explicated through narration in the form of negotiation or imposition of meaning through the medium and in the shapes of constitutional imaginaries.

The network of constitutional imaginaries can be mastered through quantum entanglement. This means that the narrative sovereign and other authoritative narrators can induce their intent in the web of constitutional imaginaries. Thus, they influence and shape the collective constitutional conscious, subconscious, and unconscious through narrative control. In that regard, the constitutional imaginaries of crisis and emergency play a central role as key nodes in the networked, emotionally loaded, intentionally entangled, and narratively represented web of constitutional meaning. This is due to the fact that crises and emergencies can be used as triggering events for quantum entanglement, collective emotion control, and production of dark constitutional anthropology, dark emotional politics, and dark constitutionalism.

4.2 Crisis and Emergency as Layered Narratives

'In the beginning was the Word, and the Word was with God, and the Word was God' (John 1:1). This is probably one of the most important and quoted verses from the Bible. It spreads the belief in the ability of the consciousness—indeed, higher consciousness—to determine the manifestation and unfolding of matter through the medium of narration. It rests upon the understanding that the world materializes through creative narration. Narration is conceived as a process of unveiling the structures of meaning and being, both ontologically and teleologically, where the creative potential of the phenomena takes material shapes in the realm of facts. This frequently happens through constitutional imaginaries as signification proxies of meaning. Hence, this verse reverses the relationship between object and subject, objectivity and subjectivity, matter and energy, intent and its projection in the objective reality. It shows the power of the consciousness and intent to master its material explications, transformations, and permutations in the realms of the real. This occurs through control over the narrative as a tool for projecting consciousness in the realm of the facts, typically using the universal language of ideas signified through imaginaries.

Indeed, the Bible speaks of the divine intent that is capable of mastering reality through its metaphysical, supreme, and non-local consciousness. Nevertheless, the constitutional ideology of Modernity operates with secular versions of such supreme and usually unrestrained creative consciousness. Most of the founding mythologies and constitutional ontologies presuppose the existence of constitutional moments,[4] moments of anomy, situations of power vacuum, state of exception[5]or similar 'Zero hours' in space–time continuum usually perceived as history, where a quasi-metaphysical phenomenon occurs and unfolds its unrestrained creative will, thus shaping the constitutional world *ex nihil.*

This axiomatic transformative supreme will belongs to the mythical entity generally labelled as 'sovereign'. The sovereign is a shape-shifter, since it may manifest itself in different forms, for example, materializing as monarch, dictator, Leviathan, 'we the people', the nation as a political entity or a transtemporal community, etc. It can even take the shape of a constitutional institution, such as the Parliament, in the case of the UK constitutional order based on parliamentary sovereignty.[6]

The 'secular God'—the sovereign—speaks and narrates through another entity that is entrenched in constitutional mythology. This is the 'constitutional legislator' as a pragmatic institutional tool for manifesting the will of the sovereign. The will of the sovereign is manifested through constitutional text and signified in constitutional texture. It results in narratives that are subject to narrative and linguistic sovereignty.[7]

Departing from the Biblical context and metaphor, it seems increasingly plausible to assume that consciousness is capable of shaping and reshaping

[4] See Bruce Ackerman, *We the People: Foundations* (Harvard University Press, 1991) 266.

[5] See Carl Schmitt, *The Concept of the Political* (University of Chicago Press, 2007) 19–80.

[6] See e.g., Michael Gordon, *Parliamentary Sovereignty in the UK Constitution: Process, Politics and Democracy* (Hart, 2015) 1–350 and Jeffrey Goldsworthy, *Parliamentary Sovereignty: Contemporary Debates* (Cambridge, 2010) 1–339.

[7] It should be noted that here I use narrative and linguistic sovereignty as concepts defining ultimate narrative control as tool for imposing meaning following Roland Barthes idea of the "death of the author and the birth of the narrator" and not as sovereignty in terms of autonomy or authorization to use a native language. For the concept of visual sovereignty see Michelle Raheja, *Reservation Reelism: Redfacing, Visual Sovereignty, and Representations of Native Americans in Film* (University of Nebraska Press, 2011) 1–360.

reality, at least to a certain extent.[8] The choice of method recalibrates its object. Constitutional phenomena can look different if approached from positivist, institutionalist, realist, socio-legal, metaphysical, semiotic, and imaginary perspectives. This is even more so if we consider the range of approaches to constitutional ontology, axiology, and teleology.

The shaping role of consciousness and imagination on the realm of facts and the realm of norms applies not only to the scientific method of research. It also concerns the methods for symbolic-imaginary signification as well as for normative construction, deconstruction, and reconstruction of legal and socio-legal reality. The former comprises the set of constitutional imaginaries shaped in the context of the range of processes for the signification of constitutional meaning. The latter includes the norm-setting function of the public power implied through legislation or jurisprudential law-making and its policy-making function that frames and forms the policy objects and phenomena.

Reductionist positivism approaches to constitutional law rest upon the belief in the predetermining role of norms on facts as well as of both norms and facts on beliefs and imaginaries. Contrary to this understanding, my claim here is that the agenda setters in the constitutional orders possess the capacity to shape the object of their activity by imposing on it the perceivable forms in which it manifests itself. In other words, the narrative frames the process of manifestation of the constitutional phenomena when they are taking shape in the realms of norms, institutions, and facts. This occurs through the conscious intention of the narrator, intuitively and intellectually managing the network of constitutional imaginaries. Norm-setting and policy-making are creative activities implying authoritative selection of the scope of reality that shall be mastered and the way it shall be conceptualized from a legal (normative and imaginary) perspective.

Thus, constitutional phenomena are not entirely objectively predetermined. They are a result of the selective deconstruction of reality and its intentional reconstruction according to a deliberate plan, ensuing in conceptual ordering and epistemic matrices. This plan is set by the agent of an imaginary setting and governance through different strategies and forms of signification and narration. The role of narrative, signification, and imaginary-setting agents can be played by the actors involved in official schemes of power (e.g., by the Parliaments, apex courts,[9] and the

[8] Benjamín Labatut, *When We Cease to Understand the World* (New York Review Books, 2021) 1–192.

[9] For the concept of apex court see Stefan Schlegel, 'Activism as Defence: The Role of Courts in Shaping the Relationship between Constitutions and International Law. A

institutions of the constituent power) or by range of political players and even theorists possessing the convincing power to persuade the audience, shape the public opinion, and produce or at least influence the constitutional imaginaries.

Thus, the constitutional phenomena, once narratively reconstructed, are being projected in the collective constitutional conscious, subconscious, and unconscious via structural significations explicated through , and unconscious via structural significations explicated through a range of signifiers. This process leads to the production of constitutional imaginaries as nodes of condensed meaning stemming from a narrative-based grid of layered cognition. In that regard, constitutional imaginaries serve as epistemic and signification nodes in a signification grid of power through meaning capable of producing constitutional ontologies and teleologies. This is especially true for the imaginaries of crisis, frequently paralleled by imaginaries of fear. They are generating triggering events that can start the unfolding of a constitutional transition and even a constitutional polytransition.

Hence, constitutional narratives are powerful instruments for influencing public opinion, forming constitutional anthropology, and shaping the constitutional conscious, subconscious, and unconscious. They are tools for predetermining reality by putting it through narratives in symbolic-imaginary frames and forms. They are also creating webs of epistemic links between the realms of the symbolic, the imaginary, the normative, and the real, where constitutional imaginaries serve as key nodes.

The constitutional narratives are normative stories. They derive their normativity from their substance and object—the constitutional phenomenon, that is narratively shaped, but also from the authority of the storyteller in case it is an office holder of a constitutional institution. The constitutional narratives predetermine the ways we perceive the world and set our epistemic and analytical perspective on the constitutional phenomena.

In that context, narration is power. It is the ultimate power to create the emotional apperception and rational comprehension of the constitutional order, the constitutional phenomena, and the multitude of their particular manifestations. The narratives are sources of authority and legitimacy. They are the instruments for the expression of linguistic and narrative

comparison of the apex Courts of Switzerland, Germany, and Austria' in M Belov (ed) *Courts and Judicial Activism under Crisis Conditions: Policy Making in a Time of Illiberalism and Emergency Constitutionalism* (Routledge, 2022) 43–61.

sovereignty. The traditional theories of sovereignty share the feature of covering, neglecting or omitting narrative and linguistic sovereignty as a key element of the supreme creative will of the sovereign. This is because they focus mostly on political and legal hegemony and domination manifested as ultimate decision-making authority and constitutional supremacy.

Narrative and linguistic sovereignty must be unveiled and explained precisely with regard to its huge potential as a world-making and 'king-making' factor in times of crisis and emergency. Narrative mastering of decisive constitutional moments and especially of political 'points of no return' in a power vacuum, constitutional polytransition, and situations of crisis and emergency through promotion of political and constitutional narratives and constitutional imaginaries is an underestimated key tool for engaging the constitutional consciousness via activation of the constitutional subconscious and unconscious. It shapes the *Weltanschauung*,[10] the *Gestalt*, and the *Zeitgeist* of the people and creates the paradigmatic and core features of the 'constitutional make-believe'.[11] It is producing constitutional magic as the necessary imaginary glue that unites the different layers of the constitutional phenomena into an emotionally and imaginatively appealing and rationally plausible 'make-believe'. The linguistic and narrative sovereignty—especially in situations of crisis and emergency—has the capacity for materializing the constitutional energy into constitutional matter and for creating, shaping, and ordering constitutional orders out of intent and narration.

The narrative and linguistic sovereignty is an excellent explanatory tool expressing the power of narration as a method for formative cognition of the world and for imposing the normativity of meaning on the constitutional phenomena. It is a way for explicating the constitutional energy (the implied potential of constitutional phenomena) and for its imprinting on the range of constitutional textures (textual, visual, performative, etc.) through narratives and imaginaries, thus shaping constitutional matter.

It should be noted that there are various forms of expressive modes for the signification of constitutional and constitutionally relevant meaning, and the textual and linguistic is only one of them. Thus, the concept of linguistic sovereignty must be expanded to the broader category of narrative sovereignty. Narrative sovereignty must include the different forms of expression of constitutional meaning through text, but also via

[10] See Wilhelm Dilthey, *Weltanschauung, Philosophie und Religion* (Legare Street Press, 2023) 1–516.

[11] See Kendall Walton, Op. cit. 1–480 and Cornelius Castoriadis, Op. cit. 160–165.

behavior, art, architecture, film, and other means for the representation of constitutional concepts. Hence, narrative sovereignty unfolds on the various plains for the signification of constitutional and constitutionally relevant meaning. It is implemented via symbolic-imaginary, emotional, visual, performative, and textual constitutionalism.[12] In this context, the constitutional imaginaries are the climax of the process of transformation of constitutional energy into a constitutional matter. Thus, they are a key element in the process of unfolding quantum constitutionalism.[13]

The explanation of the role of narrative and linguistic sovereignty for creating and controlling the narrative and the importance of the battle of narratives in times of crisis and emergency is one of the main tasks of this chapter. In that regard, the epistemic control of the socio-legal constellations and the power and authority relations as key elements of constitutional epistemology in action consists in power battles for control over the narratives and significations of the constitutional phenomena. The narratives are broader and more extensive epistemic strategies for generating normative meaning, whereas the significations are targeted inductions of meaning that reveal the constitutional imaginaries.

Hence, a crisis is an objective event, a target of policy-making, and a fact of life that may be manipulated by legal and political action. An emergency is the legal response to a crisis. Fear is an emotion that can be objectively existent, but also mastered through the politics of fear. However, apart from that, crisis, emergency and fear are narratives. They are objects of narrative policy and sovereignty shaping imaginaries of crisis and emergency. Crisis is the context of intense battles of narratives in times of emergency and transition. The control over the narratives on crisis and emergency is a key factor for the production of imaginaries and collective beliefs. Thus, it is an object of narrative and linguistic policies aiming at control over the power and authority and at producing legitimacy for change and transition. The battle for the control of narratives is a war for the hearts and minds of the people. It is a fight for shaping the official story of the materialization of the constitutional energy in constitutional matter in times of constitutional polycrisis and constitutional polytransition.

The battle of narratives and the war over the creation of a predominant narrative have occurred in all instances of the constitutional polycrisis that

[12] Martin Belov, *Constitutional semiotics. The Conceptual Foundations of a Constitutional Theory and Meta-Theory* (Hart publishing, 2022), 1–349.

[13] Ibid., 31–49.

has been unfolding since the beginning of the twenty-first century. This has happened in the context of the terrorism and security crisis, the financial crisis, the migration crisis, the COVID-19 pandemic, and the asymmetric mixture of regional wars and global cold war. These narratives have been systematically arranged around imaginaries and narratives that were emotionally engaging, visually appealing, and, at least to a certain extent, rationally plausible and convincing. Typically, these imaginaries of crisis and emergency were paralleled by imaginaries of fear. The role of the latter, being part of a fear politics, has been to promote obedience and acceptance of policies and, in the long term, to create dark anthropology based on negative emotions that is capable of sustaining dark constitutionalism.

Due to space constraints, I will not be able to expand and properly present the range of narratives that have been launched in the context of the constitutional polycrisis and constitutional polytransition. Here I shall just indicatively mention the narratives created around the imaginaries of the enemy, for example, the 'invisible enemy' in the case of the COVID-19 pandemic or the "invaders" and "aliens" in the case of terrorism and migration crisis as well as the war imaginaries for example the "war on terror," the war against "axis of the evil," the "war against the virus" etc.

4.3 The Concepts of Quantum Constitutionalism, Cloud Constitutionalism, and Quantum Entanglement through Constitutional Imaginaries

Quantum constitutionalism is an epistemic and ordering paradigm. It allows for enhanced understanding of the constitutional phenomena and their projection, manifestation, spread, unfolding, and signification in constitutional order conceived as a multidimensional reality that has spatial, temporal, but also conscious (intentional-volitional and imaginary) dimensions. The quantum approach can be used for explaining the constitutional order organized through institutions, which is the traditional understanding, or via imaginaries.

However, quantum constitutionalism can also be a more ambitious paradigm, stretching beyond the traditional institutional structure of the constitutional order. It is a theory producing a paradigm for ordering the constitutional order via a web of constitutional imaginaries serving as a constitutional neuron network and coordinated through narratives (textual, visual, performative, etc). The narratives are textual, verbal, performative, or visual stories with potential factual normativity. They are embedded in quantum entanglement.

The quantum entanglement is based on both the quantum and narrative aspects of the network of constitutional imaginaries. The quantum features refer to the permanent interplay between constitutional energy (consciousness, intent, and potential) and the constitutional matter (manifestation of the energy on the legal, socio-legal and imaginary plains of meaning). The quantum unfolding occurs through the transformation of the constitutional everywhen[14] in concrete imaginaries embedded in the time-space framework of constitutionalism. This happens through the medium of constitutional consciousness, projecting itself in the collective constitutional subconscious and unconscious and taking shapes of constitutional imaginaries.

Quantum entanglement is achieved and mastered through narratives produced as a result of narrative sovereignty. Hence, the narrative sovereign creates the initial and decisive push of the quantum entanglement, starting the quantum process of interplay between constitutional energy and constitutional matter. Usually, this happens in the context of a crisis and emergency or is at least facilitated by them. Thus, crisis and emergency are key nodes in the quantum entanglement, giving decisive pushes to the system (institutional and/or imaginary) and serving as triggering events in the quantum process. Then, multiple authoritative and semi-authoritative narrators are subsequently engaged in the process of unfolding the network of imaginaries, reproducing, further developing, and fine-tuning the quantum entanglement. They are the narrative agents of the quantum constitutional order structured as a network of constitutional imaginaries.

It must be mentioned that this organizational logic and the theory of the quantum entanglement of the quasi-neuron network of imaginaries produced through narrative sovereignty and narration are applicable to all forms of constitutional imaginaries. Thus, it constitutes a new holistic epistemic and ordering paradigm of the constitutional order. Here I am just demonstrating its epistemic and ordering capacity in the case of crisis and emergency. The specific addendum of the topic of the constitutional imaginaries of crisis and emergency to the theory of quantum constitutionalism is that it demonstrates the role of crisis and emergency as triggers of quantum transformations. This is especially valid in the context of dark

[14] More about the concept of everywhen see Ann McGrath, Laura Rademaker, Jakelin Troy (eds.) *Everywhen. Australia and the Language of Deep History* (UNSW Press, 2023) 1–324.

constitutionalism, negative emotional constitutional anthropology, and fear politics.[15]

Quantum constitutionalism is a paradigm that tries to frame the certainty about uncertainty from a constitutional perspective. It rests upon the overall logic of quantum physics applied in the context of constitutional phenomenology. Quantum constitutionalism presupposes that, by analogy to quantum physics, we can assume that constitutional phenomena are stretched between energy and matter. According to this overall quantum logic, each constitutional phenomenon contains a principal capacity that includes its essence, typical functionality, and content. This is the constitutional energy. This energy then materializes in the normative order, in the social realm, and on the plane of the collective constitutional consciousness, subconscious, and unconscious, taking the shapes of institutions, facts (mostly patterns with factual normativity), and imaginaries.

What constitutes the constitutional matter may differ according to the methodological and conceptual viewpoints. It can be the norms, the elements of the valid law, the institutions (legal positivism and institutionalism), but also the facts (socio-legal approaches), and the imaginaries (symbolic-imaginary epistemology grounded in constitutional anthropology, semiotics, semantics, and collective psychology). The definition of the constitutional energy can also vary according to the conceptual and methodological standpoint.

In my account, the constitutional energy comprises the principal characteristics of the constitutional phenomenon and the initial intent for its creation. The constitutional matter includes the modalities and patterns through which they unfold, manifest themselves, and crystallize in legal and socio-legal reality. The constitutional matter consists of the norms and institutions, the facts, the emotions and affectual attitudes, the symbols, but especially the imaginaries. The materialization of the energy also includes the imprinting and signification of intent and meaning on the various planes for the signification of constitutional and constitutionally relevant meaning. These are the plains of visual, performative, textual, and emotional constitutionalism.

Traditional institutionalist theory that predominates as an epistemological paradigm in constitutional scholarship implicitly rests upon this

[15] See Martin Belov, 'The Role of Fear Politics in Global Constitutional 'Ernstfall': Images of Fear under COVID-19 Health Paternalism' in M Belov (ed) *Populist Constitutionalism and Illiberal Democracies. Between Constitutional Imagination, Normative Entrenchment and Political Reality* (Intersentia, 2021) 187–221.

still unacknowledged concept. All theories that explain constitutional phenomena in abstract, from the viewpoint of the 'law in books', imply that there is imminent logic contained in each of the constitutional institutions, regardless of whether they are public power institutions or human rights. Then, they try to project this quasi-natural, quasi-eternal logic, pretending that it is a universal epistemic tool due to the systemic embeddedness and objectivity of constitutional phenomena. This wrong assumption is based on the merger of the constitutional energy of the phenomenon—in the case of institutionalism, this is the institution—that includes its essential abstract features with the constitutional matter consisting in the way these features materialize in the 'law in action' on the plains of empirical socio-legal reality.

Conversely, traditional socio-legal approaches to constitutional phenomena focus mostly or even exclusively on the constitutional matter. They study the manifestations of the constitutional phenomena in the socio-legal reality and their performance as part of the empirical past (the constitutional history), the empirical present, while eventually making predictions for the empirical future. This emphasis on constitutional context and empirical performance overestimates the constitutional matter while underestimating the constitutional energy.

Hence, strictly legal approaches such as institutionalism and positivism are stuck on the conceptual, principle, abstract, "energy" level of the constitutional phenomena. At the same time, socio-legal approaches are, on the contrary, overwhelmed by the constitutional matter. They are exaggerating the role of the empirical manifestations of the phenomena and the concrete shapes they take in a certain context.

In fact, both approaches are conceptually wrong but make similar epistemic failures. They are opposite in a mirroring way, but are based on the same conceptual failure. It consists of the disregard of the quantum features of cognition, the quantum dialectics of energy and matter, and the creative role of the constitutional conscious, subconscious and unconscious for shaping the certainly uncertain world of quantum constitutionalism stretched between "constitutional everywhen" and constitutional "make-believe."

Quantum constitutionalism is capable of explaining the transdimensional character of the constitutional phenomena. Thus, it is related to constitutional philosophy of time, constitutional philosophy of space, constitutional ontology, and the theory of the constitutional consciousness. This is because it explains the unfolding of constitutional phenomena in the space-time based on the certainty about the uncertainty regarding the ways the constitutional energy shall imprint itself in the realms of norms, facts, and imaginaries through the medium of the constitutional consciousness. Hence, quantum constitutionalism is a non-reductionist concept that explores constitutional phenomena in a dynamic and multi-dimensional way. It views them as fuzzy concepts embedded in a process of permanent unfolding stretched between the constitutional energy and constitutional matter, between capacity and its manifestation in the valid law, in socio-legal reality, and in the realms of the collective constitutional conscious, subconscious, and unconscious.

Quantum constitutionalism is also an ordering paradigm. It has the capacity to order the constitutional order beyond positivist, institutionalist, and legal realist matrices. Quantum constitutionalism does not deny the normative structure and institutional systematization of the constitution and constitutional law. However, it goes beyond them using multidimensionality, singularity, phenomenological organization, and cloud constitutionalism as its ordering schemes. The fundamental post-positivist and post-institutionalist claim of quantum constitutionalism that constitutional order is organized in a quantum way as a quasi-neuron network of constitutional imaginaries, which are coordinated, maintained, and developed through narratives and are entangled via narrative sovereignty, has already been explained above. In fact, this network of constitutional imaginaries is contained in cloud constitutionalism that sustains them on the basis of quantum logic.

Quantum constitutionalism operates in a multidimensional field comprising legal, empirical, and symbolic-imaginary layers of constitutional meaning. They are signified in various planes for their representation—textual, performative, visual, etc. Quantum constitutionalism rests upon the interplay between reason and emotions, intellect and intuition, conscious, subconscious, and unconscious. It organizes the constitutional order on the basis of the understanding of the entanglement between time, space, and consciousness.

The quantum entanglement of the multidimensional constitutional order and its spread in the realms of the conscious, subconscious, and unconscious produce the logical and organizational link between quantum and cloud constitutionalism. The clouds of constitutional meaning that serve as an invisible, but detectable and intelligible network of bonds between the members of the constitutional community are conceptualized through cloud constitutionalism. The collective attitudes, patterns of constitutionally relevant performance, and anthropological structures and predispositions of the members of the constitutional community create constitutional imaginaries preserved in the collective memories and the collective dreams, hopes, and fears. They crystallize in clouds of constitutional meaning. These clouds explicate the quantum characteristics of the constitutional phenomena as transtemporal networks in the constitutional imagination of the community, representing a form of higher-level transpersonal consciousness. Thus, cloud constitutionalism manifests the quantum characteristics of imagination, intent, and consciousness as driving forces of the constitutional order. At the same time, it serves as one of the organizing principles of quantum constitutionalism. In fact, cloud constitutionalism is the depot or storage of constitutional imaginaries, the latter being both driving force and result of the quantum unfolding of the constitutional phenomena in the course of the materialization of their potential or energy in the legal and socio-legal reality.

Quantum constitutionalism does not necessarily presuppose phenomenological organization of the constitutional order but can be facilitated by it. Indeed, more traditional approaches, such as the institutional one, may also be used to follow quantum logic. Constitutional institutions, regardless of whether human rights, public sphere or public power institutions, are also stretched between potential and its explication, constitutional energy and constitutional matter that reveal quantum dynamics. However, a phenomenological approach allows for focusing on the proper substance of the phenomena and not on their formal institutional shell. Institutions contribute to the legal shaping of constitutional phenomena. Nevertheless, they are too rigid and predisposed to the idea that the institutional system is rational, logical, and predictable by knowing its typical features explicated in institutional models, typologies, and schemes of power, constitutional competences, and constitutional functions.

Phenomenological organization of the constitutional order permits a more substantial, content-oriented epistemology that goes beyond the formal restraints of the institutional approach. Constitutional epistemology based on a phenomenological approach allows for multidiscursive analysis taking into account the rational, emotional, and symbolic-imaginary dimensions of the constitutional phenomena, its projection in the space-time through the collective conscious, subconscious and unconscious. It also includes the role of consciousness in the equation of the materialization of the constitutional energy in constitutional matter on the plains of the legal, the empirical, and the imaginary. The ultimate result of the quantum phenomenology is constitutional imaginaries as a point of intersection between the temporal, spatial, and conscious factors for the production of the constitutional 'make-believe'.

Quantum constitutionalism also implies singularity. This is the singularity of the collective constitutional consciousness explicated in the cloud constitutionalism through the network of constitutional imaginaries. Such singularity presupposes the intrinsic coordination between constitutional intent and its projection in the realms of the legal, the real, and the symbolic-imaginary, between experience and cognition, between rational constitutional teleology and its affectual apprehension. Singularity does not mean uniformity. Hence, there might be a multitude of constitutional imaginaries resulting from the interaction between constitutional energy and constitutional matter mastered by intent, cognition, and consciousness.

Hence, quantum constitutionalism orders the constitutional order through constitutional phenomenology, aiming at and stemming from singularity as a focal point of transdimensionality, explicated through clouds of meaning, and resulting in a multidimensional matrix stretched between energy and matter, determinacy and fuzziness, intent and its materialization and signification. This unfolding of the quantum characteristics of the constitutional order may have different appearances. It may take the shape of battles for authority and legitimacy. It is, however, ultimately a battle for mastering constitutional meaning, resulting in a battle of constitutional imaginaries.

The epistemic and ordering matrix of quantum constitutionalism consists in the interplay between the conceptual potential of the constitutional phenomenon and its manifestation through institutionalization, textualization, and socio-legal and symbolic-imaginary externalization. It demonstrates the creative, partially unpredictable, and existentially insecure tension between the intent for launching constitutional ideas and their objectivation in phenomena of the legal and empirical reality, as well as in constitutional imaginaries.

Quantum constitutionalism presumes the intelligible dynamic linking between the collective and individual constitutional conscious, subconscious, and non-conscious. It results in the conscious construction, deconstruction, and reconstruction of the institutional, normative, and material structures of the constitutional and constitutionally relevant textures through the creative intent and intuition of the constitutional agenda setters and constitutional narrators. These are operating as semi-informed and semi-autonomous agents of the constitutional order.

In this context, the constitutional order is performing as a fuzzy system based on quantum entanglement. The constitutional agenda setters, policy-makers, and narrators are semi-informed. This is because their activity is stretched between their intent, intuition, and subjective self-perception, which is typically based on interest maximization, and the determinants of the objective reality, which are quantum variables.

Hence, quantum entanglement of the constitutional order relates to the programming and signification of concepts, structures, and ideas, which are only partially dependent on operational ontological constitutional imaginaries that are trying to produce a sense of rationality, manageability, and determinacy of the process. The main operational ontological constitutional imaginaries are the "will of the sovereign," the "will of the constitutional legislator," "the will of the parliament," and even the "general will." The quantum entanglement in the context of quantum constitutionalism consists in the modelling of the legal and socio-legal reality through human reason on the basis of initial intent that projects itself in the course of unfolding of the constitutional model in the time-space continuum—in the constitutional everywhen—under the conditions of quantum uncertainty. The main aim of this quantum entanglement is to transfer and project ideas stemming from the normative (constitutional and legislative) intent of the agent of policy-making and constitutional change in the constitutional conscious, subconscious, and unconscious of the constitutionally framed community through the medium of the constitution and the constitutional law.

The constitutional quantum entanglement is organized through constitutional imaginaries signified via signifiers of textual, visual, performative, and emotional constitutionalism. These imaginaries are symbolic proxies between the reason and the emotions, the intellect and the intuition, the imagination and the behavior. They are activators and triggers of the individual and collective subconscious and unconscious. They are imprinting symbolic labels of affectual and intuitive apprehension of quantum entangled constitutional meaning.

Quantum entanglement allows for guidance of human and institutional behavior through constitutional imaginaries produced in the process of unfolding and materialization of the energy potential of the constitutional phenomenon. It allows for remote emotional control of the agents of the constitutional order (both office holders and the people) via a network of constitutional imaginaries serving as rational-emotional bridges, affectual stimuli for constitutionally relevant behavior, and emotional-imaginary proxies to human intuition. These imaginaries function in a quantum way, thus making their performance stretched between the constitutional energy and constitutional matter.

In a sense, the quantum entanglement of constitutional meaning resembles a game of encoding and decoding of constitutional intent through textual, visual, and performative proxies taking the shape of constitutional imaginaries. In this context, constitutional imaginaries function as nodes in a power field of shared enhanced consciousness. They are generated through signifiers of meaning entrenched in the official, explicit, and textually enshrined constitutional institutions. They can also be produced via signifiers of meaning stemming from visual, performative, and emotional constitutionalism, relying on activation of cognition via intellect and intuition.

In that regard, quantum constitutionalism as a paradigm for mastering the quantum potential of the constitutional phenomena and conceptualizing the certainty about uncertainty is intertwined with cloud constitutionalism as a paradigm for framing the dispersed threats of the collective constitutional consciousness, subconscious, and unconscious. Hence, quantum constitutionalism serves as a concept for grasping the creative fuzziness of the world that is stretched between creative intention, deconstructive and reconstructive assertion, and interdimensional dynamics between the symbolic, the imaginary, the normative, and the real.

4.4 Crisis and Emergency in the Context of Quantum Constitutionalism

The constitutional imaginaries approach to constitutional phenomena offers a rather different epistemological paradigm of crisis and emergency. It conceives crisis and emergency as variables that are dependent on both constitutional energy and constitutional matter organized through consciousness and intent. The key to understanding the oscillations of crisis and emergency between constitutional energy and constitutional matter is the pivotal role played by the collective constitutional consciousness, subconscious, and unconscious signified through constitutional imaginaries.

In that regard, constitutional imaginaries of crisis and emergency play a pivotal role in the epistemology of crisis and emergency in the context of quantum constitutionalism. They are the intellectual proxies that make explicit the bond between theoretical features, institutional potentialities, and empirical projections and implications. They are symbolic-imaginary shortcuts to meaning distilled on the edge between collective constitutional conscious, subconscious, and unconscious. The huge epistemic potential of constitutional imaginaries of crisis and emergency, in conjunction with their emotional load capable of activating affective attitudes of anxiety, fear, and despair or, vice versa, of security and salvation, usually grounded in a paternalistic logic of survival, makes them excellent tools for mastering the politics of fear.

Consequently, the control of the narratives of crisis and emergency is a matter of linguistic and narrative sovereignty, as explained above, which may be the key to dark emotional control. It is a well-established truth that ultimate decisions are typically imposed in times of anomy and normative vacuum. However, it is less discussed that the very moment of crisis and emergency, which can potentially culminate in such a pivotal turning point for "making order out of disorder," can be established via narratives signified in a condensed and emotionally appealing way via constitutional imaginaries. Such imaginaries must be not only intellectually plausible, but also intuitively, subconsciously, and affectively appealing.

Hence, crisis and emergency can be ambiguous terms. They can relate to phenomena of the empirical world, to normative situations when specific rules and legal regimes are activated and applied to, but also to psychological phenomena such as affects, emotions, and imaginaries. In that regard, we can distinguish between crisis as fact, emergency as a constitutional law regime, and crisis and emergency as imaginary or a set of imaginaries used to produce or sustain certain affectual attitudes towards the first two aspects outlined here.

It is not necessary that all three aspects coincide with each other. The crisis may be unfolding the reality, but without a legal response addressing them through the imposition of an emergency regime. At the same time, if the public opinion is not focused on them and is not activated via detectable and appealing imaginaries of crisis and emergency, they may not even draw much attention and may be left disregarded by the people. And, vice versa, a crisis may be staged through imaginaries in order to justify an emergency regime to be imposed, although empirically its causes and manifestations may be rather minor and unimportant beyond the deliberate activation of negative feelings, for example, anxiety, fear, and despair. This shows that the facts that constitute the crisis and the norms on the basis of which an emergency is declared are dependent variables. They are dependent on the politics of crisis, fear, and emergency that need to be signified and promoted through imaginaries activating the collective constitutional consciousness, subconscious and unconscious.

The quantum characteristics of emergency and crisis can be outlined as follows. Crisis and emergency are supposed to be objective phenomena preconditioned by facts of the empirical reality and the constitutional institutions. Typically, such facts are security threats (e.g., war, terrorism, insurgency, etc.), diseases (e.g., the COVID-19 pandemic), financial and economic failures, etc. Nevertheless, the empirical fact of crisis can be conceptualized as and subsumed under the legal phenomenon of emergency shaped by the constitution and the pubic law. In that regard, the crisis and emergency as legal and constitutional concepts have abstract shapes provided by the valid law. They also have theoretical contents based upon, but autonomous from, their legal dimension. Hence, the conceptualization of crisis and emergency by constitutional theory and constitutional law generates their energy, the abstract, typical, normative essence, and potential they possess in principle. This energy is derived from their capacity to unfold in an indiscriminate number of situations.

The crisis and emergency materialize through practice and imagination both triggered by intent and consciousness. They reveal their potential by spreading on the ground in the realm of facts, thus getting concrete manifestations in social life. They also expose their potential by materializing in constitutional imaginaries of crisis and emergency.

It is particularly important to emphasize that the imaginary dimension of crisis and emergency relates to both their energy and matter. This means that the constitutional imaginaries of crisis and emergency are containers of meaning on a very abstract level and in condensed, distilled, essential, and symbolic form. Thus, they are containers of the quantum energy of the crisis and emergency as constitutional phenomena. At the same time, they are a result of the manifestation and unfolding of the normative potential of emergency and crisis as legal phenomena on the plains of the collective constitutional conscious, subconscious, and unconscious. Hence, they are forms of constitutional matter produced by the spread of the constitutional energy of crisis and emergency as theoretical and normative-institutional phenomena.

This dual character of constitutional imaginaries of crisis and fear allows them to function as a linkage between the normative-institutional, theoretical, and socio-legal aspects and dimensions of crisis and fear. They are the crossroads of normative expectations, affectual attitudes, legal models, legal policies, and patterns of imaginary relevant behaviors that are related to the phenomena of crisis and emergency.

Emergencies and crises are usually conceived as three-dimensional phenomena that unfold in time and space and constitute a phenomenon that is allocated on the coordination scheme of the time-space. This perception does not consider the entrenchment of crisis and emergency in the collective constitutional conscious, subconscious, and unconscious. Collective consciousness in general and the collective constitutional consciousness in particular actually constitute a fourth dimension.

In such a four-dimensional world, crisis projects itself in a quantum way as both a certain and an uncertain event. There is clear certainty about the uncertainty of the emergence, content, scope, and unfolding of a crisis. That is why the constitutions operate with the implicit presumption of the temporal, spatial, ontological, essential, and contextual content of crisis. This is the reason why the legal imprints of crisis—the emergency regimes provided by the constitution—are regulated in broader shapes. The abstractness of the forms of emergency reflects this certainty about the uncertainty of the appearance and manifestation of crisis, which itself presupposes the quantum character of crisis as a socio-legal and imaginary phenomenon.

Moreover, the three-dimensional characteristics of crisis and its manifestations in space and time do not necessarily coincide with its projection in the collective consciousness as a fourth dimension. In other words, the crisis may unfold as a factual phenomenon in space and time that is fully or partially matching or even mismatching its legal model—the emergency. However, both crisis and emergency can be nonexistent in the collective consciousness due to misinformation through scarcity of information, overburdening with information and/or disinformation or the non-detection of the empirical shapes of the crisis by the collective imaginaries of the people. In that regard, collective imaginaries serve as channels for activating the collective emotions and intellectual attitudes to cope with the empirical fact of crisis and the emergency regime as its constitutional model. Hence, constitutional imaginaries of crisis and emergency are the point of intersection between the realms of the normative, the factual, and the imaginary.

4.5 Symbolic-Imaginary Conceptual Epistemology of Crisis and Emergency

It is important to conceptually clarify the relationship between crisis and emergency. The clarification should also shed light on the relationship between crisis, emergency, and related concepts such as normalcy and fear. It should be noted that while normalcy and emergency are a dichotomic couple on the conceptual level and can be institutional antipodes, fear can be related to crisis and emergency mostly on the plains of facts and imagination. The relationship between crisis and emergency appears as consequential and causal (although this is not always the case, as shall be explained below). The relationship between normalcy and emergency is conceptual, whereas the one between crisis and emergency, on the one hand, and fear, on the other, seems to be functional. In other words, intuitively, a crisis is a precondition for an emergency, an emergency is an alternative to normalcy, and fear is a result of a crisis and an emergency.

Hence, emergency and normalcy are theoretical, empirical, imaginary, but also normative concepts that frequently result in explicit or implicit ways in constitutional regimes. Constitutions typically create emergency regimes while presuming that the governance beyond them constitutes normalcy. This is because the emergency is traditionally conceived to be the exception, while normalcy should be the rule. The emergency regimes are institutionalized in types of emergency, for example, war, state of siege, state of exception, state of natural disaster, etc., provided by the constitutions and constitutional law, thus reversely defining the scope of constitutional normalcy. In this concept, normalcy is the lack of emergency, a non-emergency notwithstanding regimes, policies, and imaginaries normalizing emergency and crisis and leading to 'emergency as normalcy', for example, in times of constitutional polycrisis.

Crisis and fear are much more intellectual, imaginary, emotional, and empirical rather than institutional phenomena. Indeed, a crisis is the precondition for an emergency and is at times partially directly addressed by constitutional law. Nevertheless, the typical approach of the constitutions and constitutional law is to address a crisis indirectly through the medium of emergency shaped as emergency types and procedures. Thus, in a sense, an emergency is the institutional and legal reflection of a crisis that makes the crisis manageable through legal means. From a semiotic perspective, emergency may be the signifier of crisis. It may be the representation of crisis in the normative-institutional realm through textual signifiers provided by the constitution. Thus, we can reconstruct the legal shapes of crisis and indirectly also of constitutional fears through the context, thematic focus, and scope of the emergency. The shapes of emergency regimes provided by the constitution and the legal order implicitly represent the scope of constitutional fears and the range of crises that the constitutional and ordinary legislator attempts to predict, prevent, and remedy. From this particular perspective, an emergency may serve as a constitutional imaginary of crisis signified through the means of textual and rational constitutionalism, subsequently put in practice via performative constitutionalism when the legal provision starts to be implemented on the ground.

This logical relational network of concepts can have different practical and imaginary repercussions and manifestations. Key role for the mismatch between the principle, logical, energy aspect of these concepts and their practical unfolding and performance, producing their materialization, belongs to the constitutional imaginaries of crisis and emergency. Frequently, in conjunction with the constitutional imaginaries of fear, they rearrange the relational conceptual network, allowing for crisis to be the triggering concept of constitutional change and transition towards dark constitutionalism.

To sum up, an emergency is the legal shape and model and from a semiotic viewpoint, also the legal and textual signifier of crisis. Simultaneously, a crisis is, in principle, the factual precondition for an emergency. Crisis is the activator, triggering event, and justification for the emergency. However, these typical and conceptual relations between crisis and emergency are not necessarily immediate and automatic. In other words, a crisis does not always trigger an emergency. In many cases, a crisis unfolds and even ravages societies without the imposition of an emergency as a legal instrument for its restriction, control, and coping with its consequences. And, vice versa, an emergency can be declared without necessarily being sufficiently justified by a substantial and massive crisis. Hence, the relationship between crisis and emergency is not always symmetric, logical, objectively predetermined, and proportional. Emergencies are declared for minor crises, and major crises are not always followed by an emergency or are managed through milder emergency regimes than supposedly necessary.

For example, while migration has been considered a controllable phenomenon of the 'new normal' in the age of global mobility under the Biden administration, President Trump introduced a migration-related emergency on his first day in office. Hence, the same factual preconditions triggered diametrically opposite legal and political responses. What for Joseph Biden was normalcy was immediately reconsidered to be an emergency by Donald Trump. The same happened with the energy emergency introduced by Donald Trump in January 2025. Many further examples beyond these two more recent ones can also be derived from the 2009 financial crisis, the multitude of migration crises, and the COVID-19 pandemic.

The migration crisis has not always led to an emergency. The legal responses to migration varied from its approval and toleration to attempts at legal control and emergency regimes. They even led to the allocation of military forces (e.g., the USA in 2025) and semi-permanent reintroduction of border controls in some Schengen area Member States. In terms of imaginaries, the migrants were framed as innocent victims and objects of (frequently paternalizing) compassion, contributors to the creation of a multicultural and pluralist society. Conversely, they have also been defined and symbolically signified as 'invaders', 'aliens', and 'enemies'. Hence, on a symbolic-imaginary level, there was a clear clash between antipodal imaginaries of the victim and the criminal, the object of compassion and the object of fear.

Moreover, the pandemic crisis has been met with extraordinary measures in Scandinavia, especially in Denmark and Norway, whereas no emergency has been declared in Sweden. Discrepancies in the legal conceptualization of (factual) crisis as (legal) emergency also existed on the subnational level. Good examples are the differences between the various Swiss cantons or the mismatch between England and Scotland in the UK in their approach to the COVID-19 pandemic. The divergent legal, but especially socio–legal–political, media, and imaginary response to the COVID-19 pandemic was also visible in the EU. On the Member States level, certain countries have imposed harsh emergency regimes (e.g., Italy, Greece, and Spain). Other states have worked with more flexible and frequently changing policy responses (e.g., Poland, Hungary and Bulgaria). Last but not least, Sweden was a country where no emergency measures with a sanction character have been introduced. Hence, similar facts have been legally conceptualized, politically framed and collectively imagined in diverse and even antithetical ways.

In the search for a more moderate response to the health crisis, some countries even tried to evade the emergency for political reasons, since the emergency was very unpopular. For example, in Croatia and Bulgaria, some softer intermediate forms of epidemic quasi-emergencies (e.g., the extraordinary epidemic situation) have been introduced and even legalized by the Constitutional Courts. This happened despite the fact that they constituted an unconstitutional constitutional amendment.[16] It consisted of the introduction of a new form of emergency through legislative acts, whereas the constitutions provided for strict lists of the emergency regimes that could have been altered only via explicit constitutional amendment.

The asymmetries between crisis as a fact and emergency as a norm and legal regime are even bigger when we consider the imaginary dimension as part of the equation. There was a huge difference in the perception of the COVID-19 pandemic crisis, for example, in Italy, Greece, and Spain, where it was paralleled by massive fear, and in Bulgaria, where the anxiety was directed much more against the emergency measures than against the virus itself.[17] In many countries, for example, in the USA, UK, Bulgaria, etc., the imaginary division of the society was so deep that it created new political ideologies with constitutional relevance—the vaxxers and the anti-vaxxers. They were sustained through divergent and even antipodal imaginaries. These imaginaries were actually constitutional imaginaries because they referred to freedom, autonomy, choice and control by public power as well as to the rule of law and human rights.

The reasons for potential asymmetries between crisis and emergency from normative, empirical, and imaginary standpoints are mostly related to two factors. These are the policies for crisis management and the constitutional imaginaries of crisis and emergency. These two factors are not necessarily running in parallel but are frequently intertwined on the socio-political and macro-psychological level.

[16] For this concept see e.g., Yaniv Roznai, *Unconstitutional Constitutional Amendments. The Limits of Amendment Powers* (Oxford University Press, 2019) 1–368. For the unconstitutional constitutional amendment accomplished by the Bulgarian Constitutional Court see Martin Belov, 'Mastering emergency situations: The activist role of the Bulgarian Constitutional Court in redefining the constitutional design of war, state of siege and state of emergency' in M Belov (ed) *Courts and Judicial Activism under Crisis Conditions: Policy Making in a Time of Illiberalism and Emergency Constitutionalism* (Routledge, 2021) 171–194.

[17] See Martin Belov, 'The Influence of the COVID-19 Crisis and Its Management in Bulgaria on the Constitutional Principles' in D Valchev, S Groysman (eds) *The COVID-19 Crisis and the Future of Liberal Democracy* (University of Sofia 'St. Kliment Ohridski' Press, 2023) 58–76 and Martin Belov, 'The Role of Fear Politics in Global Constitutional 'Ernstfall': Images of Fear under COVID-19 Health Paternalism' in M Belov (ed) *Populist Constitutionalism and Illiberal Democracies. Between Constitutional Imagination, Normative Entrenchment and Political Reality* (Cambridge, Intersentia, 2021) 187–221.

Emergency is a policy tool for crisis management, whose key forms and principles are usually provided by the constitution. Nevertheless, its use and misuse are dependent on the political decisions for its activation and accomplishment, which not rarely rely on fear politics and contribute to the promotion of dark constitutionalism. Thus, a crisis is only a pre-condition for an emergency, but the declaration of an emergency regime as a legal shape of the emergency as an overall concept is subject to the discretion of the office holders of the competent institutions. This discretion concerns the moment of imposition of the emergency, its duration and forms, as well as the concrete policy and administrative measures. The interplay between the crisis as the object and the emergency as the instrument for crisis management also influences public opinion and public perception of the propriety, proportionality, efficiency, and legitimacy of emergency policies. The public opinion is formed through policies that belong to emergency constitutionalism. They are grounded in and stemming from, but also producing constitutional imaginaries of crisis and emergency. Consequently, crises and emergencies are key factors for the establishment of emergency constitutionalism as an overall phenomenon that signifies the constitutional response to them as well as for shaping the constitutional imaginaries of crisis and emergency.

Emergencies and crises are, in principle, the opposite of normalcy. They are exceptional situations that are supposed to be rare in history and limited in duration. Hence, the intuitive logic, around which the constitutional orders are built, is that the non-emergency and the lack of crisis are the rule while the crisis and the emergency are the exception. Traditionally, most constitutions refrained from trying to institutionalize crisis and emergency due to the belief that they are beyond the scope of constitutional normalcy and cannot be properly framed in legal terms.

That is why, in order to restrain crisis and emergency, the imaginary of their exceptional, temporally limited, extraconstitutional, spontaneous, and objective character has been used. Obviously, this is a composite imaginary that needs to be epistemically deconstructed in order to achieve better knowledge of its paradigmatic importance. Here, it suffices to emphasize that an emergency is traditionally imagined as a phenomenon that distorts the equilibrium and thus must be limited with regard to its temporal and spatial projections. It is also asymmetric deviation from the continuity, integrity, and cohesion of the constitutional normalcy as a transtemporal project for the organization of the constitutional order.

The opposite imaginary is the imaginary of the emergency and crisis as normalcy. The constitutional polycrisis—the multitude of overlapping and mutually reinforcing raging crises—can produce or be used to justify and stabilize the imaginary of the emergency as normalcy. Constitutional polycrisis can be a factual phenomenon. It may describe and denominate the actual processes of multiple ongoing crises that produce both a domino effect and a destructive swirl on the constitutional axiology, the institutional design, and the performance of constitutional normalcy. Thus, constitutional polycrisis may be a signifier of a constitutional normalcy in flux.

Nevertheless, constitutional polycrisis can also be a core around which constitutional imaginaries of crisis, emergency, and fear may be assembled, organized, and mobilized for the promotion of dark constitutionalism. Such imaginaries are imaginaries of constitutional apocalypse, imaginaries of destruction and decay, twilight imaginaries, and imaginaries of different versions of the Leviathan (e.g., security, pandemic, or digital Leviathan). They can be used to promote national, regional or global algorithmic technocracy[18] and security and police state capable of sustaining techno-feudalism[19] and surveillance capitalism.[20]

4.6 The Constitutional Imaginaries of Crisis and Emergency

After the conceptual introduction into the epistemology of the crisis and emergency imaginaries and the outline of their multilayered, narrative-based, and quantum character, now let's turn to the different modalities and forms through which they are represented. This part shall outline some of the most important constitutional imaginaries of crisis and emergency. This presentation is not exhaustive, but rather selective. It focuses on key examples that show the explanatory potential of the imaginary epistemology of crisis and emergency.

[18] See Martin Belov, 'Rule of Law and Democracy in Times of Transitory Constitutionalism, Constitutional Polycrisis and Emergency Constitutionalism: Towards a Global Algorithmic Technocracy?' in M Belov (ed) *Rule of Law in Crisis: Constitutionalism in a State of Flux* (Routledge, 2023) 21–47.

[19] See Yanis Varoufakis, *Technofeudalism: What Killed Capitalism* (Melville House, 2024) 1–304.

[20] See Shoshana Zuboff, *The Age of Surveillance Capitalism: The Fight for a Human Future at the New Frontier of Power* (Public Affairs, 2019) 1–704.

The representation of crisis and emergency has huge epistemic importance that results in explanatory and ordering schemes. The imaginary signs signifying crisis and emergency allow for the reconstruction of various epistemic planes for the extraction of meaning. These imaginaries can be abstractly constructed and used for theoretical modelling of crisis and emergency. Simultaneously, they can be reconstructed from the plains on which crisis and emergency are unfolding—the realms of the valid law, the socio-legal relations, and the durable and structural beliefs that are part of the constitutional anthropology.

4.6.1 Temporal Imaginaries of Crisis and Emergency

One of the most important aspects of the imaginary dimension of crisis and emergency concerns the way they are imagined as part of the space-time. Thus, the temporal and spatial shaping of crisis and emergency results in constitutional imaginaries with paradigmatic importance. The temporal imaginaries of crisis and emergency shall be explored in this section, whereas the next section shall be devoted to the spatial imaginaries of crisis and emergency.

Crisis and emergency can be imagined as topical and focused phenomena limited in time or as a prolonged and continuous crisis. Their imaginary duration allows for the distinctive counterposition between emergency and decay, apocalypse and demise, etc. They are signifiers of crisis, which have different and usually opposite temporal manifestations. Hence, momentum-based crisis, imagined as an extraordinary and singular event, differs from linear imaginaries of the crisis as a process, but also from recurrent imaginaries of crisis as cyclic and spiral-like processes. Thus, it's key to explore the main imaginary perspectives for the temporal structuring of crisis and emergency. In fact, the imaginaries are related mostly to crisis as a factual phenomenon and less to emergency as a legal and constitutional response to it.

Let's start with two antipodal imaginaries—the imaginary of the crisis and emergency as a unique and single event, and the imaginary of the crisis and emergency as a tendency and process. They frame the temporal imaginary landscapes of crisis and emergency.

Traditionally, a crisis is conceived as a single phenomenon. From this perspective, crisis, as the antipode of normalcy, appears rarely in history. However, when it occurs, it profoundly shakes the well-established constitutional order. Hence, a crisis is usually imagined as an exceptional, isolated, and unrepeated event that destroys the predominant harmony of the legal order. It goes beyond the typical fluctuations and the minor disorders that are compatible with normalcy. In that regard, a crisis is a temporal interruption of the otherwise well-ordered fabrics of constitutional space-time and a rare and exceptional break with the normalcy that is the formative concept of both the constitutional past and the constitutional future.

Hence, crisis (with or without an emergency) even functions as a precondition for the overall and principal predominance of normalcy in the unfolding of constitutional time. This is due to the fact that crises and emergencies are the indicators of non-normalcy against which we organize our criteria for normalcy. Thus, crisis is an element of the tuning and adjustment of the mutually related and interdependent regimes of constitutional emergency and constitutional normalcy. This kind of phenomenology of crisis that predominates the legal discourse and is behind the traditional shaping of the constitutional regimes of emergency is signified through the imaginary of the exceptionality of crisis and emergency.

In this context, an emergency can be imagined in twofold and contradictory ways. The first one is the imagination of the crisis as a one-time, predictable event. This imagination suggests that the crisis can be rationally and logically met with reasonable models of emergency provided in a textual and systematic manner by the constitution and the constitutional law. This imaginary of emergency as a predictable quasi-systemic phenomenon integrated in the predictive responses of a well-ordered constitutional system is deeply entrenched in rational and textual constitutionalism. Thus, it is powered by and dependent on the imaginaries of textual and rational constitutionalism. Hence, this imagination rests upon an implied symmetry between the crisis as a potential fact and the emergency as a legal response to it. This symmetry generates conceptual harmony between crisis and emergency reconciled through the means of rational constitutionalism and based on the logic that each problem has a solution.

The clearest example of such an approach to crisis and emergency is the so-called "golden (or balanced) budget rule" that was massively introduced in the EU via the six-pack, the two-pack and the Treaty on Stability, Coordination and Governance. It was subsequently implemented in the constitutional orders of the EU Member States. It rests upon the imaginary that crisis is predictable, avertible, and manageable through rational measures prescribed by the law. The "golden budget rule" as a constitutional imaginary is anti-cyclic. Thus, it frames crisis and emergency as singular events (even if they may eventually occur in the future) and not as linear or cyclic events. This approach has been criticized by many economists who were not convinced of the ability of the golden budget rule to serve as an anticyclic device preventing the negative phases of the financial and economic cycles.

This imagination is also behind the mainstream constitutional models of emergency. They cope with war, insurgency, natural disasters, etc., as single events capable of being conceptually predicted by the constitution and thus framed through constitutional, administrative, and other branches of law.

The imaginary of crisis as a one-time predictable event is the mainstream imaginary that is used for justification of the capacity of the constitutions and constitutional law to cope with crisis and emergency in a rational, logical, consequential way. It is based on the more paradigmatic imaginary of law as written reason (*ratio scripta*) and a universal tool for mastering the complexity of the world through rationalization, systematization, institutionalization, and textualization. This imaginary, however, also implies the possibility for the misuse of crisis for the sake of the introduction of emergency-as-normalcy on the basis of the 'problem-solution' fear politics promoting dark constitutionalism.

The second variant of the exceptionality imaginary of crisis and emergency suggests that crisis is not manageable by law. It is grounded in the belief that law cannot tame a crisis. Thus, an emergency is a void attempt at framing a phenomenon that cannot be mastered through any constitutional or legal provisions, either incidental and ad hoc or systematized in a model. Hence, this is an imaginary of the conceptual asymmetry between fact and norm, crisis and emergency.

This approach is in sharp contrast to the first variant, according to which a crisis can be symmetrically met with a legal response. In this former variant, emergency is the conceptually shaped constitutional regime of non-normalcy framed and imagined as an anticipated normalization of the crisis through textualization, proceduralization, and rationalization. In this first variant, there is imaginary and conceptual symmetry between crisis and emergency.

Consequently, the second variant of the exceptionality imaginary is grounded on the conceptual mismatch between crisis and emergency. Since a crisis is always an extraordinary, unique, untamable event that resembles a kind of eruption of facts similar to a super volcano, then all efforts for its legal management are doomed to failure. In this model, crisis is conceived as a one-time event of radical rupture of normalcy and clear departure from established patterns of normativity. Hence, crisis is a disruptive anomy, a unique moment of power vacuum, and a situation of fundamental antinomy and aporia. Paradoxically, it is a precondition for the normalcy, nomos, and normalcy. It serves the role of both a point of departure from the previous order and as a triggering event of the new order. Crisis as uncontrollable aporia is similar to a constitutional 'big bang' that both destroys and constructs the constitutional cosmos.

This second variant of the exceptionality imaginary of crisis contains two main sub-variants. The first one presumes human agency, whereas the second one is non-ontological, systemic, and objective. A clear example of the first sub-variant is the range of theories of exceptionalist sovereignty provided by Thomas Hobbes,[21] Carl Schmitt,[22] etc. They belong to a deeper and longer tradition of existential, exceptionalist, and decisionist thinking that has both pragmatic-rational (e.g., the theory of Niccolò Machiavelli[23]) and metaphysical (e.g., the theory of Friedrich Nietzsche[24]) variants. Despite the multitude of differences between these theories, they all suggest a pivotal role for human agency at a certain 'zero hour' in history when sovereign decisions ascribe the role of secular demiurge to the agent capable of 'making order out of disorder'.

The second sub-variant is typical for system theories of law, for example, the theories of Niklas Luhmann, Gunter Teubner, etc. Although extremely diverse and even antipodal in many of their aspects, they share in common the capacity of the system, e.g., the constitutional order, to self-adjust to the context and to rearrange after radical abruptions and crises. Hence, it is not human agency, but the intrinsic characteristics of the constitutional order that restore normalcy and push the constitutional realm away from the moment of anomy, abnormalcy, and crisis. The human agency is just an instrument of the objective systemic self-ordering of the social system and its constitutional order.

To sum up, there are three versions of the imaginary signifying the concept of crisis as a singular and unique event and representing its relationship

[21] See Thomas Hobbes, *Leviathan* (CreateSpace Independent Publishing Platform, 2017) 1–246.

[22] See Carl Schmitt, *Political Theology: Four Chapters on the Concept of Sovereignty* (University of Chicago Press, 2006) 1–70.

[23] See Niccolò Machiavelli, *The Prince* (Independently published, 2021), 1–114.

[24] See Friedrich Nietzsche, *The Complete Works of Nietzsche*, Kindle Edition. See Carl Schmitt, Op. cit., 5–16.

with emergency. These are the imaginaries of the symmetry between crisis and emergency, the imaginaries of asymmetry between crisis and emergency where crisis is tameable by human agency, and the imaginaries of asymmetry between crisis and emergency where crisis is a systemic event beyond human agency.

The imaginary of the symmetric one-time event is the one that is prevalently institutionalized in the constitutions and constitutional law. It is powering the belief in the problem-solving capacity of the emergency regimes. This imaginary is grounded in two mutually reinforcing beliefs. The first one is the belief in the crisis as extraordinary, almost once in a life time event where normalcy is conceptually and pragmatically detached from emergency. The second one is the belief in the ordering power of human reason capable of predicting the crisis and producing efficient and legitimate principle responses to it, taking the legal shape of constitutionally provided emergency regimes. Thus, the imaginary of the "crisis-emergency symmetry" can be formulated also as an imaginary of crisis as a constitutional phenomenon tameable by human reason and manageable through political action.

The imaginary of asymmetry between crisis and emergency, where crisis is tameable by human agency, is an excellent example of a powerful combination between radical realism and radical idealism. It rests upon the implicit assumption that there are two types of crisis. The first one is the low and moderate scale crisis, which can be conceived as a kind of 'business as usual'. The second one is the fundamental crisis, which is an existential game-changer. Hence, while the minor and medium-sized crises can be managed through emergency regimes (which suggests the possibility of symmetry between crisis and emergency on that level), the supreme, ultimate, and existential crisis, defined as "Ernstfall,"[25] constitutional moment,[26] etc., is beyond any kind of control. This produces the asymmetric relation between crisis and emergency. Human agency is just the factor that sets the framework and key principles of the new normalcy in the post-crisis context, but is not an instrument for coping with the crisis as such.

Hence, the imaginary of asymmetry between crisis and emergency, where crisis is tameable by human agency, can be defined also as the imaginary of the crisis as an existential event triggering constitutional ordering through exceptionality. It also presupposes the activation of imaginaries

[25] See Carl Schmitt, Op. cit., 5–16.

[26] See Bruce Ackerman, Op. cit., 266.

of sovereignty and a range of possible heroic-supremacist ontologies and foundational constitutional myths. Ontologies of heroic creation, radical departure from the past, ruptures of path-dependency, and revolutionary turns in history are grounded in retrospective transitory imaginaries.[27] They are possible strategies for the justification of the creative role of emergency activities in times of crisis. They can be supplemented by prospective transitory imaginaries producing recovery and post-crisis teleologies.

The imaginary of the asymmetry between crisis and emergency, where crisis is a systemic event beyond human agency, suggests that crisis is an objective fact. It is entirely non-manageable by the people, irrespective of whether they act prospectively by establishing emergency regimes, proactively as office holders that activate and impose them in a crisis or as agenda setters of a new post-crisis world. Hence, this imaginary can also be defined as the imaginary of the objective self-recovery of the system.

The imaginary of constitutional polycrisis constitutes the conceptual opposition to the singular, exceptional, and isolated crisis and emergency. This is especially true if constitutional polycracy is combined with constitutional polytransition.[28] Constitutional polycrisis consists of a multitude of crises that unfold sequentially or simultaneously, but ultimately in an intermingled way. Thus, they produce a cumulative effect on the constitutional order that exceeds the sum of the effects of the single crisis constituting the polycrisis. In other words, the joint effect of the crisis that overlaps and forms the polycrisis transcends the mathematical and empirical common denominator.

Hence, constitutional polycrisis can be imagined as a supercell in the network of crisis and emergency constitutionalism. It can also be imagined as a superstorm. In both cases, it produces a power vacuum capable of unlocking triggering events of power realignment, such as the above-mentioned 'Ernstfall', constitutional moment, etc.

[27] See Martin Belov, 'Constitutional Transitions and Transitional Imaginaries: Bridging Legacies of the Constitutional Past and Aspirations for the Constitutional Future', in M Belov, M Florczak-Wątor (eds) *Constitutional Traditions and Constitutional Transitions. Legal and Socio-Legal Perspectives* (Edward Elgar, 2024) and Martin Belov, 'Transitory Imaginaries in Central and Eastern Europe: Reconsidering Constitutional Tradition and Constitutional Transition from Symbolic-Imaginary Perspective', (2024) 49, 2–4, Review of Central and East European Law.

[28] See Martin Belov, 'Rule of Law in Europe in Times of Constitutional Polycrisis, Constitutional Polytransition and Democratic Discontent', 2023, 3, Diritto pubblico comparato ed europeo, Rivista trimestrale 875–884.

The 'constitutional polycrisis as supercell' imaginary may take the shape of three distinct constitutional imaginaries. These are the constitutional polycrisis as a constitutional apocalypse imaginary, the constitutional polycrisis as a point of intersection of crisis vectors imaginary, and the constitutional polycrisis as a hyperstructure on the semiotic landscape of fear constitutionalism imaginary.

The imaginary of the constitutional polycrisis as a supercell in the network of crisis and emergency constitutionalism suggests that it is the result of the accumulation of crisis tendencies that crystallize around the most important aspects of crisis and culminate at a certain moment of crisis climax. The dynamic characteristics of this imaginary stem from its ontology and the process of the emergence of the crisis and the accumulation of the supercell particles.

There are some years in constitutional history that are the climax of the accumulation of elements with revolutionary potential that produce massive socio-political eruptions. Such years are, for example, 1814, 1848, 1968, 1989, and eventually 2025. These are transformative landmark years delimiting constitutional phases of deployment of the "constitutional everywhen" on the plain of the time-space and unfolding the constitutional "make-believe." Thus, they can be symbolically defined as "magical, miraculous, years" or "annus mirabilis" since they pave the way to the future. Since the future is not always and not necessarily bright, "annus mirabilis" can be at the same time "horrible years" or "annus horribilis." Hence, the match between "annus mirabilis" and "annus horribilis" constitutes moments of constitutional polycrisis with transformative potential for the durable structures of the human condition reflected through the prism and on the plain of constitutionalism and constitutional law. Thus, the supercell metaphor implies and signifies the role of constitutional polycrisis as a node in the network of quantum constitutionalism containing the transformative potential of the constitutional singularity in the triggering moment of constitutional polytransition.

This is very similar to the constitutional imaginary of the constitutional polycrisis as a point of intersection of crisis vectors. This imaginary signifies the polycrisis as the center of a power grid. If conceptualized dynamically as a historically unfolding and/or historically repetitive phenomenon, constitutional polycrisis produces a multitude of intersections powering the energy of constitutionalism before it materializes in the form of constitutional institutions and/or constitutional imaginaries. The latter resembles a dynamic multitude of constitutional polycrisis serving as triggering events for the transformation of constitutional energy in constitutional matter and pushing the constitutional system away from its gravity center, towards which it usually tends to organize and reorganize. In other words, the constitutional polycrisis as a point of intersection of the deconstructive energy of the power grid may be conceived as the driving force of history that pushes the constitutional order away from its temporal gravity center toward a new gravity axis. Thus, constitutional history may be conceptualized as the fluctuation of constitutional orders between different gravity centers. It consists of their departure from one gravity center and parallel attraction by another that occurs in times of constitutional polycrisis through a phase that can be defined as constitutional polytransition.

Finally, constitutional polycrisis may be imagined as a hyperstructure on the semiotic landscape of fear constitutionalism. This imaginary connects constitutional polycrisis with fear politics and embeds it in what I define elsewhere as dark constitutionalism. The constitutional semiotic landscape is an imaginary grid for the signification of constitutional and constitutionally relevant meaning that involves all plains for such representation of elements of symbolic-imaginary constitutionalism through the tools of textual, visual, and performative constitutionalism.[29] The constitutional semiotic landscape is a form of constitutional non-locality that serves for signification through collective constitutional imaginaries. It can be used for signification and anthropological programming of either positive or negative emotions. Thus, it can be plain for the unfolding of dark constitutionalism based on the signification of negative emotions such as anger, hate, anxiety, fear, or despair.

In that regard, constitutional polycrisis is a signifier of a climax of negative emotional constitutionalism. It can be used to signify a constitutional Everest, demonstrating the dramatic characteristic of the events of which it is composed. Alternatively, it can also represent constitutional polycrisis as a constitutional iceberg signifying only the visible, rationally constructed and accessible part of the crisis while also suggesting the existence of an underwater part. This part is entrenched in dark constitutional anthropology. It is contained in a diffuse but entangled way through quantum conditionality in the collective constitutional conscious, subconscious, and unconscious. Constitutional polyrisis can also activate and power collective constitutional archetypes.

[29] See Martin Belov, *Constitutional semiotics. The Conceptual Foundations of a Constitutional Theory and Meta-Theory* (Hart publishing, 2022), 1–349.

4.6.2 *Spatial Imaginaries of Crisis and Emergency*

The imaginary construction of the constitutional time–space, in which crisis and emergency unfold, take shape, and project themselves, includes both imaginaries of emergency and crisis related to time and imaginaries of emergency and crisis related to space. The temporal constitutional imaginaries have just been explored. Thus, the attention here will be devoted to the spatial imaginaries of crisis and emergency.

It should be mentioned that the spatial imaginaries of emergency and crisis are related but still different from the general imaginaries of space. The constitutional imaginaries of space are based on the constitutional geometry of space shaped through territory, territoriality, and territorial politics.[30] The territorial constitutional geometry concerns the various conceptual models for the organization of the territorial structure of power. There are two main forms of constitutional imaginaries related to territorial constitutional geometry. The first one is the polygon as a form for the organization of the "squared territoriality" of the modern state (national or multicultural). The second one is the pyramid as a form that structures the power relations, jurisdictions, institutional design, and sources of law in a vertical, territory-related way. Furthermore, constitutions, constitutional law and constitutional theory use symmetry and asymmetry as instruments for symbolic, imaginary, and structural shaping of power, authority, socio-legal, and historical constellations.

The general imaginaries of space also include the imaginary territories. The imaginary territories conceptualize territory as a multilayered and multidimensional concept. The most important imaginary territories include: the territorial imaginaries of "natural habitats of nations" underpinning grand projects of nationalism especially in Europe during the 19th and twentieth century (the "great nation" projects); the imperial territories of Western Modernity and their novel, post-modern versions such as "global Britain," "Three Seas" etc.; the territories of nations without a state with significant movements aiming at secession (e.g., Catalonia, the Basque country, Scotland, Kurdistan, etc.); the 'reminiscent territories' of currently unitary states that were reunited after being previously divided between foreign countries (e.g., Poland or Romania); and the geographies of coexistence.

[30] See Martin Belov, 'Territory, Territoriality and Territorial Politics as Public Law Concepts' in M Belov (ed) *Territorial Politics and Secession. Constitutional and International Law Dimensions* (Palgrave, 2021), 15–45.

Here, the analysis is focused on the most important and powerful spatial imaginaries of crisis and emergency. These are the territorial scaling imaginaries and the cursed places and spaces.

The territorial scaling imaginaries are models for drawing the spatial framework of crisis and emergency. They define the crisis and emergency in the collective imagination as: global, regional, national, and subnational phenomena; focused and localized or non-local, expanding, or self-constraining phenomenon; territorial, transterritorial or post-territorial phenomenon.

There might be various geographies of crisis—empirical, legal, and imaginary. This is because a crisis is itself a factual, socio-legal, and imaginary phenomenon. Hence, in principle, there might be imaginaries of crisis as global, regional, national, and subnational phenomena. Global imaginaries of crisis are promoters of globalization through fear politics. They create the feeling of belongingness and togetherness against an enemy taking the shape of terrorists, viruses, financial demise, technological challenges and perils, related, for example, to AI, etc.[31]

Global imaginaries of crisis and fear are serving as producers of social cohesion through dark constitutional politics. Again, this is not the feature of global and globalist imaginaries as such. They can also be used to promote cohesion and integration on a global level through positive emotions. Initially, this was the ontological imaginary behind the League of Nations, the UN, and its organizations.

The above reflections are also applicable to regional and national imaginaries of crisis and fear. They have similar integration, cohesion, authority making, and legitimacy functions generated through negative feelings (especially fear) and dark constitutional politics. Again, regional and national integration is also achievable through positive emotions and imaginaries. Many of them are based on imaginaries of distinctiveness, exclusiveness, and even uniqueness. Examples are the American dream (in its constitutional, economic, and social versions), the Europeanness, the Euro-Atlantic Values, the "Russian world," the "German Europe"[32] etc. Frequently, these imaginaries are used for peaceful or aggressive

[31] It is interesting to cite here Pope Francis, who triggered the imaginary of the AI as phenomenon containing 'the shadow of evil'. See e.g., Joshua McElwee, 'Vatican says AI has 'shadow of evil,' calls for close oversight' available at https://www.reuters.com/technology/artificial-intelligence/vatican-says-ai-has-shadow-evil-calls-close-oversight-2025-01-28/ (last accessed on 30 January 2025 at 2 p.m. EET).

[32] See Ulrich Beck, *German Europe* (Polity, 2014), 1–112.

distinction of regional identities, usually in contrast to other regional identities. Some of these imaginaries of belongingness can be weaponized in a national (Westphalian) or neo-regional (Neo-Westphalian) context[33] in order to serve the imaginary mastering of security crises (e.g., hot, cold, or hybrid wars).

A crisis can also be imagined as focused and localized, as expanding, or as a self-constraining phenomenon. Terrorism is at the same time a global, regional, national, and local phenomenon. However, it can be imagined through topical, regional, dispersed, and universal imaginaries. The 9/11 terror attacks, the Beslan Siege, the Dubrovka theater in Moscow, the Charlie Hebdo, and the 7 October Israeli hostage-taking terror acts are hotspot terrorism imaginaries. They localize the crisis and produce imaginaries that create spaces of remembrance, horror, fear, and sorrow. These focused and localized terror hotspots are the dots and spots of a global map of terrorism as a universal phenomenon. Thus, they produce the glocal geography of crisis and fear related to terrorism.

A similar process of glocalization of crisis and fear based on both globality and locality of the phenomenon can be observed with regard to the COVID-19 pandemic. It promoted the imaginary of global apocalypse, which, at the same time, had its local hotspot—a cursed space—that was a signifier of the fear of contagion. In that regard, Wuhan in China, Daegu in South Korea, and Bergamo and Milano in Italy were drawing the image of the cursed city that spreads deadly contagion and radiates imminent apocalyptic disease.

The cursed place imaginary signifies places that are or have been stigmatized through crisis and emergency. These are places or spaces which are imagined as dangerous due to previous or continuous security, health

[33] For the Westphalian, post-Westphalian and neo-Westphalian constitutionalism see Martin Belov, 'Three Models for Ordering Constitutional Orders' (2022) 2 Pravni Zapisi, 361–387 Martin Belov, 'Constitutional Nationalism and Constitutional Globalism on the edge of Westphalian and Post-Westphalian Constitutionalism: the Bulgarian Case', in Marianti Kalyviotou (ed), *Essays in Honour of Kostas G. Mavrias*, (P.N. Sakkoulas, 2022), Vol. I, 221—251, Martin Belov, 'Judicial Dialogue – Westphalian or post-Westphalian Constitutional Phenomenon?' in: Martin Belov, (ed*) Judicial Dialogue* (Eleven, 2019), 25–51, Martin Belov, 'Global Rule of Law instead of Global Democracy? Legitimacy of Global Judicial Empire on the Edge between Westphalian and post-Westphalian Constitutionalism' in Martin Belov (ed) *The Role of Courts in Contemporary Legal Orders* (Eleven, 2019), 99–133, Martin Belov, 'The Challenges to Westphalian Constitutional Geometry in the Age of Supranational Constitutionalism, Global Governance and Information Revolution', in Martin Belov (ed) *Global Constitutionalism and Its Challenges to Westphalian Constitutional Law.* (Hart, 2018), 13–55.

or other threats. These places constitute an imaginary space of crisis and fear. Sometimes such places are concrete and real. This is, for example, the case of Bergamo or Wuhan, which have been stigmatized at the beginning of the COVID-19 pandemic and serve as signifiers of health danger in the collective memory of crisis and fear. However, cursed places may be defined in broader terms, denoting typified spaces. Such a role in the imaginaries of crisis and fear can be played by the crowded spaces (vulnerable to terror attacks), the different imagery ghettos (prone to violent criminality), or the crowded public transport (serving as a signifier of mixed fears from contagion, but also from crime and terrorism).

Crisis and emergency can be territorial, transterritorial or post-territorial phenomena. The crisis can have explicit territorial implications constrained within the imaginary 'territorial container'.[34] These are the cases of some natural disasters, for example, wildfires, earthquakes, flooding, landslides, etc. They are territorial crises and emergency topoi. They can have a transboundary dimension, but are usually confined within a certain state. Furthermore, the crisis may be transterritorial when it crosses the boundaries of two or more states and triggers an emergency in several states. Clear examples are the varieties of "spaces of flows"[35] that can be risk factors and thus determinants of transterritorial crisis and emergency, such as migration waves, epidemics, traffic impediments, etc. Finally, post-territorial crises and emergencies are related to the digital and algorithmic world and may concern data leakages, IT and AI-related crises, digital assets crises related to banking transactions or digital currencies crises, etc.

The territoriality, transterritoriality and post-territoriality of crisis and emergency have normative-institutional, socio-legal, and constitutional imaginary dimensions. The sovereignty as territorial authority for mastering crisis and emergency, and the territorial container as the ultimate scope of their unfolding are some of the important and traditionally used territorial imaginaries of crisis and emergency. The constitutional imaginary of spaces of flows can also be used as an imaginary matrix

[34] For the state as territorial container see Peter Taylor, 'The State as Container: Territoriality in the Modern World-System', in (1994) 18 *Progress in Human Geography*, 2, Peter Taylor, 'Beyond Containers: Internationality, Interstateness, Interterritoriality', in 1995 (19) *Progress in Human Geography*, 1 and Neil Brenner, 'Beyond state-centrism? Space, Territoriality and Geographical Scale in Globalization Studies' in (1999) 28 (1), *Theory and Society*, 39–78.

[35] See M Castells, *The Rise of the Network Society* (Wiley-Blackwell, 2009), 407–460 and Martin Belov, 'Rule of Law in Space of Flows', in Martin Belov (ed) *Rule of Law at the Beginning of the Twenty-First Century*. (Eleven, 2018), 97–141.

for transnational imaginaries of crisis and emergency. The post-territoriality, the digital space, and the non-physical meta-world are powerful imaginaries of non-locality that are not specifically focused on crisis and emergency. Nevertheless, the imaginary of the global digital network can be used as a paradigm in which the digital crisis can be embedded. The best example of post-territorial imaginary so far is the imaginary of the global contamination and the imaginary of the global infected community of infection and disease spreaders that emerged in the context of the COVID-19 pandemic. Similarly to this imaginary, one can expect the possible emergence of other global post-territorial and aterritorial imaginaries of crisis and fear that can be practiced in the context of fear politics. It must be mentioned that global post-territorial imaginaries can also signify very positive emotions. Examples are the imaginary of human unity, solidarity, and compassion and the imaginary of global anthropocentric equality.

4.6.3 Imaginaries of Crisis Related to the Implosion of the Constitutional Order

A constitutional crisis is usually perceived as a dramatic rupture of the constitutional order that is caused by external factors. These can be natural disasters, diseases, wars, security conflicts and threats, etc. They cause external shocks to the constitutional order that produce transformations and radical disintegrative tendencies that may lead to its explosion. They may also be triggering a radical departure from the established constitutional equilibrium, producing constitutional polycrisis and constitutional polytransition.

However, a constitutional crisis can also stem from factors that are internal to the constitutional system. Moreover, external factors can induce internal disruptive dynamics that can produce imaginaries of crisis and emergency.

Hence, three groups of such imaginaries can be outlined. These are constitutional imaginaries of crisis and emergency stemming from external threat, constitutional imaginaries of crisis and emergency stemming from internal preconditions, and mixed imaginaries of crisis and emergency related to both external and internal factors. The first group is widely explored in this chapter. That is why the focus here shall be on the imaginaries related to internal or mixed factors for crisis. They are defined as imaginaries of constitutional implosion. They are powered by the anxieties of institutional distortions, producing departures from the presumably well-established constitutional order.

Implosion of the constitutional order can be defined as stagnation of its normal performance that leads to profound dysfunctionality producing ruptures and structural cracks in the principles and the constitutional design, and non-governability, inducing as a side effect fundamental delegitimation and distrust. All these functional and structural deficiencies are a result of ordering impotence that produces constitutional stagnation and ultimately the collapse of the constitutional order. This collapse is leading to emotions and imaginaries of internal crisis and despair. Hence, the regulatory, socio-legal and imaginary collapse of the constitutional imaginaries are related. In addition, the constitutional imaginaries of crisis can function as triggers of constitutional implosion.

The implosion imaginaries are imaginaries of constitutional erosion as a side effect of external crisis, imaginaries of democratic decay and twilight, and imaginaries of the collapse of constitutionalism. They signify ruptures, cracks, and malperformance of the constitutional order, leading to imminent constitutional collapse. The ultimate result of decay and twilight is either dark constitutionalism as their stabilized form or deconstruction of the constitutional order, triggering the need to reorder constitutional disorder.

Democratic decay has multiple manifestations. It consists of democratic exclusion, lack of democratic control over the government and governance, democratic disempowerment, democratic alienation, structural democratic deficit, institutional malfunctioning and failure related to departiamentarization, growth of technocracy, etc. Democratic decay is usually related to deconstitutionalization as a process of instrumentalization of the constitution and increasing mismatch between the law in books, law in action, and law in imagination.

Signifiers of democratic decay are the architectural representations of technocracy, the visual stories of dissatisfaction with democratic performance, and manifestations of performative constitutionalism related to civic alienation. The global technofeudalism[36] and the "new middle ages"[37] are signified through the functionalist imperialism of the skyscrapers of the transnational corporations and the sterile austerity of the architecture of the governmental buildings of the late twentieth and early twenty-first century.

[36] Varoufakis, Op. cit.

[37] See Alain Minc, *Le nouveau moyen age*, (Le Grand Livre Du Mois, 1994).

They represent democratic detachment, which does not immediately result in democratic implosion. Key narrative on democratic implosion serving as a textual signifier of its imaginaries is the democratic absenteeism. The empty square and the empty ballot box are among the important imaginaries of democratic implosion via alienation and decay. This imagination is powerfully developed by Jose Saramago in his novel "Seeing."[38]

Indeed, art, literature, and architecture are abundant with significations and representations of inclusion, participation, and democratic activism. The imaginaries of deliberative and participatory democracy (e.g., the deliberative crowd, the public square and the street as correctives of political government, and the constitutional crowdsourcing network), the imaginaries of democratic parliamentary representation (e.g., the imaginary of the Parliament as the temple of the ultimate secular God—the nation, chess board, mirror, and national agora) are key imaginary pillars that are enabling and supporting the democratic thriving and normalcy. Democratic implosion, however, has been to a lesser extent an object of textual, but especially visual representation. It is mostly signified through performative constitutionalism in the form of imaginaries of civic disobedience and revolution. Hence, democratic implosion is imagined in negative and in opposition to democratic thriving and normalcy. It is signified mostly through performative signifiers in the politically deviant behavior of alienation, dissatisfaction, and frustration.

Thus, it seems that the implosion imaginaries, different from revolutionary, populist, and disobedience imaginaries, are part of the missing imaginary constitution. They need to be reconstructed through comparative and reflective dichotomic differentiation from the imaginaries of participation, empowerment, and inclusion. Part of the explanation of this fact is the desire of the actors of visual, textual, emotional, and performative constitutionalism to promote trust in the constitutional order through positive signification of imaginaries of democratic prosperity instead of decay. Thus, constitutional decadence has remained part of the "shadow constitutionalism."[39]

Imaginaries of constitutional twilight[40] are more common. Nevertheless, they have been entrenched mostly in the anti-populism discourse that

[38] See Jose Saramago, *Seeing* (Mariner Books, 2007) 1–320.

[39] See Martin Belov, *Constitutional semiotics. The Conceptual Foundations of a Constitutional Theory and Meta-Theory* (Hart publishing, 2022), 55–61.

[40] See also Petra Dobner and Martin Loughlin (eds) *The Twilight of Constitutionalism?* (OUP 2010), 1–370.

predominated the period of constitutional polycrisis at the beginning of the twentieth century and especially the decade between 2015 and 2025. Despite their importance, populist imaginaries[41] are not the only form of twilight imaginaries. Constitutional twilight as a signifier of democratic implosion and democratic deconstitutionalization is represented not just by populist, but also through elitist and technocratic imaginaries.[42]

Constitutional crisis related to implosion of the constitutional order can also be signified through imaginaries of chaos and anarchy. Chaos can be imagined as both the antipode of order, and thus as the ultimate form of anomy, but also as a creative source in which the new order is embedded, waiting to be born through the push of the initial ontological creation. In that regard, the imaginary of the crisis as chaos is a signifier of the first, destructive phase of constitutional implosion. It can be imagined as democratic dissolution through supreme power, for example, internal or external elites, or as a collapse due to the dark, destructive force of the masses. However, chaos can be the natural context for constitutional rebirth. The constitutional rebirth is embedded in ontological metaphysics. That is why it is signified through a range of ontological myths and mythologies signifying the reestablishment of the constitutional order, the reinstatement of golden traditions, etc. A powerful constitutional mythology and imaginary of the reestablishment of democratic traditions has unfolded, for example, in the Central and Eastern European states after the fall of communism.

4.6.4 *The Signification of Crisis and Emergency as Symbolic-Imaginary Dissociation, Alienation, and Disgrace*

Crisis and emergency are occasions for symbolic-imaginary labelling of places, spaces, and people. This is done through textual, visual, and performative signifiers used to signify danger, fear, anxiety, frustration, and despair. Thus, the constitutional imaginaries of crisis and emergency are

[41] Jiří Přibáň, Journal of Law and Society, Volume 50, Issue S1, Supplement: Political Constitutions in Transnational Society: Socio-Legal and Interdisciplinary Perspectives, September 2023, 26–44 and Paul Blokker, 'Shifting constitutional imaginaries: is the liberal-legal imaginary unsettled by populism?' in Martin Belov and Monika Florczak-Wątor (eds) *Constitutional Traditions and Constitutional Transitions. Legal and Socio-Legal Perspectives*, (Edward Elgar, 2024), 35–57.

[42] See Martin Belov, 'Imaginaries of Representation: There and Back Again' in M Belov (ed) *Representative Democracy in Flux. Deconstructive Narratives from a Legal and Constitutional Perspective* (Routledge, 2025).

usually used in conjunction with constitutional imaginaries of fear and other negative emotions. They jointly induce dark emotions in the collective constitutional conscious, subconscious, and unconscious and shape dark constitutional anthropology. Thus, they contribute to the production of dark constitutionalism.

The cursed places imaginaries have already been studied above. That is why the analysis here shall be focused on the person-related imaginaries of stigmatization, marginalization, and exclusion.

There is a range of strategies and tactics for symbolic-imaginary stigmatization, marginalization, and exclusion in the context of crisis and emergency. The most important of them are the territorial stigmatization producing cursed places and spaces and indirectly cursed events and activities (e.g., the infamous football match in Bergamo, Italy that symbolically kick-started the COVID-19 pandemic in Europe) and the personal stigmatization based on origin (e.g., persons from families which members have been involved in terrorist activities), beliefs (e.g., anti-vaxxers), mode of life (e.g., ways of life non-compliant with the combat against climate change), etc. The result of the latter is the symbolic-imaginary personal condemnation leading to various categories of cursed people. These can be migrants, contaminated people, conspirators and fake news spreaders, the enemies of the public order in general, where public order includes national security, public health, etc.

These strategies can have a wide range of goals pursued separately or jointly. The most important of them are the symbolic-imaginary dissociation, alienation, and disgrace. They altogether aim at bestowing fear and other negative emotions through forms of dark constitutionalism.

The symbolic-imaginary dissociation is accomplished through separative constitutional imaginaries. They are based on the distinction between "friend" and "enemy," "us," and "them," "good" and "bad" places, spaces or people, etc. Constitutional dissociation can be used for demarcation of unwished social strata and even for symbolic-imaginary signification of cursed people, places, and spaces.

Symbolic dissociation imaginaries are based on fear. This fear can concern an objective process, for example, war, military incursion, invasion, migration wave, financial or economic collapse, technological disaster or disease, health epidemic or pandemic. The fear can also be related to the essence of the enemy—the aliens, the foreigners, the invaders, the defectors, the elites, or vice versa, the masses, etc. In any case, they produce feelings, emotional predispositions, affectual relations to someone or something that must be separated, restrained, limited, and ousted.

Fences and walls are good examples of migratory symbolic-imaginary stigmatization. The Berlin wall or the new walls built around the world produce separative imaginaries and delimit the 'cursed beyond' spaces, places, and realms. The wearing or non-wearing of masks during the pandemic was also used as a form of signification of belonging to the two extreme camps—the believers in the imminent and present danger of the COVID-19 virus, or the believers that it was a form of psyop. Thus, they served as imaginaries of symbolic dissociation, creating two conflictual imaginary communities. Indeed, the masks had a pragmatic purpose to possibly limit contamination, but also served as demarcation lines between the healthy and the sick, signifying the peril of contamination.

The extreme example of imaginary dissociation signifiers was the yellow stars that were put on the people of Jewish origin and the stars of David on their properties. They were visual signifiers of the "we-them" divide, drawing visual demarcation lines between the members of the community and the others, the enemies, and the disturbers of social order and cohesion.

Dissociation imaginaries are thriving in times of crisis. The natural chaos of crisis, its essence as rupture and crack in the overwhelming fabric of normalcy, triggers an emotional need to point out "good" and "bad," "friends," and "enemies," saviors and contributors to the danger. Indeed, unity can also be used as a tool for mastering a crisis. Crisis management based on solidarity and compassion can be the best solution for efficient and legitimate crisis and emergency policy-making. Unfortunately, the flourishing of dark emotions in times of crisis is frequently used as intuitive preconditions for emergency policy-making grounded in dark constitutional politics. Moreover, the setting up of a crisis, based on the production of crisis affects, emotions, and feelings, is a typical strategy for justification of the "emergency as normalcy." The "imperialist European North" vs. the "lazy and irresponsible European South" in the context of the 2009 financial crisis, the multitude of separative imaginaries in times of security threat, for example, the suspicion against the Japanese in the US during World War II and the Muslims in the context of the War on Terror since 9/11, and the clash between the vaxxers and the antivaxxers in the COVID-19 pandemics are some of the telling examples.

The alienation strategies aim at societal disentanglement and individual alienation from the pursuit of common constitutional projects. They aim at the deconstruction of the personal, social, and political bonds between the people. Thus, they may lead to radical individualism, egoism, solipsism, and even survivalism. Some of the important alienation imaginaries are the solitary and solipsistic individual and the crisis and emergency survivor. They are grounded in excessive rationalism, secularism, and pragmatism, radical detachment from meta-legal ontologies and teleologies, consumerism, and egoism. They thrive on the radical detachment of the human existence from both meta-rational sources of justification of the human life and collectivist, solidarity-based imaginaries of socio-political inclusion. In that regard, the alienation imaginaries are antagonistic to both imaginaries of higher metaphysical purpose of human life, for example, post-mortal salvation of the soul, rebirth, redemption, etc. and imaginaries of higher social and political purpose of human life, such as related to the integration and contribution to a common socio-political, moral, and constitutional project.

Alienation imaginaries were widespread during the times of the health crisis produced by the COVID-19 pandemic. They were powered by the unbearable horror of the uniqueness of human life reduced to material pleasures and preconditioned on physical life and health. The concentration of the purpose of human life on mere existence and consumerist pleasures was misused for the promotion of dark imaginaries, serving to unfold the politics of fear. Hence, alienation imaginaries were encouraged by the spiritual and social profanation of the human life reduced to physical existence.

The disgrace strategies are resulting in imaginaries of embarrassment, ridicule, and stigmatization. Despite the variations in their ontology, aim and content, they can be generally unified under the concept of disgrace imaginaries for the sake of conciseness. One of the main instruments for the production of disgrace imaginaries is labelling. Labelling is not restricted to a certain political group, specific ideology, or region. Instead, it is a signifying tool used to humiliate, dishonor and defame the political opponent. For example, the Daily Mail on its front page published on 4 November 2016 defined the UK Supreme Court judges as 'enemies of the people'. Conversely, many politicians and political acts are labelled as 'populist'. While many of them are populist, others are just signified as such as a strategy for decrying the political opponent.

To sum up, there is a clear logical, conceptual, and pragmatic bond between symbolic-imaginary dissociation, alienation, and disgrace strategies as part of the overall and overarching strategy for symbolic-imaginary stigmatization, marginalization, and exclusion in the context of crisis and emergency. These imaginaries are prolific and mushrooming in times of crisis and transition. Constitutional polycrisis and constitutional polytransition, with the multitude of divisive lines and battles for truth, narrative authority and sovereignty that they foster, are the perfect context for the use and misuse of dissociation, alienation, embarrassment, ridicule, stigmatization, and, ultimately, disgrace imaginaries. Their spread and flourishing are facilitated by the post-modern condition of post-truth, the digital augmented reality and the context of memefication,[43] as well as the visual and emotional turns in constitutionalism.[44] Thus, symbolic-imaginary representations of stigmatization through labelling are an engine of symbolic-imaginary battles over the crisis and emergency narrative.

4.7 Crisis as an Opportunity, Salvation, or Element of the Constitutional Fabric of Quantum Constitutionalism: Imaginaries of Crisis Beyond Emergency Regimes and Fear Constitutionalism

It has been reaffirmed above that a crisis is typically considered a negative phenomenon that distorts the normal functioning of the constitutional order. In principle, this seems intuitively, logically, normatively, and empirically true. However, there are three groups of arguments that contravene that otherwise generally reasonable suggestion. They are different from the imaginary of the constitutional polycrisis as normalcy or "the new normal." They integrate crisis as an element of the quantum unfolding of constitutional phenomenology in the time-space and conceptualize it as a necessary or even desirable element with regard to constitutional transition and constitutional change. Thus, they can be defined as integrative imaginary conceptualizations of crisis. They are still preserving its exceptionality and keeping its character as a concept that is opposite to normalcy.

The three integrative imaginary conceptualizations of crisis are the crisis-as-salvation imaginary, the crisis-as-opportunity imaginary, and the imaginary of crisis as an element of the fabrics of constitutional

[43] See Martin Belov, Constitutional semiotics. The Conceptual Foundations of a Constitutional Theory and Meta-Theory (Hart publishing, 2022), 211–216.

[44] See Martin Belov, 'Constitutional semiotics as a post-positivist and post-modern approach to constitution and constitutionalism based on the linguistic, visual and emotional turns' in Anne Wagner, Sarah Marusek (eds) *Research Handbook on Legal Semiotics* (Edward Elgar, 2023) 105–119.

"space-time" mastered through consciousness, intelligibility, and intent. They are independent and different from each other. Thus, they are grouped together only in contrast to the predominant understanding of crisis as a purely disruptive event, detached from the overall process of unfolding of normalcy throughout the constitutional history. Moreover, the third imaginary—the imaginary of the crisis as an element of the fabrics of constitutional "space-time" —is an element of the quantum approach to crisis and emergency described above. It is mentioned also here in order to better emphasize its perception of crisis as an element entrenched in the general process of development of the constitutional order in the time–space. Hence, it is substantially different from the imaginary of the crisis as salvation imaginary and the imaginary of the crisis as opportunity.

The crisis is imagined as an opportunity by sovereignist and political decisionism theories. They are structured around the assumption that a crisis is a necessary precondition for the emergence of the new post-crisis order. The state of exception is the required context for triggering deep structural change of the constitutional order. It is necessary in order to produce the new post-crisis normalcy. Hence, proper order can be made only through substantial and structural disorder. Such logic, policy strategy, and conceptualization of the constitutional history and the constitutional process are preconditioned on the imaginary of crisis in a multitude of its manifestations: the imaginary of the crisis as rebirth, the imaginary of the crisis as a chance for reestablishment and conceptual, axiological or institutional reconstruction of the constitutional and socio-political order, etc.

The imaginary of crisis as salvation is counterintuitive. This is so because the traditional legal and constitutional logic excludes the option of achieving something positive (salvation) out of something negative (crisis). However, salvation is not a simple positive development. Instead, it is the entry into a new age and a new world beyond the conceptual constraints of the older one. In line with this reasoning, the destruction of the chains of the old world is possible only through an exceptional, apocalyptic, and revolutionary event serving as a point of departure from the status quo and as a fundamental structural rupture in the constitutional space-time fabric.

Hence, the imaginary of crisis as salvation is based on a range of possible justifications. The first one includes the activation of apocalyptic imaginaries. Messianic thinking and apocalyptic conceptualization of the world suggest that the crisis is the necessary climax of the historic process and/or precursor of its development towards a final point of no return. Thus, crisis is entangled with such a deterministic and final approach to constitutionalism where constitutional history necessarily ends after the ultimate and supreme crisis that is followed by radical destruction or, possibly, salvation. There are many religious and secular versions of the imaginary of crisis-as-salvation. They cannot be studied in detail due to space constraints. Some of them have already been explored above.

The imaginary of the crisis as salvation is also part of some strands of revolutionary constitutionalism.[45] The revolution serves as the ultimate game-changer of the historical process. It is conceptualized and imagined as a kind of 'supreme and final crisis', 'the master crisis' or "crisis of the crisis." According to these theories, it has a liberating effect because it tears apart the historic process into two phases—the dark past that is (or ought to be) swept away by the crisis and the glorious and bright future. The revolutionary crisis as salvation is used in various theoretical paradigms—Marxism, Trotskyism, the theoretical legitimations of the big revolutions of the Enlightenment, etc.

The imaginary of crisis as an element of the fabric of constitutional 'space-time' in which constitutionalism is embedded and unfolds is a powerful paradigm for the general conceptualization of constitutional phenomena, the constitutional order, and the role and function of crisis for both constitutional history and the constitutional "make-believe." In this context, crisis is part of the constitutional polyphony produced by the unfolding of the constitutional cycles organizing the constitutional "time–space–consciousness" matrix. Here, crisis is an element of the logic of constitutional renewal stemming from the quantum logic of pulsing constitutionalism. The constitutional pulsations that generate and sustain the constitutional cycles are powered by crisis as triggering events. The constitutional pulsations that are producing the durable logic of the constitutional history and the projections of the constitutional phenomena in it oscillate between constitutional energy and constitutional matter.

The imaginary of crisis as an element of the fabrics of constitutional 'space-time' and the spatial-temporal matrix of constitutionalism raises again paradigmatic questions that have been explored above. Is a crisis a regular event following predictable or at least traceable and describable

[45] For the concept of revolutionary constitutionalism see Richard Albert, *Revolutionary Constitutionalism: Law, Legitimacy, Power* (Hart, 2020), 1–424, Gary Jacobsohn and Yaniv Roznai *Constitutional Revolution* (Yale University Press, 2020), 1–384, Bruce Ackerman, *Revolutionary Constitutions: Charismatic Leadership and the Rule of Law* (Belknap Press, 2019), 1–472.

cycles, or is it a sporadic and unpredictable phenomenon? Here again, the paradigmatic problem of the symmetry and asymmetry as a typical modus of the unfolding of the constitutional energy in constitutional matter arises. If a crisis is a symmetric element of the overall constitutional process, then it is traceable and predictable in case the general routine and logic of the historic unfolding of crisis can be discovered and intellectually mastered. This is, for example, the rationale behind the balanced (or golden) budget rule, which was introduced as an anti-cyclical crisis-preventive mechanism. If a crisis is an asymmetric phenomenon, then it constitutes an unpredictable rupture of normalcy or at least an exceptional event that can be contextually discovered and analyzed, but does not follow some general trend, rule, or logic. This is the general assumption behind nature-driven crises such as natural disasters and health crises.

The imaginary of crisis as an element of the fabrics of constitutional 'space-time' and the fabrics of constitutionalism suggests that the crisis is not a synchronized and imminently predictable phenomenon. Thus, it is not purely symmetric—at least not in a way that can be institutionalized in the valid law as a positively provable element of the constitutional history. However, a crisis has an overall cyclic logic and produces general symmetry of its projections on the plains of the imaginary and the real. The very concept of emergency as a legal model for mastering crisis suggests the symmetry-as-predictability of the crisis. Hence, a crisis is a constitutive element of the overall mosaic of the constitutional history. Indeed, the financial crisis, the migration crisis, and even the wars manifest themselves in cycles, thus producing partially symmetrical patterns of their unfolding. Hence, they are partially normalized as elements of the conceptual framing of constitutional time and space. This is an important factor behind the imagination of the crisis as an element of the fabric of constitutional "space–time" and the fabric and matrix of constitutionalism.

4.8 Conclusions

This chapter exposed the manifestations of the crisis as singular or networked, causal or quantum, symmetric or asymmetric, objective or policy-driven phenomena. It has outlined a narrative-based quantum theory of constitutional imaginaries, demonstrated against the example of crisis and emergency. The quantum characteristics of the imaginaries of crisis and emergency have been embedded in the conceptual matrix that includes quantum entanglement, cloud constitutionalism, constitutional consciousness, and philosophy of space and time. Quantum constitutionalism has been used as a paradigm for conceptual framing of the certainty about the uncertainty of the unfolding of consciousness and intent as the main drivers of constitutional make-believe. In the context of a networked imaginary-based structuring of the constitutional order, quantum entanglement has been exposed as an instrument for the projection of the intent of the narrative sovereign and authoritative and quasi-authoritative narrators on the plains of the constitutional conscious, subconscious, and unconscious. It has been shown that crises and emergencies may be used as a driving force of quantum entangled dark constitutionalism.

The constitutional geometry of crisis and emergency is unfolding on the plains of the normative, the legal, the real, and the imaginary. It is perceived by the constitutionally framed socio-legal community through imaginaries. In that context, the people are conceptualized as emotional agents deriving the meaning of constitutional phenomena through constitutional imaginaries and engagement in narrative games. Hence, crises and emergencies are not only facts and legal models, but nodes in the network of constitutional consciousness. They are communicated between the people or between the people and the authorities through textual, visual, and performative signifiers of meaning, processed as narratives and resulting in constitutional imaginaries. The different types of constitutional imaginaries of crisis and fear that have been outlined above are signifiers of entangled meaning revealed through narratives. In that regard, they are less forms of objective, stable, and imminent meaning rather than results of battles for control of the narratives. Hence, the specific forms in which the imaginaries of crisis and fear manifest themselves are a product of narrative sovereignty.

References

Ackerman, B. *Revolutionary Constitutions: Charismatic Leadership and the Rule of Law*. Belknap Press, 2019

Ackerman, B. *We the People: Foundations*. Harvard University Press, 1991

Albert, R. *Revolutionary Constitutionalism: Law, Legitimacy, Power*. Hart, 2020

Albert, R., & Roznai, Y. (eds.) *Constitutionalism Under Extreme Conditions: Law, Emergency, Exception*. Springer, 2020

Beck, U. *German Europe*. Polity, 2014

Belov, M. (ed.) *Rule of Law in Crisis: Constitutionalism in a State of Flux*. Routledge, 2023

Belov, M. "Constitutional Nationalism and Constitutional Globalism on the Edge of Westphalian and Post-Westphalian Constitutionalism: The Bulgarian Case" in Kalyviotou, M. (ed.) *Essays in Honour of Kostas G. Mavrias*. Vol. I. P.N. Sakkoulas, 2022, 221–251

Belov, M. "Constitutional Semiotics as a Post-positivist and Post-modern Approach to Constitution and Constitutionalism Based on the Linguistic, Visual and Emotional Turns" in Wagner, A., & Marusek, S. (eds.) *Research Handbook on Legal Semiotics*. Edward Elgar, 2023, 105–119

Belov, M. "Constitutional Transitions and Transitional Imaginaries: Bridging Legacies of the Constitutional Past and Aspirations for the Constitutional Future" in Belov, M., & Florczak-Wątor, M. (eds.) *Constitutional Traditions and Constitutional Transitions. Legal and Socio-Legal Perspectives*. Edward Elgar, 2024, 13–35

Belov, M. "Global Rule of Law Instead of Global Democracy? Legitimacy of Global Judicial Empire on the Edge Between Westphalian and Post-Westphalian Constitutionalism" in Belov, M. (ed.) *The Role of Courts in Contemporary Legal Orders*. Eleven, 2019, 99–133

Belov, M. "Imaginaries of Representation: There and Back Again" in Belov, M. (ed.) *Representative Democracy in Flux. Deconstructive Narratives from a Legal and Constitutional Perspective*. Routledge, 2025, 17–49

Belov, M. "Judicial Dialogue—Westphalian or Post-Westphalian Constitutional Phenomenon?" in Belov, M. (ed.) *Judicial Dialogue*. Eleven, 2019, 25–51

Belov, M. "Mastering Emergency Situations: The Activist Role of the Bulgarian Constitutional Court in Redefining the Constitutional Design of War, State of Siege and State of Emergency" in Belov, M. (ed.) *Courts and Judicial Activism under Crisis Conditions: Policy Making in a Time of Illiberalism and Emergency Constitutionalism*. Routledge, 2021, 171–194

Belov, M. "Rule of Law and Democracy in Times of Transitory Constitutionalism, Constitutional Polycrisis and Emergency Constitutionalism: Towards a Global Algorithmic Technocracy?" in Belov, M. (ed.) *Rule of Law in Crisis: Constitutionalism in a State of Flux*. Routledge, 2023, 21–47

Belov, M. "Rule of Law in Europe in Times of Constitutional Polycrisis, Constitutional Polytransition and Democratic Discontent" 3 *Diritto pubblico comparato ed europeo*, 2023, 875–884

Belov, M. "Rule of Law in Space of Flows" in Belov, M. (ed.) *Rule of Law at the Beginning of the Twenty-First Century*. Eleven, 2018, 97–141

Belov, M. "Territory, Territoriality and Territorial Politics as Public Law Concepts" in Belov, M. (ed.) *Territorial Politics and Secession. Constitutional and International Law Dimensions*. Palgrave, 2021, 15–45

Belov, M. "The Challenges to Westphalian Constitutional Geometry in the Age of Supranational Constitutionalism, Global Governance and Information Revolution" in Belov, M. (ed.) *Global Constitutionalism and Its Challenges to Westphalian Constitutional Law*. Hart, 2018, 13–55

Belov, M. "The Conceptual Shapes of Constitutional Polycrisis: Deconstruction, Asymmetries and Post-Modern Anxieties of Constitutional Normalcy" 70 *Irish Jurist*, 2023, 393–410

Belov, M. "The Influence of the Covid-19 Crisis and Its Management in Bulgaria on the Constitutional Principles" in Valchev, D., & Groysman, S. (eds.) *The Covid-19 Crisis and the Future of Liberal Democracy*. University of Sofia "St. Kliment Ohridski" Press, 2023, 58–76

Belov, M. "The Role of Fear Politics in Global Constitutional 'Ernstfall': Images of Fear under COVID-19 Health Paternalism" in Belov, M. (ed.) *Populist Constitutionalism and Illiberal Democracies. Between Constitutional Imagination, Normative Entrenchment and Political Reality*. Intersentia, 2021, 187–221

Belov, M. "Three Models for Ordering Constitutional Orders" 2 *Pravni Zapisi*, 2022, 361–387

Belov, M. "Transitory Imaginaries in Central and Eastern Europe: Reconsidering Constitutional Tradition and Constitutional Transition from Symbolic-Imaginary Perspective" 49 *Review of Central and East European Law*, 2024, 161–189

Belov, M. *Constitutional Semiotics. The Conceptual Foundations of a Constitutional Theory and Meta-Theory*. Hart, 2022

Belov, M. *Courts and Judicial Activism under Crisis Conditions: Policy Making in a Time of Illiberalism and Emergency Constitutionalism*. Routledge, 2021

Blokker, P. "Shifting Constitutional Imaginaries: Is the Liberal-Legal Imaginary Unsettled by Populism?" in Belov, M., & Florczak-Wątor, M. (eds.) *Constitutional Traditions and Constitutional Transitions. Legal and Socio-Legal Perspectives*. Edward Elgar, 2024, 35–57

Brenner, N. "Beyond State-Centrism? Space, Territoriality and Geographical Scale in Globalization Studies" 28(1) *Theory and Society*, 1999, 39–78

Castells, M. *The Rise of the Network Society*. Wiley-Blackwell, 2009

Castoriadis, C. *The Imaginary Institution of Society*. Polity Press, 1987

Dilthey, W. *Weltanschauung, Philosophie und Religion*. Legare Street Press, 2023

Goldsworthy, J. *Parliamentary Sovereignty: Contemporary Debates*. Cambridge University Press, 2010

Gordon, M. *Parliamentary Sovereignty in the UK Constitution: Process, Politics and Democracy*. Hart, 2015

Greene, A. *Permanent States of Emergency and the Rule of Law. Constitutions in an Age of Crisis*. Hart, 2018

Hobbes, T. *Leviathan*. CreateSpace Independent Publishing Platform, 2017

Jacobsohn, G., & Roznai, Y. *Constitutional Revolution*. Yale University Press, 2020

Labatut, B. *When We Cease to Understand the World*. New York Review Books, 2021

Machiavelli, N. *The Prince*. Independently published, 2021

McElwee, J. "Vatican Says AI Has 'Shadow of Evil,' Calls for Close Oversight" *Reuters*, 28 January 2025. https://www.reuters.com/technology/artificial-intelligence/vatican-says-ai-has-shadow-evil-calls-close-oversight-2025-01-28/ (accessed 30 January 2025, 14:00 EET)

McGrath, A., Rademaker, L., & Troy, J. (eds.) *Everywhen. Australia and the Language of Deep History*. UNSW Press, 2023, 1–324

Minc, A. *Le nouveau moyen âge*. Le Grand Livre du Mois, 1994

Nietzsche, F. *The Complete Works of Nietzsche*. Kindle Edition
Přibáň, J. "Political Constitutions in Transnational Society: Socio-Legal and Interdisciplinary Perspectives" 50(S1) *Journal of Law and Society*, 2023, 26–44
Raheja, M. *Reservation Reelism: Redfacing, Visual Sovereignty, and Representations of Native Americans in Film*. University of Nebraska Press, 2011
Roznai, Y. *Unconstitutional Constitutional Amendments. The Limits of Amendment Powers*. Oxford University Press, 2019
Saramago, J. *Seeing*. Mariner Books, 2007
Schlegel, S. "Activism as Defence: The Role of Courts in Shaping the Relationship Between Constitutions and International Law. A Comparison of the Apex Courts of Switzerland, Germany, and Austria" in Belov, M. (ed.) *Courts and Judicial Activism under Crisis Conditions: Policy Making in a Time of Illiberalism and Emergency Constitutionalism*. Routledge, 2022, 43–61
Schmitt, C. *Political Theology: Four Chapters on the Concept of Sovereignty*. University of Chicago Press, 2006
Schmitt, C. *The Concept of the Political*. University of Chicago Press, 2007
Taylor, P. "The State as Container: Territoriality in the Modern World-System" 18(2) *Progress in Human Geography*, 1994; "Beyond Containers: Internationality, Interstateness, Interterritoriality" 19(1) *Progress in Human Geography*, 1995
Varoufakis, Y. *Technofeudalism: What Killed Capitalism*. Melville House, 2024
Walton, K. *Mimesis as Make-Believe. On the Foundations of Representational Arts*. Harvard University Press, 1993
Zuboff, S. *The Age of Surveillance Capitalism: The Fight for a Human Future at the New Frontier of Power*. Public Affairs, 2019

PART II

Emergency, Identity, Interpretation

CHAPTER 5

Constitutional Interpretation of Emergencies: Sustainability of Typical Arguments Over Time

Djordje Gardasevic and Dora Pavković

5.1 Introduction

One of the basic issues regarding emergencies is the perception of unpredictability of both their causes and their consequences. In Federalist No. 23, A. Hamilton famously stated that: "… it is impossible to foresee or define the extent and variety of national exigencies, or the correspondent extent and variety of the means which may be necessary to satisfy them."[1] To this, Hamilton added that "the circumstances that endanger the safety of nations are infinite, and for this reason no constitutional shackles can wisely be imposed on the power to which the care of it is committed."[2]

This chapter is produced as part and funded by the European Union-NextGenerationEU, through the National Recovery and Resilience Plan of the Republic of Bulgaria, project No bg-rrp-2.004-0008.

[1] Alexander Hamilton, 'Federalist No. 23 (The Necessity of a Government as Energetic as the One Proposed to the Preservation of the Union)' (1787).

[2] Ibid.

M. Belov (ed.), *Constitutional Polycrisis and Emergency Constitutionalism*, Federalism and Internal Conflicts,
https://doi.org/10.1007/978-3-032-06516-2_5

Similar views can be found with other classical authors such as J. Locke, J. J. Rousseau, A. V. Dicey, C. Schmitt, and C. L. Rossiter.[3]

In brief, this, firstly, means that emergencies are qualified by uncertainties as to what can cause them. Despite generally accepted definitions in constitutional documents (e.g., war, imminent threat to constitutional order, severe natural disasters, etc.), the perception is that real emergencies can never truly be foreseen. As such, real emergencies are often perceived as sui generis situations with no real historical precedent (e.g., world wars, War on Terrorism, COVID-19 pandemic, etc.). This, secondly, means that if such emergencies could not have been foreseen, new tools to combat them are required. Consequently, this leads to the invention of new mechanisms either through judicial interpretation of law or through the adoption of new emergency measures designed for novel circumstances.

Our aim in this paper is to show that a series of normative approaches to emergencies, regarding specific roles of particular constitutional institutions and seen in a historical perspective, very often revolves around some similar opposing arguments. By saying this, we do not mean to suggest that there is no value in new normative views on what should be done, which are expected to appear with every new global crisis. To the contrary, a great deal of new theoretical work that came with COVID-19 produced highly important and fresh insights into how constitutional systems do and should react to emergencies.

By presenting our observations here, we want to suggest that from the theoretical point of view, emergencies are not, or at least not any more, *terra incognita* that inevitably leads to the necessity of introducing states of exception of any degree. In addition, we want to suggest that any discussion on specific roles of governmental branches in emergencies very often must take into account some typical basic questions. This way, we would also like to claim that, despite the postulate of unpredictability of their causes and consequences, crises inevitably provoke divergences of

[3] This basic proposition that emergencies cannot fully be foreseen, or qualification about their unprecedented nature that comes to surface with every new major crisis, is the usual conclusion or a starting point for new debates. This is very clear also with most recent authors. See, for instance: Elena Griglio, 'Parliamentary Oversight under the COVID-19 Emergency: Striving Against Executive Dominance' (2020) 8(1–2) The Theory and Practice of Legislation 49, DOI: 10.1080/20508840.2020.1789935; Jan Petrov, 'The COVID-19 Emergency in the Age of Executive Aggrandizement: What Role for Legislative and Judicial Checks?' (2020) 8(1–2) The Theory and Practice of Legislation 71, https://doi.org/10.1080/20508840.2020.1788232; Ladislav Vyhnánek and others, 'The Dynamics of Proportionality: Constitutional Courts and the Review of COVID-19 Regulations' (2024) 25(3) German Law Journal 386.https://doi.org/10.1017/glj.2023.96 accessed 1 February 2025.

constitutional interpretation on some quite common grounds that, as such, can be expected.

In the following part of this paper, we will first give an overview of typical normative arguments on emergencies in theory (2. arguments in theory). To this, we will add some selected examples from the case-law (3. arguments in case-law).

5.2 Arguments in Theory

In the following part of this chapter, we will first give some general observations on possible interpretative approaches to emergencies and then, in some more detail, examine the work of selected modern authors. In references, we will point to some links to previous theoretical points, in order to show the continuity in the detection of essential elements of debates on emergencies.

5.2.1 A Note on Possible Interpretations of Emergencies in Theory

From a methodological point of view, one very inspiring way of thinking about the emergency role of particular branches of government comes with a possible division of theories of emergencies in the American literature.[4] Even though we will not use the following division as the only guidance for some references we intend to make, we find the systematic approach of the American authors worth taking into account for our purposes here.

Thus, in the realm of American theories, executive unilateralists argue for the functional supremacy of the executive, seek wide executive discretionary powers to cope with crises and ask for deference of the legislature and judiciary, claiming that the executive is composed of security experts and enjoys the benefits of secrecy, expediency and efficiency.[5] Civil

[4] For our prior presentation of some of the classical arguments in emergency theories, including the division in the American emergency theories, see also: Djordje Gardasevic, 'American Lessons Learned—European Future Rethought' (2016) 66 *Zbornik Pravnog Fakulteta u Zagrebu* 61; Djordje Gardasevic, 'Activism of the Croatian Constitutional Court and COVID A Bridge Too Far' in Martin Belov (ed), *Courts and Judicial Activism under Crisis Conditions: Policy Making in a Time of Illiberalism and Emergency Constitutionalism* (Routledge 2022), doi: 10.4324/9781003200666-14; Djordje Gardasevic, 'Constitutional Interpretation and COVID-19 in Croatia' in Saša Zagorc and Samo Bardutzky (eds), *Ustava na robu izrednega stanja* (Univerza v Ljubljani, Pravna fakulteta 2024).

[5] Mark Tushnet, 'Controlling Executive Power in the War on Terrorism' (2005) 118 *Harv. L. Rev.* 2673; Richard A Posner, *Not a Suicide Pact: The Constitution in a Time of*

libertarians claim that in crises, courts play a special role because they are not politically accountable, they perform their functions with the benefit of an ex post facto view, and they must present structured reasoning that binds them in future cases.[6] Democratic formalists especially emphasize the role of the Congress as an appropriate forum for representative, free and democratic debate and deliberation that produces both an ex ante legislative regulation or ex post control of emergency measures.[7] Finally, proponents of the process-based approach focus on institutional emergency coordination between political branches and claim that the judicial review mainly focuses on checking whether the president and Congress have reached a consensus and undertaken a joint action.[8]

Apart from this, we would like to point out some other considerations we deem important for our work. Thus, one of the basic postulates about emergencies is that they lead to the concentration of powers in the hands of the executive branch.[9] This "Hamiltonian"

National Emergency (Oxford University Press 2006); John Yoo, *The Powers of War and Peace: The Constitution and Foreign Affairs after 9/11* (University of Chicago Press 2006); Eric A Posner and Adrian Vermeule, *Terror in the Balance—Security, Liberty and the Courts* (Oxford University Press 2007).

[6] David Cole, 'Judging the Next Emergency: Judicial Review and Individual Rights in Times of Crisis' (2002–03) 101 *Mich L Rev* 2565; David Cole, 'The Priority of Morality: The Emergency Constitution's Blind Spot' (2004) 113 *Yale LJ* 1753; Burt Neuborne, 'The Role of Courts in Time of War' (2005) 29 *NYU Rev L & Soc Change* 555; Posner (n 5); Geoffrey R Stone, 'Civil Liberties v National Security in the Law's Open Areas' (2006) 86 *BU L Rev* 1315; Posner and Vermeule (n 5); Geoffrey R Stone, 'National Security v Civil Liberties' (2007) 95 *Cal L Rev* 2203. For a conceptual view on the role of courts in crisis conditions, with an emphasis on judicial activism, see also: Martin Belov, 'Introduction' in Martin Belov (ed), *Courts and Judicial Activism under Crisis Conditions: Policy Making in a Time of Illiberalism and Emergency Constitutionalism* (Routledge 2022), doi: 10.4324/9781003200666-1.

[7] Bruce Ackerman, 'The Emergency Constitution' (2004) 113 *Yale LJ* 1029; William E Scheuerman, 'Emergency Powers and the Rule of Law After 9/11' (2006) 14 (1) *J Polit Philos* 61; Bruce Ackerman, *Before the Next Attack: Preserving Civil Liberties in an Age of Terrorism* (Yale University Press 2006).

[8] Samuel Issacharoff and Richard H Pildes, 'Emergency Contexts without Emergency Powers: The United States' Constitutional Approach to Rights During Wartime' (2004) 2(2) *Intl J Const L* 296, https://doi.org/10.1093/icon/2.2.296 accessed 1 February 2025.

[9] Yet another usual consequence of emergencies is also the vertical concentration of powers. This has been observed in both the classical and modern theory. Thus, already C. L. Rossiter observed that "federalism and local self-government...present distinct barriers to effective crisis action, and in a great they will be broken down." In their turn, O. Gross and F.

approach[10] may easily be qualified as the starting point for any discussion because it is the most usual way of thinking about emergencies, either as a normative proposal or as an object of criticism that leads to alternative normative views. As usual, this postulate has a twofold nature.

On the one hand, there stands a positive claim that executive crisis concentration of powers is a (historical) fact, part of reality which must be taken into account in any relevant discussion on the whole topic of emergencies. On the other hand, there appears a normative (principally unilateralist) claim that executive concentration of powers is actually a preferable path to follow.

As for the positive claim, it is clear that historical experiences are relevant for discussions on emergencies in several ways.[11] C. L. Rossiter, for instance, made an important methodological input that a more comprehensive view of how different branches really did act in emergencies is indispensable. In fact, he presented his own model of emergency powers only after having made an extensive overview of emergency experiences in five different states.[12]

More recently, E. Posner and A. Vermeule argued that from historical experiences on how different branches acted in emergencies, one can discern two differing views. This way, they suggest that history may be seen either as an instance of "political and constitutional failure" or an instance of "political and constitutional success," which consequently leads to the adoption of either "civil libertarianism" or the "deferential"

Ní Aoláin claimed that "...in federal states one of the first "victims" of exigencies and crises is the principle of federalism". Clinton L Rossiter, *Constitutional Dictatorship: Crisis Government in the Modern Democracies* (Princeton University Press 1948) 5, 289; Oren Gross and Fionnuala Ní Aoláin, *Law in Times of Crisis: Emergency Powers in Theory and Practice* (Cambridge University Press 2006) 59–60. For quite a recent view on the interplay between local and central authorities in dealing with emergencies, see, among other sources: James G. Hodge Jr., 'National Legal Paradigms for Public Health Emergency Responses' (2021) 71 American University Law Review 65.

[10] Alexander Hamilton, 'Federalist No. 70 (The Executive Department Further Considered)', March 18, 1788; Alexander Hamilton, 'Federalist No. 74 (The Command of the Military and Naval Forces, and the Pardoning Power of the Executive)' March 25, 1788.

[11] For a view that history may thus be used both in favor of and against a given interpretive stance and that sometimes a recourse to history may yield contradictory positions, see: Kevin Y L Tan, 'Interpreting the Constitution: The Use and Abuse of History' (2022) 20(5) *International Journal of Constitutional Law* 1958, https://doi.org/10.1093/icon/moac115.

[12] Rossiter (n 9). Such a comprehensive comparative overview, as a precondition for further proposals, is visible with contemporary authors as well.

view.[13] While Posner and Vermeule affirm deference, explaining that throughout history it was successful, others emphasize historical emergency executive "overreactions" and claim that they later led to regret.[14]

In the same context, one especially important methodological input comes with detailed analyses of the historical record pertaining to the operation of branches other than the executive. Thus, for instance, G. R. Stone and D. Cole argue that the long-standing practice of American judges to defer to other governmental branches in emergencies was characteristic until the 1950s. According to them, this stance was later reversed either through "rejection" of the "logical" presumption of deference by the newly developed case-law or through various forms of political excuse for past mistakes or overreactions.[15]

The overall importance of the evaluation of historical data, as an element of positive analysis that at the same time serves as a precondition for further normative claims, is clearly visible with modern authors as well.

Thus, for instance, A. L. Tyler argues that, save a few exceptions, historical deference of the US Supreme Court has changed "at least to some extent, during the COVID-19 pandemic."[16] E. Griglio puts a similar argument as it relates to legislatures, namely that parliaments during the COVID-19 crisis did play a significant role in controlling the executive.[17] T. Ginsburg and M. Versteeg assert that "contrary to the conventional wisdom, courts, legislatures, and subnational governments have played important roles in constraining national executives."[18] In further working out those claims related directly to the COVID-19 pandemic, they also

[13] Posner and Vermeule (n 5) 3–4

[14] Geoffrey R Stone, 'War Fever' (2004) 69 *Mo L Rev* 1131; Geoffrey R Stone, *Perilous Times: Free Speech in Wartime (From the Sedition Act of 1798 to the War on Terrorism)* (WW Norton & Co 2004) 12–14; David Cole, 'No Reason to Believe: Radical Skepticism, Emergency Power, and Constitutional Constraint' (2008) 75 *U Chi L Rev* 1329. See also: David Cole, 'The New McCarthyism: Repeating History in the War on Terrorism' (2003) 38(1) *Harv CR-CL L Rev* 1. For recent work taking into account the executive overreach, see: Griglio (n 3); Petrov (n 3)

[15] See: Stone, 'National Security v Civil Liberties' (no 6); Cole, 'Judging the Next Emergency: Judicial Review and Individual Rights in Times of Crisis' (n 6). For another view, that the legislative branch in emergencies has also usually played a deferential role see: Posner and Vermeule (n 5) 47

[16] Amanda L Tyler, 'Judicial Review in Times of Emergency: From the Founding through the COVID-19 Pandemic' (2023) 109(3) *Va L Rev* 489, 555

[17] Griglio (n 3)

[18] Tom Ginsburg and Mila Versteeg, 'The Bound Executive: Emergency Powers during the Pandemic' (2021) 19 Int'l J Const L 1498

state that courts played an important role in scrutinizing governmental actions from both procedural and substantive points of view, as well as demanding that the executive take action. On the other hand, according to them, legislators devised quick legislative solutions, provided authority and oversight and declared or extended a state of emergency.[19]

Obviously, a historical record that shows examples of concrete judicial or legislative impact on emergency decision-making may serve as a good basis for claiming that such a model of conduct is also a desirable one. In other words, such positive claims lead further to normative propositions on the appropriate emergency role of either courts or legislatures in the future.[20]

5.2.2 Modern Views

We start with an overview of modern theoretical proposals on emergencies with R. Albert and Y. Roznai.[21] Their research is basically focused on one of the essential issues related to emergencies: how to protect the existing constitution from being altered under circumstances of pressure?[22] The specific segment of their work is thus related to the question of unamendability of the constitutional document. Unamendability here serves the purpose of protecting the constitution, but aware of the fact that a crisis may have demands of its own, Albert and Roznai seek alternative ways to ensure that a constitution is properly adapted to the exigencies of an emergency moment. They propose three separate solutions to the problem: the judicial review of constitutional amendment, a self-destruction trigger, and an escalating sunset rule.

By definition, emphasizing judicial review is primarily connected to civil libertarianism, but Albert and Roznai are not keen to take that specific course: they are expressly concerned about the democratic legitimacy of courts to review constitutional amendments, the danger of courts

[19] ibid 1500

[20] Thus, A. L. Tyler further advocates the "Business As Usual Model" and a distinguished emergency role for courts, E. Griglio does the same for parliaments, and T. Ginsburg and M. Versteeg for both courts and parliaments.

[21] Richard Albert and Yaniv Roznai, 'Emergency Unamendability: Limitations on Constitutional Amendment in Extreme Conditions' (2022) 81 *Md L Rev* 243

[22] The question of how to preserve the constitution from being altered in cases of turmoil has a long history, dating back to Roman times where it was deemed as one of the essential features of the institution of dictatorship. See: Rossiter (n 9); Gross and Ní Aoláin (n 9)

overstepping their powers, as well as the danger of judges to "rally around the flag" when faced with an emergency.[23] Therefore, the two authors are relying on two other solutions. The concept of the "self-destruction trigger" finds its basis in the idea that "constitutional designers could permit amendments in periods of emergency but require that any emergency amendment expire automatically after a certain period of time."[24] On the other hand, the "escalating sunset rule," "does not automatically repeal the emergency amendment, but it does require a higher threshold to extend its application after a predetermined duration."[25] Both of those alternative views are intrinsically linked to the stream of democratic formalism. Albert and Roznai propose a scheme that would be a part of a constitutional document, thus a product of ex ante deliberations of "constitutional designers" and a tool later on to be used by "constitutional actors," that is, federal and state bodies participating in the amendment process.

Alan Greene's approach to emergencies seems to belong to the same category.[26] In the specific part dealing with the distribution of emergency powers among several branches of government, Greene puts into question "the standard assumption that prevails in national security emergencies that executives are best placed to act."[27] Instead of that, he contends "that in a pandemic, there is no reason to assume that the executive should be privy to sensitive information that the legislature cannot also hear; nor, once the emergency powers are in effect, that the legislature is unable to scrutinize the executive and hold it to account."[28] To the contrary, Greene argues that "while it may ostensibly appear difficult for legislatures

[23] Albert and Roznai (no 21) 252–253. For previous accounts on the "rally around the flag" problem, see: Gross and Ní Aoláin (n 9) 64.

[24] Albert and Roznai (no 21) 254.

[25] ibid. It is notable that both proposals owe something to previously crafted ideas on the so-called "sunset clauses" embedded in the American emergency legislation and the so-called "supermajoritarian escalator". For one, among several prior suggestions for introduction of sunset clauses in emergency legislation, see: Stone, 'War Fever' (no 14) 1141–1142. For previous analyses of the "sunset clauses" in the American PATRIOT ACT, see: Stewart A Baker and John Kavanagh (eds), *Patriot Debates: Experts Debate the USA PATRIOT Act* (American Bar Association Publishing 2005). For the concept of the "supermajoritarian escalator" see: Ackerman, 'Before the Next Attack: Preserving Civil Liberties in an Age of Terrorism' (n 7) 80–83.

[26] Alan Greene, *Emergency Powers In A Time Of Pandemic* (Bristol University Press 2020).

[27] Ibid 3

[28] Ibid. In his earlier analysis of the importance of access to information, B. Ackerman also pointed that in the emergency context the executive would have enormous incentives to keep

to sit during a pandemic where the virus is airborne and spreads easily in closed spaces with large groups of people, states' experiences during the COVID-19 pandemic demonstrate that there are innovative ways to facilitate this."[29]

From the structural point of view, Greene's position in its entirety is very clear. Starting from the Roman paradigm,[30] his proposal for a highlighted role of the legislature builds on unavoidable elements of discussion. Those include time limits on legislation (sunset clauses), requirements for Parliament to be recalled and for subsequent legislative approval and oversight of executive emergency powers, including the role of parliamentary committees.[31] While acknowledging that in times of crisis, including the case of a pandemic, there indeed exists a substantial temptation to delegate

some information secret and that "The legislature cannot act effectively if it is at the mercy of the executive for information". Ackerman, 'Before the Next Attack: Preserving Civil Liberties in an Age of Terrorism' (n 7) 84–85. For another recent proposal that legislature (Congress) and public should also have access to expert knowledge necessary to control emergency policy choices, see: Barry Sullivan, 'Expert Knowledge, Democratic Accountability, and the Unitary Executive' (2023) 92 *Fordham L Rev* 575. Besides this, it is worth saying that the "technical" question of access to information has a somewhat deeper meaning for models of emergency powers. In our view, it touches upon one of the most favorable claims of executive unilateralists, which is that the executive possesses particular (expert) knowledge that the other two branches do not have. T. Ginsburg and M. Versteeg give a good illustration of this link: "While a pandemic undoubtedly constitutes a crisis, it is far from clear that crisis governance should be the same in a pandemic as in a national security crisis. A key difference is that, during a pandemic, information is highly dispersed, and there is no need for secrecy in formulating the response. Under these circumstances, courts and legislatures may see no need to defer to the executive; to the contrary, they may possess some institutional advantages in dictating (part of) the response. Ginsburg and Versteeg (no 18) 1501

[29] Greene (no 26) 4. Here, Greene also deals with the conventional account that "the executive is often seen as the branch most suited to act in a crisis, owing to its ability to respond swiftly, decisively, and to hear secret information." Ibid 3. For a remainder of Greene's argument of stressing the importance of the role of a legislature in pandemic, that we reconstruct here, see especially: ibid 93–118. In addition, we should add that the problem of a difficulty for legislatures to sit during emergencies belongs to one of classical arguments. In this context, already J. Locke stated that "…for since in some governments the law-making power is not always in being, and is usually too numerous, and so too slow for the dispatch requisite to execution." See: John Locke, *The Works of John Locke in Nine Volumes* (12th edn, Rivington 1824) vol 4

[30] The Roman model of emergency powers is a classical element of discussion in various theories based on "democratic formalism" premises. It has also been an object of extensive evaluation with numerous writers, including C. L. Rossiter, C. J. Friedrich, B. Ackerman, O. Gross and F. Ní Aoláin.

[31] Active participation of legislatures in emergency contexts is one of essential elements of discussion for democratic formalists. C. L. Rossiter claims: "It is in the debates, the

law-making powers to the executive, he proceeds to argue that this may be clear at the beginning, but not so clear as the crisis progresses. Like with other notable authors, the passage of time for Greene plays an important role in validating the role of the legislature, especially when one takes into account difficulties in firmly establishing the exact point at which exceptional measures should end.[32] Ginsburg and Versteeg argue that emergencies require the joint and cooperative action of all branches of government. In their view, therefore, both courts and parliaments play significant roles. The basis of their argument is that different "...branches have different epistemic bases and distinct institutional advantages."[33] This way, "courts are institutionally well equipped to demand well-reasoned justifications, and to identify individual interests that may suffer as a result of collective policies," while "legislatures provide distinct advantages as arenas for policy debate, and for being the ultimate loci of democratic legitimacy in a representative democracy."[34]

committees, and the roll-calls of the House and Senate that the doctrinaire criteria of constitutional dictatorship advanced in this chapter can take on practical significance." Rossiter (n 9) 309–310. On the other hand, in reference to the recall, B. Ackerman states: "The executive should be given power to act unilaterally only for the briefest period—long enough for the legislature to convene and consider the matter, but no longer. If the legislature is already in session, one week seems long enough; if not, two weeks is sufficient." Ackerman, 'Before the Next Attack: Preserving Civil Liberties in an Age of Terrorism' (n 7) 84–85. The problem of a legislature that needs to convene in time has been an object of discussion at least since the American Civil War. Ackerman also argues that parliamentary committees have a significant role in emergencies, especially for opposition political parties who through committees may influence the oversight of the executive. Ibid 83–87

[32] In fact, Greene here touches upon two big themes of emergencies. As for the relevance of passage of time and the correspondingly growing importance of a legislative oversight (the "supermajoritatian escalator") see also the proposals of B. Ackerman. On the other hand, the problem of determining the end of emergencies has long preoccupied various scholars and starting with the Roman model of dictatorship, as a paradigm thereof. See also a comparable "problem of separation" and temporal distinctions, in: Gross and Ní Aoláin (n 9) 174–180. For another comparable approach to emergencies, and COVID-19 especially, in line with basic premises of democratic formalism, and with an emphasis on ex ante parliamentary regulation, see also: Griglio (n 3).

[33] Ginsburg and Versteeg (no 18) 1534.

[34] Ibid. Generally, Ginsburg and Versteeg are addressing on of the most salient questions related to emergencies: which particular branch of government is best positioned to deal with them, in terms of its institutional capacities and expertise? Naturally, executive unilateralists have long claimed that this is the executive while civil libertarians and democratic formalists have long defended the advantages of judiciary and legislatures. For several

Even though Ginsburg and Versteeg are aware that "interactions among multiple institutions introduce complexities, as the response may take longer to develop and may be altered a number of times,"[35] they argue that cooperation has many advantages. According to them, "first, it may produce better reason-giving, forced by the back and forth between different branches. Second, the fact that multiple branches of government were involved in formulating the response might demonstrate a consensus among institutions with their own distinct bases of legitimacy. Third, it is possible that any single actor is more likely to be wrong, and that when multiple actors are involved, the risk of a colossal mistake is lower."[36]

Stressing specific roles of courts and legislatures in enhancing the effectiveness and legitimacy of emergency action, J. Petrov[37] starts with pointing to some very important and already classical settings regarding emergencies. Besides taking into account the "Hamiltonian" advantages of the executive, he refers to insights from the "panic," "democratic failure," and "ratchet" theories as well as to the "rallying around the flag" problem.[38] He also points to the fact that emergency concentration of powers in the executive results from the fact that the executive "has what responding to an emergency needs: hierarchical

arguments supporting the emergency role of courts (absence of political accountability, benefits of an ex post facto judicial review, the obligation of courts to produce well-reasoned decisions, the fact that they are not working under pressure of the moment), see: Stone, 'National Security v Civil Liberties' (no 6) 2209; Cole, 'Judging the Next Emergency: Judicial Review and Individual Rights in Times of Crisis' (n 6). For another previous view that legislatures have the advantage of being elected representative bodies that provide free and democratic decision-making, which is the best option for controlling emergency actions, see: Scheuerman (n 7) 75–77. As for the emergency role of courts to identify and properly treat individual interests through "microadjudication", see: Ackerman, 'Before the Next Attack: Preserving Civil Liberties in an Age of Terrorism' (n 7).

35 Ginsburg and Versteeg (no 18) 1534.

36 Ibid. For a similar argument, that reliance on different constitutional actors which have "different democratic pedigrees" (or, as Ginsburg and Versteeg put it "own distinct bases of legitimacy") in emergencies indeed is important, see: Issacharoff and Pildes (no 8) 298 https://doi.org/10.1093/icon/2.2.296 accessed 1 February 2025. For previous accounts of the problem that emergencies require measures to be taken by "rational" actors who do not make systematic errors, see: Posner and Vermeule (n 5) 29–31, 59–86 (The Panic Theory). G. F. Stone too seriously takes the argument that one of the reasons for judicial deference could be a danger of judicial error, which in an emergency could be catastrophic. See: Stone, 'National Security v Civil Liberties' (no 6) 2203

37 Petrov (n 3)

38 On these three theories, see: Posner and Vermeule (n 5)

structure with a clear division of ranks and responsibilities, access to expertise, and qualities that allow for swift and decisive action for protecting the nation."[39]

However, the COVID-19 emergency is yet another completely new situation, with "several distinctive features", and Petrov explains the following: "It is a public health emergency on a global scale with virtually every individual potentially affected. There is no clearly defined external enemy or evil-doer who must be stopped, but an invisible virus spreading through interpersonal contact, respiratory droplets and contaminated surfaces."[40] This fact immediately opens the door for envisaging a new role for courts and parliaments. Like with Ginsburg and Versteeg, Petrov's approach is a comprehensive one, including all branches, because an increase in the efficiency of governance may best be achieved if "competences are assigned to those authorities that are best suited to carrying them out" and "Each branch of power has its integrity and distinctive character."[41] Legislature is particularly important because it "stands out as the representative branch," "parliaments are important deliberative fora where different political ideas can be heard and discussed," and "the parliamentarians can voice the views and concerns of their constituents affected by the emergency measures."[42] On the other hand, the judiciary also has its particular advantages in dealing with emergencies in resolving individual disputes over emergency policies, in checking the executive and in clarifying the imperfect emergency policies.[43]

In fact, Petrov very firmly argues that joint action of courts and legislatures is important also because "They can also improve the feasibility of emergency measures by identifying and/or rectifying eventual legal

[39] Petrov (n 3) 75

[40] Ibid. For a classical claim on the impossibility to define emergencies ex ante, see the Federalist no. 23. On the other hand, the American theoretical debate on the nature of the "War on Terrorism" once again revived the old question of whether to define new emergency as a sui generis situation ("War–Crime" debate). See generally: Ackerman, 'Before the Next Attack: Preserving Civil Liberties in an Age of Terrorism' (n 7); Posner (n 5); Yoo (no 5); Michel Rosenfeld, 'Judicial Balancing in Times of Stress: Comparing the American, British, and Israeli Approaches to the War on Terror' (2006) 27 *Cardozo L Rev* 2079

[41] Petrov (n 3) 78

[42] Ibid 78–79.

[43] Ibid 80–81.

deficiencies, inconsistencies and contradictions" embedded in emergency measures "made in a rush and under pressure."[44]

A. L. Tyler gives one particularly strong stance in defense of the "Business as Usual" approach to emergencies. Justifying a distinctive role that courts should keep in emergencies, she offers a number of important arguments that support her general claim.[45] Those arguments may be divided into four categories.

In the first category, Tyler argues that a normative proposal for a strong emergency role of the judiciary relies on some rather definitional elements of emergencies themselves. Consequently, she claims that, on one side, people may not agree as to whether there is an emergency, and on the other, that emergencies no longer have clear start and end points. Whereas in relation to the first consideration, she, quite rhetorically, raises a question, "Will every situation inevitably be treated as sui generis?", in relation to the second, straightforwardly claims: "The long and short of it is that drawing neat lines between emergencies and 'normal' times today is an elusive objective. And if a state of emergency of one kind or another is our new normal, then why shouldn't the normal constitutional rules apply? And, for that matter, be judicially enforceable?"[46] The second category of Tyler's arguments is principally based on the historical record. In this context she basically claims that when courts stand down or defer to the political branches there will be downsides because the political branches will not self-police, that there will be overreactions on the side of those managing crises, that all those lessons from the past must not be neglected and that there is no plausible ground for claiming that government will disobey binding court decisions.[47] In the third category, Tyler is basically building up a counterfactual argument and claims that many cases "in which the Court has deferred to the political branches would not have been disastrous had they come out differently."[48] Finally, in the fourth category, Tyler presents an interpretive argument, claiming that numerous constitutional principles and norms should not be "adapted" in wartime

[44] Ibid 78. For previous accounts on the problem of "rational" actors who do not make systematic errors see: n 36.

[45] For a comprehensive view on the "Business As Usual" model, see: Gross and Ní Aoláin (n 9) 86–109. For this part of overview of A. L. Tyler's arguments see: Tyler (no 16) 562–582.

[46] Tyler (no 16) 562, 567.

[47] Ibid 567–577.

[48] Ibid 577.

according to determinations of both politically accountable branches, and at the expense of the judiciary.[49]

Before we move on to the survey of the relevant case-law, we would like to make one additional comment in this chapter. As we indicated above, the "core" of the process-based approach lies in the proposition that courts focus on questions of institutional decision-making and that their analysis thus is process-oriented. In addition, S. Issacharoff and R. Pildes do suggest that, in that context, one of the important questions (for courts reviewing emergency measures) is how specific the legislature's (congressional) participation in emergency decision-making must be.[50] With full reservation that pure analogies are not possible, we would like to suggest that some of the most recent approaches also put significant focus on procedural aspects of emergency actions.[51]

5.3 Arguments in Case-Law

Even though executive unilateralist arguments in strict form do not appear in the analyzed decisions of the European constitutional courts,[52] some courts favored the government's broad discretion and practiced a higher degree of judicial deference. One such example can be found in a decision Pl. ÚS 106/20 of the Czech Constitutional Court (hereinafter: CCC). First of all, the CCC highlighted the importance of the role played by the government, saying that "one must accept a wide degree of discretion for

[49] Ibid. 579–582. We have already pointed to some points of discussion with other authors that are clearly visible in Tyler's approach as well (e.g., definition of an emergency, its sui generis characters, the problem of overreactions in crises, the issue of a rational emergency actor). Additionally, in comparison to Tyler's argument that "emergencies no longer have clear start and end points", consider the Ackerman's argument on the impossibility to determine when, as opposed to classical wars, the "War on Terrorism" would end. Ackerman, 'Before the Next Attack: Preserving Civil Liberties in an Age of Terrorism' (n 7) 6.

[50] Issacharoff and Pildes (no 8) 326 https://doi.org/10.1093/icon/2.2.296 accessed 1 February 2025.

[51] For a "semi-procedural review," that postulates the necessity for emergency policymakers to follow certain procedural steps, see: Vyhnánek and others (n 3). For another account that stresses the importance of courts to seek reasoned justifications from political branches in crises, see also: Conor Casey, 'Business as Usual? Irish Courts, the Constitution, and COVID-19' (2021) 2 *Percorsi Costituzionali/Constitutional Paths* 337, https://ssrn.com/abstract=3924138 accessed 1 February 2025.

[52] For arguments regarding executive unilateralist approach by the Croatian Constitutional Court, see: Gardasevic, 'Constitutional Interpretation and COVID-19 in Croatia' (n 4)

the Government."[53] Secondly, the CCC practices self-restraint, mentioning that it "cannot enter the field of political decision making by requiring an optimal, most suitable, or best solution".[54] However, the Government is somewhat restricted,[55] and in the end, the CCC annulled the resolution in question even though it exercised a lot of constraint due to the Government not being able to justify its actions and "support its measure with rational arguments."[56] Therefore, the CCC required justification and evidence, applying, as some authors argue, procedural rationality review.[57] Criticizing the fact that the CCC at the same time claims restraint while "it rejects as insufficient the grounds that the Government presented in its statements," one justice argued for a higher degree of judicial deference in his dissenting opinion.[58]

Similar arguments regarding deference and broad discretion for the government are also presented in a Decision No. PL. ÚS 22/2020-104 of the Slovak Constitutional Court and Decision 23/2021 of the Hungarian Constitutional Court (hereinafter: HCC). Discussing the need to declare a state of emergency in the context of COVID-19, the Slovak Constitutional Court claimed that "the government is in a better position" to assess this, and therefore has a degree of political discretion.[59] It further noted that "the government, not the judiciary, bears the burden of primary responsibility for the security situation in the country."[60] The HCC follows this line as well, claiming that it has "neither the power nor the means" to assess which measures are necessary to combat the pandemic.[61]

[53] Czech Constitutional Court, Judgment no. Pl. ÚS 106/20 of 9 February 2021, [87].

[54] Czech Constitutional Court, Judgment no. Pl. ÚS 106/20 of 9 February 2021, [87]

[55] For example, the Government enacts individual measures based on a parliamentary statute, and must present reasoning behind specific measures. See: Czech Constitutional Court, Judgment no. Pl. ÚS 106/20 of 9 February 2021, para [76], [77]

[56] Czech Constitutional Court, Judgment no. Pl. ÚS 106/20 of 9 February 2021, [91].

[57] Vyhnánek and others (n 3) 399

[58] Czech Constitutional Court, Judgment no. Pl. ÚS 106/20 of 9 February 2021, Dissenting opinion of Justice Jaroslav Fenyk. For a similar view, advocating for more deference, see also the Czech Constitutional Court, Judgment no. Pl. ÚS 106/20 of 9 February 2021, Dissenting opinion of Justice Josef Fiala.

[59] Slovak Constitutional Court, Decision—Finding No. PL. ÚS 22/2020 of 14 October 2020, [71]

[60] Slovak Constitutional Court, Decision—Finding No. PL. ÚS 22/2020 of 14 October 2020, [71]

[61] Hungarian Constitutional Court, Decision 23/2021 (VII. 13.) of 22 June 2021, [28]

The "power and responsibility to introduce the necessary extraordinary measures," according to the HCC, belongs to the government.[62]

Some European courts also argued for a broader discretion during emergencies, but favored the discretion and the central role of the legislative rather than the executive branch. For example, the Federal Constitutional Court of Germany (hereinafter: FCC) claimed that "the legislator's margin of appreciation" in the case in question was broad, since the overall pandemic situation is characterized by its dangerous and unpredictable nature.[63] Similarly, the Austrian Constitutional Court (hereinafter: ACC) held that "the legislator enjoys a wide margin of appreciation when combating the economic consequences of the COVID-19 pandemic."[64]

In another decision, the FCC stressed that due to "factual uncertainties" based on which the measures are adopted, the legislator is required to "monitor further developments" and amend the law in accordance with new information.[65] As the pandemic persists and the longer the intrusive measures remain in force, "the more it is incumbent upon the legislator to ensure that its decisions are based on sufficiently reliable assessments", claims the FCC.[66] This idea—as more information is available, the legislative's (or the executive's) discretion is becoming more and more narrow, while judicial scrutiny is intensifying[67]

[62] Hungarian Constitutional Court, Decision 23/2021 (VII. 13.) of 22 June 2021, [28]

[63] Federal Constitutional Court of Germany, Order of the First Senate of 19 November 2021—1 BvR 781/21—paras. 1–306, [205]

[64] Austrian Constitutional Court, decision G-202-2020 of 14 July 2020, [2.4.2.3.] Though according to Stöger, the executive had a dominant role during the pandemic, its ordinances were enacted on a statutory basis provided by the parliament. See: Klaus Stöger, 'Austria: Legal Response to COVID-19' in Jeff King and others (eds), *The Oxford Compendium of National Legal Responses to COVID-19* (OUP) https://oxcon.ouplaw.com/display/10.1093/law-occ19/law-occ19-e28?rskey=Eos6sC&result=2&prd=OCC19 accessed [4 February 2025]

[65] Federal Constitutional Court of Germany, Order of the First Senate of 19 November 2021—1 BvR 971/21—paras. 1–222, [123], [198]

[66] Federal Constitutional Court of Germany, Order of the First Senate of 19 November 2021—1 BvR 971/21—paras. 1–222, Headnotes.

[67] According to Kaiser, judicial review conducted by German courts became more robust with the increase in the knowledge on the pandemic, see: Anna-Bettina Kaiser and Robert Hensel, 'Federal Republic of Germany: Legal Response to COVID-19' in Jeff King and others (eds), *The Oxford Compendium of National Legal Responses to COVID-19* (OUP) https://oxcon.ouplaw.com/display/10.1093/law-occ19/law-occ19-e2, accessed [4 February 2025]Indeed, in the above-mentioned decision of the FCC, the court restricted itself

—is also not new, and can also be detected in the decisions of some other European courts.[68]

Argumentative invocations in line with the concept of democratic formalism can also be traced across the case-law. By giving his account of the situation, one judge of the Slovenian Constitutional Court (hereinafter: SCC) presents classic arguments thereof, arguing that by being elected, the parliament enjoys democratic legitimacy and should "regulate in advance on a general and abstract level" the measures needed to deal with the pandemic.[69] Thus, as the democratic formalist argument goes, during emergencies, a legislative body is an appropriate forum for democratic debate, and an ex ante legislative regulation is favored.[70]

Finally, although a somewhat rare occurrence, there are examples of civil libertarian reasoning among the judges of European courts. A good example is portrayed by judges Mežnar and Šugman Stubbs of SCC, who assert that finding the balance between providing health care and protecting human rights is done *first* by the government and the legislature, but the final say belongs to the Constitutional Court.[71] Furthermore, they stated that fundamental rights must rigorously be assessed in times of emergency, in terms of proportionality, necessity, and

to assessing whether the legislator's prognosis on the suitability or necessity of measures is merely tenable, indicating a less strict judicial review. See: Federal Constitutional Court of Germany, Order of the First Senate of 19 November 2021—1 BvR 971/21—paras. 1–222, [115], [123]

[68] See, for example: Czech Constitutional Court, decision Pl. ÚS 106/20, [79], [81]. The influence of the "time factor" on the "possibility (and quality) of the measure's justification" in the context of this decision is noticed by Vyhnánek and others. See: Vyhnánek and others (n 3) 400. For a similar reasoning, see also: Slovenian Constitutional Court, Decision no. U-I-83/20 of 27 August 2020, [50]; see also: Toma Birmontiene, 'The Main Trends in Constitutional Jurisprudence Developed by Constitutional Courts During the COVID-19 Pandemic' in Rainer Arnold and José Cremades (eds), *Rule of Law and the Challenges Posed by the Pandemic: Contributions to the World Law Congress 2021 in Barranquilla* (Springer 2023)

[69] Slovenian Constitutional Court, Decision no. U-I-79/20 of 13 May 2021, Partially concurring, partially dissenting opinion of Judge Dr Rajko Knez.

[70] According to Birmontiene, the importance of parliament's involvement to determine the limits of fundamental rights and freedoms was highlighted by the Slovak Constitutional Court in its decision PL. ÚS 13/2020, as well. See: Birmontiene (no 68) 91

[71] Slovenian Constitutional Court, Decision no. U-I-83/20 of 27 August 2020, Separate opinion of judge Dr. Špelce Mežnar joined by judge dr. Katja Šugman Stubbs.

non-discrimination.[72] Although not always as assertive, some courts across Europe managed to set some standards for the protection of human rights even during emergencies and showed that even in such uncertain times, there is a place for judicial review.[73]

5.4 Conclusion

In the overall course of history, human knowledge constantly builds upon its earlier discoveries. This process is as important from the purely scientific as from the social point of view. Whereas in the former sense it may be self-evident, in the latter it means that every new generation must repeat and learn some lessons from the past, in order to maintain and improve its own institutions for the future.

In the foregoing text, we have tried to suggest that normative theories on emergencies very often focus on certain specific issues that have been objects of analysis for a long time. By pointing to this, we have also tried to suggest that emergencies are not, as is often claimed, phenomena that

[72] Slovenian Constitutional Court, Decision no. U-I-83/20 of 27 August 2020, Separate opinion of judge Dr. Špelce Mežnar joined by judge dr. Katja Šugman Stubbs. Judges show their disagreement with the majority decision, stating that it "unfortunately … does not follow this path". Similar view on the level of judicial scrutiny is expressed by Bardutzky and Zagorc, who claim that proportionality test was "watered down … compared to the manner in which it [the court, op. a] usually exercises it" see: Samo Bardutzky and Saša Zagorc, 'Slovenia: Second Wave of Challenges to Constitutionalism' (VerfBlog, 19 March 2021) https://verfassungsblog.de/slovenia-second-wave-of-challenges-to-constitutionalism/ accessed [4 February 2025]

[73] For instance, Steuer claims that the Slovak Constitutional Court "displayed some capacity to invalidate measures with a potential to undermine democracy", see: Max Steuer, 'Slovakia's Democracy and the COVID-19 Pandemic: When Executive Communication Fails' (VerfBlog, 9 March 2021) https://verfassungsblog.de/slovakias-democracy-and-the-covid-19-pandemic-when-executive-communication-fails accessed [4 February 2025]. Furthermore, for Austria, Stöger says that the ACC "proved to be the most effective remedy against an 'unchained' executive" while, according to Lachmayer, both parliaments and courts were able to limit the government from obtaining "total control". See: Stöger (no 64); Konrad Lachmayer, 'Muddling through Mutation Times or the Return of Federalism in Austria: From COVID-19 Response to the Vaccination Campaign' (VerfBlog) https://verfassungsblog.de/muddling-through-mutation-times-or-the-return-of-federalism-in-austria/ accessed [4 February 2025]. Though, it must be noted that a strict version of proportionality test was not used by any court, according to Vyhnánek and others. See: Ladislav Vyhnánek and others (n 3) 393

go beyond human understanding and the capabilities of an appropriate legal regulation.

In this context, we would like to stress that in the specific area of states of emergencies, historical and comparative analyses bring some insights of utmost importance. Taking into account those facts, one can more easily detect challenges that come along with every new emergency.

References

Ackerman, B., 'The Emergency Constitution' (2004) 113 *Yale Law Journal* 1029

Ackerman, B., *Before the Next Attack: Preserving Civil Liberties in an Age of Terrorism* (Yale University Press, 2006)

Albert, R. and Roznai, Y., 'Emergency Unamendability: Limitations on Constitutional Amendment in Extreme Conditions' (2022) 81 *Maryland Law Review* 243

Austrian Constitutional Court, Decision G-202-2020 of 14 July 2020

Baker, S.A. and Kavanagh, J. (eds), *Patriot Debates: Experts Debate the USA PATRIOT Act* (American Bar Association Publishing, 2005), 3–97

Bardutzky, S. and Zagorc, S., 'Slovenia: Second Wave of Challenges to Constitutionalism' (*VerfBlog*, 19 March 2021) https://verfassungsblog.de/slovenia-second-wave-of-challenges-to-constitutionalism/ accessed 4 February 2025

Belov, M., 'Introduction' in M. Belov (ed), *Courts and Judicial Activism under Crisis Conditions: Policy Making in a Time of Illiberalism and Emergency Constitutionalism* (Routledge, 2022), 1–17

Birmontienė, T., 'The Main Trends in Constitutional Jurisprudence Developed by Constitutional Courts During the COVID-19 Pandemic' in Rainer Arnold and José Cremades (eds), *Rule of Law and the Challenges Posed by the Pandemic: Contributions to the World Law Congress 2021 in Barranquilla* (Springer, 2023), 87–96

Casey, C., 'Business as Usual? Irish Courts, the Constitution, and COVID-19' (2021) 2 *Percorsi Costituzionali / Constitutional Paths* 337

Cole, D., 'Judging the Next Emergency: Judicial Review and Individual Rights in Times of Crisis' (2002–03) 101 *Michigan Law Review* 2565

Cole, D., 'No Reason to Believe: Radical Skepticism, Emergency Power, and Constitutional Constraint' (2008) 75 *University of Chicago Law Review* 1329

Cole, D., 'The New McCarthyism: Repeating History in the War on Terrorism' (2003) 38(1) *Harvard Civil Rights–Civil Liberties Law Review* 1

Cole, D., 'The Priority of Morality: The Emergency Constitution's Blind Spot' (2004) 113 *Yale Law Journal* 1753

Czech Constitutional Court, Judgment no. Pl. ÚS 106/20 of 9 February 2021

Czech Constitutional Court, Judgment no. Pl. ÚS 106/20 of 9 February 2021, Dissenting opinion of Justice Jaroslav Fenyk

Czech Constitutional Court, Judgment no. Pl. ÚS 106/20 of 9 February 2021, Dissenting opinion of Justice Josef Fiala

Federal Constitutional Court of Germany, Order of the First Senate of 19 November 2021—1 BvR 781/21—paras. 1–306

Federal Constitutional Court of Germany, Order of the First Senate of 19 November 2021—1 BvR 971/21—paras. 1–222

Gardašević, Đ., 'Activism of the Croatian Constitutional Court and COVID-19: A Bridge Too Far' in Martin Belov (ed), *Courts and Judicial Activism under Crisis Conditions: Policy Making in a Time of Illiberalism and Emergency Constitutionalism* (Routledge, 2022), 194–212

Gardašević, Đ., 'American Lessons Learned—European Future Rethought' (2016) 66 *Zbornik Pravnog Fakulteta u Zagrebu* 61

Gardašević, Đ., 'Constitutional Interpretation and COVID-19 in Croatia' in Saša Zagorc and Samo Bardutzky (eds), *Ustava na robu izrednega stanja* (Univerza v Ljubljani, Pravna fakulteta, 2024), 363–379

Ginsburg, T. and Versteeg, M., 'The Bound Executive: Emergency Powers during the Pandemic' (2021) 19 *International Journal of Constitutional Law* 1498

Greene, A., *Emergency Powers in a Time of Pandemic* (Bristol University Press, 2020)

Griglio, E., 'Parliamentary Oversight under the COVID-19 Emergency: Striving Against Executive Dominance' (2020) 8(1–2) *The Theory and Practice of Legislation* 49

Gross, O. and Ní Aoláin, F., *Law in Times of Crisis: Emergency Powers in Theory and Practice* (Cambridge University Press, 2006)

Hamilton, A., 'Federalist No. 23' (1787)

Hamilton, A., 'Federalist No. 70: The Executive Department Further Considered', 18 March 1788

Hamilton, A., 'Federalist No. 74: The Command of the Military and Naval Forces, and the Pardoning Power of the Executive', 25 March 1788

Hungarian Constitutional Court, Decision 23/2021 (VII. 13.) of 22 June 2021

Issacharoff, S. and Pildes, R.H., 'Emergency Contexts without Emergency Powers: The United States' Constitutional Approach to Rights During Wartime' (2004) 2(2) *International Journal of Constitutional Law* 296

Kaiser, A.-B. and Hensel, R., 'Federal Republic of Germany: Legal Response to COVID-19' in Jeff King and others (eds), *The Oxford Compendium of National Legal Responses to COVID-19* (Oxford University Press) https://oxcon.ouplaw.com/display/10.1093/law-occ19/law-occ19-e2 accessed 4 February 2025

Lachmayer, K., 'Muddling through Mutation Times or the Return of Federalism in Austria: From COVID-19 Response to the Vaccination Campaign' (*VerfBlog*) https://verfassungsblog.de/muddling-through-mutation-times-or-the-return-of-federalism-in-austria/ accessed 4 February 2025

Neuborne, B., 'The Role of Courts in Time of War' (2005) 29 *NYU Review of Law & Social Change* 555
Petrov, J., 'The COVID-19 Emergency in the Age of Executive Aggrandizement: What Role for Legislative and Judicial Checks?' (2020) 8(1–2) *The Theory and Practice of Legislation* 71
Posner, E.A. and Vermeule, A., *Terror in the Balance: Security, Liberty and the Courts* (Oxford University Press, 2007)
Posner, R.A., *Not a Suicide Pact: The Constitution in a Time of National Emergency* (Oxford University Press, 2006)
Rosenfeld, M., 'Judicial Balancing in Times of Stress: Comparing the American, British, and Israeli Approaches to the War on Terror' (2006) 27 *Cardozo Law Review* 2079
Rossiter, C.L., *Constitutional Dictatorship: Crisis Government in the Modern Democracies* (Princeton University Press, 1948)
Scheuerman, W.E., 'Emergency Powers and the Rule of Law After 9/11' (2006) 14(1) *Journal of Political Philosophy* 61
Slovak Constitutional Court, Decision—Finding no. PL. ÚS 22/2020 of 14 October 2020
Slovenian Constitutional Court, Decision no. U-I-79/20 of 13 May 2021
Slovenian Constitutional Court, Decision no. U-I-79/20 of 13 May 2021, Partially concurring, partially dissenting opinion of Judge Dr. Rajko Knez
Slovenian Constitutional Court, Decision no. U-I-83/20 of 27 August 2020
Slovenian Constitutional Court, Decision no. U-I-83/20 of 27 August 2020, Separate opinion of Judge Dr. Špelca Mežnar joined by Judge Dr. Katja Šugman Stubbs
Steuer, M., 'Slovakia's Democracy and the COVID-19 Pandemic: When Executive Communication Fails' (*VerfBlog*, 9 March 2021) https://verfassungsblog.de/slovakias-democracy-and-the-covid-19-pandemic-when-executive-communication-fails accessed 4 February 2025
Stöger, K., 'Austria: Legal Response to COVID-19' in Jeff King and others (eds), *The Oxford Compendium of National Legal Responses to COVID-19* (Oxford University Press, 2021) https://oxcon.ouplaw.com/display/10.1093/law-occ19/law-occ19-e28?rskey=Eos6sC&result=2&prd=OCC19 accessed 4 February 2025
Stone, G.R., 'Civil Liberties v National Security in the Law's Open Areas' (2006) 86 *Boston University Law Review* 1315
Stone, G.R., 'National Security v Civil Liberties' (2007) 95 *California Law Review* 2203
Stone, G.R., 'War Fever' (2004) 69 *Missouri Law Review* 1131
Stone, G.R., *Perilous Times: Free Speech in Wartime (From the Sedition Act of 1798 to the War on Terrorism)* (W.W. Norton & Co, 2004)

Sullivan, B., 'Expert Knowledge, Democratic Accountability, and the Unitary Executive' (2023) 92 *Fordham Law Review* 575

Tan, K.Y.L., 'Interpreting the Constitution: The Use and Abuse of History' (2022) 20(5) *International Journal of Constitutional Law* 1958

Tushnet, M., 'Controlling Executive Power in the War on Terrorism' (2005) 118 *Harvard Law Review* 2673

Tyler, A.L., 'Judicial Review in Times of Emergency: From the Founding through the COVID-19 Pandemic' (2023) 109(3) *Virginia Law Review* 489

Vyhnánek, L. et al., 'The Dynamics of Proportionality: Constitutional Courts and the Review of COVID-19 Regulations' (2024) 25(3) *German Law Journal* 386

Yoo, J., *The Powers of War and Peace: The Constitution and Foreign Affairs after 9/11* (University of Chicago Press, 2006)

CHAPTER 6

Constitutional Identity and States of Exception

Alan Greene

6.1 Introduction

Doctrines of constitutional identity have emerged in several European states as a means of checking and constraining the supremacy of EU law. Drawing upon a perceived need to protect fundamental constitutional norms and national values, constitutional identity relies upon what has been termed a "manufactured homogeneity."[1] This chapter argues that this notion of an idealized or manufactured homogeneity paves the way for a productive comparative conceptual analysis between constitutional identity and states of exception, in particular, the understanding of states of exception articulated by Carl Schmitt. By understanding constitutional identity through this lens of exception, the utility of constitutional identity can be revealed, but also, importantly, its fundamental dangers. These dangers relate not just to the harmony of EU law but also to other fundamental democratic principles that ought to be embodied in a liberal

This chapter is produced as part and funded by the European Union-NextGenerationEU, through the National Recovery and Resilience Plan of the Republic of Bulgaria, project No bg-rrp-2.004-0008.

[1] Julian Scholtes, 'Abusing Constitutional Identity' (2021) 22 German Law Journal 534, 553.

M. Belov (ed.), *Constitutional Polycrisis and Emergency Constitutionalism*, Federalism and Internal Conflicts,
https://doi.org/10.1007/978-3-032-06516-2_6

constitutionalist order. However, constitutional identity's other function as a means of delineating the limits of the constitutional amendment power also reveals its potential to limit constitutional abuse. Moreover, instances where constitutional identity and emergency powers have collided demonstrate that constitutional identity has the potential to tame and control emergencies, repudiating a Schmittian reading of the Constitution as a blank check statute in a time of crisis.[2] Like emergencies or states of exception, invocation of the concept of constitutional identity therefore demands critical interrogation, not just of what has been categorized but of who is doing the categorizing.

Part I of this chapter delineates the key elements of states of emergency and states of exception. It briefly describes Carl Schmitt's emphasis on the state of exception as key to understanding the locus of sovereignty in a given legal order, as well as the precarious contingency of this legal order. Part II then introduces constitutional identity, demonstrating that it shares many of the similar elements of Schmitt's conception of states of exception, not least its propensity towards a 'pure' identitarian basis of the state and *Volk*. Part III unpacks some of the key insights to be drawn from this conceptual comparison between emergencies and constitutional identity; specifically, the potential for both concepts to act as both a danger to and in defense of core constitutionalist concepts, as well as the need to shift focus away from the categorized towards the categorizer.

6.2 Emergencies and States of Exception

States of emergency tend to sound alarm bells amongst defenders of constitutionalism. A state of emergency, by definition, permits what would otherwise be impermissible. They usher in powers that are antithetical to quintessential constitutionalist values such as human rights, the separation of powers and the rule of law. They can undermine democracy by circumventing deliberative decision-making processes and sidelining accountability mechanisms. These dangers of emergency powers are underlined by high-profile historical examples of the abuse of constitutional emergency provisions. From Julius Caesar's debasement of the office of Dictatorship of the Roman Republic to Hitler's use of Article 48

[2] David Dyzenhaus, *Legality and Legitimacy: Carl Schmitt, Hans Kelsen and Hermann Heller in Weimar* (Oxford University Press, 1997) 52–53.

of the Weimar Constitution to usher in the Third Reich, one would be remiss not to approach the question of emergency powers with caution. Thus, in *Federalist No. 70,* Alexander Hamilton remarked that:

> Every man least conversant in Roman history knows how often that republic was obliged to take refuge in the absolute power of a single man, under the formidable title of dictator, as well against the intrigues of ambitious individuals who aspired to tyranny, and the seditions of whole classes of the community whose conduct threatened the existence of all government, as against whole classes of the community whose conduct threatened the existence of all government, as against the invasions of external enemies who menaced the conquest and destruction of Rome.[3]

Owing to this danger, the US Constitution does not explicitly provide for formal declarations of a state of emergency. The one exception to this is the permitted suspension of habeas corpus in time of war.[4] This constitutional silence, however, did not constrain Abraham Lincoln's wielding of vast executive power during the Civil War, with the legality of his actions, particularly at the outbreak of the war, concerning the enlargement of the army without Congressional approval, being highly questionable.[5]

Likewise, in *Re Korematsu,* the US Supreme Court contorted the provisions of the US Constitution so as to permit the detention without trial of all Japanese-US citizens living on the US Pacific Coast for the duration of World War II.[6] Such "business as usual models" of emergency accommodation lose the all-important "quarantining effect" of formally declared states of emergency as fidelity to the rule of law and constitutional rights yield to inexorable necessity and claims that "The Constitution is not a suicide pact."[7]

Emergencies raise profound questions about *inter alia*: what constitutes an emergency; who gets to decide that an emergency exists; when, if ever, does an emergency end; what actions are permissible or impermissible;

[3] Hamilton, Madison, Jay, *The Federalist Papers* (Clinton Rossiter ed, Signet Classics 2003) 422.

[4] Article 1, Section 9, Clause 2, US Constitution.

[5] See Clinton Rossiter, *Constitutional Dictatorship: Crisis Government in the Modern Democracies* (first published 1948, Routledge 2002) Ch 2.

[6] *Re Korematsu* (1944) 323 US 214.

[7] *Terminiello v City of Chicago* (1949) 337 US 1, 37 (Jackson J dissenting); see also RA Posner, *Not a Suicide Pact: The Constitution in a Time of Emergency* (Oxford University Press, 2006).

and what safeguards, if any, are necessary on emergency powers. To capture these issues, I have thus defined a state of emergency as:

> A crisis identified and labelled by a state to be of such magnitude that it is deemed to cross a threat severity threshold, necessitating urgent, exceptional, and, consequently, temporary actions by the state not permissible when normal conditions exist.[8]

This definition is necessarily broad and vague. It also seeks to place the decision-maker—the state institution or actor tasked with declaring an emergency—at the heart of the question.

6.2.1 States of Emergency: Who Decides?

Typically, constitutions vest the power to declare a state of emergency in the executive. Even where a constitution places the power in the legislature, it may also include provisions allowing for the executive to act in the event that the legislature cannot sit, or it empowers the executive to act for a short period of time before legislative approval is required.[9] The prominent role of the executive in times of emergency arises for two key reasons. Firstly, the executive is the body of government most capable of acting swiftly and decisively. It is usually shorn of formally entrenched decision-making procedures, and it invariably consists of ideologically aligned personnel, which reduces the extent of disagreement and the risk of decision-making paralysis.[10] Secondly, particularly in areas of national security, the executive can also claim a degree of expertise that the legislature or judiciary may lack. Such information may be based on national security briefings from state security and intelligence agencies, the disclosure of which in court or a public sitting of the legislature would be inappropriate, or would compromise national security.[11] For this reason,

[8] Alan Greene, *Permanent States of Emergency and the Rule of Law: Constitutions in an Age of Crisis* (Hart Publishing, 2018) 30. I do not mean to use this definition in a legally prescriptive sense; ie as a type of definition to be incorporated into positive law. Rather, I use this definition in a descriptive sense—to describe the phenomenon of a state of emergency so as to enable us to study it.

[9] It is this propensity for the executive to gain in power in a time of emergency that Rossiter referred to emergency powers as a 'constitutional dictatorship'. See Rossiter (n 5).

[10] Greene (n 8) 24–25.

[11] Oren Gross and Fionnuala Ní Aoláin, *Law in Times of Crisis: Emergency Powers in Theory and Practice* (Cambridge University Press, 2006) 65.

the legislature and the judiciary often defer to the executive's assessment of the situation and confer on it a broad array of discretion, which is then subjected to weakened oversight. The judiciary has a further, third reason for deference to the executive in a time of emergency; namely, its democratic deficit. Under this perspective, the response to an emergency should be conducted by those whom the people have elected, and who the people can hold accountable in the event of failure or abuse of power.[12] The judiciary, therefore, may consider itself ill-suited to this task. Indeed, in Lord Atkin famously remarked that in an emergency, the judiciary tends to be "more executive-minded than the executive."[13] For these reasons, emergencies raise profound questions as to the scope of executive power and its potential for abuse.

This prominent role for the executive, coupled with the vague and nebulous concept of emergency, is integral to Carl Schmitt's theory as to the nature of what he terms 'states of exception'. For Schmitt, emergencies must be necessarily vague, and therefore, it is impossible for law to try to define them in any meaningful sense.[14] Even where the law sets out certain parameters regarding the state of emergency, the Sovereign will still act if it deems necessary. This shift in language I use here from "executive" to Sovereign is deliberate, for Schmitt bases his definition on what constitutes the sovereign in a legal order upon his theory of the exception. He then deploys this in a scathing critique of liberalism and parliamentary democracy.[15] For Schmitt, an emergency or state of exception acts as a litmus test that reveals the true nature of political power in a legal order. Liberalism may claim that all state power is exercised through law, with the epitome of this theory being Hans Kelsen's identity thesis and his claim that the state is synonymous with the legal order.[16] However, emergencies show that this is impossible. Schmitt contends that this liberal fiction can only be established after Sovereign power has been exercised to create the necessary political stability upon which a legal order can be founded. As such, liberal constitutionalism takes up the reins only after

[12] Ibid.

[13] Fiona de Londras and Fergal F Davis, 'Controlling the Executive in Times of Terrorism: Competing Perspectives on Effective Oversight Mechanisms' (2010) 30 (1) Oxford Journal of Legal Studies 19, 26; Posner (n 7) 24.

[14] *Liversidge v Anderson* [1942] AC 206, 244 (Atkin L).

[15] Dyzenhaus (n 2) 32–37.

[16] See generally Hans Kelsen, *Pure Theory of Law* (University of California Press, 1967) and Hans Kelsen, *General Theory of Law and State* (Harvard University Press, 1949).

the state is up and running.[17] This political stability has, in turn, been created by the sovereign making the irrational decision between friend and enemy. It is only through the banishment or exclusion of the enemy that the requisite stability required for a stable legal order to be founded can be created. This power of the sovereign to distinguish between friend and enemy is the clearest expression of sovereign power. However, even once the state is up and running and liberal democracy is convincing itself that all state power is exercised through law, emergencies can erupt; that is, the stability brought about by the sovereign distinction between friend and enemy breaks down.[18] Liberal parliamentary democracy was particularly prone to this risk, Schmitt contended, owing to its rejection of the friend–enemy distinction. Liberalism, therefore, either lacked the means to defend itself, or hypocritically took such necessary measures, but then it would deny that it did so, or contort itself in such a way as to legitimate it. For Schmitt, therefore, in an emergency, a sovereign power is required again to make this necessary distinction between friend and enemy and to restore the stability required for the operation of the legal order. The Sovereign, therefore, once again steps in and exercises its dormant power—a power identical to that which it exercises to enable the founding of the legal order in the first instance. For this reason, Schmitt contends that sovereignty or political power exists *prior* to the legal order and further, that this power reveals itself in a time of emergency or state of exception. He therefore declares that "Sovereign is he who decides on the exception."[19]

6.3 From States of Exception to Constitutional Identity

It would be remiss to speak of Schmitt and not mention that he was considered the Crown jurist of the Third Reich. This dark past must be acknowledged, particularly in light of his claims as to the degree of stability necessary to enable the founding of a legal order. To deliver this

[17] Carl Schmitt, *The Concept of the Political* (G Schwab trans, University of Chicago Press 2005) 38; Greene (n 8) 72; David Dyzenhaus, '"Now the Machine Runs Itself": Carl Schmitt on Hobbes and Kelsen' (1994) 16(1) Cardozo Law Review 1, 11–12

[18] Ibid.

[19] Carl Schmitt, *Political Theology: Four Chapters on the Concept of Sovereignty* (G Schwab Trans, University of Chicago Press 2005) 1.

stability, Schmitt posits a degree of commonality or homogeneity amongst a *Volk* which constitutes the basis of the state.[20] Schmitt's insistence in this regard thus paves the way for repugnant conceptions of the people based on race, xenophobia, or religious or ideological purity. It is also this insistence upon homogeneity or commonality that paves the way for a comparison to be drawn between states of exception and constitutional identity.

Constitutional identity has emerged as a salient topic of concern amongst courts and court-watchers alike. In a European context, constitutional identity has risen to prominence in the context of debates concerning limits to the supremacy of EU law. In this European context, Scholtes suggests that constitutional identity operates as "a form of argument that occupies the interstitial space between national and European constitutional orders, and thus helps negotiate the allocation of authority between them."[21] Arguments concerning constitutional identity thus operate as a space for the negotiation of authority, and constitutional identity needs to be understood as an argument concerning the allocation of authority between competing constitutional sites.'[22] This concept of national identity is hardwired into the Treaty on European Union (TEU):

> The Union shall respect the equality of Member States before the Treaties as well as their national identities, inherent in their fundamental structures, political and constitutional, inclusive of regional and local self-government. It shall respect their essential State functions, including ensuring the territorial integrity of the State, maintaining law and order and safeguarding national security. In particular, national security remains the sole responsibility of each Member State.[23]

This reference to national identity opens up space for disagreement over what national identity actually entails. According to Schnettger, as national identity is an imagined concept, albeit one based upon shared views as to its content across a community, it follows that "only the community whose identity is being examined can determine its content."[24] However,

[20] Schmitt (n 17) 38–45.

[21] Scholtes (n 1) 540.

[22] Ibid., 541.

[23] Article 4(2) TEU. https://eur-lex.europa.eu/resource.html?uri=cellar:2bf140bf-a3f8-4ab2-b506-fd71826e6da6.0023.02/DOC_1&format=PDF

[24] Anita Schnettger, 'Article 4(2) TEU as a Vehicle for National Constitutional Identity in the Shared European Legal System' in Christian Calliess and Gerhard van der Schyff (eds) *Constitutional Identity in a Europe of Multilevel Constitutionalism* (Cambridge University Press 2019) 9, 15.

as the ECJ is the ultimate arbiter regarding the interpretation of treaties, this raises questions concerning the appropriate authority to adjudicate the meaning of national identity in Article 4(2) TEU. Schnettger contends that the EU has the right to define the general framework of what the Member States' national identity, inherent in their fundamental structures, political and constitutional, could be. However, within this general framework, it is the Member States' right to specify what it actually is.[25]

The doctrine of constitutional identity has been specifically deployed by EU states as a check on the supremacy of EU law. For instance, the German BVerfG has invoked constitutional identity to question whether the outright monetary transaction (OMT) program of the European Central Bank (ECB) exceeded the ECB's treaty mandate.[26] Similar invocations against the supremacy of EU law can also be seen by Italy,[27] Ireland,[28] and even the UK prior to Brexit.[29] Aspects of these constructions of constitutional identity may seem benign, such as Germany's emphasis on the inherent dignity of the individual, or Ireland's protection of democracy and the separation of powers.[30] However, the most dangerous manifestations of constitutional identity or "abusive constitutional identity" in EU states can be seen in Hungary and Poland. In Hungary, the self-identified[31] illiberal government of Viktor Orbán invoked Hungary's constitutional identity to justify hostile migration policies in the face of a so-called migrant crisis facing the EU.[32] These policies clearly violated EU

[25] Ibid., 15

[26] BverfG 2 BvR 2728/13 et al, order of 7 February 2014; Federico Fabbrini and András Sajó, 'The dangers of constitutional identity' (2019) 25 European Law Journal 457, 459.

[27] Ibid.

[28] *Costello v Government of Ireland* [2022] IESC 44; Oran Doyle, 'Constitutional Identity, Legal Autonomy and Sovereignty: *Costello v Government of Ireland* [2022] IESC 44' (2023) 19(4) European Constitutional Law Review 715.

[29] R (*HS2 Alliance) v Secreatary of State for Transport and another* [2014] UKSC 3; Paul Craig, 'Constitutional Identity in the United Kingdom: An Evolving Concept' in Calliess and van der Schyff (n 24) 284, 284–288.

[30] Fabbrini and Sajó (n 26) 473; Doyle (n 28).

[31] See Hamai Gábor, 'Illiberalism in East-Central Europe' in András Sajó, Renáta Uitz and Stephen Holmes (eds), *Routledge Handbook of Illiberalism* (Routledge, 2022) Ch 51; Wojciech Brzozowski, 'Whatever works: Constitutional interpretation in Poland in times of populism' in Fruzsina Gárdos-Orosz and Zoltán Szente (eds), *Populist Challenges to Constitutional Interpretation in Europe and Beyond* (Routledge, 2021), 174, 177.

[32] Gábor ibid; R Daniel Keleman and Laurent Pech, 'The Uses and Abuses of Constitutional Pluralism: Undermining the Rule of Law in the Name of Constitutional Identity in Hungary and Poland' (2019) 21 Cambridge Yearbook of European Legal Studies 59, 66.

law; however, Orbán claimed that compliance with these policies would debase Hungary's constitutional identity. Hungary's constitutional court duly obliged and declared that:

> If human dignity, another fundamental rights, the sovereignty of Hungary (including the extent of the transferred competences) or its self-identity based on its historical constitution and be presumed to be violated due to the exercise of competences based on Article (E) (2) of the Fundamental Law, the Constitutional Court may, in the course of exercising its competences, examine the existence of an alleged violation on the basis of a relevant petition.[33]

This judicial pronouncement was subsequently entrenched by way of constitutional amendments in 2018.[34] These changes included a clause stating that a fundamental obligation of the state was to protect "our self-identity rooted in our historical constitution;" clauses purporting to clarify the supremacy of EU law only to the extent that they are 'consistent with the fundamental rights and freedoms laid down in the Basic Law, and shall not limit Hungary's inalienable right of disposal related to its territorial integrity, population, form of government and governmental organization'; and (3) the addition of a clause providing that all bodies of the State shall protect the constitutional self-identity of Hungary.[35]

Meanwhile, in Poland, the election of the Law and Justice Party (PiS), which won control of both the presidency and parliament, led Warsaw into a direct confrontation with the EU and Council of Europe, with the so-called migrant crisis playing a pivotal role in this confrontation. The Polish government also implemented radical reforms to the judiciary, increasing executive control over the appointments process and undermining judicial independence and the separation of powers. PiS drew direct comparisons between itself and Orbán's Fidesz party, with their project described as 'an accelerated and condensed version' of what Fidesz accomplished in Hungary.[36] These reforms, which constituted no less

[33] Keleman and Pech, ibid, 67.

[34] Ibid, 68

[35] Ibid.

[36] Wojciech Sadurski, 'How Democracy Dies (in Poland): A Case Study of Anti-Constitutional Populist Backsliding' [2018] Revista Formul Judecatorilor 104, 106.

than a full-frontal attack on the rule of law, were condemned by both the European Court of Justice and European Court of Human Rights.[37]

This European experience of constitutional identity reveals its Schmittian DNA. The emphasis on 'a minimum amount of homogeneity of the constituted community' echoes Schmitt's contention that a relatively homogenous Volk is required to provide the requisite stability upon which a legal order can be founded.[38] This necessarily entails a friend-enemy distinction to be drawn by the Sovereign. Fabbrini and Sajó thus argue that:

> Once (even in the strict terms of legal dogmatics) constitutional identity becomes a form of national identity, it is open to a Schmittian interpretation for whom the constitution and its state offer the capacity for people to realise 'otherness' to other people.[39]

The utilization of constitutional identity by states such as Poland and Hungary to exceptionalize their respective illiberal constitutional orders against EU integration underlies this. In the hands of populist authoritarians, constitutional identity can thus be deployed to construct both the 'pure people' and the 'corrupt elite' whom they are pitted against.[40] As a result, Kelemen and Pech conclude that autocrats in Hungary and Poland were 'simply carrying arguments about constitutional identity to their logical conclusions.'[41] Further, according to Kelemen and Pech, this problem also affects notions of constitutional pluralism. Constitutional identity, they claim, is closely related to constitutional pluralism as the latter recognizes multiple sources of constitutional authority and seeks to eschew a formal hierarchy between competing sources of authority, such as between the EU and domestic legal orders. It follows that this repudiation of hierarchy creates the potential space for constitutional identity to be deployed against the supremacy of EU law.[42] They therefore conclude

[37] See *Reczkowicz v Poland* App no. 43447/19, (22 July 2021); *Dolińska-Ficek and Ozimek v Poland* App No 49868/19 and 57511/19, (8 November 2021);*AK and Others v Sąd Najwyższy, CP v. Sąd Najwyższy and DO v Sąd* Najwyższy [GC], C-585/18, C-624/18 and C-625/18, 19 November 2019; *AB and Others v Krajowa Rada Sądownictwa and Others*, C-824/18, 2 March 2021.

[38] Fabbrini and Sajó (n 26) 466.

[39] Ibid, 465.

[40] See Cas Mudde, 'The Populist Zeitgeist' (2004) 39(4) Government and opposition 541.

[41] Kelemen and Pech (n 32) 65.

[42] Ibid 61.

that 'some ideas are inherently dangerous, and constitutional pluralism/identity is certainly one of them.'[43]

The innate Schmittian nature of constitutional identity also extends to the aforementioned notion of vagueness, which appears to be inherent to all constructions of constitutional identity. Analyzing the Irish Supreme Court's development of the concept, Doyle contends that Irish constitutional identity appears to consist of the following elements: democracy, separation of powers, non-abrogation of the Constitution through treaty-making, fundamental constitutional values/principles, state sovereignty, and the protection of rights.[44] This list, he remarks, "appears almost as broad as the Constitution itself."[45] Fabbrini and Sajó's analysis thus concludes that this vagueness is a feature rather than a glitch of constitutional identity. Highlighting the difficulty of identifying a 'hard core' of inviolable constitutional norms, they suggest that constitutional identity could even refer to all constitutional provisions, as seems to be the case, for instance, in France.[46] Even when a list of unamendable provisions is contained in a constitution, such as in Italy's case, this still did not prevent courts from extending that list.[47]

This argument has strong echoes of Schmitt's proposed interpretation of Article 48 of the Weimar Constitution—that constitution's emergency clause, which was used extensively throughout Weimar's short life and ultimately became the legal vehicle for the passing of Hitler's enabling act. While Article 48 did contain an express list of constitutional norms that could be derogated from in a time of emergency, Schmitt argued that this list could not be exhaustive as other constitutional norms such as those pertaining to the federal character of the Weimar Republic and the division of power between the central government and the Länder must also, necessarily, be abrogated in a crisis.[48] The concept of constitutional identity, therefore, is equally vague and can potentially encompass aspects beyond these expressly enumerated provisions. For this reason, Fabbrini and Sajó contend that the notion of constitutional identity is too vague

[43] Ibid.

[44] Doyle (n 28) 725–726.

[45] Ibid 726.

[46] Fabbrini and Sajó (n 26) 468.

[47] Ibid

[48] Greene (n 8) 155–156; Marc de Wilde, 'The State of Emergency in the Weimar Republic: legal Disputes over Article 48 of the Weimar Constitution' (2010) 78 Legal History Review 135, 141.

to satisfy the requirements of the rule of law.[49] In this EU context, constitutional identity may operate as "an arbitrary escape hatch," capable of being deployed at a judicial whim to derogate from EU obligations and undermine the legal and political cohesion of the Union.[50]

6.4 States of Exception and Constitutional Identity: Inherently Dangerous Concepts?

Drawing comparisons between states of exception and doctrines of constitutional identity helps to reveal some of the dangers associated with these concepts. In turn, this raises further questions as regards their utility. As noted, several commentators expressly reject the concept of constitutional identity as a result of these dangers. Similar objections to the legal provision of emergency powers can also be found, not least because of the dangers such clauses can pose to constitutions and international human rights treaties. For this reason, many people cautioned against the formal use of emergency powers in response to the COVID-19 pandemic, arguing instead that any necessary pandemic measures could be enacted within the ordinary constitutional and human rights frameworks.[51] The dangers with such "business as usual" approaches, however, are that rather than raising human rights and constitutional norm protection up to the level that one sees in a state of normalcy, these protections are themselves recalibrated so as to permit the previously impermissible.[52] In turn, such a recalibration

[49] Fabbrini and Sajó (n 26) 466–469;

[50] Scholtes (n 1) 545; Andras Sajó and Renáta Uitz, *The Constitution of Freedom: An Introduction to Legal Constituitonalism* (Oxford University Press, 2017) 470.

[51] See Kanstantsin Dzehtsiarou, 'Article 15 derogations: Are they really necessary during the COVID-19 pandemic?' [2020] EHRLR 359; Tom Hickman, 'The Coronavirus Pandemic and Derogation from the European Convention on Human Rights'[2020] EHRLR 593. For arguments in favor of derogation from a human rights perspective see A Greene, 'Derogating from the European Convention on Human Rights in Response to the Coronavirus Pandemic: If Not Now, When?' [2020] EHRLR 263; A Greene, 'On the Value of Derogations from the ECHR in Response to the COVID-19 Pandemic: A Rejoinder' [2020] EHRLR 526; and A Greene, 'Derogations, Deprivation of Liberty and the Containment Stage of Pandemic Responses' [2021] EHRLR 263.

[52] Oren Gross, 'Chaos and Rules: Should Responses to Violent Crises always be Constitutional?' (2002–2003) 112 Yale Law Journal 1011, 1043–1052. See text to n 5 above regarding the US Constitution's failure to provide for emergency powers nevertheless being unable to constrain Lincoln's actions at the start of the Civil War, or the detention of US citizens of Japanese dissent during World War II.

lacks the requisite quarantining effect of a formal declaration of a state of emergency, which could limit the utility of any such precedent in the future.[53] However, is there any equivalent of the "quarantining effect" of a doctrine of constitutional identity? Is there anything that would justify this context, or are we solely left with just its dangerous potential? One way in which this question can be answered is to think of what alternatives to constitutional identity could be developed.

6.4.1 Balance as an Alternative to Constitutional Identity?

As an alternative to constitutional identity, Fabbrini and Sajó propose that the idea of an inviolable national constitution founded upon national identity be rejected, and instead, courts should consider the matter in terms of balancing and proportionality, i.e., accepting that a proportionate restriction of the constitutional identity can be tolerated.[54] Certainly, notions of balance and proportionality are familiar judicial tools; however, examination of 'balance' in the context of emergencies and national security reveals that it too is not immune from abuse and contortion. Ashworth thus argues that:

> The very conceptualization of this [balanced] approach, in particular the imagery of balance is dubious… the balanced response thesis tends to assume a hydraulic relationship between human rights safeguards and the promotion of security, that is that as one goes up the other goes down, and vice versa.[55]

This security–liberty dichotomy fails to appreciate the degree to which human rights are necessary for the provision of security or, relatedly, how measures enacted in the name of security may turn out to be counter-productive.[56] Counter-terrorism and national security are replete

[53] Alan Greene, *Emergency Powers in a Time of Pandemic* (Bristol University Press, 2020) 25–28.

[54] Fabbrini and Sajó (n 26) 470.

[55] Andrew Ashworth, 'Security, Terrorism and the Value of Human Rights' in Ben Goold and Liora Lazarus (eds), *Security and Human Rights* (Hart Publishing, 2007) 203, 208. See also Mark Neocleous, 'Security, Liberty and the Myth of Balance: Towards a Critique of Security Politics' (2007) 6 Contemporary Political Theory 131; Jeremy Waldron, 'Security and Liberty: The Image of Balance' (2003) 11(2) Journal of Political Philosophy 191.

[56] See Imran Swan, 'COUNTERBLAST: Terror in the Eye of the Beholder: The 'Spycam' Saga: Counter-Terrorism or Counter-Productive?' (2011) 50 Howard Journal of Criminal Justice 199.

with instances of counter-productive counter-terrorism where measures invoked in the name of security had the opposite effect. For instance, the files leaked by the whistle-blower Edward Snowden as to the extent of the United States's covert security and spying apparatus also revealed that much of this security framework relied upon 'backdoors' inserted into encryption programs so as to allow NSA access.[57] These deliberate vulnerabilities were then exploited by criminals to engage in data theft and other online crimes.

The metaphor of 'balance' can also have a particularly pernicious rhetorical effect. To invoke balance is to seek to lay claim to the middle ground. This middle ground is conceptualized as the legitimate position to take with any alternative position classified as extreme.[58] This powerful framing device can have an adverse effect on public debate and legal reasoning, as any counter-position to the so-called "balanced approach" is placed on the back foot in terms of legitimacy, and critics are required to carry out more intellectual labor to convince. An illustrative example of this can be seen from the early days of the COVID-19 pandemic in the UK. Appearing on BBC News on 10 March 2020, the Deputy Chief Medical Officer, Dr Jenny Harries, debated with former Conservative Party MP Rory Stewart as to whether the UK needed to implement a lockdown. Responding to Stewart's claim that the UK should lockdown, she stated that:

> I would beg to differ on a scientific basis with Mr Stewart because our advice in this country is founded entirely on scientific evidence. We have modelers working almost hourly at the moment looking at cases as they arise and looking at the effects of various different interventions including some of the ones which Mr Stewart and your reporters have mentioned. But actually, what we're trying to do is get a really balanced response, maximizing the safety of the public, maximizing the effectiveness of the health service but minimizing the disruption to people's lives and particularly to the economy and businesses.[59]

This was at a time when the rest of Europe was beginning to implement lockdowns. Just two days later, on 12 March, Irish Taoiseach Leo Varadkar

[57] 'Snowden leaks: US and UK crack online encryption' *BBC News* (6 September 2013) https://www.bbc.co.uk/news/world-us-canada-23981291 accessed 14 February 2025.

[58] Ashworth (n 55).

[59] 'BBC Breakfast' (10 March 2020) https://x.com/BBCBreakfast/status/1237310362992685057?s=20 accessed 14 February 2025.

announced that all schools, colleges and childcare facilities in Ireland would close.[60] Far from the UK taking a 'balanced approach', its refusal to lockdown stood as a stark outlier to the rest of Europe. This refusal was subsequently condemned by a House of Commons Select Committee as "one of the UK's worst ever public health failures."[61]

Therefore, while notions of balance and proportionality may sound superficially attractive and viable alternatives to concepts of constitutional identity, there is no guarantee that these more familiar judicial concepts cannot be deployed in such a way as to have damaging effects on both the relations between the EU and domestic states, and in terms of resisting an authoritarian trajectory within a state's domestic legal order. On a related note, balance and proportionality raise the question of who decides and reviews whether the calibration struck between the competing authorities of the EU and the domestic constitution. Again, lessons from emergencies are instructive in this regard for constitutional identity.

6.4.2 States of Emergency and Constitutional Identity: Who Decides?

As noted, one way in which constitutional identity mirrors Schmitt's analysis of states of exception is through his claim that exceptions are so inherently vague that it is impossible to control or constrain the power to declare a state of emergency through law. As emergencies are by definition unforeseen, they cannot be exhaustively defined; moreover, even where emergencies are legally defined and a situation is considered to fall outside of these contours, the Sovereign will invariably act anyway if they consider it necessary. Vagueness of definition, therefore, is integral to emergencies, and for Schmitt, it is the key to identifying *who* the sovereign is.

Drawing parallels between states of exception and constitutional identity, in turn, demands that we shift focus away from what has been labelled as "an emergency" or "constitutional identity" and instead focus on *who* is doing the labelling and invoking the concept of emergency or constitutional identity. Ostensibly, in the case of emergencies, the question of who decides should not necessarily be of concern, as an emergency's existence should be objectively verifiable. This stems from the emergency's close link to necessity and the invocation of the idea that there is no viable

[60] Alan Greene, *Emergency Powers in a Time of Pandemic* (BUP, 2020) 1.

[61] House of Commons Health and Social Care, and Science and Technology Committees, *Coronavirus: Lessons Learned to Date* (HC 92, 12 October 2021) < https://committees.parliament.uk/publications/7496/documents/78687/default/> accessed 14 February 2025.

choice available but the course proposed. However, some emergencies are more objective than others. For instance, I have argued that the COVID-19 pandemic was the closest the World has seen in many years to an objectively verifiable emergency.[62] The existence of an airborne virus capable of spreading rapidly and causing severe illness and death is not a matter of debate. Moreover, while some uncertainty in the early days of the emerging pandemic centered on the efficacy of pandemic measure responses, such as masking or lockdown, we subsequently were able to specifically mathematically model the impact of these measures. Thus, lockdowns could be mathematically demonstrated to reduce the transmission rate of the virus. In contrast, the necessity and efficacy of national security measures such as those declared in the aftermath of a terrorist attack are more difficult, if not impossible, to objectively verify or measure.

A similar question as to objective necessity also arises in terms of economic states of emergency. I have argued elsewhere that economic crises do not necessarily satisfy the conditions required for a formal state of emergency or deference to the executive.[63] Economic crises can certainly wreak havoc upon a given constitutional order. Moreover, there is often a need to act swiftly in a given crisis, not least to prevent the phenomenon of contagion. Even the language of contagion and emergency speaks volumes about the manner in which economic crises are often conceptualized. The difficulty arises, however, in the claim made—usually by the executive—that a specific response is necessary; that is, that there is no other choice. However, as economic matters or crises are often polycentric issues, it is difficult, if not impossible, to get universal agreement that a specific response is required. Indeed, ideological opponents may argue the polar opposite, with one side arguing that increased state spending is required and the other arguing that austerity is the cure.[64]

The point, therefore, is that who is invoking the concept of emergency matters as it invariably reveals much about their ideological preferences as it does about the phenomenon invoked to justify the emergency response. Translating this observation to constitutional identity, we can, in turn, see

[62] See Greene, 'Derogating from the European Convention on Human Rights in Response to the Coronavirus Pandemic: If Not Now, When?' (n 51).

[63] See Alan Greene, 'Questioning Executive Supremacy in an Economic State of Emergency' (2015) 35(4) Legal Studies 594.

[64] Ibid, 614–615.

why who invokes the concept of constitutional identity matters too. As previously noted, it is invariably the executive who increases in power in a time of emergency. This has profound dangers, as the executive is arguably the most dangerous branch. In contrast, it is the "least dangerous branch" —the judiciary—that has developed and utilized the concept of constitutional identity.[65] However, the most egregious abuses of this concept of constitutional identity seen in Poland and Hungary come from judiciaries where constitutional reforms were enacted, significantly weakening judicial independence. In this regard:

> The legal doctrine of constitutional identity claims to refer to the constitution only, but in reality, partly because of the ambiguity of the term, it is open to identitarian concerns of the judges.[66]

Relatedly, Polzin argues that when identifying the bounds of constitutional identity, "Such material limits are not derived from the constitution itself but from (doubtful) theoretical assumptions underpinning a general theory of constitutions, namely the idea of constitution as a harmonious legal order or the fundamental decision of an absolute and non-regulable figure of constituent power."[67] It is submitted, therefore, that it is not the indeterminacy of constitutional identity that results in the arbitrariness of its use per se; rather, this indeterminacy is itself symptomatic of the fact that abusive constitutional identity is a manifestation of the executive's claim to best speak for the state, channeled through a pliant judiciary.[68] In turn, it is not clear that concepts like balance or proportionality would be any less of a conduit for identitarian and authoritarian populist ideals than national identity in the hands of a captured judiciary. Balance and proportionality are vehicles for judicial deference towards the executive, and, moreover, these more legally quotidian concepts vis-à-vis constitutional identity could cloak these judgments in an additional layer of legitimacy.

[65] See Alexander Bickel, *The Least Dangerous Branch: The Supreme Court at the Bar of Politics* (2nd ed Yale University Press, 1986).

[66] Fabbrini and Sajo (26) 466.

[67] Monika Polzin, 'Constitutional identity, unconstitutional amendments and the idea of constituent power: The development of the doctrine of constitutional identity in German constitutional law' (2016) 14(2) International Journal of Constitutional Law 411, 421.

[68] Fabbrini and Sajó (n 26) 458

6.4.3 *Defensive Constitutional Identity*

It is submitted therefore that *who* invokes the concept of constitutional identity matters. Up until now, I have told an exclusive European story of constitutional identity, with this narrow focus underlining the doctrine's dangerous potential. However, beyond this European specificity, constitutional identity has arisen in cases concerning an inviolable core of a constitution. This notion of an inviolable is then deployed in a theory of unconstitutional constitutional amendment, conceptualizing constitutional amendment powers as a constituted power rather than as an expression of the constituent power that created the constitution in the first instance. Abandoning constitutional identity, therefore, could result in the loss of a concept that can be used to resist a slide towards authoritarianism, including attempts to utilize emergency powers in pursuit of this agenda. An illustrative example of this can be seen in India where, in a series of clashes between the Indian Supreme Court and Indira Gandhi's government, the Court ruled that the Indian parliament could not amend the constitution in such a way as to abolish its 'essential features'.[69] In this context, constitutional identity was deployed by the Indian Supreme Court as a way to control and constrain the excesses of the executive branch. Indeed, these excesses were exercised through emergency powers.

A similar historical attempt at this can be seen in the Irish Free State case of *The State (Ryan v Lennon)* the famous dissenting judgment of Kennedy CJ.[70] This case centered on the legality of constitutional amendments enacted by the parliament of the Irish Free State during the interim period following the enactment of the 1922 Constitution whereby it could be amended via the ordinary legislative procedure rather than the proposed referendum procedure that would enter into effect after this period. The Oireachtas (Ireland's bicameral legislature) then used this power to extend the period during which it could amend the constitution by way of ordinary legislation, and then inserted the infamous Article 2A into the 1922 constitution. This amendment allowed for the establishment of military tribunals whenever the Executive Council is of the opinion that circumstances render it expedient."[71] They had the power to issue any sentence,

[69] Greene (n 8) 84.

[70] [1935] IR 170; see also A Greene, 'The Supreme Legislative Authority Speaking as the Mouthpiece of the People": Constituent Power and the Irish Free State' in and Laura Cahilane and Donal Coffey (eds), *The Centenary of the Irish Free State Constitution* (Palgrave MacMillan, 2024) 47.

[71] Constitution (Amendment No. 17) Act 1931.

including death, for any offence. The background to this amendment was to confront remnants of the "Anti-Treaty" Irish Republican Army (IRA), which the state considered to still pose a threat owing to their refusal to reject violence as a means of opposing the partitioning of Ireland following the ratification of the Anglo–Irish Agreement in 1921.

While the majority of the Supreme Court took a highly positivist approach to reject the concept of an unconstitutional constitutional amendment, Kennedy CJ drew heavily from natural law to read into the constitution express limits to this amendment power:

> ...all lawful authority comes from God to the people, and it is declared by Article 2 of the Constitution that "all powers of government and all authority, legislative, executive and judicial, in Ireland are derived from the people of Ireland..." it follows that every act, whether legislative, executive or judicial, in order to be lawful under the Constitution must be capable of being justified under the authority thereby declared to be derived from God. From this it seems clear that, if any legislation of the Oireachtas (including any purported amendment of the Constitution) were to offend against that acknowledged ultimate Source from which the legislative authority has come through the People to the Oireachtas, as for instance, if it were repugnant to the Natural Law, such legislation would be necessarily unconstitutional and invalid and it would be, therefore absolutely null and void and inoperative.[72]

In this way, Kennedy CJ reads the constitution in a highly normative light, echoing concepts that we see in conceptions of constitutional identity today. He then deploys this in an attempt to constrain the introduction of emergency powers, which even the state's lawyers in *Ryan v Lennon* referred to as 'repellent to the instincts of every lawyer'.[73]

This idea of constitutional identity can be deployed to underline the importance of the fact that emergency powers are temporary. Permanent emergency powers are justified by so-called permanent states of emergency. Usher in permanent changes to the status quo. These changes, it is contended, may go to the very basis of the constitutional norms such as human rights, the separation of powers and the rule of law. If such aberrations from these norms are no longer temporary, then to what extent can we claim that the state embody these norms? It is for this reason that I have argued that permanent emergencies which usher in permanent

[72] *Ryan* (n 70) 204–205 (Kennedy CJ).

[73] Ibid 194.

suspension or permanent changes of these fundamental norms amount to a proxy-constitutional amendment.[74] Claims that these norms are merely in abeyance lack grounding in reality when this abeyance is perpetual. It is to contort the meaning of constitutionalism in a way that embodies Schmitt's critique of liberalism as emptying the rule of law and constitutionalism of any meaningful value, so as to cling to the fiction that the state still has a commitment to these norms.

Consequently, emergency powers must be conceptualized as temporary in order to avoid this proxy-constitutional amendment scenario. Failure to do so results in the constitution being amended in a manner not envisaged, and so, to all intents and purposes, a permanent state of emergency operates, similar to an exercise of constituent power by destroying the suspended constitutional norms. Emergency powers must be conceptualized as constituted powers to prevent this outcome and this necessarily entails constitutional safeguards on the decision to declare a state of emergency and its consequences. Through this perspective, the utility of constitutional identity as a means of constraining emergency powers reveals itself. If constitutional identity can be used to ensure that the constitutional amendment power is understood as inferior to the constituent power, the same applies to emergency powers. Consequently, rejecting constitutional identity out of fear of vindicating Carl Schmitt could, ironically, deny us the necessary tools to ensure that emergency powers do not create a Schmittian state of exception.

6.5 Conclusions

The concept of the "polycrisis" was popularized in the aftermath of the COVID-19 pandemic, as public health measures enacted to confront the pandemic raised questions as to their economic implications and, in turn, whether emergency economic measures would be required to address the pandemic and the impact of these public health measures. Such economic pressures can, in turn, trigger political instability, protests, and public order challenges. The impact of the pandemic on global supply chains demonstrated the global extent of this and economic crises' particular resistance to geographical containment. Against this forefront of immediate crises or crises that demand a fire-fighting response from the state, climate change

[74] Greene (n 8) Ch 3.

looms large. There is evidence to suggest that climate change will play a role in future pandemics and their frequency, owing to the resulting decrease in biodiversity and increased contact between humans and hitherto unknown viruses and pathogens.[75] COVID-19's impact on global supply chains is also, worryingly, a harbinger of things to come as climate change adversely affects the stability of food production, which can cause inflationary spikes. The extent of this risk is demonstrated by the fact that in 2024, the European Commission established the European Olive Oil and Table Olives Market Observatory in response to olive oil production in the EU falling 24% below the five-year average harvest in the 2023/24 season. This has been attributed to 'recent extreme weather events such as droughts, wildfires, and unseasonable temperatures.'[76] The worrying implications of all of this are that exceptional events such as pandemics, supply-chain shocks, terrorism, and political unrest are not that exceptional and may, in fact, become more common in the future. In this light, it may be more important than ever that we are equipped with the intellectual and legal tools necessary to resist the abuse of emergency powers.

The Schmittian similarities between constitutional identity and emergency powers is both a cause for concern and key to understanding the values and limitations of both concepts. The idea of constitutional identity shares many of the components of Schmitt's notion of the state of exception; specifically, his emphasis upon a relatively homogenous *Volk* as necessary for the establishment of a legal order, and the inherent vagueness of the concept as leaving space for the arbitrary whims of the person invoking the notion of constitutional identity or state of exception. At their most dangerous, they are both concepts that attempt to disguise arbitrary sovereign power under the cloak of legal doctrine. However, when utilized effectively, they can constitute a manifestation of, and defense of, key constitutional values such as democracy, the separation of powers and the rule of law. Ultimately, abuse of both constitutional identity and emergency powers is a symptom of a deeper constitutional malaise that we must be mindful of. However, in confronting and addressing this malaise, we

[75] See Aliana Pfenning-Butterworth et al, 'Interconnecting global threats: climate change, biodiversity loss, and infectious diseases' (2024) 8(4) Lancet Planet Health 1; Odette K Lawler et al, 'The COVID-19 pandemic is intrinsically linked to biodiversity loss and ecosystem health' (2021) 5(11) The Lancet Planetary Health 840.

[76] https://agriculture.ec.europa.eu/media/news/european-commission-launches-market-observatory-olive-oil-and-table-olives-sector-2024-11-11_en#:~:text=However%2C%20recent%20extreme%20weather%20events,average%20in%20the%20last%20harvest.

should not deny ourselves the potential legal tools that can assist in such a confrontation.

References

Ashworth, A. "Security, Terrorism and the Value of Human Rights" in Goold, B., & Lazarus, L. (eds.) *Security and Human Rights*. Hart Publishing, 2007, 203

Bickel, A. *The Least Dangerous Branch: The Supreme Court at the Bar of Politics*. 2nd ed. Yale University Press, 1986

Brzozowski, W. "Whatever Works: Constitutional Interpretation in Poland in Times of Populism" in Gárdos-Orosz, F., & Szente, Z. (eds.) *Populist Challenges to Constitutional Interpretation in Europe and Beyond*. Routledge, 2021, 174

Craig, P. "Constitutional Identity in the United Kingdom: An Evolving Concept" in Calliess, C., & van der Schyff, G. (eds.) *Constitutional Identity in a Europe of Multilevel Constitutionalism*. Cambridge University Press, 2019, 284–302

de Londras, F., & Davis, F.F. "Controlling the Executive in Times of Terrorism: Competing Perspectives on Effective Oversight Mechanisms" 30(1) *Oxford Journal of Legal Studies*, 2010, 19

de Wilde, M. "The State of Emergency in the Weimar Republic: Legal Disputes over Article 48 of the Weimar Constitution" 78 *Legal History Review*, 2010, 135

Doyle, O. "Constitutional Identity, Legal Autonomy and Sovereignty: Costello v Government of Ireland [2022] IESC 44" 19(4) *European Constitutional Law Review*, 2023, 715

Dyzenhaus, D. "Now the Machine Runs Itself: Carl Schmitt on Hobbes and Kelsen" 16(1) *Cardozo Law Review*, 1994, 1

Dyzenhaus, D. *Legality and Legitimacy: Carl Schmitt, Hans Kelsen and Hermann Heller in Weimar*. Oxford University Press, 1997

Dzehtsiarou, K. "Article 15 Derogations: Are They Really Necessary During the COVID-19 Pandemic?" *European Human Rights Law Review*, 2020, 359

Fabbrini, F., & Sajó, A. "The Dangers of Constitutional Identity" 25 *European Law Journal*, 2019, 457

Greene, A. "Derogating from the European Convention on Human Rights in Response to the Coronavirus Pandemic: If Not Now, When?" *European Human Rights Law Review*, 2020, 263

Greene, A. "Derogations, Deprivation of Liberty and the Containment Stage of Pandemic Responses" *European Human Rights Law Review*, 2021, 263

Greene, A. "On the Value of Derogations from the ECHR in Response to the COVID-19 Pandemic: A Rejoinder" *European Human Rights Law Review*, 2020, 526

Greene, A. "Questioning Executive Supremacy in an Economic State of Emergency" 35(4) *Legal Studies*, 2015, 594

Greene, A. "The Supreme Legislative Authority Speaking as the Mouthpiece of the People: Constituent Power and the Irish Free State" in Cahilane, L., & Coffey, D. (eds.) *The Centenary of the Irish Free State Constitution.* Palgrave Macmillan, 2024, 47
Greene, A. *Emergency Powers in a Time of Pandemic.* Bristol University Press, 2020
Greene, A. *Permanent States of Emergency and the Rule of Law: Constitutions in an Age of Crisis.* Hart Publishing, 2018
Gross, O. "Chaos and Rules: Should Responses to Violent Crises Always Be Constitutional?" 112 *Yale Law Journal*, 2002–03, 101
Gross, O., & Ní Aoláin, F. *Law in Times of Crisis: Emergency Powers in Theory and Practice.* Cambridge University Press, 2006
Hamai, G. "Illiberalism in East-Central Europe" in Sajó, A., Uitz, R., & Holmes, S. (eds.) *Routledge Handbook of Illiberalism.* Routledge, 2022, ch. 51, 813–821
Hamilton, A., Madison, J., & Jay, J. *The Federalist Papers.* Rossiter, C. (ed.) Signet Classics, 2003, 422
Hickman, T. "The Coronavirus Pandemic and Derogation from the European Convention on Human Rights" *European Human Rights Law Review*, 2020, 593
Kelemen, R.D., & Pech, L. "The Uses and Abuses of Constitutional Pluralism: Undermining the Rule of Law in the Name of Constitutional Identity in Hungary and Poland" 21 *Cambridge Yearbook of European Legal Studies*, 2019, 59
Kelsen, H. *General Theory of Law and State.* Harvard University Press, 1949
Kelsen, H. *Pure Theory of Law.* University of California Press, 1967
Lawler, O.K. et al. "The COVID-19 Pandemic Is Intrinsically Linked to Biodiversity Loss and Ecosystem Health" 5(11) *The Lancet Planetary Health*, 2021, 840
Mudde, C. "The Populist Zeitgeist" 39(4) *Government and Opposition*, 2004, 541
Neocleous, M. "Security, Liberty and the Myth of Balance: Towards a Critique of Security Politics" 6 *Contemporary Political Theory*, 2007, 131
Pfenning-Butterworth, A. et al. "Interconnecting Global Threats: Climate Change, Biodiversity Loss, and Infectious Diseases" 8(4) *Lancet Planetary Health*, 2024, 1
Polzin, M. "Constitutional Identity, Unconstitutional Amendments and the Idea of Constituent Power: The Development of the Doctrine of Constitutional Identity in German Constitutional Law" 14(2) *International Journal of Constitutional Law*, 2016, 411
Posner, R.A. *Not a Suicide Pact: The Constitution in a Time of Emergency.* Oxford University Press, 2006
Rossiter, C.L. *Constitutional Dictatorship: Crisis Government in the Modern Democracies.* First published 1948, reissued Routledge, 2002
Sadurski, W. "How Democracy Dies (in Poland): A Case Study of Anti-Constitutional Populist Backsliding" *Revista Forumul Judecatorilor*, 2018, 104

Sajó, A., & Uitz, R. *The Constitution of Freedom: An Introduction to Legal Constitutionalism*. Oxford University Press, 2017

Schmitt, C. *Political Theology: Four Chapters on the Concept of Sovereignty*. Translated by G. Schwab. University of Chicago Press, 2005

Schmitt, C. *The Concept of the Political*. Translated by G. Schwab. University of Chicago Press, 2005

Schnettger, A. "Article 4(2) TEU as a Vehicle for National Constitutional Identity in the Shared European Legal System" in Calliess, C., & van der Schyff, G. (eds.) *Constitutional Identity in a Europe of Multilevel Constitutionalism*. Cambridge University Press, 2019, 9–37

Scholtes, J. "Abusing Constitutional Identity" 22 *German Law Journal*, 2021, 534

Swan, I. "Counterblast: Terror in the Eye of the Beholder: The 'Spycam' Saga: Counter-Terrorism or Counter-Productive?" 50 *Howard Journal of Criminal Justice*, 2011, 199

Waldron, J. "Security and Liberty: The Image of Balance" 11(2) *Journal of Political Philosophy*, 2003, 191

CHAPTER 7

Justifying Legislation in the Face of Environmental and Climate Crises: The French Case and the Classical Constitutional Failure

Laurianne Allezard

7.1 Introduction

The justification of legislation has never been a prerequisite for the validity of the law. The validity of a law lies in its conformity with the Constitution, not in the extra-legal reasons that may have led to its adoption. However, in a context of polycrisis—particularly in light of the climate crisis, but also more broadly the environmental crisis—the justification of legislative choices is regaining relevance. The year 2024 marked a turning point in climate and environmental litigation. The ECtHR,[1] ITLOS,[2] and the

This chapter is produced as part and funded by the European Union-NextGenerationEU, through the National Recovery and Resilience Plan of the Republic of Bulgaria, project No bg-rrp-2.004-0008.

[1] Verein KlimaSeniorinnen Schweiz and Others v Switzerland [2024] ECHR 304, App no 53600/20 (ECtHR, Grand Chamber, 9 April 2024)

[2] Request for an Advisory Opinion submitted by the Commission of Small Island States on Climate Change and International Law (Request for Advisory Opinion submitted to the Tribunal), Advisory Opinion, 21 May 2024, ITLOS Reports 2024,

M. Belov (ed.), *Constitutional Polycrisis and Emergency Constitutionalism*, Federalism and Internal Conflicts,
https://doi.org/10.1007/978-3-032-06516-2_7

ICJ[3] (in ongoing proceedings) have all highlighted an increasing expectation that political action be coherent with the realities of the climate crisis. The EctHR, particularly, and some constitutional[4] and administrative courts[5] have demonstrated that a state may be held liable for inaction regarding scientific consensus. In essence, they suggest that given the available scientific facts and knowledge, a state could and should have done more. The contours of such a state responsibility remain difficult to determine precisely. In particular, regarding the question of who within the State is responsible, and at what point in the decision-making process. Is it the government? The legislature? Constitutional or administrative courts? Or does it result from a broader institutional inertia shared across the branches of the State? What can constitutional courts do in this context?

The legislative process, in particular, appears to lack certain safeguards to ensure that the government and the legislator are held accountable in the face of the climate and environmental crisis. This chapter argues that one possible avenue for improvement lies in the obligation of justification of laws and the mechanisms for reviewing them. Indeed, across constitutional democracies, legislative choices appear to be increasingly drawn into a "pull of justification" —to use David Dyzenhaus's phrase[6]—that demands greater transparency and persuasive reasoning. The greater the interference with rights, particularly individual rights, the stronger the demand for justification becomes.[7] As Patricia Popelier has aptly noted, "the rationality of the legislator, once a legal axiom tied to parliamentary sovereignty, is no longer an irrebuttable presumption."[8] The current

[3] Request for an Advisory Opinion submitted by the United Nations General Assembly on the Obligations of States in respect of Climate Change, Oral Proceedings, International Court of Justice, 2–13 December 2024, Verbatim Records 2024/38–2024/54

[4] Urgenda Foundation v The State of the Netherlands (Ministry of Economic Affairs and Climate Policy) [2019] ECLI:NL:HR:2019:2007, Supreme Court of the Netherlands, 20 December 2019;

[5] Neubauer et al. v Germany [2021] BVerfG, 1 BvR 2656/18, 24 March 2021; 2020Hun-Ma389 et al. (consolidated), Constitutional Court of Korea, 29 August 2024

[6] D Dyzenhaus, 'Proportionality and Deference in a Culture of Justification' in G Huscroft, B Miller and G Webber (eds), *Proportionality and the Rule of Law: Rights, Justification, Reasoning* (Cambridge University Press 2014) 254.

[7] P Ondřejek, 'Threshold of Justification of Emergency Regulations: On Coherentism Requirement for the Justification of Measures Adopted in the Czech Republic during the COVID-19 Pandemic' (2021) 2 *Journal of the Polish Section of IVR* 46.

[8] Ibid.

trend thus moves towards enhancing the quality of legislation—and, in turn, its public perception—through the promotion of better regulation tools[9] within the legislative process: expert input, impact assessments, and empirical data.

Thus, what emerges on the horizon is a widening gap between the reality of the climate and environmental crisis and the constitutional safeguards intended to ensure that political decision-making is rational. In turn, it is the responsibility of the state as a whole that is called into question by the lack of rational justification in lawmaking.

In France, one observes a general inertia within the legislative process in response to the broader trend toward increased justification of legislation. The legislature is only formally required to justify its laws, but the constraint placed upon it remains limited and stops short of threatening its margin of political discretion. However, this obligation remains largely "legal"[10] in nature and seldom extends into the scientific domain—despite the potential benefits of doing so.[11] The Constitutional Council typically refrains from scrutinizing this lack of substantive justification. As President Laurent Fabius and his predecessors have argued, delving into "a luxury of detail"[12] would amount to overstepping the institution's role. In this respect, France continues to embody a form of theoretical conservatism, in which factual evidence argued for or against the law remains under the control of the political sphere. Accordingly, the assessment and management of emergencies fall within the exclusive competence of elected representatives. The Schmittian doctrine of exceptionalism[13]—which grants discretion to the government in times of emergency—remains influential in France, privileging the operability and effectiveness of law over its quality, even in areas where science offers clear answers. This logic persists even in response to crises that are, in reality, structural rather than exceptional,

[9] Ibid.

[10] Thomas Perroud, 'Les Études d'impact Dans l'action Publique En France: Perspective Critique et Propositions' (2018) 35 Politiques et Management public 215.

[11] Ibid

[12] L Fabius, 'If we were to enter into a luxury of details, if we were to enter into the facts, then we would go beyond our role. We must not go into details that would be unnecessary' (speech at the University of Nantes, 24 May 2019)

[13] Carl Schmitt, *Political Theology: Four Chapters on the Concept of Sovereignty* (MIT Press 1985).

but continue to be perceived as emergencies—such as the climate and environmental crises.

That is why, in this chapter, I have chosen to focus on the French case—an extreme yet paradigmatic example of political, and even theoretical, resistance to a more rationally justified legislative process. This case encapsulates the various underlying reasons behind the reluctance to align more closely with scientific knowledge. It also helps to illuminate, for instance, the visceral reaction of the Swiss Parliament to the ECtHR's climate ruling, in which national discretion and sovereign political choice were invoked in response.

This chapter seeks to explore how the French government justifies bills submitted to Parliament, which account for 80 to 90% of enacted legislation, and how it navigates between overlapping crises, emergencies, and competing interests. The aim is to identify the types and degrees of justification that emerge from this process. To that end, the chapter examines a selection of recent climate- and environment-related laws that have been reviewed by the Constitutional Council. Drawing on parliamentary debates, written observations submitted by the government, the members of Parliament who brought the case, external contributions, and the Constitutional Council's decisions themselves, this chapter offers an assessment of the value of governmental rational justifications and highlights potential areas for improvement.

The chapter is organized into three parts. First, it provides an overview of the existing obligations surrounding the rationalization of legislation. Second, it analyses how the justification of laws often serves to reinforce the government's general policy direction and strategic priorities. Third, it considers how scientific knowledge is mobilized as a tool for legitimising legislation, without necessarily becoming a criterion for its constitutionality. In sum, the aim is to examine how the primary function of the obligation to justify—namely, to constrain political decision-makers based on facts—has been transformed into an argument that ultimately serves political authority.

7.2 A Constitutional Obligation to Rationalize Legislation Without Safeguards

The obligation to rationalize legislation has, over time, acquired constitutional status in France (2.1), but it is accompanied by only a very limited degree of judicial enforceability (2.2).

7.2.1 A Gradual Constitutional Recognition

The political and constitutional development of legislative rationalization in France has already been extensively studied.[14] Efforts to improve the quality of legislation have gradually reinforced the scientific justification—and, more broadly, the rhetorical legitimacy—of the legislator, and more precisely of the government behind the bill, notably through the establishment of an obligation to systematically attach an impact assessment to each draft law. Initiated in 1976 in the field of environmental law,[15] this requirement was formally introduced in 1995 with the aim of providing "a precise analysis of the expected benefits and the multiple implications of the text,"[16] and was extended to all government bill proposals in 1998.[17] Since the 2008 constitutional reform[18] prescribed by the organic law of 15 April 2009,[19] the presentation of impact assessments has become a constitutional obligation. In this way, the preparatory works accompanying draft legislation have gradually acquired normative significance.

The degree of urgency underlying the justification for a law has a direct impact on the practical scope of the obligation. In its decision of 9 April 2009, the Constitutional Council limited the binding nature of impact assessments in order to preserve the continuity of national life, should such requirements hinder the proper conduct of the legislative process.[20] The

[14] B-L Combrade, *L'obligation d'étude d'impact des projets de loi* (Dalloz, Nouvelle Bibliothèque des Thèses 2017).

[15] Loi n° 76-629 du 10 juillet 1976 relative à la protection de la nature [Law No 76-629 of 10 July 1976 on the Protection of Nature].

[16] Circulaires du Premier ministre des 26 juillet et 21 novembre 1995 relatives à l'expérimentation d'une étude d'impact accompagnant les projets de loi et de décret en Conseil d'État [Prime Minister's Circulars of 26 July and 21 November 1995 on the Pilot Scheme for Impact Assessments Accompanying Bills and Draft Decrees Submitted to the Conseil d'État].

[17] See Circulaire du 26 janvier 1998 relative à l'étude d'impact des projets de loi et de décret en Conseil d'État [Circular of 26 January 1998 on Impact Assessments], in which the Prime Minister sought to generalize the use of impact assessments for all government bills, excluding enabling acts, ratification laws, and international agreement legislation.

[18] Loi constitutionnelle n° 2008-724 du 23 juillet 2008 de modernisation des institutions de la Ve République [Constitutional Law No 2008-724 of 23 July 2008 on the Modernization of the Institutions of the Fifth Republic]. Article 39 of the Constitution.

[19] Loi organique n° 2009-403 du 15 avril 2009 relative à l'application des articles 34-1, 39 et 44 de la Constitution [Organic Law No 2009-403 of 15 April 2009 on the Implementation of Articles 34-1, 39 and 44 of the Constitution].

[20] Conseil constitutionnel, Decision No 2009-579 DC of 9 April 2009, *Loi organique relative à l'application des articles 34-1, 39 et 44 de la Constitution* (France) [Organic Law Implementing Articles 34-1, 39 and 44 of the Constitution].

fact that an impact assessment is incomplete at the time of a bill's submission cannot, in itself, prevent the bill from being adopted.[21] Moreover, the Organic Law provides exemptions from the impact assessment obligation, including for laws extending states of emergency. The underlying rationale is that the urgency of decision-making in such circumstances does not allow for an assessment that is sufficiently robust and comprehensive, or simply that the initial exceptionalism justified by the emergency persists.

7.2.2 A Limited Constitutional Review

Since 2008, the Constitutional Council has been formally required to ensure that legislation complies with this obligation. Given the limited guidance provided by the 2009 Organic Law, the Council has been tasked with interpreting both the scope of the obligation and the extent of its own competences in this regard.[22]

The Constitutional Council could, however, intervene on two distinct levels: first, by assessing the quality of the impact assessment itself, and second, by evaluating the extent to which the legislator's choices align with the findings of that assessment.

A specific procedure is planned by the constitution as a tool available to the parliamentary opposition to prevent a bill from being placed on the legislative agenda. Under Article 39 of the Constitution, the Constitutional Council must rule within eight days on whether the drafting process of the bill complies with the 2009 Organic Law—namely, whether the impact assessment and the justification for the bill meet the required standards. If the Council is not seized under this procedure, it forfeits the opportunity to declare the bill inadmissible due to an inadequate impact assessment. Moreover, if it is seized solely on the basis of Article 39, the Constitutional Council is not authorized to review the substantive constitutionality of the bill. It is therefore limited to evaluating whether the impact assessment is sufficiently detailed.

On the basis of Article 39, in a decision dated 22 April 2024, the Constitutional Council was called upon to review the impact assessment accompanying a framework law on agricultural sovereignty, which sought to address the ongoing economic and ecological crises affecting both the agricultural sector and the State more broadly. In its written observations,

[21] Conseil constitutionnel, Decision No 2001-448 DC of 25 July 2001, *Loi organique relative aux lois de finances* (France) [Organic Law on Finance Acts], cons 75, 79 and 80.

[22] Perroud (n 10).

the government reiterated that the Council exercises only a formal review and is not entitled to assess the substance of the law, which falls within its political discretion. However, it appears that the boundary between formal review and artificial review is exceedingly thin. The Council limits itself to verifying whether the impact assessment and the government's reasoning address certain expected points—namely, the objectives pursued by the law, the alternative options considered apart from the proposed measure, and the government's stated rationale.[23] In addition, it merely confirms whether the economic and financial consequences of the bill,[24] as well as the state's objectives,[25] have been outlined with sufficient clarity, but not whether they are accurate regarding the concrete situation. In doing so, the Court places its trust in the government's good judgment. This results in the Constitutional Council reviewing only the informational quality of the impact assessment and the legislative rationale, without assessing the completeness or reliability of the information provided. As Bertrand-Léo Combrade notes, "To date, in every instance where the Constitutional Council has been asked to rule on the inadequacy of an [impact assessment], it has ruled in favor of the government, even when the violation of the Organic Law of 15 April 2009 was manifest."[26] In fact, external contributors to the 2024 decision nonetheless identified clear deficiencies in the impact assessment, including a total omission of the environmental impacts.[27] Thus, the very purpose of the impact assessment—to inform Parliament in its entirety, in both its political and deliberative dimensions, and to guide debates toward greater rationality and less ideology—may be undermined.

Turning now to the standard procedure for reviewing the substantive constitutionality of legislation—Article 61 of the Constitution—the

[23] Conseil constitutionnel, Decision No 2024-14 FNR of 22 April 2024, *Présentation du projet de loi d'orientation pour la souveraineté en matière agricole et le renouvellement des générations en agriculture* [Draft Framework Law for Agricultural Sovereignty and Generational Renewal in Farming], pt 7.

[24] Ibid. Pt 8

[25] Ibid. Pt 9

[26] Bertrand-Léo Combrade, 'Le Gouvernement Argumente, l'étude d'impact Passe (Commentaire de La Décision N° 2023-13 FNR Du 20 Avril 2023, Présentation Du Projet de Loi Relatif à La Programmation Militaire Pour Les Années 2024 à 2030 et Portant Diverses Dispositions Intéressant La Défense)' [2023] Revue française de droit constitutionnel 966.

[27] External contribution by the Syndicat de la magistrature in *Conseil constitutionnel*, Decision No. 2024-14 FNR of 22 April 2024, *Présentation du projet de loi d'orientation pour la souveraineté en matière agricole et le renouvellement des générations en agriculture.*

Constitutional Council applies the same limited scrutiny to the accompanying impact assessment and the scientific reasoning of the government in general regarding the motives of the law. The required degree of justification remains purely formal. In a decision concerning a law that sought to reintroduce the occasional use of neonicotinoids in the event of a health crisis affecting sugar beet crops,[28] the claimant members of the National Assembly pointed to clear inaccuracies in the impact assessment, while the senators argued that the justification of the law was insufficient to justify lowering the level of legal protection afforded to the environment. The government, for its part, once again invoked the limited nature of judicial review over environmental protection measures, referring to previous decisions and thereby locking the judge into established precedent[29]—even though the circumstances and known risks have evolved, and environmental protection has since gained greater legal and constitutional recognition. The Constitutional Council ultimately endorsed the government's political argument, which claimed to pursue a form of "humanist ecology"[30] that balances environmental concerns with other interests, at the legislator's discretion.

Thus, the Council has never fully seized the opportunity offered by the organic law and continues to exercise only a "purely formal and procedural"[31] review. Such restricted review confers a predominantly political, rather than legal, character on legislative justification. It illustrates where current justifications fall short and where the rational foundation of legislation might need to be rethought.

7.3 An Opportunistic Justification of Legislative Motives

According to the Constitutional Council's well-known and consistent formula: "The limitations imposed by the legislature on the exercise

[28] Conseil constitutionnel, Decision No 2020-809 DC of 10 December 2020, *Loi relative aux conditions de mise sur le marché de certains produits phytopharmaceutiques en cas de danger sanitaire pour les betteraves sucrières* [Law on the Marketing Conditions of Certain Plant Protection Products in Case of Health Hazards for Sugar Beets],

[29] Government submissions (*Observations du gouvernement*), 18 April 2024

[30] Dominique Perben, *Senate Official Journal* (*JO Sénat*), 23 June 2004.

[31] Céline Fercot, 'Données empiriques et contrôle de constitutionnalité des lois: le Conseil constitutionnel sur la réserve' (2020) 173 Revue française d'administration publique 95. 100

of (this) right must be connected to constitutional requirements or justified by *a ground of general or public interest*[32] and proportionate to the *objective pursued.*"[33] The general interest has traditionally served as a basis for derogating from constitutional principles and as a justification for limiting the guarantee of fundamental rights.[34] Even though the legislator is presumed to act in the general interest,[35] "more than ever, the general interest occupies a central place in the process of reconciling constitutional principles."[36] The increasing reliance on the general interest[37] has not, however, prompted any clarification of its definition.[38] It should also be noted that crises or emergencies introduce an additional argument often used to reinforce legislative choices: the existence of a 'threat' or a "danger"[39] that demands an immediate response. In such cases, the legislator engages in a process of balancing

[32] See Margherita Pieraccini, 'The Public Interest in Environmental Decision-Making: A Pragmatist Turn' (2024) 36 Journal of Environmental Law 363.

[33] See Conseil constitutionnel, Decision No 2020-809 DC of 10 December 2020, Loi relative aux conditions de mise sur le marché de certains produits phytopharmaceutiques en cas de danger sanitaire pour les betteraves sucrières [Law on the Marketing Conditions of Certain Plant Protection Products in Case of Health Hazards for Sugar Beets], §14.Conseil constitutionnel, Decision No 2022-991 QPC of 13 May 2022, Association France nature environnement et autres (France) [Exemption for Certain Watermills from Obligations Ensuring Ecological Continuity of Watercourses], §6.

[34] Conseil constitutionnel, Decision No 2021-825 DC of 13 August 2021, *Loi portant lutte contre le dérèglement climatique et renforcement de la résilience face à ses effets* (France) [Law on Combating Climate Change and Strengthening Resilience to Its Effects], §7.

[35] European Commission for Democracy through Law (Venice Commission), *Parameters on the Relationship between the Parliamentary Majority and the Opposition in a Democracy: a Checklist* CDL-AD(2019)015 (24 June 2019) 6: "Both the majority and the opposition have to act based on the same joint and responsible commitment to the public interest of the citizens, who are the legitimate source of democratic power."

[36] D Ribes, 'Le réalisme du Conseil constitutionnel' (2007) 22 *Cahiers du Conseil constitutionnel* (Dossier : Le réalisme en droit constitutionnel).

[37] G Merland, 'L'intérêt général, instrument efficace de protection des droits fondamentaux?' (2004) 16 *Cahiers du Conseil constitutionnel* (prix de thèse 2003).

[38] See D Truchet, 'La notion d'intérêt général: le point de vue d'un professeur de droit' (2017) Légicom: Revue du droit de la communication des entreprises et de la communication publique 5.

[39] Conseil constitutionnel, Decision No 2020-809 DC of 10 December 2020, *Loi relative aux conditions de mise sur le marché de certains produits phytopharmaceutiques en cas de*

competing interests.[40] privileging one crisis over another within a broader context of polycrisis.

The general interest (3.1) and/or the urgency (3.2) thus become decisive standards in the proportionality review—but these are not legal standards per se. As such, they prevent the absolute application of one right over another, or of a binding state obligation regarding scientific consensus.

7.3.1 A Discretionary Balancing of Interests

Max Weber held that decisions are legitimate when made in the interest of all.[41] Yet the management of polycrisis inevitably involves sacrificing one interest in favor of another. In practice, the legislator tends to prioritize certain interests over others. The key issue, as the European Court of Human Rights has repeatedly emphasized in cases concerning environmental pollution, is to maintain a "fair balance" that respects all competing interests.[42]

Typically, this involves a conflict between general interests related to environmental or public health concerns and those linked to economic objectives.[43] While health and environmental protection have been recognized by the Constitutional Council as constitutionally valuable objectives and as legitimate public interests, they are not granted absolute protection. The Council has stated that "the protection of the environment must be pursued on an equal footing with the other fundamental interests of the Nation."[44] However, any limitations imposed on the right to live in a balanced and healthy environment must be justified by a general interest.[45] Crucially, however, the definition of the Nation's fundamental interests is

danger sanitaire pour les betteraves sucrières [Law on the Marketing Conditions of Certain Plant Protection Products in Case of Health Hazards for Sugar Beets]

[40] See on this point PA Hall, 'Policy Paradigms, Social Learning, and the State: The Case of Economic Policy-Making in Britain' (1993) 25 *Comparative Politics* 275–296.

[41] See M Weber, *Le savant et le politique*, Plon, 1995.

[42] For instance : Fadeyeva v Russia App no 55723/00 (ECtHR, 9 June 2005)

[43] Ex : Conseil constitutionnel, Decision No 2019-823 QPC of 31 January 2020, *Union des industries de la protection des plantes* [Union of the Plant Protection Products Industry]

[44] Ibid.

[45] Conseil constitutionnel, Decision No 2023-1066 QPC of 26 October 2023, *Société TotalEnergies Renouvelables France*(France) [TotalEnergies Renewables France], pt 7.

left entirely to the discretion of the government that justifies the law, or to the legislator itself.

First, with regard to the updating of the legislative list of the Nation's fundamental interests by the legislator: this is not merely a matter of invoking the general interest to justify restricting a right, but rather involves enshrining in law the definition of a new "major public interest." In a law on Food Sovereignty and Generational Renewal in Agriculture submitted to the Constitutional Council for review,[46] the aim was to add "the protection, enhancement, and development of agriculture and fisheries... insofar as they guarantee the Nation's food sovereignty" as a public interest, alongside forest exploitation. The claimant members of Parliament criticised the vagueness and lack of clarity surrounding the notions of "major public interest" and "fundamental interest of the Nation," arguing that such ambiguity undermines the constitutional objective of legal accessibility and intelligibility.[47] According to these opposing deputies, "there already exists an abundance of expressions in positive law that refer to the general interest." Despite the ambiguity surrounding both the definition and invocation of these terms, the Constitutional Council found that the concepts of major public interest and fundamental national interest, as expressed in the law in question, were not "unintelligible."[48] Yet inserting new interests into legislation has implications that go beyond the regulatory level, and the Constitutional Council would be mistaken never to examine the constitutional relevance of such interests. For instance, recognizing forest exploitation as a fundamental interest in law may have two constitutional consequences: either the Constitutional Council will systematically reject any future legislative changes that contradict this interest—thus effectively elevating it to constitutional status—or it will accept such changes, thereby diluting the meaning of "fundamental" and weakening its normative force. A degree of ambiguity remains as to what the Council should or may do, and this indeterminacy ultimately benefits the legislator, who retains broad discretion in determining which interests to pursue—even at the expense of others.

[46] Conseil constitutionnel, Decision No 2025-876 DC of 20 March 2025, *Loi d'orientation pour la souveraineté alimentaire et le renouvellement des générations en agriculture* (France) [Framework Law on Food Sovereignty and Generational Renewal in Agriculture].

[47] Point 5

[48] Point 11

Secondly, beyond the potential expansion of the legislative list of general or fundamental national interests, the government remains free.[49] To find other general interests, even if that interest has never been previously invoked. On a case-by-case basis, during proportionality review, the government may advance a new interest in place of an older one previously used to justify another law. It may reverse the hierarchy between competing interests at will, following political opportunism. There is thus no established hierarchy among interests. They function as 'joker' arguments, opportunistically invoked by the government to justify a law proposal. As a result, there is neither substantive nor temporal coherence in the use of these interests or in how they are balanced against one another.

Routinely, the Constitutional Council has passively accepted new general interests put forward by the government to justify legislation, such as in 2020: "ensuring the competitive operation of the electricity market" and "guaranteeing price stability in that market."[50] The Council refrains from taking a position on the substance of the matter. In its ruling on the law authorizing the reintroduction of neonicotinoids,[51] the general interest advanced by the government was strongly contested by opposition members of Parliament. They criticised it for favoring certain economic actors within the sugar beet industry. According to the government, the objective was to save the sugar sector, which it claimed contributes to France's food sovereignty—specifically, to protect sugar-processing companies, since beet farmers can switch crops. In reality, this meant defending five major groups, three of which own 21 out of France's 23 sugar factories. Beekeepers, who suffer the ecological consequences of reintroducing neonicotinoids, were not considered to be contributing to national food sovereignty. In its defence, the government simply ignored the objection raised by the claimants, arguing that the method it had chosen—seed coating—is less harmful to bees than spraying. However, as the opposing deputies demonstrated, no scientific study confirms this claim. The government also failed to address the fact that such practices contaminate the soil for up to twenty years—well beyond the 120-day exemption period

[49] Merland n(34)

[50] Conseil constitutionnel, Decision No 2022-843 DC of 12 August 2022, *Loi portant diverses dispositions de vigilance sanitaire* [Law on Various Provisions of Health Vigilance]

[51] Conseil constitutionnel, Decision No 2020-809 DC of 10 December 2020, *Loi relative aux conditions de mise sur le marché de certains produits phytopharmaceutiques en cas de danger sanitaire pour les betteraves sucrières*

permitted under the European regulation[52]—thereby affecting future crops and biodiversity. In doing so, it overlooked other interests which are arguably of a general nature, first and foremost, public health.

Most recently, the interest of future generations has emerged in the jurisprudence of the French Constitutional Council. The Council has taken a step in this direction, though without yet recognizing an enforceable right that individuals may invoke.[53] In addition to lacking direct justiciability, it does not currently appear that, in the context of the climate crisis, the interest of future generations is likely to prevail over shorter-term interests.

In short, the Constitutional Council remains indifferent to the definition of the general interest.[54] At present, the nature of the interests at stake—economic versus ecological, collective versus individual, national versus global, present versus future—does not give rise to an ordered or principled reconciliation. In the absence of a clearly established hierarchy among interests, a potential substitute could be the emergence of a hierarchy of threats. A long-term emergency or structural crisis that requires sustained intervention might offer a more secure framework for balancing interests. Yet for now, it is the most immediate and pressing emergency that justifies the prioritization of one interest over another.

7.3.2 *A Balancing of Emergencies Favoring the Short Term*

The management of emergencies, traditionally a prerogative of the government and the legislator, functions not as a rational justification, but rather as a political argument in support of legislative measures. In a context of polycrisis—and thus of overlapping and competing emergencies—this argument becomes even more vulnerable to political discretion.

The notions of "threat," "risk," and "danger" are even more indeterminate than that of the general interest, as they require a personal and political assessment of a threshold of severity and cannot be defined

[52] Article 53 of Regulation (EC) No. 1107/2009

[53] Conseil constitutionnel, Decision No 2023-1066 QPC of 27 October 2023, *Association Meuse nature environnement et autres* (France) [Association Meuse Nature Environnement and Others], pt 7.

[54] Merland n(34) « Juridiquement fondé, le contrôle par le Conseil constitutionnel de l'appréciation législative de l'intérêt général est-il politiquement souhaitable? Le Conseil ne semble pas le penser. Un des soucis récurrents qu'il exprime à travers ses décisions est de présenter sa mission comme étant d'une nature juridictionnelle.»

by any exhaustive legal list. They fall within what has been described as "ambiguous determinations" with "limited normativity"—tools that are ambivalent, uncertain, and at times incoherent.[55] In practice, French legal scholarship has observed that "the notion of urgency is frequently invoked by the legislator to justify the suspension of certain guarantees or the restriction of certain rights."[56] Threats thus serve as key factors shaping the balancing of competing interests. The Constitutional Council is consistently quick to accept restrictions on certain interests previously recognized as general in nature, when justified by the exception created by a perceived threat. For example, while legislation must serve the general interest of environmental protection, this requirement may be set aside "in the case of a serious threat to the security of gas supply."[57]

In that instance, the government sought to establish a permanent regulatory framework for LNG terminals, which—according to its position—"is only intended to be applied in the context of a severe energy crisis and as long as the security of the natural gas supply is under threat." As such, the law raised the greenhouse gas emissions threshold previously set by an earlier statute. The justification rested on the argument that the framework, while not eliminating the climate impact, would mitigate it—particularly, as the opposition pointed out, because a floating LNG terminal would reduce reliance on coal-fired power plants. According to the government, this framework helps to minimise the risk of failing to meet constitutional requirements related to the continuity of national life and public service. In this way, the legislator engages in balancing competing risks and threats, based on the urgency it chooses to prioritize. In this case, it favored the management of immediate emergency over that of the long-term crisis—overlooking the fact that addressing the emergency in this way may actually contribute to worsening the underlying crisis.

In the decision concerning the rescue of the sugar beet industry, the Constitutional Council, as previously noted, upheld the general interest invoked: the temporary reauthorization of neonicotinoids to address the

[55] See P de Montalivet, 'Les objectifs de valeur constitutionnelle' (2006) 20 *Les Cahiers du Conseil constitutionnel.*

[56] JF de Montgolfier, 'L'urgence et le Conseil constitutionnel' (2017) 54 *Les Nouveaux Cahiers du Conseil constitutionnel* (Dossier : La Constitution et le temps).

[57] Conseil constitutionnel, Decision No 2022-843 DC of 12 August 2022, *Loi portant diverses dispositions de vigilance sanitaire.*

serious threats facing sugar beet cultivation.[58] The referring members of Parliament contested the claim that the Nation's food sovereignty was at risk, arguing that France is a major exporter and retains sufficient capacity to ensure its own autonomy. In this case, the appeal to sovereignty does not concern the concept in its entirety but rather the economic strength of a sector that is important, yet not essential or overarching. The threat to the environment, once again, was downplayed by the government, which framed it as a necessary trade-off to protect the industry.[59]

At a deeper level, what emerges is a hierarchy of crises based on the degree of urgency attributed to each. Under normal circumstances, the environmental and climate crisis takes precedence. However, as soon as an immediate emergency arises, this hierarchy is reversed, and the mere invocation of a threat serves as sufficient justification—without any requirement to demonstrate the existence of that threat or its severity. There thus exists a temporal hierarchy among crises, over which the government in France retains full discretion and control.

The balancing of emergencies determines the balancing of interests—and vice versa. Their relationship, in turn, governs the reconciliation of constitutional principles, rights, and freedoms. The government is neither required to prove the existence of an emergency nor to justify why one fundamental interest should prevail over another. Similarly, the government is not obliged to establish the severity threshold of a threat or danger. In practice, no objective tools are used to determine such a threshold. Justification, in this context, is merely informative and declaratory; it is by no means binding or mandatory.

7.4 A Scientific Justification in Distress

Scientific knowledge—even in the case of scientific consensus—serves as an argumentative resource for the government and, more broadly, in parliamentary debates, but it plays no role in the Constitutional Council's assessment of constitutionality. It is used to legitimise legislation, but not to determine its constitutionality (4.1). And often, legislative derogations

[58] Conseil constitutionnel, Decision No 2020-809 DC of 10 December 2020, *Loi relative aux conditions de mise sur le marché de certains produits phytopharmaceutiques en cas de danger sanitaire pour les betteraves sucrières*, § 20

[59] It is interesting to compare this reasoning with the General Court and CJEU's approach in Bayer CropScience AG v European Commission (T-429/13) EU:T:2018:280 and Bayer CropScience AG and Bayer AG v European Commission (C-499/18 P) EU:C:2021:367.

from environmental protection and climate change mitigation are deemed constitutional because their concrete implementation is assessed on a case-by-case basis, left to the discretion of administrative authorities, which are free to interpret scientific knowledge in making their decisions. A law is thus considered constitutional because the scientific justification for its application is delegated to other institutions (4.2).

7.4.1 A Lack of Alignment Between Legislation and Scientific Knowledge

A decision is still deemed valid based on its legal foundation, not its effects.[60] Scientific justification has never been a prerequisite for the exercise of political power. As Hannah Arendt famously wrote, it is "opinion, not truth, [that] is one of the indispensable foundations of all power."[61] And despite the existence of rational obligations, a legal norm cannot be "the product of an objective 'calculation.'"[62] This is why, as David L. Faigman has noted, "absolute certainty has never been a criterion for constitutional decision-making."[63] Indeed, courts have traditionally[64] refrained from intervening in situations marked by scientific uncertainty regarding the evolution of the issue addressed by legislation, thereby leaving such matters in the hands of the political branches.

This explains the Constitutional Council's consistent position in *ordinary times*: "It is not for the Constitutional Council, which does not have a general power of assessment and decision-making comparable to that of Parliament, to question, in light of the state of knowledge, the provisions thus adopted by the legislator."[65] In other words, the Council does not require the legislator to align its decisions with scientific knowledge—nor

[60] S Salles, 'Le conséquentialisme dans la jurisprudence du Conseil constitutionnel' (2016) 53 *Les Nouveaux Cahiers du Conseil constitutionnel* 75–80.

[61] H Arendt, *La crise de la culture* (Gallimard 1972) [*Between Past and Future: Eight Exercises in Political Thought*] 296

[62] J Chevallier, 'Peut-on rationaliser la production du droit?' in *L'Union européenne et l'idéal de la meilleure législation*(Pedone 2013)

[63] DL Faigman, 'Normative Constitutional Fact-Finding: Exploring the Empirical Component of Constitutional Interpretation' (1991) 139 *University of Pennsylvania Law Review* 541. 607

[64] EH Meazell, 'Scientific Avoidance: Toward More Principled Judicial Review of Legislative Science' (2008) 84 *Indiana Law Journal* 239, 252–53

[65] Conseil constitutionnel, Decision No 2019-823 QPC of 31 January 2020, *Union des industries de la protection des plantes* (France) [Union of the Plant Protection Products Industry], §9.

does it require the government to act in accordance with that knowledge, even when it is uncontested. In a 2019 decision concerning bone testing used to determine whether young foreign nationals were minors, the Council dismissed the scientific arguments presented by the referring deputies.[66] Despite growing controversy over the reliability of such tests, and in the absence of alternative methods, the Council upheld the government's choice. As Céline Fercot noted in her commentary on the decision, the judge "did not sanction the failure to take into account both 'the state of knowledge and techniques' and 'the evolution of scientific, medical, and epidemiological data.'"[67] In sum, under normal circumstances, the benefit of the doubt is granted to the government's choice.

In times of urgency, the Constitutional Council has reiterated its interpretative restraint, stating that it will uphold the reasoning of the legislator so long as the measure is not, "in light of current scientific and technical knowledge, manifestly inappropriate to its objectives."[68] On paper, the Council appears to reserve the option to intervene; in practice, however, it has never found that a legislative measure contradicted the available scientific evidence.[69] As previously noted, in fulfilling its obligation to rationalize legislation, the government refers to the state of scientific knowledge by consulting experts and specialized authorities, and incorporates these findings into the preparatory works accompanying the draft law. The Constitutional Council reviews the government's procedural approach, but not the substance of the scientific reasoning itself. As a result, no oversight exists over how the government selects scientific knowledge or how it frames that knowledge to support its legislative argumentation when submitting a bill to Parliament.

Yet the government does selectively use scientific knowledge that supports its policy objectives.[70] In the case of the construction of a floating

[66] Conseil constitutionnel, Decision No 2018-768 QPC of 21 March 2019, *M. Adama S.*

[67] Fercot (n 23) 105.

[68] DC Conseil constitutionnel, Decision No 2023-1066 QPC of 27 October 2023, *Association Meuse Nature Environnement et autres* (France) [Association Meuse Nature Environment and Others].

[69] S Nutley, I Walter and H Davies, *Using Evidence: How Research Can Inform Public Services* (Policy Press 2007) 7. "The term 'evidence' is broader still and signifies any facts or information used to make decisions"

[70] Their motivations carry an inherent risk of selectively using evidence to suit predetermined outcomes, leading to what has been described as "the arbitrary cherry-picking of evidence" or "policy-based evidence gathering". See A Sharman and J Holmes, 'Evidence-Based Policy or Policy-Based Evidence Gathering? Biofuels, the EU, and the 10% Target' (2010) 20(5) *Environmental Policy and Governance* 309.

LNG terminal, for instance, its assessment of environmental impact mitigation omits any mention of the American origin of the LNG, 80% of which is derived from shale gas—whose extraction and import has been banned in France since 2011 due to its highly polluting nature. The government also fails to account for the carbon cost of transatlantic transportation, as well as the extraction and processing phases. It falls to the referring members of Parliament to introduce these scientific elements into the debate, thereby fully informing parliamentary deliberations and attempting to influence the outcome of the vote. By excluding these calculable scientific factors, the government avoids having to justify, for example, why between 2021 and 2022, the U.S. share of the French LNG import market rose from 22% to 48%, even though the decline in imports from Russia was not the only significant change. Similar reductions were seen in long-standing trade partners such as Algeria (from 25% to 12%) and Nigeria (from 18% to 4%). The government makes no effort to justify its political choices with quantitative evidence.

In the law concerning the rescue of the sugar beet sector, the government's justification relied on demonstrating that the adopted measure was the least harmful option. In response, the referring deputies highlighted serious shortcomings and clear inaccuracies in the impact assessment. The senators, in particular, presented scientific data contradicting the government's reasoning, citing peer-reviewed scientific studies and expert opinions from CNRS researchers. They pointed to a "convergence of scientific studies." This constituted a clash of arguments, in which scientific data were deployed as persuasive tools that the Senate, through its referral to the Constitutional Council, attempted to transform into constitutional constraints. To that end, they invoked the precautionary principle. However, the government responded that the precautionary principle applies only in cases of scientific uncertainty. Since, in its view, there was scientific certainty regarding the environmental harm caused by neonicotinoids, the principle did not apply. As such, the matter was cast as a political choice falling exclusively within the government's discretion. In this case, scientific justification served primarily to bypass the only legal tool capable of asserting scientific rationality over political rationality.

Similarly, members of Parliament identified serious misinterpretations of scientific data in the government's justification of the law. As previously noted, the decision to use seed coating rather than spraying was based on incomplete data. Coating is a preventive—and therefore systematic—treatment, whereas spraying is curative and occasional. From the deputies' perspective, the former actually increases the risk and, as already highlighted, contaminates the soil for up to twenty years. In their response to the government's written observations, the deputies argued that the government relied on a general opinion by ANSES concerning the methodology for evaluating phytopharmaceutical products, rather than on a specific assessment of neonicotinoids. In addition, they demonstrated that the government had fundamentally misinterpreted EFSA's February 2018 findings—ironically, the very conclusions that led to the EU-wide ban on the use of neonicotinoids as seed coatings.

The nature of the crisis does not prompt a shift in the standards of justification. The climate crisis—global and long-term—does not require laws addressing it to be grounded in the well-established scientific consensus. The climate crisis and emergency do not give rise to new obligations in terms of rational legislative justification. On the contrary, when scientific bodies such as the High Council on Climate issue assessments contradicting the ambitions of legislation aimed at reducing greenhouse gas emissions, the government is under no legal obligation to align its legislative agenda with the more accelerated pace of reform recommended by those experts. And yet, in the Grande-Synthe ruling, the Conseil d'État relied on these very studies to order the government to adopt additional measures to meet the Paris Agreement target of a 40% reduction in GHG emissions by 2030.[71] One might be led to believe that administrative justice is more rational than constitutional justice—perhaps precisely because the former is meant to serve the general interest, while the latter is intended to uphold the will of the people, despite the evolving nature of the rule of law.[72]

Legislation is presumed to be the result of a political compromise emerging from adversarial debate, in which scientific knowledge now serves as one argument among others. In the two aforementioned decisions, the Constitutional Council maintained its usual limited review, suggesting that even informative justification—that is, the mere mention of scientific

[71] CC 2021-825 QPC Conseil constitutionnel, Decision No 2021-825 DC of 13 August 2021, *Loi portant lutte contre le dérèglement climatique et renforcement de la résilience face à ses effets* [Law on Combating Climate Change and Strengthening Resilience to Its Effects].

[72] It should be recalled that the Constitutional Council is not the judge of the general interest, unlike the administrative judge. See V. F. Rangeon, *L'idéologie de l'intérêt général* (Economica, 1986).

knowledge without adherence to it—is not required to be accurate.[73] Such an approach results in a distorted debate and a misleading adoption of the law, which continues to rest on ideological balances and misses the opportunity to appeal to greater reason. Thus, scientific reasoning behind a law serves a persuasive rather than a binding function.

7.4.2 *The Delegation of Scientific Justification to the Implementation of the Law*

In the absence of constitutional review concerning the degree of scientific rationality of legislation, a trend has emerged whereby laws are upheld precisely because they defer scientific justification to a level below the legislative. Two main pathways can be identified: delegation to administrative authorities, or to the regulatory power, often with the involvement of other actors—particularly from the economic and scientific sectors—who will assess the law's application on a case-by-case basis. The constitutionality of the law is thus made contingent upon its proper implementation by these authorities, rather than its initial legislative content.

In the 2024 decision on agricultural sovereignty, the law states that "environmental impacts must be assessed during the drafting of the ordinances,[74] in order to ensure the preservation of protected species and their habitats in the conduct of human activities." Under this law, the government is authorized to adopt ordinances modifying the criminal liability regime for certain environmental offences—that is, it may revise how such infractions are prosecuted, effectively leading to the decriminalization of some practices. As a result, scientific justification by the legislator regarding environmental impacts becomes superfluous and necessarily broad, since it is the regulatory authority that will ultimately assess the scientific situation. Once again, it is unclear whether these expert assessments will be binding on the regulatory authority. The referring deputies criticised the creation of this exceptional regime, which they believe undermines the right to an effective legal remedy. They argued that "the first option to consider [...] would be to provide the Environmental Authority with

[73] N Wagner, S Velander, L Biber-Freudenberger and T Dietz, 'Effectiveness Factors and Impacts on Policymaking of Science-Policy Interfaces in the Environmental Sustainability Context' (2023) 125 *Environmental Science & Policy* 145.

[74] The Government is authorized to adopt measures by ordinance to adapt the system of sanctions for certain environmental offences, specifically to amend—towards decriminalization—the framework for penalising such offences.

the necessary resources and staffing to process initial and modified applications,"[75] thereby suggesting the transfer of greater powers to this independent administrative authority due to its expert status.

In the decision concerning radioactive waste storage,[76] the law provides that the authorization for commissioning the storage facility must be based on a report from the National Agency for Radioactive Waste Management, an opinion from a specific commission, and an opinion from the Nuclear Safety Authority, which is transmitted to the Parliamentary Office for the Evaluation of Scientific and Technological Choices. This Office then evaluates and reports its findings to the relevant committees of the National Assembly and the Senate. The bill states that the government shall take into account the Office's recommendations when drafting the legislation on the reversibility of storage. The Nuclear Safety Authority issues the final authorization for full commissioning. In this case, the scientific component is more clearly structured and involves a greater number of independent administrative authorities. Accordingly, the Constitutional Council upheld the constitutionality of the law, considering these expert consultations to constitute part of the legal safeguards surrounding its implementation. Nevertheless, the law does not specify to what extent the government is required to follow the advice of these authorities and the Parliamentary Office. Another important point concerns the responsibility of these expert bodies, which, even if their opinions are not binding, still have the capacity to significantly influence the actions of the regulatory authority and other relevant actors.[77]

In sum, the law permits derogations to be authorized based on the perceived opportunity, assessed on a case-by-case basis.

In the case of the sugar beet law, an alternative form of deferred review by other types of authorities was chosen. The administrative authorities were tasked with issuing the authorization for the derogation based on the opinion of a monitoring committee specifically created by the law. Upon

[75] Observations of the France Insoumise—NUPES parliamentary group, Conseil constitutionnel, Decision No 2024-14 FNR of 22 April 2024, *Présentation du projet de loi d'orientation pour la souveraineté en matière agricole et le renouvellement des générations en agriculture*

[76] Conseil constitutionnel, Decision No 2024-14 FNR of 22 April 2024, *Projet de loi d'orientation pour la souveraineté en matière agricole et le renouvellement des générations en agriculture* (France) [Framework Law on Agricultural Sovereignty and Generational Renewal in Farming]

[77] L Allezard, 'La responsabilité du fait des actes de droit souple : impasse ou angle-mort du contentieux administratif?' (2022) *Revue française de droit administratif* 259–270.

examining the composition of this committee, it becomes clear that it is made up of representatives of the interests at stake—namely, the sugar industry—alongside elected officials and experts. It is therefore not a body of scientific expertise, but a mixed entity intended to reduce the debate to a group representative of the competing interests. Scientific argumentation carries no greater weight than other types of considerations. Moreover, there are no established rules regarding the procedures for debate, drafting, or the adoption of the committee's opinion. The debate, initially held in Parliament, is shifted to a case-by-case basis within a non-transparent structure. As the referring deputies noted in response to the government, the opinion of this monitoring committee "in no way constitutes a deontological or scientific safeguard comparable to the public opinion of ANSES, which this mechanism replaces with respect to derogations." A legislative justification that relies on delegating the responsibility of scientific assessment to administrative authorities thus creates legal uncertainty—subject to the proper discretion of those authorities, with limited avenues for appeal, often only available after the decision has been made and potential harm has already occurred.

This choice has scientific merit. Such a mechanism of shifting review to the regulatory level ostensibly offers flexibility proportionate to the evolving nature of scientific knowledge. The idea is no longer to consult regulatory authorities solely at the upstream stage to legitimise a definitive legislative choice, but rather to render that choice more adaptable over time, with regulatory bodies serving as safeguards throughout the process. The constitutionality of the law is thus conditioned on this delegation, justified either by these authorities' scientific expertise or by their capacity to reach a compromise acceptable to stakeholders. However, it must be noted that the responsibility and accountability of such authorities remain ill-defined, which does not fully secure their discretionary decisions.

Nonetheless, this logic is not applied consistently. In the 2025 decision, certain provisions of the challenged law stated that political actors must refrain from "prohibiting the use of phytopharmaceutical products authorized by the EU." The referring deputies argued that this provision preemptively removes the discretion of administrative authorities to "draw the logical consequences from advancements in scientific knowledge regarding the health or environmental risks of a given phytopharmaceutical product." In doing so, they claimed, the provision effectively nullifies the precautionary principle. Yet the Constitutional Council did not find this to be unconstitutional. In short, in this case, the delegation of scientific justification to the administrative authority was simply and entirely revoked, as the law expressly prohibited any scientific justification and merely aligned itself with EU law.

Ultimately, the only rational and reassuring development made by the Constitutional Council regarding the legislature's duty to justify a law concerns the limitation of the law's impact. Since the decision on sugar beet cultivation, the Council has exercised review over the justification of such measures through three sets of safeguards. First, any derogation from environmental protection must be time-limited—even though, in this particular case, the duration of soil pollution casts doubt on the effectiveness of that time limit. Second, the derogation may only be implemented under specific conditions. Third, the final safeguard concerns the conditions governing the use of the products in question. These conditions, which constitute the core of these safeguards, are assessed on a case-by-case basis by the administrative authority responsible for implementing the derogation, and ultimately, where competent, by the administrative courts. In sum, constitutional law does not ensure the systematic scientific justification of derogations.

7.5 Conclusion: A Need for a Structural Turn

In France, the justification of legislation serves an informative role and, at best, a persuasive one—intended to influence parliamentary debate and voting. In a theoretical perspective, the question of conformity with scientific knowledge thus remains a matter of legitimacy, not legality—a political rather than legal issue. The French legal tradition, grounded in positivism, continues to maintain a clear separation between positive law and factual elements, even in a context that increasingly calls for bridging that gap. In this respect, it follows the logic of the CJEU, which holds that national courts may not substitute their own assessment of scientific facts for that of the competent authorities.[78]

Yet, particularly in the context of the climate crisis and with recent developments at the ECtHR, we are witnessing a new potential shift

[78] *Court of Justice of the European Union*, *Pesticide Action Network Europe v College voor de toelating van gewasbeschermingsmiddelen en biociden* [2024] EU:C:2024:350 (*PAN Europe v College*), joined cases C-308/22 and C-316/24 P, judgment of 25 April 2024.

from legitimacy derived solely from parliamentary vote toward "alternative"[79] forms that incorporate greater scientific rationality—a shift that, in effect, "places legitimacy within legality."[80] And the constitutional courts are today the only tipping point at which legislative justification could shift from a tool of legitimation and persuasion to one of constraint. But, the Constitutional council stays in line with its "proclaimed and asserted self-restraint," and avoids "the danger" of being seen as a "third chamber."[81] A constitutional judge who demands a higher degree of justification from the legislature inevitably "puts their own legitimacy at stake and must endure the scrutiny of *droit savant*."[82] Yet, despite this sword of Damocles, this posture is gradually evolving among national courts.[83] In 2020, the Chief Justice of the Irish Supreme Court stated, in a landmark climate litigation case, that what once belonged to the political realm now falls within the domain of law.[84] This marks a key development: the shift of climate and environmental governance from the political sphere to the legal one. However, this move toward the legal constraint of rationalization is not without difficulty. The Czech example is particularly instructive in this regard.

The Czech Constitutional Court has developed its own doctrine by systematically applying a "rationality review" whenever scientific elements are invoked to justify restrictions on fundamental rights and freedoms.[85] In striking down such restrictions in the context of the COVID-19 pandemic, the Court explicitly affirmed the necessity of providing "sufficiently

[79] P Popelier, 'Le droit constitutionnel en contexte' (2013) 70 *Revue interdisciplinaire d'études juridiques*149

[80] Truchet (n 35)6.

[81] Merland n(34) quotes Doyen Roussillon

[82] Salles n(58)

[83] Neubauer et al. v Germany [2021] BVerfG, 1 BvR 2656/18, 24 March 2021; 2020Hun-Ma389 et al. (consolidated), Constitutional Court of Korea, 29 August 2024

[84] Supreme Court of Ireland, *Friends of the Irish Environment CLG v. The Government of Ireland, Ireland and the Attorney General*, Appeal No: 205/19, 31 July 2020: "I also conclude that the issues are justiciable and do not amount to an impermissible impingement by the courts into areas of policy. What might once have been policy has become law by virtue of the enactment of the 2015 Act."

[85] Zdeněk Červínek, 'Proportionality or Rationality in Socio-Economic Rights Adjudication? Case Study of the Czech Constitutional Court's Judgment in Compulsory Vaccination Case' [2018] Social Science Research Network. This practice closely echoes an approach developed outside Europe, as the South African Constitutional Court exercises a 'reasonableness' review of legislation. See Constitutional Court of South Africa, *Government of the Republic of South Africa and Others v Grootboom and Others*(CCT 11/00, 4 October 2000).

rational grounds" to legitimise such measures in the eyes of the public.[86] In doing so, it rejected the traditional idea that authority alone confers legitimacy, asserting instead that legitimacy now derives from knowledge. The Czech Constitutional Court thus pits a culture of justification against a culture of authority.[87] However, this doctrinal shift has not been accepted among the Czech constitutional judges themselves, with some viewing this form of review as overly activist.[88]

If we approach the issue faced by constitutional courts from the opposite direction, the question becomes: where should the legitimacy of legislation—and its possible evolutions—be situated? Should it lie in its justification in accordance with scientific reality, or in the origin of its production and the mechanisms of its control? Within the current constitutional structure, treating scientific fact as a binding element for the justification and validity of legislation may still be considered illegitimate—and indeed, remains subject to criticism. A lasting shift toward greater judicial power in this regard appears unattainable. The resolution to this legitimacy paradox may thus lie not in a silent shift in the distribution of competences, but in the evolution of the constitutional structure itself. In the current framework, neither the government, the legislature, nor the judiciary possesses sufficient control over scientific facts, nor the legitimacy to claim authority over them. The French approach, which reduces scientific facts to a matter of political discretion, amounts either to an abdication or a resignation in the face of complexity. In the end, since no institutional actor holds the required expertise, it is left to the people, through their representatives, to make the choice.[89]

It appears, however, that the debate on this issue is fundamentally flawed. As shown throughout this chapter, the role of the Constitutional Council in the context of the environmental and climate crisis is not to

[86] Constitutional Court of the Czech Republic, Decision Pl. ÚS 106/20 of 9 February 2021, §94. See on this P Ondřejek, 'Threshold of Justification of Emergency Regulations: On Coherentism Requirement for the Justification of Measures Adopted in the Czech Republic during the COVID-19 Pandemic' [2021] Archiwum Filozofii Prawa i Filozofii Społecznej 42.

[87] Ibid, 49

[88] See dissending opinion Jaroslaw Fenyk and Josef Friala in Decision Pl. ÚS 106/20 of 9 February 2021.

[89] See the legitimacy of the production and use of evidence should be understood as a process that science and politics build upon mutually. Kano, H., & Hayashi, T. I. (2021). A framework for implementing evidence in policymaking: Perspectives and phases of evidence evaluation in the science-policy interaction. *Environmental Science and Policy, 116*, 86–95.

interpret scientific facts or to substitute its own judgment for that of scientific experts, but rather to apply existing scientific consensus—whether on climate change or the well-documented harmful effects of pesticides. This is not a response to a sudden, unforeseen emergency, but to a long-term crisis that must be addressed with urgency. Moreover, it is a crisis involving issues that demand continuous and systematic legal attention. It is therefore essential not to conflate the *emergency* with the *urgency of* the crisis. In this respect, the Schmittian exceptionalist distribution of competences between the political decision-maker and the judge proves ill-suited. For all these reasons, this chapter concludes that it is now necessary to initiate a change in the constitutional structure to incorporate scientific facts as a new form of counter-power alongside existing checks and balances. Such a shift would necessarily entail a theoretical rupture within legal science itself, moving away from positivism and conditioning the validity of law not only on its formal normativity but also on its substantive justification.[90] The emerging European New Legal Realism—particularly as developed in the work of Luc J. Wintgens[91]—offers a timely and robust scientific framework that this chapter invites legal scholars to explore.[92]

It is therefore time to rethink the way laws are made, because we are no longer dealing with emergencies that disrupt the normal functioning of society, but with structural crises that demand a transformation of that very functioning. If legislative justification were effectively guaranteed, it could serve as a crucial safeguard against the risks posed by political alternation and the rise of climate and environmental denialism or backsliding. In this sense, it would offer a chance to overturn the grim meaning that the old saying has taken on in this context: Fiat justitia, et pereat mundus—"Let justice be done, though the world perish."

[90] Over the past three decades, the relationship between law and science has become an increasingly prominent subject of scholarly inquiry. SA Cole, 'Science, Technology, Society and Law' (2017) 13 *Annual Review of Law and Social Science* 351; DS Caudill and LH LaRue, *No Magic Wand: The Idealization of Science in Law* (Rowman & Littlefield 2006).

[91] Luc J. Wintgens, *Legisprudence: A New Theoretical Approach to Legislation* (Hart Publishing 2006).

[92] Victoria Nourse and Gregory Shaffer, "Varieties of New Legal Realism: Can a New World Order Prompt a New Legal Theory?" (2009) 95 *Cornell Law Review* 61

References

Allezard, L. "La responsabilité du fait des actes de droit souple : impasse ou angle-mort du contentieux administratif?" Revue française de droit administratif, 2022, 2, 259–270

Arendt, H. Truth and Politics. In *Between Past and Future: Eight Exercises in Political Thought*, 223–259. London: Penguin Books, 2006. First published 1967.

Caudill, D.S., and LaRue, L.H. *No Magic Wand: The Idealization of Science in Law*. Rowman & Littlefield, 2006

Červínek, Z. "Proportionality or Rationality in Socio-Economic Rights Adjudication? Case Study of the Czech Constitutional Court's Judgment in Compulsory Vaccination Case." Social Science Research Network, 2018

Chevallier, J. "Peut-on rationaliser la production du droit?" In *L'Union européenne et l'idéal de la meilleure législation*. Pedone, 2013, 17–28

Cole, S.A. "Science, Technology, Society and Law." Annual Review of Law and Social Science, 13, 2017, 351

Combrade, B-L. "L'impact limité du contrôle du Conseil constitutionnel sur l'évaluation préalable des projets de loi." JCP A, 3, 2020, 2044

Combrade, B-L. "Le Gouvernement argumente, l'étude d'impact passe (Commentaire de la décision n° 2023-13 FNR du 20 avril 2023, présentation du projet de loi relatif à la programmation militaire pour les années 2024 à 2030 et portant diverses dispositions intéressant la défense)." Revue française de droit constitutionnel, 2023, 966

Combrade, B-L. *L'obligation d'étude d'impact des projets de loi*. Dalloz, Nouvelle Bibliothèque des Thèses, 2017

Dyzenhaus, D. *The Constitution of Law: Legality in a Time of Emergency*. Cambridge University Press, 2006

Faigman, D.L. "Normative Constitutional Fact-Finding: Exploring the Empirical Component of Constitutional Interpretation." University of Pennsylvania Law Review, 139, 1991, 541–607

Faigman, D.L. *Constitutional Fictions: A Unified Theory of Constitutional Facts*. Oxford University Press, 2008

Fercot, C. "Chronique—contrôle de proportionnalité et expertise scientifique." Revue française de droit constitutionnel, 117, 2019

Fercot, C. "Données empiriques et contrôle de constitutionnalité des lois : le Conseil constitutionnel sur la réserve." Revue française d'administration publique, 173, 2020, 95–100

Kano, H., and Hayashi, T.I. "A Framework for Implementing Evidence in Policymaking: Perspectives and Phases of Evidence Evaluation in the Science-Policy Interaction." Environmental Science and Policy, 116, 2021, 86–95

Meazell, E.H. "Scientific Avoidance: Toward More Principled Judicial Review of Legislative Science." Indiana Law Journal, 84, 2008, 239–253

Merland, G. "L'intérêt général, instrument efficace de protection des droits fondamentaux?" Cahiers du Conseil constitutionnel, 16, 2004

Montalivet, P. de. "Les objectifs de valeur constitutionnelle." Cahiers du Conseil constitutionnel, 20, 2006

Montgolfier, J.F. de. "L'urgence et le Conseil constitutionnel." Les Nouveaux Cahiers du Conseil constitutionnel, 54, 2017

Nourse, V., and Shaffer, G. "Varieties of New Legal Realism: Can a New World Order Prompt a New Legal Theory?" Cornell Law Review, 95, 2009, 61

Nutley, S., Walter, I., and Davies, H. *Using Evidence: How Research Can Inform Public Services.* Policy Press, 2007

Ondřejek, P. "Threshold of Justification of Emergency Regulations: On Coherentism Requirement for the Justification of Measures Adopted in the Czech Republic during the COVID-19 Pandemic." Journal of the Polish Section of IVR, 2, 2021, 46

Perroud, T. "Les Études d'impact dans l'action publique en France : perspective critique et propositions." Politiques et Management public, 35, 2018, 215

Pieraccini, M. "The Public Interest in Environmental Decision-Making: A Pragmatist Turn." Journal of Environmental Law, 36, 2024, 363

Popelier, P. "Legislation and the Principle of Proportionality." Legisprudence, 3, 2012, 170

Rangeon, V.F. *L'idéologie de l'intérêt général.* Economica, 1986

Ribes, D. "Le réalisme du Conseil constitutionnel." Cahiers du Conseil constitutionnel, 22, 2007

Salles, S. "Le conséquentialisme dans la jurisprudence du Conseil constitutionnel." Les Nouveaux Cahiers du Conseil constitutionnel, 53, 2016, 75–80

Schmitt, C. *Political Theology: Four Chapters on the Concept of Sovereignty.* MIT Press, 1985

Sharman, A., and Holmes, J. "Evidence-Based Policy or Policy-Based Evidence Gathering? Biofuels, the EU, and the 10% Target." Environmental Policy and Governance, 20(5), 2010, 309

Truchet, D. "La notion d'intérêt général: le point de vue d'un professeur de droit." Légicom: Revue du droit de la communication des entreprises et de la communication publique, 2017, 5–11

Wagner, N., Velander, S., Biber Freudenberger, L., and Dietz, T. "Effectiveness Factors and Impacts on Policymaking of Science Policy Interfaces in the Environmental Sustainability Context." Environmental Science & Policy, 125, 2023, 145

Weber, M. *Économie et société, vol.* 1. Plon, 1971

Wintgens, L.J. *Legality and Legitimacy: Normative Aspects of Public Law.* Ashgate, 2002

PART III

Crisis and Emergency in Multilevel and Consociational Constitutional Orders

CHAPTER 8

Emergency Constitutionalism, Federalism, and Pluralism

Francesco Palermo

8.1 Emergencies and Threats to Constitutions

Emergency is the Constitution's worst enemy. Whether constitutions explicitly regulate emergency powers or not,[1] when critical situations occur, the overall trends are always the same: fundamental rights are limited and a centralization of power takes place, both horizontally (from parliaments to governments)[2] and vertically (from the subnational to the central level).[3] All that can, of course, happen to different degrees, for longer or shorter periods of time, with heavy or limited stress on the system

This chapter is produced as part and funded by the European Union-NextGenerationEU, through the National Recovery and Resilience Plan of the Republic of Bulgaria, project No bg-rrp-2.004-0008. The paper is also one of the products of the PRIN2022 Project "Swinging Peripheries and Centers in Europe (SPACE): Comparative Legal Dimensions of Territory", CUP B53D23010910006.

[1] Elliot Bulmer, 'Emergency Powers' (2018) International IDEA Constitution-Building Primer 18, https://www.idea.int/publications/catalogue/emergency-powers.

[2] Tom Ginsburg and Mila Versteeg, 'The bound executive: Emergency powers during the pandemic' (2021) 19 I•CON 5, 1498.

[3] Nico Steytler (ed.), *Comparative Federalism and COVID-19. Combating the Pandemic* (Routledge 2022).

M. Belov (ed.), *Constitutional Polycrisis and Emergency Constitutionalism*, Federalism and Internal Conflicts,
https://doi.org/10.1007/978-3-032-06516-2_8

of the sources of law, but it happens.[4] Lately, this is happening all the more frequently, presenting a multiple, concentric threat to the rule of law, also due to the growing democratic discontent produced by such polycrisis.[5]

The pandemic made the threats inherent in every emergency situation more visible to a broader audience. Constitutions were generally ill-prepared to face the unexpected and unprecedented challenge posed by COVID-19, just as most health care systems were. And like health care systems, also constitutions need some adjustment after the pandemic to better cope with similar challenges in the future. Unlike private law, where the instrument of insurance exists to help protect against damages resulting from the realization of the anticipated risk, public law has entrusted the definition of situations dangerous to the system and the means of dealing with them to the interpretation (sometimes to mere common sense) developed by institutions, and only recently has begun to create autonomous instruments of risk regulation with the aim of mitigating adverse effects.[6]

As Carl J. Friedrich put it, "there is no object in arguing against such emergency powers on the ground that they endanger the constitutional morale, and hence the maintenance of the constitutional order".[7] For this reason, the Venice Commission reminds that "*de facto* state of emergency should be avoided, and emergency rule should be officially declared",[8] as normally they provide some safeguards against abuses, like the preservation of certain rights and the upholding of democratic procedures. In democratic societies, the divide between acceptable and intolerable emergency interventions rests in the preservation of the rule of law, in the first place of judicial review, and of pluralism. The regulation and the use of emergency powers, and more generally the management of crises, can therefore serve as an indicator of democratic functioning or decay.[9]

[4] Cosmin Cercel, Gian Giacomo Fusco and Simon Lavis (eds.), *States of Exception. Law, History, Theory* (Routledge 2021).

[5] Martin Belov, 'Rule of Law in Europe in Times of Constitutional Polycrisis, Constitutional Polytransition and Democratic Discontent' (2023) 3 Diritto pubblico comparato ed europeo, 875.

[6] Richard A. Posner, *Catastrophe. Risk and Response* (Oxford University Press 2004).

[7] Carl J. Friedrich, *Constitutional government and democracy: Theory and practice in Europe and America* (Ginn 1950) 595–596.

[8] Venice Commission (European Commission for Democracy through Law), 'Emergency Powers', CDL-STD(1995) 012, 1995, www.venice.coe.int/webforms/documents/default.aspx?pdffile=CDLSTD(1995)012-e, 6.

[9] Pasquale Pasquino, 'Emergency Powers' (2023) Elgar Encyclopedia of Comparative Law, 3–10.

All constitutions tend to be (some more, some less) "good weather constitutions" (*Schönwetter-Verfassungen*, as the Weimar constitution was called to indicate that it was working well in ordinary times but was unfit to face crises). The challenge is to better prepare them in order to tame the adverse effects of emergency conditions, be they a pandemic, terrorism, economic turmoil, the balance between mass migration and fundamental rights, secession, climate change, the populist challenge, or geopolitical tensions. All that has already popped up in the first quarter of the new millennium, challenging the constitutional order, and is likely to spill over in the future. Shall we conclude that constitutions are simply overstressed and accept that this can happen and just hope for the best, or shall we acknowledge that the historical *raison d'être* of constitutionalism is to, step by step, constitutionalize phenomena that were previously in the exclusive realm of politics, progressively subjugating them to legal (more: constitutional) regulations? If so, there is a lot of work ahead in order to reinforce the banks of the river and to avoid floods in case of bad weather.

Unfortunately, a couple of years down the road from the pandemic, very few constitutions have been amended with regard to the exercise of emergency powers. And in the few cases in which that happened, the checks and balances have generally been reduced rather than expanded. This is in the first place the case of authoritarian regimes, such as the Russian Federation, where the law on emergencies from 2001 has not been used during the main emergencies that affected the country since its adoption (the second Cechen war and the COVID-19 pandemic) as it provides for some balances and controls, and the authoritarian regime did not want to be bound in any respect.[10] At the same time, a constitutional reform significantly increasing the President's powers (and duration of mandate) has been adopted in the midst of the pandemic, in 2020.[11] But the phenomenon is to some extent also noticeable in democratic contexts, such as Finland, where Article 23 of the Constitution was amended in 2022 to strengthen the Government's powers in cases of emergency.[12] In Germany, a constitutional reform has been adopted in late 2024 in order to improve the resilience of the Federal Constitutional Court avoiding

[10] Alexander N. Domrin, *The limits of Russian Democratisation: Emergency powers and states of emergency* (Routledge 2006).

[11] Derek Hutcheson and Ian McAllister, 'Consolidating the Putin Regime: The 2020 Referendum on Russia's Constitutional Amendments' (2021) 6:3 Russian Politics, 362.

[12] Mikko Värttö, 'Parliamentary oversight of emergency measures and policies: A safeguard of democracy during a crisis?' (2024) 10:1 European Policy Analysis, 84.

that a populist qualified minority can torpedo the functioning of the most significant body for constitutional protection: while this is an appropriate move in the right direction, it is simply prompted by the fear that an extremist party might influence the appointment of federal constitutional judges.[13] In general, nowhere has a regulatory shift taken place from an emergency approach to a risk management and regulation paradigm.

One of the constitutional areas more severely affected by emergencies in general, and by the COVID-19 pandemic in particular, is that of the vertical division of powers. Fighting a pandemic requires quick and coordinated action. The reason why horizontal and vertical centralization happens is that national governments are better suited to take such action. This is what has happened everywhere. In such a context, deconcentration of powers has a hard time, and the political (often also academic) narrative around the asserted inefficiency of a territorial division of powers in emergency situations gained momentum in many countries. Why have separate health care systems, with different authorities introducing potentially different regulations? How is it acceptable to come up with different solutions in different parts of the territory if people in the same country are "all in the same boat?" How is it even thinkable that the protection of rights, including the more existential one, the right to life, can vary based on the territory where people live? More levels of government mean negotiation and dialog: why bother with that in times of crisis? Isn't a centralized, unitary response much more effective after all? Such criticism has been voiced not only in countries where the "federal spirit,"[14] that is, a rooted culture, tradition and acceptance of federalism is lacking, but also where it is undoubtedly present. In the United States, in the midst of the pandemic, the (not particularly refined) expression by a Californian scholar, Jonathan Zasloff, that "federalism is for suckers"[15] has become quite popular, including in the media.

This paper contends that the opposite is true, and it is precisely an effective vertical division of powers that can help better protect constitutions and the fundamental rights they provide for, by guaranteeing the

[13] Simon Willaschek, 'Das Resilienzrisiko: Zur geplanten Einführung eines Ersatzwahlmechanismus für Verfassungsrichter*innen ohne rechtliche Absicherung des Zweidrittelquorums' (2024) 11/12 VerfBlog, 1.

[14] Michael Burgess, *In Search of the Federal Spirit* (Oxford University Press 2012).

[15] Jonathan Zasloff, 'Federalism is for Suckers' (2020) LegalPlanet, https://legal-planet.org/2020/04/20/federalism-is-for-suckers/.

efficiency of the response to emergencies. Furthermore, as control by the sole political institutions might not be sufficient to face the abuse of (emergency) powers prompted by (poly)crises, it is argued that participatory tools can be a powerful instrument to deconcentrate power and to increase democratic legitimacy of decision-making.

8.2 What Is Different in Federal Systems?

Important studies have shown that, in the first place, the territorial setup of a country is just one of many variables that might determine the response to an emergency.[16] Not only factors such as demography, geography, living conditions, etc.,[17] but also legal and institutional elements such as the form of government, the (pervasiveness of) judicial review, the administrative structure, the civil protection system, profoundly influence the capacity of different countries (and territories) to tackle emergencies[18] more than the territorial organization. Even if federalism was to blame for poor action against emergencies, criticism should remain within limits, as many other factors play a role in determining the effectiveness or inefficiency of responses. However, the prejudiced approach to federalism might sometimes lead to confusing the level of the analysis and thus to wrong conclusions: for instance, since 7 of the 10 most populous states in the world are federal, one may be superficially led to believe that in the pandemic the territorial layout affects infections when the issue is the number (and territorial concentration) of inhabitants, and the quality of the health systems.

Secondly, when it comes to the regulation of emergencies, every country, including federal or highly decentralized ones, has sufficient means to concentrate powers in case of unexpected events, thus avoiding inconsistent

[16] Nico Steytler (n 3); Arianna Vedaschi, Chiara Graziani, 'Post-Pandemic Constitutionalism: COVID-19 as a Game-Changer for "Common Principles"?' (2022) 44:4 University of Pennsylvania Journal of International Law, 815; Arianna Vedaschi (ed.), *Governmental Policies to Fight Pandemic* (Brill/Nijhoff 2024).

[17] David Cameron, 'The Relative Performance of Federal and Non-federal Countries During the Pandemic' (2021) Forum of Federations, Occasional Paper no. 50 https://forumfed.org/document/the-relative-performance-of-federal-and-non-federal-countries-during-the-pandemic-number-50/.

[18] Angelo Jr Golia, Laura Hering, Carolyn Moser and Tom Sparks, 'Constitutions and Contagion. European Constitutional Systems and the COVID-19 Pandemic' (2020) Max Plank MPIL Research Paper Series no. 42.

regulations and uncoordinated action.[19] This is done through explicit rules for each different degree of emergency: such rules are either provided for in the constitution (the most interesting example in this regard is probably the Spanish constitution, where Article 116 provides for three different degrees of emergency actionable by the central government under the control of and for the duration set by the parliament, allowing for a temporary centralization of powers), or in sectoral disciplines. For example, in Germany, although the possibility of operating a parallel constitution for the state of defence is provided for at the constitutional level (Art. 115a-l Basic Law), the pandemic was tackled through a sectoral ordinary law, the Infection Act, which provides the federal government with the tools to coordinate the actions of the *Länder* and impose actions derogatory to the division of powers among levels of government; the Infection Act has been amended during and after the pandemic to make it more efficient, increasing the coordinating power in the hands of the federal government while granting that the latter cannot interfere from the top down with the powers of the *Länder*.

While the effect of power concentration in the hands of the central government is similar between federal and non-federal countries, a fundamental qualitative difference is represented by the decision-making level. Normally, in federal systems, centralization for emergency reasons is agreed upon and decided by the subnational actors, who provisionally transfer certain powers to the center for the sake of coordination and efficiency (see further the chapter by Sören Keil in this volume). To the contrary, in decentralized but not federal countries, the centralization of subnational powers is typically decided by the center, normally without an effective involvement of the subnational entities.

Third, emergencies in general and the pandemic in particular, boost the theory of federalism as a laboratory. In a number of countries, including in particular the US and Brazil,[20] the inaction at the federal level has been countered by the proactiveness of several subnational entities. In Brazil, in the first months of the pandemic, the governors in 24 of the 27 states rebelled against then-President Bolsonaro and refused to lift the restrictions, constructively proposing a list of coordinated measures to fight the

[19] Oren Gross, 'Constitutions and Emergency Regimes', in Tom Ginsburg and Rosalind Dixon (eds), *Comparative Constitutional Law* (Edgar Elgar 2011), 334.

[20] Daniel Béland, Philip Rocco, Catarina Ianni Segatto and Alex Waddan, 'Trump, Bolsonaro, and the framing of the COVID-19 crisis: How political institutions shaped presidential strategies' (2021) 184:4 World Affairs, 413.

pandemic.[21] In response, the President issued a provisional act to enlarge his powers. In Mexico, too, governors have used their relative autonomy as a defence mechanism against the federal government, which has been reluctant, at least initially, to take decisive measures to contain the spread of the disease.

8.3 Federalism, States of Emergency, and Exceptions Confirming the Rule

Most importantly, the comparative practice of the fight against the pandemic (a more general observation with regard to other emergencies would require a wider and deeper analysis, although likely leading to similar results) tells that in federal systems (those that call themselves federal, therefore showing a stronger and shared federal culture), resort to the state of emergency is much rarer than in unitary systems or in those with non-federal decentralization. Federal systems that during the pandemic have resorted to the declaration of a state of emergency at the federal level have been only Ethiopia (which, however, was in an emergency situation for reasons other than combating the pandemic, with the Tigray crisis and armed intervention in the fall of 2020), South Africa (which is unanimously considered a federal state, but it should be remembered that it does not define itself as such in its constitution), Mexico, and, as of January 2021, Malaysia. In Argentina, the state of emergency was already in place (as of 2019) at the time of the pandemic outbreak, to deal with the economic crisis.

In the other federal countries, the pandemic has been managed with ordinary tools, which allow for the centralization of functions under the federal executive, but without the need to resort to a national state of emergency, using sector legislation and therefore without disrupting the powers of subnational entities. Not even in the face of the devastating resurgence of the virus in spring 2021 did countries such as India and Nepal resort to these instruments. Nor have Germany, Austria, Belgium, Switzerland, Brazil, Russia, Pakistan, or others. The intensity of the centralization of emergency management in the federal executive varied, of course, among different jurisdictions, even according to the degree of

[21] Emilio Peluso Neder Meyer and Thomas Bustamante, 'Authoritarianism Without Emergency Powers: Brazil Under COVID-19' (2020) VerfBlog 4/08 https://verfassungsblog.de/authoritarianism-without-emergency-powers-brazil-under-covid-19/.

already existing centralization of the system (like in the aforementioned Russian case), as does the degree of conflict between the national government and the federated entities. However, from a constitutional point of view, it seems highly significant that federal systems, on the one hand, do not preclude centralization of the line of command, and on the other hand allow this to take place through ordinary procedures, without derogating from the constitutional order.

In this regard, the cases of the U.S. and Canada are interesting exceptions confirming the rule of a more limited range (and more limited potential damage) of national states of emergency in federal systems as opposed to non-federal ones. In the United States, a national emergency was declared in March 2020 under Sections 201 and 202 of the National Emergencies Act (later extended by then-President Biden to February 2021), which grants special powers to the president but does not alter the constitutionally mandated division of powers, nor can it do so, merely assigning coordination functions of an extraordinary nature in the head of the president with regard to the activities of federal institutions and agencies. Thus, it was not even possible to regulate at the federal level the obligation (or not) to wear masks, because the matter remains in the jurisdiction of the states, and the declaration of national emergency had the sole effect of reorganizing the functions of the entities operating in the federal sphere. As it has been rightly pointed out, "the slow U.S. response was not due to constitutional infirmities of federalism but to party polarization and lack of preparation."[22]

Furthermore, the attitude of then-President Trump to deny the pandemic and to refuse to take stronger measures may have strengthened the position of the states as a counterbalance to the federal power.[23] Similarly, in Australia, in the absence of a constitutional emergency provision, "responding to the emergency created by the pandemic was merely another application of the federal division of power" and "most of the subnational governments invoked general emergency powers under legislation, while emergency powers invoked by the center dealt only with matters within its direct control."[24]

[22] John Kincaid and J. Wesley Leckrone, 'Federalism and the C-19 Crisis in the Unites States of America' (2020) Forum of Federations http://forumfed.org/2020/04/john-kincaid-and-j-wesley-leckrone-federalism-and-covid-19/.

[23] David Cameron (n 17).

[24] Cheryl Saunders, 'How Federations Responded to COVID-19' (2021) 7 Constitutional INSIGHTS, 4.

Even more interesting for the purpose of this study is the case of Canada.[25] In February 2022, the Emergency Act (1988) was first used to address protests due to COVID-19 restrictions. Protests started after the Public Health Agency of Canada announced that, as of January 15, 2022, certain groups of foreign nationals, who had previously been exempted from the vaccination requirement for entry into Canada, would be required to be fully vaccinated and that unvaccinated Canadian truck drivers would not be denied entry into the country, but would have to meet strict requirements. Following these measures, a group of individuals prepared to travel across Canada to protest in Ottawa under the slogan "Freedom Convoy 2022." On February 14th, 2022, a Public Order Emergency was proclaimed under the Emergency Act (EA) to deal with the repercussions of the Freedom Convoy, and then revoked just one week later, on February 23rd, 2022. The EA's invocation was consequently challenged before the Federal Court, a national trial court based in Ottawa that adjudicates legal disputes arising in federal jurisdiction. In January 2024, the Federal Court issued an important decision (2024 FC 42) based on a number of criteria. The most relevant one for our purposes involves issues about federalism. The judges accepted the claim brought by the province of Alberta that the executive "has to respect the principles of federalism" (para. 227) and that "federal disagreement with provincial decisions not to exercise particular powers is not a sufficient basis to conclude that the situation exceeded the capacity or authority of the provinces or could not be effectively dealt with under existing law" (para. 234). Inaction by the provinces does not imply incapacity, so the executive cannot invoke the EA "because it is convenient, or because it may work better than other tools at their disposal or available to the provinces" (para. 253).

While the case will be finally adjudicated by the Supreme Court, the wording of the Federal Court is extremely telling about the understanding and the interpretation of the principle of federalism as a strong limitation to the use of emergency powers.

It can be concluded that federal structures not only do not pose a legal hurdle when certain urgent decisions have to be made with the overarching purpose of protecting public health and national security. More importantly, despite the significant differences among federal systems in terms of allocation of powers, distribution of financial resources and rules

[25] Nicola Abate, 'The emergence of emergency in Canada: What can democratic institutions do?' (2024) Diritti comparati, 1.

on coordination,[26] While it is always possible to streamline procedures and to shorten the line of command in exceptional cases, in federal systems, this tends to be possible in a more regular way rather than derogating from the constitutional order. Furthermore, it follows that federalism is, at least in principle, a tool that tends to better safeguard the constitutional order as it is and ought to be and to make it more resistant against (ab)use of emergency powers stripping subnational actors of their constitutional role in a multilevel system.

8.4 Federalism and Pluralism

8.4.1 The Challenge of Participation

Not only does federalism overall promote the use of ordinary instruments in crisis situations, but it also supports the preservation of the rule of law. It also creates a more favorable environment for pluralism (next to the rule of law, the other cornerstone of constitutionalism) as it supports participation of a broader range of actors in decision-making and thus increases the legitimacy of decisions, which is key in moments of crisis.

One of the most significant challenges faced by contemporary constitutionalism is how to combine pluralism with good and effective governance. Put differently: how is it possible to make decisions in a manner that is democratic, transparent, inclusive, and effective, taking into account different claims, different interests, and different legitimacies? Growing complexity is simply part of the natural and inevitable evolution of contemporary societies; consequently, institutions and procedures must become increasingly articulated and sophisticated. In plain words, contemporary constitutionalism requires much more elaborate rules than in the past in order to continue to be legitimate.[27]

In recent times, frustration with regard to the lack of effective participation through representative bodies and the structural limits of direct democracy created what can be described as a "dam effect:" like a river blocked by a dam, the water tends to flow in alternative, often unnatural ways. Therefore, alternative channels need to be built in order not to

[26] Rupak Chattopadhyay et al (eds), *Federalism and the Response to COVID-19. A Comparative Analysis* (Routledge 2022); Cheryl Saunders (n 24).

[27] See already the pioneering work by Carole Pateman, *Participation and Democratic Theory* (Cambridge University Press 1970).

waste the water; such a dispersion not only dissipates the water with all its negative consequences, but also makes the dam itself rather useless, and the decision-making process is frequently blocked. Contemporary democracies cannot pretend that the dam does not exist, nor can they claim that it will be destroyed by the flooding water. Rather, they are tasked with the challenge of developing effective alternative channels for the water and making the best use of the water trapped by the dam.

Starting in the 1980s and accelerating in more recent years, especially at the local level, several spontaneous practices have been initiated in order to overcome some of the structural deficits of classical decision-making.[28] The different forms of such experimental practices and instruments have commonly been classified by scholars into two main groups: participatory and deliberative democracy,[29] although some also include a third genus, associative democracy.[30] Rather than engaging in terminological and definitional issues, it seems more useful to consider deliberative and participatory exercises as a common phenomenon, aiming at complementing (rather than substituting) the classical forms of representative and direct democracy. In essence, what matters is the development of complementary forms that are trying to overcome, or at least to integrate and dilute, the main feature common to both representative and direct democracy: the majority principle. Participatory and deliberative democracy (which can be labelled as alternative or complementary decision-making tools) aim at expanding the number of involved actors, anticipating and preventing conflicts, as well as including relevant stakeholders and collective knowledge as early as possible in the decision-making process. The aim is to avoid, prevent, or at least prepare, to the extent possible, majority decisions, and, consequently, to limit opposition to the decision eventually taken by absorbing such opposition at the earliest possible stage, thereby establishing a more pluralistic and participative decisional process.[31]

[28] Graham Smith, *Democratic Innovations. Designing Institutions for Citizen Participation* (Cambridge University Press, 2010).

[29] Jürg Steiner, *The Foundations of Deliberative Democracy: Empirical research and normative implications* (Cambridge University Press, 2012).

[30] Paul Hirst, *Associative Democracy* (Cambridge University Press, 1995).

[31] Martina Trettel, 'The politics of deliberative democracy. A comparative survey of the "Law in action" of citizen participation' (2015) 1(94) Revista de Derecho Político, 85.

8.4.2 *The Role of Federalism: From Government to Governance*

Why is federalism tremendously relevant for these challenges? Inevitably, federalism must address pluralism. Pluralism is, in fact, the backbone of federalism,[32] since federalism is at odds with any state organization aimed at protecting only one interest, such as the interest of the leader in autocratic states, that of the dominant denomination in religious states, that of the majority nation in nationalistic states, etc.

When the idea of federalism was first born, it was a philosophical approach to political organization, serving essentially economic and military purposes.[33] In legal terms, the early idea of federalism was closer to international rather than constitutional law, aimed at bringing together sovereign units that alone were no longer competitive in economic and military terms; this has been the case for historic federations, notably, the U.S., Switzerland, and Germany.

The more federal states established themselves (nineteenth century) and significantly increased in number (twentieth century), the more federalism became noteworthy not only to political philosophers and political scientists, but also to constitutional lawyers and economists.[34] In the twenty-first century, the challenge is not so much the creation of new federations as the federal idea has been sufficiently explored, and new federations are rather rare. Instead, the critical test that remains is the effective management of pluralism and its inherent complexity. This is why federalism is being used in recent times predominantly to accommodate minority claims, much more than for territorial governance reasons.[35]

The main complexity challenge to the accommodation of contemporary pluralism is the claim for the participation of a number of actors that are not institutional in nature. Consequently, federalism can no longer be seen as a pure institutional interplay, a system accommodating the coexistence of institutions belonging to different tiers of government. Decision-making is now enriched by the presence of individuals or groups (interest groups, lobbies, NGOs, etc.).

[32] Nicholas Aroney, George Duke and Stephen Tierney, 'A Theory of Plural Constituent Power for Federal Systems' (2024) 13:3 Global Constitutionalism, 591.

[33] Stephen Tierney, *The Federal Contract* (Oxford University Press 2022).

[34] Thomas Hueglin and Alan Fenna, *Comparative Federalism: A Systematic Inquiry* (Broadview Press 2006), 3.

[35] Nicolò P Alessi and Martina Trettel (eds), *Federalism and the Law of Diversity. The theoretical contribution of federalism to the explanation of emergent models for the accommodation of diversity* (Brill/Nijhoff 2025).

Indeed, federalism is still an institutional principle, that is, it is a mode of organizing state structures in a way that preserves the plurality of levels of government and their decision-making autonomy. As such, it does not per se include citizens in decision-making more than other systems, even though citizens in federations are involved more often, at the very least through various levels of election. Moreover, the wider subnational and local autonomy, the more these levels of government can experiment with forms of participatory democracy. But, as such, participation is certainly a different phenomenon from federalism.

Federalism is, however, the most powerful and, thus far, the most tested tool for institutional pluralism. It addresses exactly what is at the core of all claims for a more participatory decision-making: by multiplying decisions, federalism attenuates and complements the majority principle, and thus divides powers, keeping them under control. Deciding by majority—but at different levels—fragments and limits the potential abuses of the majority principle and therefore produces a counter-majority, a pluralistic effect. For this reason, it can be argued that federalism is the oldest instrument for dividing and diffusing power, even though others have followed, such as judicial review of legislation, rigidity of constitutions, and others. Being the organizational principle that regulates government at multiple levels and actors, federalism is the most developed form of institutional pluralism. Therefore, it is the best-suited instrument to serve as a basis for developing governance theories and practices that meet the requirements of contemporary democratic pluralism. Furthermore, in its innate connection with pluralism lies the link between federalism and participatory democracy; the latter is a contemporary manifestation of the claim for pluralism, of which federalism is perhaps the oldest. In other words, federalism can be identified as the institutional side of pluralism, similarly to what participatory democracy is on the societal or even on the individual side. Both are expressions of pluralism: institutional and societal, respectively.

Federalism and its by-products (regionalism, devolution, and the like) developed at a time when the claims for pluralism were limited to the institutional sphere (government). It was neither the individual nor organized "civil society" who claimed a share in power and the right to effectively participate in decision-making, but existing institutions. Conversely, participatory forms of democracy become essential in a period when institutional pluralism is no longer sufficient; the full extent of interests in society cannot be channeled through (subnational, national, supranational) institutions and claims are therefore extended to other and more direct forms of participation, no longer necessarily mediated by institutions (governance).[36]

If the analogy is correct, it can be concluded that federalism—with its institutions, procedures, structured relations, and mechanisms for the prevention and resolution of conflicts—can provide inspiration for the development of a theory and (more importantly) procedural solutions for the growing demands for pluralist (participatory, inclusive, multilevel) democracy. The German scholar Peter Häberle once famously described regionalism as the younger brother of federalism[37]: federalism might thus have more little brothers than just regionalism, including, in particular, complementary decision-making processes. Federalism, with its history and its machinery, could be assessed in order to identify how instruments and procedures for accommodating pluralism and participation could be designed and developed. Put differently, federalism might represent one of the most relevant democratic innovations despite being quite an old and consolidated concept and toolkit, and not being normally considered in this perspective.[38]

8.5 Federalism, Pluralism, and the Fight against Exceptionalism

Recent crises, from emergencies to quests for more participatory decision-making, have revealed an overall need for most constitutions to be refined with regard to how power is managed, both in ordinary times and especially in emergency situations. In such polycrisis scenarios, constitutional law is called upon to provide instruments that safeguard the backbones of constitutionalism: democracy, the rule of law and pluralism. Federalism is one of the most significant of such instruments as it promotes (rather: forces) decision by many, which is, per se, at odds with the excessive concentration of powers (especially in vertical terms), that is, the immediate consequence of a crisis situation.

[36] Fulvio Cortese, Marco Dani and Francesco Palermo, 'Back to Government? The Pluralistic Deficit in the Decisionmaking Process and Before the Courts' (2005) 12:2 Indiana Journal of Global Legal Studies, 409.

[37] Peter Häberle, *Europäische Rechtskultur* (Suhrkamp 1997), 233.

[38] Stephen Elstub and Oliver Escobar (eds), *Handbook of Democratic Innovation and Governance* (Edward Elgar 2019).

Metaphorically, it can be argued that federalism is the grandfather of most other instruments for the constitutional management of pluralism. Federalism can be seen as the founder of a company that produces a whole set of tools that aim at managing ever more sophisticated pluralistic claims and, by doing so, safeguards constitutionalism and its values. Having become old, federalism increasingly operates through proxies, and spreads its genes through its grandsons and daughters, who have been inheriting the company. The family remains the same, and so the company's products: constitutional tools to accommodate pluralism as the backbone of constitutionalism. But the actors evolve, change, and bring with them some important elements or legacies of the progenitor while adding new features and elements and modernizing the company.

In other words, federalism is as critical as ever before in an era marked by the ever more frequent recurrence of subsequent crises, which represent a threat to constitutionalism and its founding values: rule of law, democracy and pluralism. The importance of federalism lies in its being the prototype of institutional regulation of pluralism. As a matrix, it can hardly be used in its original and traditional form, but it remains the prototype that inspires all other tools, as it has been the first one to deal with the challenges of a pluralizing society. Initially, federalism provided pluralism in an institutional way only; now it increasingly does so also with regard to societal actors. The claim, however, remains the same: accommodating different needs and interests within a unitary constitutional framework, in order to avoid an excessive concentration of power. No other constitutional tool has more potential than federalism as a conceptual and practical matrix for providing the answers required by contemporary societies, since federalism is the most consolidated and sophisticated tool for regulating institutional and procedural complexity.

This chapter has shown that, in general terms, federal culture and working federal institutions, including notably intergovernmental relations and participatory procedures, do contribute to combat the idea that in times of crisis everything should be done differently and by fewer actors. To the contrary, it should be a goal that each player can function as normally as possible, even in a crisis, and can do what they normally do (and therefore do best) as much as possible. In contrast, being shuffled around and reinvented when nerves are on edge should be avoided as much as possible. As the idea of doing things differently during crises is particularly dangerous for constitutionalism, contrasting it can be one of the great contributions of federalism to rescue constitutionalism in times of crisis. Especially considering that crises such as climate change will become the rule in the coming years and decades, the challenge will be to deal with problems in an ordinary, not extraordinary way, and to come up with solutions that are as democratically legitimate as possible, thus inclusive and participatory, so as to limit disaffection, alienation and opposition to the extent possible.

Too easy resort to (often vaguely formulated) emergency powers represents a threat to democratic systems. It creates an imbalance of power in favor of the national executive and therefore generates high costs on all levels: for society, for the economy, for institutions. As it is likely that new emergencies will continue to emerge on the planet, it is essential to strengthen the resilience of constitutions and to better regulate and limit the impact of emergency measures. Federalism not only contributes to the safeguard of pluralism, but it also helps the establishment of a culture that considers it normal to work together, also in emergency situations: among institutions and between institutions and further societal actors by means of procedures that allow broader participation in decision-making. For this reason, updating constitutions to make them more resilient in times of (quasi-)permanent crisis is essential, and so is considering the key contribution of federal instruments, including in shaping participatory processes.

The advantage of federal systems lies in the ability to centralize and differentiate as needed, and in the presence of procedures that ensure these processes in a cognizable way and through cooperation rather than imposition. It is the quality of cooperation that makes the difference between complex arrangements that have responded efficiently and those that have not. Symphonic music is different from music for solo instruments. It is more articulate, more sophisticated, more powerful. If a musician splints, her mistake is easier to cover up. And the fact that she may splint is no reason to eliminate orchestras or make the conductor play everything: musicians without a conductor may play worse, but a conductor without musicians does not play at all.

References

Abate, N. "The Emergence of Emergency in Canada: What Can Democratic Institutions Do?" *Diritti comparati*, 2024. https://www.diritticomparati.it/the-emergence-of-emergency-in-canada-what-can-democratic-institutions-do/ (last access 23 Oct 2025)

Alessi, N.P.P., and Trettel, M. (eds.). *Federalism and the Law of Diversity: The Theoretical Contribution of Federalism to the Explanation of Emergent Models for the Accommodation of Diversity*. Leiden/Boston: Brill/Nijhoff, 2025

Aroney, N., Duke, G., and Tierney, S. "A Theory of Plural Constituent Power for Federal Systems." *Global Constitutionalism*, 13:3, 2024, 591–611

Béland, D., Rocco, P., Segatto, C.I., and Waddan, A. "Trump, Bolsonaro, and the Framing of the COVID-19 Crisis: How Political Institutions Shaped Presidential Strategies." *World Affairs*, 184:4, 2021, 413–440

Belov, M. "Rule of Law in Europe in Times of Constitutional Polycrisis, Constitutional Polytransition and Democratic Discontent." *Diritto pubblico comparato ed europeo*, 3, 2023, 875–884

Bulmer, E. *Emergency Powers.* International IDEA Constitution-Building Primer 18, Stockholm, 2018. https://www.idea.int/publications/catalogue/emergency-powers (last access 23 Oct 2025)

Burgess, M. *In Search of the Federal Spirit.* Oxford University Press, Oxford, 2012

Cameron, D. *The Relative Performance of Federal and Non-Federal Countries During the Pandemic.* Forum of Federations, Occasional Paper 50, 2021. https://forumfed.org/document/the-relative-performance-of-federal-and-non-federal-countries-during-the-pandemic-number-50/ (last access 23 Oct 2025)

Cercel, C., Fusco, G.G., and Lavis, S. (eds.). *States of Exception: Law, History, Theory.* Routledge, London, 2021

Chattopadhyay, R. et al. (eds.). *Federalism and the Response to COVID-19: A Comparative Analysis.* Routledge, London, 2022

Cortese, F., Dani, M., and Palermo, F. "Back to Government? The Pluralistic Deficit in the Decisionmaking Process and Before the Courts." *Indiana Journal of Global Legal Studies*, 12:2, 2005, 409–413

Domrin, A.N. *The Limits of Russian Democratisation: Emergency Powers and States of Emergency.* Routledge, London, 2006

Elstub, S., and Escobar, O. (eds.). *Handbook of Democratic Innovation and Governance.* Edward Elgar, Cheltenham, 2019

Friedrich, C.J. *Constitutional Government and Democracy: Theory and Practice in Europe and America.* Ginn, Boston, 1950

Ginsburg, T., and Versteeg, M. "The Bound Executive: Emergency Powers During the Pandemic." *I•CON*, 19:5, 2021, 1498–1535

Golia, A. Jr, Hering, L., Moser, C., and Sparks, T. *Constitutions and Contagion: European Constitutional Systems and the Covid-19 Pandemic.* Max Planck MPIL Research Paper Series 2020/42, 2020

Gross, O. "Constitutions and Emergency Regimes." In Ginsburg, T., and Dixon, R. (eds.). *Comparative Constitutional Law.* Edward Elgar, Chaltenham, 2011, 334–355

Häberle, P. *Europäische Rechtskultur.* Suhrkamp, Frankfurt, 1997

Hirst, P. *Associative Democracy.* Cambridge University Press, Cambridge, 1995

Hueglin, T., and Fenna, A. *Comparative Federalism: A Systematic Inquiry.* Broadview Press, Toronto, 2006

Hutcheson, D., and McAllister, I. "Consolidating the Putin Regime: The 2020 Referendum on Russia's Constitutional Amendments." *Russian Politics*, 6, 2021, 362–376

Kincaid, J., and Leckrone, J.W. "Federalism and the Covid-19 Crisis in the United States of America." Forum of Federations, 2020. http://forumfed.org/2020/04/john-kincaid-and-j-wesley-leckrone-federalism-and-covid-19/ (last access 23 Oct 2025)

Pasquino, P. "Emergency Powers." *Elgar Encyclopedia of Comparative Law*, Cheltenham: Elgar, 2023

Pateman, C. *Participation and Democratic Theory*. Cambridge University Press, Cambridge, 1970

Peluso Neder Meyer, E., and Bustamante, T. "Authoritarianism Without Emergency Powers: Brazil Under COVID-19." *VerfBlog*, 8 April 2020. https://verfassungsblog.de/authoritarianism-without-emergency-powers-brazil-under-covid-19/ (last access 23 Oct 2025)

Posner, R.A. *Catastrophe: Risk and Response*. Oxford University Press, Oxford, 2004

Saunders, C. *How Federations Responded to Covid-19*. Melbourne Forum on Constitution-Building, Constitutional Insights 7, 2021

Smith, G. *Democratic Innovations: Designing Institutions for Citizen Participation*. Cambridge University Press, Cambridge, 2010

Steiner, J. *The Foundations of Deliberative Democracy: Empirical Research and Normative Implications*. Cambridge University Press, Cambridge, 2012

Steytler, N. (ed.). *Comparative Federalism and Covid-19: Combating the Pandemic*. Routledge, London, 2022

Tierney, S. *The Federal Contract*. Oxford University Press, Oxford, 2022

Trettel, M. "The Politics of Deliberative Democracy: A Comparative Survey of the 'Law in Action' of Citizen Participation." *Revista de Derecho Político*, 1:94, 2015, 85–114

Värttö, M. "Parliamentary Oversight of Emergency Measures and Policies: A Safeguard of Democracy During a Crisis?" *European Policy Analysis*, 2023, 84–100

Vedaschi, A. (ed.). *Governmental Policies to Fight Pandemic*. Brill/Nijhoff, Leiden/Boston, 2024

Vedaschi, A., and Graziani, C. "Post-Pandemic Constitutionalism: Covid-19 as a Game-Changer for 'Common Principles'?" *University of Pennsylvania Journal of International Law*, 44:4, 2022, 815–905

Venice Commission (European Commission for Democracy through Law). *Emergency Powers*, CDL-STD(1995) 012, 1995. www.venice.coe.int/webforms/documents/default.aspx?pdffile=CDLSTD(1995)012-e (last access 23 Oct 2025)

Willaschek, S. "Das Resilienzrisiko: Zur geplanten Einführung eines Ersatzwahlmechanismus für Verfassungsrichter*innen ohne rechtliche Absicherung des Zweidrittelquorums." *VerfBlog*, 12 November 2024 (last access 23 Oct 2025)

Zasloff, J. "Federalism Is for Suckers." *LegalPlanet*, 20 April 2020. https://legal-planet.org/2020/04/20/federalism-is-for-suckers/ (last access 23 Oct 2025)

CHAPTER 9

Insights on Multilevel Governance Effects on Crisis Governance During the COVID-19 Pandemic

Soeren Keil

9.1 Introduction

COVID-19 has been a challenge for all countries around the globe in 2020 and 2021—until various vaccines helped to mitigate the situation. Before that, the commonly known Coronavirus pandemic had developed from an initial health crisis in China into a global health emergency, as well as an economic crisis as a result of several lockdowns, the breakdown of global supply chains and the abrupt end of economic interconnectedness in the wake of the crisis. Moreover, in several countries, from Hungary to the Philippines, COVID-19 measures became a real threat to already fragile democratic institutions through the increased centralization of powers in the hands of the executives. While the military coups in Myanmar and Mali, amongst others, did not primarily occur because of COVID-19

This chapter is produced as part and funded by the European Union-NextGenerationEU, through the National Recovery and Resilience Plan of the Republic of Bulgaria, project No bg-rrp-2.004-0008. This project uses data and insight from the EU Horizon project LEGITIMULT, GA no. 101061550. It also benefited from funding from the Swiss Federal Department for Economic Affairs, Education and Research for the same project.

M. Belov (ed.), *Constitutional Polycrisis and Emergency Constitutionalism*, Federalism and Internal Conflicts,
https://doi.org/10.1007/978-3-032-06516-2_9

management, their handling by democratic elites contributed to the justification of the generals to stage the military power grab. Whilst these two countries are on one side of the extreme of democratic recession during the COVID-19 pandemic, data by International IDEA confirms that all countries around the world faced substantial democratic challenges—and an overall democratic recession, during the pandemic management period.[1]

In many countries, the COVID-19 crisis governance also posed a challenge to existing competence distributions and intergovernmental relations. This did not only apply to formally federal countries, but also those which have undergone, and continue to undergo, substantial decentralization reforms in recent decades. It is these dynamics that are at the heart of this paper. Looking at evidence from 31 European countries (The EU's 27-member states plus Iceland, Norway, the United Kingdom and Switzerland), this discussion will examine how multilevel governance (MLG) has affected the crisis response and what lessons have been learned. The starting point of the paper is David Cameron's initial assessment of COVID-19 management by federal countries. He argued back in 2022 that "there is no structural impediment to high performance on the part of federal countries. As in the case of their non-federal cousins, federal countries can be found all across the performance scale, with some at or near the very top."[2] In other words, some federations performed very well, while others did not. This, of course, begs the question of the impact of federalism—and MLG more generally—on performance during the COVID-19 pandemic. Whilst it is impossible to measure exactly how governance structures made a difference in the overall pandemic management and performance, as factors such as health care funding, age and general health of the population, the speed of government decisions, and compliance by the population, amongst others, all affect performance in terms

[1] International IDEA monitored the global situation in terms of COVID-19 measures and subsequent challenges to democracy in their Global Monitor of COVID-19's impact on Democracy and Human Rights, which is available at: https://www.idea.int/gsod-indices/covid19globalmonitor

[2] David Cameron, 'The Relative Performance of Federal and Non-Federal Countries During the Pandemic' in Rupak Chattopadhyay et.al. (eds) *Federalism and the Response to COVID-19—A Comparative Analysis* (Routledge 2022).

For a more challenging first comparison during the pandemic, see for example: Jen Gaskell and Gerry Stoker: Centralized or multi-level: Which Governance Systems are having a 'good' pandemic? *British Politics and Policy at LSE,* [2020], see: https://blogs.lse.ac.uk/politicsandpolicy/governance-systems-covid19/

of access death rates, this paper nevertheless argues that MLG mattered and continues to matter.[3] To avoid complex questions about the performance of MLG countries, which require data and analytical insights that go beyond this contribution, the paper will look at the relevance of MLG structures in numerous areas.[4] First, it will deal with the question of emergency constitutionalism and the varieties that can be observed when calling for an emergency in the context of COVID-19. Second, the paper deals with the centralization hypothesis, the initial institutional rearrangements seen across Europe, and how they affected not only the crisis response but also MLG. Third, the paper deals with subsequent divergence in crisis responses within and across countries, as the COVID-19 pandemic held on, but more information and less centralized decision-making allowed for increased divergence. In the conclusion, the paper will highlight why an assessment of MLG dynamics in crisis situations is important—and what lessons many countries have learned in the wake of the crisis.

9.2 COVID-19, MLG, and Emergency Constitutionalism

Emergency constitutionalism is widely discussed in the academic literature.[5] As discussed across other contributions in this volume, it refers to the legal framework that democratic countries use in cases of national, regional and local emergencies. This, foremost, focuses on constitutional provisions, but can go beyond this initial framework to also include the wider 'law by the book' provisions, such as pandemic laws, natural disaster guidelines and legal provisions to deal with emergencies at a regional or local level.

[3] On the relevance of MLG, see: Brendan Carroll, Lars Brummel, Dimiter Toshkov, and Kutsal Yesilkagit. "Multilevel governance and responses to the COVID-19 pandemic: a systematic literature review." *Regional & Federal Studies* 35, [2025], 305.

[4] For a more detailed discussion on governance factors affecting crisis governance during Covid-19, see: Dimiter Toshkov, Brendan Carroll and Kutsal Yesilkagit "Government capacity, societal trust or party preferences: what accounts for the variety of national policy responses to the COVID-19 pandemic in Europe?", *Journal of European Public Policy 29,* [2021], 1009, DOI: 10.1080/13501763.2021.1928270

[5] Martin Belov 'Rule of Law and Democracy in Times of Transitory Constitutionalism, Constitutional Polycrisis and Emergency Constitutionalism: Towards a Global Algorithmic Technocracy?' in: Martin Belov (ed) *Rule of Law in Crisis: Constitutionalism in a State of Flux*, (Routledge, 2023).

During the COVID-19 pandemic, we find a variety of emergency provisions used by European states. Several countries activated national emergency provisions in their constitutions, such as Belgium, Czechia, Estonia, Finland, Iceland, Italy, Latvia, Lithuania, and Slovakia. Others, such as Spain (state of alarm) or Portugal (state of calamity) and Luxembourg (state of crisis), activated similar provisions in their constitutions, albeit with different names. Several European countries also declared national health emergencies. Switzerland, for example, declared a state of an extraordinary situation, Slovenia declared a state of a national pandemic, and France declared a state of a health emergency in the wake of the COVID-19 pandemic. A final group of countries did not declare a constitutional emergency situation; countries such as Germany, Austria and Denmark did not enact a formal declaration of an emergency, though they implemented substantial restrictive measures. The most well-documented case of a non-declaration of an emergency is the Swedish case, where the responsible health authority departed from other European countries and abstained from implementing lockdowns and severe restrictions throughout the pandemic.[6]

In addition to the variation that can be observed at the national level, there is also severe divergence when looking at the regional level. In Germany, for example, only the Free State of Bavaria declared a regional state of emergency, while the states of Brandenburg, Saxony, Hamburg, Saxony-Anhalt, Schleswig-Holstein, and Thüringia all declared an epidemic state of emergency. However, Länder such as North Rhine-Westphalia, Saarland, Lower Saxony or Hesse did not declare any emergency, either of regional nature or specifically related to an epidemic.[7] A similar pattern is visible in Switzerland, where cantons such as Aargau, Basel District and Vaud declared a cantonal emergency, while Thurgau, Valais and Zurich followed the national level in declaring an extraordinary situation. Cantons such as Fribourg and Geneva referred to an extraordinary state of affairs and a state of necessity, respectively, while Nidwalden and

[6] Evangelia Petridou "Politics and administration in times of crisis: Explaining the Swedish response to the COVID-19 crisis". [2022] *European Policy Analysis 6*.147.

See also Jostein Askim and Thomas Bergström "Between Lockdown and Calm Down. Comparing the Covid-19 Responses of Norway and Sweden" [2021]. *Local Government Studies 48*, 291. https://doi.org/10.1080/03003930.2021.1964477.

[7] For a discussion of the German case, see:

Nathalie Behnke and Christian Person "Föderalismus in der Krise- Restriktivität und Variation der Infektionsschutzverodnungen der Länder" [2022] D*MS-Der Moderne Staat—Zeitschrift für Public Policy, Recht und Management* 15, 62.

Obwalden did not formally declare an emergency situation, but activated the cantonal command staff provisions. Other cantons, such as Basel-City and Appenzell Inner-Rhodes, did not declare any cantonal or health emergency.[8] This diverse legal activism in Germany and Switzerland, however, has not resulted in substantial divergence when it came to the implementation of measures. Here we see a high degree of coordination in Germany, especially at the beginning of the crisis,[9] and a high degree of centralization at the beginning in the Swiss case.[10] However, this pattern is also not consistent for all federal and regional states across Europe. For example, in the United Kingdom, neither the national level nor the regions (Scotland, Wales and Northern Ireland) declared a health or national emergency. In Austria, too, we see no variance between national and Länder level, while in Belgium, the regions played a vital role in crisis management, but there is no national declaration of an emergency.

This variety can be explained by a number of factors. First, legal provisions and existing rules played a major role in the initial and later treatment of the COVID-19 crisis by decision-makers. Where constitutional provisions allowed for a declaration of a state of emergency, this was often used. In cases with no, or restricted emergency provisions, such as in the German Basic Law, where emergency constitutional provisions are limited to the case of a foreign military attack, we see reliance on other legal provisions, such as infection protection legislation or, as was used extensively in the Swiss case, pandemic laws. Second, in some cases, we also see a shift from one status to another. Bulgaria, for example, first declared a national state of emergency in mid-March 2020, before specifying this through the declaration of an epidemic state of emergency in mid-April of the same year. Likewise, Estonia declared a state of emergency in mid-March 2020, only to downgrade this in December 2020 to a health emergency. Portugal moved from a state of calamity to a state of contingency by the end of August 2021, while Romania changed from a

[8] For a discussion of the Swiss case, see Stefanie Rusch and Bernhard Waldmann "Kantonale Notrechtssysteme—Eine Vergleichende Übersicht des Intrakonstitutionellen Notrechts in den Kantonen" [2024], *Jusletter*, 3, 1.

[9] For Germany, see for example: Nathalie Behnke and Steffen Eckhard. "A systemic perspective on crisis management and resilience in Germany." *dms–der moderne staat–Zeitschrift für Public Policy, Recht und Management 15* [2022], 3.

[10] For centralization in Switzerland at the beginning of the crisis, see Eva Maria Belser and Simon Mazidi. "Der Schweizer Föderalismus in Zeiten der Pandemie: Wie krisenfest ist die vertikale Gewaltenteilung?." In Europäisches Zentrum für Föderalismusforschung (Ed.) *Jahrbuch des Föderalismus 2021*, (Nomos 2021).

national state of emergency to a state of alert. There was, in other words, a lot of variety in how countries handled the legal framing of the crises, not only between countries, but within countries over a period of time. These shifts in emergency constitutionalism that framed COVID-19 governance also highlight the importance of time limits to emergencies and the need for proportionality in the application of emergency provisions. The more the world knew about COVID-19, and the closer new treatments and options for vaccines came, the more we saw a fading out of emergency provisions in the majority of countries. There are, of course, also very different implications for the use of emergency provisions. If we look at the extent of measures used in countries such as Germany, Spain, Switzerland, and Austria, we notice that the major policy preferences are significantly aligned, despite different legal frameworks and constitutional provisions. Lockdown arrangements, financial support, limitations to contacts, and distancing rules, travel restrictions, and protection mechanisms for the most vulnerable population (including, e.g., in care homes) looked very different across many European countries, though the degree of restrictions, the time frame and their enforcement differed.[11]

The issue of timing is also interesting for another reason. There is a growing recognition that when emergencies occur, it is important to act fast and decisively to protect the population and address the challenge of the emergency. In light of this, it is often argued that centralized countries are better equipped to act fast and put in place uniform actions that will mitigate the crisis.[12] However, research on COVID-19 has demonstrated that the argument that centralized countries react quicker—and more efficiently does not hold. Nathalie Behnke demonstrates this for the case of Germany,[13] and Eva Maria Belser demonstrates how the cantons were able to react quickly in Switzerland, and additionally put pressure on the Confederation to implement border closures and tougher restrictions across the country.[14] Additionally, countries that responded immediately

[11] For a comparison of lockdown policies and their impact, see: Emanuele Lindo Secco and Stefano Conte. "To lockdown or not to lockdown: analysis of the EU lockdown performance vs. COVID-19 outbreak." *Frontiers in Medical Technology* 4 [2022].

[12] Arjan Boin et. Al. *The politics of crisis management* (Cambridge University Press 2017).

[13] Nathalie Behnke "Föderalismus in der (Corona-) Krise?Föderale Funktionen, Kompetenzen und Entscheidungsprozesse" [2020] *Aus Politik und Zeitgeschehen*, see: https://www.bpb.de/apuz/314343/foederalismus-in-der-corona-krise

[14] Eva Maria Belser "Existierte die Schweiz während der Pandemie? Die Eigenheiten der Schweiz und ihre Eignung für den Krisenfall", in Frank Rühli/Andreas Thier (eds.), *Weissbuch Corona, Die Schweiz nach der Pandemie, Befunde—Erkenntnisse—Perspektiven,* (NZZ Libro 2021).

with strong centralization measures did not manage to contain the spread of the pandemic, or manage patient loads better. Instead, as highlighted by numerous comparative studies, it is less the degree of centralization and decentralization that mattered at the beginning of the COVID-19 countries, but more the ability of different levels of governance to coordinate, work together and cooperate in their respective crisis management.[15]

9.3 COVID-19, Centralization, and Institutional Re-Alignment

There is a widely accepted centralization thesis in the crisis management literature.[16] The thesis assumes that in crisis situations, quick and coherent decisions are vital—and can only be delivered through centralized institutions. In order to achieve this, both decision-making processes and administrative implementation structures need to align under one authority to ensure timely, efficient and coherent results, which also enjoy a high degree of trust and acceptance by the population.[17] Decentralized crisis responses are often seen as too slow because they require a variety of actors to agree on common rules when these are needed quickly. Policy formulation might not only be delayed, but instead of robust decisions, involvement of a multitude of actors might water down decisions, substantially affecting the efficiency of important crisis responses. Moreover, decentralized approaches might lead to policy divergence in decision-making (with

[15] Davide Vampa "COVID-19 and territorial policy dynamics in Western Europe: comparing France, Spain, Italy, Germany, and the United Kingdom." [2021] *Publius: The Journal of Federalism* 51, 601.

See also for an assessment of coordination in federal countries:

Yvonne Hegele and Johanna Schnabel "Explaining Intergovernmental Coordination during the COVID-19 Pandemic: Responses in Australia, Canada, Germany, and Switzerland" [2022] *Publius—The Journal of Federalism*, 51, 537.

For a discussion on the failure of coordination in Italy and Spain, see:

Paola Mattei and Eloisa Del Pino "Coordination and health policy responses to the first wave of COVID-19 in Italy and Spain" [2021] *Journal of Comparative Policy Analysis: Research and Practice* 23, 274.

[16] See for example: Paul 't Hart, Uriel Rosenthal, and Alexander Kouzmin. "Crisis decision making: The centralization thesis revisited." *Administration & Society* 25, [1993]:,12.

[17] For a discussion of the centralization thesis in practice, see: James Douglas, Ringa Raudla, Tiina Randma-Liiv, and Riin Savi. "The impact of greater centralization on the relevance of performance information in European governments during the fiscal crisis." *Administration & Society* 51, [2019], 1020.

different rules applying to different parts of a country) and in implementation (with the same set of rules implemented differently across internal legal orders), which not only confuses populations but might also lower popular trust in the overall response capacity of decision-makers. The more divergence is visible for people in crisis situations, the more compliance might be affected, as it is difficult to understand why one set of rules applies to one territorial area in a country, but not to another.[18] In addition, decentralized approaches might not work in practice. For example, strict lockdowns in one region might be counteracted by a neighboring region keeping its shops and businesses open, thereby promoting people from the region with stricter rules to simply travel to the neighboring region.[19] This can be a challenge, particularly in situations where territorial units are relatively small and internal boundaries are easy to cross. As COVID-19 has demonstrated, at the beginning of a crisis, quick decisions are needed. Indeed, a short amount of days has had a substantial impact on access death figures, with countries implementing earlier and stricter measures performing substantially better than those that delayed any robust action.[20]

However, proponents of decentralized crisis management have countered some of the above-mentioned arguments. They point out that decentralized approaches might allow for better, that is, more focused responses. During COVID-19, for example, different parts of countries were affected at different points in time, so allowing more robust and time-effective actions in one part, while limiting the severe economic and social welfare effects of strict measures in another part of a country, is a distinct advantage of a decentralized response.[21] Moreover, supporters of

[18] At the beginning of the COVID-19 crisis, leading public administration and crisis management experts revisited some of these assumptions, concluding that the emerging governance patterns were very complex and that a variety of other issues matters for effective conflict management as well. See: Arjen Boin, Martin Lodge and Marte Luesink "Learning from the COVID-19 crisis: An Initial Analysis of National Responses", *Policy Design and Practice 3* [2020] 189.

[19] For a wider discussion of the centralization hypothesis and the implications for crisis management, see: Arjen Boin *The Politics of Crisis Management—Public Leadership under Pressure* (2nd ed. Cambridge University Press 2017).

[20] Waleed Al-Salem, Paula Moraga, Hani Ghazi, Syra Madad, and Peter J. Hotez. "The emergence and transmission of COVID-19 in European countries, 2019–2020: a comprehensive review of timelines, cases and containment." *International health* 13, [2021], 383.

[21] Nico Steylter "Introduction" in: Nico Steylter (Ed.). *Comparative Federalism and COVID-19—Combating the* Pandemic (Routledge 2021).

decentralized solutions have emphasized how the inclusion of multiple actors usually increases both the quality and the acceptability of decisions. Federal and decentralized systems require elites and veto players from very different political constellations to come together, which has played an important role in countries such as Germany, to break the dominance of the then Christian Democratic—Social-Democrat national coalition, and allow voices from smaller parties, poorer (and richer) regions and more densely populated and more rural Länder to voice their concerns, objections, and proposals in the management of the crisis. This has had little to no impact on the quality and coherence of any decisions taken, but it did enhance participation—and thereby acceptability and trust in decision-making at the beginning of the pandemic.[22] Finally, proponents of decentralized solutions have pointed out, including with reference to COVID-19, that crises are usually not static, one-time events, but unfold dynamically over time. Indeed, as governments learned more about the virus, infections and who is most at risk, strategies adjusted. Decentralized solutions allow to take into account this dynamic development within a country more effectively by addressing different infection rates through different measures, allowing openings and the end of measures in areas with high vaccine rates, and tailoring measures depending on local and regional conditions—an issue that for example became vitally important in Switzerland in the duration of the crisis response, despite the initial centralization, and partial marginalization of the cantons.[23]

Even strong supporters of the centralization hypothesis have since realized that the responses across Europe during COVID-19 were a lot more diverse, without necessarily a clear pattern in the better performance of quick centralization.[24] While all countries in Europe have seen a dominance of executive decision-making in response to the COVID-19 crisis (without necessarily completely marginalizing parliaments),[25] we do

[22] Fabian Hattke and Helge Martin. "Collective action during the Covid-19 pandemic: The case of Germany's fragmented authority." *Administrative Theory & Praxis* 42, [2020] 614.

[23] Eva Maria Belser, Bernhard Waldmann, and Andreas Stöckli. "Der schweizerische Föderalismus funktioniert auch im Krisenmodus." *IFF Newsletter 2/2020* [2020].

[24] For an assessment of the interplay of different factors of crisis governance during COVID-19, and a slight adjustment of the centralization hypothesis, see: Arjen Boin, Allan McConnell, and Paul 't Hart *Governing the Pandemic—The Politics of Navigating a Mega-Crisis* (Palgrave 2021).

[25] Elena Griglio. "Parliamentary oversight under the Covid-19 emergency: striving against executive dominance." *The Theory and Practice of Legislation* 8, [2020] 49.

not, per se, see the same pattern when it comes to the centralization of decision-making and implementation in multilevel systems.

Research has demonstrated that effective crisis governance has less to do with quick centralization and more to do with the coordination between different levels of government. Hegele and Schnabel, for example, demonstrate in their comparison of the reaction of numerous Western states, that the issue is not about centralization and decentralization, but that coordination affected the efficiency of crisis governance the most.[26] There are also substantial differences in this assessment between federal and unitary states. Not all federal states were able to utilize existing coordination mechanisms at the beginning for the crisis,[27] which explains the high degree of centralization in Switzerland, while countries such as Belgium, despite their federal nature, were characterized by the absence of strong intergovernmental mechanisms, which became a major challenge for cooperation[28]—an issue that also affected regional states such as Spain and Italy.[29] Other federations, such as Germany, build on a long tradition of executive cooperation amongst multiple governance levels. The conference between the Länder Minister Presidents and Chancellor Angela Merkel consequently played a vital role in the management of the crisis, ensuring both coherence and acceptability of measures adopted during the first phase of the pandemic.[30] It was only when the first lockdown ended, and variation amongst the Länder became more obvious as a result of

[26] Yvonne Hegele and Johanna Schnabel. "Federalism and the management of the COVID-19 crisis: centralisation, decentralisation and (non-) coordination." *West European Politics* 44, [2021],1052.

[27] Johanna Schnabel and Yvonne Hegele "Explaining Intergovernmental Coordination during the COVID-19 Pandemic: Responses in Australia, Canada, Germany, and Switzerland", Publius- The Journal of Federalism, 51 [2021], 537.

[28] Patricia Popelier and Peter Bursens. "Managing the COVID-19 Crisis in a Divided Belgian Federation - Cooperation against all odds" in Nico Steylter (Ed.). *Comparative Federalism and COVID-19—Combating the Pandemic* (Routledge 2021).

For an overall assessment of Belgian Covid-19 management from a federal perspective, see: Jeroen Luyten and Erik Schokkaert. "Belgium's response to the COVID-19 pandemic." *Health Economics, Policy and Law* 17, [2022] 37.

[29] See for example: Mattia Casula and Serafin Pazos-Vidal "Assessing the Multi-level Government Response to the Covid-19 crisis: Italy and Spain Compared", *International Journal of Public Administration 44* [2021], 994.

[30] Sabine Kuhlmann and Jochen Franzke. "Multi-level responses to COVID-19: crisis coordination in Germany from an intergovernmental perspective." *Local Government Studies* 48 [2022] 312.

increased individual Länder responsibility in the management of the crisis and its handling in the summer of 2020, that both divergence and political competition between different actors amongst the Länder and within them became more pronounced[31]—with negative consequences on the public acceptability of divergent measures. While coordination challenges increased in Germany, as a result of increased competition and divergent visions for the handling of the pandemic in Germany in the second part of 2020, in Switzerland and countries such as Belgium and Spain, intergovernmental coordination improved over time, ensuring better COVID-19 governance as the pandemic developed.

This dynamic assessment of intergovernmental coordination, polarization and governance innovation over time is an important element of the COVID-19 management in federal and regional states in Europe. It does, of course, not apply to all states, with countries such as the United Kingdom struggling with intergovernmental coordination throughout the crisis, but particularly after initial joint coordination reverted to the autonomy of Scotland, Wales and Northern Ireland to take individual measures in the handling of the crisis.[32] Instances of convergence and divergence in intergovernmental coordination during COVID-19 also need to be contextualized for the specific context. As research by Paul Anderson and his co-authors has recently demonstrated, in the United Kingdom, Belgium, and Spain, contested intergovernmental relations, and divergent Covid-19 management strategies between regional and national levels can also be explained by regionalist minority nationalist governments using the pandemic as a tool to demonstrate their ability to handle a crisis and steer the region successfully through such a demanding period. Here, COVID-19 management becomes a tool of regional state-making, while it is designed to undermine the crisis governance of the Union.[33]

[31] Antonios Souris, Sabine Kropp, and Christoph Nguyen. "Attributing blame: how political parties in Germany leverage cooperative federalism." *West European Politics* 47, [2024] 1529.

See also: Christian Person, Nathalie Behnke, and Till Jürgens. "Effects of territorial party politics on horizontal coordination among the German Länder–An analysis of the COVID-19 pandemic management in Germany." *German Politics* 33, [2024] 246.

[32] Paul Anderson. "The COVID-19 pandemic in the United Kingdom: a tale of convergence and divergence." In: Nico Steylter (Ed.). *Comparative Federalism and Covid-19—Combating the Pandemic* (Routledge 2021).

[33] Paul Anderson, Coree Brown Swan, Carles Ferreira, and Judith Sijstermans. "State making or state breaking?' Crisis, COVID-19 and the constitution in Belgium, Spain and the United Kingdom." *Nations and Nationalism* 30, [2024]:110.

In traditionally more unitary systems, we are also observing important developments hinting at the importance of intergovernmental cooperation and coordination. In the Netherlands, for example, regions played a major part in handling the crisis, and initial variation is visible in the handling of the pandemic between those regions that followed the national government's initial plan of herd immunity and those that implemented mitigating measures.[34] In the Scandinavian countries, too, regional variety matters. In Norway, for example, it is possible to observe an initial nationally coordinated response, which is followed by substantial local autonomy for the municipalities in the handling of the pandemic, including the rights to impose localized lockdowns and implement a series of divergent measures, which resulted in some tensions between the different layers of governance.[35] In traditionally centralized France, too, regions, provinces, and municipalities played a major role in the handling of the crisis—despite traditionally more hierarchical relations between Paris and the rest of the country, and an initial response to the pandemic that was described as presidential hyper-centralization.[36]

There are a number of important conclusions that can be drawn from the discussion above. First, multilevel governance clearly mattered during the management of the COVID-19 pandemic. It mattered in those states that have traditionally been characterized by federal and regional structures, though many (but not all) faced challenges of centralization and hyper-activism of the executive at the expense of parliamentary control. Second, throughout the handling of the pandemic, there is an important observation about the increased importance of regional and local levels. Many countries reverted to more "traditional" decision-making after the initial COVID-19 phase was over, which meant that responsibilities for social welfare, economic development or security arrangements became, once again, a regional or local responsibility. In light of this, divergent policy decisions and implementation are observable. While this helped in some cases mitigate the consequences of COVID-19 infections and

[34] Lieke Michaela Hoekman, Marlou Marriet Vera Smits, and Xander Koolman. "The Dutch COVID-19 approach: regional differences in a small country." *Health Policy and Technology* 9, [2020] 613.

[35] Annette Fosse, Anders Svensson, Ingvill Konradsen, and Birgit Abelsen. "Tension between local, regional and national levels in Norway's handling of COVID-19." *Scandinavian Journal of Public Health* 51, [2023] 995.

[36] Céline Du Boys, Marius Bertolucci, and Robert Fouchet. "French inter-governmental relations during the COVID-19 crisis: between hyper-centralism and local horizontal cooperation." *Local Government Studies* 48, [2022] 251.

measures by regionalizing and localizing lockdowns, for example, it did nevertheless increase levels of confusion, frustration and eventually also distrust amongst the population. Rising opposition against strict COVID-19 measures therefore becomes a major feature in most European countries in the second half of 2020.[37] This also results in shifting patterns in public trust in different levels of government, as recently discussed by colleagues at the University of Antwerp.[38]

Moreover, neither the centralization thesis nor the arguments of proponents of decentralization can fully be confirmed or rejected. Whilst it is true that intergovernmental coordination and the quality of multilevel governance coordination were key factors impacting the performance of crisis governance, there are nevertheless examples of quick centralization (Switzerland, the United Kingdom, Spain, Norway) and instances of decentralized approaches (Germany, Belgium, Italy). In each category, however, we find countries that have managed the pandemic reasonably well, as well as cases that struggled with substantial access death rates and severe COVID-19 impact on the healthcare system and society as a whole. In order to fully assess which governance techniques, measures and adjustments worked, further comparative studies are required. This is even more important because there is a clear dynamic in the crisis response across all European countries. Initial centralization in Switzerland was reversed when the cantons became important actors again in the easing of measures and the management of the next stage of the pandemic in the later months of 2020. Likewise, allowing divergent policies amongst the German Länder in the summer of 2020 did not prevent another nationwide lockdown a few months later and the reversal to more coordinated actions, despite growing political and popular contestation.

Finally, it is important to go back to the initial discussion on legal frameworks. While the earlier discussion demonstrated a multitude of legal frameworks adopted and used by European countries, we find a high degree of convergence in the measures adopted between countries, and also between regions and municipalities within countries. There was relative agreement on how to manage the pandemic, despite the severe impact of the initial

[37] Nocholas Charron, Victor Lapuente, and Andres Rodrigues-Pose "Uncooperative society, uncooperative politics or both? Trust, polarization, populism and COVID-19 deaths across European regions." *European Journal of Political Research* 62, no. 3 (2023): 781.

[38] Jakob Frateur, Peter Bursens, Patricia Popelier, and Susana Coroado. "How to explain citizens' declined political trust during the COVID-19 pandemic: a time-series qualitative comparative analysis (TsQCA)." *Comparative European Politics* [2025] https://doi.org/10.1057/s41295-025-00412-z.

containment and mitigation measures on human and fundamental rights, democracy and economic performance. Legal frameworks were adopted as needed—as is demonstrated by the continued adjustment of pandemic laws in Denmark and Germany throughout the COVID-19 pandemic, for example.[39] The pre-existing legal framework mattered—it defined who is in charge of what and how countries should react. Moreover, where institutionalized and part of the existing legal regulations, intergovernmental coordination, including through intergovernmental councils, was vitally important in the handling of the crisis.[40] However, countries also demonstrated remarkable abilities of adaptation and changes, as well as new forms of governance innovation, in order to deal with the unprecedented governance and management of the pandemic. These innovations in cooperation, in divergent governance approaches, and in institutional learning should not be neglected when assessing the governance of the crisis as a whole.

9.4 Learning from COVID-19: New MLG Discussions Across Europe

The COVID-19 pandemic has resulted in a renewed focus on the impact of multilevel governance institutions and processes during crisis periods. More than half a decade after the start of the pandemic, many inquiry bodies, expert commissions and academic publications have attempted to assess what worked and what did not work during the pandemic crisis management and in the governance of the crisis. Some of these so-called lessons-learned exercises have emphasized the importance of decentralized decision-making, implementation and intergovernmental coordination,[41]

[39] For Germany, see: Sabine Kropp and Johanna Schnabel "Germany's response to COVID-19 Federal coordination and executive politics". In: Nico Steylter (Ed.). *Comparative Federalism and Covid-19—Combating the Pandemic* (Routledge 2021).

[40] Johanna Schnabel, Rahel Freiburghaus, and Yvonne Hegele. "Crisis management in federal states: the role of peak intergovernmental councils in Germany and Switzerland during the COVID-19 Pandemic." *dms–der moderne staat–Zeitschrift für Public Policy, Recht und Management* 15, [2022] 42.

[41] Thomas Bossert, Gregory P. Marchildon, and Dian Kusuma. "Decentralization and COVID-19 Policies." In *Effective Pandemic Response: Linking Evidence, Intervention, Politics, Organization, and Governance A World Scientific Reference on Pandemics: Volume 2: Institutions, Politics, the Organization of Public Health Systems, and Governance in Pandemic Response: Perspectives from Theory and Practical Concepts*, (World Scientific Publishing 2025).

while others—such as the UK COVID inquiry—have questioned the usefulness of decentralized approaches to crisis management.[42] The debate over centralized versus decentralized approaches is therefore far from over, and will also continue for future crisis managers. Nevertheless, there are important multilevel implications that can be learned from the handling of COVID-19.

First, the question of centralized versus decentralized approaches might be the wrong question when looking into the management of crisis situations. Instead, as the discussion in the previous section has demonstrated, a more relevant question would focus on the sequencing of when to take decisions in a more centralized way to ensure coherence, how to ensure coherence in approaches that recognize decentralized decision-making and implementation structures, and when to follow a more divergent approach, allowing territorial units to take different measures in order to mitigate the crisis. Furthermore, discussions on centralization versus decentralization are also overshadowed by the fact that traditional countries in either category followed different crisis governance pathways. While Switzerland was heavily centralized during the first stage of the crises (after the Swiss government was initially very hesitant to impose country-wide measures), countries such as the Netherlands, Denmark, France and Norway saw a high involvement of regional and local levels of government in the management of the COVID-19 pandemic, especially in later phases of the crises after the summer of 2020. The question, therefore, is first and foremost not if centralized or decentralized approaches are better in mitigating a pandemic such as COVID-19, but first and foremost what the advantages and disadvantages of the different approaches are, how they unfolded, and at what point in time during a crisis it might be sensible to centralize and when to decentralize. Moreover, in order to implement any decisions, it is fundamentally important to pay much more attention to the role of intergovernmental relations, coordination between local, regional and national levels (and the European Union level). In order to do so, crisis governance needs to consider new frameworks for intergovernmental interactions during crises, possibly even ensuring new policy coordination formats to allow for these processes to happen in systems with weak intergovernmental practices and structures.

[42] Coree Brown Swan, Paul Anderson, and Judith Sijstermans. "Politics and the Pandemic: The UK Covid-19 Inquiry and Devolution." *The Political Quarterly* [2024] https://doi.org/10.1111/1467-923X.13473

Second, any crisis governance response, independent of the level of action, needs to focus much more on public trust[43] in order to ensure effective crisis mitigation, public compliance with restrictive measures and ultimately the success of any mitigating measures.[44] Pandemic populism has become a global phenomenon, which continues to affect institutional stability and democratic governance in many countries.[45] Since it is not a question of "if" but "when" the crises might hit European countries, sincerely engaging with COVID-19 misinformation, ensuring clear and transparent communication lines, and providing a framework for mitigating measures, which are understandable, easy to understand, inclusive, and proportionate, will remain a major challenge for years to come. Growing distrust in decision-making processes, in elites, and in media information has contributed to alienation from democratic governance and rising anti-democratic, authoritarian and anti-liberal movements, which have given rise to populist parties now playing a major role in the governments of many countries in Europe (including in Italy and the Netherlands, where they are leading these governments in 2025). While wider debates will be required about the crisis of democracy and how COVID-19 played into this,[46] what has become clear is that a global trend of democratic decline is continuing and that even established liberal democracies in Europe are now continuously challenged.[47] Multilevel governance might play an important role in this debate, as people have shown to trust in their local and regional governance responses more than in national responses at different stages of the crises (though initially trust

[43] On the conceptualization of trust and its relevance in COVID-19 management (and the multilevel governance perspective), see: Jakob Frateur, Peter Bursens, Susana Duarte Coroado, Patricia Popelier "Literature Review WP5: Legitimate Crisis Governance and Trust" LEGITIMULT Working Paper [2023] https://legitimult.eu/wp-content/uploads/2023/06/Del-5.1-Working-paper-Literature-review-and-methodology.pdf

[44] Jia Liu, Yasir Shahab, and Hafiz Hoque. "Government response measures and public trust during the COVID-19 pandemic: evidence from around the world." *British Journal of Management* 33, [2022] 571.

[45] Mattia Zulianello and Petra Guasti. "The demand and supply of pandemic populism: A global overview." *Government and Opposition* [2023] 1.

[46] See e.g.: Sarah Repucci, and Amy Slipowitz. "Democracy in a Year of Crisis." *Journal of Democracy* 32, [2021] 45.

[47] On the linkages between the global recession of democracy and COVID-19, see: Christopher Hartwell, "The Decline of Economic and Political Freedom After COVID-19: A New Authoritarian Dawn?." *Politics and Governance* 12 [2024].

was highest in national governments).[48] Moreover, regional and local governance is generally seen as more responsive to citizen needs, providing more tailor-made solutions to local people, and ensuring a higher degree of accountability.[49] Tailor-made solutions and accountability will remain key features in any future crisis governance, so enhancing the effective interplay of multiple layers of governance and ensuring citizens' understanding of decisions (per se and when variation occurs) will remain major challenges for all levels of governance for future crises.

A third lesson learned relates to emergency constitutionalism. In the age of emergency that we are living in, legal frameworks and their application to emergency governance remain highly salient.[50] The divergencies of constitutional frameworks used (as demonstrated at the beginning of this chapter), and the divergent responses across Europe, highlight a rethink and re-evaluation of how crises need to be framed constitutionally and legally more generally. Surprisingly, we do not observe large-scale emergency clauses and provisions being revised, revisited and rewritten. There is no trend towards shifting constitutional frameworks on emergency governance. Having said this, there are numerous revisions of pandemic laws and emergency health frameworks that have been ongoing in recent years as a result of lessons learned from the COVID-19 pandemic.[51] In this regard, it is also important to briefly mention the role of Courts during the pandemic and its aftermath. Courts in numerous countries have limited government legislation, crisis mitigation measures and have declared illegal processes in which decisions were taken, or substantial limitations of human and fundamental rights when these did not seem appropriate or proportionate. Courts have also counterbalanced centralization and executive dominance during the pandemic and have given a voice to those who felt disproportionately negatively affected by crisis mitigation measures, even when they did not declare all (or even major) decisions as illegal and

[48] Jakob Frateur, Peter Bursens, Patricia Popelier, and Susana Coroado. "How to explain citizens' declined political trust during the COVID-19 pandemic: a time-series qualitative comparative analysis (TsQCA)." *Comparative European Politics* [2025] https://doi.org/10.1057/s41295-025-00412-z.

[49] Maria de Lourdes Melo Zurita, Brian Cook, Louise Harms, and Alan March. "Towards new disaster governance: Subsidiarity as a critical tool." *Environmental Policy and Governance* 25, [2015] 386.

[50] Kushagr Bakshi "Crisis Constitutionalism." *ICL Journal* 18, [2024] 203.

[51] Arianna Vedaschi and Chiara Graziani. "New dynamics of the "post-COVID-19 era": A legal conundrum." *German Law Journal* 24, [2023] 1612.

wrong.[52] Courts remained in many instances strong defenders of both human rights and democratic governance—countering the dangers of authoritarian takeover and creeping de-democratization in the midst of a health crisis. Yet, lessons too will need to be learned about the performance of courts, their ability to play the role of an effective counterweight against centralization, executive takeover and substantial limitations to fundamental human rights. In cases such as Hungary, the courts were unable to prevent executive dominance and fundamental limitations to human rights. In other cases, such as in Germany, courts at all levels of governance have checked and limited the extent of government intervention.

The next crisis is very much upon us. With an ongoing war in Ukraine (as of May 2025), growing concerns over climate change, global economic insecurity as a result of the return of Donald Trump to the U.S. Presidency, and global fears of a conflict between the U.S. and China, an escalation of the India-Pakistan conflict, a worsening of the world-wide refugee crisis and new challenges to energy, raw materials and food security, together with the ever-existing danger of a new pandemic—we are only ever one step away from the next governance challenge.

While the World Health Organization has managed to get its member states to agree on an international pandemic agreement in May 2025[53] to avoid the lack of coordination and the breakdown of global supply chains seen during the COVID-19 pandemic, other crises and challenges remain lingering and unaddressed. The framing and improvement of crisis governance will remain a challenge for years to come. Thinking about the role of multilevel governance in this process is important in order to enhance the effectiveness, legitimacy and public trust of any crisis governance measures.

References

Al-Salem, W., Moraga, P., Ghazi, H., Madad, S., & Hotez, P.J. "The emergence and transmission of COVID-19 in European countries, 2019–2020: a

[52] For an example of the role of courts, and the challenges they faced, see the discussion of the British case in: Barry Godfrey, Jane C. Richardson, and Sandra Walklate. "The crisis in the courts: Before and beyond Covid." *The British Journal of Criminology* 62, [2022] 1036.

[53] World Health Organization. World Health Assembly adopts historic Pandemic Agreement to make the world more equitable and safer from future pandemics. WHO Press Release, [2025] https://www.who.int/news/item/20-05-2025-world-health-assembly-adopts-historic-pandemic-agreement-to-make-the-world-more-equitable-and-safer-from-future-pandemics

comprehensive review of timelines, cases and containment." *International Health* 13, [2021], 383

Anderson, P. "The COVID-19 pandemic in the United Kingdom: a tale of convergence and divergence." In Steylter, N. (ed.) *Comparative Federalism and Covid-19—Combating the Pandemic.* Routledge, [2021], 142–159

Anderson, P., Brown Swan, C., Ferreira, C., & Sijstermans, J. "State making or state breaking? Crisis, COVID-19 and the constitution in Belgium, Spain and the United Kingdom." *Nations and Nationalism* 30, [2024], 110

Askim, J., & Bergström, T. "Between Lockdown and Calm Down. Comparing the Covid-19 Responses of Norway and Sweden." *Local Government Studies* 48, [2021], 291. https://doi.org/10.1080/03003930.2021.1964477 (last access 15 Oct 2025)

Bakshi, K. "Crisis Constitutionalism." *ICL Journal* 18, [2024], 203

Behnke, N. "Föderalismus in der (Corona-) Krise? Föderale Funktionen, Kompetenzen und Entscheidungsprozesse." *Aus Politik und Zeitgeschehen*, [2020]. https://www.bpb.de/apuz/314343/foederalismus-in-der-corona-krise

Behnke, N., & Eckhard, S. "A systemic perspective on crisis management and resilience in Germany." *dms—der moderne staat—Zeitschrift für Public Policy, Recht und Management* 15, [2022], 3

Behnke, N., & Person, C. "Föderalismus in der Krise—Restriktivität und Variation der Infektionsschutzverordnungen der Länder." *dms—der moderne staat—Zeitschrift für Public Policy, Recht und Management* 15, [2022], 62

Belov, M. "Rule of Law and Democracy in Times of Transitory Constitutionalism, Constitutional Polycrisis and Emergency Constitutionalism: Towards a Global Algorithmic Technocracy?" In Belov, M. (ed.) *Rule of Law in Crisis: Constitutionalism in a State of Flux.* Routledge, 2023

Belser, E.M. "Existierte die Schweiz während der Pandemie? Die Eigenheiten der Schweiz und ihre Eignung für den Krisenfall." In Rühli, F., & Thier, A. (eds.) *Weissbuch Corona, Die Schweiz nach der Pandemie, Befunde—Erkenntnisse—Perspektiven.* NZZ Libro, [2021], 124–141

Belser, E.M., & Mazidi, S. "Der Schweizer Föderalismus in Zeiten der Pandemie: Wie krisenfest ist die vertikale Gewaltenteilung?" In Europäisches Zentrum für Föderalismusforschung (ed.) *Jahrbuch des Föderalismus 2021.* Nomos, [2021], 67–84

Belser, E.M., Waldmann, B., & Stöckli, A. "Der schweizerische Föderalismus funktioniert auch im Krisenmodus." *IFF Newsletter* 2, [2020]

Boin, A., et al. *The Politics of Crisis Management.* Cambridge University Press, 2017

Boin, A., Lodge, M., & Luesink, M. "Learning from the COVID-19 crisis: An Initial Analysis of National Responses." *Policy Design and Practice* 3, [2020], 189

Boin, A., McConnell, A., & 't Hart, P. *Governing the Pandemic—The Politics of Navigating a Mega-Crisis.* Palgrave, 2021

Bossert, T., Marchildon, G.P., & Kusuma, D. "Decentralization and COVID-19 Policies." In *Effective Pandemic Response: Linking Evidence, Intervention, Politics, Organization, and Governance. A World Scientific Reference on Pandemics: Volume 2*, edited by Berman, P., Patrick, D., Larnder, A. & Ruck, C. Singapore: World Scientific Publishing, [2025], 123–144

Brown Swan, C., Anderson, P., & Sijstermans, J. "Politics and the Pandemic: The UK Covid-19 Inquiry and Devolution." *The Political Quarterly*, [2024]. https://doi.org/10.1111/1467-923X.13473 (last access 15 Oct 2025)

Cameron, D. "The Relative Performance of Federal and Non-Federal Countries During the Pandemic." In Chattopadhyay, R., et al. (eds.) *Federalism and the Response to Covid-19—A Comparative Analysis.* Routledge, [2022], 15–34

Carroll, B., Brummel, L., Toshkov, D., & Yesilkagit, K. "Multilevel governance and responses to the COVID-19 pandemic: a systematic literature review." *Regional & Federal Studies* 35, [2025], 305

Casula, M., & Pazos-Vidal, S. "Assessing the Multi-level Government Response to the Covid-19 crisis: Italy and Spain Compared." *International Journal of Public Administration* 44, [2021], 994

Charron, N., Lapuente, V., & Rodrigues-Pose, A. "Uncooperative society, uncooperative politics or both? Trust, polarization, populism and COVID-19 deaths across European regions." *European Journal of Political Research* 62, no. 3, [2023], 781

de Lourdes Melo Zurita, M., Cook, B., Harms, L., & March, A. "Towards new disaster governance: Subsidiarity as a critical tool." *Environmental Policy and Governance* 25, [2015], 386

Douglas, J., Raudla, R., Randma-Liiv, T., & Savi, R. "The impact of greater centralization on the relevance of performance information in European governments during the fiscal crisis." *Administration & Society* 51, [2019], 1020

Du Boys, C., Bertolucci, M., & Fouchet, R. "French inter-governmental relations during the Covid-19 crisis: between hyper-centralism and local horizontal cooperation." *Local Government Studies* 48, [2022], 251

Fosse, A., Svensson, A., Konradsen, I., & Abelsen, B. "Tension between local, regional and national levels in Norway's handling of COVID-19." *Scandinavian Journal of Public Health* 51, [2023], 995

Frateur, J., Bursens, P., Coroado, S.D., & Popelier, P. "Literature Review WP5: Legitimate Crisis Governance and Trust." *LEGITIMULT Working Paper*, [2023]. https://legitimult.eu/wp-content/uploads/2023/06/Del-5.1-Working-paper-Literature-review-and-methodology.pdf (last access 15 Oct 2025)

Frateur, J., Bursens, P., Popelier, P., & Coroado, S. "How to explain citizens' declined political trust during the COVID-19 pandemic: a time-series qualitative comparative analysis (TsQCA)." *Comparative European Politics*, [2025]. https://doi.org/10.1057/s41295-025-00412-z

Gaskell, J., & Stoker, G. "Centralised or multi-level: Which Governance Systems are having a 'good' pandemic?" *British Politics and Policy at LSE*, [2020]. https://blogs.lse.ac.uk/politicsandpolicy/governance-systems-covid19/ (last access 15 Oct 2025)

Godfrey, B., Richardson, J.C., & Walklate, S. "The crisis in the courts: Before and beyond Covid." *The British Journal of Criminology* 62, [2022], 1036

Hartwell, C. "The Decline of Economic and Political Freedom After Covid-19: A New Authoritarian Dawn?" *Politics and Governance* 12, [2024]

Hattke, F., & Martin, H. "Collective action during the Covid-19 pandemic: The case of Germany's fragmented authority." *Administrative Theory & Praxis* 42, [2020], 614

Hegele, Y., & Schnabel, J. "Explaining Intergovernmental Coordination during the Covid-19 Pandemic: Responses in Australia, Canada, Germany, and Switzerland." *Publius—The Journal of Federalism* 51, [2022], 537

Hegele, Y., & Schnabel, J. "Federalism and the management of the COVID-19 crisis: centralisation, decentralisation and (non-) coordination." *West European Politics* 44, [2021], 1052

Hoekman, L.M., Smits, M.M.V., & Koolman, X. "The Dutch COVID-19 approach: regional differences in a small country." *Health Policy and Technology* 9, [2020], 613

Kropp, S., & Schnabel, J. "Germany's response to COVID-19: Federal coordination and executive politics." In Steylter, N. (ed.) *Comparative Federalism and Covid-19—Combating the Pandemic*. Routledge, [2021], 84–94

Kuhlmann, S., & Franzke, J. "Multi-level responses to COVID-19: crisis coordination in Germany from an intergovernmental perspective." *Local Government Studies* 48, [2022], 312

Liu, J., Shahab, Y., & Hoque, H. "Government response measures and public trust during the COVID-19 pandemic: evidence from around the world." *British Journal of Management* 33, [2022], 571

Luyten, J., & Schokkaert, E. "Belgium's response to the COVID-19 pandemic." *Health Economics, Policy and Law* 17, [2022], 37

Mattei, P., & Del Pino, E. "Coordination and health policy responses to the first wave of COVID-19 in Italy and Spain." *Journal of Comparative Policy Analysis: Research and Practice* 23, [2021], 274

Person, C., Behnke, N., & Jürgens, T. "Effects of territorial party politics on horizontal coordination among the German Länder—An analysis of the COVID-19 pandemic management in Germany." *German Politics* 33, [2024], 246

Petridou, E. "Politics and administration in times of crisis: Explaining the Swedish response to the COVID-19 crisis." *European Policy Analysis* 6, [2022], 147

Popelier, P., & Bursens, P. "Managing the Covid-19 Crisis in a Divided Belgian Federation—Cooperation against all odds." In Steylter, N. (ed.) *Comparative Federalism and Covid-19—Combating the Pandemic*. Routledge, [2021], 88–105

Repucci, S., & Slipowitz, A. "Democracy in a Year of Crisis." *Journal of Democracy* 32, [2021], 45

Rusch, S., & Waldmann, B. "Kantonale Notrechtssysteme—Eine Vergleichende Übersicht des Intrakonstitutionellen Notrechts in den Kantonen." *Jusletter* 3, [2024], 1

Schnabel, J., Freiburghaus, R., & Hegele, Y. "Crisis management in federal states: the role of peak intergovernmental councils in Germany and Switzerland during the COVID-19 Pandemic." *dms—der moderne staat—Zeitschrift für Public Policy, Recht und Management* 15, [2022], 42

Secco, E.L., & Conte, S. "To lockdown or not to lockdown: analysis of the EU lockdown performance vs. COVID-19 outbreak." *Frontiers in Medical Technology* 4, [2022]

Souris, A., Kropp, S., & Nguyen, C. "Attributing blame: how political parties in Germany leverage cooperative federalism." *West European Politics* 47, [2024], 1529

Steylter, N. "Introduction." In Steylter, N. (ed.) *Comparative Federalism and Covid-19—Combating the Pandemic.* Routledge, [2021], 1–12

't Hart, P., Rosenthal, U., & Kouzmin, A. "Crisis decision making: The centralization thesis revisited." *Administration & Society* 25, [1993], 12

Toshkov, D., Carroll, B., & Yesilkagit, K. "Government capacity, societal trust or party preferences: what accounts for the variety of national policy responses to the COVID-19 pandemic in Europe?" *Journal of European Public Policy* 29, [2021], 1009. DOI: 10.1080/13501763.2021.1928270

Vampa, D. "COVID-19 and territorial policy dynamics in Western Europe: comparing France, Spain, Italy, Germany, and the United Kingdom." *Publius: The Journal of Federalism* 51, [2021], 601

Vedaschi, A., & Graziani, C. "New dynamics of the 'post-covid-19 era': A legal conundrum." *German Law Journal* 24, [2023], 1612

World Health Organization. "Press Release." [2025]. https://www.who.int/news/item/20-05-2025-world-health-assembly-adopts-historic-pandemic-agreement-to-make-the-world-more-equitable-and-safer-from-future-pandemics (last access 15 Oct 2025)

Zulianello, M., & Guasti, P. "The demand and supply of pandemic populism: A global overview." *Government and Opposition*, [2023], 1

CHAPTER 10

Coping with Crises in a Multilevel Constitutional Order: The Example of the European Union

Gavin Barrett

10.1 Crises: Inherent in the Development of the European Union?

The European Union has, over time, been the location of a great number of events understood, narrated and responded to as crises or emergencies. Each decade had its share—for example, the failure of the European Defence Community (and with it any hope of a European Political Community) in 1954, the "empty-chair" crisis in 1965–6, the

This chapter is produced as part and funded by the European Union-NextGenerationEU, through the National Recovery and Resilience Plan of the Republic of Bulgaria, project No bg-rrp-2.004-0008.

Thanks are expressed to Professor Martin Belov for the original invitation to write on this topic, to Dr. Alan Greene for alerting me to what would otherwise have been an overlooked source, to all the participants in *Constitutional Polycrisis and Emergency Constitutionalism*, a seminar held on 4 April 2025 in Sofia, Bulgaria that led to this book, and to the organizers and participants in *The Area of Freedom, Security and Justice in the context of war in the EU's neighbourhood*, a conference held on 28–29 April 2025 at the Centre for European Integration, University College Cork, which provided the opportunity to further develop the ideas herein.

M. Belov (ed.), *Constitutional Polycrisis and Emergency Constitutionalism*, Federalism and Internal Conflicts,
https://doi.org/10.1007/978-3-032-06516-2_10

"eurosclerosis" that blighted the 1970s and so on. Over time, the role of such crises has not decreased. There appears to be an increasing number of them. Moreover, they are now of a different order of magnitude, in terms of their implications for the Union and its Member States, with the Great Financial Crisis (the combined sovereign debt and banking crises from 2008 onwards), the COVID-19 crisis and the crisis stemming from the Russian invasion of Ukraine in February 2022 all being examples of polycrises (or "cluster" crises),[1] and coinciding in time with other crises such as Brexit, the rule of law and the climate crisis. Europe may thus fairly be described as "in a stage of accelerating turbulence and crises."[2]

This chapter seeks to consider some of the implications of such events for the European Union's legal order. Famously, and somewhat prophetically, the Union's intellectual godfather, Jean Monnet, predicted that "Europe will be forged in crises, and will be the sum of the solutions adopted for those crises," a view so often repeated that it has by now become almost a cliché. The anticipation that the architecture of the European integration process would gradually be constructed as a result of the overcoming of particular challenges and difficulties is also implicitly reflected in the Schuman Declaration (authored in large measure by Jean Monnet), according to which "Europe will not be made all at once, or according to a single plan. It will be built through concrete achievements, which first create a de facto solidarity." The integration process envisaged here was one where the union "evolves gradually, and often under the pressure of events, when it needs to adapt to a changed reality."[3] One way or another, Europe has been in a state of permanent evolution since these beginnings, with developments in its legal order often driven by or accelerated by the need to rise to the challenge of particular crisis or emergency events. As Riddervold *et al* have argued, understanding EU crises and EU

[1] On the concept of polycrisis, see Martin Belov, "The conceptual shapes of constitutional polycrisis: deconstruction, asymmetries and post-modern anxieties of constitutional normalcy" in Gavin Barrett (ed.) *Law in a Time of Crises* (2023) LXX The Irish Jurist (new series) (Special Edition) 393.

[2] Marianne Riddervold, Jarle Trondal and Akasemi Newsome, "European Union Crisis: An Introduction" in Marianne Riddervold, Jarle Trondal and Akasemi Newsome (eds.), *The Palgrave Handbook of EU Crises* (Palgrave Macmillan, London 2021) 3 at 7, quoting Christopher Ansell, Jarle Trondal and Morten Øgård, *Governance in Turbulent Times* (Oxford University Press, 2017).

[3] Vestert Borger, *The Currency of Solidarity—Constitutional Transformation during the Euro Crisis* (Cambridge University Press, 2020), xix.

responses is thus key to our understanding of the EU more generally.[4] And even were their seemingly particularly strong driving force at EU level not the case, the interaction between law and emergency is, as Bellinghi has argued, a fundamental issue that cannot be ignored by *any* legal order based on the rule of law.[5]

10.2 Defining Crises

In engaging in a discussion of crisis or emergency politics or law in the EU, much of course depends on what definition is given to "crisis" or "emergency". Too wide a definition will stretch the concept of crisis beyond its useful limits.[6] No definition of either "crisis" or "emergency" is to be found in the Treaties themselves, although some academic definitions have been attempted. Boin *et al* have suggested that crises involve "events or developments widely perceived by members of relevant communities to constitute urgent threats to core community values and structures."[7] This is useful in that it emphasizes that a degree of subjectivity is inherent in the idea of crisis—for what may appear a crisis to one may appear normal to others. To Rosenthal *et al*, a crisis means "a serious threat to the basic structures or the fundamental values and norms of a system, which under time pressure and highly uncertain circumstances necessitates making vital decisions."[8] Key properties have been identified as being threat, urgency and uncertainty[9]—hence a crisis will involve a threat to some fundamental value or vital system manifesting itself, and an urgent response being needed in an uncertain situation. For de Witte, the concept of an emergency is a useful narrowing device, since, for him, a *crisis* can be slow-burning and appear only gradually (like the rule of law crisis) and be handled with the normal resources of EU law, like the climate crisis, whereas an *emergency* involves

[4] Riddervold *et al*, n.2, 4.

[5] Guido Bellinghi, "Neither Normalcy nor Crisis: The Quest for a Definition of Emergency under EU Constitutional Law" (2025) European Journal of Risk Regulation 1, 3.

[6] Riddervold *et al*, n.2, 7.

[7] Arjen Boin, Paul 't Hart and Allan McConnell, "Crisis exploitation: political and policy impacts of framing contests" (2009) 16 Journal of European Public Policy 81

[8] Uriel Rosenthal, Michael Charles, Paul 't Hart *Coping with Crises: The Management of Disasters, Riots, and Terrorism* (Charles C Thomas, 1989) quoted in Riddervold *et al*, n.2, 7.

[9] See Arjen Boin, Paul 't Hart, Eric Stern and Bengt Sundelius, *The Politics of Crisis Management: Public Leadership Under Pressure* (Cambridge University Press, 2009) at 3–4.

sudden threats to the core values and structures of the EU and its Member States.[10] Bellinghi has identified an embryonic somewhat similar tendency to distinguish between crisis and emergency in the case law of the European Court of Justice, noting that in *Slovak Republic and Hungary v Council of the European Union*,[11] the Court used the word 'crisis' to refer to the broader situation of distress that had prevailed in Member States since 2014, whereas the emergency that had triggered recourse to Article 78(3) TFEU was a sharp sudden increase in the inflow of third country nationals over a short period of time during July and August in 2015.[12] However, drawing neat lines between crises and emergencies is no easy task. Both the Treaties and implementing legislation cloud the distinction and use the words interchangeably. Hence, Article 144 TFEU refers to the concept of a "sudden crisis" rather than an emergency[13] and recent legislation, which might have been classed as emergency legislation, categorizes terrorist attacks and natural disasters as "crises."

10.3 The Role of Emergency Constitutionalism in European Union Law

The traditional concept of a state of emergency appears in any case to have no application to the European Union. Emergency constitutionalism is a classical subject of scholarly debate, and the interaction between law and emergency has been a "fundamental issue of modern constitutional theory"[14]—but not insofar as concerns supranational entities. A state of emergency is normally connected to a state and its right of self-preservation: the concept is a highly controversial, if arguably necessary, part of any national constitutional order. Its lack of applicability to the European Union derives from two reasons. One is that the European Union is bound by the doctrine of limited powers. It has no inherent power, but rather only such powers as the Member States give it. Secondly, the European Union has

[10] Bruno de Witte, "EU Emergency Law and its Impact on the EU Legal Order—European Crises and EU Emergency Law" (2022) 59 Common Market Law Review 3, 4.

[11] Joined Cases C-643/15 and C-647/15 *Slovak Republic and Hungary v Council of the European Union* EU:C:2017:63

[12] Bellinghi, n. 5, 19.

[13] This language arguably also serves to give implicit recognition of the notion of a non-sudden crisis.

[14] Bellinghi, n. 5, 3.

no express general emergency clause and no general emergency regime—the rules laid down in the Treaties must be adhered to, crisis or not, and neither the Treaties themselves nor the Charter of Fundamental Rights of the EU (in this respect, unlike the European Convention on Human Rights[15]) can be derogated from on a general basis.[16]

In practice, therefore, in a crisis situation, the *rhetoric* of emergency is used and the *modus operandi* deployed by the EU and its Member States may be new—but no breach of normal European Union law will occur and general legal dynamics will not be suspended. That much said, it is fair to say that a whole series of steps taken by the European Union in crisis situations have "oscillated on the very edge of legality"[17] Examples include Member State bailouts of otherwise insolvent States; the setting up of bailout funds such as the European Financial Stabilisation Mechanism, the European Financial Stability Facility and the European Stability Mechanism; European Central Bank initiatives such as the Outright Monetary Transactions programme or asset purchase programmes such as the Public Sector Purchase Programme or the Pandemic Emergency Purchase Programme, several of which were the subject of major, if ultimately unsuccessful legal challenges before the European Court of Justice.[18]

If it is true that there is no equivalent to a state of emergency in European Union law, it is also true that there are a number of provisions in the Treaties that are of potential significance in crisis or emergency situations—Treaty articles that, as one writer puts it, show awareness "that unforeseen events can happen and that the EU's institutional system

[15] Article 15(1) of which allows contracting states to derogate from certain rights guaranteed by the Convention in exceptional circumstances, more specifically during a time of "war or other public emergency threatening the life of the nation."

[16] Note, however, the 2023 proposal by the European Parliament of the insertion into the Treaties of a state of emergency clause that would allow the Parliament and the Council to declare the existence of an 'emergency' and grant 'extraordinary powers' to the European Commission, commented on by Guido Bellenghi, "The European Parliament's Proposal for an EU State of Emergency Clause: A Comparative and Constitutional Analysis" (2024) 20 Croatian Yearbook of European Law and Policy 1; Merijn Chamon, "The EU's Dormant Economic Policy Competence: Reliance on Article 122 TFEU and Parliament's Misguided Proposal for Treaty Revision" (2024) 49 European Law Review 166. See *European Parliament resolution of 22 November 2023 on proposals of the European Parliament for the amendment of the Treaties* (2022/2051(INL)) (OJ C/2024/4216, 24.7.2024)

[17] Vojtěch Belling, "Legality and Legitimacy of the EU 'Emergency Governance'—On the Application of the State of Emergency in the European Union" (2018) 73 Zeitschrift für öffentliches Recht 271, 280.

[18] Note in particular the *Pringle, Gauweiler* and *Weiss* rulings.

should have tools to deal with them"[19] or, as another terms them, "various horizontal frameworks that seek to comprehend, and enable the Union to respond to, crises and disasters in a more holistic manner."[20]

Three kinds of such Treaty provisions may be identified.[21] First, there are Treaty provisions that essentially *clear the way for Member States to act in an emergency.* Thus, under Article 144(1) TFEU, where a sudden crisis in the balance of payments occurs and a Council decision to grant mutual assistance is not immediately taken, a Member State with a derogation may, as a precaution, take the necessary protective measures.[22]

Another example is that Articles 346 to 348 TFEU contain provisions which acknowledge, in effect, that there are measures which a Member State may have to take in the interests of security, or as Article 347 TFEU puts it:

> measures which a Member State may be called upon to take in the event of serious internal disturbances affecting the maintenance of law and order, in the event of war, serious international tension constituting a threat of war, or in order to carry out obligations it has accepted for the purpose of maintaining peace and international security.

Notably too, the various Treaty free movement provisions all contain security-related exceptions.[23]

[19] de Witte, n. 10, 10.

[20] Michael Dougan, "From 'Crisis' to 'Resilience' in EU Internal Market Law: Foundations, Techniques and Challenges" (2024) 51 Legal Issues of Economic Integration 317 at 320.

[21] Using the taxonomy provided by de Witte, n. 10.

[22] Various restrictions apply. Such measures must cause the least possible disturbance in the functioning of the internal market and must not be wider in scope than is strictly necessary to remedy the sudden difficulties which have arisen. Moreover, under Article 144(2), the Commission and the other Member States are to be informed of such protective measures not later than when they enter into force. Furthermore, subject to certain procedural requirements, under Article 144(3), the Council may decide that the Member State concerned shall amend, suspend or abolish the protective measures referred to above.

[23] See e.g., Article 36 TFEU (concerning goods), Article 45(3) TFEU concerning workers, Article 65(1) TFEU concerning capital and Article 52 TFEU (relating to establishment and also applied to services by Article 62). See further Julien Sterck, "A Time of Crises and the Emergence of a European Public Order" in Gavin Barrett (ed.), n. 2 at 49 and Panos Koutrakos "Public Security Exceptions", chapter 10 in Panos Koutrakos, Niamh Nic Shuibhne and Phil Syrpis (eds.), *Exceptions from EU Free Movement Law - Derogation, Justification and Proportionality* (Hart, 2016)

Secondly, there are Treaty provisions which *require Member States to act in solidarity with one another in times of crisis or emergency*. Hence, Article 222(1) requires EU Member States to act jointly in a spirit of solidarity if a Member State is the object of a terrorist attack or the victim of a natural or man-made disaster. Article 222(2) further requires that, should a Member State be the object of a terrorist attack or the victim of a natural or man-made disaster, the other Member States shall assist it at the request of its political authorities.[24]

Similarly, Article 42(7) TEU provides that "if a Member State is the victim of armed aggression on its territory, the other Member States shall have towards it an obligation of aid and assistance by all the means in their power, in accordance with Article 51 of the United Nations Charter."[25]

Thirdly, there are provisions that provide for *action on the part of the European Union*. De Witte distinguishes in this regard between (a) articles in the Treaties which provide a legal basis allowing the EU to take action to address crises or unforeseen situations—what we might call provisions directed at crises—and (b) articles providing general (*i.e.*, non-crisis-linked) legal bases in the Treaties which can nonetheless be used to adopt legislation to deal with crises either *ex ante* (by setting up a governance framework which can be triggered in a crisis) or *ex post facto* (by dealing with a crisis if and when it occurs).

10.3.1 Provisions Directed at Crises

Some—rather sporadic—provisions in the Treaties are designed to provide for Union action in the event of a crisis. Hence Art. 78(3) TFEU provides that

> in the event of one or more Member States being confronted by an emergency situation characterised by a sudden inflow of nationals of third countries, the Council, on a proposal from the Commission, may adopt provisional measures for the benefit of the Member State(s) concerned. It shall act after consulting the European Parliament.

[24] Note that Article 222 also imposes obligations on the EU itself and provides for EU-level coordination of Member State actions.

[25] It is specifically provided that this should not prejudice the specific character of the security and defence policy of certain Member States, a provision which seems to have been intended as a protection for neutral states.

Article 78(3) has been used to provide the legal basis for a number of prominent measures. One recent example is the 2024 Crisis and Force Majeure Regulation,[26] which establishes a framework enabling Member States to respond to crisis situations in the area of asylum and migration. Another example consisted of the 2015 relocation decisions, which sought to relieve frontline states like Italy and Greece from some of the burden of a sudden rise in the number of asylum seekers and migrants, which threatened to overwhelm their reception capacity by transferring a number of them to other states.[27]

Another provision designed to provide for Union action in the event of a crisis is Article 107(3)(b) TFEU, which authorizes the Commission to consider as compatible with the internal market what would otherwise be illegal state aid, where it is compatible with the internal market, where this is undertaken to remedy a serious disturbance in the economy of a Member State. This was deployed both in the Great Financial Crisis to permit state aid to banks during the financial crisis and during the COVID-19 crisis to allow for economic aid to the private sector.[28]

A further example of such a Treaty provision is Article 122 TFEU, which provides that.

[26] Regulation (EU) 2024/1359 of the European Parliament and of the Council of 14 May 2024 addressing situations of crisis and force majeure in the field of migration and asylum and amending Regulation (EU) 2021/1147 (OJ L, 2024/1359, 22.5.2024). This is a component of the 'Pact on Migration and Asylum'.

[27] Council Decision (EU) 2015/1523 of 14 September 2015 establishing provisional measures in the area of international protection for the benefit of Italy and of Greece (OJ L 239/146, 15.9.2015); Council Decision (EU) 2015/1601 of 22 September 2015 establishing provisional measures in the area of international protection for the benefit of Italy and Greece (OJ L 248/80, 24.9.2015). The latter decision was upheld by a Grand Chamber of the European Court of Justice in Joined Cases C-643/15 and C-647/15 *Slovak Republic and Hungary v Council of the European Union* EU:C:2017:63, analysed in Bruno de Witte and Evangelia Tsourdi, "Confrontation on relocation - the Court of Justice endorses the emergency scheme for compulsory relocation of asylum seekers within the European Union: *Slovak Republic and Hungary v. Council*" (2018) 55 CMLRev 1457. Both of these decisions have since expired.

[28] See de Witte, n. 10, 8; European Commission, *Communication from the commission — Temporary Community framework for State aid measures to support access to finance in the current financial and economic crisis* (OJ C 83/1, 7.4.2009) (which was followed by several other such measures); European Commission, *Communication from the Commission Temporary Framework for State aid measures to support the economy in the current COVID-19 outbreak* (OJ C 91I/1, 20.3.2020) (which was subsequently amended on several occasions).

1. Without prejudice to any other procedures provided for in the Treaties, the Council, on a proposal from the Commission, may decide, in a spirit of solidarity between Member States, upon the measures appropriate to the economic situation, in particular if severe difficulties arise in the supply of certain products, notably in the area of energy.
2. Where a Member State is in difficulties or is seriously threatened with severe difficulties caused by natural disasters or exceptional occurrences beyond its control, the Council, on a proposal from the Commission, may grant, under certain conditions, Union financial assistance to the Member State concerned. The President of the Council shall inform the European Parliament of the decision taken.

This actually comprises two emergency-directed provisions, the second a more specific example of the first. Both have been highly significant in recent crises. The first paragraph (apparently originally intended to focus on energy security) has been given an expansive interpretation and used variously as the legal basis for emergency measures obliging Member States to keep minimum stocks of oil and petroleum products; as the legal basis for a permanent programme providing for EU emergency support in the event of a Member State being struck by disasters (either natural or man-made); and even more broadly as the legal foundation for the provision of financial support for health measures taken by Member States to combat the COVID-19 pandemic as well as for establishing a framework to ensure the supply of crisis-relevant medical countermeasures in the event of an EU-level public health emergency.[29]

Article 122(2) - a narrower interpretation of which might have led one to think applied only to events analogous to natural disasters - has in practice been used to provide the legal basis for a wide range of measures, a first wave of which helped the EU to climb gradually out of the morass of the sovereign debt crisis (such as the EFSF, which paved the way for the European Stability Mechanism). It was then deployed again as the legal

[29] *Ibid.;* Council Directive 2009/119/EC of 14 September 2009 imposing an obligation on Member States to maintain minimum stocks of crude oil and/or petroleum products (OJ L 265/9, 9.10.2009); Council Regulation (EU) 2016/369 of 15 March 2016 on the provision of emergency support within the Union (OJ L 70, 16.3.2016, p. 1); Council Regulation (EU) 2020/521 of 14 April 2020 activating the emergency support under Regulation (EU) 2016/369, and amending its provisions taking into account the COVID-19 outbreak (OJ L 117/3 15.4.2020); and Council Regulation (EU) 2022/2372 of 24 October 2022 on a framework of measures for ensuring the supply of crisis-relevant medical countermeasures in the event of a public health emergency at Union level (OJ L 314/64, 6.12.2022). *Top of FormBottom of Form*

basis for some of the most important measures that were used to counter the economic effects of the coronavirus pandemic, such as the €100 billion European instrument for temporary Support to mitigate Unemployment Risks in an Emergency (SURE), and the €648 billion Next Generation EU programme (more specifically the 2020 European Union Recovery Instrument (EURI) Regulation, which is a key element of NGEU's legal superstructure).[30]

Mention has already been made of the Article 222 TFEU "solidarity clause" in the text above as a provision that requires Member States to act in solidarity with one another in times of crisis or emergency. However, Article 222 also fits into the present discussion of provisions in the Treaties designed to provide for Union action in the event of a crisis, since Article 222 also imposes obligations on the EU itself and provides for EU-level coordination of Member State actions.[31]

[30] Council Regulation (EU) 2020/2094 of 14 December 2020 establishing a European Union Recovery Instrument to support the recovery in the aftermath of the COVID-19 crisis (OJ L 433I/23, 22.12.2020). There was some academic questioning of the extent to which EURI was really a crisis-related measure, and therefore appropriately based on Article 122 TFEU. See de Witte, n. 10, 10 at footnote 31.

[31] Article 222 provides that

1. The Union and its Member States shall act jointly in a spirit of solidarity if a Member State is the object of a terrorist attack or the victim of a natural or man-made disaster. The Union shall mobilise all the instruments at its disposal, including the military resources made available by the Member States, to:
   (a) prevent the terrorist threat in the territory of the Member States;
      - protect democratic institutions and the civilian population from any terrorist attack;
      - assist a Member State in its territory, at the request of its political authorities, in the event of a terrorist attack;
   (b) assist a Member State in its territory, at the request of its political authorities, in the event of a natural or man-made disaster.
2. Should a Member State be the object of a terrorist attack or the victim of a natural or man-made disaster, the other Member States shall assist it at the request of its political authorities. To that end, the Member States shall coordinate between themselves in the Council.
3. The arrangements for the implementation by the Union of the solidarity clause shall be defined by a decision adopted by the Council acting on a joint proposal by the Commission and the High Representative of the Union for Foreign Affairs and Security Policy. The Council shall act in accordance with Article 31(1) of the Treaty on European Union where this decision has defence implications. The European Parliament shall be informed.

Deriving its origins in the terrorist attacks in Madrid in March 2004, what became Article 222 has been used to provide a legal basis for a decision laying down the rules and procedures for the operation of the solidarity clause and aimed at ensuring that all parties concerned at national and EU levels work together to respond quickly, effectively and consistently in the event of terrorist attacks or natural or man-made disasters.[32]

10.3.2 General Legal Bases Which Can Be Used to Adopt Crisis-Related Legislation

It will be noticed that under most of the above specific crisis provisions, decision-making power is put in the hands of the Council, thus enhancing executive power in crisis situations. It will also be noted that the provisions are rather sporadic in nature. One consequence of the absence of further such provisions has probably been the use of general legal bases for the adoption of crisis-related legislation. As will be seen presently, such legal bases are now being used with increasing frequency to create frameworks designed to ensure that the EU and its Member States have sufficient resilience to deal with crisis and emergency situations. Given its importance, the topic of resilience will be returned to in the text below. In considering the use of 'normal' legal bases for the adoption of emergency measures, de Witte distinguishes between emergency prevention measures and emergency management measures—the former being used to set in place a governance framework that can be triggered when a sudden crisis occurs later on, the latter being measures adopted to deal with a crisis if and when it occurs, whether through the implementation of a preventive framework or the adoption of self-standing measures—although he admits himself that this distinction is a rather fluid one, since a framework measure may

> For the purposes of this paragraph and without prejudice to Article 240, the Council shall be assisted by the Political and Security Committee with the support of the structures developed in the context of the common security and defence policy and by the Committee referred to in Article 71; the two committees shall, if necessary, submit joint opinions...

[32] Council Decision 2014/415/EU of 24 June 2014 on the arrangements for the implementation by the Union of the solidarity clause (OJ L 192/53, 1.7.2014)

be amended on an *ad hoc* basis to deal with some unforeseen circumstance or emergency.[33]

10.4 The Reality of Reactions to Crises in the European Union: Some Preliminary Points

Before considering the reality of how the European Union has responded to crises over the years, a number of preliminary observations can be made. One is that responses to crises can vary from one such event to another. Hence, the severe austerity imposed on bailout states during the Great Financial Crisis in exchange for bailouts was not replicated during the financial crisis. While loans formed part of Next Generation Europe, so too did grants, and the loans themselves were not on the same punitive conditions. The European Union can muddle through a crisis: it can 'fail forward' by adopting inadequate measures that nonetheless see development in the EU itself (the temporarily successful but nonetheless inadequate European Financial Stabilisation Mechanism, and European Financial Stability Facility being examples of this). It can also 'head forward' by adopting successful measures such as the European Central Bank's Outright Monetary Transactions programme, the creation of which was so successful in calming bond market turbulence during the Great Financial Crisis that it did not actually need to be implemented.

Overall, further integration does appear to be happening in the EU because of crises—the development of both the European Banking Union and the European Health Union in response to the Great Financial Crisis and the COVID-19 pandemic being examples of this. Interestingly, however, the benefits derived from crisis-driven actions may not be as directly related to the crisis itself as one might have expected. Thus, for example, the financial assistance provided under Next Generation Europe—adopted in response to economic devastation wreaked by the coronavirus—provided benefits which have accrued largely after the pandemic itself passed and which did not bear any necessary relation to the economic damage wreaked by COVID-19, but rather related to pre-existing economic difficulties. Similarly, the adoption of the European Arrest Warrant in extraordinarily short order in response to the 9/11 attack had little to do with the issues raised by the attack itself (which was planned and executed entirely

[33] de Witte, n. 10, 11–12

outside the European Union), even if it would later prove valuable in the fight against cross-border crime generally, including terrorist offences.

A further preliminary point is that EU responses to crises can fail and sometimes do. The ongoing rule of law crisis has been tackled with a barrage of strategies by the European Union, ranging from Commission prosecutions under Article 258 TFEU, to a Rule of Law Framework, to annual rule of law reports, to major developments in European Court of Justice case law to a financial conditionality mechanism to the attempted deployment of the procedures provided for under Article 7 TEU. Yet none of these has yet been sufficient to solve the ongoing difficulties in this field.

Moreover, even where a solution is ultimately found to a crisis, the wrong response may initially be adopted. Hence, during the COVID-19 crisis, the adoption of effective EU-wide action in a range of areas was preceded by an initial retreat by Member States into ineffective and counterproductive nationally-oriented solutions. Again, during the Great Financial Crisis, a moralistic, punitive and ultimately self-defeating approach was adopted vis-à-vis Greece when a more generous approach would have probably been more politically and economically effective, and ended up being adopted later on in any case.[34]

One issue that arises is whether the European Union itself could fail on the foot of a crisis. This question might seem far-fetched: the European Union has after all survived multiple crises over several decades. However, the EU is now beset by challenges. These include the rule of law crisis, which finds EU Member States are moving ever further down the road towards autocracy. Not alone do present mechanisms seem inadequate to the task of coping with this, but further, Member States seem unlikely to be able to amend the Treaties to provide a better mechanism to deal with this problem because of the unanimity rule. Additionally, and perhaps less obviously, Dougan has pointed out that the Internal Market faces the ongoing risk of fragmentation in any fresh crisis, with the danger that Member States may engage in protectionism or an uncoordinated free-for-all (without even the need for this to involve any illegality as such—merely unilateral conduct that may disrupt the Internal Market ecosystem). The same writer observes that vulnerabilities revealed by recent polycrises appear more specific to the EU than to the US, to Canada or to the UK.[35]

[34] See generally here Jean Pisani-Ferry, *The Euro Crisis and its Aftermath* (Oxford University Press, Oxford, 2011).

[35] Dougan, n. 20, 331.

It can not be ruled out that the European Union may one day be overwhelmed by the scale of such challenges facing it. On the other hand, it may be that the European Union is sufficiently growing in resilience that it is now better able to cope with polycrises: the economic and monetary challenges given rise to by the COVID-19 crisis were, after all, arguably better dealt with than those generated by the Great Financial Crisis, and using the expertise gained in the earlier crisis.[36] To take one example of this, the quantitative easing programme used by the European Central Bank in the coronavirus crisis owed much in terms of its conception, and its political acceptability, to the experience gained in the sovereign debt crisis. Also to be noted is the gradual adoption of an approach based on the concept of resilience at the sub-Treaty level as part of its response in dealing with polycrises or cluster crises, a topic which is returned to in the text below.[37]

10.5 Some of the More Prominent Reactions to Crises in the European Union

The various reactions of the European Union to crises over the years have been many and varied, and could not possibly all be enumerated here. However, it does seem possible to mention some of the more eye-catching reactions which have featured among the European Union's responses. In no particular order, these have included.

- *resort to international law measures* such as the Fiscal Stability Treaty and the European Stability Mechanism Treaty,[38] Both of which featured in the response of the EU to the Great Financial Crisis, including using these to impose obligations on European Union institutions in non-EU Treaties (something the Fiscal Stability Treaty does[39]);

[36] For analysis of how the EU dealt with the economic consequences of the COVID-19 and Ukraine crises, see Federico Fabbrini, *EU Fiscal Capacity—Legal Integration after COVID-19 and the War in Ukraine* (Oxford University Press, Oxford, 2022)

[37] See more generally on this topic, Dougan, n. 20.

[38] Such resort has been referred to as 'multilateral emergency politics', distinguishing it from the use of EU measures of various kinds, which has been referred to as 'supranational emergency politics'.

[39] See Articles 3(1) and (2), 4, 5(1) and (2), 6, 8(1) and (2), 12(1), (4) and (5) and 13 of the Fiscal Stability Treaty.

- *new and expanded interpretations of primary law*—seen during the Great Financial crisis in the rulings in *Pringle*, *Gauweiler* and *Weiss*, *concerning the legal bases of the European Stability Mechanism, the Outright Monetary Transactions and the Public Sector*; and also in the construction of the entire edifice of the Single Supervisory Mechanism (the key element of European Banking Union) on the narrow legal basis provided by Article 127(6) TFEU according to which the Council may "confer specific tasks upon the European Central Bank concerning policies relating to the prudential supervision of credit institutions and other financial institutions with the exception of insurance undertakings."
- *a trend towards greater use of soft law, and within this trend a greater use of "harder," more specific soft law, side by side with the replacement of existing soft law with hard law*—something seen in the aspects of the EU reactions to both the COVID and the Great Financial Crisis; and
- in the field of hard law, *a trend towards the use of regulations*, which can enter into force quickly, and do not require transposition into national legal systems

10.6 Some Particularly Significant Trends

A number of trends in, or features of, the way in which the European Union deals with crises appear particularly significant, however.

- *Action in Areas Normally Linked with National Policies*

Recent times have seen considerable levels of action in areas normally linked to national policies. One thinks of the large-scale movement of the European Union into the health policy field during the COVID-19 crisis. Another example was the move into borrowing at federal level in the European Union in order to finance Next Generation EU, the response of the European Union to the economic challenges created by COVID-19. In this way, a certain degree of centralization has taken place in areas in which the European Union has heretofore had only a coordinating or supporting role.[40]

[40] According to Article 5 TFEU, the Member States shall coordinate their economic policies within the Union and to this end the Council shall adopt measures. According to Article

- *Changes in Political Paradigms*

Dealing with multiple crises has led to major changes in political paradigms associated with the EU. The ECB now clearly acts in ways that would have been unthinkable before the Great Financial Crisis, in particular through its deployment of various quantitative easing programmes.

It has been further argued by Borger that the Great Financial Crisis has brought about a profound upgrading of the fundamental joint commitment—the political contract—underlying the Union, and more specifically, a fundamental transformation of the currency union, characterized by a widening of its stability conception.[41]

According to this view, the European Union's role differs fundamentally from that it enjoyed at the time of the entry into force of the Maastricht Treaty. The transformation described is a political one, only partly reflected in the law, and more specifically in European Court of Justice rulings in cases such as *Pringle, Gauweiler* and *Weiss*.[42] Other writers, such as Schmidt may be more modest in their claims,[43] but there can be little doubt that the European Union has changed very considerably since the Great Financial Crisis and that these changes owe an immense amount to the EU reaction to that crisis.

10.6.1 The Advent of a Resilience Approach to Dealing with Crises

Awareness of the need for a more holistic and consistent approach to dealing with repeated crises has increased in recent years. A major consequence

6 TFEU, the Union shall have competence to carry out actions to support, coordinate or supplement the actions of the Member States in the area of protection and improvement of human health;

[41] See generally Borger, n. 3.

[42] Case 370/12 *Pringle v Government of Ireland and others* EU:C:2012:756; Case C-62/14 *Gauweiler and others v Deutscher Bundestag* EU:C:2015:400; Case C-493/17 *Weiss and others* EU:C:2018:1000.

[43] See Vivien Schmidt, "Economic Crisis Management in the EU: from past Eurozone mistakes to future promise beyond the COVID-19 pandemic", Chapter 1 in Anna Wetter Ryde (ed.) *EU Crisis Management* (Report 1op, April 2022, Swedish Institute for European Policy Studies).

of this, as Dougan has identified,[44] is that "resilience" has now become a key concept in European Union policy discourse. Indeed, it is one identified by the Commission as forming "a new compass for EU Policies".[45] A resilience agenda has gathered momentum during the years of polycrisis.[46] The Council for its part, declared in the light of the COVID-19 crisis that

> in the future, the EU must also be ready to face acute crises of a different nature, which could be multi-faceted, of a hybrid nature, have cascading effects or occur simultaneously. This will require improved cross-sectoral and cross-border crisis management, including risk analysis and strategic foresight for better anticipatory action, prevention, preparedness and response, in an all-hazards approach, in order to inform longer-term action to build resilience to challenges. Available EU mechanisms, including their interaction with global mechanisms, should be regularly reviewed by the Council in order to ensure they remain fit for purpose.[47]

A multifaceted and deliberate approach to resilience has thus become an explicit overarching strategy, structuring the Union's preparation for and response to crises. There are various aspects to this—dissuading Member States from uncoordinated unilateral reactions, improving forward planning and intelligence gathering and reduction of strategic dependencies on third countries all form part of resilience.[48] Legislation forms a particularly important element. This is therefore a theme returned to below.

[44] See generally in relation to resilience, Dougan, n. 20. As the same author points out, the European Council has linked resilience to the wider goal of building EU sovereignty. See the Versailles Declaration made by the informal meeting of the Heads of State or Government, 10 and 11 March 2022 (*i.e.*, just after the Russian invasion of Ukraine) in which the European Council embedded resilience in the broader sovereignty goal. On the broader theme of European sovereignty, see Gavin Barrett, Jean-Philippe Rageade, Peter-Christian Müller-Graff and Viktor Vadász (eds.), *European Sovereignty: The Legal Dimension* (Springer, January 2025).

[45] *Strategic Foresight—Charting the Course towards a More Resilient Europe*, (2020 Strategic Foresight Report), Communication from the Commission to the European Parliament and the Council, (COM/2020/493 final, Brussels 9.9.2020)

[46] Dougan, n. 20 at 329.

[47] Council of the European Union, *Council conclusions on enhancing preparedness, response capability and resilience to future crises* (14276/21) (Brussels, 23 November 2021) at para. 5 thereof.

[48] Dougan, n. 20 at 318.

10.6.2 The Institutional Impact of Crises

The institutional impact of crises has been considerable: institutional innovation has formed part and parcel of the EU reaction to crisis events. The *creation* of new networks, institutions, entities and unions during the Great Financial Crisis, such as the European System of Financial Supervision,[49] the European Stability Mechanism and the European Banking Union all stand as testament to this reality. The *development* of other pre-existing institutions or entities, such as the ECB (with the additional roles in quantitative easing, bailout administration, and banking supervision being assigned to it or assumed by it) and the Eurogroup, was also a feature of the Great Financial Crisis. As Fromage *et al* summarize,

> in reaction in particular to the Great Financial Crisis, the institutional involvement of EU institutions and bodies, and the coordination between EU and Member State actors, were reinforced significantly, mostly by creating new EU bodies (in particular, European agencies) or by giving new powers to existing institutions (in particular, the ECB).[50]

The COVID-19 crisis also led to an intense process of institution-building.[51] Hence, the European Centre for Disease Prevention and Control was upgraded,[52] with the ultimate objective of making it a real European Health Agency. So too was the European Medicines Agency,[53] including through the setting up of the COVID-19 EMA Pandemic Task Force and the creation of a permanent EMA Emergency Task Force. Another development involved the Health Security Committee, which now has representation

[49] The ESFS is a network centered around the three European Supervisory Authorities (ESAs), the European Systemic Risk Board and national supervisors.

[50] Diane Fromage, Adrienne Héritier and Paul Weismann, "EU Regulatory Responses to Crises" in Diane Fromage, Adrienne Héritier and Paul Weismann (eds.), *EU Regulatory Responses to Crises- Adaption or Transformation* (OUP, Oxford, 2025)

[51] See here Andreas Eriksen and Michelle Everson "Health Policy: A Cautionary Tale of Constitutional Slippage and Polity Building between Crisis and Nation Building", chapter 4 of Diane Fromage, Adrienne Héritier and Paul Weismann (eds.), *EU Regulatory Responses to Crises- Adaption or Transformation* (OUP, Oxford, 2025).

[52] See now Regulation (EU) 2022/2370 of the European Parliament and of the Council of 23 November 2022 amending Regulation (EC) No 851/2004 establishing a European centre for disease prevention and control OJ L 314/1 (6.12.2022).

[53] See now Regulation (EU) 2022/123 of the European Parliament and of the Council of 25 January 2022 on a reinforced role for the European Medicines Agency in crisis preparedness and management for medicinal products and medical devices OJ L20/1 (31.1.2022)

in its high-level working group at the level of Deputy Health Ministers, capable of triggering common EU-level responses, and an enhanced role in coordinating risk communication in addition to a strengthened mandate to enforce coordinated responses.[54] A further institutional innovation has been the creation of an entirely new authority—the European Health Emergency Preparedness and Response Authority (HERA), to provide a structure to deal with future pandemics.[55]

Other COVID-19 crisis-related innovations have been the recent creation of specifically crisis- and emergency-related bodies such as the Commission-managed Emergency Response and Coordination Centre,[56] which was established with the aim of ensuring 24/7 operational capacity in pursuit of the objectives of the Union Civil Protection Mechanism and is supposed in particular to coordinate, monitor and support in real-time the response to emergencies at Union level and to work to promote a cross-sectoral approach to disaster management.

Moving away from institutional arrangements deriving from the COVID-19 crisis to more generalised institutional crisis-related developments, the Integrated Political Crisis Response[57] was developed to enable both timely coordination and a response at the Union political level to crises, whether these originate inside or outside the Union or not, where these have a wide-ranging impact or are of political significance.[58] As such, it can be seen as part of the resilience approach, which will be returned to later in the text.

10.7 Pathologies of Crisis Politics

Crisis-linked insitutional developments are normally aimed at output legitimacy and more specifically at ensuring exit from a crisis situation of the EU and its Member States. They also tend to go hand in hand with

[54] See now *e.g.*, Regulation (EU) 2022/2371 of the European Parliament and of the Council of 23 November 2022 on serious cross-border threats to health and repealing Decision No 1082/2013/EU OJ L 314/26 (6.12.2022)

[55] As to which, see Commission Decision of 16.9.2021 establishing the Health Emergency Preparedness and Response Authority Brussels, C(2021) 6712 final 16 September 2021

[56] This was created by Article 7 of Regulation (EU) 2021/836 of the European Parliament and of the Council of 20 May 2021 amending Decision No 1313/2013/EU on a Union Civil Protection Mechanism (OJ L 185, 26.5.2021)

[57] Council Implementing Decision (EU) 2018/1993 of 11 December 2018 on the EU Integrated Political Crisis Response Arrangements (OJ L 320, 17.12.2018)

[58] See Article 1 of the Preamble to Council Implementing Decision (EU) 2018/1993

expertocracy, depoliticization and increased executive federalism (including increased cooperation between the EU and Member State actors). In other words, they are negative from the standpoint of input legitimacy and tend to involve "executive drift"—the gradual concentration of power in executive institutions, going hand-in-hand with deparliamentarization. Legitimacy questions are therefore raised.

Somewhat paradoxically, however (and as writers such as Borger and van Middelaar[59] have noted), the Great Financial Crisis in particular saw a shift from a rules-based approach to economic and monetary union to an approach involving political choices. Overall, therefore, we have seen somewhat contradictory outcomes from crises—a growth in expertocracy and depoliticization, but also, at least when it has come to the the single currency as this has emerged from the Great Financial Crisis and subsequent crises, an increase in politicization, with responses often driven by the European Council.

10.8 A New Dawn in Dealing with Crises? Resilience Legislation

Dealing with crisis and emergency situations through Treaty change and constitutional innovation—which must surely have formed an important part of the reaction to crises that Monnet originally anticipated—has become more difficult with the gradual increase in the number of Member States and the simultaneous retention of the requirement of unanimous agreement of the Member States in order for Treaty change to occur. It has already been noted in the text above[60] that an expansive interpretation by the Court of Justice of existing Treaty provisions has been one form of constitutional pressure valve, allowing for needed flexibility to cope with crises. However, many of the reactions and changes resulting from crises and emergencies discussed in the text above involve not constitutional-level change, but rather changes that take place at sub-Treaty level, either in the form of legislation, or through soft law or through institutional innovations or else involve the use of international legal instruments outside the purview of EU law. In this context, one of the most significant recent developments which may enable the European Union to cope with crises as they arise while forestalling, to at least some extent, the need for Treaty change must surely be recent moves towards resilience structures

[59] Borger, n. 3; Luuk van Middelaar, *Alarums and Excursions—Improvising Politics on the European Stage* (Agenda Publishing, Newcastle upon Tyne, 2019)

[60] See para. 5 of text above.

and legislation.[61] A very recent example of such a move (and indeed as yet the broadest example of the legislative aspect of this approach) is the package of laws adopted in October 2024 and collectively referred to as the Internal Market Emergency and Resilience Act (IMERA).

10.9 The Internal Market Emergency and Resilience Act (IMERA)

The impetus for adopting the Internal Market Emergency and Resilience Act (IMERA) was provided by the occurrence of recent crises such as the COVID-19 pandemic and the war in Ukraine. The Act's objective is to secure the movement across the EU without interruption of essential goods (as well as that of services and persons) in the event of any crisis, in addition to ensuring that critical supplies will be available whenever the EU is confronted by an emergency. The IMERA package includes the main regulation,[62] a so-called omnibus regulation[63] and a directive.[64] All three were adopted together on 9 October 2024, and will be in effect by 30 May 2026.[65] IMERA seeks to introduce both a comprehensive preparedness and a comprehensive crisis-response architecture into the single market. Its system is intended to be a *lex generalis* applying when no

[61] See generally, Dougan, n. 20.

[62] Regulation (EU) 2024/2747 of the European Parliament and of the Council of 9 October 2024 establishing a framework of measures related to an internal market emergency and to the resilience of the internal market and amending Council Regulation (EC) No 2679/98 (OJ L, 2024/2747, 8.11.2024).

[63] Regulation (EU) 2024/2748 of the European Parliament and of the Council of 9 October 2024 amending Regulations (EU) No 305/2011, (EU) 2016/424, (EU) 2016/425, (EU) 2016/426, (EU) 2023/988 and (EU) 2023/1230 as regards emergency procedures for the conformity assessment, presumption of conformity, adoption of common specifications and market surveillance due to an internal market emergency (OJ L, 2024/2748, 8.11.2024)

[64] Directive (EU) 2024/2749 of the European Parliament and of the Council of 9 October 2024 amending Directives 2000/14/EC, 2006/42/EC, 2010/35/EU, 2014/29/EU, 2014/30/EU, 2014/33/EU, 2014/34/EU, 2014/35/EU, 2014/53/EU and 2014/68/EU as regards emergency procedures for the conformity assessment, presumption of conformity, adoption of common specifications and market surveillance due to an internal market emergency (OJ L, 2024/2749, 8.11.2024)

[65] Under Article 48 of Regulation (EU) 2024/2747, that regulation is to apply from 29 May 2026. Under Article 7 of Regulation Regulation (EU) 2024/2748, that regulation is also to apply from 29 May 2026. Under Article 11 of Directive (EU) 2024/2749, Member States are to adopt and publish the measures necessary to comply with the Directive by 29 May 2026 and are to apply them from 30 May 2026.

specific sectoral measures are in place. Its main elements are well summarized on the Commission website as including the following:

- *a contingency planning framework* prepares for potential crises by establishing crisis protocols, training, drills, and an early warning system for disruptions in the functioning of the single market.
- *a Single market vigilance framework* monitors critical supply chains of goods and services before disruptions escalate, allowing early crisis response.
- *an emergency framework* will be activated during a crisis. This framework ensures the free flow of goods, services and persons, prohibiting EU countries from imposing certain restrictions and requiring transparency in their actions. It also enables Commission-led procurement of crisis-relevant goods with EU country participation. This toolbox includes *exceptional measures* to ensure that essential goods are available when needed most. These measures allow the Commission to request information from companies, to place priority orders with companies and to speed up the procedures for placing essential products on the market (as specified in the Omnibus acts).[66]

It will be immediately noticed that this package includes elements which have been discussed in the text above as typical of the responses of the EU to crisis situations, and thus involves an approach which builds on the experience of dealing with multiple emergencies and crises over time. It combines several different approaches simultaneously. It involves institutional creativity, of which the IMERA Board is the most important manifestation. It involves the use of hard law and, more specifically, the use of regulations (*viz.*, the main regulation and the omnibus regulation) in order to secure its aims. It involves a strong role for the executive, particularly the Commission, but also for national market surveillance authorities and, if there is little reference to soft law, the various measures at least make extensive reference to and demonstrate reliance on standards concerning goods that have been implemented via Commission implementing legislation.[67]

[66] See "Internal Market Emergency and Resilience Act", European Commission website at https://single-market-economy.ec.europa.eu/single-market/internal-market-emergency-and-resilience-act_en.

[67] Soft law (such as guiding principles) and administrative measures form important elements of other measures designed to ensure Internal Market resilience, *e.g.*, in the transport field. See Dougan, n. 20, 321.

IMERA is not equivalent to an emergency constitutional procedure involving suspension from the normal operation of the law, but is rather a *lex specialis* involving, for instance, provision for derogation from assessment procedures for conformity with normal EU standards for goods in times of crisis, and mutual recognition for national decisions doing this.[68]

Dougan has pointed out that the various policy initiatives grouped together around the concept of resilience "may well be a contemporary response to years of 'cluster crisis'—but they are also a continuation and indeed magnification of much deeper and longer-term trends in the evolution of the Internal Market".[69] To this extent, IMERA can be regarded as the confluence of two streams: single market law on the one hand, and the EU's efforts to prepare for and meet the challenges which future crises may bring, on the other. IMERA has been far from the only such measure or even the last such crisis-relevant measure attempting to deal with resilience: other recent 'resilience' legislation designed to cope with crises in some shape or form includes the NIS 2 Directive (which, *inter alia*, seeks to ensure a uniform approach to cybersecurity attacks on important entities in critical sectors),[70] the Critical Entities Resilience Directive (CER) (which seeks to safeguard essential services by ensuring that critical entities can withstand, react to and recover from non-cyber related crises such as sabotage or national disasters)[71] and the Digital Operational Resilience Act (DORA), which seeks to ensure that the financial sector can prevent and recover from disruption related to information and communications technology, particularly where this relates to cybersecurity.[72]

[68] See in this regard *e.g.*, Recital 13 of Regulation (EU) 2024/2748.

[69] Dougan, n. 20, 325.

[70] See Directive (EU) 2022/2555 of the European Parliament and of the Council of 14 December 2022 on measures for a high common level of cybersecurity across the Union, amending Regulation (EU) No 910/2014 and Directive (EU) 2018/1972, and repealing Directive (EU) 2016/1148 (OJ L 333, 27.12.2022).

[71] See Directive (EU) 2022/2557 of the European Parliament and of the Council of 14 December 2022 on the resilience of critical entities and repealing Council Directive 2008/114/EC (OJ L 333, 27.12.2022)

[72] Note also the Cyber Resilience Act (CRA) which seeks to ensure that products with digital elements remain cybersecure throughout their lifetime through proper design, maintenance and vulnerability management. This is obviously also resilience-related, although not as linked to crisis prevention and management as the measures mentioned in the text above. The CRA entered into force on 10 December 2024. Its main obligations will apply from 11 December 2027. (See Regulation (EU) 2024/2847 of the European Parliament and of the Council of 23 October 2024 on horizontal cybersecurity requirements for products with digital elements and amending Regulations (EU) No 168/2013 and (EU) 2019/1020 and Directive (EU) 2020/1828 (Cyber Resilience Act) (OJ L, 2024/2847, 20.11.2024)).

That the EU is using secondary legislation and the novel institutional and executive arrangements found in and associated with these measures, rather than Treaty law, to forestall and cope with crises is an interesting development. A comprehensive approach to deal with potential crises in such technical fields could not in any case have been provided for in the Treaties—in other words, at constitutional level (and given the impossibility in present political circumstances of securing broad-based Treaty change, even making framework provision in the Treaty, or providing explicit legal bases for this kind of measure might have proven impracticable). It does show, however, that Europe continues to be forged in crises, and will be the sum of the solutions adopted for those crises—but that the smithy of Europe's soul in which such forging takes place may well frequently be henceforth in places other than in its constitutive Treaties.

References

Books, Reports and Journal Special Editions

Ansell, C., Trondal, J., and Øgård, M. *Governance in Turbulent Times.* Oxford University Press, Oxford, 2017

Barrett, G. (ed.). *Law in a Time of Crises.* LXX *The Irish Jurist* (new series), Special Edition, Thomson Reuters, Dublin, 2023

Barrett, G., Rageade, J.-P., Müller-Graff, P.-C., and Vadász, V. (eds.). *European Sovereignty: The Legal Dimension.* Springer, Heidelberg, January 2025

Belling, V. "Legality and Legitimacy of the EU 'Emergency Governance'—On the Application of the State of Emergency in the European Union." *Zeitschrift für öffentliches Recht*, 73, 2018, 271

Boin, A., 't Hart, P., Stern, E., and Sundelius, B. *The Politics of Crisis Management: Public Leadership Under Pressure.* Cambridge University Press, Cambridge, 2009

Borger, V. *The Currency of Solidarity—Constitutional Transformation during the Euro Crisis.* Cambridge University Press, Cambridge, 2020

Brack, N., and Gürkan, S. (eds.). *Theorising the Crises of the European Union.* Routledge, Abingdon, 2021

Buhari, D., Kaunert, C., and Gulmez, S.B. (eds.). *Transforming Europe through Crises—Thin, Thick, Parochial and Global Dynamics.* Routledge, Abingdon, 2023

Cotta, M., and Isernia, P. (eds.). *The EU Through Multiple Crises.* Routledge, Abingdon, 2021

European Commission. *Strategic Foresight—Charting the Course towards a More Resilient Europe (2020 Strategic Foresight Report).* Communication from the

Commission to the European Parliament and the Council, COM/2020/493 final, Brussels, 9 September 2020

Fabbrini, F. *EU Fiscal Capacity—Legal Integration after COVID-19 and the War in Ukraine.* Oxford University Press, Oxford, 2022

Fromage, D., Héritier, A., and Weismann, P. (eds.). *EU Regulatory Responses to Crises—Adaptation or Transformation.* Oxford University Press, Oxford, 2025, 177–202

Karkowska, R., Korzeb, Z., Matysek-Jędrych, A., and Niedziółka, P. *Banking, Risk and Crises in Europe—From the Global Financial Crisis to COVID-19.* Routledge, Abingdon, 2023

Koutrakos, P., Nic Shuibhne, N., and Syrpis, P. (eds.). *Exceptions from EU Free Movement Law—Derogation, Justification and Proportionality.* Hart, Oxford, 2016, 190–217

Pisani-Ferry, J. *The Euro Crisis and its Aftermath.* Oxford University Press, Oxford, 2011

Riddervold, M., Trondal, J., and Newsome, A. (eds.). *The Palgrave Handbook of EU Crises.* Palgrave Macmillan, London, 2021

Rosenthal, U., Charles, M., and 't Hart, P. *Coping with Crises: The Management of Disasters, Riots, and Terrorism.* Charles C Thomas, Springfield, Illinois, 1989

Sandbu, M. *Europe's Orphan—The Future of the Euro and the Politics of Debt.* Princeton University Press, Princeton, 2017

van Middelaar, L. *Alarums and Excursions—Improvising Politics on the European Stage.* Agenda Publishing, Newcastle upon Tyne, 2019

Wetter Ryde, A. (ed.). *EU Crisis Management.* Report 1op, April 2022, Swedish Institute for European Policy Studies, Stockholm

Zeitlin, J., and Nicoli, F. (eds.). *The European Union Beyond the Polycrisis—Integration and Politicisation in an Age of Shifting Cleavages.* Routledge, Abingdon, 2020

Articles and Book Chapters

Barrett, G. "Law in a Time of Crises—An Introduction." In Barrett, G. (ed.), *Law in a Time of Crises.* LXX *The Irish Jurist* (new series), Special Edition, 2023 (Thomson Reuters, Dublin) 1

Bauerschmidt, J., and Quaglia, L. "Financial Regulation and Supervision: Crisis as Catalyst for Institutional and Policy Reforms." In Fromage, D., Héritier, A., and Weismann, P. (eds.), *EU Regulatory Responses to Crises—Adaptation or Transformation.* Oxford University Press, Oxford, 2025, ch. 3, 37

Bellenghi, G. "Neither Normalcy nor Crisis: The Quest for a Definition of Emergency under EU Constitutional Law." *European Journal of Risk Regulation*, 2025, 1

Bellenghi, G. "The European Parliament's Proposal for an EU State of Emergency Clause: A Comparative and Constitutional Analysis." *Croatian Yearbook of European Law and Policy*, 20, 2024, 1

Belov, M. "The Conceptual Shapes of Constitutional Polycrisis: Deconstruction, Asymmetries and Post-modern Anxieties of Constitutional Normalcy." In Barrett, G. (ed.), *Law in a Time of Crises.* LXX *The Irish Jurist* (new series), Special Edition, 2023 (Thomson Reuters, Dublin) 393

Boin, A., 't Hart, P., and McConnell, A. "Crisis Exploitation: Political and Policy Impacts of Framing Contests." *Journal of European Public Policy*, 16, 2009, 81

Brack, N., and Gürkan, S. "Introduction—European Integration (Theories) in Crisis?" In Brack, N., and Gürkan, S. (eds.), *Theorising the Crises of the European Union.* Routledge, Abingdon, 2021, ch. 1

Chamon, M. "The EU's Dormant Economic Policy Competence: Reliance on Article 122 TFEU and Parliament's Misguided Proposal for Treaty Revision." *European Law Review*, 49, 2024, 166

de Witte, B. "EU Emergency Law and Its Impact on the EU Legal Order—European Crises and EU Emergency Law." *CMLRev*, 59, 2022, 3

de Witte, B. "The European Union's COVID-19 Recovery Plan: The Legal Engineering of an Economic Policy Shift." *CMLRev*, 58, 2021, 635

de Witte, B., and Tsourdi, E. "Confrontation on Relocation—The Court of Justice Endorses the Emergency Scheme for Compulsory Relocation of Asylum Seekers within the European Union: Slovak Republic and Hungary v. Council." *CMLRev*, 55, 2018, 1457

Delhomme, V., and Hervey, T. "The European Union's Response to the COVID-19 Crisis and (the Legitimacy of) the Union's Legal Order." *Yearbook of European Law*, 41, 2022, 41

Dermine, P. "Article 122 TFEU and the Future of the Union's Emergency Powers." *EU Law Live*, 25 January 2024

Dougan, M. "From 'Crisis' to 'Resilience' in EU Internal Market Law: Foundations, Techniques and Challenges." *Legal Issues of Economic Integration*, 51, 2024, 317

Eriksen, A., and Everson, M. "Health Policy: A Cautionary Tale of Constitutional Slippage and Polity Building between Crisis and Nation Building." In Fromage, D., Héritier, A., and Weismann, P. (eds.), *EU Regulatory Responses to Crises—Adaptation or Transformation.* Oxford University Press, Oxford, 2025, ch. 4, 63

Fromage, D., Héritier, A., and Weismann, P. "EU Regulatory Responses to Crises." In Fromage, D., Héritier, A., and Weismann, P. (eds.), *EU Regulatory Responses to Crises—Adaptation or Transformation.* Oxford University Press, Oxford, 2025, ch. 9, pp. 177-202

Fromage, D., Héritier, A., and Weismann, P. "Introduction: The Crisis-induced Development of EU Rule-making." In Fromage, D., Héritier, A., and Weismann, P. (eds.), *EU Regulatory Responses to Crises—Adaptation or Transformation.* Oxford University Press, Oxford, 2025, ch. 1, pp. 1-7

Koutrakos, P. "Public Security Exceptions." In Koutrakos, P., Nic Shuibhne, N., and Syrpis, P. (eds.), *Exceptions from EU Free Movement Law—Derogation, Justification and Proportionality.* Hart, 2016, ch. 10, pp. 190-217

Kreuder-Sonnen, C. "The Case for an EU Emergency Constitution." In Wetter Ryde, A. (ed.), *EU Crisis Management*. Report 1op, April 2022, Swedish Institute for European Policy Studies, ch. 3, pp. 59-74

Markakis, M., Kafka, C., and Papadopoulou, L. "Accountability and Democratic Legitimacy in European Union Economic Governance: From the Euro Crisis to the Pandemic and Beyond." In Barrett, G. (ed.), *Law in a Time of Crises*. LXX *The Irish Jurist* (new series), Special Edition, 2023 (Thomson Reuters, Dublin), 68

Riddervold, M., Trondal, J., and Newsome, A. "European Union Crisis: An Introduction." In Riddervold, M., Trondal, J., and Newsome, A. (eds.), *The Palgrave Handbook of EU Crises*. Palgrave Macmillan, London, 2021, ch. 1, 3

Schmidt, V. "Economic Crisis Management in the EU: From Past Eurozone Mistakes to Future Promise beyond the COVID-19 Pandemic." In Wetter Ryde, A. (ed.), *EU Crisis Management*. Report 1op, April 2022, Swedish Institute for European Policy Studies, ch. 1, pp. 19-39

Schoeller, M., and Weismann, P. "Economic and Monetary Union: Incremental Adaptation under Legal and Political Constraints." In Fromage, D., Héritier, A., and Weismann, P. (eds.), *EU Regulatory Responses to Crises—Adaptation or Transformation*. Oxford University Press, Oxford, 2025, ch. 2, 8

Sterck, J. "A Time of Crises and the Emergence of a European Public Order." In Barrett, G. (ed.), *Law in a Time of Crises*. LXX *The Irish Jurist* (new series), Special Edition, 2023 (Thomson Reuters, Dublin), 49-57

van den Brink, T. "Two Crises On: Convergence in Economic Performance Policies in the Economic and Monetary Union in the Light of Next Generation EU and the Creation of the Macroeconomic Imbalance Procedure." In Barrett, G. (ed.), *Law in a Time of Crises*. LXX *The Irish Jurist* (new series), Special Edition, 2023 (Thomson Reuters, Dublin) 111-30

Weiler, J. "In the Face of Crisis: Input Legitimacy, Output Legitimacy and the Political Messianism of European Integration." *European Integration*, 34, 2012, 825

Wetter Ryde, A. "Introduction: How Should the EU Govern in an Emergency?" In Wetter Ryde, A. (ed.), *EU Crisis Management*. Report 1op, April 2022, Swedish Institute for European Policy Studies, 11

White, J. "Before the Next Emergency." In Wetter Ryde, A. (ed.), *EU Crisis Management*. Report 1op, April 2022, Swedish Institute for European Policy Studies, ch. 2, pp. 40-58

Zeitlin, J., Nicoli, F., and Laffan, B. "Introduction: The European Union beyond the Polycrisis? Integration and Politicization in an Age of Shifting Cleavages." In Zeitlin, J., and Nicoli, F. (eds.), *The European Union Beyond the Polycrisis—Integration and Politicisation in an Age of Shifting Cleavages*. Routledge, Abingdon, 2020, ch. 1, pp. 1-14

Judicial Decisions

Case C-62/14 *Gauweiler and others v Deutscher Bundestag* EU:C:2015:400

Case 370/12 *Pringle v Government of Ireland and others* EU:C:2012:756
Joined Cases C-643/15 and C-647/15 *Slovak Republic and Hungary v Council of the European Union* EU:C:2017:63
Case C-493/17 *Weiss and others* EU:C:2018:1000

CHAPTER 11

Constitutionalism amid Crisis: Adopting and Adapting Power-Sharing Settlements

Allison McCulloch

11.1 Introduction

Consociational power-sharing is designed to bring together ethnic majorities and minorities in shared governing institutions across all levels of the state. Frequently adopted as a way to end war, support democratization, and repair community relations, it can be considered a leading governance arrangement for responding to political crises and emergency conditions. Yet, once up and running, power-sharing can also beget a political crisis. Patterns of protracted government formation processes or cyclical political crises that bring the government to the brink can be identified across the power-sharing universe. In Northern Ireland, the power-sharing executive is estimated to have been non-functioning for around 40% of its existence.[1] Belgium went some 652 days without forming a government after its 2018 elections. Lebanon appointed its new president in January 2025 after the position sat vacant for more than two years; it took even longer

This chapter is produced as part and funded by the European Union-NextGenerationEU, through the National Recovery and Resilience Plan of the Republic of Bulgaria, project No bg-rrp-2.004-0008.

[1] Pivotal Public Policy Forum, "Governing Northern Ireland Without an Executive" [2022] Pivotal Briefing, 1 September.

M. Belov (ed.), *Constitutional Polycrisis and Emergency Constitutionalism*, Federalism and Internal Conflicts,
https://doi.org/10.1007/978-3-032-06516-2_11

to assemble its Council of Ministers following the 2022 election. Power-sharing governments, that is, rarely seem to work.

Power-sharing has also proven to be a difficult system to reform. In 2019, citizens took to the streets in the hundreds of thousands in Lebanon and Iraq to demand political reforms and the end of sectarian government. It has not happened. The European Court of Human Rights has issued multiple rulings on the discriminatory features of the Bosnian constitution, namely its 3-person presidency and its upper house. No changes have been made. John Nagle describes this phenomenon as "zombie power-sharing." As he puts it, "rather than transformation and change, consociations tend to develop ossified properties rendering them resistant to practically any reform."[2] Many power-sharing systems now appear "stuck" with a set of institutions that have long outlived their usefulness yet are seemingly incapable of moving beyond them. In other cases, power-sharing risks ending or eroding due to authoritarian revival. These represent instances of power-sharing's adaptation problem.

Nonetheless, many contemporary peace processes have followed a "power-sharing oriented mediation,"[3] or the idea that the decision to recommend the sharing of power will have already been made at the earlier stages of a mediation process. Indeed, power-sharing was on the table—at least as an abstract or aspirational concept—since 2012 for Syria, where the Geneva process, from Kofi Annan's 6-point plan to UN Security Council Resolution 2254, aims at a negotiated and inclusive political transition. Power-sharing has been a central dimension to any reunification of the two parts of Cyprus for decades.[4] Power-sharing has informed attempts to build peace in Yemen, with the former UN special envoy noting, "power-sharing is the only way to end war in Yemen."[5] Agreement has remained elusive or been surpassed by facts on the ground. That is, they represent instances of the power-sharing adoption problem.

[2] John Nagle, "Consociationalism is Dead! Long Live Zombie Power-Sharing!" [2020] 20(2) *Studies in Ethnicity and Nationalism*, 137.

[3] Irene Costantini and Ruth Hanau Santini, "Power Mediators and the 'Illiberal Peace' Momentum: Ending Wars in Libya and Syria" [2022] 43(1) *Third World Quarterly*, 131.

[4] Neophytos Loizides and John McGarry, "The UN in 21st Century Cyprus: Meditration, Mediation-lite and Beyond" [2022] 27 *International Negotiation*.

[5] Quoted in Simon Mabon and Allison McCulloch, Power-Sharing: Why Is It Still Central in the Efforts to End the Wars in Syria and Yemen? [2022] Foreign Policy Centre.

This chapter takes as its starting point the fact that power-sharing agreements are often negotiated within a context of crisis and urgency: the kinds of emergency conditions that exist at war's end, after authoritarian collapse, or in the context of deep ethnic divisions. This constitutional moment is marked by lines of division that are raw and vexatious, and often operates on expedited timelines that are meant to heighten the sense of urgency to get a deal done. Peace negotiations or other political transitions thus frequently include the writing of a new constitution or the significant amendment of the extant constitutional order to provide for joint governing institutions, such as executive power-sharing, group autonomy, proportionality and veto powers. What impact do these starting conditions—writing or revising constitutional documents under the extreme conditions of the fog of war or amidst fraught ethnic relations—have on the functionality and adaptability of these new constitutional rules?

In what follows, I investigate the consequences of adopting new constitutional rules in crisis conditions, the interplay between these starting conditions and system functionality over time, and the capacity for constitutional change. To do so, I draw from a collection of interviews with international mediators, advisors, academic experts, civil society activists and others who have closely followed or participated in the negotiation, adoption and/or implementation processes in a range of power-sharing cases.[6] Interviews focused on a set of thematic clusters: how power-sharing is put on the agenda in negotiations and by whom, the dynamics at the table, the role of external actors, opportunities for citizen inclusion, and the interplay between domestic and international versions of power-sharing propositions. Then, employing a "lifecycle approach"[7] and illustrative case examples, I engage in textual analysis of foundational texts (e.g., constitutions, comprehensive peace agreements, autonomy statutes, high-level ad hoc agreements) to investigate the problems that emerge over the life of power-sharing agreements. Here, I focus on two

[6] The interviews were conducted in the context of two projects: "Citizen Inclusion in Power-Sharing Settlements" (Open Research Area 7) and "Power-Sharing for Peace? Between Adoptability and Durability in Lebanon, Syria, and Iraq" (Swiss Network for International Studies). Several of the interviews cited in this chapter were jointly conducted with Soeren Keil.

[7] Allison McCulloch and Joanne McEvoy, "The Power-Sharing Lifecycle across the Global South" in Eduardo W. Aboultaif, Soeren Keil and Allison McCulloch (eds.), *Power-Sharing in the Global South: Patterns, Practices and Potentials* (Palgrave Macmillan 2024).

contrasting—and potentially contradictory—trade-offs in the adoption of power-sharing rules that redound to adaptability. The first is that provisions may be struck with 'constructive ambiguity' in mind. Constructive ambiguity is an important part of negotiations, whereby "actors deliberately adopt language that is vague and can simultaneously mean different things to different people."[8] This can help to elicit agreement, glossing over substantial differences between parties and making power-sharing provisions acceptable at the constitutional table.

The second relates to the perceived "stickiness" or rigidity of power-sharing provisions. Jai Kwon Jung, for example, argues that power-sharing suffers from "institutional rigidity"—"once power-sharing is agreed upon, it becomes difficult to make changes to the initial set-up."[9] Donald Horowitz concurs, suggesting that such arrangements "tend to rigidify conflicts and do not lend themselves to renegotiation. Most agree that consociational institutions, once established, are sticky."[10] Such stickiness is often a product of the adoption process in that power-sharing settlements are negotiated at the very point at which group identities are the most politically salient and polarized. Under conditions of insecurity, group representatives are unlikely to settle for anything other than a strong guarantee of their share in power. That is, negotiated transitions from war to democracy, or from majority control to shared power, are more likely to produce corporate or predetermined power-sharing rules, in the form of reserved seats, quotas and other group-specific rights. Together, constructive ambiguity and institutional stickiness might be necessary to reach a new constitutional agreement, but they create problems of adaptability later on. In this chapter, I consider three such adoption-to-adaptation problems: ambiguous provisions can give way to serious disagreements about their meaning; some clauses of an agreement needed to elicit agreement are ignored thereafter; and some provisions become seemingly "unreformable," leaving divided societies "stuck" with anachronistic rules and institutions.

[8] Christine Bell and Kathleen Kavanaugh, "'Constructive Ambiguity' or Internal Self-determination? Self-determination, Group Accommodation, and the Belfast Agreement." [1998] 22(4) *Fordham International Law Journal*, 1345.

[9] Jai Kwan Jung, "Power-sharing and Democracy Promotion in Post-civil War Peace-building" [2012] 19(3) *Democratization*, 486.

[10] Donald L. Horowitz, "Ethnic Power Sharing: Three Big Problems" [2014] 25(2) *Journal of Democracy*, 12.

11.2 Prescribing Power-Sharing in Constitution-Making Processes

Since 1989, more than 100 peace agreements have compelled some kind of constitutional change, such as the adoption of a new constitution, the establishment of an interim constitution or other transitional provisions, or the promise of changes to an extant constitutional order.[11] As described by Asli Ozcevik and Tarik Olcay, "regardless of whether constitutional change is explicitly promised, almost all peace agreements, as 'constitutions in embryo,' include provisions on constitutional matters, ranging from political power-sharing to changes in intra-state and state borders, and from national identity to human rights guarantees."[12]

Constitution-writing and -amending processes, particularly when embedded in wider peace processes or in transitions from autocracy to democracy, are profoundly fraught moments whose outcomes are often contingent on prevailing power dynamics. Given the complexities of inter-group relations—as noted above, lines of division are raw and vexatious at the point of negotiation—some degree of power-sharing is often part of the mediated peace agreement. Indeed, since the end of the Cold War, power-sharing has become a go-to response to ending conflict and mediating deep divisions.

In a 2007 influential article about Iraq's power-sharing constitution, John McGarry and Brendan O'Leary posit liberal consociation as "political prescription." They position the institutional rules of Iraq's 2005 constitution (negotiated on an expedited timeline with American pressure) not only as promising for Iraq, but also as a model for other divided places. Indeed, McGarry and O'Leary explicitly frame their analysis of Iraq's constitution in terms of what prescriptive lessons it offers to other places: "Progress in Iraq requires the maintenance and extension of the principles of liberal consociation already present in Iraq's federation…This is as likely to be true for Sri Lanka, Sudan and Cyprus as it is for Iraq."[13] While they

[11] Jordan Kyle and Danielle Resnick, "Securing the Peace or Renegotiating the Political Settlement? Understanding Popular Support for Post-Conflict Constitutions" [2024] 31(8) *Democratization*, 1645.

[12] Asli Ozecelik and Tarik Olcay, "(Un)constitutional Change Rooted in Peace Agreements" [2021] 18(4) *International Journal of Constitutional Law*, 1378.

[13] John McGarry and Brendan O'Leary, "Iraq's Constitution of 2005: Liberal Consociation as Political Prescription" [2007] 5(4) *International Journal of Constitutional Law*, 670.

focus specifically on liberal forms of power-sharing in this article, a general prescriptive tone frequently dominates in the literature. In the introduction to his co-edited volume with Joanne McEvoy—aptly subtitled "An Advocate's Introduction"—O'Leary reminds us that "power-sharing is one of the most important instances of enhanced 'inclusion'…It is a standard prescription for protracted national, ethnic, and communal conflicts in deeply divided places."[14] Acknowledging that "no sensible advocate of power sharing sees it as a panacea," he nonetheless offers a robust defense of the model against its critics. Arend Lijphart has at times been even more direct: for divided places, it is either "consociational democracy or no democracy at all."[15]

O'Leary's positioning of power-sharing as an instance of 'enhanced inclusion' finds resonance in internationally mediated processes and other forms of constitutional assistance. The *UN Manual for Mediators*, the *Secretary-General Report on Strengthening the Role of Mediation*, and the *UN Guidance on Gender and Inclusive Mediation Strategies*, as well as other UN mediation documents, all frame the consideration of governance choices around ideas of power-sharing, suggesting it serves as a kind of "go-to" response or cognitive template for how to design governing institutions. The *Manual for Mediators,* for example, states: "Of critical importance is finding a model for power-sharing that fits the unique characteristics of the situation." Insights, according to the *Manual*, can be learned from other cases that have pursued similar arrangements and the UN's Mediation Support Unit regularly develops thematic analysis on power-sharing and other issues (e.g., to support the UN Mission in Iraq, MSU drew up analytical and advisory papers on power-sharing, drawing lessons and good practices from Northern Ireland, Bosnia-Herzegovina, Cyprus, Belgium, Andorra, Switzerland, Italy, and India). Understandings of power-sharing in these policy documents continue to view it as a template for bringing parties together to find common solutions and political institutions. That is, it is perceived to be an appropriate response to the kinds of emergency conditions that characterize political transitions.

[14] Brendan O'Leary, "Power-Sharing in Deeply Divided Societies: An Advocate's Introduction" in Joanne McEvoy and Brendan O'Leary (eds.) *Power Sharing in Deeply Divided Places* (University of Pennsylvania Press 2013), 8.

[15] Arend Lijphart, *Power-Sharing in South Africa* (University of California Press 1985), 102.

11.3 The "Adoption/Adaptation Problem"

Under what conditions do power-sharing agreements come into being? First, it is important to recognize that power-sharing is agreed in different contexts and with different incentives. As one international advisor to the constitutional negotiations in Iraq noted, "I don't think it's possible to say that there is one path through which power sharing broadly arrives on the agenda."[16] Yet, a number of macro-political factors were repeatedly highlighted in the interviews when asked what might elicit or impede agreement. This includes: the political willingness of elites to make compromises, economic considerations, the security-territory calculus (e.g., prospect of victory via military means), path dependence, the inclusion or exclusion of key constituencies in negotiations, state capacity to subsequently deliver on agreed-upon provisions, and the involvement of external actors, whose shifting interests and priorities within the wider geopolitical environment significantly influence the dynamics of the conflict.[17]

For a power-sharing agreement to come into being, preferences must converge between different sets of actors within distinct arenas, many of which will start negotiations with "asymmetrical preferences"[18] on the use of power-sharing as a form of government. Successful agreements often require a combination of domestic acceptance and international backing to overcome security dilemmas, support democratization and ensure long-term peace. Indeed, many research participants noted that while the challenge of getting local actors to commit to power-sharing solutions is extraordinarily difficult, the role of regional and international actors adds another layer of complexity. As one international advisor noted about Yemen:

> So, I think it depends on the historical moment we're referring to. Like Yemen 10 years ago: it was the default; Yemen today: it's not even considered. And it was the default I feel...because there was a minimum of consensus in the region or nationally, that solution should be found through dialogue, mediation and negotiated settlements. We don't have this consensus now. And so, I don't think the region has a consensus that this conflict should be resolved through dialogue. If you don't have that, then power sharing doesn't come up the ladder of solutions.[19]

[16] Interview, August 2023.

[17] Allison McCulloch, *et al.*, "Power-Sharing for Peace? Between Adoptability and Durability in Lebanon, Syria, and Iraq" [2024] swisspeace Working Paper.

[18] Horowitz, n10.

[19] Interview, September 2023.

Specifically, the adoption problem stands the best chance of resolution when three conditions are met: when domestic actors come to see power-sharing as the way to solve their collective disputes; when there is convergence between international actors in support of a power-sharing solution, and when key international actors reinforce the commitment to power-sharing amongst their domestic proxies.[20] Michael Kerr's description of the solution to mutual coexistence in Lebanon seems particularly apt in this context: "finding that narrow piece of common ground where nobody is happy but where everyone can live."[21] This effectively encapsulates the small window of opportunity that exists for overcoming the adoption problem.

Power-sharing proposals offer a degree of flexibility that can help to induce parties towards a settlement. Such proposals allow mediators to avoid taking sides between conflict actors or between different international legal norms; they also allow conflict actors to claim some measure of victory (or at least not outright defeat) in constitutional negotiations.[22] Power-sharing, as an institutional package consisting of some configuration of coalition governments, proportionality, autonomy and vetoes, lends itself to the exchange of concessions. Yet, because it often brings together parties with "asymmetrical preferences"[23] or "irreconcilable differences,"[24] it frequently entails the elision of those differences in foundational texts or ambiguously worded provisions that the different sides to a conflict can live with, or conversely, it requires rigid guarantees in order to counter the effects of mistrust between parties.

Constructive ambiguity, a term frequently attributed to Henry Kissinger, plays an important role in negotiations, the premise of which is that "ambiguously worded text can create opportunities for advancing the interests of both parties, under the assumption that tackling the most difficult issues in an unambiguous way would cause a breakdown in negotiations."[25] As applied to peace negotiations, there are several advantages,

[20] McCulloch et al, n17.

[21] Michael Kerr, *Imposing Power-Sharing: Conflict and Coexistence in Northern Ireland and Lebanon* (Irish Academic Press 2005), 175.

[22] Allison McCulloch and Joanne McEvoy, "The International Mediation of Power-Sharing Settlements," [2018] 53 (4), *Cooperation and Conflict,* 467.

[23] Horowitz, n10.

[24] Michael Byers, "Still Agreeing to Disagree: International Security and Constructive Ambiguity" [2021] 8(1) *Journal on the Use of Force and International Law*, 91.

[25] Elie Friedman, "Evasion Strategies in International Documents: When 'Constructive Ambiguity' Leads to Oppositional Interpretation" [2017] 14(4) *Critical Discourse Studies,* 385.

including: it can facilitate progress towards an overall agreement without the risk of a particularly contentious or controversial issue scuppering the deal; in the context of ongoing violence, the preference may be to "push for the earliest possible agreement and to defer time-consuming issues," and it can allow the different sides to "can allow both parties to claim that a concession has been obtained on an important issue, thereby easing negotiators' relations with their constituencies." Indeed, this was the case with the Good Friday Agreement, where constructive ambiguity over the final constitutional status of Northern Ireland, as well as the requirements on paramilitary decommissioning, helped to facilitate the acceptance of the agreement by negotiators at the table and by voters in dual referendums in Northern Ireland and the Republic of Ireland.[26] Michael Byers also highlights how constructive ambiguity is "sometimes used to paper over irreconcilable differences so that at least some agreement between the negotiating parties can be achieved."[27] Further, negotiated agreements will necessarily entail some ambiguities not only because they bring together "complex issues, divergent interests, and tight time constraints" but also because ambiguities are "unavoidable when crafting general rules that will later be applied to specific situations."[28]

Constructive ambiguity may elicit agreement, making power-sharing provisions acceptable in the moment, but translating them into practice can give way to serious disagreements about how to put such provisions into effect, leaving some clauses of an agreement unimplemented or simply ignored. Such agreements are written in the midst of urgency and crisis, under considerable time constraints, and with a variety of different actors and interests jockeying for power, none of whom are likely to be satisfied with the final product. As one mediation support actor noted, "It's about postponing the decision about who controls the state by sharing the state and all the resources of the state. In order to keep those who have the power to return to conflict satisfied.... [It is] a way of kicking the can down the road."[29] This echoes David Mitchell's observation, which is that.

> constructive ambiguity has a perilous double-edged character and may create more problems than it solves. The 'constructive' element refers to the

[26] David Mitchell, "Cooking the Fudge: Constructive Ambiguity and the Implementation of the Northern Ireland Agreement, 1998–2007" [2009] 24(3) *Irish Political Studies*, 323

[27] Byers, n24, 93.

[28] Byers, n24, 93.

[29] Interview, September 2023.

> immediate advancement of a political objective; in the longer term it may in fact be destructive. By deferring difficult issues and masking concessions, parties agree to create time and space in the hope that the necessary ground might be traversed—from violence to democracy, enmity to co-operation, suspicion to trust—without preventing accommodation on certain issues in the short term.[30]

The notion of institutional stickiness, the second adoption solution under consideration, stems from the circumstances of insecurity and mistrust that characterize inter-group relations during constitution-writing or amending processes in divided settings. Group representatives will aim to lock in guarantees of their share of power—through corporate provisions such as reserved seats and ethnic quotas in legislative, executive, and bureaucratic spaces and through group-based autonomy provisions—during the writing stage.[31] At the amendment stage, representatives will often be unwilling to forsake previously agreed-upon group rights. As Ozan Varol argues, even "increasingly obsolete constitutional provisions can become increasingly difficult to alter," a phenomenon he calls constitutional stickiness.[32] Indeed, it remains unclear how to initiate the transition to another political arrangement beyond power-sharing without jeopardizing the gains of peace and stability. This is why some scholars argue that power-sharing blocks the transition to more "normal" politics—where bread and butter issues, rather than ethnicized ones, dominate and where political institutions can be organized on a more majoritarian basis.[33] Certainly, parties in power-sharing systems often find it difficult to work together, but at the same time they are either not willing to change a set of rules under which they benefit or, because they have so little in common in terms of how they envision the role of the state, they cannot agree on new institutional rules—hence, the stickiness problem.

Siobhan Byrne has made the case that power-sharing denotes an action verb: it's power-*sharing*, not power-*shared*.[34] As such, it requires sustained

[30] Mitchell, n26, 323.

[31] Allison McCulloch, *Power-Sharing and Political Stability in Deeply Divided Societies* (Routledge, 2014).

[32] Ozan O. Varol, "Constitutional Stickiness," [2016], 49, *University of California, Davis Law Review*, 906.

[33] Horowitz, n10; Jung, n19; Nagle n2.

[34] Siobhan Byrne, "Feminist Reflections on Discourses of (power) + (sharing) in Power-Sharing Theory." [2020] 41(1) *International Political Science Review*, 58.

commitment and recommitment to ensuring functional performance. This, it would seem, is a difficult ask. Having delivered short-term benefits in the realm of security and stability, a point is reached at which more power-sharing cannot deliver further peace dividends, and in fact may be harmful to the very solution it seeks. Rather than rendering itself "superfluous" as anticipated by Lijphart,[35] the end of power-sharing democracy is more likely to come about via authoritarian revival, conflict resumption, or regression on minority rights. Still, other cases are "sticky," locking—or attempting to lock in—a specific balance of power even in the face of political and demographic shifts.

Drawing on a set of illustrative examples, let me now turn to some adoption solutions that later become adaptation problems. First, agreed-upon provisions end up unimplemented or ignored. Second, they become the source of serious contestation in the implementation period, with the distance in meaning between the parties leading to a stalemate. Third, the strong guarantees needed to elicit agreement are subsequently "unreformable," even in the face of dysfunctional political dynamics.

11.3.1 Ignored or Unimplemented Provisions

Some constitutional provisions may be necessary to facilitate the overall adoption of a constitutional settlement, but then they may languish in the implementation period. An illustrative example of this comes from Lebanon, where power is shared between Maronite Christians, Sunni Muslims, and Shia Muslims, with 18 different sects receiving constitutional recognition. A 1989 peace agreement, negotiated in Taif, Saudi Arabia, helped to facilitate the end of a 14-year civil war. Yet, significant provisions, agreed as part of the Taif Accords, have never been implemented: provisions for a Senate as well as the eventual de-confessionalization of parliament. De-confessionalism—or the notion of moving away from sect-based representation—was given a sense of priority in the negotiations in recognition that confessionalism had exacerbated tensions leading up to the civil war.[36]

[35] Arend Lijphart, *Democracy in Plural Societies: A Comparative Exploration* (Yale UP 1977).

[36] Eduardo W. Aboultaif, *Power-Sharing in Lebanon: Consociationalism since 1820* (Routledge 2019). See also Allison McCulloch, et al."Power-Sharing Between Adoptability and Durability: Insights from Lebanon and Iraq" [2025] OnlineFirst, *Regional and Federal Studies*, 1

Per the agreement, a committee was to be set up with a mandate to consider how best to move towards deconfessionalization. From there, once a non-confessional parliament was elected, a Senate would be established with equal communal representation. The Senate's role would be restricted to the consideration of issues deemed to be of national importance ("crucial issues"). Despite a few false starts, neither the committee nor the Senate has been established. As Kerr describes, "it remained as an aspiration for many, but no one sect was actually ready to put it into effect."[37] Ambiguous wording on Article 11.A.7—it provides neither a timeline nor a roadmap on how to bring these provisions to life—is often noted as a major stumbling block.[38] As one research participant noted, "There's no real timeline there because there's no incentive for the local class to actually do those reforms because it would undermine their own authority and control of the system…All too often, the implementation is kind of left to the political elites' own devices rather than an attached monitoring mechanism that is part of the settlement."[39] Ambiguous language served as an adoption solution, but the inability to initiate its practice effect turned it into an adaptation problem.

The idea of the eventual abolition of political sectarianism is an example of an "aspirational pathway"[40] from power-sharing, which, if implemented, would have facilitated constitutional adaptation and potentially even the move to a more 'normal' kind of politics. This kind of aspirational clause, imbued with ambiguity, is intended to support the parties, allowing them to collectively articulate the speed of the transition, to defer particularly difficult and contentious issues to a later date when the stakes are not as high, and to reach a more readily consensus once the crisis conditions of adoption have passed. But this ambiguity creates a downstream problem: without a specified end date to the agreement, it has languished in perpetual transition, and political elites have been able to avoid constitutional change.

[37] Kerr, n21, 166. See also, Fouad Younes, *Abolishing Sectarianism in Lebanon* Policy Paper (Arab Association of Constitutional Law 2022).

[38] Stephan Rosiny, "A Quarter Century of 'Transitory Power-Sharing': Lebanon's Unfulfilled Ta'if Agreement of 1989 Revisited" [2015] 17(4) *Civil Wars*, 485; McCulloch et al, n18.

[39] Interview, Beirut-based NGO program officer, November 2023.

[40] Allison McCulloch, "Pathways from Power-Sharing" [2017] 19(4) *Civil Wars*, 405.

Taif Agreement, Lebanon, 1989

Article II.A.7. Chamber of Deputies
With the election of the first Chamber of Deputies on a national, not sectarian, basis, a senate shall be formed and all the spiritual families shall be represented in it. The senate powers shall be confined to crucial issues.

Article II. G. Abolition of Political Sectarianism
Abolishing political sectarianism is a fundamental national objective. To achieve it, it is required that efforts be made in accordance with a phased plan. The Chamber of Deputies election the basis of equal sharing by Christians and Muslims shall adopt the proper measures to achieve this objective and to form a national council which is headed by the president of the republic and which includes, in addition to the prime minister and the Chamber of Deputies speaker, political, intellectual, and social notables. The council's task will be to examine and propose the means capable of abolishing sectarianism, to present them to the Chamber of Deputies and the cabinet, and to observe implementation of the phased plan.

11.3.2 Serious Contestation over the Meaning of Provisions

A second challenge is that ambiguous clauses can give rise to serious contestation over their meaning in either the short or long term. It may subsequently come to light that parties have contrasting interpretations over how to give practical effect to the clause, with the provision amenable to different means of uptake. The clause on multi-ethnic government formation in Fiji's now-defunct 1997 constitution is an illustrative example of this kind of contestation, or how an adoption solution translated into an adaptation problem.

Fiji's constitution-making process emerged in the wake of the country's ongoing coup-proneness (e.g., two back-to-back coups in 1987), ethnic tensions between Indigenous Fijians and Indo-Fijians, and a desire to "establish and consolidate a national consensus on how the country should be governed" so as to "put aside the divisions and the bitterness of [the] 1987 coups and subsequent policies of discrimination."[41] While not written with the same sense of urgency that typically characterizes "peace-agreement constitutions,"[42] there were nonetheless several ambiguous clauses, most notably Article 99, which mandates that parties with more than 10% of seats must be invited to the cabinet. The clause was intended to create multi-ethnic governments, but as Michael Green notes, there were many holes: "There was no clear formula for deciding Cabinet

[41] Yash Ghai, "The Implementation of the Fiji Islands Constitution," in A. Harmon Akram-Lodhi (ed.), *Confronting Fiji Futures* (ANU Press e-view 2000), 25.

[42] Ozecelik and Olcay, n12.

allocations among qualified parties; there were no rules for the conduct of Cabinet; there was no limit on Cabinet membership; and the processes for selecting Ministers from qualified parties were vague, apart from a requirement for the Prime Minister to consult the leaders of those parties."[43] It was also unclear "whether 'their numbers in the House' referred to the qualifying 10% + parties, or to the total 71 members."[44]

Indeed, the constitutional experiment was short-lived, subject to abrogation following another coup in 2006 and a return to military rule that lasted until 2013. Article 99 was the subject of several court challenges in the interim. After the 1999 victory of the Indo-Fijian Fiji Labour Party (FLP), incoming prime minister, Mahendra Chaudhry, formed a multi-ethnic coalition; however, this was mainly with Indigenous Fijian parties that had not met the 10% threshold. Chaudhry did invite Soqosoqo ni Vakavulewa ni Taukei (SVT)—the only Indigenous party to surpass the threshold—but the SVT responded with a series of conditions on participation that were eventually rebuffed by the government.[45] A coup abruptly ended the government's tenure.

New elections were held in 2001 with the return to civilian rule. This time, it was the SVT that won the election, with the FLP now the party to whom the invitation to cabinet was to be extended. SVT leader Laisenia Qarase did so in the most perfunctory of ways, noting that he found the prospect of a coalition "unworkable" and that he had already invited other "like-minded parties" to join.[46] Ultimately, the new government did not include any FLP members. The decision to exclude the FLP was adjudicated by the Supreme Court, which found the government to have acted unconstitutionally. In the wake of the court ruling, "Qarase conformed to

[43] Michael Green, "Fiji's Short-Lived Experiment in Executive Power-Sharing, May-December 2006" [2009] *State, Society and Governance in Melanesia* Discussion Paper 2009/2, 1–2.

[44] Jon Fraenkel, "Mandatory Power-sharing in Coup-prone Fiji" in Allison McCulloch and John McGarry (eds), *Power-Sharing: Empirical and Normative Challenges* (Routledge 2017), 110. See, also, Brij V. Lal, "Fiji's Constitutional Conundrum," [2010] 92 (372) *The Round Table,* 671.

[45] According to Jon Fraenkel, "the SVT responded by setting conditions on participation, including demands for four ministerial portfolios, for three of the nine prime ministerial nominations to the Senate and that all of the Rabuka government's diplomatic and state-owned enterprise appointees be allowed to complete their terms of office" (Fraenkel, n44, 110).

[46] Fraenkel, n44.

the letter, but not the spirit, of the law by offering the FLP token portfolios in an expanded Cabinet," which the FLP declined.[47] The government subsequently fulfilled its mandate without adhering to the provisions of Article 99. The government formed following the 2006 election brought together the SVT and FLP, as anticipated by Article 99, but was plagued by tensions between the coalition partners and lasted only six months in office before another military coup upended the entirety of the constitutional experiment. The return to democracy was deferred to 2013, with a constitution without any power-sharing provisions.

Constitution, Fiji, 1997

Article 99: Appointment of the Prime Minister [...]

(3) The Prime Minister must establish a multi-party Cabinet in the way set out in this section comprising such number of Ministers as he or she determines.

(4) Subject to this section, the composition of the Cabinet should, as far as possible, fairly represent the parties represented in the House of Representatives.

(5) In establishing the Cabinet, the Prime Minister must invite all parties whose membership in the House of Representatives comprises at least 10% of the total membership of the House to be represented in the Cabinet in proportion to their numbers in the House.

11.3.3 *Sticky or Unreformable Institutions*

Bosnia and Herzegovina has one of the most complex constitutions in the world, with a presidency shared between representatives of three constituent peoples, reserved seats for the different communities, a heavily decentralized federal system, and veto points spread throughout every level of state. The constitution—largely written by American lawyers in English, with no official version in any of the local languages—was appended as an annex to the 1995 Dayton Peace Accords, which ended a three-and-a-half-year war. Its architects have claimed it was only meant to be temporary; according to James Pardew, a key member of the American negotiations team at Dayton, "it was a document made in compromise. It was never imagined to be absolute and the only solution for the future of Bosnia and Herzegovina. It was a starting point."[48] Yet, the constitution has proven highly resistant to reform efforts.

[47] Green, n43.

[48] See https://www.rferl.org/a/bosnians-unhappy-with-permanence-of-the-dayton-s-temporary-solution-/30325778.html

There have been several rounds of high-level talks designed to reform the constitution towards a less ethnically rigid framework—the 2006 "April package" talks, the Prud talks in 2008, and the Butmir process in 2009, among them—but all have failed to reach agreement.[49] These efforts were designed to redistribute competencies between the state and entity level, introduce a weaker presidency and stronger government and prime minister, and reduce the powers of the second chamber, the House of Peoples.[50] Alongside these high level talks, the European Court of Human Rights has issued six rulings that call for the reform to the three-person collective presidency and House of Peoples, election to which violate the rights of "Others" (small minorities such as members of the Jewish, Roma, and Albanian minorities), citizens unwilling to declare an affiliation with a constituent people, Bosniaks living in the Republika Srpska, and Serbs living in the Federation of Bosnia-Herzegovina. These rulings have also failed to elicit any agreed-upon constitutional reforms.

One explanation for such stickiness considers the "symbolic weight" of the institutions. As Karlo Basta argues,

> The symbolic content of different institutional options, internalized by the general population(s) and their political representatives, presents a fundamental obstacle to constitutional compromise in Bosnia and Herzegovina. Any deviation from either the civic (for the Bosniaks) or the ethnic (for the Serbs and Croats) institutional model is cons trued as a threat not only to group interests, but to collective identities.[51]

This recalls Peter Hall and Rosemary Taylor's argument about institutions more broadly, which is that they "influence behaviour by providing the cognitive scripts, categories, and models that are indispensable for action… Institutions influence behaviour not simply by specifying what one should do but also by specifying what one can imagine doing in a given context."[52] This logic ran through many of the interviews I conducted in Bosnia and Herzegovina, where everyone agreed on the need to reform the Dayton

[49] Aleksandra Zdeb, "Prud and Butmir Processes in Bosnia and Herzegovina: Intra-Ethnic Competition from the Perspective of Game Theory" [2017] 16(4) *Ethnopolitics*, 367.

[50] Valentino Grbavac, "Who Watches the Watchmen? External Actors and Consociational Democracy in Bosnia and Herzegovina" [2024] PhD Dissertation, University of Edinburgh.

[51] Karlo Basta, "Imagined Institutions: The Symbolic Power of Formal Rules in Bosnia and Herzegovina" [2016] 75(4) *Slavic Review*, 965

[52] Peter Hall and Rosemary Taylor, "Political Science and the Three New Institutionalisms" [1996] 44(5) *Political Studies*, 948.

system, but no one could agree on how to do so or what might replace it. As one high-ranking international actor bluntly put it: "There's no way you can get out of the power-sharing agreement without another war in this country."[53] They further stated: "The point is there is no consensus on what the constitutional framework of Bosnia is now, and it's very dangerous to open constitutional reform when the current understanding is not settled." That is, the 'cognitive script' of the Dayton arrangement has proven resilient. A leading country expert also noted the challenge of moving beyond power-sharing: "nobody has come up with a clearly defined agenda, even those who claim to be for a civic state.... Okay, what do you mean by that? And does that include Serbs and Croats? And if so, how do you allay the fears that may or may not be legitimate, but are there. And if you don't go over the hump on that, it's no sale."[54] Ultimately, the case of Bosnia and Herzegovina highlights how choices made at earlier stages lock in institutional rules, imbuing them with 'constitutional stickiness.'[55]

Dayton Peace Accords, Annex 4 (constitution), Bosnia & Herzegovina, 1995

Article V: Presidency
The Presidency of Bosnia and Herzegovina shall consist of three Members: one Bosniac and one Croat, each directly elected from the territory of the Federation, and one Serb directly elected from the territory of the Republika Srpska.

Article IV: Parliamentary Assembly
9. House of Peoples. The House of Peoples shall comprise 15 Delegates, two-thirds from the Federation (including five Croats and five Bosniacs) and one-third from the Republika Srpska (five Serbs).

a The designated Croat and Bosniac Delegates from the Federation shall be selected, respectively, by the Croat and Bosniac Delegates to the House of Peoples of the Federation. Delegates from the Republika Srpska shall be selected by the National Assembly of the Republika Srpska.
b Nine members of the House of Peoples shall comprise a quorum, provided that at least three Bosniac, three Croat, and three Serb Delegates are present.

11.4 Conclusion

Power-sharing and political crisis are ineluctably related. Power-sharing is, above all, a response to crisis: it represents a set of political institutions

[53] Interview, November 2023.

[54] Interview, November 2023.

[55] See Varol, n32 on 'constitutional stickiness' and its consequences.

put in place to end or prevent violent conflict, to transition from autocracy to democracy, and to forge more constructive intergroup relations. This means that there is often a sense of urgency to reaching such a solution. More often than not, power-sharing comes too late—amid widespread devastation, loss of life, and economic and social upheaval. Power-sharing, however, also begets crisis: it brings together reluctant partners, follows a fairly cumbersome decision-making process, one that often results in deadlock and immobilism. Finally, power-sharing also risks becoming the crisis, whether it is the failure to adopt such a system, for that system to function well, or to be able to reform, adapt, or move beyond it. Yet, despite this association with crisis, power-sharing still exists as a go-to model for governance in divided settings, functioning as a "moral or cognitive template"[56] through which governance options continue to be filtered at the constitution-making table.

Can the kinds of crises these adoption-to-adaptation problems throw up be mitigated? Some scholars have advocated for incrementalist approaches to constitution-writing in divided societies as a way to take the heat out of a constitutional moment characterized by emergency conditions. Hanna Lerner, for example, suggests that it may be preferable to move "explosive issues" out of the constitution-making arena, where the stakes are high and divisions between communities are at their most salient, and into "the realm of ordinary politics" to be handled by future political institutions when the crisis has dissipated. In so doing, she highlights the benefits of using ambiguous, ambivalent or even contradictory language in constitutional documents.[57] Shamshad Parsalay has extended this line of inquiry, calling for "dialogic incrementalism," which involves elite-level negotiation at the pre-constitutional stage, the use of incremental tools during the drafting stage, and ongoing elite conversation in the post-ratification stage.[58] Deliberative constitutionalism, where the principles of deliberative democracy, such as the establishment of citizens' assemblies and other mini-publics, can help "a polity work through specific social controversies," might be another way forward.[59] The notion of

[56] Hall and Taylor, n52.

[57] Hanna Lerner, "Constitution-Writing in Deeply Divided Societies: The Incrementalist Approach," [2010] 16 (1), *Nations and Nationalism*, 82.

[58] Shamshad Parsalay, "Dialogic Incrementalism in Deeply Divided Societies," [2024] 22 (2), *International Journal of Constitutional Law*, 318.

[59] Hoi L. Kong and Ron Levy, "Deliberative Constitutionalism," in Andre Bächtiger (ed), *The Oxford Handbook of Deliberative Democracy* (Oxford UP, 2018).

"living consociationalism" where constitutional reform proceeds through staggered iterations, with minor changes adapted through less demanding procedures and major reforms through more onerous procedures, represents another potential strategy.[60]

International mediators and domestic constitutional designers have frequently turned to consociational power-sharing in their bids to end war, support democratization, and repair community relations in the world's most divided places. Yet, a set of adoption solutions—namely the tendency to employ constructive ambiguity on especially contentious provisions and the desire for parties to lock in their share of power via sticky provisions—later become adaptation problems, including ignored or unimplemented provisions, serious contestation over shared meanings, and seemingly "unreformable" provisions. Without the ability to mitigate their worst effects, these adoption-to-adaptation challenges may put the long-term performance of power-sharing as a form of constitutionalism amid crisis into doubt.

References

Aboultaif, E.W. *Power-Sharing in Lebanon: Consociationalism since 1820.* Routledge, 2019

Basta, K. "Imagined Institutions: The Symbolic Power of Formal Rules in Bosnia and Herzegovina." *Slavic Review*, 75:4, 2016, 944

Bell, C., and Kavanaugh, K. "'Constructive Ambiguity' or Internal Self-determination? Self-determination, Group Accommodation, and the Belfast Agreement." *Fordham International Law Journal*, 22:4, 1998, 1345

Byers, M. "Still Agreeing to Disagree: International Security and Constructive Ambiguity." *Journal on the Use of Force and International Law*, 8:1, 2021, 91

Byrne, S. "Feminist Reflections on Discourses of (power) + (sharing) in Power-Sharing Theory." *International Political Science Review*, 41:1, 2020, 58

Cochrane, F., Loizides, N., and Bodson, T. *Mediating Power-Sharing: Devolution and Consociationalism in Divided Societies.* Routledge, 2018

Costantini, I., and Hanau Santini, R. "Power Mediators and the 'Illiberal Peace' Momentum: Ending Wars in Libya and Syria." *Third World Quarterly*, 43:1, 2022, 131

Fraenkel, J. "Mandatory Power-sharing in Coup-prone Fiji." In McCulloch, A., and McGarry, J. (eds.) *Power-Sharing: Empirical and Normative Challenges.* Routledge, 2017, 103

[60] Feargal Cochrane, Neophytos Loizides, and Thibaud Bodson, *Mediating Power-Sharing: Devolution and Consociationalism in Divided Societies* (Routledge 2018).

Friedman, E. "Evasion Strategies in International Documents: When 'Constructive Ambiguity' Leads to Oppositional Interpretation." *Critical Discourse Studies*, 14:4, 2017, 385

Ghai, Y. "The Implementation of the Fiji Islands Constitution." In Akram-Lodhi, A.H. (ed.) *Confronting Fiji Futures.* ANU Press e-view, 2000, 21

Grbavac, V. "Who Watches the Watchmen? External Actors and Consociational Democracy in Bosnia and Herzegovina." PhD Dissertation, University of Edinburgh, 2024

Green, M. "Fiji's Short-Lived Experiment in Executive Power-Sharing, May–December 2006." *State, Society and Governance in Melanesia Discussion Paper*, 2009/2, 2009

Hall, P., and Taylor, R. "Political Science and the Three New Institutionalisms." *Political Studies*, 44:5, 1996, 936

Horowitz, D.L. "Ethnic Power Sharing: Three Big Problems." *Journal of Democracy*, 25:2, 2014, 5

Jung, J.K. "Power-sharing and Democracy Promotion in Post-Civil War Peace-building." *Democratization*, 19:3, 2012, 486

Kerr, M. *Imposing Power-Sharing: Conflict and Coexistence in Northern Ireland and Lebanon.* Irish Academic Press, 2005

Kong, H.L., and Levy, R. "Deliberative Constitutionalism." In Bächtiger, A. (ed.) *The Oxford Handbook of Deliberative Democracy.* Oxford UP, 2018, 625

Kyle, J., and Resnick, D. "Securing the Peace or Renegotiating the Political Settlement? Understanding Popular Support for Post-Conflict Constitutions." *Democratization*, 31:8, 2024, 1645

Lal, B.V. "Fiji's Constitutional Conundrum." *The Round Table*, 92:372, 2010, 671

Lerner, H. "Constitution-Writing in Deeply Divided Societies: The Incrementalist Approach." *Nations and Nationalism*, 16:1, 2010, 82

Lijphart, A. *Democracy in Plural Societies: A Comparative Exploration.* Yale University Press, 1977

Lijphart, A. *Power-Sharing in South Africa.* University of California Press, 1985

Lijphart, A. *Thinking About Democracy.* Routledge, 2008

Loizides, N., and McGarry, J. "The UN in 21st Century Cyprus: Mediation, Mediation-lite and Beyond." *International Negotiation*, 27, 2022, 131

Mabon, S., and McCulloch, A. "Power-Sharing: Why it is Still Central in the Efforts to End the Wars in Syria and Yemen?" *Foreign Policy Centre*, 2022

McCulloch, A. "Pathways from Power-Sharing." *Civil Wars*, 19:4, 2017, 405

McCulloch, A. *Power-Sharing and Political Stability in Deeply Divided Societies.* Routledge, 2014

McCulloch, A., and McEvoy, J. "Conclusion: The Power-Sharing Lifecycle across the Global South." In Aboultaif, E.W., Keil, S., and McCulloch, A. (eds.) *Power-Sharing in the Global South: Patterns, Practices and Potentials.* Palgrave Macmillan, 2024, 353

McCulloch, A., and McEvoy, J. "The International Mediation of Power-Sharing Settlements." *Cooperation and Conflict*, 53:4, 2018, 467

McCulloch, A., et al. "Power-Sharing for Peace? Between Adoptability and Durability in Lebanon, Syria, and Iraq." *Swisspeace Working Paper*, 2024

McCulloch, A., Keil, S., Aboultaif, E. W., and Ammar, S. "Power-Sharing Between Adoptability and Durability: Insights from Lebanon and Iraq." *Regional and Federal Studies* OnlineFirst, 2025, 1

McGarry, J., and O'Leary, B. "Iraq's Constitution of 2005: Liberal Consociation as Political Prescription." *International Journal of Constitutional Law*, 5:4, 2007, 670

Mitchell, D. "Cooking the Fudge: Constructive Ambiguity and the Implementation of the Northern Ireland Agreement, 1998–2007." *Irish Political Studies*, 24:3, 2009, 321

Nagle, J. "Consociationalism is Dead! Long Live Zombie Power-Sharing!" *Studies in Ethnicity and Nationalism*, 20:2, 2020, 137

O'Leary, B. "Power-Sharing in Deeply Divided Societies: An Advocate's Introduction." In McEvoy, J., and O'Leary, B. (eds.) *Power Sharing in Deeply Divided Places*. University of Pennsylvania Press, 2013

Ozecelik, A., and Olcay, T. "(Un)constitutional Change Rooted in Peace Agreements." *International Journal of Constitutional Law*, 18:4, 2021, 1375

Pivotal Public Policy Forum. "Governing Northern Ireland Without an Executive." *Pivotal Briefing, 1 September*, 2022

Rosiny, S. "A Quarter Century of 'Transitory Power-Sharing': Lebanon's Unfulfilled Ta'if Agreement of 1989 Revisited." *Civil Wars*, 17:4, 2015, 485

Shamshad Parsalay. "Dialogic Incrementalism in Deeply Divided Societies." *International Journal of Constitutional Law*, 22:2, 2024, 318

United Nations. *A Manual for UN Mediators*. Mediation Support Unit, Department of Political Affairs, 2010

United Nations. *Guidance on Gender and Inclusive Mediation Strategies*. Department of Political and Peacebuilding Affairs, 2017

United Nations. *Strengthening the Role of Mediation in the Peaceful Settlements of Disputes, Conflict Prevention and Resolution, Report of the Secretary-General* (A/66/811)

Varol, O.O. "Constitutional Stickiness." *University of California, Davis Law Review*, 49, 2016, 906

Younes, F. *Abolishing Sectarianism in Lebanon Policy Paper*. Arab Association of Constitutional Law, 2022

Zdeb, A. "Prud and Butmir Processes in Bosnia and Herzegovina: Intra-Ethnic Competition from the Perspective of Game Theory." *Ethnopolitics*, 16:4, 2017, 367

PART IV

Populism, Emergency, Crisis

CHAPTER 12

Populism and the Transformations in the Global Economic Constitution

Marta Vicente and Catarina Santos Botelho

12.1 Introduction

This chapter seeks to illuminate the concept of populism by examining it through an economic perspective. Populism is a multifaceted and frequently misinterpreted concept that reflects anti-establishment feelings, marked by a moral divide between the "genuine people" and a corrupt elite. The literature clearly establishes that populism arises as a societal response to globalization and neoliberal legality.[1] It is often seen as a result of the shortcomings and challenges posed by the so-called global economic constitution. Multiple crises endured in the last decades have inflicted new areas of tension within the domestic constitution itself and in relation to regional and transnational constitutionalism.[2] The growing

This chapter is produced as part and funded by the European Union-NextGenerationEU, through the National Recovery and Resilience Plan of the Republic of Bulgaria, project No bg-rrp-2.004-0008.

[1] Chantal Mouffe, *For a Left Populism* (Verso 2018) 12.

[2] Catarina Botelho and Nuno Garoupa, 'Regulating Parties by Constitutional Rules in Liberal Democracies' (2023) 24 German Law Journal 1648, 1657.

M. Belov (ed.), *Constitutional Polycrisis and Emergency Constitutionalism*, Federalism and Internal Conflicts,
https://doi.org/10.1007/978-3-032-06516-2_12

distrust of established political and economic elites has paved the way for populism.[3]

In some cases, democratic backsliding emerges as the result of weakening democracies through illiberal movements. Yet, populist endeavors should not be demeaned nor confined to exclusionary or xenophobic concepts of "the people," characteristic of right-wing populism. Populism, especially left-wing populism, is deeply critical of the role that counter-majoritarian institutions, independent agencies, central banks, and investment tribunals have played in curtailing the capacity of states to regulate their own economy. The latter trend has led both states and international organizations, such as the European Union, to *reassert power over politics*, by way of withdrawing from international organizations, non-ratifying international agreements or transforming international dispute settlement.

The chapter discusses the assumption found in existing literature that some populisms are better than others. In this light, not all variants of populism seem to deserve the same pejorative assessment. One's stance on the global economic constitution appears to be crucial. Critiques and proposed transformations in the neoliberal constitution significantly influence perceptions of populism, shaping whether it is seen in a positive or negative light. The chapter seeks to clarify this debate by dissecting the role played by the economic constitution in the moral assessment of populism.

The remainder of the chapter proceeds as follows. Part 2 reviews the literature on the concept of populism and the principal debates around its meaning. Part 3 delves into the premises of the global economic constitution and the ways right-wing and left-wing varieties of populism envision such a constitution. Part 4 dissects the changes to the global economic constitution associated with (right-wing and left-wing) populist movements and highlights their primary pitfalls.

12.2 Democratic Erosion and Illiberalism

12.2.1 What Is Populism?

The expressions "populism" and "populist" are all over the place. They are used so often and in such different scenarios that their meaning is getting blurrier. One may use the label "populism" to address serious threats to democracy, but also to lazily take down some idea or policy that one

[3] Roger Eatwell and Matthew Goodwin, *National Populism—The Revolt Against Liberal Democracy* (Penguin Random House 2018) 30.

strongly disagrees with. One thing, though, is sure: "populism" and "populist" are expressions that carry a strong pejorative meaning.

In a nutshell, populism equals anti-establishment or the defense of the people against the morally corrupt elites. Besides, populism is portrayed as an exacerbation of "political anxieties"[4] (*e.g.*, "anxiety about ethnic and cultural change")[5] And negative emotions, such as anger, resentment and dissatisfaction. However, one can wonder whether the label 'populism' is misused or an empty concept that merely vents one's frustration with current politics.

In today's world, populism has become a ubiquitous term that emerges in a "complete conceptual chaos."[6] Furthermore, populism is often confused with demagoguery or with the act of being popular and appealing to the people. It is a melting pot of apparently contradicting concepts, such as democratic or antidemocratic, liberal or illiberal, left-wing or right-wing.[7] Is such a bricolage of competing principles and ideals a valid concept in academia? Where do we draw the line between populism and popular?

The definition of populism is not an easy one. Like the definition of democracy, it is easier to agree on a few of its main traits than on its conceptual definition. Hence, scholars have tried to build a theory of populism by putting together a series of traits of a populist leader. One of the most relevant traits is *anti-elitism*.[8] Populist leaders are critical of elites. The "us versus them" or "good versus evil" rhetoric is not based on objective criteria but anchored in a profound moral division between "us," the real people, versus "them," the morally inferior, corrupt elite.[9] Such "exclusionary tendency" is evident.[10]

For right-wing populism, the divide is between "us," mostly the white Christians, and 'them," the incoming migrants, refugees and the ethnic and religious minorities (like the Roma or the Muslims). For left-wing populism, the divide is instead "us," the "Main Street" against "them," the "Wall Street"[11] Or the capitalists that "put profits before the people" in order to satisfy the neoliberal economic system."[12]

[4] Jan-Werner Müller, *What Is Populism?* (Penguin Random House 2017) 7.

[5] Eatwell and Goodwin (n 3) 34.

[6] Müller (n 4) 10.

[7] ibid 10.

[8] ibid 10.

[9] Eatwell and Goodwin (n 3).

[10] Paul Blokker, 'Populism as a Constitutional Project' (2019) 17 International Journal of Constitutional Law 535, 537.

[11] Müller (n 4) 8.

[12] Eatwell and Goodwin (n 3) 37.

Still, it is important to stress that, notwithstanding several populist experiences on the left (*v.g.*, in Latin America) or on the right (*v.g.*, current scenario in Europe), populism lacks ideological density, and a populist party may very well act as a "catch-all party," switching from right to left, and vice versa. That is why many scholars stress that populism is a "thin-centered ideology"[13] that showcases "incredible ideological flexibility."[14] Hence, instead of focusing on the political side (left or right), we should focus on what is absent: a coherent ideology. To Théo Fournier, populism is not a "common ideology," but "a common strategy for implementing various distinct ideologies."[15] More than an ideology, populism appears as a heroic and messianic mission to rescue the people from the corrupt elite.[16] Greater than a "way of competing for power", populism is a "way of ***doing*** politics."[17]

Such a clear-cut division brings out the second common characteristic: populism is ***antipluralistic.*** Popular leaders claim to represent the "real people," that being the non-corrupt elite, the authentic, pure and righteous people.[18] Still, this direct representation is not without costs: only the selected people are really the people. Populists do not represent all the people in their inherent heterogeneity, but only the homogeneous people—"People-As-One"[19]—or, if one prefers, the ones that accept their worldview. That is why Müller, Martinico and several other scholars argue that populism is always a form of identity politics.[20]

Another very important trait of populism is the banalization of political merits. Populist leaders offer easy (and often unreasonable) answers to hard and complex topics. For example, the Venezuelan President Nicolás

[13] Cass Mudde, 'The Populist Zeitgeist" (2004) 39 Government and Opposition 541, 543.

[14] Giuseppe Martinico, *Filtering Populist Claims to Fight Populism—The Italian Case in a Comparative Perspective* (Cambridge University Press 2022) 13.

[15] Théo Fournier, 'From Rhetoric to Action, a Constitutional Analysis of Populism' (2019) 20 German Law Journal 362, 363.

[16] Paul Blokker, 'Shifting Constitutional Imaginaries: Is the Liberal-Legal Imaginary Unsettled by Populism', in Martin Belov and Monika Florczak-Wator (eds), *Constitutional Traditions and Constitutional Transitions* (Elgar 2024) 54.

[17] Eatwell and Goodwin (n 3) 44.

[18] Müller (n 4) 3.

[19] Blokker, 'Shifting Constitutional Imaginaries: Is the Liberal-Legal Imaginary Unsettled by Populism' (n 16) 50.

[20] Martinico (n 14). 15, Müller (n 4). 80, and Marta Marchlewka and others, 'Populism as Identity Politics: Perceived In-Group Disadvantage, Collective Narcissism, and Support for Populism' (2018) 9 Psychological and Personality Science 151.

Maduro tackled inflation by sending the army to the stores and ordering them to lay stickers with lower prices on products.[21]

Populism is often signaled in protest parties, and many argue that such parties will lose their strength once in government, as they drop their anti-elitist stance. However, this hope may very well be an illusion, as history shows that several populist leaders were able to remain in power.[22] Accordingly, populists may still find vague enemies to accuse or foreign/international ones (*e.g.*, Chávez kept blaming the USA for any shortcomings of the Bolivarian Revolution)[23] so that they can keep the protesting tone alive. Also, when in power, populist parties will discredit non-partisan NGOs, the vocal civil society and the academics that do not play along. Besides, they will openly engage in mass clientelism, corruption and in the colonization of the state, by placing loyalists in strategic civil service functions, in the courts and in the media (see the examples of Fidesz in Hungary and PiS in Poland).[24]

12.2.2 Janus-Faced Populist Regimes: Populist Regimes as Illiberal Democracies or Authoritarian States

After the Fall of the Berlin Wall, Francis Fukuyama anticipated that the world was nearing the "end of history" after the consolidation of the liberal democracy model.[25] Yet, "history had not read the script"[26] and the reality was quite different and revealed "an era of great turmoil and uncertainty."[27] Is populism anti-democratic per se or a danger to democracy? Will a populist party in power turn the state into an authoritarian state, or will it remain a democracy?

The doctrine is divided. To Jan-Werner Müller, populism is not only a danger to liberalism but also a danger to democracy that ultimately becomes a "degraded form of democracy."[28] Under this understanding,

[21] Müller (n 4) 13.

[22] Ibid 41.

[23] Ibid 42.

[24] Ibid 44–45.

[25] Francis Fukuyama, *The End of History and the Last Man* (Free Press 1992).

[26] Eatwell and Goodwin (n 3) 84.

[27] Paul Blokker, 'Populist Constitutional Politics and Civil Society Fundamentalism', in Mark Tushnet and Dimitry Kochenov (eds), *Research Handbook on the Politics of Constitutional Law* (Elgar 2023) 638.

[28] Müller (n 4) 6.

populist leaders in power do not prefer the path of rupturing with democracy, as "the costs of open authoritarianism are simply too high," mainly due to the vigilance of the international community.[29]

With a distinct perspective, Jeffrey Alexander argues that populism is only fatal to democracy when combined with extremism.[30] Similarly, to Paul Blokker, populist democratic backsliding "reveals unresolved conflicts over the form and substance of constitutional democracy."[31] In fact, many people "are actually not giving up on democracy," but feel "animosity towards established politicians" and long for a greater say in the decisions that affect their daily lives.[32] With this in mind, many scholars suggest that "far from being antidemocratic," populism "is a response to contradictions within liberal democracy."[33] As Margaret Canovan points out, populism follows our democratic systems "like a shadow," therefore, provided that we have liberal democracy, we will concomitantly have populism.[34]

The term "illiberal democracy" became very popular after 1989 to describe regimes that still respect elections but do not perform well on the quality of democracy, mainly regarding the respect of the rule of law, human rights and checks and balances.[35] One can wonder if illiberal democracies are mere "deviations from a 'normal path' of democratic politics and democratic societies."[36] Some view the label "illiberal democracy" as a euphemism that downplays the populist attack on democracy and perceives populist leaders as mere opponents of liberalism instead of distorters of the democratic process.[37] As these scholars do not foresee the concept of democracy as capable of such a lato sensu approach, they prefer other designations, such as "defective democracy."[38]

[29] Ibid 50.

[30] Jeffrey Alexander, 'Introduction. The Populist Continuum from Within the Civil Sphere to Outside It', in J Alexander, P Kivisto and G Sciortino (eds), *Populism in the Civil Sphere* (Polity 2020).

[31] Blokker, 'Populist Constitutional Politics and Civil Society Fundamentalism' (n 27) 636.

[32] Eatwell and Goodwin (n 3) 30–32.

[33] Ibid 48.

[34] Margaret Canovan, 'Trust the People! Populism and the Two Faces of Democracy' (1999) 47 Political studies 2.

[35] Müller (n 4) 50–51.

[36] Blokker, 'Shifting Constitutional Imaginaries: Is the Liberal-Legal Imaginary Unsettled by Populism' (n 16) 35.

[37] Müller (n 4) 50–60.

[38] Wolfgang Merkel *et al.* (eds) *Defekte Democratien* (2003) *apud* Müller (n 4).

Although populism may open the eyes of politicians to many sectors of the society feels totally unrepresented, it is "not a corrective to liberal democracy in the sense of bringing politics 'closer to the people' or even reasserting popular sovereignty."[39] Post-War constitutions tried to prevent totalitarian setbacks, by setting generous catalogs of rights, strong political institutions, judicial independence, rights-based judicial review, effective checks and balances mechanisms and openness to international and regional human rights law. Nonetheless, the doctrinal constitutional arena will not remain the same after the populist overhaul of last decades. As Paul Blokker sharply points out, populism has unsettled "hegemonic understandings of constitutionalism."[40] For this reason, the "illiberal political project"[41] relates not necessarily to a critic of political and economic liberalism but to a strong aversion to the "liberal-legal project more in general."[42] To tackle this, one must adopt a broader perspective and envision constitutionalism "in a historical and wider, cultural and semantic context as of great importance and utility."[43]

12.2.3 Constitutions as Shields

Are constitutionalism and populism irremediable apart or can there be a sort of populist constitutionalism? Some scholars consider these two concepts antithetical categories, as populism challenges the rule of law.[44] Others suggest that populism and constitutionalism share common traits or categories, such as the revolutionary Jacobinism,[45] therefore signaling "a (largely implicit) constitutional theory" within populism.[46] To

[39] ibid 103.

[40] Blokker, 'Shifting Constitutional Imaginaries: Is the Liberal-Legal Imaginary Unsettled by Populism' (n 16) 37.

[41] Blokker, 'Populist Constitutional Politics and Civil Society Fundamentalism' (n 27) 634.

[42] Blokker, 'Shifting Constitutional Imaginaries: Is the Liberal-Legal Imaginary Unsettled by Populism' (n 16) 55.

[43] Ibid 39.

[44] Antonino Spadaro, 'Costituzionalismo versus Populismo (Sulla c.d. Deriva Populistico-Plebiscitaria Delle Democrazie Costituzionali Contemporanee)', in G Brunelli, A Pugiotto, P Veronesi (eds), *Scritti in onore di Lorenza Carlassare*, vol V (Jovene Editore 2009).

[45] Martinico (n 14). Luigi Corrias, 'Populism in a Constitutional Key: Constituent Power, Popular Sovereignty and Constitutional Identity' (2016) 12 European Constitutional Law Review 6, 8.

[46] Corrias (n 45) 8.

Paul Blokker, populist constitutionalism enshrines a "a competing political force regarding the definition of constitutional democracy," built on unrestrained "popular sovereignty," "extreme majoritarianism," "instrumentalism," and legal skepticism or "legal resentment."[47] Likewise, David Landau concedes that "populist constitutions" are the ones emphasizing direct or participatory democracy, such as some Latin American constitutions.[48] In contrast, Giuseppe Martinico believes that populist constitutionalism stretches the concept of constitutionalism "too far"[49] and argues that "there is no populist constitutional theory at all" but instead an "instrumental and cherry-picking approach to the constitution endorsed by populists."[50]

Furthermore, the exploitation of constitutions by populist leaders has been quite evident throughout history. Théo Fournier describes this manipulation with a metaphor of a "parasite slowly spreading in the constitutional world,"[51] in which "constitutional democracy would be the host and populism would be the parasite."[52] Indeed, populist leaders instrumentalize constitutions to keep populist leaders in power. The classic example is increasing the number of mandates of the head of state. Another example is judicial reform leading to significant court-packing. Hence, populism frequently mimics the language of constitutionalism, attempting to redesign it in a sort of "constitutional counter-narrative,"[53] "constitutional counter-revolution,"[54] or "counter-constitutionalism"[55] move.

Can constitutions shield democracy from populism? At first stance we would think affirmatively as constitutions were built to preserve democracy, the rule of law and fundamental rights. Yet, the answer may not be straightforwardly positive, since "abusive constitutionalism" may,

[47] Blokker, 'Populism as a Constitutional Project' (n 9) 540–541.

[48] David Landau, 'Populist Constitutions'' (2018) 85 The University of Chicago Law School Review 521, 523.

[49] Martinico (n 13) 22.

[50] Ibid 27.

[51] Fournier (n 14) 363.

[52] Fournier (n 15) 364.

[53] Martinico (n 13) 11.

[54] Gábor Halmai, 'Rule of Law Backsliding and Memory Politics in Hungary' (2023) 19 European Constitutional Law Review 602, 613.

[55] Kim Lane Scheppele, 'The Social Lives of Constitutions'', in Paul Blokker and Chris Thornhill (eds), *Sociological Constitutionalism* (Cambridge University Press 2017) 35.

instead of promoting pluralism, "serve to eliminate it."[56] Martin Belov's concept of transitology comes as an interesting addition. We were used to think about democratic transition as a movement from totalitarianism and authoritarianism to democracy.[57] This happened in Latin America and Southern Europe after WWII (Portugal in 1974, Spain in 1975, and Brazil in 1985) and in Central and Eastern Europe (Bulgaria in 1990 and Poland and Romania in 1991) after the fall of the Berlin Wall. Yet, in recent times of "illiberalism, democratic backsliding, and constitutional polycrisis," transitology can reverse its trend and become a return to a non-democratic past.[58]

How should we deal with populism and protoauthoritarian leaders? Some consider the "cordons sanitaires," excluding populist parties from the democratic debate. Others disagree, either for philosophical reasons or for pragmatic reasons.[59] The philosophic reason is that excluding parties from the democratic arena can be interpreted as cynic or a profound contracting, as to preserve democracy one had to engage in a non-democratic behavior: the exclusion of a party. In either event, shifting the discussion about politics leaders from politics to "social psychology" and envisioning populist voter as "potential patients for a political sanatorium" is "deeply condescending."[60]

There is an inevitable paradox in, as Müller puts it, responding "to the populist will to exclusion by excluding the populist"[61] and, if populist parties are represented in Parliament, all the citizens who voted for them.[62] The pragmatic reasons are very evident, as excluding populists will only promote the martyr effect and it will confirm what populists have been ratting on their supporters from the beginning: the "others" don't want to listen to us nor to debate vital societal issues that concern many people. Ultimately constitutional courts and electoral courts might play a relevant role in scrutinizing the internal democracy of populist political parties.

[56] Müller (n 3) 5.

[57] Martin Belov, 'Constitutional Transitions and Transitional Imaginaries: Bridging Legacies of the Constitutional Past and Aspirations for the Constitutional Future', in Martin Belov and Monika Florczak-Wator (eds), *Constitutional Traditions and Constitutional Transitions* (Elgar 2024) 13.

[58] Ibid 14.

[59] For a discussion, see Botelho and Garoupa (n 2) 1648.

[60] Müller (n 4) 16.

[61] Ibid 5.

[62] Ibid 112.

12.3 Economic Populism and the Global Economic Constitution

Part 2 dealt with the definition of populism and its roots. It depicted populism as "thin" ideology which is capable of absorbing different political projects and ideologies.[63]

This part approaches economic populism. It is well-settled in the literature that populism can be framed as a reaction of the society against globalization and the "political economy of modern capitalism".[64] Populism is a consequence of neoliberalism's failures and pitfalls. Yet, by economic populism, the authors are not willing to stress the economic roots of a concept, but rather to explore, in Dani Rodrik's account, what it means to be populist *in the economic sense*.[65] In other words, we seek to discuss whether populism stands for a distinguishable set of economic proposals and what their impact is on the economic constitution. Populism assumes that the economic order became insulated from democracy and is now protected by a global economic constitution based on supranational commitments to free trade and property rights protection.[66] If that is the case, populism may disrupt the legal foundations of such global order and formally or informally change the economic constitution.

Therefore, this section starts by approaching the current understanding of the global economic constitution. It then delves into the idea of economic populism, carving-out the importance of the economic element in the moral assessment of populism.

12.3.1 The Global Economic Constitution

The economic constitution is the set of fundamental rules that shape a polity's economic system.[67] It is revealing of the existing (or non-existing)

[63] Landau (n 48) 524.; Massimo La Torre, 'On Populism as a "Spectre" and an Unmanageable Concept', in Ingeborg van der Geest, Henrike Jansen and Bart van Klink (eds), *Vox Populi* (Elgar 2020) 29.

[64] Bojan Bugaric, 'The Two Faces of Populism: Between Authoritarian and Democratic Populism' (2019) 20 German Law Journal 390, 392.

[65] Dani Rodrik, 'Is Populism Necessarily Bad Economics?' (2018) 108 AEA Papers and Proceedings 196.

[66] Mouffe (n 1) 12. ("These transformations have led to a situation that we call "post-democracy" to indicate the erosion of the two pillars of the democratic ideal: equality and popular sovereignty").

[67] David G Gerber, 'Constitutionalizing the Economy: German Neo-Liberalism, Competition Law and the "New" Europe' (1994) 42 American Journal of Comparative Law 25, 44.

balance between market and state within a given community. Wolf Sauter defines it as "the coherent set of principles forming the basis of an effective body of economic law that allows conflicts over public intervention in the market to be resolved." The presence (or absence) of such principles in the formal constitution furnishes an indication as to the type of economic model a polity endorses, or at least an indication as to the economic models which are set aside. Therefore, the explicit recognition of social rights, the definition of the functional content of property rights and freedom to conduct business, or the provision of guarantees against expropriation and nationalization signal the rejection of classic liberalism and socialist models.[68]

Yet, the formal constitution tells only half the story. The essential features of the economic model are also the product of "the inseparable connection between constitutional law and social order."[69] A structural element of the global economic constitution comes from the association between the rule of law and economic development, enshrined in the so-called "rule of law promotion." Starting from the 1990s, the orthodox approach to welfare merged the "essentials" of neoliberalism with a series of reforms influenced by German ordo-liberalism and new institutional economics.

Under this framework, economic growth became reliant on good governance policies, which redefine and emphasize the role of the State as a neutral arbiter responsible for setting and safeguarding the "rules of the game" while facilitating market operations. This facilitation involves creating a stable regulatory environment characterized by protections for private property rights, combating corruption, and ensuring judicial independence from political influence.[70]

[68] Rosalind Dixon, 'Fair Market Constitutionalism: From Neo-Liberal to Democratic Liberal Economic Governance' (2022) 20 Oxford Journal Legal Studies 1, 2., stressing that most constitutions contain an implicit endorsement of a specific economic model.

[69] Gunther Teubner, 'Transnational Economic Constitutionalism in the Varieties of Capitalism' (2015) 1 Italian Law Journal 219.

[70] On rule of law promotion, see Tor Krever, 'The Legal Turn in Late Development Theory: The Rule of Law and the World Bank's Development Model' (2011) 52 Harvard International Law Journal 287; and Dani Rodrik, 'Goodbye Washington Consensus, Hello Washington Confusion? A Review of the World Bank's Economic Growth in the 1990s: Learning from a Decade of Reform' (2006) 44 Journal of Economic Literature 973.

One of the central tenets of the rule of law agenda is the concept of "lock-in" mechanisms, which aim to ensure that political or economic decisions made to attract investment remain insulated from abrupt political shifts. Such mechanisms function as safeguards, fostering a stable environment that reassures investors by demonstrating a commitment to consistency in policies like macroeconomic strategies and public utilities' privatization.[71] By adopting such constraints, governments signal credibility and reliability to both domestic and international stakeholders, prioritizing developmental stability over short-term political opportunism. These are the three "Cs" of capital: consistency, confidence and credibility.[72]

This invisible constitution places further limits on state action in the economy, by preventing, delaying or adjusting democratic options, such as taxation, environmental measures or prohibitions on the use of certain substances in agriculture or industrial processes. Under this narrative, the economic constitution of neoliberalism is aimed at insulating the economic policies from democratic scrutiny through a range of "lock-in" institutions, particularly central banks, regulatory agencies, WTO law, investment treaties and international arbitration.

Investment treaty arbitration, for example, allows investors to directly submit claims against the states in international tribunals, circumventing domestic courts and putting governments under market supervision. Indeed, if governments must pay compensation every time they change policies with detrimental effect to foreign investments—be it the termination of offshore oil production, the introduction of tobacco plain-package policies or the shut-down of nuclear power plants—democratic preferences will be chilled and delayed.[73] Investment treaties tend to encroach

[71] A 1997 World Bank Report echoes this sentiment, stating: "a number of possible lock-in mechanisms are available, all with the same basic logic: to provide checks that restrain any impulse to depart from announced commitments (...) experience suggests that long-term goals are better served by sticking to self-imposed restraints and living with the rigidities they inflict." ('World Development Report 1997. The State in a Changing World').

[72] Stephen Gill, 'Market Civilization, New Constitutionalism and World Order', in Stephen Gill and A Claire Cutler (eds), *New constitutionalism and world order* (Cambridge University Press 2015).

[73] Kyla Tienhaara and others, 'Investor-State Dispute Settlement: Obstructing a Just Energy Transition' [2022] Climate Policy 1.

more on the sovereignty of a state's economy compared to traditional trade agreements.[74]

The ongoing influence of these commitments over domestic legislation has been described as an instance of "constitutionalization," a term used to illustrate the process of submitting state action to the universal authoritative standards of legitimacy of liberal-legal constitutionalism without the symbolic and democratic dimensions of constitutionalism. More pejoratively, this is what Claire Cutler and Stephen Gill have labeled "new constitutionalism," to depict the *de facto* global constitution of neoliberalism.[75] This constitution has given rise to "a new transnational economic orthodoxy,"[76] which far from being neutral toward economic policy, exhibits a blatant "neoliberal bias," based on deregulation, liberalization, fiscal austerity, and strong property rights.[77]

As advanced by Mark Tushnet and David Law, the *de facto* global constitution led to the inevitable "convergence" of domestic constitutional law, especially by means of strong property rights and a neutral and universal understanding of the rule of law.[78] Under the latter, national interest and political preferences are downsized in the process of balancing, unless they are

[74] Dani Rodrik, 'Populism and the Economics of Globalization' [2018] Journal of International Business Policy <https://www.nber.org/papers/w23559> accessed 28 February 2025.

[75] Stephen Gill and Claire Cutler, 'New Constitutionalism and World Order: General Introduction', in Stephen Gill and A Claire Cutler (eds), *New constitutionalism and world order* (Cambridge University Press 2015).

[76] Neil Walker, 'Where's the "e" in Constitution? A European Puzzle', in Achilles Skordas, Gábor Halmai, and Lisa Mardikian (eds), *Economic Constitutionalism in a Turbulent World* (Elgar 2023).

[77] Bojan Bugaric, 'The Neo-Liberal Bias of the EU Constitutional Order: A Critical Analysis', in Mark Tushnet and Dimitry Kochenov (eds), *Research Handbook on the Politics of Constitutional Law* (Elgar 2023)., arguing that the EU has systematically privileged the interests of capital against the pursuit of "autonomous welfare policies." In the case of the European Union, the Author points out that "the ruling parties' obsession with fiscal austerity" triggered "a lost decade" of economic stagnation and "poisonous ultra-nationalism." A critique that resonates with the one made following the austerity crisis by authors such as Christian Joerges and Christian Kreuder-Sonnen (see Christian Joerges and Christian Kreuder-Sonnen, 'European Studies and the European Crisis: Legal and Political Science between Critique and Complacency' (2017) 23 European Law Journal 118.). See also Helena Alviar García, 'Neoliberalism as a Form of Authoritarian Constitutionalism', in Helena Alviar García and Günter Frankenberg (eds), *Authoritarian Constitutionalism Comparative Analysis and Critique* (Elgar 2019).

[78] Mark Tushnet, 'The Inevitable Globalization of Constitutional Law' [2009] 49 985.

backed by technical and scientific evidence.[79] For instance, in Germany, public perception about the safety of nuclear energy was found to be insufficient to validate the anticipated shutdown of nuclear power plants. Internationalist constitutions, which give both treaties and customary law direct effect and hierarchical superiority over domestic law, further exacerbate said convergence, since national courts will inevitably mirror international adjudication or risk facing international responsibility and financial pressure.[80]

This strand of literature pictures the *de facto* global constitution of neoliberalism in very partisan terms. Be as it may, it is undeniable that much of what has been called economic populism—from the right and from the left of the political spectrum—is a reaction to the so-called neoliberal or global economic constitution. It is a reaction, in other words, to the process of *embedded disconnection* between the economic constitution and popular sovereignty.

12.3.2 Economic Populism

As explained in Part 2, defining populism is highly problematic. Populism is usually sketched as a regime premised on a friend-enemy logic[81]—the "people" versus the "elites"—which accommodates multiple political orientations. The literature uses the expression "varieties of populism" to emphasize the geographical, political and social diversity of the "enemies" of the people.[82] Others, as explained, associate populism with authoritarian and predominantly right-wing regimes, excluding the possibility of democratic or "good" versions of populist as well as the theoretical possibility of some kind of "populist constitutionalism."[83]

[79] Anthea Roberts and Nicolas Lamp, *Six Faces of Globalization. Who Wins, Who Loses, and Why It Matters* (Harvard University Press 2021) 108–109.

[80] Pierre-Hughes Verdier and Mila Veersteeg, 'International Law in National Legal Systems: An Empirical Investigation' (2015) 109 American Journal of International Law 514.; Tom Ginsburg, Svitlana Chernykh and Zachary Elkins, 'Commitment and Diffusion: How and Why National Constitutions Incorporate International Law' [2008] University of Illinois Law Review 201.

[81] Paul Blokker, 'Varieties of Populist Constitutionalism: The Transnational Dimension' (2019) 20 German Law Journal 332, 333.

[82] Mark Tushnet, 'Varieties of Populism' (2019) 20 German Law Journal 382., and Rodrik, 'Populism and the Economics of Globalization' (n 74)., approaching right-wing and left-wing populisms.

[83] Gábor Halmai, 'Populism, Authoritarianism and Constitutionalism' (2019) 20 German Law Journal 296.

In this sense, focusing on the way several political movements approach the issue of economic constitution looks helpful. Rightly or wrongly, such economic mindset influences the assessment of certain varieties of populism (as "good" populism or "bad" populism). Plus, for those who are uncapable of admitting "good" versions of populism, economic proposals may impact the qualification of a political movement as *populist* in the first place.

One possible distinction is the one between right-wing and left-wing populism. From a constitutional theory standpoint, it seems central to understand, firstly, whether criticism and reform of the global economic constitution comes exclusively from the left of the political spectrum, and secondly, whether and why left-wing populisms are traditionally seen under more benign eyes than right-wing versions.

Right-wing populists, on the one hand, are said to emphasize the ethnological or national cleavage and target immigrants and foreign countries as the enemies of the people. In this scenario, economic anxiety is directed against newcomers with dissimilar cultural and religious identities and tends to endorse some version of "economic sovereigntism." The latter can be summarized as a "fight for prosperity of national community," which requires the reassertion by the state of its "sovereign authority and exclusive authority over borders, laws and international interactions."[84]

Mark Tushnet claims that the economic programs of right-wing populists are compatible with the neoliberal constitution premised on privatization and liberalization of trade and investment.[85] Andrew Arato and Gábor Halmai exemplify this assertion with the case of Hungary, claiming that Fidesz is not against globalization and has pursued, since the enactment of the 2011 constitution, a neoliberal economic agenda.[86]

However, international case-law involving Hungary does not exactly endorse this assumption. In UP v. Hungary, international investment tribunals were asked to assess a package of measures taken by Hungary under

[84] Gilles Ivaldi and Oscar Mazzoleni, 'Economic Populism and Sovereigntism: The Economic Supply of Europena Radical Right-Wing Populist Parties' (2020) 21 European Politics and Society 202, 203.

[85] Tushnet (n 80) 387.

[86] Andrew Arato and Gábor Halmai, 'Economic Constitutionalism, the Challenge of Populism and the Role of the Constituent Power', in Achilles Skordas, Gábor Halmai, and Lisa Mardikian (eds), *Economic Constitutionalism in a Turbulent World* (Elgar 2023) 87. Ivaldi and Mazzoleni (n 82) 210. also recognize that some right-wing parties have endorsed conventionally neoliberal policies, such as the introduction of a flat tax.

the government of Fidesz, which were aimed at evicting foreign owned companies from the voucher meal market. The package was enacted on behalf of the mandate that meal voucher should "stay in Hungary and serve a public purpose" rather than being transferred out of the country.[87] Similarly, in Könyv-Tár Kft. And Others v. Hungary, the European Court on Human Rights assessed a 2012 decision by Hungary under the government of Fidesz to create a public monopoly on the schoolbook distribution sector.[88]

Hence, the association between right-wing populism and the so-called neoliberal constitution is not always present. On the contrary, as Roberts and Lamp underline, one of the most voiceful narratives against globalization and free trade establishment comes precisely from right-wing populists. This is particularly salient in the United States, where right-wing populists blame the elites and the establishment narrative—based on the advantages of trade and investment liberalization—for the devastating effects over blue-collar jobs and communities. The critique is that, irrespective of whether trade and investment liberalization are overall economically advantageous, low-skilled non-college-educated workers are undoubtedly worse-off as the result of globalization.[89]

Under these premises, right-wing populism may generate protectionist (mercantilist) economic policies—such as tariffs and withdrawal from investment agreements—which can hardly be detached from economic security policies. Unconstrained networks and economic interdependence fueled by globalization have decreased since the coronavirus pandemic. Regardless of whether the world has entered an era of *deglobalization*, that means that states are increasingly perceiving some economic competitors as posing a threat to national security interests. The idea of "weaponizing" the world economy shares the "friend-enemy" and "scapegoatism" *rationale* of populism.

[87] UP and C.D Holding Internationale v. Hungary ICSID Case no. ARB/13/35 (ICSID, 9 October 2018).

[88] Könyv-Tár Kft. And Others v. Hungary App. no. 21623/13 (ECtHR,16 October 2019).

[89] Roberts and Lamp (n 79). 78, associating such anti-trade right-wing narrative with Donald Trump and his backlash against NAFTA, the Transpacific Partnership, Mexico and China; and Rodrik, 'Populism and the Economics of Globalization' (n 74)., highlighting that trade generically produces losers and that people react differently to joss loss caused by domestic and international competition.

In contrast, Rodrik stresses that, in Europe, right-wing populism has been channeled against immigration and cosmopolitism, but not necessarily against free trade. This is arguably because European countries managed, through their welfare states, to redistribute the gains from free trade and mitigate social inequality.[90] Support for free trade, however, is not at odds with economic sovereignty. The "tacking back control" narrative uphold by Brexit supporters was not anti-trade. On the contrary, Brexit would enable Britain to expand liberalization in a way that the European Union, owing to its institutional and jurisdictional constraints, was uncapable of achieving.[91]

Left-wing populists, on the other hand, are said to emphasize the social / income cleavage, by condemning the social inequality caused by free trade, globalization and neoliberal austerity policies. It targets as enemies not only the corrupt domestic elites (*v.g.* the Banks, the billionaires) but also the multinational corporations and the international system that allows them to concentrate power and wealth and prevent governments from acting on behalf of the people's best interest.

In fact, opposition to investment agreements such as the TTIP (Transatlantic Trade and Investment Partnership) or CETA (Comprehensive and Economic Trade Agreement) came originally from the left. In 2015, pressure from left-wing circles led the German Minister of Economy to halt the negotiations of the TTIP. The European Commission decided to carry out a public consultation that resulted in a renewed model of dispute settlement.[92] They feared that Investment-state dispute settlement and vague standards of treatment, such as the fair and equitable treatment or the protection against indirect expropriation, could jeopardize much-needed environmental, public health and social reforms.[93]

Left-wing populism calls for the elimination of "veto points," in other words, for the elimination or withdrawal from institutions that "locked-in" the structures of neoliberalism—such as international arbitration, regulatory agencies, central banks or strong forms of judicial review—and

[90] Rodrik, 'Populism and the Economics of Globalization' (n 74).

[91] Rodrik, 'Populism and the Economics of Globalization' (n 74).; also Ivaldi and Mazzoleni (n 84) 211.

[92] Arato and Halmai (n 86). Konrad Popławski, 'Germany's Stance on the TTIP. Background, Interests and Concerns' (2015) 52 OSW Studies <https://www.osw.waw.pl/en/publikacje/osw-studies/2015-03-24/germanys-stance-ttip-background-interests-and-concerns> accessed 28 February 2025.

[93] Ivaldi and Mazzoleni (n 84) 211.

prevented the economy from pursuing the well-being of the people.[94] Prioritizing the welfare of the people means, in some instances (*v.g.* Latin America), to open the floor to direct democracy, by fostering referenda and public consultations on economic projects with social and environmental consequences.[95]

As explored in Part 2, a group of scholars challenge the idea that populism should be synonymous with authoritarian or autocratic governments. Under this strand of thought, a distinction can be made between authoritarian right-wing forms of populism and left-wing emancipatory and inclusive forms of populism.[96] While both share anti-establishment and anti-elitist features of populism and the need to regain control over the economy, the right-wing version not only is anti-pluralist but also constitutes a threat to the basic principles of liberal democracies.

The left-wing version, it is posited, aspires to a more democratic and socially inclusive exercise of public power, which is responsive *vis-a-vis* economic inequality produced by the neoliberal agenda. This version argues to be perfectly in line with liberal constitutional democracy. As Gábor Halmai suggests, populism is not inherently hostile to the values of constitutionalism.[97] Emancipatory versions of populist—which, on Bojan Bugaric's account, come exclusively from the left of the spectrum—seek to "resuscitate" key tenets of democratic constitutionalism from the "moneyed elites," which threaten "the very nature of democratic republic."[98] Under this version, far from being anti-cosmopolitan, left-wing populism may even incorporate a transnational imaginary, in the sense that rebuilding liberal democracies demands a post-national effort against transnational enemies and globalized elites.[99] Similarly, Rodrik highlights that constraints imposed by international agreements or by the neoliberal

[94] Tushnet (n 82) 384.

[95] Robert Howse, 'Epilogue: In Defense of Disruptive Democracy—A Critique of Anti-Populism', (2019) 17 International Journal of Constitutional Law, 641., 648); Alviar García (n 77) 51.

[96] Mouffe (n 1)., 18 ("Right-wing populism claims that it will bring back popular sovereignty and restore democracy, but this sovereignty is understood as "national sovereignty" and reserved for those deemed to be true "nationals" (...). Left populism on the contrary wants to recover democracy to deepen and extend it").

[97] Halmai (n 83) 311.

[98] Bugaric (n 64) 391.

[99] Blokker, 'Varieties of Populist Constitutionalism: The Transnational Dimension' (n 81) 345.; Mouffe (n 1) 19.

orthodoxy can jeopardize democracy by constraining governments' ability to act decisively in times of social and economic upheaval.[100]

Previous lines corroborate that, under some accounts, changes to the economic constitution do not contribute to populism's bad reputation. Quite the opposite, amending or rebuilding the neoliberal economic constitution allows for a more nuanced understanding of populism and may even shape its definition. It highlights the positive and progressive aspects of populism. The economic constitution is, under this stance, preponderant in forging a moral perspective over populism's proposals and achievements. To sum up, if "good" populism exists, as some literature suggests, it is because of the economic constitution. The next section explores some of the transformations to the global economic constitution brought in by populism. It seeks to alert that, contrary to the literature depicted above, both right-wing and left-wing populist's proposals may endanger the rule of law and its most critical achievements.

12.4 Populist Changes to the Economic Constitution

Part 4 analyses in more detail typical populist's changes to the economic constitution. As explained, both right-wing and left-wing populism hold criticism over the global economic constitution and partake similar proposals.[101] The study focuses on three changes: the weaponization of the world economy, the demise of the rule of law as a neoliberal and authoritarian agenda, and the withdrawal from the international economic system. The analysis will hopefully shed some light on whether populist critiques and reforms to the global economic constitution align with liberal constitutional principles.

12.4.1 The "Weaponization" of the World Economy

Populist movements share a certain disenchantment with economic globalization and free trade. They accuse economic elites of being responsible for the decline of the people's well-being and the dropping wages of ordinary citizens.[102] However, the anti-globalization narrative encapsulates very different reactions, ranging from the backlash against the rule

[100] Rodrik, 'Is Populism Necessarily Bad Economics?' (n 65) 198.

[101] Mouffe (n 1) 14.

[102] Dixon (n 68) 5.

of law *agenda* and reassertion of the state's control over international dispute settlement, to economic sovereignty and economic protectionism, as observed in the Hungarian case.

The global pandemics and Russia's invasion of Ukraine reinforced the so-called "geoeconomic narrative," which emphasizes the need to take into consideration national security concerns in economic regulation. As Anthea Roberts and Nicolas Lamp explain, post-cold-war era was shaped by growing economic interdependence and strong trade and investment ties between the states.[103] These times are over, since states are becoming increasingly aware of the need of self-sufficiency and economic decoupling, on the one hand, and the dangers of receiving foreign investments which may compromise security in the provision of public services, on the other.[104] This is the case of Chinese investments in critical infrastructure and strategic industries, which are deemed crucial for the maintenance of public order, such as 5G, chips, energy networks or artificial intelligence software.[105]

The EU is an example of this growing awareness. The EU overlooked the geopolitical risks associated with economic choices, particularly its dependence on Russian gas and the need for Chinese raw materials to perform the most aspired clean energy transition.[106] It concentrated its efforts, instead, on anti-trust compliance and preventing market concentration. Yet, in 2019, the EU approved Regulation No. 2019/452, on foreign direct investment screening. In 2020, the European Commission alerted its Member States to the risks faced by the EU's openness toward foreign investment. Member States responded to the challenge by introducing and reinforcing existing investment screening mechanisms, which allow government officials to scrutinize and block foreign transactions that are likely to affect national security.

[103] Roberts and Lamp (n 79) 123.

[104] Carlos Esplugues Mota, 'A More Targeted Approach to Foreign Direct Investment: The Establishment of Screening Systems on National Security Grounds' (2018) 15 Brazilian Journal of International Law 440, 444.

[105] Cheng Bian, 'Foreign Direct Investment Screening and National Security: Reducing Regulatory Hurdles to Investors through Induced Reciprocity' (2021) 22 Journal of World Investment & Trade 561, 572.

[106] Henry Farrell and Abraham Newman, *Underground Empire. How America Weaponized the World Economy* (Penguin Random House 2023) 116., explaining that "The EU relied on America for security, Russia for energy, and China for trade. (…) When European politicians worried about global trade and supply chains, they focused on economics, not security risk".

Mikko Rajavuori and Kaisa Huhta describe this movement as "a recalibration in the relationship between open investment climate and protection of essential security interests."[107] Henry Farrell and Abraham Newman highlight the pivotal role played by the United States in the "weaponization of the world economy."

Although screening foreign direct investment is a worldwide course which has been endorsed by both populist and non-populist governments, the literature points to the very thin line between national security and protectionist concerns over the economy. Investment screening is usually not carried out on economic grounds, in the sense that it is not way of protecting the economic interests of the host state against outside competitors.[108] However, it blurs the line between economy and security.[109] When it comes to public services and fundamental freedoms, economic and non-economic interests inevitably intertwine and overlap.[110] For Pawel Gadocha, Regulation no. 2019/452 works as a "political declaration of the EU regulator reflecting growing economic nationalism and protectionism in Europe."[111] Cheng Bian links investment screening with "protectionist and populism movements", depicting screening as an instance of short-term interests and zero-sum games in the international arena.[112] Populist governments may adversely take advantage of the geoeconomic narrative to favor national champions in detriment of foreign companies.

[107] Mikko Rajavuori and Kaisa Huhta, 'Investment Screening: Implications for the Energy Sector and Energy Security' (2020) 144 Energy Policy 10.

[108] Zenobia Chan and Sophie Meunier, 'Behind the Screen: Understanding National Support for a Foreign Investment Screening Mechanism in the European Union' 17 The Review of International Organizations 2022 518.

[109] ibid 517. In Anthea Roberts and Nicolas Lamp's words, "if economic security is national security [quoting Trump], how can we draw the line between protection, which is allowed, and protectionism, which is prohibited? If national security is defined to mean that a country must be economically prosperous and self-sufficient, including at surge capacity during wartime, the concept can be used to justify protective/protectionism measures across an enormous range of industries, from steel manufacturing to tent making" – Roberts and Lamp (n 79) 130.

[110] Danielle Gallo, 'On the Content and Scope of National and European Solidarity under Free Movement Rules: The Case of Golden Shares and Sovereign Investments' (2016) 1 European Papers 823, 837.

[111] Paweł Mateusz Gadocha, 'Assessing the EU Framework Regulation for the Screening of Foreign Direct Investment—What Is the Effect on Chinese Investors?' (2020) 6 The Chinese Journal of Global Governance 36.

[112] Bian (n 105) 588.

Be as it may, economic protectionism and security interests have invaded the world economy. As the Draghi Report alerts, "the previous global paradigm is fading. The era of rapid world trade growth looks to have passed."[113] The material constitution no longer points to free trade and openness toward foreign investment. It points to each state's (or supranational organization) undeniable right and duty to seek "strategic sovereignty" and protect economy against Chinese, Russian and even American villains.

12.4.2 The Demise of the Rule of Law as Neoliberal Legality

The rule of law is a fundamental principle of constitutionalism, overtly enshrined in the text of multiple constitutions and supranational and international treaties. It is associated with the respect for human rights and the non-arbitrary exercise of public power.[114] The Venice Commission describes the rule of law, irrespective of its historical and cultural provenience, as "the prevailing organizational model" of states and constitutional organizations. Predictability, legal certainty, equality under the law, right to access an independent and impartial court and due process of law make part of the proposed definition.[115]

Despite this apparent universality, important critiques have been directed at the rule of law. The rule of law is accused of having championed a type of non-democratic (post-democratic), one-sided and westernized constitutionalism which depicts the constitution as a framework of fundamental principles guaranteed by apex courts and counter majoritarian institutions.[116] In this sense, the rule of law has played a foundational role in the governance of capitalism by exporting the neoliberal

[113] The future of European competitiveness, Part A, A competitiveness strategy for Europe, September 2024, available online at https://commission.europa.eu/document/download/97e481fd-2dc3-412d-be4c-f152a8232961_en (access on 27 February 2025).

[114] Ian Hurd, 'The International Rule of Law and the Domestic Analogy' (2015) 4 Global Constitutionalism 365, 397.; Simon Chesterman, 'An International Rule of Law' (2008) 56 American Journal of Comparative Law 331, 342.; Michael Rosenfeld, 'Constitutional Identity', in Michael Rosenfeld and András Sajó (eds), *The Oxford Handbook of Comparative Constitutional Law* (Oxford University Press 2012) 1313.

[115] Commission de Venise, Liste des critères de l'État de Droit, Adoptée par la Commission de Venise à sa 106e session plénière (Venise, 11–12 mars 2016), available at https://www.venice.coe.int/webforms/documents/default.aspx?pdffile=CDL-AD(2016)007-f (access on 27 February 2025).

[116] Blokker, 'Populism as a Constitutional Project' (n 10) 335.

legality worldwide.[117] It channeled into the international arena a set of quasi-constitutional economic arrangements which overemphasize the need to create a stable and friendly business environment at the expense of human rights obligations and the promotion of social welfare.

The neoliberal constitution is premised, among other relevant traits, on a broad definition of property, which includes contractual rights, claims to money and commitments (having monetary value) made by the states. It hinges on the commodification of nature, i.e. the emergence of new dematerialized intangible forms of property, such as emission rights or fishing rights, and the privatization of public utilities.[118] This definition, endorsed under constitutional law, international economic law and international human rights law, is accused of excessively broadening the range of rights granted to economic operators.[119]

The embeddedness of public law into private law legal imagination—it is said—explains the emphasis placed on the principle of *pacta sunt servanda* and the protection of investors' legitimate expectations. To David Schneiderman, "the State ceases to serve the public interest but is expected to behave along the lines of imagined private actors," avoiding political or electoral considerations.[120] Investors' reliance on a promise or assurance made by the government is analyzed from a purely transactional private law mindset. As Nicola Perrone puts it, "the private law dimension of neoliberalism shapes public action by promoting legal techniques that block, minimize or make state intervention excessively costly."[121] The legal actions taken by tobacco companies against Uruguay and Australia for implementing plain packaging policies based on public health issues are

[117] Christopher May, 'The Rule of Law as the Grundnorm of the New Constitutionalism', in Stephen Gill and A Claire Cutler (eds), *New constitutionalism and world order* (Cambridge University Press 2015) 63.

[118] Claire Cutler, 'New Constitutionalism and the Commodity Form of Global Capitalism', in Stephen Gill and A Claire Cutler (eds), *New constitutionalism and world order* (Cambridge University Press 2015) 50.; and Christina Godt, 'Regulatory Property Rights—a Challenge', in Christina Godt (eds), *Regulatory Property Rights* (Martinus Nijhof 2017) 37.

[119] Nicola Perrone, *Investment Treaties and the Legal Imagination. How Foreign Investors Play By Their Own Rules* (Oxford University Press 2021) 18.

[120] David Schneiderman, 'Hayek's Dream: International Investment Law and the Denigration of Politics' (2022) 35 Leiden Journal of International Law 743, 746.

[121] Nicola Perrone, 'The International Investment Regime after the Global Crisis of Neoliberalism: Rupture or Continuity?' (2016) 23 Indiana Journal of Global Legal Studies 603, 609.

frequently cited as examples of this obstruction. Pre-commitments to the rule of law are accused of obstructing any meaningful democratic reform.[122]

Criticism also extends to the principle of proportionality. The latter has been used for balancing the states' right to regulate the economy and investors' expectations. However, only technical, neutral regulations that are backed by scientific evidence enter the balancing stage. To the critics, then, proportionality is merely another device of the neoliberal toolkit, which undermines the democratic right of the people to change economic policies.[123]

Critics go even further to suggest that, by excluding popular-democratic and parliamentary influence over central aspects of economic policy, liberal constitutionalism became authoritarian and undemocratic. In other words, neoliberal legality has disrupted the nature of the constitutional system.[124]

Questioning the rule of law and its emphasis on predictability, legal certainty and proportionality is certainly an important mutation of the global economic constitution. However, it remains uncertain which rules would replace the so-called neoliberal legality. It was proposed that the principle of proportionality is unnecessary when it comes to safeguarding companies from the state's authority to regulate for the public good. The state has a constitutional duty to protect the human rights of the people. Human rights obligations, Steven Ratner says, should assume something like "a Rawlsian lexical priority" and always trump investors' rights and expectations. This is so because states are not under the legal obligation to abide by commitments made to companies, which are legal persons, not individuals.[125] Alternatively, states could return to the Calvo doctrine,[126]

[122] May (n 117).

[123] Perrone (n 120) 624. ("Proportionality aims to reach a balance, but this balance is struck in the shadow of the contractualization of foreign investment relations and the legitimate expectations doctrine").

[124] Alviar García (n 77).

[125] Steven Ratner, 'Fair and Equitable Treatment and Human Rights: A Moral and Legal Reconciliation' (2022) 25 Journal of International Economic Law, 568, 576.; and Perrone (n 120) 624.

[126] Christopher Campbell, 'House of Cards: The Relevance of Legitimate Expectations under Fair and Equitable Treatment Provisions in Investment Treaties' (2013) 30 Journal of International Arbitration 361., 377; Arnaud de Nanteuil, *International Investment Law* (Elgar 2020) 349.

under which foreigners would enjoy the same rights as nationals but not superior rights.[127]

12.4.3 *Withdrawing from the International Economic System*

Withdrawing from the international economic system can be seen as a particular example of the wider relationship between populism and multilateralism. Changes to foreign policy triggered by populism are sector-specific and vary across the political spectrum.[128] As seen, populists form a heterogenous group of movements. Erik Voeten argues that backlashes against international courts and tribunals have taken place in countries under populist governments.[129] Besides, although they do not necessarily pursue economic protectionism, there is a consistent trend showing that both right-wing and left-wing populists followed a strategy of disengagement with international economic institutions. For instance, the United States under Trump have withdrawn from the Transpacific Partnership and imposed the renegotiation of NAFTA. Ecuador and Indonesia terminated their investment agreements containing arbitration clauses (investor-state dispute settlement). Bolivia, Ecuador and Venezuela have withdrawn from the ICSID Convention (International Center for the Settlement of Investment Disputes).[130]

Reassertion of control over international dispute settlement in the economic domain is not necessarily performed through exiting the system. For instance, following the European Court on Human Rights' ruling in Yukos v. Russia,[131] the Russian parliament issued legislation that granted

[127] Jose E Alvarez, 'The Return of the State', (2011) 20 Minnesota Journal of International 223, 241.

[128] Agnese Pacciardi, Kilian Spandler and Fredrik Söderbaum, 'Beyond Exit: How Populist Governments Disengage from International Institutions', (2024) 100 International Affairs 2025, 2032.

[129] Erik Voeten, 'Populism and Backlashes against International Courts' (2020) 18 Perspective on Politics 407.

[130] Sergio Puig and Gregory Shaffer, 'Imperfect Alternatives: Institutional Choice and the Reform of Investment Law' (2018) 112 The American Journal of International Law 361, 365.

[131] Oao Neftyanaya Kompaniya Yukos v. Russia, Application no. 14902/04, Judgment (Former First Section), 20 September 2011; Oao Neftyanaya Kompaniya Yukos v. Russia, Application no. 14902/04, Judgment (Just satisfaction), 31 July 2014. The ECtHR condemned Russia to pay a compensation of EUR 1,866,104,634, owing to a violation of Yukos' right to property and right to due process under the ECHR.

Russian courts the right not to implement its judgments.[132] But, of course, joining or leaving an international organization, as well as ratifying or terminating a treaty, are 'essential acts of sovereignty,' which align with the populist mindset of viewing international institutions as constraints placed upon popular sovereignty and democracy.[133]

This mindset is shared by both right-wing and left-wing populism. In right-wing populism, it aligns with the desire to defy the establishment and the global international liberal elites, by imposing commercial war and competition instead of cooperation. In left-wing populism, it is believed that international economic dispute settlement is a "power grab" that benefits multinational companies. As Anthea Roberts and Nicolas Lamp posit, opposition to TTIP and CETA in Germany was not about trade, but rather about fear that these investment agreements would give large North American and Canadian corporations the right to directly sue an European state for measures taken in the public interest.[134] In this sense, by either sabotaging or pulling out of international institutions, they claim to be reinstating the "will of the people" in opposition to a system that is allegedly controlled by global elites.[135]

Interestingly, the European Union's decision to withdraw from the Energy Charter Treaty (in 2024)[136] and, more importantly, not to sign the modernized Energy Charter Treaty following negotiations that the EU itself has initiated can arguably be described as populist move.[137] In fact, both the European Union and its Member States have rejected or conditionally accepted the conclusion of investment agreements with third states. They did so by assessing international economic agreements under the well-known doctrine of constitutional

[132] Voeten (n 128) 407.

[133] Bernardett Lehoczki, 'Populist Sovereigntism and International Cooperation: The Case of Brazil and Hungary' (2024) 30 Contemporary Politics 177, 181.

[134] Roberts and Lamp (n 79) 114.

[135] Pacciardi, Spandler and Söderbaum (n 127) 2027.

[136] Council Decision on the approval of the withdrawal of the European Atomic Energy Community from the Energy Charter Treaty, Brussels, 4 March 2024, available at https://data.consilium.europa.eu/doc/document/ST-6514-2024-INIT/en/pdf (access on 28 February 2025).

[137] Critically, see Nikos Lavranos, 'Why the EU Violated Art. 21 TEU by Not Signing the Modernized ECT Text' <https://arbitrationblog.kluwerarbitration.com/2024/12/21/why-the-eu-violated-art-21-teu-by-not-signing-the-modernized-ect-text/>.

identity, or in the case of the European Union, under the principle of autonomy of EU law.[138]

To be more precise, in Costello v. The Government of Ireland, the Irish Supreme Court rejected the conclusion of CETA on the grounds that the powers given under the treaty amounted to the "ceding of legislative sovereignty." To the Irish Supreme Court, "what undermines sovereignty is that the right to make laws is alienated and that the national judiciary may be overruled in an enforceable manner by a foreign tribunal." In a similar vein, the Court of Justice in Opinion 1/17, on the compatibility of CETA with the EU primary law, concluded that the agreement could undermine "the capacity of the Union to operate autonomously within its unique constitutional framework," which goes by saying that it could undermine policy choices taken by the EU's democratic institutions.[139]

Withdrawing from the international economic system undoubtedly impacts the global economic constitution. Not so much because some constitutions or supranational treaties provide obligations to access certain international organizations, but fundamentally because it means that the *last word* on the validity and temporal implementation of economic measures remains within the realm of the polity and not within counter majoritarian non-elected institutions."[140]

[138] Delving into these doctrines is, of course, beyond our topic. We assume, though, that autonomy is a principle through which the Court of Justice has sought to protect the EU's constitutional integrity *vis-à-vis* international law. See Angelos Dimopoulos, 'Constitutional Fundamentals of EU Investment Policy', in Stephan Schill and Christian Tams (eds), *International Investment Protection and Constitutional Law* (Elgar 2022). Constitutional identity, similarly, is a doctrine brough forward by the German Constitutional Court and later summoned by other Member States' courts, which severs, within each polity's constitutional framework, a core of values and principles which cannot be amended nor transferred to supra national institutions. This is so because giving away such attributes, such as democratic self-government or statehood, amounts to a new formal exercise of constituent power, which arguably could only be performed under the guise of a new constitution. On the topic, see for instance Ana Bobic, *The Jurisprudence of Constitutional Conflict in the European Union* (Oxford University Press 2022) 138.

[139] Opinion 1/17 [2019] ECLI:EU:C:2019:341, para. 149–153.

[140] The literature discusses the relationship between populism and non-legalist /non-judicial forms constitutionalism, including political constitutionalism. Blokker understands the debacle against counter majoritarian (domestic and international) institutions as "a populist version" of the critique raised against legal constitutionalism in the form of "political constitutionalism". Blokker, 'Populism as a Constitutional Project' (n 10). 547. To Martinico (n 14) 21., there are important differences between populism and political constitutionalism, especially because the latter is grounded on parliamentary sovereign whereas the former endorses a "pre-political understanding of the people".

That is not to say, for sure, that all backlash against counter majoritarian institutions, such as the ones which support the global economic constitution, are necessarily populism or bad populism. But one should not forget that international courts and tribunals often help to protect groups against whom there is a pre-existing (justified or unjustified) prejudice.[141] The latter may feel the legitimate need to resort to international institutions offering supplemental protection in comparison with domestic or regional constitutions.[142]

12.5 Conclusion

Populism is a complex and often misused term that embodies anti-establishment sentiments, characterized by a moral divide between the "real people" and a corrupt elite. It lacks a coherent ideology, functioning instead as a flexible strategy that can adapt across the political spectrum. Populist leaders often simplify complex issues, engage in identity politics, and maintain power by creating enemies and undermining dissent, as seen in various global contexts.

The relationship between constitutionalism and populism is complex, with some scholars arguing they are fundamentally opposed, while others suggest a form of "populist constitutionalism" exists. Premised on this assumption, the text has delved into the concept of populism *in an economic sense*, seeking to ascertain whether populism stands for a unique set of economic proposals and how these proposals affect the global economic constitution.

Populist movements express a particular dissatisfaction with economic globalization and free trade. They hold economic elites accountable for the deterioration of the public's well-being and the stagnation of average citizens' wages. A group of scholars argues against equating populism solely with authoritarian or autocratic regimes. They emphasize the need to differentiate between authoritarian right-wing populism and left-wing populism. Although both types share characteristics such as anti-establishment sentiments and a desire to reclaim control over the economy, right-wing

[141] Voeten (n 128) 408.

[142] On the role of international institutions, particularly investment agreements, as "supplemental constitutions", see Joshua Paine, 'Investment Protection Standards as Global Constitutional Law', in Stephan Schill and Christian Tams (eds), *International Investment Protection and Constitutional Law* (Elgar 2022).

populism poses a danger to the foundational tenets of liberal democracies. In contrast, left-wing populism—it is said—seeks a more democratic and socially inclusive approach to governance, aiming to address economic inequalities exacerbated by neoliberal policies.

In this light, changes to the global economic constitution are not responsible for populism's negative accounts. On the contrary, it is the revision of the neoliberal economic framework that, according to some authors, points to a more favorable understanding of populism and influences its very definition. Our study examined this assumption by exploring three significant changes in the global economic framework that have been linked to (good or bad, left or right-wing) populism: the weaponization of the world economy, the demise of the rule of law as neoliberal legality, and the withdrawal from the international economic system.

We conclude that some of these changes are problematic in the sense that, by attacking neoliberal legality and institutions, economic populism may annihilate the supplementary role of international economic institutions and wipe out the fundamental *acquis* of liberal constitutionalism, such as the rule of law and the principle of proportionality.

References

Alexander, J. "Introduction. The Populist Continuum from Within the Civil Sphere to Outside It." In Alexander, J., Kivisto, P., and Sciortino, G. (eds.) *Populism in the Civil Sphere*. Polity, 2020, 1-16

Alvarez, J.E. "The Return of the State." *Minnesota Journal of International Law*, 20, 2011, 223

Alviar García, H. "Neoliberalism as a Form of Authoritarian Constitutionalism." In Alviar García, H., and Frankenberg, G. (eds.) *Authoritarian Constitutionalism Comparative Analysis and Critique*. Elgar, 2019, 37-56

Arato, A., and Halmai, G. "Economic Constitutionalism, the Challenge of Populism and the Role of the Constituent Power." In Skordas, A., Halmai, G., and Mardikian, L. (eds.) *Economic Constitutionalism in a Turbulent World*. Elgar, 2023, 87-108

Belov, M. "Constitutional Transitions and Transitional Imaginaries: Bridging Legacies of the Constitutional Past and Aspirations for the Constitutional Future." In Belov, M., and Florczak-Wator, M. (eds.) *Constitutional Traditions and Constitutional Transitions*. Elgar, 2024, 13-34

Bian, C. "Foreign Direct Investment Screening and National Security: Reducing Regulatory Hurdles to Investors through Induced Reciprocity." *Journal of World Investment & Trade*, 22, 2021, 561

Blokker, P. "Populism as a Constitutional Project." *International Journal of Constitutional Law*, 17, 2019, 535
Blokker, P. "Varieties of Populist Constitutionalism: The Transnational Dimension." *German Law Journal*, 20, 2019, 332
Blokker, P. "Populist Constitutional Politics and Civil Society Fundamentalism." In Tushnet, M., and Kochenov, D. (eds.) *Research Handbook on the Politics of Constitutional Law*. Elgar, 2023, 634–657
Blokker, P. "Shifting Constitutional Imaginaries: Is the Liberal-Legal Imaginary Unsettled by Populism." In Belov, M., and Florczak-Wator, M. (eds.) *Constitutional Traditions and Constitutional Transitions*. Elgar, 2024, 35-55
Bobic, A. *The Jurisprudence of Constitutional Conflict in the European Union*. Oxford University Press, 2022
Botelho, C., and Garoupa, N. "Regulating Parties by Constitutional Rules in Liberal Democracies." *German Law Journal*, 24, 2023, 1648
Bugaric, B. "The Two Faces of Populism: Between Authoritarian and Democratic Populism." *German Law Journal*, 20, 2019, 390
Bugaric, B. "The Neo-Liberal Bias of the EU Constitutional Order: A Critical Analysis." In Tushnet, M., and Kochenov, D. (eds.) *Research Handbook on the Politics of Constitutional Law*. Elgar, 2023, 386-409
Campbell, C. "House of Cards: The Relevance of Legitimate Expectations under Fair and Equitable Treatment Provisions in Investment Treaties." *Journal of International Arbitration*, 30, 2013, 361
Canovan, M. "Trust the People! Populism and the Two Faces of Democracy." *Political Studies*, 47, 1999, 2
Chan, Z., and Meunier, S. "Behind the Screen: Understanding National Support for a Foreign Investment Screening Mechanism in the European Union." *The Review of International Organizations*, 17, 2022, 513
Chesterman, S. "An International Rule of Law." *American Journal of Comparative Law*, 56, 2008, 331
Corrias, L. "Populism in a Constitutional Key: Constituent Power, Popular Sovereignty and Constitutional Identity." *European Constitutional Law Review*, 12, 2016, 6
Cutler, C. "New Constitutionalism and the Commodity Form of Global Capitalism." In Gill, S., and Cutler, A.C. (eds.) *New Constitutionalism and World Order*. Cambridge University Press, 2015, 45-62
Dimopoulos, A. "Constitutional Fundamentals of EU Investment Policy." In Schill, S., and Tams, C. (eds.) *International Investment Protection and Constitutional Law*. Elgar, 2022, 180-220
Dixon, R. "Fair Market Constitutionalism: From Neo-Liberal to Democratic Liberal Economic Governance." *Oxford Journal of Legal Studies*, 20, 2022, 1
Eatwell, R., and Goodwin, M. *National Populism—The Revolt Against Liberal Democracy*. Penguin Random House, 2018

Esplugues Mota, C. "A More Targeted Approach to Foreign Direct Investment: The Establishment of Screening Systems on National Security Grounds." *Brazilian Journal of International Law*, 15, 2018, 440

Farrell, H., and Newman, A. *Underground Empire: How America Weaponized the World Economy*. Penguin Random House, 2023

Fournier, T. "From Rhetoric to Action, a Constitutional Analysis of Populism." *German Law Journal*, 20, 2019, 362

Fukuyama, F. *The End of History and the Last Man*. Free Press, 1992

Gadocha, P.M. "Assessing the EU Framework Regulation for the Screening of Foreign Direct Investment—What Is the Effect on Chinese Investors?" *The Chinese Journal of Global Governance*, 6, 2020, 36

Gallo, D. "On the Content and Scope of National and European Solidarity under Free Movement Rules: The Case of Golden Shares and Sovereign Investments." *European Papers*, 1, 2016, 823

Gerber, D.G. "Constitutionalizing the Economy: German Neo-Liberalism, Competition Law and the 'New' Europe." *American Journal of Comparative Law*, 42, 1994, 25

Gill, S. "Market Civilization, New Constitutionalism and World Order." In Gill, S., and Cutler, A.C. (eds.) *New Constitutionalism and World Order*. Cambridge University Press, 2015, 29-44

Gill, S., and Cutler, C. "New Constitutionalism and World Order: General Introduction." In Gill, S., and Cutler, A.C. (eds.) *New Constitutionalism and World Order*. Cambridge University Press, 2015, 1-22

Ginsburg, T., Chernykh, S., and Elkins, Z. "Commitment and Diffusion: How and Why National Constitutions Incorporate International Law." *University of Illinois Law Review*, 2008, 201

Godt, C. "Regulatory Property Rights—a Challenge." In Godt, C. (ed.) *Regulatory Property Rights*. Martinus Nijhoff, 2017, 13-43

Halmai, G. "Populism, Authoritarianism and Constitutionalism." *German Law Journal*, 20, 2019, 296

Halmai, G. "Rule of Law Backsliding and Memory Politics in Hungary." *European Constitutional Law Review*, 19, 2023, 602

Howse, R. "Epilogue: In Defense of Disruptive Democracy—A Critique of Anti-Populism." *International Journal of Constitutional Law*, 17, 2019, 641

Hurd, I. "The International Rule of Law and the Domestic Analogy." *Global Constitutionalism*, 4, 2015, 365

Ivaldi, G., and Mazzoleni, O. "Economic Populism and Sovereigntism: The Economic Supply of European Radical Right-Wing Populist Parties." *European Politics and Society*, 21, 2020, 202

Joerges, C., and Kreuder-Sonnen, C. "European Studies and the European Crisis: Legal and Political Science between Critique and Complacency." *European Law Journal*, 23, 2017, 118

Krever, T. "The Legal Turn in Late Development Theory: The Rule of Law and the World Bank's Development Model." *Harvard International Law Journal*, 52, 2011, 287

La Torre, M. "On Populism as a 'Spectre' and an Unmanageable Concept." In van der Geest, I., Jansen, H., and van Klink, B. (eds.) *Vox Populi*. Elgar, 2020, 29-42

Landau, D. "Populist Constitutions." *University of Chicago Law School Review*, 85, 2018, 521

Lavranos, N. "Why the EU Violated Art. 21 TEU by Not Signing the Modernized ECT Text." https://arbitrationblog.kluwerarbitration.com/2024/12/21/why-the-eu-violated-art-21-teu-by-not-signing-the-modernized-ect-text/, 2024, accessed 29 April 2025

Lehoczki, B. "Populist Sovereigntism and International Cooperation: The Case of Brazil and Hungary." *Contemporary Politics*, 30, 2024, 177

Marchlewka, M., et al. "Populism as Identity Politics: Perceived In-Group Disadvantage, Collective Narcissism, and Support for Populism." *Psychological and Personality Science*, 9, 2018, 151

Martinico, G. *Filtering Populist Claims to Fight Populism—The Italian Case in a Comparative Perspective*. Cambridge University Press, 2022

May, C. "The Rule of Law as the Grundnorm of the New Constitutionalism." In Gill, S., and Cutler, A.C. (eds.) *New Constitutionalism and World Order*. Cambridge University Press, 2015, 63-76

Mouffe, C. *For a Left Populism*. Verso, 2018

Mudde, C. "The Populist Zeitgeist." *Government and Opposition*, 39, 2004, 541

Müller, J.-W. *What Is Populism?* Penguin Random House, 2017

Nanteuil, A. de. *International Investment Law*. Elgar, 2020

Pacciardi, A., Spandler, K., and Söderbaum, F. "Beyond Exit: How Populist Governments Disengage from International Institutions." *International Affairs*, 100, 2024, 2025

Paine, J. "Investment Protection Standards as Global Constitutional Law." In Schill, S., and Tams, C. (eds.) *International Investment Protection and Constitutional Law*. Elgar, 2022, 255-305

Perrone, N. "The International Investment Regime after the Global Crisis of Neoliberalism: Rupture or Continuity?" *Indiana Journal of Global Legal Studies*, 23, 2016, 603

Perrone, N. *Investment Treaties and the Legal Imagination: How Foreign Investors Play By Their Own Rules*. Oxford University Press, 2021

Popławski, K. "Germany's Stance on the TTIP. Background, Interests and Concerns." *OSW Studies*, 2015. https://www.osw.waw.pl/en/publikacje/osw-studies/2015-03-24/germanys-stance-ttip-background-interests-and-concerns, accessed 28 February 2025

Puig, S., and Shaffer, G. "Imperfect Alternatives: Institutional Choice and the Reform of Investment Law." *The American Journal of International Law*, 112, 2018, 361

Rajavuori, M., and Huhta, K. "Investment Screening: Implications for the Energy Sector and Energy Security." *Energy Policy*, 144, 2020
Ratner, S. "Fair and Equitable Treatment and Human Rights: A Moral and Legal Reconciliation." *Journal of International Economic Law*, 25, 2022, 568
Roberts, A., and Lamp, N. *Six Faces of Globalization: Who Wins, Who Loses, and Why It Matters.* Harvard University Press, 2021
Rodrik, D. "Goodbye Washington Consensus, Hello Washington Confusion? A Review of the World Bank's Economic Growth in the 1990s: Learning from a Decade of Reform." *Journal of Economic Literature*, 44, 2006, 973
Rodrik, D. "Is Populism Necessarily Bad Economics?" *AEA Papers and Proceedings*, 108, 2018, 196
Rodrik, D. "Populism and the Economics of Globalization." *Journal of International Business Policy*, 2018. https://www.nber.org/papers/w23559, accessed 28 February 2025
Rosenfeld, M. "Constitutional Identity." In Rosenfeld, M., and Sajó, A. *The Oxford Handbook of Comparative Constitutional Law.* Oxford University Press, 2012, 756–776
Scheppele, K.L. "The Social Lives of Constitutions." In Blokker, P., and Thornhill, C. *Sociological Constitutionalism.* Cambridge University Press, 2017, 35-66
Schneiderman, D. "Hayek's Dream: International Investment Law and the Denigration of Politics." *Leiden Journal of International Law*, 35, 2022, 743
Spadaro, A. "Costituzionalismo versus Populismo (Sulla c.d. Deriva Populistico-Plebiscitaria Delle Democrazie Costituzionali Contemporanee)." In Brunelli, G., Pugiotto, A., and Veronesi, P. (eds.) *Scritti in onore di Lorenza Carlassare*, Vol. V. Jovene Editore, 2009, 2007-2042
Teubner, G. "Transnational Economic Constitutionalism in the Varieties of Capitalism." *Italian Law Journal*, 1, 2015, 219
Tienhaara, K., et al. "Investor-State Dispute Settlement: Obstructing a Just Energy Transition." *Climate Policy*, 2022, 1
Tushnet, M. "The Inevitable Globalization of Constitutional Law." 49, *Virginia Journal of International Law*, 2009, 985
Tushnet, M. "Varieties of Populism." *German Law Journal*, 20, 2019, 382
Verdier, P.-H., and Veersteeg, M. "International Law in National Legal Systems: An Empirical Investigation." *American Journal of International Law*, 109, 2015, 514
Voeten, E. "Populism and Backlashes against International Courts." *Perspectives on Politics*, 18, 2020, 407
Walker, N. "Where's the 'e' in Constitution? A European Puzzle." In Skordas, A., Halmai, G., and Mardikian, L. (eds.) *Economic Constitutionalism in a Turbulent World.* Elgar, 2023, 11-37
World Bank. World Development Report 1997: The State in a Changing World, 1997. http://hdl.handle.net/10986/5980, accessed 29 April 2025

CHAPTER 13

Contexts of Crisis: Sovereign Power, Constitutional Change, and Dictatorship in Interwar Romania

Cosmin Cercel

13.1 Introduction

The legal and constitutional history of the interwar period enables us to scrutinize with a sobering critical gaze the conceptualization and praxis of constitutional categories. Such a reflection is necessary for understanding not only the historical trajectory of these foundational notions of constitutional discourse, but also for a caveat concerning the limitations of constitutional law in addressing crisis as well as its interconnection to politics, economics and society.

For instance, the theory of emergency and emergency powers, as a distinct field at the interstices of constitutional law, international human rights law and political science, carries on as a matter of basic knowledge the temporary and essentially conservative character of emergency.[1] This

This chapter is produced as part and funded by the European Union-NextGenerationEU, through the National Recovery and Resilience Plan of the Republic of Bulgaria, project No bg-rrp-2.004-0008.

[1] John Ferejohn and Pasquale Pasquino, 'The Law of the Exception: A Typology of Emergency Powers', (2004) 2 *International Journal of Constitutional Law* 210.

M. Belov (ed.), *Constitutional Polycrisis and Emergency Constitutionalism*, Federalism and Internal Conflicts,
https://doi.org/10.1007/978-3-032-06516-2_13

is, of course, not only a restatement of the *opinio juris* existing in international human rights law,[2] for what is left of in our current historical epoch that we are traversing, but runs deeper into various attempts of theorizing emergency powers as far as the beginning of modernity. The Paris Minimum Standards in Situations of Emergency[3] and Article 15 of the ECHR[4] both hold that the emergency is to be temporarily limited and that it should not impede or interfere with constitutional change. The idea of an inner limitation of the emergency is also retroactively projected over its history: Roman dictatorship, as the ur-type instrument of tackling turmoil, was constantly read[5] under the lenses of a self-limitation, first by the object of its action, which would always determine a level of proportionality,[6] and second, by temporal limitations. As a result, the emergency, as a politico-legal institution aimed to address a crisis, is considered to be doubly bound: internally by the proportionality of the institutional reaction, and temporarily, by being an essentially temporary regime.[7] As Ferejohn and Pasquino emphatically wrote, 'the purpose is fundamentally conservative: it is aimed at resolving the threat to the system in such a way that the legal/constitutional system is restored to its previous state."[8]

However, already these historical readings of the previous uses and theorizations of this institution, as reductive and mythical as they are, already point towards a specific tension within the very core of the concept: emergency can or has the potential of changing the constitutional order. Cincinnatus can turn into Caesar. Perhaps one of the best iterations of this tension that lies at the core of emergency powers thinking was offered by Carl Schmitt in his historically refined distinction between commissarial

[2] Richard B. Lillich, 'The Paris Minimum Standards of Human Rights Norms in a State of Emergency', (1985) *American Journal of International Law* 79: 1072–1081, 1073; Subrata Roy Chowdhury, *Rule of Law in a State of Emergency: The Paris Minimum Standards of Human Rights Norms in a State of Emergency* (Pinter Publishers, 1989).

[3] Art 15 ECHR.

[4] Nomi Claire Lazar, "Making Emergencies Safe for Democracy: The Roman Dictatorship and the Rule of Law in the Study of Crisis Government", (2006) Constellations 13: 506–521.

[5] Théodore Reinach, *De l'état de siège et des institutions du salut public* (F Pichon, 1885) 16; Clinton Rossiter, *Constitutional Dictatorship: Crisis Government in the Modern Democracies* (Princeton University Press, 1949) 23–24;

[6] Rossiter, *Constitutional Dictatorship*, 24. Oren Gross and Fionnuala Ni Aolain, *Law in Times of Crisis: Emergency Powers in Theory and Practice*, (Cambridge University Press, 2006) 262

[7] Gross and Ni Aolain, *Law in Times of Crisis*, 22.

[8] Ferejohn and Pasquino, 'The Law of the Exception', 210.

dictatorship and sovereign dictatorship.[9] Whereas the commissarial dictator is acting on the basis of a commission, finding its powers granted in the constitution that it aims to protect, the sovereign dictatorship finds its legitimation and grounding in a constitution that is yet to be. As he writes,

> From the perspective of sovereign dictatorship, the entire existing order is a situation that the dictatorship will resolve through its own actions. Dictatorship does not suspend an existing constitution through a law based on the constitution—a constitutional law; rather, it seeks to create conditions in which a constitution—a constitution that it regards as the true one—is made possible. Therefore, dictatorship does not appeal to an existing constitution, but to one that is still to come.[10]

In other words, the sovereign dictatorship operates an avowed alteration of the constitutional order. Sure, the German theorist soon to become a Nazi collaborator was writing this in 1921, in the context of the German revolution—an era of constant crisis and social turmoil that witnessed the fall of the Empire, occupation, revolutions and constitutional change.[11] Yet, as misleading as he might have been about the contained nature of commissarial dictatorship,[12] Schmitt was pointing towards an important tension within the practice of emergency and its potential to actually alter constitutional arrangements.

We can note that in many respects the historical thesis he proposes is enmeshed in his ideological defense of the imagined *jus publicum Europaeum*[13] allegedly prevailing before the French Revolution and the rise of liberalism. For him, the contained dictatorship is in the past: the French revolution and the later rise of liberal constitutions had muddled so far constitutional concepts to the point that they enabled the possibility of a sovereign dictatorship: a dictatorship that is not really one, as it defends a constitution that is not yet there: But, while the commissary dictatorship is authorized by a constituted organ and has an identity in the existing constitution, sovereign dictatorship exists only *quoad exercitium* [in relation to what it does], and it derives directly from the amorphous *pouvoir*

[9] Carl Schmitt, *Dictatorship* (Cambridge: Polity, 2014 [1921]), 111.

[10] Ibid, 119.

[11] Gopal Balakrishnan, *The Enemy: An Intellectual Portrait of Carl Schmitt* (London: Verso, 2000) 28–30.

[12] Schmitt appears to be conscious of the close interrelation between the two: 'The commissary dictator is the unconditional commissar of action of a pouvoir constitué, and sovereign dictatorship is the unconditional commission of action of a pouvoir constituant': Schmitt, *Dictatorship*, 127.

[13] Carl Schmitt, *Theory of the Partisan* (New York: Telos Press 2007 [1962]) 11.

constituant.[14] With it, an era of absolute hostility,[15] was opened, and the Soviet revolution was the embodiment of this type of dictatorship.[16]

Yet, other classical theorists of emergency powers have noted this transformative potential of emergency. For Clinton Rossiter, even when acting within the boundaries of the constitution, an emergency *alters* constitutional arrangements with a view to tackling a crisis.[17] A constitutional dictatorship is therefore fundamentally connected to this alteration, which is needed to address the external danger to the constitutional order. In a similar vein, writing before the era of the World Wars, Théodore Reinach was emphasizing the *fictional* dimension at the core of the French legislation of the state of siege, which was potentially becoming a political tool in the hands of the legislative and, at times, the executive.[18]

Contemporary literature has also perceived the capacity of emergency to alter and transform constitutional arrangements. As Alan Greene noted, this transformative potential it carries is constantly unrecognized, while of course, it is there: "permanent states of emergency today, (...) are potentially transformative but this transformative dimension is never expressly acknowledged".[19] This is not only the specific inertia that emergency measures have, and their possibility of being embedded within the constitutional order, but the very possibility that an accumulation of emergency-based legislation, and a specific type of emergency-based legal interpretation, does affect the existing constitutional arrangements, actually giving rise to a silent or explicit constitutional change.

The traditional historical example of the nineteenth century is that of Napoléon III, his rule by state of siege and transgressions of the 1848 constitution, culminating with the coup d'état of 1852.[20] The twentieth century has known countless examples of the appropriation of emergency powers that culminated in a new regime or constitutional change. The most visible and highly analyzed was the Reichstag fire decree, coming in

[14] Schmitt, *Dictatorship*, 127.

[15] The same theme of regression is recurrent in Schmitt's reading of both constitutional and international public law: Schmitt, *Theory of the Partisan*, 20.

[16] Schmitt, Dictatorship, 179.

[17] Rossiter, Constitutional Dictatorship,15.

[18] Reinach, *De l'état de siège*, 109–111.

[19] Alan Greene, *Permanent States of Emergency and the Rule of Law: Constitutions in an Age of Crisis*, (London: Hart, 2018) 212.

[20] Cosmin Cercel, 'Marx's concept of dictatorship', in Umut Oszu and Paul O'Connell, *Research Handbook on Law and Marxism* (Cheltenham: Edward Elgar, 2020), 61–76.

a context of long use of emergency legislation, and enabling Hitler to take power.[21] Formally, and regardless of Nazi claims to revolution, the Weimar constitution was still in the background,[22] while the prerogative state was taking hold over legal structures and forms.[23] Against this historical evidence, the experience of emergency and its disruptive potential has constantly been placed symbolically within an outside—the interwar period, the Nazi takeover, and regimes of the Global South. However, and this is the main argument line of this study, we need to be able to reconstruct and recuperate this history within the frames of constitutional history—of course, by pointing towards the dangers and difficulties it raises for both legal theory and legal history—but as a part of the ways in which constitutional discourse operates.

Having this in mind, we need to re-evaluate the experience of the interwar period not only as a caveat for a *worse* status of constitutional rule, but as a period of multiple crises that have fueled an unprecedented practice of emergency legislation and rule by emergency powers that is reminiscent of our continuous poly-crisis. In other words, the aim is to recuperate and rethink this history as a *darker legacy* of law,[24] by overcoming a widespread "reluctance to a glance in the mirror"[25] that stifled our understanding of constitutional concepts as essentially 'neutral' and able to contain authoritarian rule. The focus on Romania should not be understood as a part of an essentially national history—it is not about a specific *Sonderweg*, and even though it is less about a history of the nation-state that was in the making at that time. Rather than focusing on the internal—mostly pertaining to myth-history and myth-making—justifications, the aim of this intervention is to uncover the operation of emergency in response to various contexts that were multi-layered in their nature. It is therefore a contribution to a history of constitutional, legal and political practices that

[21] Simon Lavis, 'The Exception of the norm in the Third Reich: Rereading the Nazi constitutional state of exception' in Cosmin Cercel, Gian-Giacomo Fusco and Simon Lavis (eds.) *States of Exception: Law, History, Theory* (Abingdon: Routledge 2021), 92–118.

[22] Ibid., 97.

[23] Ernst Fraenkel, *The Dual State: A Contribution to the Theory of Dictatorship* (New York: Octagon Books, 1969 [1942]), 142.

[24] Christian Joerges and Navraj Singh Ghaleigh (eds.) *Darker Legacies of Law in Europe* (Oxford: Hart Publishing, 2003).

[25] Michael Stollleis, 'Reluctance to glance in the mirror: The Changing Face of German Jurisprudence after 1933 and post-1945', in Christian Joerges and Navraj Singh Ghaleigh (eds.) *Darker Legacies of Law in Europe* (Oxford: Hart Publishing, 2003) 1–18.

takes place at the interstices of various actors—from state authorities to law officials, but also social forces and political movements, many of them acting within and beyond the borders of the nation-state. As I shall try to substantiate, the point is precisely to critically analyze and consider in a deconstructive manner the inner reasons and the internal perspective that sustained the uses of emergency, and ultimately contributed to the radical transformation—if not dissolution—of the constitutional order.

13.2 Origins of the State of Siege: From the Long Nineteenth Century to the Age of Extremes

Before I proceed with an analysis of the contexts giving rise to emergency, and reflect on the legal, political and institutional layers and processes that supported the operation of emergency, a number of preliminary observations are needed. First, a periodization, marking the substance of the historical argument I shall develop, would enable us to situate better the nature and functioning of these mechanisms. Second, several contextual observations pertaining to both Romanian legal history and the trajectory of the Romanian state prior to the interwar era will enable us to offer a more refined understanding of the role of the institutional responses to crisis.

My analysis starts with the interwar period and considers the uses of emergency regulations—most importantly, the state of siege and the government by decree—under the constitutional framework of 1866. This period of relatively short time, between 1918 and 1923, is marked by a continuation of emergency measures that were grounded in World War I and subsisted before the adoption of the new constitution in 1923. They are mainly concerned with tackling military threats and related to state-building, while being subsequently directed towards internal order maintenance, tackling especially leftist movements, from revolutionary communist to social democratic trade unionism. The constitutional reform of 1923 while affecting the legal technique and the political status of emergency through accommodation, did not produce a break with this contextual determination: the state of siege remained an instrument used to quell militarily the Soviet-backed uprising of Tatar Bunary in 1924, Bulgarian independentism in Southern Dobruja, as well as to entrench the policing of political movements, directed especially against the leftist circles. Between 1928 and 1933, a relatively calm period opens in the history of this institution, with emergencies enacted only in border areas. The golden age of the state of siege starts in February 1933, with a return to the militarized quelling of strikes. However, faced with an increasingly menacing far-right and against the background of rising German revisionism, the emergency is being slowly directed towards the revolutionary part of the far-right, while the political establishment is moving towards a stronger right-wing authoritarian regime. The last period we examine is the constitutional reform of 1938, which, as I shall substantiate, is nothing short of a constitutionalized state of siege.

The main legal mechanism of emergency in interwar Romania was the state of siege. With origins in French legislation—under the most articulated form in that of 1849,[26] produced in the wake of the proletarian June rising, quelled by General Cavaignac[27]—the Romanian version had a rather tortuous constitutional life that will make the substance of this investigation. As a preliminary observation, it is useful to note that its original form was part of a statute passed in 1864, under the rule of Alexandru Ioan Cuza, in a rather complex political context marked by internal instability and international—especially Russian—opposition to the unification of the two Principalities, Wallachia and Moldavia.[28]

The core legal effect of the state of siege, which distinguishes it within the plethora of emergency measures, is the transfer of order-maintaining, police and judicial powers from civilian authorities to military ones under the conditions of the "siege." In the Romanian context of 1864, the state of siege could have been declared by the Prince himself, with the only inner limitation pertaining to the "imminent danger for order and public safety."[29] Upon its declaration, the transfer of powers from civilian to military authorities operated, with military courts' jurisdiction being extended to crimes committed by civilians against the State order,

[26] Loi du 9 août 1849 sur l'état de siège, *Bulletin des lois*, No. 186, 146. See also, 'Rapport fait par M. Alex. Fourtanier, au nom de la commission chargée d'examiner le projet de loi sur l'état de siége', in *Comptes Rendus des Séances de l'Assemblée Nationale Legislative*, Vol II (Paris : Panckouke, 1849) 127–131.

[27] Assemblée nationale, 'Décret par lequel l'Assemblée nationale se maintient en permanence, met Paris en état de siège, et délègue les pouvoirs exécutifs au général Cavaignac' 24 juin 1848, in *Collection complète des lois, décrets, ordonnances, réglements, et avis du Conseil d'Etat*, Jean-Baptiste Duvergier ed. (Paris: Charles Noblet, 1848), 354.

[28] Paul E. Michelson, *Romanian Politics, 1859–1871: From Prince Cuza to Prince Carol* (Iasi: Centre for Romanian Studies, 1998); Keith Hitchins, *Rumania 1866–1947* (Oxford: Oxford University Press, 1994), 11.

[29] Legea pentru starea de asediu din 10 Decembrie 1864 in *Codul general al României*, Vol. II (Bucharest : Alcalay, 1907) 117–118.

the constitution, and public safety.[30] Moreover, a number of limitations on the exercise of public freedoms—such as freedom of movement, assembly and freedom of speech. It is useful to note that at that time the country was ruled by a special fundamental law, which was in essence a Statute developing the provisions of the Paris Convention of 1858, settling the international status of the Romanian principalities and their internal organization.[31]

From its very beginning, both formally and substantially, the state of siege is intimately connected to internal-national politics and concerns about the stability of the country, as it is with international considerations related to the equilibrium of powers within the region. Even though the United Principalities were still under the sovereign rule of the Ottoman Empire, their internal autonomy was under the joint guarantee of the Crimean War victors.[32] This is important to note insofar as the state of siege is part of a series of legal and institutional developments that were determined by the relation between the Ottomans, the Russian Empire and Austria ever since the early nineteenth century. First, it was about securing autonomy for the principalities, then about entrusting them with a national army with the purpose of quelling rebellions and ensuring a level of internal stability that aligned with the predicaments of free trade in the region.

The contingent historical developments determining the need for a regular procedure for addressing internal strife go back to the time of the beginnings of modernity in the region: a theatre of war between Russia and the Ottoman Empire, the status of the Principality was nonetheless regulated under conditions of peace, with the Ottomans retaining sovereign rights and Russia exercising a de facto protection[33] over the Christian principalities ever since 1774.[34] This was concretized in the duty of the Ottoman not to have a military presence over the territory unless called in by the local aristocratic *estates* and receiving a confirmation from the Russian consul in

[30] Convention signée à Paris pour l'organisation des Principautés Unies de Valachie et Moldavie', in *Recueil des Traités de la France*, Vol. VII (Paris : Durand and Pedone-Lauriel, 1880) 483–484.

[31] Ibid.

[32] Art. 2–Art.3, Ibid.

[33] Roderic H. Davison, '"Russian Skill and Turkish Imbecility": The Treaty of Kuchuk Kainardji Reconsidered', (1976) 35 *Slavic Review* 463, 465–467.

[34] Treaty of Perpetual Peace and Amity between Russia and Turkey, signed at Kuçuk Kainardji [Küçük Kaynarca], 10(21) July 1774, in *Parry's Consolidated Treaties Series*, Vol. 45 (Oxford University Press 2017), 379.

Bucharest.[35] For a short period of time, the country lacked a regular military presence, which fueled not only banditry but also the possibility of rebellion.

A first instance of the *practice* of the state of siege can be found in the context of the revolution of 1821, itself part of the broader Greek War of Independence. Faced with a rise in the local population in Western Wallachia, the provisional government in Bucharest entrusted *full powers* to one of the prominent aristocrats to raise a corps of mercenaries and quell the rebellion, and otherwise to engage in negotiations and pardon the rebels.[36] Meanwhile, Bucharest was placed under siege, meaning that a permanent guard of the city was established, and night curfews were implemented, with a prohibition of opening public houses and cafés during the night.[37] Interestingly, once the revolutionaries occupied the town, order was maintained by means of *ad hoc* military regulations.[38]

The formation of a permanent local militia, following the Treaty of Adrianople in 1829 and the implementation of the Organic Regulation, created a clear attribution in the ranks of the military to deal with insurgencies and internal strife.[39] For its part, the revolution of 1848 offered not only the first organization of provisional revolutionary rule but also important attributions to the military with a view to maintaining order and containing revolutionary fervor.[40] By 1852, under the restoration of the aristocratic rule, a new regulation was drafted as a *supplement* to the Code of Military Justice, under the title *For the state of encirclement.*[41] It

[35] The consequences of this normative framework became visible on the occasion of the 1821 uprising: See 'Doc. No. 134: A. Pini replies to the committee that he does not assume responsibility for the call of Turkish troops within the country' in *Rascoala din 1821: documente interne*, Vol. I, ed. Andrei Otetea (Bucharest: Editura Academiei Republicii Populare Romine, 1959), 238.

[36] 'Doc. No. 151: The Committee sends high *vornic* Constantin Samurcas with full powers in Oltenia to appease the uprising' in *Rascoala din 1821*, 259.

[37] 'Doc. No. 130: The ruling aristocrats take guard measures in Bucharest', in *Rascoala din 1821*, 232–233.

[38] 'Doc. No. 275: Tudor Vladimirescu asks the provisional government to establish a special tribunal at Cotroceni, composed of three judges, to judge the felonies and thefts committed by the pandurs', in *Rascoala din 1821*,433–424.

[39] Art. 412, *Regulamentul Organic al Valahiei* in *Regulamentele organice ale Valahiei și Moldovei*, eds. Paul Negulescu and George Alexianu (Bucharest: Eminescu, 1944) 1–170, 138.

[40] See, Constantin Căzănișteanu, M. Cuccu and E. Popescu, *Aspecte militare ale revoluției de la 1848* (Bucharest: Editura Militară) 25–40.

[41] 'Supliment la Condica Penală Ostășeacă—Pentru starea de împresurare', in *Asezamant ostasesc pentru straja pamanteasca a Valahii din 1832*, ed. Stefan Gr. Berechet (Iasi : Institutul de Arte Grafice Tatarasi) 95–97.

essentially offered a series of provisions that entrusted the Prince, with the assent of the Council of Ministries, to send a member of the General Staff to address disturbances and restore order in parts of the territory by declaring them encircled and putting them under military control, extending military attributions over civilian order maintaining ones and extending military jurisdiction over a series of crimes concerning loyalty, public safety and public peace. This legislation is considered to have been dormant; however, in 1863, one year before the 1864 law was passed, reports on a Polish army of volunteers' incursion in the Principalities, giving rise to a skirmish with the Romanian army in Costangalia (today's Bessarabia), indicate a military operation that followed the same practice.[42]

This genealogy of the state of siege, with origins in a practice that owes much to a context of aristocratic restoration and revolutionary counteraction, as well as to a peripheral status at the border of empires, is important in order to reconstruct its articulation at the intersection of law, politics and military doctrine. Not only is the state of siege in its incipient forms a useful tool to prevent disorder and to sustain a specific social structure, but it is also a way in which autonomy is secured under the conditions of international treaties between the Great Powers. The military and its rule are the experience of this modernity in the making of the principalities. The specific use of the military and its inner regulations, not only during longer periods of foreign occupation, but also by the revolutionary risings, underline a specific presence of the army that is not essentially repressive, but also transformative.

Moreover, under the conditions of the two revolutions of the nineteenth century—1821 and 1848—martial law and military regulations are used specifically to contain violence and to distinguish between the legitimate revolution and the illegitimate one. This was indeed strategic, insofar as it was meant to prevent—and in reality, it just delayed—foreign intervention. But it also had a politically *positive* role, that of producing a specific type of legitimacy, one that was grounded in the preservation of order and peace, in both their material and symbolic meanings. Before entering the sphere of the law, the state of siege was already a tested political practice and part of the military doctrine.

Before the First World War, the state of siege was used on three occasions: as a partial siege in the Southern counties as a support for the

[42] Dumitru P. Ionescu and Emil Puşcaşu, 'Lupta de la Constagalia (iunie 1863)', (1996) 7 *Revista Istorică* 757, 759–761.

military campaign of the war of independence (1877–1878), in response to the peasant uprising of 1907 and during the Second Balkan War. The declaration, especially in 1907, did not fail to spark controversy and by its wartime declaration in 1915–1916, a small body of literature concerning its constitutional status developed. In essence, owing to the provisions of Article 127, 128, and 129 of the 1866 Constitution, the opinion of this small body of the doctrine was that the Law of 1864 was unconstitutional and could not serve as a basis for the declaration of the state of siege: at best it could provide some guide for the actions of the military, but it did not offer a ground for the accommodation of this emergency measure within the legal framework. The point was that it was at best unconstitutional and at worst "inexistent."[43] If indeed there was a ground to support the possibility of the declaration of the state of siege, it could have rested only on the doctrine of necessity, insofar as in situations of "imminent danger, the law of necessity is imposed, and itself it does not know any law, and it becomes law."[44]

The only legal way of addressing such actions was by a statute of the parliament. If the parliament was in recess, it was the duty of the executive to take the measures required by necessity and once the danger was no longer, to respond both legally and politically for the legitimacy of its actions, which stayed as a matter of constitutional law, "an *usurpation*."[45] To this effect, the legal mechanism adopted by the Romanian state was rather peculiar: during the time of neutrality in the First World War, a law for the declaration of the state of siege was passed by the Parliament, authorizing the King to declare it by decree, under the conditions prescribed by the legislation of 1864.[46] Subsequently, once Romania joined the war on the side of the Entente, the King declared the state of siege, referring directly to the statute of 1864. Another decree, issued in 1918, prorogued the state of siege until 'it would be considered that peace was restored,"[47] according to the statute of 1864, yet without overstepping the limits of the enabling act of 1916, referring to the restoration of the European peace.

[43] Iuliu Dragomirescu, 'Starea de asediu', (1914) 43 *Dreptul* 417, 418.

[44] Constantin Dissescu, *Drept constituțional* (Bucharest : SOCEC, 1915) 482.

[45] Ibid. [emphasis added].

[46] Legea stărei de asediu of 14 August 1916, M. Of.,No. 107,14 August 1916.

[47] Decretul Regal Nr. 1626 din 30 Iunie 1918 pentru modificarea Decretului Nr. 2798 din 14 August 1916, relativ la starea de asediu, M. Of., No. 79bis, 1 July 1918.

13.3 Legal "Siege" and the European Civil War

There are two points that are central in this excursus for the purposes of our analysis: first, there is the subsistence of the legislation of 1864 as a guide for the operation of the state of siege and second, the nature of the state of siege as a response to specific contexts of crisis. While the origins of the Statute of 1864 regulating the state of siege are somewhat clear, being connected to a Bonapartist regime grounded in a veneer of *popular legitimacy*[48] and a historical trajectory that emphasized the role of the military as a guarantee of internal order, its survival within the regime of a liberal constitutional monarchy is somewhat obscure.

As a matter of formal constitutional status, the statute is no longer active as such, insofar as it contradicts the provisions of the constitution concerning access to natural justice, and the prohibition of the suspension of constitutional guarantees, as well as the transitional clause concerning the enactment of the constitution of 1866.[49] However, the provisions of the statute carry on, as a guide for state action and the operation of the transfer of attributions from civilian authorities to military ones, as early as 1878 and distinctly in the context of the peasant uprising of 1907, with the statute being furtively activated within the constitutional order as an *extraconstitutional* mechanism through the doctrine of necessity.

In this sense, the state of siege is *transfigured*[50] as a legal device that loses its formal binding character, yet is articulated as a practice that guides military and law officials' actions as a matter of interpretation, before regaining through judicial review its binding force for the parts of the provisions concerning the transfer of authority. This transfiguration offers an important insight into the relation between the law and the contexts of crisis that will follow.

Prior to the First World War, there were three notable declarations of the state of siege: two pertaining to war, and one to internal order. The wartime measures of 1877[51] were introduced at the request of the Grand Duke Nicholas, who led the Russian forces, as the Russian Army

[48] Manuel Guțan, 'Avatarurile autoritarismului domnesc la mijlocul secolului al XIX lea : între absolutism luminat și cezarism democratic' in Manuel Guțan *et al.*, *Șefii de stat: dinamica autoritară a puterii politice în istoria constituțională românească* (Bucharest: Universul Juridic, 2020) 149–244, 215–222.

[49] Dissescu, *Drept constituțional*, 482.

[50] Rafał Mańko, 'Legal Survivals and the Resilience of Juridical Form' (2023) *Law and Critique* https://doi.org/10.1007/s10978-023-09357-2.

[51] High Princely Decree No. 1219 of 26 May 1877, M. Of. No. 117, 26 May 1877.

was lacking the necessary personnel to prosecute exactions against the Army and acts perpetrated by the military forces.[52] Those of 1907 were taken by the Parliament, facing a growing peasant uprising that was fueled by unequal and unfair tenancy agreements and a fragmentation of rural property.[53] It is useful to note that the declaration by the Parliament was already preceded by blatantly unlawful declarations of the state of siege operated by representatives of the government in the territory (*prefects*).[54]

What we are facing within this experience is nothing but a survival of a politico-legal practice with a military content that has already been shaped by the history of the nineteenth century, that of a mechanism of repressing dissent that is understood as a threat to sovereign power and carries on a class content in protecting the landowners in their tensions with the peasantry.

When, during the First World War, the state of siege was enacted within the 34 counties of the country at that time, it was meant as a measure supporting the war effort and bolstering the cohesion of the army. However, by the time of the Armistice, it became an important instrument in organizing the repression of strikes and public dissent and in countering attempts of Russian deserters to foment an insurrection. This points out to the inner malleability of the institution of the state of siege in its response to contexts: declared in order to support the war effort of a country that was just relinquishing its neutral status, and used especially for a measure of protecting military operations by tackling treason, dissent, espionage, and potential sabotage it is turned into an instrument of policing political action and to some extent producing national mobilization. As a commentator of the events wrote with regard to the Romanian response to the October Revolution and the former Russian Empire's forces aiming to bring about a communist rising:

> The Romanian High Command immediately set Romanian reserves behind the portions of the front still held by Russian troops; they greatly strengthened the state police (gendarmes); they divided Moldavia up into military districts, each of which was entrusted to a military unit; every infraction of the regulations of the High Command was severely punished; no Russian

[52] Doc. No. 803 (cyphered telegram of 31 May 1877), in *Documente privind istoria României: Războiul pentru independență*, ed. Mihai Roller, Vol. III (Bucharest: Editura Academiei RPR, 1953) 431.

[53] Emil Cernea, *Criza dreptului în România la anul 1907* (Bucharest : Editura Universității București 2001) 103–104.

[54] Ibid., 103.

troops, even unarmed, might approach Jassy; none might leave the front or return into Russia without surrendering their arms.[55]

Notwithstanding the important shift in the state of siege at the time of the October Revolution and the turn it had produced in blending once again law, military and order-maintenance, the political undertones of its uses were present from its very beginning in altering the constitutional protections supporting a frail, but nonetheless existent element of liberal legalism. Already in 1907, the military repression was devised under the operation of the state of siege in support of existing proprietary relations concerning leases of the land to peasants. Later on, during the early stages of the war, it was used for censoring the social democratic press.[56]

By the end of the War, going through the short period of forced peace with the Central Powers, the state of siege was already meant to tackle different types of contexts, ranging from purely military ones to more politically marked ones by the use of censorship and by tackling crimes against the state. The confusion produced by the various elements that are united by the state of siege through the operation of the legal fiction is important in order to seize the inherently constitutional potential that the siege already contained in its wartime practice. Not only is confusion produced between war powers and police powers, and a conceptual and practical line of continuity is revealed between the two,[57] but military operations and the presence of military administration in the newly acquired territories also expose the military as a bearer of a minimum or original constitutionality.

For instance, in the context of the Romanian intervention in quelling the Hungarian Revolution in 1919, a military occupation entrusted with minimum relief and administration powers was in place.[58] Different forms of control at the borders between occupation and formal state of siege were in place in Bessarabia, Transylvania, Banat, Bukovina and Southern Dobruja with various degrees of discretion entrusted to the military commanders. Understanding the legal status of these operations involves a plurality of

[55] Charles Upson Clark, United Roumania (New York: Dodd, Mead and Co., 1932), 173.

[56] Corneliu Pintilescu, 'The Impact of the October Revolution, Social Turmoil and the Resort to the State of Siege in Interwar Romania', (2023) 14 *History of Communism in Europe* 89, 96.

[57] Cosmin Cercel, 'The "Right" Side of the Law: State of Siege and the Rise of Fascism in Interwar Romania', 2 (2013) *Fascism* 205.

[58] Clark, *United Romania*, 204–212.

layers going from the national to the international, against the background of what historians have called the *European Civil War*.[59] Within this specific apparent normative vacuum, in which contested sovereignties existed alongside affirmations of sovereign power, the state of siege remains a guideline for the internal extension of the Romanian constitutional sphere, and, alongside military legislation, the only normative guide.

This state of siege is revealing for the role of the military within the constitutional arrangements, and it reproduces the specific extra-constitutionality of the legal institution: by means of necessity, the state of siege ensures both the continuity of constitutional order and produces the conditions of its application. While outside the recognized territory, the military is bound to fight primarily the Soviet revolution and various national independentist movements; within the borders, it aims to tackle left-wing movements. This ranges from military operations on an important scale, especially in the region of Khotyn and in various corners of Bessarabia,[60] to quell strikes, exercise censorship and bring before martial courts political dissenters.[61]

As early as 1920, while the enabling law was still in force, a Decree suspended the application of the state of siege on the whole territory with the exception of the border regions.[62] In theory, this was meant to herald an end to the emergency regime of wartime measures. However, in October 1920, a new state of siege alongside censorship was declared by decree in Bucharest, following strikes.[63] This continuation of the state of siege was defended by the Supreme Court on the basis that, regardless of the temporal limits instituted in the enabling law of 1916 concerning the restauration of the European peace, and the conclusion of Versailles Treaty, it was only the body that enabled the declaration of the state of siege that held the authority to consider the existence of peace.[64] In a legal sense, the country was carrying on its wartime provisions within the historical conditions of the *European civil war*.

[59] Enzo Traverso, *Fire and Blood The European Civil War*, 1914–1945 (London: Verso, 2017), 71.

[60] Charles Upson Clark, *Bessarabia, Russia and Roumania on the Black Sea* (New York: Dodd, Mead & Co., 1927) 241–243.

[61] Pintilescu, 'The Impact of the October Revolution…', 93–95.

[62] Decret Regal Nr. 2939 din 15 Iulie 1920 relativ la restrângerea stării de asediu, *M. Of.*, No. 83, 16 July 1920.

[63] Decret Regal Nr. 4209 din 21 Octombrie 1920, pentru declararea stării de asediu în București și instituirea cenzurei, *M. Of.*, No. 159, 21 October 1920.

[64] Gr D Grecul, *Starea de asediu actuală* (Bucharest: Curierul Judiciar, 1928), 6–7.

The entry into force of the constitution of 1923 changed the legal landscape of the state of siege by integrating this practice—somewhat ambiguously—within the constitutional order and discourse. In fact, Article 128 contained the provision that was considered by constitutionalists as a contradiction in terms: "this constitution cannot be suspended either in whole or in part. In case of state danger, it can be instituted by law the general or partial state of siege."[65] In principle, regardless of whether the state of siege in practice was effectively suspending the constitution, by subverting the separation of powers and by affecting the exercise of fundamental rights guaranteed by the constitution—such as freedom of assembly, freedom of press, inviolability of the domicile and freedom of movement—the new provision made one thing clear. It grounded the state of siege within the constitution and, at a minimum, granted a power to the parliament to enable the executive to declare the state of siege. Yet, one should not disregard the fact that the very constitutional provisions were passed while a partial state of siege was in place in Transylvania,[66] which should put things into perspective as to the extent to which the state of siege was accommodated or tamed by the constitutional layer.

The most significant use of the state of siege during the 1920s, against a background of constant emergencies, was undoubtedly in the repression of the Tatar Bunar uprising.[67] Within the context of what Romanian authorities described as a Soviet-backed rebellion, the military quelled the insurrection in a number of skirmishes in South-Eastern Bessarabia and brought before martial courts no less than four hundred suspects indicted for rebellion, manslaughter, murder, theft or willful destruction of property. The trials, through the sheer number of suspects brought before the court, the extension of military jurisdiction over civilians, and the international context—ranging from negotiations between USSR and Romania over the recognition of the borders that were halted, to the assassination of Matteoti in Italy as well as similar developments in Yugoslavia, Bulgaria and Hungary—became a *cause celebre* for sections of the European left. French communist writer, Henri Barbusse, as well as a French lawyer, Henri Torrès and Italian lawyer Ezio Riboldi, were present at the proceedings in support of the defenders.[68]

[65] Art 128 Constitution of Romania of 1923,

[66] Decret regal Nr. 131 din 16 Ianuarie 1923 referitor la lărgirea stărei de asediu în Ardeal,

[67] Cosmin Cercel, 'Unearthing the Dark Side of the Law. Narratives of Law and Authority in the Tatarbunar Trials', (2023) 14 *History of Communism in Europe* 111.

[68] Ibid., 116.

Under these circumstances, being under a non-negligible public scrutiny, the activity of the courts was somewhat curbed. As one of the defending lawyers in the trial, and longstanding defender of fundamental rights, Constantin Costa-Foru noted in the ensuing anti-communist repression: "it is sad that from the War onwards the state of siege has been embedded; but it does not mean at all the loss of constitutional guarantees for citizens with regards to the respect due to personhood and the right to be defended according to civil laws even when before military courts."[69]

In the following years, the state of siege was used in Southern Dobruja, allegedly in response to *commitadjii* activism, and throughout the country in order to allegedly curb electoral violence. By 1928, foreign commentators described Romania as living "under a virtual martial law,"[70] all geared and honed to serve the political purposes of the ruling National Liberal Party. Faced with a mounting opposition that was poised to spill outside the established constitutional limits, the NLP backed down from its authoritarian position, and the National Peasant Party won the December elections with a resounding majority. One of the pledges of the new government was to curb the use of emergency, and during the following five years, the state of siege was restricted to a very limited territory. Areas of 10–15 kilometers on the borders were still subjected to this regime; however, municipalities are exempted from its operation, the censorship was no longer in force, and the jurisdiction of military courts was limited only to crimes against the state and the constitutional order.

13.4 Normalizing the Exception: Constitutional Change and the Rise of Fascism

Yet this period of legal and constitutional normality—as fragmented as it was by the subsistence of *siege* directly originating in the statute voted under the conditions of World War I—will also be marked by two major crises. A first crisis is of economic origins, and it was determined by accumulated debts driven by military expenditure and the efforts of building a local industry. It later morphed, under the effects of the financial meltdown of 1929, into a significant slump, insofar as French creditors who had

[69] Constantin G. Costa-Foru, *Abuzurile și crimele siguranței statului* (Bucharest: Triumful, 1925), 5.

[70] Joseph S. Roucek, 'Social Background of Roumanian Politics' (1932) 10 *Social Forces* 419, 424.

traditionally supported Romania during the interwar reconstruction were also facing difficulties. Faced with efforts in repayment, the government was forced to implement a moratorium from the foreign lenders, including austerity measures by limiting spending in the public sector, called expressively the "sacrificial curve."[71] They affected especially workers in the extractive sectors—mining and oil extraction—and railway workers.

This crisis was also doubled by a constitutional one: in 1926, the Crown Prince Carol was forced to renounce the throne following the estrangement with his wife and his scandalous lifestyle. King Ferdinand, his father, died in the same year, as well as the leader of NLP, leaving the political elites in a state of disarray. A regency council was installed, and the Crown Prince, then living in exile as a private citizen, plotted a return on several occasions with the support of the Peasants' Party. Ultimately, his return succeeded in 1930, in an odd plot: all the members of the Regency Council agreed to his return, he had obtained the assent of the Prime Minister, yet the agreement was formally illegal and unconstitutional as it circumvented the renunciation act and interfered with the succession to the throne.[72] This return—in many respects that of a charismatic leader rather than of a constitutional monarch—added a new layer of strain to the political and economic conditions of the country, insofar as the King was poised to run the state "as a business,"[73] and aimed to gain the support of the far-right movement.

In 1933, the NPP-led government, now again holding a majority in the Parliament, felt compelled to pass a new bill enabling the declaration of the state of siege in response to the strikes by railway and oil workers. In the words of the promoter of the bill, the government "has to take exceptional measures," which were possible "only under a state of siege."[74] The new statute did not differ significantly from the one passed in 1916: it enables the government to declare the state of siege under the conditions of the statute of 1864, and the modifying provisions of the Royal Decree of 1916, giving, though, a discretionary power to determine what specific attributions shall be transferred to the military authorities.[75]

[71] 'La situation économique et financière' in Ministère des Affaires Etrangères, *Bulletin périodique de la presse roumaine: du 2 février au 18 mars 1933*, No. 111, 25 March 1933, 5–7.

[72] Cosmin Cercel, 'Reversing Liberal Legality: Romania's Path to Dictatorship, 1930–1938', (2020) 2 *Journal of Romanian Studies* 23, 33.

[73] 'Le prince Carol proclamé roi', Ministère des Affaires Etrangères, Bulletin périodique de la presse roumaine: du 26 mai au 25 juin 1930, No. 92, 3 July 1930, 4.

[74] Pintilescu, 'The Impact of the October Revolution…', 102.

[75] Lege pentru autorizarea starei de asediu din 4 Februarie 1933, *M. Of.*, No. 29, 4 Februarie 1933.

The repression of the railway workers followed swiftly, being taken under the pretense that Soviet and communist actions were underway against the Romanian state. However, this was not the case: as analysis of the Commintern communications of the time proves, a revolution in Romania was not on the agenda at that time.[76] Rather, the true context determining the enabling of the emergency powers was the social disruption produced by the economic conditions.

By the end of the year, it will become clear that the main contender to the authority of the state was not the communist movement, as declared and feared publicly by the authorities, but the rising far-right Legion of the Archangel Michael. Initially a group affirming itself as a strike breaking force during the early 1920s, operating under the conditions of the state of siege, and supporting the state power in quelling the strikes, it developed as an autonomous youth movement within the antisemitic League of National Christian Defense (LANC) through the 1920s, militating against the Constitution of 1923 and the equal rights granted to foreign nationals. It did so through open violent means, with its leader standing trial for murder and attempted murder, rebellion, manslaughter and delicts against public peace and state of siege legislation on several occasions, being each time pardoned by the jury or amnestied by the King.[77] In 1927 the movement cut ties with LANC, and built itself as an increasingly redoubtable political force operating both within electoral politics as well as a paramilitary force and a "civil society" movement determined to produce a radical change by mobilizing support and changing the society through work camps, campaigns in support of the peasantry and "equitable," Romanian commerce, driven to limit the perceived Jewish domination in internal trade.[78]

The Legion did not renounce its recourse to violence even after it secured places in the parliament, and the press was constantly reporting scuffles with the Gendarmerie, as well as campaigns of intimidation directed mainly against citizens of Jewish origins and left-wing groups. In response, the liberal Prime Minister, IG Duca, dissolved the Legion before

[76] Cristina Diac, 'Scapegoats or Agents of State Dissolution? The Comintern, the Romanian Communists, and the Grivița Strike in February 1933', 14 *History of Communism in Europe* 131, 153.

[77] Cosmin Cercel, 'Fascist Claims to sovereign power' 33 *Contemporary European History* 1273, 1279.

[78] Rebecca Ann Haynes, 'Work Camps, Commerce, and the Education of the "New Man" in the Romanian Legionary Movement', 51 (2008) *The Historical Journal* 943.

the elections of December 1933, aiming to stave off its rise. In retaliation, a Legionary "death squad" assassinated him on the 30th of December. This gave rise to a new Decree Law, which was passed by the King and the government, as the Parliament was in recess, and the enabling powers passed in February were deemed limited in scope.[79]

Following this decree, the state of siege will become a constant presence in the life of the country. A specific procedure was followed until 1938: every six months, the Parliament prorogued the enabling powers, then the government or the King declared the state of siege, which was effective for this duration. The provisions are very similar, with the state of siege being generally declared on parts of the territory, and only on two occasions on the whole country. The now ritualistic reference to the Statute of 1864—and the transfer of order-maintaining, police powers and jurisdictional attributions from civil authorities to military ones continue to be present.

Within the historical trajectory of this normalization of the emergency, there are two moments of particular importance, marking the transformative potential of the emergency and underlying its specific ambiguity between law, politics and military considerations. First, a judgment of the United Sections of the Supreme Court in a constitutional review on a criminal appeal, filed by the representative of the Skoda company in Romania, affirms that the state of siege is imposing a constitutional regime of exception, yet is fully consistent with the constitution, and it is a mere application of the powers entrusted to the Parliament and the government.[80] Otherwise said, the state of siege, and its subsequent distribution of power, is not outside the constitutional order, and it does not change or suspend its application. In a word, it is *accommodated* by the constitutional order.

A second, significant development concerns the drafting and enactment of the Criminal Code, titled *the Criminal Code Carol II*.[81] While not explicitly connected to the institution of the state of siege, it introduced as a matter of regular legislation the legal developments passed as a matter of emergency during the 1920s, especially the criminalization of preparatory acts—directly connected to the repression of communist and anarchist activism of the early 1920s—as well as a series of amendments of

[79] Decretul Lege Nr. 3376 din 30 Decembrie 1933, M. Of. No. 301, 30 December 1933.

[80] (ICCJ-SU) Judgment of 24 May 1934, No. 17 (on a criminal appeal by Bruno Szeletzky), in (1935) 5 *Curierul Judiciar* 27 January 1935, 71–73.

[81] Cosmin Cercel, 'The Enemy Within: Criminal Law and Ideology in Interwar Romania' in Stephen Skinner (ed.) *Fascism and Criminal Law: History, Theory, Continuity* (Oxford: Hart, 2015) 101–126.

the criminalization of the acts constituting offenses against the state and the constitutional order. It also banned the unlawful wearing of military uniforms and aimed to tackle political violence. The enabling law of the state of siege passed in March 1937 took stock of these legal changes, and explicitly attributed crimes against the state and constitutional order to military courts, alongside murder, manslaughter, assault and battery when the latter were committed due to beliefs and the political convictions or the nationality of the victims.[82] The crimes against the state were to be judged in summary trials according to the rules for "caught in the act" offenses. Last, criminal delicts such as contempt of authority or assault were also passed temporarily within the remit of the military jurisdictions.

By 1938, the state of siege was not only an integral part of the still nominally liberal constitutional order, but was on the point of becoming a central criminal *cum* military dispositive for addressing crisis, political disruption and more generally the growing and diffuse dissent in society. It is significant to note that within this context, not only does the state of siege become a regular and ostensible presence in the daily life of the polity, but some of its features enter within the sphere of regular legality, becoming embedded in the legal system.

An important shift is to be noted concerning the danger that was aimed to be tackled by this form of repression: while traditionally, as we could observe through this investigation, the state of siege was meant to address revolutionary actions, from within the ranks of the leftist circles, during this period of time, it is directed primarily against the fascist Legionary movement. Following the assassination of Prime Minister Duca, the Legion started to attack the King and his mistress, alongside the groups of politicians around the King—his camarilla—as early as 1935.[83] It also grew in presence across the country and was particularly emboldened by the rise of fascism elsewhere and the participation of its members in the Spanish Civil War.[84] Corruption scandals and a general sense of suspicion towards the King and his meddling in politics, as well as a generalization of political violence, marked the political spectrum.[85]

[82] Lege pentru prelungirea stării de asediu din 15 Martie 1937, M. Of,, 15 March 1937.

[83] Rebecca Ann Haynes, 'Reluctant Allies? Iuliu Maniu and Corneliu Zelea Codreanu against King Carol II of Romania', (2007) 85 *Slavonic and East European Review* 106, 111.

[84] Roland Clark, *Holy Legionary Youth: Fascist Activism in Interwar Romania* (Ithaca: Cornell University Press, 2015), 204–205.

[85] Cosmin Cercel, 'Darker Legacies of Anti-corruption: Fascist Criticisms of the Law in Interwar Romania', (2024) 20 *International Journal of Law in Context* 529.

In a generalized confusion, political parties of the opposition decided to protect the free character of the elections by expressing their shared support for resisting the interference of the executive in what was called the pact of electoral non-aggression, whose heralds were the former Prime Minister Iuliu Maniu (NPP) and the leader of the Legion, Zelea Codreanu.[86] The result of the election was a standstill, as the National Liberals refused to enter a coalition with either the NPP or the Legion. The King invited another fascist party under the rule of ultranationalist and antisemitic poet Octavian Goga to form a government, thus increasing the political crisis. Pieces of antisemitic legislation,[87] as well as dissolution and ban of leftist journals, followed.[88] Protests from Romania's formal allies, France and the UK, halted the law on the review of citizenship of Jewish nations. Threats of invasion from the Soviet Union, and the prospect of a fascist union, prompted the King to ask for Goga's resignation,[89] dissolve the Parliament and declare the state of siege as a measure that was no longer temporarily limited.[90]

In his first proclamation, the King explicitly stated that he was determined to "lay down the supreme law, which is the salvation of the country."[91] For its part, Article 6 of the Royal Decree passed on 11 February introducing the state of siege on the whole territory of the country, read: "the state of siege will be lifted when it is deemed appropriate."[92] In this way, the limited, yet present and important parliamentary scrutiny over the enabling of emergency powers was dealt with by legal means. Two weeks later, a new constitution was presented for popular assent.[93] It significantly increased the King's formal powers (on the basis of already existing informal practices under the constitution of 1923), doing away

[86] Haynes, 'Reluctant Allies', 119.

[87] Order of the Council of Ministers No. 4036 concerning the suppression of newspapers, M. Of., No. 302, 31 December 1937.

[88] Royal Decree concerning the revision of citizenship of 21 January 1938, M. Of., 22 January 1938.

[89] Paul A. Shapiro, 'Prelude to Dictatorship in Romania: the National Christian Party in Power, December 1937–February 1938,' (1974) 8 Canadian-American Slavic Studies 45–88, 80.

[90] Decretul Regal Nr. 856 din 11 Februarie 1938 pentru înființarea stărei de asediu în toată țara, M. Of., No. 34, 11 February 1938.

[91] 'Le premier ministère Miron Cristea', Ministère des Affaires Etrangères, *Bulletin périodique de la presse roumaine: du 9 février au 28 avril 1938*, No. 92, 17 May 1938, 8.

[92] Decretul Regal Nr. 856

[93] The Constitution of Romania of 1938 in M. Of. No 48, 27 February 1938.

with the traditional separation of powers and instituting the principle of the unitary nature of power, insofar as the constitution declared the King to be *the Head of State*.[94] Moreover, fundamental rights, while still present within the body of the constitution, were preceded by citizen duties, insofar as the accent moves from political freedoms grounding a political citizenship, to subjecthood towards the King and Nation.

Shortly after the enactment of the Constitution, a decree-law containing the provision of the Law for the Defense of Order Within the State[95] was issued. Not only was it directly inspired by the ongoing practice of the state of siege, but it was meant to complement it as a foundational part of the new constitutional regime. The text was meant to tackle political violence, and it criminalized a number of specific actions that would have otherwise been protected under freedom of assembly and freedom of speech, already altered by the constitution under the general proviso that they were meant to be exercised according to the laws of the country. The Decree tackled thus, propaganda aimed at a regime or constitutional change, political propaganda in cult places, marching in military formations, forming clandestine organizations, pledging oaths of allegiance outside the legal provisions, organizing paramilitary armed formations, etc. The most significant provision, contained towards the end of the Decree, declared "the dissolution of all political organizations."[96] Another Decree-law instituted the Front of National Rebirth as the sole political organization within the state, sealing in this way the formal turn of the regime into an authoritarian rule organized around the person of the Monarch.[97]

What is of particular importance in this final sequence of the history of the state of siege, is that it provided both the material and symbolic grounding of the new regime: from 1933 at least up to 1938 the constitutional state of siege operated as transformative and disruptive force: the so-called commissarial dictatorship was already, and perhaps has been from the very beginning the vector of a constitutional change. Even within the new constitutional arrangements, the state of siege carried on as the legal and material structure on which the authoritarian regime could build its institutional patchwork of a formal constitution, and the haphazard and

[94] Paul Negulescu, Principiile fundamentale ale constituției din 27 februarie 1938 (Bucharest, Atelierele Zanet Corlățeanu, 1939) 90.

[95] Decret lege Nr 1556 din 14 Aprilie 1938, M. Of. No. 88, 15 April 1938.

[96] Art 13, Ibid.

[97] Royal Decree of 30 March 1938 in M.Of. No 75, 31 March 1938.

frenzied production of Decree laws on various criminal law or political organizational matters.

13.5 Conclusion: Survival and Transfiguration of "Siege"

The historical analysis of the state of siege within the interwar years in Romania is able to reveal this institution as containing the formal and, in a specific way, the material conditions of a full-fledged constitutional change and turn towards an authoritarian order. This is because, first the state of siege was the legal and constitutional loophole through which by being fully within a constitutional regime, another regime of legality was able to be produced: this was ostensible in the largely discretionary powers exercised by military and civilian authorities in wartime and insurrectional contexts: summary trials, military orders applicable to civilian populations adding to the provisions of criminal law without statutory basis, extrajudicial killings, illegal declarations of the state of siege. But the question goes, of course, beyond limit-cases: even in standard and limited operations of siege, the constitutional protections and the exercise of fundamental rights were affected as a matter of formal legal practice and as a matter of principle.

Constant use was not only bound to alter constitutional arrangements, but also revealed something deeper about their inner stability and nature. It would be a stretch to observe that the inner material constitution was ultimately relying on the state of siege, but it is important to note how the insinuation of the state of siege within the regular practice of the state was able to effectively rewrite constitutional practices to the point of replacing the whole order. In many respects, this was possible because of the specific operation of the "siege:" a legal fiction and a screen between contexts of crisis and the constitutional order, meant to contain, through an exception[98] the corrosive effect of the context. Yet, looked at historically, the situation is much more complex: the legal fiction is not purely an outside, but a different way of addressing crisis, in many respects a much more direct and malleable one than the regular operation of the law: unprincipled, ambiguous, elusive and apparently "easy" to grasp. It is a legal operation with distinct legal effects, that posits as its only guiding principle the

[98] Giorgio Agamben, Agamben, *State of Exception* (University of Chicago Press, 2005), 17–18.

"salvation of the country" or "the elimination of state danger." In it, legal simplicity is doubled by the direct material effects of the military force: the siege is to be fought with military discipline and organization. This, of course, produces a series of symbolic, legal and political confusions as to what counts as siege, danger, and what are the limits of the activity of the military and of the public authorities in declaring the siege, which will fall back on their institutional and class ideology.

In this respect, the history of this practice comes full circle in the 100 years we cover in this sequence: the military institution was, from its very beginnings, structured in the Romanian principalities as the 'force on which authority would rest its trust,'[99] meant to deal primarily with potential rebellions against the aristocratic rule. In full modernity—some would call it even hypermodernity due to its palingenetic overtones,[100] and pledges to full reframing of the polity—it is the only safe ground for sovereign discretion, the "supreme law." Looking at its legal practice, one thing is striking: the state of siege was the name given to an institution that, as a matter of constitutional law, had a disputed existence for almost six decades—between 1866 and 1923—and an obscure one for the rest of its life, insofar as only a limited constitutional provision referred to it. However, each and every declaration would refer to the legal conditions of the statute of 1864, which was, as a matter of constitutional transition against the dispositions of the 1866 constitution, and never formally reintegrated into the legal order.

Quilting together a patchwork of criminal law measures, military practice, and political considerations, the state of siege not only travelled from historical contexts as different as the French June uprising of 1848 to the Wallachian restauration of 1852, but has also survived in its logic and name from the times of restauration to the hybrid hyper-modernism of 1930s authoritarianism.

References

Balakrishnan, G. *The Enemy: An Intellectual Portrait of Carl Schmitt*. London: Verso, 2000

Căzănişteanu, C., Cuccu, M., and Popescu, E. *Aspecte militare ale revoluţiei de la 1848*. Bucharest: Editura Militară

[99] Art. 379, Regulamentul Organic al Valahiei.

[100] Roger Griffin, *Modernism and Fascism: The Sense of a Beginning under Mussolini and Hitler* (Basingstoke: Palgrave Macmillan 2007), 220–224.

Cercel, C. "Darker Legacies of Anti-corruption: Fascist Criticisms of the Law in Interwar Romania." *International Journal of Law in Context*, 20, 2024, 529
Cercel, C. "Fascist Claims to Sovereign Power." *Contemporary European History*, 33, 1273
Cercel, C. "Marx's Concept of Dictatorship." In Oszu, U., and O'Connell, P. (eds.) *Research Handbook on Law and Marxism*. Cheltenham: Edward Elgar, 2020, 61–76
Cercel, C. "Reversing Liberal Legality: Romania's Path to Dictatorship, 1930–1938." *Journal of Romanian Studies*, 2, 2020, 23
Cercel, C. "The 'Right' Side of the Law: State of Siege and the Rise of Fascism in Interwar Romania." *Fascism*, 2, 2013, 205
Cercel, C. "The Enemy Within: Criminal Law and Ideology in Interwar Romania." In Skinner, S. (ed.) *Fascism and Criminal Law: History, Theory, Continuity*. Oxford: Hart, 2015, 101–126
Cercel, C. "Unearthing the Dark Side of the Law. Narratives of Law and Authority in the Tatarbunar Trials." *History of Communism in Europe*, 14, 2023, 111
Cernea, E. *Criza dreptului în România la anul 1907*. Bucharest: Editura Universității București, 2001
Clark, C.U. *Bessarabia, Russia and Roumania on the Black Sea*. New York: Dodd, Mead & Co., 1927
Clark, C.U. *United Roumania*. New York: Dodd, Mead and Co., 1932
Clark, R. *Holy Legionary Youth: Fascist Activism in Interwar Romania*. Ithaca: Cornell University Press, 2015, 204–205
Costa-Foru, C.G. *Abuzurile și crimele siguranței statului*. Bucharest: Triumful, 1925, 5
Davison, R.H. "'Russian Skill and Turkish Imbecility': The Treaty of Kuchuk Kainardji Reconsidered." *Slavic Review*, 35, 1976, 463
Diac, C. "Scapegoats or Agents of State Dissolution? The Comintern, the Romanian Communists, and the Grivița Strike in February 1933." *History of Communism in Europe*, 14, 2023, 131
Dissescu, C. *Drept constituțional*. Bucharest: SOCEC, 1915
Dragomirescu, I. "Starea de asediu." *Dreptul*, 43, 1914, 417
Ferejohn, J., and Pasquino, P. "The Law of the Exception: A Typology of Emergency Powers." *International Journal of Constitutional Law*, 2, 2004, 210
Fraenkel, E. *The Dual State: A Contribution to the Theory of Dictatorship*. New York: Octagon Books, 1969
Grecul, G.D. *Starea de asediu actuală*. Bucharest: Curierul Judiciar, 1928
Greene, A. *Permanent States of Emergency and the Rule of Law: Constitutions in an Age of Crisis*. London: Hart, 2018, 212
Gross, O., and Ni Aolain, F. *Law in Times of Crisis: Emergency Powers in Theory and Practice*. Cambridge: Cambridge University Press, 2006
Guțan, M. "Avatarurile autoritarismului domnesc la mijlocul secolului al XIX lea: între absolutism luminat și cezarism democratic." In Guțan, M., et al. *Șefii de*

stat: dinamica autoritară a puterii politice în istoria constituțională românească. Bucharest: Universul Juridic, 2020, 149–244
Haynes, R.A. "Reluctant Allies? Iuliu Maniu and Corneliu Zelea Codreanu against King Carol II of Romania." *Slavonic and East European Review*, 85, 2007, 106
Haynes, R.A. "Work Camps, Commerce, and the Education of the 'New Man' in the Romanian Legionary Movement." *The Historical Journal*, 51, 2008, 943
Hitchins, K. *Rumania 1866–1947*. Oxford: Oxford University Press, 1994
Ionescu, D.P., and Pușcașu, E. "Lupta de la Constagalia (iunie 1863)." *Revista Istorică*, 7, 1996, 757
Joerges, C., and Ghaleigh, N.S. "Preface and Acknowledgements'. In Joerges, C., and Ghaleigh, N.S. (eds.) *Darker Legacies of Law in Europe*. Oxford: Hart Publishing, 2003, ix–xi.
Lavis, S. "The Exception of the Norm in the Third Reich: Rereading the Nazi Constitutional State of Exception." In Cercel, C., Fusco, G.-G., and Lavis, S. (eds.) *States of Exception: Law, History, Theory*. Abingdon: Routledge, 2021, 92–118
Lazar, N.C. "Making Emergencies Safe for Democracy: The Roman Dictatorship and the Rule of Law in the Study of Crisis Government." *Constellations*, 13, 2006, 506
Lillich, R.B. "The Paris Minimum Standards of Human Rights Norms in a State of Emergency." *American Journal of International Law*, 79, 1985, 1072
Mańko, R. "Legal Survivals and the Resilience of Juridical Form." *Law and Critique*, 2023. https://doi.org/10.1007/s10978-023-09357-2
Michelson, P.E. *Romanian Politics, 1859–1871: From Prince Cuza to Prince Carol*. Iasi: Centre for Romanian Studies, 1998
Negulescu, P. *Principiile fundamentale ale constituției din 27 februarie 1938*. Bucharest: Atelierele Zanet Corlățeanu, 1939, 90
Pintilescu, C. "The Impact of the October Revolution, Social Turmoil and the Resort to the State of Siege in Interwar Romania." *History of Communism in Europe*, 14, 2023, 89
Reinach, T. *De l'état de siège et des institutions du salut public*. Paris: F. Pichon, 1885
Rossiter, C. *Constitutional Dictatorship: Crisis Government in the Modern Democracies*. Princeton University Press, 1949, 23–24
Roucek, J.S. "Social Background of Roumanian Politics." *Social Forces*, 10, 1932, 419
Schmitt, C. *Dictatorship*. Cambridge: Polity, 2014
Schmitt, C. *Theory of the Partisan*. New York: Telos Press, 2007
Shapiro, P.A. "Prelude to Dictatorship in Romania: the National Christian Party in Power, December 1937–February 1938." *Canadian-American Slavic Studies*, 8, 1974, 45
Stollleis, M. "Reluctance to Glance in the Mirror: The Changing Face of German Jurisprudence after 1933 and Post-1945." In Joerges, C., and Ghaleigh, N.S. (eds.) *Darker Legacies of Law in Europe*. Oxford: Hart Publishing, 2003, 1–18
Traverso, E. *Fire and Blood: The European Civil War, 1914–1945*. London: Verso, 2017

Legal Materials

(ICCJ-SU) *Judgment of 24 May 1934, No. 17* (on a criminal appeal by Bruno Szeletzky). In *Curierul Judiciar*, 5, 27 January 1935, 71–73

"Convention signée à Paris pour l'organisation des Principautés Unies de Valachie et Moldavie." In *Recueil des Traités de la France*, Vol. VII. Paris: Durand and Pedone-Lauriel, 1880, 483–484

Constitution of Romania of 1923

Constitution of Romania of 1938. M. Of. No. 48, 27 February 1938

Decret lege Nr 1556 din 14 Aprilie 1938. M. Of. No. 88, 15 April 1938

Décret par lequel l'Assemblée nationale se maintient en permanence, met Paris en état de siège, et délègue les pouvoirs exécutifs au général Cavaignac, 24 juin 1848. In Duvergier, J.-B. (ed.) *Collection complète des lois, décrets, ordonnances, réglements, et avis du Conseil d'Etat.* Paris: Charles Noblet, 1848

Decret Regal Nr. 131 din 16 Ianuarie 1923 referitor la lărgirea stărei de asediu în Ardeal

Decret Regal Nr. 2939 din 15 Iulie 1920 relativ la restrângerea stărei de asediu. M. Of., No. 83, 16 July 1920

Decret Regal Nr. 4209 din 21 Octombrie 1920, pentru declararea stărei de asediu în București și instituirea cenzurei. M. Of., No. 159, 21 October 1920

Decretul Lege Nr. 3376 din 30 Decembrie 1933. M. Of. No. 301, 30 December 1933

Decretul Regal Nr. 1626 din 30 Iunie 1918 pentru modificarea Decretului Nr. 2798 din 14 August 1916, relativ la starea de asediu. M. Of., No. 79bis, 1 July 1918

Decretul Regal Nr. 856 din 11 Februarie 1938 pentru înființarea stărei de asediu în toată țara. M. Of., No. 34, 11 February 1938

European Convention of Human Rights

High Princely Decree No. 1219 of 26 May 1877. M. Of. No. 117, 26 May 1877

Lege pentru autorizarea starei de asediu din 4 Februarie 1933. M. Of., No. 29, 4 February 1933

Lege pentru prelungirea stării de asediu din 15 Martie 1937. M. Of., 15 March 1937

Legea pentru starea de asediu din 10 Decembrie 1864. In *Codul general al României*, Vol. II. Bucharest: Alcalay, 1907, 117–118

Legea stărei de asediu of 14 August 1916. M. Of., No. 107, 14 August 1916

Loi du 9 août 1849 sur l'état de siège. Bulletin des lois, No. 186, 146. See also, "Rapport fait par M. Alex. Fourtanier, au nom de la commission chargée d'examiner le projet de loi sur l'état de siége." In *Comptes Rendus des Séances de l'Assemblée Nationale Legislative*, Vol. II. Paris: Panckouke, 1849, 127–13

Order of the Council of Ministers No. 4036 concerning the suppression of newspapers. M. Of., No. 302, 31 December 1937

Regulamentul Organic al Valahiei. In Negulescu, P., and Alexianu, G. (eds.) *Regulamentele organice ale Valahiei și Moldovei.* Bucharest: Eminescu, 1944, 1–170

Royal Decree concerning the revision of citizenship of 21 January 1938. M. Of., 22 January 1938
Royal Decree of 30 March 1938. M. Of. No 75, 31 March 1938
Supliment la Condica Penală Ostăşeacă—Pentru starea de împresurare. In Berechet, S. Gr. (ed.) *Asezamant ostasesc pentru straja pamanteasca a Valahii din 1832*. Iasi: Institutul de Arte Grafice Tatarasi, 95–97
Treaty of Perpetual Peace and Amity between Russia and Turkey, signed at Kuçuk Kainardji [Küçük Kaynarca], 10(21) July 1774. In *Parry's Consolidated Treaties Series*, Vol. 45. Oxford University Press, 2017

Archival Sources

"Le premier ministère Miron Cristea." *Ministère des Affaires Etrangères, Bulletin périodique de la presse roumaine: du 9 février au 28 avril 1938*, No. 92, 17 May 1938, 7–11
"Doc. No. 134: A. Pini replies to the committee that he does not assume responsibility for the call of Turkish troops within the country." In Otetea, A. (ed.) *Rascoala din 1821: documente interne*, Vol. I. Bucharest: Editura Academiei Republicii Populare Romine, 1959, 238
"Doc. No. 151: The Committee sends high vornic Constantin Samurcas with full powers in Oltenia to appease the uprising." In Otetea, A. (ed.) *Rascoala din 1821: documente interne*, Vol. I. Bucharest: Editura Academiei Republicii Populare Romine, 1959, 259
"Doc. No. 130: The ruling aristocrats take guard measures in Bucharest." In Otetea, A. (ed.) *Rascoala din 1821: documente interne*, Vol. I. Bucharest: Editura Academiei Republicii Populare Romine, 1959, 232–233
"Doc. No. 275: Tudor Vladimirescu asks the provisional government to establish a special tribunal at Cotroceni, composed of three judges, to judge the felonies and thefts committed by the pandurs." In Otetea, A. (ed.) *Rascoala din 1821: documente interne*, Vol. I. Bucharest: Editura Academiei Republicii Populare Romine, 1959, 433–424
Doc. No. 803 (cyphered telegram of 31 May 1877). In Roller, M. (ed.) *Documente privind istoria României: Războiul pentru independență*, Vol. III. Bucharest: Editura Academiei Republicii Populare Romîne, 1953, 431
"Le prince Carol proclamé roi." *Ministère des Affaires Etrangères, Bulletin périodique de la presse roumaine: du 26 mai au 25 juin 1930*, No. 92, 3 July 1930, 3–6
"La situation économique et financière." In *Ministère des Affaires Etrangères, Bulletin périodique de la presse roumaine: du 2 février au 18 mars 1933*, No. 111, 25 March 1933, 5–7

CHAPTER 14

Militant Constitutionalism in Times of Polycrisis: The EU Perspective

Antonia Baraggia

14.1 Introduction: From Militant Democracy to Militant Constitutionalism

Militant democracy, a concept[1] that was notoriously coined in the aftermath of the First World War, given the rise of fascist regimes, and which is now back on the stage, vis-à-vis the crisis of constitutional democracy in many countries worldwide. Militant democracy is built on an oxymoron: democracy should be able to defend itself from the threats coming from the democratic process, even putting in place illiberal measures to prevent a subversion of the democratic order. As is the case with other paradoxical concepts, the journey toward a deep understanding of the heart of darkness of militant democracy is an intriguing but insidious one.

We can understand the difficulty in grasping the essence of militant democracy if we consider that, despite tons of papers addressing the concept

This chapter is produced as part and funded by the European Union-NextGenerationEU, through the National Recovery and Resilience Plan of the Republic of Bulgaria, project No bg-rrp-2.004-0008.

[1] K. Loewenstein, 'Militant Democracy and Fundamental Rights', in [1937] 31(3) *The American Political Science Review* 417.

M. Belov (ed.), *Constitutional Polycrisis and Emergency Constitutionalism*, Federalism and Internal Conflicts,
https://doi.org/10.1007/978-3-032-06516-2_14

and its different variations, there is no normative theory about militant democracy. As Muller argues, "there is no model of militant democracy that might straightforwardly be adopted by a newly consolidated democracy, and there exist no clear general normative guidelines as to how liberals should take their own side in an argument without ceasing to be liberals."[2]

Indeed, we can identify different models of militant democracy. First, we have the prototypical model, the German one, where the Basic Law constitutionalized provisions of militant democracy, introducing the ban of parties deemed unconstitutional and the restriction of free speech rights for individuals acting against democracy. Moreover, the Basic Law empowered the Constitutional Court with the task of judging the unconstitutionality of a political party, a function that, after being dormant for some years, has regained the stage with the proceedings against the National Democratic Party of Germany (NPD) and more recently against Alternative for Deutschland (AFD). From this prototype—aimed at protecting democracy from extremist forces, we can further distinguish other models—constitutionally explicit or not—of militant democracy.

An interesting example is given by countries that adopted militant democracy to protect national or constitutional identity. This is the case of Turkey, with the famous case of the ban of the Refah Party, upheld by the ECtHR in 2003, and the case of France, with the ban of headscarves in schools and other restrictions on religious symbols in the public sphere. The idea of militant democracy has also been applied within European democracies in the fight against terrorism and Islamic extremism.[3] More recently, militant democracy has been used to address the different responses of legal systems—both national and supranational—to the rule of law crisis[4] and the rise of populism and of autocratic tendencies.

In this vein, the term militant democracy can be used in order to encompass not only the traditional tools related to the concept but, more generally, the use of different instruments by counter-majoritarian institutions or supranational bodies to tackle processes of democratic backsliding and to protect liberal democratic constitutions from actors and forces against this model. This broader understanding of militant democracy

[2] J.-W. Müller, 'Militant Democracy', in M. Rosenfeld, A. Sajó (eds), *The Oxford Handbook of Comparative Constitutional Law* (OUP 2012).

[3] K. Roach, 'Anti-Terrorism and Militant Democracy: Some Western and Eastern Responses' in A. Sajo (ed), *Militant Democracy* (Eleven International Publishing, 2004).

[4] J.-W. Müller, 'Defending Democracy within the EU' [2013] *Journal of Democracy* 24(2) 138.

refers, for example, to the use of the doctrine of unconstitutional constitutional amendment,[5] the use of identity clauses, or—at the supranational level—to the use of Art. 7 TEU or, more recently, to the development of a regime of conditionality to protect the rule of law.

This new use of the concept of militant democracy, which departs from the essence of the original, narrower meaning, is the focus of this chapter. I do not underestimate the relevance of the classical category of militant democracy, which remains a cornerstone of the legal debate on how to defend the democratic order. What I argue, however, is that militant democracy is anchored in a classic understanding of the rise of authoritarian regimes rooted in extremism and violence—while it is not well suited to representing the defense against new forms of authoritarian regimes, variously identified as *autocratic legalism* or *abusive constitutionalism*, that is, threats to constitutional democracy that occur gradually, without clear breaches of the constitutional system.

In this chapter, I will look at the responses of the different legal systems to this authoritarian turn, linking the idea of militancy not only to protect democracy, but more generally the constitutional order. Militant constitutionalism is a term already advanced by the literature. As explained, "militant constitutionalism addresses any constitutional design feature that aims at safeguarding constitutionalism."[6] Militant constitutionalism and militant democracy differ in several relevant features, "such as their timing (militant democracy tries to prevent non-democrats from acquiring power, whereas militant constitutionalism tries to contain the damage even if enemies of the rule of law have acquired political power), the actors charged with their implementation (the government versus actors well beyond the government), and the means employed to reach their goal (bans on extreme parties, media accountability, as well as limits on the freedom of assembly and protecting the constitution from self-serving amendments)."[7]

If we observe the reaction of the legal system to these trends, we can identify new tools, different from the ban of political parties or the limitation of rights: new forms of defensive constitutionalism may be traced in the use of the eternity clauses, the unconstitutional constitutional amendment

[5] Y. Roznai, *Unconstitutional Constitutional Amendments. The Limits of Amendment Powers* (OUP 2017).

[6] J. Gutmann, S. Voigt, 'Militant constitutionalism: a promising concept to make constitutional backsliding less likely?' in [2023] 195 *Public Choice* 377, 378.

[7] *Ivi*, 378–379.

doctrine, the use of identity clauses, and, at the supranational level, in the use of regimes of conditionality for the protection of the rule of law.

This contribution will look at the development of militant constitutionalism in the realm of the EU, with a focus on the nature and the implications of the rule of law conditionality regulation (n. 2020/2092) and the use of the concept of European identity by the CJEU. I will proceed as follows: first, I will address the question of whether the EU is moving toward a militant constitutional model; second, I will highlight the new role of the concept of European identity in the legal reasoning of the CJEU, which sets the basis for the development of a regime that I define as militant identity; third, I will argue that the use of conditionality may be considered a tool of militant constitutionalism; and, finally, I will look at some recent cases and show that they seems to move toward a militant conception of EU values.

14.2 Is the EU Moving toward a Militant Constitutional Model?

The European Union is increasingly adopting elements that align with the principles of militant constitutionalism as it navigates the complexities of safeguarding democratic values within its Member States.[8] Facing challenges such as the rise of populism, nationalism, and democratic backsliding in countries like Hungary and Poland, the EU has enhanced its legal and political mechanisms to protect its foundational principles. Instruments like Article 7 of the Treaty on European Union (TEU) and the Rule of Law Mechanism, which ties funding to adherence to the EU values, illustrate this shift. These mechanisms reflect a proactive stance in addressing threats to democracy and the rule of law, suggesting a move towards militancy in defense of its values and, as the CJEU stated, of its identity.

In particular, Regulation 2020/2092[9] and its application has marked the EU's new path in protecting its *identity*. I argue that with Regulation 2020/2092, the EU has moved significantly towards a militant constitutional model driven to protect the "constitutional identity" of the EU.

[8] T. Theuns, 'Is the European Union a militant democracy? Democratic backsliding and EU disintegration' [2024] *Global Constitutionalism* 13(1) 104.

[9] Regulation (EU, Euratom) 2020/2092 of the European Parliament and of the Council of December 16, 2020 on a general system of conditionality for the protection of the Union's budget.

This has marked a constitutional moment of the EU that will reshape the role of the EU vis-à-vis the Member State, redefining the constitutional balance of the EU.

In order to grasp this implication, it is necessary to dig into the genesis and the implication of the rule of law conditionality mechanism, which establishes a conditionality regime aimed at suspending European funding to a Member State if violations of the principle of the rule of law are found to undermine or seriously threaten to undermine in a sufficiently direct manner the sound financial management of the Union budget or the protection of its financial interests.

This conditionality mechanism was approved in December 2020, at the same time as the Union's 2021–2027 multi-year budget, at the end of a troubled process, which began in 2018 with a Commission proposal that was significantly amended due to critical considerations by both the Council Legal Service and the European Parliament regarding the compatibility of the foreshadowed conditionality regime with the Union's primary law.

Moreover, the actual approval of the regulation was at the crossroads of political dynamics and more strictly legal aspects inherent in the regulation. On the one hand, it proposes to address one of the most pressing constitutional issues for the Union: the sanctioning of those Member States that ignore, and indeed defy, respect for the fundamental values of the EU;[10] those same values whose acceptance had been at the heart of the Copenhagen criteria for EU accession.[11] This is an extremely sensitive issue, touching subtle strings relating to the very nature of the Union, the relations between the Union and the Member States, and the constitutional tensions that have been exacerbated as relations with Hungary and, till 2023, Poland, have deteriorated.[12]

[10] W. Sadurski, *Poland's Constitutional Breakdown* (OUP 2019); A. Di Gregorio, 'L'Ungheria e i valori europei. Un matrimonio difficile' (*Associazione DPCE*, 17 September 2018) <http://www.dpce.it/l-ungheria-e-i-valori-europei-un-matrimonio-difficile.html>; G. Halmai, 'Abuse of constitutional identity: the Hungarian constitutional court on interpretation of article E (2) of the fundamental law' [2018] *Review of Central and East European Law* 43(1) 23.

[11] C. Pinelli, 'Conditionality and Enlargement in Light of the EU Constitutional Developments' [2004] 10 *European Law Journal* 3; K.E. Smith, 'The Evolution and Application of EU Membership Conditionality' in M. Cremona (ed), *The Enlargement of the European Union* (OUP 2003).

[12] N. Kirst, 'Rule of Law Conditionality: The Long-awaited Step Towards a Solution of the Rule of Law Crisis in the European Union?' [2021] *European Papers* 101; A. Baraggia,

In this context, the Union has moved, and is still moving, along the delicate line between the need, on the one hand, to protect the fundamental values of the system and, on the other hand, to respect the sovereignty and constitutional identity of the member countries. This tension is intrinsic to the European constitutional balance, and there are many cases of conflict in a context characterized by legal pluralism. However, it has never been posed in such oppositional terms as to justify recourse, albeit unsuccessfully, to the Article 7 procedure, which sanctions systemic violations of the Union's values by Member States, and which was activated in the Hungarian case in 2018.[13]

Article 2 of Regulation 2020/2092 provides, first, a broad definition of the fundamental concept of the rule of law, which includes the principle of legality, legal certainty, prohibition of arbitrariness of executive power, effective judicial protection, including access to justice, guarantee of independent and impartial courts, separation of powers and the principle of non-discrimination and equality before the law. This is particularly relevant because, for the first time, the value of the rule of law has declined, at the regulatory level, in a series of punctual principles that represent the so-called operationalization of the principle in question.

The subsequent Art. 3 of the regulation details some situations that may indicate the existence of a violation of the *rule of law* and thus lead to the activation of the mechanism: threats to the independence of the judiciary; failure to prevent or sanction arbitrary or illegitimate decisions made by public authorities or failure to ensure the absence of conflicts of interest; limiting the availability and effectiveness of legal remedies, for example, through restrictive procedural rules and failure to enforce judgments or limiting the effectiveness of investigations, prosecutions or sanctions for violations of law.

M. Bonelli, 'Linking Money to Values: the new Rule of Law Conditionality Regulation and its constitutional challenges' [2020] 23(2) German LJ 131; M. Fisicaro, 'Rule of Law Conditionality in EU Funds: The Value of Money in the Crisis of European Values' [2019] *European Papers* 695.

[13] G. Halmai, 'The alternatives to a bite or a bark: after launching Article 7 TEU against the Hungarian government', in U. Belavusau, A. Gliszczyńska-Grabias (eds), *Constitutionalism under stress: essays in honor of Wojciech Sadurski* (OUP 2020).

This circumscribed nature of the text of the regulation can be seen as a defeat[14] by those who expected the introduction of a robust and comprehensive mechanism to address the crisis of the rule of law, capable also of extending to sanctioning violations of fundamental rights and democracy by Member States. However, the literature on conditionality,[15] especially that which has questioned the effectiveness of conditionality regimes, has shown that for conditions to be effective, they must be clear, precise, formally codified, and enforceable in concrete, defined cases. Paradoxically, then, while the regulation's linkage to violations of the rule of law that reverberate on the Union budget might narrow the scope of conditionality under consideration, in reality, this limitation results in a positive feature that can strengthen the legitimacy of the conditionality regime, without affecting the sovereignty of Member States or the principle of conferral.

Despite being built on such a fragile equilibrium, Regulation 2020/2092 can be considered in the realm of militant constitutionalism insofar as it is aimed at sanctioning the threats posed by Member States to one of the core values (i.e., the identity) of the EU enshrined in Art. 2 TUE.

14.3 The EU Identity: The Court of Justice Contribution to Defining Militant Constitutionalism in the EU

The link between the rule of law regulation and the EU identity has been made explicit by the CJEU, in the Cases C-156/21 and C-157/21, where it confirmed the compatibility of the regulation with the Treaties and EU law, thus paving the way for the adoption of the Commission's Guidelines, published in March 2022 and also making the mechanism fully operational.[16] The two—almost twin—rulings, responding promptly to the

[14] K.L. Scheppele, L. Pech, S. Platon, *Compromising the Rule of Law while Compromising on the Rule of Law* (*Verfassungsblog.de*, 13 December 2020) <https://verfassungsblog.de/compromising-the-rule-of-law-while-compromising-on-the-rule-of-law/>

[15] M. Blauberger, V. van Hüllen, 'Conditionality of EU funds: an instrument to enforce EU fundamental values?' [2021] 43(1) *Journal of European Integration* 1.

[16] Communication from the Commission, C (2022) 1382 final, Guidelines on the application of Regulation (EU, Euratom) 2020/2092 on a general system of conditionality for the protection of the Union's budget, Brussels (Brussels), March 2, 2022.

complaints of Member States (9 by Hungary and 11 by Poland), provide the Court with an opportunity to underscore the nature and *telos* of the European Union—and also its *militant* attitude—while recognizing the inherent limits of the EU concerning the prerogatives of states. In other words, the Court of Justice outlines the contours within which relations between the EU and its member states are developed, marked by respect for the fundamental values of the Union that were accepted and shared by the states at the time of their voluntary accession to the European project.

If, however, one reads the judgments in a diachronic perspective, one realizes that they enshrine a reading of the values of the Union and the role of institutions in protecting them that begins already, consciously, in the strand that has concerned the issue of the independence of the judiciary: above all, the cases of the Portuguese judges,[17] *Repubblika*,[18] and LM.[19] This has been a slow progression that has led to the sanctioning of the normative and not just merely value-political nature of the Union's values under Article 2 TEU: these values, intrinsically connected to each other, become, in fact, the vector of binding norms for states, failure to comply with which can be sanctioned at the jurisdictional level.

However, even in this expansive reading of the meaning of the values of Article 2 TEU, which the Court supports, it is common ground that the Union can act to protect them provided that other provisions of the treaties grant it competence to do so. This is one of the most sensitive aspects of the regulation in question, and it is no coincidence that much of the tensions that have arisen over the crisis of the rule of law in the Union have had as their theater precisely the debate about the limits of the Union's competences and, conversely, respect for national sovereignty and identity.

It is not surprising, then, that one of the strongest claims made by Hungary and Poland concerned precisely the question of the legal basis of the regulation. As mentioned above, the regulation, which lays down the rules necessary to protect the Union budget in the event of violations of the principles of the rule of law in the Member States, is based on Article 322 TFEU. The latter requires the European Parliament and the Council to adopt, by means of regulations, the financial rules determining, in particular, the procedure to be followed for the establishment and implementation of the budget, as well as for the presentation of the accounts and the auditing of the accounts.

[17] *Associação Sindical Dos Juízes Portugueses* (C-64/16) ECLI:UE:C:2018:117.

[18] *Czech Republic* (C-896/19), ECLI:EU:C:2021:311.

[19] *PPU LM*, C-216/18 ECLI:EU:C:2018:586.

In order to assess the appropriateness of the legal basis, according to the Court, several factors should be considered, including the purpose and content of the measure and the legal framework in which the new mechanism is placed. On this point, according to Hungary and Poland, "the ultimate goal of this regulation is to enable the Commission and the Council to examine whether the principles of the rule of law are respected by the Member States and, in the event of violations of these principles, to impose sanctions through the Union budget."[20]

In other words, the issue at stake can be summarized in the opposing view of the mechanism under consideration as an instrument aimed at protecting the EU budget from a violation of the rule of law that may harm the sound financial interest of the EU, or rather as an instrument aimed at protecting and sanctioning violations of the rule of law through the EU budget. To address these issues, the Court provides a "systemic" reading of the articles relating to the EU budget and financial interests, namely Articles 310, 315, 316, and 317 TFEU in conjunction with Article 322 TFEU: the latter must be interpreted to ensure the principle of sound financial management, including by Member States in the implementation of the EU budget.[21]

It is precisely the protection of sound financial management, therefore, that becomes the objective of the regulation in question, which, as the Court repeats on several occasions, aims to "protect the Union budget in the event of violations of the principles of the rule of law in the Member States" in a sufficiently direct manner, and not to sanction such violations as such, whatever their gravity.[22]

In sum, the Court recognizes that respect for the rule of law is an essential prerequisite for sound financial management. However, only violations of the rule of law that *sufficiently directly harm* the interests of the Union can be sanctioned. This inseparable link between violations of the rule of law and damage to the EU budget weakens and narrows the scope of the conditionality mechanism. However, it is believed that it is precisely this requirement that legitimizes the mechanism, allowing it to fall within the perimeter of the EU's competencies.

[20] *Hungary v. Parliament and Council* (C-156/21) ECLI:EU:C:2021:974 at 109.

[21] *Poland v. Parliament and Council* (C-157/21) ECLI:EU:C:2021:975 at 119; *Hungary v. Parliament and Council* (C-156/21) ECLI:EU:C:2021:974 para. 105.

[22] *Poland v. Parliament and Council* (C-157/21) ECLI:EU:C:2021:975, para. 124; *Hungary v. Parliament and Council* (C-156/21) ECLI:EU:C:2021:974 para. 110.

Indeed, the EU can act to protect the values of Article 2 TEU, but it can do so only on the basis of those provisions of the Treaties that give it the competence to take such action. What remains to be considered, however, even in light of this assertion, is, as argued by Hungary and Poland in their actions, the legitimacy of a *horizontal conditionality* regime, that is, conditionality linked to the value of the rule of law in general and not instead closely linked to the objectives of a specific program, EU action, or sound financial management of the EU budget.

The link between the nature of conditions and the purpose of a given program is a requirement for the legality of conditionality schemes, a requirement already widely recognized in federal studies on conditionality, elaborated in the so-called "unconstitutional conditions doctrine"[23] by the U.S. Supreme Court. The Court of Justice, however, seems to take a different path: in fact, it recognizes the legitimacy of such a *horizontal conditionality* when it states that the conditions at stake can be linked to the value of the rule of law in Article 2 TEU, which must be respected in all areas of Union action. As the Court argues, based on the literal tenor of the regulation, the notion of the 'rule of law,' as defined for the purposes of the application of that regulation, "is to be understood in the light of the other values and principles of the Union enshrined in Article 2 TEU." It follows that respect for such values and principles—as participating in the very definition of the value of the "rule of law" contained in Article 2 TEU or, as is evident from the second sentence of that article, intimately linked to a society respecting the rule of law—may be required under a horizontal conditionality mechanism such as that established by the contested regulation.[24]

This broad statement, when viewed beyond the context of this regulation, is of utmost importance for the future development of the EU, as it could pave the way for the adoption of new forms of conditionality—having a legal basis in a primary law rule—to also protect the other Article 2 TEU values, which must be considered as a whole as they form the foundation of the EU legal order and "define the very identity of the Union as a common legal order."[25]

[23] *South Dakota v. Dole*, 483 U.S. 203, 1987.

[24] *Hungary v. Parliament and Council* (C-156/21) ECLI:EU:C:2021:974, para. 136.

[25] *Hungary v. Parliament and Council* (C-156/21), para. 127.

14.4 Towards a Militant Constitutional Identity?

The Court of Justice thus inaugurated, after an incremental process,[26] a new constitutional phase in the relations between the Union and the Member States, on the one hand through reference to the identity of the European Union as a common legal order, and, on the other hand, through recognition of the normative nature of the values of Article 2 TEU, which "are embodied in principles that entail legally binding obligations on member states."[27] In particular, the Court states, "respect for the principles of the rule of law constitutes an obligation of result to be achieved by the member states, which derives directly (...) from their membership in the European Union."[28]

Never had it gone so far as to use such terminology in reference to Article 2 TEU. Moreover, this stark configuration of the normative value of Article 2 TEU has broad implications beyond the rule of law. It could also relate to principles outside the values of Article 2 TEU, such as non-discrimination and the principle of equality. The Luxembourg court on the point makes clear: "although Article 2 TEU refers separately to the rule of law as a value common to the member states and to the principle of non-discrimination, it is clear that a member state whose society is characterized by discrimination cannot be regarded as guaranteeing respect for the rule of law within the meaning of that common value."[29]

Recognition of the applicability of the values of Article 2 TEU thus leads the Court to define the nature, structural features and ultimate reason why the Union stands, particularly by playing the delicate strings of the concept of identity. According to the Court, the values enshrined in Article 2 TEU are "an integral part of the very identity of the European Union as a common legal order. Therefore, the European Union must be able to defend those values, within the limits of its powers under the Treaties."[30]

[26] A. von Bogdandy, P. Bogdanowicz, I. Canor, G. Rugge, M. Schmidt, M. Taborowski, 'A Potential Constitutional Moment for the European Rule of Law: The Importance of Red Lines' in A. von Bogdandy, P. Bogdanowicz, I. Canor, C. Grabenwarter, M. Taborowski M. Schmidt (eds), *Defending Checks and Balances in EU Member States* (Springer 2021).

[27] *Hungary v. Parliament and Council* (C-156/21) ECLI:EU:C:2021:974, para. 232.

[28] *Poland v. Parliament and Council* (C-157/21) ECLI:EU:C:2021:975, para. 169; *Hungary v. Parliament and Council* (C-156/21) ECLI:EU:C:2021:974, para. 231.

[29] *Hungary v. Parliament and Council* (C-156/21) ECLI:EU:C:2021:974, para. 229.

[30] *Hungary v. Parliament and Council* (C-156/21) ECLI:EU:C:2021:974, para. 127; *Poland v. Parliament and Council* (C-157/21) ECLI:EU:C:2021:975, para. 145.

This argument seems to envisage a shift of the EU if not toward a model of militant democracy, at least toward a model of militant constitutionalism, characterized by the development of instruments aimed at protecting the order itself from drifts that could undermine its foundation. The conceptualization of European identity is placed in tension with national identities so that, in case of conflict, European identity cannot be contradicted or denied by national identities: as has been argued, in light of this case law, there is no room for unconstitutional identities in the EU.[31] And in case of conflict, the mechanism of conditionality can be triggered, which thus appears to be a defensive mechanism of the core values of the Union.

In this sense, conditionality seems to be consecrated by the Court as an instrument of militant constitutional nature, in defense of the identity of the Union, which is added—without eluding them—to other instruments available to the European institutions for the protection of fundamental values, including Article 19 TEU, Article 47 of the Charter of Fundamental Rights and, of course, Article 7 TEU. One could object that the ultimately financial character of the *rationale* of the regulation—necessary for the respect of the Union's competences—makes the mechanism in question part of an instrument aimed at protecting the financial interests of the Union and not to directly protect from rule of law violations. As Advocate General Sánchez-Bordona effectively reminds us in his conclusions in cases C-156/21 and C-157/21, the regulation straddles "the boundary between financial conditionality and the guarantee of the rule of law" (point IV), thus not being able to be configured as an instrument *to* defend the rule of law *tout court*. However, I think that this is the formal, legalistic account of the nature of the conditionality regime, necessary to "save" it under the EU law principle of conferral and in the conditionality decision, "the Court of Justice has interpreted the rule of law within the EU in keeping with the checks and balances laid down in the Treaties".[32]

[31] P. Faraguna, T. Drinóczi, 'Constitutional Identity in and on EU Terms' (*Verfassungsblog.de*, 21 February 2022), <https://verfassungsblog.de/constitutional-identity-in-and-on-eu-terms/>; P. Faraguna, *Constitutional Identity and General International Law*, in G. Puma (ed.), *Diritto internazionale e sistema delle fonti. Tra modello accentrato e modello diffuso del controllo di costituzionalità* (Cacucci, 2020).

[32] K. Lenaerts, 'On checks and balances: The rule of law within the EU', [2023] 29(2) *Columbia Journal of European Law* 25.

14.5 New Developments toward a Militant Constitutional Model

The rule of law crisis represented a key context for offering the CJEU the opportunity to explicitly introduce the reference to the concept of European identity. However, from the CJEU decisions, we cannot grasp the content of the European identity: which features of the EU define the boundaries of this notion? How can we describe the substance of the European identity? The CJEU in the rule of law conditionality case law gave no precise answer to these questions, but there are already relevant cases that may offer the chance to the CJEU to engage with the definition of EU identity and its role as a militant tool.

Key under this perspective is Case C-808/21 and C-814/21, decided by the CJEU in November 2024, addressing the rights of EU citizens residing in Member States of which they are not nationals, specifically concerning their ability to join political parties and stand as candidates in municipal and European Parliament elections.

The European Commission initiated infringement proceedings against the Czech Republic (Case C-808/21) and Poland (Case C-814/21), alleging that both Member States violated EU law by restricting membership in political parties exclusively to their nationals. The central issue in both cases was whether restricting political party membership to nationals was compatible with the rights of EU citizens under Articles 20, 21, and 22 TFEU, read in conjunction with Article 12 of the EU Charter of Fundamental Rights. The Commission argued that this restriction indirectly affected the right of EU citizens to stand as a candidate in municipal and European Parliament elections, since the fact that EU citizens residing in a Member State, but not being nationals of that Member State, cannot be members of a political party and thus cannot enjoy the many advantages that such membership entails, in particular in terms of public profile, human and financial resources, organizational infrastructure and access to the media, undermines their ability to successfully and effectively stand for election under the same conditions as Member State nationals.

Poland and the Czech Republic emphasized that a Member State cannot be compelled to permit EU citizens to engage permanently and without limitation in its political life, or to influence the results of national parliamentary and presidential elections through participation in the political party system, as would happen if they were granted the right to join a political party. Indeed, the organization of national political life, to which political parties contribute, is part of national identity, within the meaning of Article 4(2) TEU.

In light of this, the Court determined the scope of Article 22 TFEU in order to assess whether the difference in treatment on grounds of nationality introduced by Polish and Czech legislation, as regards the possibility of becoming a member of a political party, is prohibited by that provision or may potentially be justified by reasons relating to respect for a Member State's national identity. In this assessment, the Court emphasized that effective participation in European and municipal elections necessitates equal access to political party membership, as political parties play a crucial role in representative democracy.[33] This interpretation aligns with Article 10 of the Treaty on European Union (TEU), which states that the EU operates on the principle of representative democracy. By linking Articles 10 TEU and 22 TFEU, the Court reinforced the notion that democracy is a fundamental value of the EU, as enshrined in Article 2 TEU.

These judgments build upon the methodology established in the "Portuguese Judges" case, where the ECJ affirmed that Member States must uphold the rule of law to ensure effective judicial protection in areas covered by EU law. Similarly, in the recent cases, the Court applied this approach to the value of democracy, suggesting that Member States are obligated to protect structures essential for democratic participation, such as political parties. As it has been argued, "the CJEU operationalizes the citizens' right directly enshrined in Article 10(3) TEU to transform Article 10(1) and (2) into legal obligations, namely, to ensure that the citizen is directly represented in the European Parliament."[34]

The implications of these rulings are also significant concerning the relationship between national constitutional identity protected by Art. 4 (2) TEU and the European identity. This complex relationship has been addressed by the Court, confirming the approach adopted in the decisions

[33] "It follows, next, that those EU citizens enjoy that right 'under the same conditions' as nationals of the Member State in which they reside. By referring to the conditions governing the right to vote and to stand for election applicable to nationals of the Member State of residence of such an EU citizen, Article 22 TFEU prohibits that Member State from making the exercise of that right by that EU citizen subject to conditions other than those applicable to its own nationals."

[34] M. Schuler, 'Paving the Way for an Enforcement of Democracy under Article 10 TEU? The Court's Judgments in Cases C-808/21 Commission v Czechia and C-814/21 Commission v Poland' (*European Law Blog*, 20 November 2024). https://www.europeanlawblog.eu/pub/fsca541k/release/2>.

on the rule of law conditionality mechanism. The Polish and the Czech authorities invoked Art. 4 (2) TEU in order to challenge the legitimacy of the Commission infringement procedure. However, the Court stated that "Article 4(2) TEU must be read in the light of provisions of the same rank, in particular Articles 2 and 10 TEU, and cannot exempt Member States from the obligation to comply with the requirements arising from those provisions."[35] In particular, "Article 2 TEU is not merely a statement of policy guidelines or intentions, but contains values which are an integral part of the very identity of the European Union as a common legal order, values which are given concrete expression in principles containing legally binding obligations for the Member States".[36]

According to the Court, Article 10(1) TEU provides that the functioning of the European Union is to be founded on the principle of representative democracy, which gives concrete form to the value of democracy referred to in Article 2 TEU. Along this reasoning, the CJEU linked clearly representative democracy as an expression of the binding values of Art. 2 TEU. In this vein, the Court suggests that EU law may have a say in national measures affecting political party membership, even in purely internal situations. We are witnessing a substantive expansion of the scope of application of Art. 2 TEU that could impact scenarios where a Member State seeks to ban certain political parties, as such actions might conflict with EU citizens' rights to participate in the democratic life of the Union.

The ECJ's decisions in Cases C-808/21 and C-814/21 not only affirm the rights of mobile EU citizens to participate fully in their host Member States' political processes, but also pave the way for a stronger enforcement of democratic values throughout the EU, while utilizing European identity as a limit to the Member States' unconstitutional constitutional identity. However, the use of Art. 2 TEU in these cases remains indirect: Art. 2 TEU is not invoked autonomously as a standing rule, but to support other principles and rights protected by the treaties, namely the principle of democracy in Art. 10 and 22 TEU. The justiciability of Art. 2 TEU remains uncertain, making the possibility of using it directly as a militant instrument today quite remote. Nevertheless, a case is currently pending before the CJEU that may represent a turning point for the militant use of Art. 2 TEU.

[35] *European Commission v. Czech Republic* (C-808/21) ECLI:EU:C:2024:962, para. 155.

[36] *European Commission v. Czech Republic* (C-808/21) ECLI:EU:C:2024:962, para. 157.

14.6 Case C-769/22: Art. 2 TEU Becoming "Militant"?

Case C-769/22, Commission v. Hungary, represents a pivotal moment in the European Union's legal framework, marking the first instance where the European Commission initiated infringement proceedings against a Member State primarily based on an alleged violation of the fundamental values enshrined in Article 2 TEU. This case underscores the EU's commitment to upholding its core principles, including respect for human dignity, freedom, democracy, equality, the rule of law, and human rights.

In June 2021, the Hungarian Parliament enacted Act LXXIX of 2021, commonly referred to as the "Child Protection Act." While ostensibly aimed at safeguarding minors, the law introduced provisions that prohibit the dissemination of content portraying or promoting gender identities differing from the sex assigned at birth, sex reassignment, or homosexuality to individuals under 18. The legislation also mandates that such content be restricted to late-night broadcasting hours and excludes it from classifications as public interest media or socially beneficial advertising.

The European Commission contends that these measures contravene several EU laws and principles, including Directive 2010/13/EU on audiovisual media services, by imposing unjustified restrictions on content dissemination; Directive 2000/31/EC on electronic commerce, by limiting the free movement of information society services; Directive 2006/123/EC on services in the internal market, by creating discriminatory barriers to service provision; Article 56 TFEU, which guarantees the freedom to provide services across Member States; Articles 1, 7, 11, and 21 of the Charter of Fundamental Rights of the European Union, which protect human dignity, private and family life, freedom of expression, and non-discrimination. Moreover, the Commission argues that the Hungarian law violates Article 2 TEU, asserting that the legislation undermines the EU's foundational values.

The case was brought before the Court of Justice of the European Union (CJEU) in December 2022. Given the gravity and unprecedented nature of the allegations, the CJEU convened in its full court formation to hear the case in November 2024. Notably, sixteen Member States intervened in support of the Commission, highlighting the collective concern over potential breaches of EU values.

This case raises critical questions about the enforceability of Article 2 TEU. Traditionally, Article 2 has been viewed as a declaratory provision, outlining the EU's values without direct legal enforceability. However, the Commission's approach in this case challenges that notion, seeking to establish Article 2 as a standalone basis for infringement proceedings.[37]

In Case C-769/22, the Commission explicitly relies on Article 2 TEU as a freestanding legal norm, arguing that Hungary's "Child Protection" legislation is incompatible with the fundamental values of the Union, particularly human dignity, equality, and non-discrimination. This challenges the long-standing understanding that values must be operationalized through more concrete obligations (like directives or specific Treaty provisions) to be judicially enforced.

If the Court of Justice of the European Union (CJEU) accepts the Commission's position, it would affirm that Article 2 TEU has normative autonomy—that it is not merely a preamble-like statement of values, but a directly justiciable provision capable of grounding legal obligations. This would signify a doctrinal evolution, potentially allowing direct judicial enforcement of values in situations where no specific secondary law exists or has been violated and enabling the Commission to target systemic threats to EU values in ways that Article 7 TEU, which is highly political and requires unanimity, often cannot.

Such a reading would strengthen the EU's legal order and tools to confront democratic backsliding, marking a transformation of Art. 2 TEU into a militant tool. However, this turn would have a significant transformative impact on the relationship between the CJEU and national authorities, and more profoundly will determine a new federal balance in the EU.[38] The use of Art. 2 TEU as a self-standing provision would expand the Court's jurisdiction, potentially in many matters of domestic constitutional relevance, transforming it into a militant tool, like identity clauses in national constitutions, but this turn would also undermine the legitimacy of the Court vis-à-vis domestic authorities, potentially triggering new conflicts and resistance by national courts.

[37] M. Bonelli, M. Claes, 'Crossing the Rubicon? The Commission's use of Article 2 TEU in the infringement action on LGBTIQ+ rights in Hungary' [2023] 30(1) *Maastricht Journal of European and Comparative Law* 3.

[38] L. Spieker, 'EU Values Before the Court of Justice. Foundations, Potential, Risks'. Oxford: Oxford University Press (2023).

14.7 Concluding Remarks: The Persistent Aporias of Militant Constitutionalism in the EU

In conclusion, the Court of Justice's interpretation of the values enshrined in Article 2 TEU signals a significant constitutional shift in the relationship between the European Union and its Member States. By affirming the legally binding nature of these values, particularly the rule of law and democracy, the Court has highlighted the Union's responsibility to protect its foundational principles. This development brings the Union closer to a model of militant constitutionalism, where the protection of core values becomes a central concern, reinforced by instruments such as conditionality, Article 7 TEU, and other mechanisms designed to uphold the integrity of the Union's legal order.

While the financial dimension of conditionality may appear to obscure its broader constitutional purpose, it is clear that its real substance lies in safeguarding the Union's fundamental values, including respect for democracy, the rule of law, and non-discrimination. This dual function of conditionality, blending financial and constitutional concerns, reinforces the Union's capacity to defend its identity and legal order in the face of challenges posed by Member States. As such, conditionality can be seen as a crucial instrument in the Union's ongoing effort to prevent constitutional erosion and to ensure that the foundational values of European integration remain intact. The Court's development of this jurisprudence not only reaffirms the centrality of European identity but also places it in tension with national identities, setting the stage for a more assertive Union in defending its core principles. While the balance between national sovereignty and Union values remains delicate, the expanding use of conditionality as a tool for militant constitutionalism reflects a growing commitment to protecting the EU's fundamental legal and political order.

In the same vein, we can read the judgments in Cases C-808/21 and C-814/21, which reflect a significant evolution in the role of the European Union in protecting democracy, particularly regarding the rights of mobile EU citizens. By affirming that restrictions on political party membership based on nationality violate EU citizens' rights, the Court reinforced the notion that democracy, as enshrined in Article 2 TEU, is a fundamental value that must be safeguarded across the Union.

Even more groundbreaking (at least potentially) is Case C-769/22, which could mark the constitutional turning point where Article 2 TEU shifts from a normative compass to an enforceable legal rule. If the Court recognizes Article 2 as a justiciable provision, it will expand the legal toolkit available to the EU to safeguard its fundamental values, especially in the face of populist and authoritarian legislative trends, fostering a model of militant constitutionalism. However, at the same time, it will force a redefinition of the balance between national autonomy and supranational values enforcement, which will significantly alter the constitutional equilibrium of the EU.

References

Baraggia, A. and Bonelli, M., 'Linking Money to Values: the new Rule of Law Conditionality Regulation and its constitutional challenges' [2020] 23(2) German LJ 131

Blauberger, M. and van Hüllen, V., 'Conditionality of EU funds: an instrument to enforce EU fundamental values?' [2021] 43(1) Journal of European Integration 1

Bonelli, M. and Claes, M., 'Crossing the Rubicon? The Commission's use of Article 2 TEU in the infringement action on LGBTIQ+ rights in Hungary' [2023] 30(1) Maastricht Journal of European and Comparative Law 3

Di Gregorio, A., 'L'Ungheria e i valori europei. Un matrimonio difficile' (Associazione DPCE, 17 September 2018, last access on 9 October 2025, last access on 9 October 2025) http://www.dpce.it/l-ungheria-e-i-valori-europei-un-matrimonio-difficile.html

Faraguna, P. and Drinóczi, T., 'Constitutional Identity in and on EU Terms' (Verfassungsblog.de, 21 February 2022) https://verfassungsblog.de/constitutional-identity-in-and-on-eu-terms/

Faraguna, P., *Constitutional Identity and General International Law*. In Puma, G. (ed.), *Diritto internazionale e sistema delle fonti. Tra modello accentrato e modello diffuso del controllo di costituzionalità*. Cacucci, 2020

Fisicaro, M., 'Rule of Law Conditionality in EU Funds: The Value of Money in the Crisis of European Values' [2019] European Papers, Vol. 4, No. 3, 695

Gutmann, J. and Voigt, S., 'Militant constitutionalism: a promising concept to make constitutional backsliding less likely?' [2023] 195 Public Choice 377

Halmai, G., 'Abuse of constitutional identity: the Hungarian constitutional court on interpretation of article E) (2) of the fundamental law' [2018] Review of Central and East European Law 43(1) 23

Halmai, G., 'The alternatives to a bite or a bark: after launching Article 7 TEU against the Hungarian government'. In Belavusau, U. and Gliszczyńska-Grabias, A. (eds.), *Constitutionalism under Stress: Essays in Honor of Wojciech Sadurski*. OUP 2020

Kirst, N., 'Rule of Law Conditionality: The Long-awaited Step Towards a Solution of the Rule of Law Crisis in the European Union?' [2021] European Papers 101

Lenaerts, K., 'On checks and balances: The rule of law within the EU' [2023] 29(2) Columbia Journal of European Law 25

Loewenstein, K., 'Militant Democracy and Fundamental Rights' [1937] Am. Pol. Sci. Rev. 31(3) 417

Maduro, M.P. and Menezes Queiroz, B., 'A Hard Law Approach to States Systemic Violations of Article 2 of the Treaty of the European Union: Reasons and Means'. In Fisher, E., King, J. and Young, A. (eds.), *The Foundations and Future of Public Law: Essays in Honour of Paul Craig*. OUP 2020

Müller, J.-W., 'Defending Democracy within the EU' [2013] Journal of Democracy 24(2) 138

Müller, J.-W., 'Militant Democracy'. In Rosenfeld, M. and Sajó, A. (eds.), *The Oxford Handbook of Comparative Constitutional Law*. OUP 2012

Pinelli, C., 'Conditionality and Enlargement in Light of the EU Constitutional Developments' [2004] 10 European Law Journal 3

Roach, K., 'Anti-Terrorism and Militant Democracy: Some Western and Eastern Responses'. In Sajo, A. (ed.), *Militant Democracy*. Eleven International Publishing, 2004

Roznai, Y., *Unconstitutional Constitutional Amendments. The Limits of Amendment Powers*. OUP 2017

Sadurski, W., *Poland's Constitutional Breakdown*. OUP 2019

Scheppele, K.L., Pech, L. and Platon, S., *Compromising the Rule of Law while Compromising on the Rule of Law* (Verfassungsblog.de, 13 December 2020, last access on 9 October 2025) https://verfassungsblog.de/compromising-the-rule-of-law-while-compromising-on-the-rule-of-law/

Schuler, M., 'Paving the Way for an Enforcement of Democracy under Article 10 TEU? The Court's Judgments in Cases C-808/21 Commission v Czechia and C-814/21 Commission v Poland' (European Law Blog, 20 November 2024, last access on 9 October 2025) https://www.europeanlawblog.eu/pub/fsca541k/release/2

Smith, K.E., 'The Evolution and Application of EU Membership Conditionality'. In Cremona, M. (ed.), *The Enlargement of the European Union*. OUP 2003, 105-140

Spieker, L.D., *Berlaymont is back: The Commission invokes Article 2 TEU as self-standing plea in infringement proceedings over Hungarian LGBTIQ rights violations*. EU Law Live, 22 February 2023

Spieker, L.D., *EU Values Before the Court of Justice. Foundations, Potential, Risks*. Oxford: Oxford University Press 2023

Theuns, T., 'Is the European Union a militant democracy? Democratic backsliding and EU disintegration' [2024] Global Constitutionalism 13(1) 104

von Bogdandy, A., Bogdanowicz, P., Canor, I., Rugge, G., Schmidt, M. and Taborowski, M., 'A Potential Constitutional Moment for the European Rule of Law: The Importance of Red Lines'. In von Bogdandy, A., Bogdanowicz, P., Canor, I., Grabenwarter, C., Taborowski, M. and Schmidt, M. (eds.), *Defending Checks and Balances in EU Member States*. Springer 2021

CHAPTER 15

The Judicial Overhaul in Israel Before and After October 7: The Amalgamation of Constitutional Crisis & Security Crisis

Yaniv Roznai

15.1 Introduction

In the span of a year, Israel has faced two crises of historic magnitude: a profound constitutional crisis triggered by the 2023 'judicial overhaul' (so-called governance reform) and a devastating national security emergency following the October 7 massacre by Hamas. While each of these events could independently strain a democratic system, the convergence of the two has exacerbated the threats to Israel's liberal democratic institutions. This chapter explores the interrelation between these crises and argues that the security emergency did not, as one might expect, cause the government to abandon or suspend its controversial constitutional reforms. Instead, it served as a smokescreen and facilitator for the continuation—and even intensification—of the judicial overhaul.

This chapter is produced as part and funded by the European Union-NextGenerationEU, through the National Recovery and Resilience Plan of the Republic of Bulgaria, project No bg-rrp-2.004-0008. Researcher under the International Mobility Programme - Assesing Constitutional Crisis Impact and Security (IMP-ACCTS) - Project Proposal TNE23-00057 - CUP B61/24000450006.

M. Belov (ed.), *Constitutional Polycrisis and Emergency Constitutionalism*, Federalism and Internal Conflicts,
https://doi.org/10.1007/978-3-032-06516-2_15

The judicial overhaul, spearheaded by Justice Minister Yariv Levin, has been presented as a 'governance reform' to recalibrate the balance of powers between the judiciary and the political branches of government. However, legal scholars and civil society actors argue that it represents an instance of "abusive constitutionalism" designed to entrench executive power and weaken judicial oversight.

Following the October 7 attacks, many assumed that such domestic power struggles would be set aside in favor of national unity. Paradoxically, perhaps, the post-attack environment has allowed the overhaul to proceed largely unchecked, under the radar of public attention preoccupied with war and hostages. This chapter traces the development of the overhaul before and after October 7, situates it within the broader theoretical framework of populist constitutionalism and security-driven populism, and explains how wartime dynamics enabled the persistence and deepening of the constitutional crisis.

15.2 The 2023 Judicial Overhaul

On January 4, 2023, Israel's Minister of Justice Yariv Levin presented a plan to radically reshape the judiciary, which he called a "governance reform." The reform was pitched as a measure to restore balance between the branches of government, against the backdrop of the increasing power of the Israeli Supreme Court and allegations of judicial activism.[1] However, critics identified the judicial overhaul as a textbook case of abusive constitutionalism—a set of reforms aimed not at improving governance but at consolidating power in the executive branch and weakening checks and balances.[2]

The proposal included several core components:

[1] For such arguments, see e.g. Yechiel Oren-Harush, The Case for Israel's Judicial Reform' Hashiloach (2025), https://hashiloach.org.il/the-case-for-the-judicial-reform-en/; Aharon Garber, 'Why Judicial Reform in Essential' Kohelet, https://www.kohelet.org.il/en/article/why-judicial-reform-is-essential/

[2] See e.g. Yaniv Roznai, Rosalind Dixon & David E. Landau, 'Judicial Reform or Abusive Constitutionalism in Israel', 56 Israel Law Review (2023), 292; Suzie Navot, 'An Overview of Israel's 'Judicial Overhaul': Small Parts of a Big Populist Picture' (2023) 56(3) Israel Law Review 482; Ittai Bar-Siman-Tov, Tamar Hostovsky Brandes, Eliav Lieblich, Yaniv Roznai, & Adam Shinar, 'Scholactivism in the Service of Counter-populism: The Case of the Constitutional Overhaul in Israel' (2025) 22(4) International Journal of Constitutional Law 1059.

First, the proposed reform would limit judicial review by requiring a supermajority of 12 out of 15 Supreme Court justices to strike down legislation that violates Basic Laws that function as Israel's quasi-constitutional framework. It would also include an override mechanism that would allow a majority of 61 Members of Knesset to override decisions of unconstitutional legislations and re-enact unconstitutional legislation. Additionally, it would bar the Court from reviewing Basic Laws altogether. This would effectively allow a parliamentary majority to insulate constitutional legislation from any judicial scrutiny.

Second, the reform proposed altering the composition of the Judicial Selection Committee to give the ruling coalition effective control over judicial appointments. Under Israel's current hybrid model, the committee includes representatives from all three branches of government, as well as the Bar Association and requires a supermajority of 7 out of the 9 in a manner that provides veto to the coalition and Justices of the Supreme Court for such appointments. The proposed changes would ensure a majority of members aligned with the executive, thereby eroding the independence of the judiciary.[3]

Third, the proposal would transform the role of legal advisors to government ministries from independent professionals to politically appointed positions whose advice would no longer be binding. This would reduce legal oversight and encourage the politicization of legal interpretation within the executive.

Fourth, the reform sought to abolish the reasonableness doctrine, which allows courts to review administrative decisions and strike them down for being manifestly unreasonable. The government framed this as a democratic correction, but legal scholars warned that it would eliminate one of the few tools for reviewing executive discretion in appointments and administrative actions.[4]

The legal and academic response was swift and severe. Law professors acted collectively and individually against various elements of the judicial overhaul.[5] Former presidents of the Supreme Court and retired Attorneys

[3] Guy Lurie, 'The Attempt to Capture the Courts in Israel' (2023) Israel Law Review 456.

[4] Mordechai Kremnitzer, 'Releasing the Government from Acting Reasonably; or, the Government Says Goodbye to Reasonableness' (2023) 56(3) Israel Law Review 343. Contra, on Israel's unique reasonableness doctrine, see Yoav Dotan, 'Impeachment by Judicial Review: Israel's Odd System of Checks and Balances' (2018) 19(2) Theoretical Inquiries in Law 705.

[5] Bar-Siman-Tov, Hostovsky Brandes, Lieblich, Roznai, & Shinar (n 2).

General issued statements warning of the collapse of democratic governance, and the serving President of the Supreme Court, Esther Hayut, warned that "should the planned changes as they were presented come to fruition, the nation's 75 the year will be remembered as the year when its democratic identity received a fatal blow."[6]

Levin's proposal was accompanied by a broader discursive strategy. Coalition leaders framed the judiciary as an unelected elite obstructing the will of the people, invoking populist tropes of "the real majority" versus "the privileged elite minority." This rhetorical move mirrors patterns observed in other cases of populist constitutionalism, where attacks on judicial institutions are justified through appeals to majoritarianism. It was also accompanied by 'abusive borrowing', justifying various features of the judicial overhaul by their existence in other countries while ignoring other balancing mechanisms, the political culture or the overhaul structure.[7]

The public reaction to the judicial overhaul was unprecedented. Public protests erupted across Israel, including massive weekly demonstrations and sector-specific resistance from academics, economic sectors, high-tech leaders, and IDF reservists.[8] The depth and breadth of the backlash led President Isaac Herzog to propose a compromise framework, known as the "People's Framework," calling for broad consensus on constitutional changes, however this proposal was rejected by the coalition.[9]

[6] *Public Address by The President of the Supreme Court of Israel, [Justice] Esther Hayut, at the Conference of the Israeli Association of Public Law*, Israel Policy Forum (Jan. 12, 2023), http://tinyurl.com/3mm764ex (unofficial translation). On President's Hayut's role, see Yaniv Roznai and Shani Schnitzer, 'Navigating the judicial ship through stormy waters: President Esther Hayut and the Israeli constitutional crises, 2018–23' (2025) 23(1) , International Journal of Constitutional Law 179.

[7] On the judicial overhaul as a populist project, see Yaniv Roznai, 'From the 'Hungarian Blitz' to the 'Polish Salami': Populism, The Gaza War and The Judicial Overhaul in Israel'. In Takao Suami, Keisuke Kondo, Kaoru Obata (eds.), *The Cambridge Handbook of Global Crisis and Global Legal Ordering*. Cambridge Unviersity Press. (forthcoming).

[8] See Doron Shultziner, 'The Movement Against Democratic Backsliding in Israel' (2023) 38(3) Sociological Forum 896; Yaniv Roznai, 'We the Fourth Branch? The People as an Institution Protecting Democracy', in Vicki Jackson and Madhav Khosla (eds.), *Redefining Comparative Constitutional Law: Essays for Mark Tushnet* (Oxford University Press 2024) 293.

[9] Office of the President, 'People's Directive—From a crisis to a constitutional opportunity: The President's proposed constitutional framework for settling the relations between the branches of government in Israel by broad consensus', www.mitve-haam.org/_files/ugd/f35a26_8eb0f820ae1b4d32bd178cc2b7cf4352.pdf; Isabel Kershner, 'Israeli Government Rejects Presi-

Despite massive public opposition, the coalition advanced parts of the plan. Mainly, after negotiations between the coalition and opposition under the auspices of the President of the state have failed, on July 24, 2023, the government enacted a constitutional amendment to Basic Law: The Judiciary according to which: "no court of law, including the High Court of Justice, may consider and/or pass judgment on the reasonableness of any 'decision' of the Cabinet, the prime minister, or any minister; nor may a court give an order on the said matter based on its purported unreasonableness."[10] The amendment was enacted on strict party-lines, with all members of the coalition voting in favor, while all members of the opposition walking out of the vote in protest, following an expedited and one-sided legislative process.[11] This amendment was struck down by the Supreme Court on January 1, 2024 for violating core democratic values as rule of law and separation of power. This 738-page landmark judgement was the first case in which the Supreme Court invalidated a section of a Basic Law.[12]

15.3 The October 7 Massacre and the Formation of the Unity Government: "Together We Win!"

On the morning of October 7, 2023, Hamas launched an unprecedented and coordinated attack on Israel from the Gaza Strip. Thousands of militants infiltrated Israeli territory, while rockets rained down on civilian centers. The attack resulted in the deaths of over 1,200 Israelis, including civilians and soldiers, and led to the abduction of more than 240 individuals into Gaza. It marked the deadliest day in Israeli history since

dent's Judicial Compromise' The New York Times (March 15, 2023), https://www.nytimes.com/2023/03/15/world/middleeast/israel-herzog-judicial-compromise.html?smid=url-share

[10] David Kretzmer et al., 'Israel's Recent "Unreasonableness Amendment" and its Implications', Israel Law Professors Forum for Democracy (July 28, 2023), https://www.lawprofs-forum.org/post/israel-s-recent-unreasonableness-amendment-and-its-implications

[11] Ori Aronson, Ittai Bar-Siman-Tov, Eden Israely Levy, Ronit Levine-Schnur, Doreen Lustig, and Issachar Rosen-Zvi, 'Procedural Norms for Enacting Basic Laws and Knesset Committee Initiatives', 48 Tel Aviv University Law Review (2025) 5 https://ssrn.com/abstract=4566393 (Hebrew).

[12] HCJ 5658/23 Movement for Quality Government v. the Knesset, Nevo Legal Database (Jan. 1, 2024) (Isr.).

the establishment of the state and has been widely described as Israel's "9/11 moment."[13]

The failure of Israeli intelligence and defense institutions to anticipate and prevent the assault sparked immediate public outrage and exposed grave vulnerabilities in the country's security architecture.[14] As a direct consequence, the political landscape in Israel shifted dramatically. The government, under Prime Minister Benjamin Netanyahu, faced widespread criticism for prioritizing the judicial overhaul and other political objectives at the expense of national security.[15]

In response to the national trauma and the exigencies of war, a temporary unity government was formed. On October 12, 2023, opposition leaders Benny Gantz and Gadi Eizenkot joined the government under a wartime coalition agreement, and a new small war cabinet was established. This arrangement was intended to project a sense of national cohesion and facilitate unified decision-making during a time of existential crisis.[16]

However, the unity government was limited in scope and time-bound. It focused exclusively on managing the military campaign in Gaza and did not extend to other areas of governance, including the judicial overhaul. Although it was agreed by Netanyahu and Gantz that as long as the war is taking place, no judicial overhaul legislation will be discussed in the Knesset.[17] However, while the formation of the unity government momentarily quelled political infighting, it did not result in the suspension of the constitutional reform agenda. As Adam Shinar correctly notes, "the coalition agreement was limited to legislation, which meant that the overhaul could continue, or at least not disappear, in other forms… So,

[13] Newspaper headlines: 'Human Shiled Horror' and Israel's '9/11 moment' BBC (October 8, 2023). ee Seth J. Frantzman, The October 7 War: Israel's Battle for Security in Gaza (Wicked Son, 2024) part 2.

[14] See e.g. Avner Barnea, 'Israeli Intelligence Was Caught Off Guard: The Hamas Attack on 7 October 2023—A Preliminary Analysis' (2024) 37(3) International Journal of Intelligence and Counter Intelligence 1056.

[15] See, for example, Sheera Frenkel, 'Israelis Are Angry at Netanyahu, but Chances of His Ouster Are Slim' The New York Times (Dec. 5, 2023), https://www.nytimes.com/2023/12/02/world/middleeast/israel-netanyahu-hamas-war.html?smid=url-share

[16] Jeremy Sharon, 'Netanyahu, Gantz agree to Form Emergency Unity Government' The Times of Israel (Oct. 11, 2023), https://www.timesofisrael.com/liveblog_entry/netanyahu-gantz-agree-to-form-emergency-unity-government/

[17] Barak Ravid, 'Israel's Netanyahu forms unity government with ex-Defense Minister Gantz' Axios (Oct. 11, 2023), https://www.axios.com/2023/10/11/hamas-israel-war-gantz-netanyahu-unity-government

although the overhaul was officially "shelved," it has not disappeared. Levin and others have already declared that once the war is over, they will return to implement their program. In the meantime, the government has been taking small sub-constitutional measures intended at weakening veto points, as will be discussed below, that also further the overarching goal of the overhaul—increasing executive power at the expense of the Court and civil service."[18]

In fact, the formation of the unity government arguably provided political cover for continued executive action. Furthermore, in June 2024, Gantz and Eisenkot resigned from the cabinet because Netanyahu did not present a post-war plan for Gaza by the previous day, meeting a previously announced deadline. Accordingly, the special war cabinet was dissolved. This further allowed the government, politically, to continue with the judicial overhaul. As the public and media focused on the war effort, significant legal and institutional changes advanced without broad scrutiny or opposition. This phenomenon illustrates how security crises can serve to entrench executive authority rather than curtail it, especially in hybrid regimes with weak constitutional safeguards.

15.4 The Judicial Overhaul Continues

Following the October 7, 2023, Hamas attacks, Israel's political landscape underwent significant changes, particularly concerning the judiciary and democratic institutions. This section examines key developments, including the refusal to appoint a Supreme Court president according to the seniority rule, the non-appointment of Supreme Court vacancies, the politicization of the Judicial Selection Committee, and other related issues.

15.4.1 Refusal to Appoint a Supreme Court President According to the Seniority Rule

Traditionally, Israel's Supreme Court president is appointed based on seniority. However, Justice Minister Yariv Levin deviated from this practice by refusing to appoint Justice Isaac Amit, the most senior judge, as president. Instead, Levin proposed appointing Justice Yosef Elron, a

[18] Adam Shinar, 'Constitutional Overhaul, the War in Gaza, and the Puzzle of Civic Mobilization in Israel' (2024) 26 German Law Journal 1, 11, https://doi.org/10.1017/glj.2024.37

conservative judge, which was met with resistance from Acting President Uzi Vogelman and other justices. This refusal led to a prolonged vacancy in the court's leadership, prompting the High Court to order Levin to proceed with the appointment, emphasizing that the delay was unlawful and detrimental to the judiciary's functioning. After the appointment of Justice Amit as the court's President in a meeting that Levin boycotted, the Justice Minister declined to sign the official announcement of the appointment and vowed to boycott Amit as president of the Supreme Court in protest at how the court, sitting as the High Court of Justice, ordered him to hold a vote for a new president after he refused to do so for over a year.[19]

15.4.2 Non-Appointment of Supreme Court Vacancies

Since October 2023, four Supreme Court seats have remained unfilled due to the Justice Minister's refusal to convene the Judicial Selection Committee, in additional to Levin's insistence on appointing two ultra-conservative candidates, Dr. Aviad Bakshi and Dr. Raphael Bitton, two of the chief architects of the 2023 judicial overhaul plan. This inaction has raised concerns about the court's capacity to function effectively in light of its caseload and maintain its independence. The prolonged vacancies are unprecedented and have been criticized as a means to exert political pressure on the judiciary. Furthermore, Yuval Shany and Amichai Cohen note that because three judges out of the four who retired since October 2023 have been members of the so-called "liberal camp," the policy of non-appointment has resulted, in and of itself, in a conservative shift in the court's orientation.[20]

[19] Jeremy Sharon and Sam Sokol, 'High Court orders Levin to appoint new court president; he calls its ruling undemocratic' The Times of Israel (Sep. 8, 2024), https://www.timesofisrael.com/high-court-orders-levin-to-appoint-new-supreme-court-president-says-refusal-unlawful; Eliav Breuer, 'Isaac Amit appointed permanent High Court chief justice as 15-month saga ends' The Jerusalem Post (Jan. 26, 2025), https://www.jpost.com/israel-news/article-839327; Jeremy Sharon, 'Levin declines to sign official announcement of new Supreme Court president' The Times of Israel (February 3, 2025), https://www.timesofisrael.com/levin-declines-to-sign-official-announcement-of-new-supreme-court-president/

[20] See Yuval Shany and Amichai Cohen, 'Israel's Renewed Judicial Overhaul' Israel Democracy Institute (March 04, 2025), https://en.idi.org.il/articles/58607

15.4.3 Politicization of the Judicial Selection Committee

In March 2025, the Knesset passed legislation altering the composition of the Judicial Selection Committee, increasing political influence over judicial appointments. The law was introduced by Levin and Foreign Minister Gideon Sa'ar as an ostensible compromise over previously proposed legislation that would have given the coalition almost complete control over all judicial appointments. The new law, which will come into effect in the next Knesset, changes the composition of the Judicial Selection Committee and allows the governing coalition to have greater control over the committee, effectively diminishing the role of legal professionals. It replaces the two representatives of the Israel Bar Association with one lawyer to be directly chosen by the coalition and another to be chosen by the opposition. Additionally, it removes any influence of the three judges on the committee over appointments to the Supreme Court while granting the coalition and opposition vetoes. In the event that there are two empty slots on the Supreme Court and the coalition and opposition sides veto all of each other's nominations for a year, the justice minister can activate a deadlock-breaking mechanism whereby both sides nominate three candidates, and the other side must choose at least one. Critics argue that this change undermines judicial independence and is part of a broader strategy to weaken checks and balances within the Israeli government.[21]

15.4.4 Changes to the Ombudsperson for the Judiciary

The Knesset also passed a law changing the selection process for the state ombudsman for judges, granting lawmakers more influence over the appointment. This move has been perceived as an attempt to intimidate judges and compromise their independence, as the ombudsman plays a crucial role in overseeing judicial conduct.[22]

[21] Sam Sokol, 'Knesset passes law greatly boosting political control over appointment of judges' The Times of Israel (March 27, 2025), https://www.timesofisrael.com/knesset-passes-law-greatly-boosting-political-control-over-judicial-appointments/

[22] Jeremy Sharon and Sam Sokol, 'Coalition passes judicial overhaul law taking over appointment of judges' ombudsman' The Times of Israel (March 4, 2025), https://www.timesofisrael.com/coalition-passes-judicial-overhaul-law-taking-over-appointment-of-judges-ombudsman/

15.4.5 *Controversies Surrounding the Civil Service Commissioner*

Another point of struggle was over the appointment of the Civil Service Commissioner—a central 'gatekeeper' in Israel. The Civil Service Commissioner is a crucial official in Israel's public administration. Appointed by the government but expected to act independently, the Commissioner oversees the appointment, discipline, and regulation of civil servants. This includes preventing politicization of the public service and ensuring appointments are based on merit.

The Israeli government has decided that the next Civil Service Commissioner will be appointed by the cabinet. The Attorney General, Gali Baharav Miara, has made it clear to the High Court of Justice that the government's decision to change its previous decision concerning the manner by which the Civil Service Commissioner is chosen (through a professional process) is illegal.[23] The High Court of Justice ruled that the appointment process was illegal, stating that it failed to ensure the independence and apolitical nature of the position.[24] An additional hearing will be held at the Hight Court of Jusitce on this matter. This incident highlights concerns about the politicization of senior civil service roles.

15.4.6 *Efforts to Weaken the Israel Bar Association*

The government has introduced legislation aimed at weakening the Israel Bar Association, which plays a significant role in judicial appointments (two members out of nine in the Judicial Selection Committee). The law enables the Justice Minister and the Knesset Constitution, Law and Justice Committee to determine, in part, how the Israel Bar Association may use its own funds. It also hands the justice minister authority to set the bar association's membership fees. Amit Becher, the head of the Israel Bar Association, said in response to the bill passing that "the legislative process was accompanied by attempts to intimidate and blackmail the bar association and me, so we would enable the thwarting of the selection

[23] 'AG opposes PM choosing Civil Service Commissioner' Globes (Sep 8, 2024).

[24] Sarah Ben-Nun, 'Gov't process for appointing civil service commissioner illegal—High Court' Jerusalem Post (May 12, 2025), https://www.jpost.com/breaking-news/article-853716?utm; Gidi Weitz, 'Netanyahu's Civil Service Chief Pick Under Scrutiny Amid Recommendation Letter Scandal' Haaretz (March 8, 2025), https://www.haaretz.com/israel-news/2025-03-08/ty-article/.premium/netanyahus-civil-service-chief-pick-under-scrutiny-amid-recommendation-letter-scandal/00000195-751b-d0f8-a1f7-7ddb8cc50000

of a Supreme Court president and allow the selection of judges Levin wants."[25] This law may influence the ability of the bar to fulfil its function, according to the law, to "protect the rule of law, human rights and the fundamental values of the State of Israel."

15.4.7 Politicization of the Police

Since October 7, 2023, concerns over the politicization of the Israel Police have intensified, particularly following the enactment of Amendment No. 37 to the Police Ordinance, commonly referred to as the "Ben-Gvir Law." This amendment, passed in December 2022, granted the Minister of National Security—Itamar Ben-Gvir—expanded authority over the police, including the power to set general policies and principles of operation, encompassing investigative priorities.

This shift undermines the independence of the police force and opens the door to political interference in law enforcement activities. Petitions were filed with the Supreme Court, contending that the amendment violates democratic principles and the rule of law.[26]

On January 10, 2024, the Supreme Court issued an interim order prohibiting the Minister from interfering in police operations related to demonstrations, emphasizing the importance of maintaining the professional discretion of the police in operational matters. Further, on January 2, 2025, by a majority of five justices to four, the Supreme Court struck down a key component of law—the clause regarding authority over police investigations policy. Other clauses granting the minister more general authorities were upheld by the court.[27]

15.4.8 Threats to Independent Media

Since October 7, 2023, Israel has experienced a significant erosion of press freedom, marked by heightened government control over media narratives

[25] ToI Staff, 'Coalition passes law limiting bar association's control of its finances' The Times of Israel (January 23, 2025), https://www.timesofisrael.com/coalition-passes-law-limiting-bar-associations-control-of-its-finances/

[26] Eran Shamir-Borer and Mirit Lavi, 'The Independence of the Israel Police and the Limits of Political Intervention in Its Operations' (June 19, 2024), https://en.idi.org.il/articles/54565

[27] Jeremy Sharon, 'High Court annuls legislation that gave Ben Gvir Strong influence over police probes' The Times of Israel (January 2, 2025), https://www.timesofisrael.com/high-court-annuls-legislation-that-gave-ben-gvir-heavy-influence-over-police-probes/

and increased suppression of dissenting voices. The Israeli government enacted legislation empowering it to shut down foreign media outlets deemed threats to national security, leading to the closure of Al Jazeera's operations within Israel and the occupied West Bank. Additionally, the government ordered a boycott of the newspaper Haaretz, ceasing all official communications and advertising with the publication due to its critical coverage of the Israel–Hamas war. These actions, among others, have drawn criticism from press freedom advocates, who view them as attempts to silence critical voices and undermine democratic principles.[28]

15.4.9 Proposals to Limit Human Rights Organizations

Since October 7, 2023, the Israeli government has intensified efforts to restrict the activities of human rights organizations, particularly those focusing on Palestinian rights. One significant legislative proposal under debate in the Knesset aims to impose an 80% tax on foreign government funding to Israeli NGOs and to bar such organizations from accessing Israeli courts. This bill primarily targets groups monitoring human rights in Gaza and the West Bank. While proponents, like Likud lawmaker Ariel Kallner, contend that foreign-funded NGOs undermine Israel's legitimacy and aid its enemies, critics argue that it seeks to silence dissent and could devastate civil society.[29]

15.4.10 Ban Political Parties

Since October 7, 2023, the Israeli government has intensified efforts to limit or ban political parties, particularly those representing Arab citizens. In late 2024, a bill was introduced to amend Section 7A of the Basic Law: The Knesset, aiming to expand the criteria for disqualifying candidates and party lists. The proposed changes would allow disqualification based on minimal or past expressions interpreted as support for armed struggle against Israel, even if such support was for isolated acts by individuals

[28] Sara Fischer, 'Israeli government votes to boycott Haaretz' Axios (Nov 25, 2024), https://www.axios.com/2024/11/25/israeli-government-votes-to-boycott-haaretz; Nathan Klabin, 'Press Freedom in Israel Endangered by Legislative Push, Critics Say' The-medialine (December 15, 2024), https://themedialine.org/life-lines/press-freedom-in-israel-endangered-by-legislative-push-critics-say

[29] Gerry Shih and Claire Parker, 'Israel moves to tighten control of aid and rights groups' The Washington Post (May 6, 2025), https://www.washingtonpost.com/world/2025/05/06/israel-gaza-aid-groups-regulations

rather than organized groups. Notably, the bill also seeks to remove the Supreme Court's authority to review disqualification decisions, transferring final say to the Central Elections Committee.[30]

Critics argue that these legislative moves disproportionately target Arab-led parties and candidates, threatening minority representation and democratic principles. While proponents claim these measures are necessary for national security, opponents view them as steps toward authoritarianism, potentially undermining Israel's democratic framework.[31]

In summary, the period following October 7, 2023, has seen significant actions by the Israeli government that have raised concerns about the erosion of judicial independence, the politicization of key institutions, and threats to democratic principles and the rule of law in Israel.

15.5 How Is This Happening? Security, Distraction, and Populist Strategy

The post-October 7 constitutional acceleration in Israel raises a fundamental question: how is this happening, especially under conditions of national trauma and war? While many observers assumed that the attack would postpone, or even cancel, the judicial overhaul, the opposite occurred. To explain this paradox, this section identifies several overlapping dynamics that help account for the government's conduct: the fog of war; scapegoating the judiciary; incrementalism; sub-constitutional changes; diverted public attention; and the weaponization of humanitarian legalism.

15.5.1 Under the Fog of War

One of the key explanations for the persistence of the judicial overhaul is the so-called fog of war. Historically, crises have often served as catalysts for the expansion of executive power and even for constitutional revolutions.[32] Carl Schmitt famously argued that "sovereign is he who decides on

[30] Amir Fuchs, 'New Bill Proposed Expands the Criteria for Disqualification of Electoral Lists' Israel Democracy Institute (November 28, 2024), https://en.idi.org.il/articles/57319?

[31] Noam Sheizaf, 'Netanyahu Remains Unpopular at Home—This Is How He Could Win a Coming Election. His party is pushing a bill that would suppress turnout among Arab Israeli voters' Foreign Policy (February 6, 2025), https://foreignpolicy.com/2025/02/06/netanyahu-unpopular-israel-election-gaza

[32] Clinton L. Rossiter, *Constitutional Dictatorship: Crisi Government in the Modern Democracies* (Princeton University Press 1948); Oren Gross and Fionnuala Ní Aoláin, *Law*

the exception."[33] In Israel, which is anyway in a constant and continuing state of emergency, the ongoing war created a continuous state of exception—blurring the lines between emergency governance and regular policymaking. The Israeli government leveraged the urgency and uncertainty generated by the October 7 attacks to operate with minimal scrutiny. With the public preoccupied with war, bereavement, and the hostage crisis, the executive branch exploited the moment to push forward policies that would ordinarily (as occurred pre-Oct. 7) provoke substantial backlash.

15.5.2 *Blaming the Judiciary and Legal Advisers for October 7*

In the immediate aftermath of the attack, prominent coalition members—including Likud MKs and Ministers—openly suggested that judicial constraints were responsible for Israel's intelligence failure. Ministers claimed that fears of legal repercussions had stymied preventive actions. Some government-aligned media outlets insinuated that legal advisers and High Court decisions had encouraged Hamas. Yair Netanyahu, the Prime Minister's son, amplified these sentiments by sharing posts on social media blaming the High Court, IDF, and Shin Bet for the October 7 failures. He claimed that changes in the IDF's rules of engagement, influenced by the High Court, allowed Hamas terrorists to approach the Gaza border more easily. These assertions have sparked significant controversy and criticism within Israeli society, with many viewing them as attempts to deflect responsibility from the political leadership.[34]

In response to these allegations, there has been a surge in public demand for a comprehensive, independent investigation into the events leading up to October 7. While Netanyahu has expressed support for an "objective"

in Times of Crisis: Emergency Powers in Theory and Practice (CUP 2006). On limits to constitutional change during emergencies, see Richard Albert & Yaniv Roznai, 'Emergency Unamendability: Limitations on Constitutional Amendment in Extreme Conditions' (2021) 81(1) Maryland Law Review 243.

[33] Carl Schmitt, *Political Theology. Four Chapters on the Concept of Sovereignty* (MIT Press 1985) 5.

[34] See e.g. ToI Staff, 'Minister blames Hamas's Oct. 7 onslaught on attorney general, High Court justices' The Times of Israel (December 25, 2024), https://www.timesofisrael.com/minister-blames-oct-7-onslaught-on-attorney-general-high-court-justices; ToI Staff, 'Yair Netanyahu shares posts casting blame for Oct. 7 on courts, security services' The Times of Israel (November 19, 2023), https://www.timesofisrael.com/yair-netanyahu-shares-posts-casting-blame-for-oct-7-on-courts-security-services/

commission of inquiry, he has resisted calls for a state commission, which would be appointed by the Supreme Court's chief justice, perhaps due to concerns that such an inquiry could implicate him and his government in the failures that allowed the attack to occur.[35]

15.5.3 *Governing by Many Small Increments*

On January 4, 2023, Justice Minister Yariv Levin proudly announced, on national TV, his big plan for judicial overhaul. In many ways, this was a wake-up call for the liberal camp. This time, rather than push through major transformative constitutional reforms, the Israeli government, post-October 7, adopted a strategy of many small, seemingly technical laws. This incrementalism makes it more difficult for the public, scholars and the media to keep track of all the maneuvers and to mobilize against any one measure.

This is consistent with what scholars term "stealth authoritarianism," where executives undermine democracy not through dramatic acts, but through accumulations of technical rule changes, that, in isolation, may appear marginal but cumulatively reshape the democratic architecture.[36] This tactic raises various challenges to legal doctrines aiming to protect the constitutional order against radical unconstitutional constitutional reforms.[37]

15.5.4 *Sub-Constitutional Overhaul: Bypassing Formal Amendment*

In contrast with its previous, pre-Oct. 7 modus operandi, a major feature of the government's strategy has been its reliance on sub-constitutional reforms—through ordinary statutes, ministerial regulations, and administrative practices—rather than formal constitutional amendments. This approach avoids the political costs and visibility associated with changing Basic Laws, and allows the government to achieve nearly similar outcomes through lower-profile avenues.

[35] Gershom Gorenberg, 'Netanyahu Doesn't Want the Truth to Come Out' The Atlantic (March 14, 2025), https://www.theatlantic.com/international/archive/2025/03/israel-inquiry-october-7/682041

[36] Ozan O. Varol, 'Stealth Authoritarianism' (2014–2015) 100 Iowa Law Review 1673.

[37] See Yaniv Roznai & Tamar Hostovsky Brandes, 'Democratic Erosion, Populist Constitutionalism, and the Unconstitutional Constitutional Amendments Doctrine', 14(1) Law & Ethics of Human Rights (2020), 19; Tamar Hostovsky Brandes & Yaniv Roznai, 'When the First Brick falls of the Fortress of Democracy: How Should Courts Deal with The First Slice of the "Salami" Tactic for Eroding Democracy?', (2025) 19 Asian Journal of Comparative Law 535 doi:10.1017/asjcl.2025.7

For instance, rather than constitutionally changing the composition of the judicial selection committee (or, until this formal change), the Justice Minister misuses its administrative powers by not convening the committee, and the Knesset weakens the Bar Association, which has two representatives in the committee. Also, as aforementioned, the Knesset changed the law regarding the ombudsman of the judiciary, which may undermine judicial independence in other ways. And instead of formally changing the role and status of legal advisors in governmental departments, the ministers simply ignore their advice at will. These changes serve to erode checks and balances in ways functionally equivalent to constitutional change.

15.5.5 Absence of Media and Public Attention

Wartime conditions severely curtailed the media's ability to investigate, criticize, and contextualize domestic policies. News coverage prioritized developments in the Gaza Strip, hostage diplomacy, the war with Iran, and the northern front with Hezbollah. Issues of constitutional governance, which had dominated Israeli discourse until October 2023, receded from view.

Meanwhile, public attention and empathy were largely focused on the hostages and their families. Civil society efforts that had previously coordinated large-scale demonstrations redirected resources toward humanitarian relief and solidarity. As a result, the judicial overhaul resumed with much less resistance than before, even though the institutional implications were no less profound.[38]

15.5.6 Allegations That the Judiciary Aids Hamas

One of the most chilling turns in post-October 7 political discourse has been the accusation that the judiciary and legal community are aiding Hamas. The trigger for this narrative was a series of High Court petitions and legal advisory decisions concerning humanitarian aid to Gaza.[39]

[38] See e.g. 'How Israel's judicial reform protesters shifted focus to aiding victims of Hamas' PBS News (November 5, 2023), https://www.pbs.org/newshour/show/how-israels-judicial-reform-protesters-shifted-focus-to-aiding-victims-of-hamas

[39] Dahlia Scheindlin, "The High Court Stands With Hamas': Israel's Hard Right Is Intensifying Its Attack on the Judiciary' Haaretz (January 6, 2025), https://www.haaretz.com/israel-news/haaretz-today/2025-01-06/ty-article/.highlight/the-high-court-is-hamas-israels-hard-right-is-intensifying-its-attack-on-the-judiciary/00000194-3c81-d18c-a7bd-bcd9ebe30000

Eventually, on March 27, 2025, a three-judge panel of the Israeli Supreme Court rejected a petition challenging the legality of Israel's policy relating to the facilitation and provision of humanitarian aid in the Gaza Strip during the Gaza war. The Court decided that, whereas Israel is obligated under international law and Israeli law to allow and facilitate humanitarian aid, such obligations are relative in nature, and the petitioners failed to establish that those obligations were generally violated during the Gaza war.[40]

Nonetheless, the fact that the Supreme Court heard the petitions and gave interim measures allowed the government to weaponize international legal obligations and turn judicial independence and the rule of law into a political liability. More broadly, it reveals how populist governments can fuse security discourse with anti-legal sentiment, portraying independent adjudication as betrayal in times of war.

15.6 Why Is It Happening? Social Dynamics behind the Overhaul's Persistence

The persistence and acceleration of Israel's judicial overhaul in the aftermath of October 7 cannot be explained by institutional dynamics alone. Sociopolitical and psychological processes also played a key role, particularly those associated with national trauma, political identity, and collective fears. This section examines several interrelated dynamics: the rally-round-the-flag syndrome, the centrality of the hostage issue, the limitations of the protest movement's liberal framing, the political taboos surrounding military service, and security-based populism.

15.6.1 Rally-Round-the-Flag Syndrome

In times of national crisis, societies often exhibit what political scientists term the "rally-round-the-flag" effect: a temporary surge in support for incumbent leaders and a suspension of political dissent.[41]

[40] See y Yuval Shany and Amichai Cohen, 'Limited Protection: Israel's High Court of Justice Rejection of Gaza Humanitarian Aid Petition' Just Security (April 1, 2025), https://www.justsecurity.org/109731/israel-court-rejects-gaza-aid-petition/

[41] See generally, Yuval Feinstein, *Rally 'round the Flag': The Search for National Honor and Respect in Times of Crisis* (Oxford University Press, 2022); William D. Baker and John R. Oneal, 'Patriotism or Opinion Leadership?: The Nature and Origins of the "Rally 'Round the Flag'" Effect' (2001) 45(5) Journal of Conflict Resolution 661.

Following October 7, this phenomenon was evident in the Israeli public's initial embrace of national unity and the formation of a wartime coalition government. Political critique—particularly against the executive—was widely perceived as inappropriate, even unpatriotic.[42]

This atmosphere provided the government with the breathing room to resume its domestic agenda without sustained opposition or large protests. Attempts to challenge the judicial overhaul were reframed as undermining national cohesion during wartime. In this context, concerns about checks and balances were cast as distractions from the existential threat posed by Hamas and Hezbollah.

15.6.2 *The Centrality of Hostages*

The ongoing plight of Israeli hostages held by Hamas became an emotional and moral epicenter for the national discourse. Public attention, media coverage, and civil society activism converged around the demand for their release. Families of the hostages emerged as new moral authorities, further sidelining broader discussions about institutional reform.

The focus on hostages, while deeply justified on humanitarian grounds, inadvertently diverted energies away from monitoring or resisting the judicial overhaul. Large segments of civil society—previously active in anti-reform protests—rechanneled their organizing capacity toward humanitarian advocacy. This shift left a vacuum in legal-political mobilization.

15.6.3 *The Limits of Liberal Protest Framing*

A deeper explanation for the weakening of anti-overhaul protests lies in the ideological framing of the movement itself. Adam Shinar has argued that the protests were largely mobilized around liberal universalist values such as judicial independence, minority rights, and democratic norms. While these principles are essential, the framing often avoids engaging with more contentious, structural issues—particularly the occupation and systemic inequality faced by Arab-Palestinian citizens of Israel. This omission had

[42] Shingo Hamanaka, 'Anger, Anxiety, and the Star of David: An Experimental Survey of the Rally Phenomenon', in Aiko Nishikida, Chie Ezaki and Toshiya Tsujita, *"Fragile Stability" as a Political Background of October 7: Current and Foreseeable Issues in the Israeli-Palestinian Conflict* (Springer 2025) 87

practical consequences.[43] Many Arab Israelis perceived the protests as a Jewish intra-communal affair rather than a shared democratic struggle. They were thus less likely to participate in or support the movement.[44] According to Shinar:

> the protest movement was directed at structural and institutional features of the overhaul, but without a deep commitment to equality and human rights. As such, the movement was lacking from the beginning, for it failed to acknowledge the tensions inherent in Israel's constitutional identity as a Jewish and democratic state, believing it could focus on the "democratic" part, while neglecting to address the "Jewish" element and its relationship with Israel's democracy. Specifically, the protests' focus on abstract values in order to draw diverse participants effectively excluded Israeli Palestinians, who, as a minority group, faced unique issues not shared by the Jewish population. Indeed, the protests' insistence on the rule of law and equality often rang hollow to a group whose inclusion in the Israeli body politic has been questioned. Thus, when the war began, with government measures mostly affecting Israeli Palestinians, whether directly or indirectly, the protest movement failed to rally in their support. This also explains why some of the gains made by the protest movement diminished during the war, because the target of the government's repressive policies was the very public that was largely excluded or distanced itself from the protest movement.[45]

In other words, the previous insistence on neutrality vis-à-vis the occupation or the Jewish/Arab divide undercut its capacity to oppose postwar repression.

15.6.4 Taboo around Military Service Boycotts

During the height of the judicial reform protests in 2023, one of the most potent tools of resistance was the threat by IDF reservists to refuse service.

[43] Shinar (n 18)

[44] See Mohammed S. Wattad, Ephraim Lavie, Mora Deitch, and Meir Elran, 'Why Don't Arab Citizens Join the Protest Movement against the Proposed Judicial Overhaul?' (2023), INSS Insight No. 1703, https://www.researchgate.net/profile/Mora-Deitch/publication/370099508_Why_Don't_Arab_Citizens_Join_the_Protest_Movement_against_the_Proposed_Judicial_Overhaul/links/643ecde2e881690c4be1f3b8/Why-Dont-Arab-Citizens-Join-the-Protest-Movement-against-the-Proposed-Judicial-Overhaul.pdf

[45] Shinar (n 18) 3.

This tactic garnered significant media attention and brought pressure on the government.[46]

However, after October 7, this strategy became politically and morally untenable. The scale and brutality of the Hamas attacks led many Israelis to view military service as sacrosanct.[47] Accusations soon surfaced that previous threats of refusal had emboldened Hamas by signaling national weakness. In this climate, any suggestion of leveraging military service for political protest was met with hostility, if not outright criminalization.[48]

As a result, the most effective pressure point used by the protest movement in 2023 was now defused. With reservists returning to active duty and protest leaders unwilling to advocate military disobedience during wartime, the government faced little organized resistance from within the security establishment.

15.6.5 Security-Based Populism in Israel Post-October 7

Populism has traditionally emerged in response to economic hardship, cultural conflict, or social inequality. European and American populists often mobilize support by emphasizing economic anxiety or anti-immigration sentiment. Security-based populism in Israel differs from its counterparts in other democracies. in the Israeli context, a distinct form of security-driven populism has evolved—one that prioritizes national survival over liberal-democratic norms. Israeli populism hinges on existential fears linked to the ongoing Israeli–Palestinian conflict, regional instability, and the memory of historical trauma. As Levi and Agmon observe:

> what distinguishes Israeli populism from many of its foreign equivalents—namely, its political content. As mentioned above, we argue that while

[46] See Ayelet Harel, 'Refusal to serve in the Israel Defense Forces reserves in an era of anti-democratic judicial reform' (2024) 10(4) Critical Military Studies 562; Guy Ziv, 'Military Reservists and the Resistance To Netanyahu's Legal Overhaul' (forthcoming 2025) Middle East Policy https://doi.org/10.1111/mepo.12810

[47] See Gabriel Colorado, 'From protest to duty: How Gaza war recast the Israeli reservist ethos' The Jerusalem Post (May 5, 2025), https://www.jpost.com/israel-news/defense-news/article-852752

[48] 'Violent militia': MK calls to outlaw 'Brothers in Arms' JNS (November 20, 2024), https://www.jns.org/violent-militia-mk-calls-to-outlaw-brothers-in-arms/

populism typically feeds on cultural and economic anxieties, its Israeli variant is security-driven, as it mainly exploits fears related to national security.[49]

This form of populism has proven particularly potent in the wake of the October 7, 2023, Hamas attacks, which were the deadliest assault on Israel in decades. It is much easier to establish a Schmittian 'enemy–friend' distinction when there is a 'real' enemy with whom there is an armed conflict that constitutes a security threat. The Israeli government, led by a right-wing coalition, seized upon the security emergency not to pause its controversial judicial overhaul, but rather to justify its continuation and accelerate broader illiberal transformations. The heightened security discourse allowed the government to entrench executive authority, delegitimize judicial and legal constraints, and limit civil liberties—all under the banner of safeguarding the nation.

15.7 Conclusion

The Hamas attack on October 7, 2023, which resulted in the deaths of over 1,200 Israelis and the abduction of hundreds more, created a massive rupture in Israeli political life. One might have expected that the horrors of October 7, 2023, and the ensuing war in Gaza would have frozen, if not entirely abandoned, the contentious judicial overhaul in Israel. A nation under existential threat, grappling with unprecedented violence, and striving for national unity would presumably shelve divisive domestic reforms. Security is more important than obsessions with the judicial system, and thus, this tragedy might have prompted a pause in the internal constitutional conflict. Yet the opposite occurred. The security crisis acted as an accelerant for the governing coalition's populist agenda as the constitutional crisis deepened, and the populist government's efforts to weaken judicial independence, control key institutions, and consolidate power accelerated. The Israeli story thus demonstrates how the security crisis can enable and facilitate a populist constitutional project.

This chapter has demonstrated that the convergence of a security crisis with an ongoing constitutional transformation was neither coincidental nor contradictory. On the contrary, the security emergency created the political, social and psychological conditions that facilitated and legitimized further assaults on the rule of law. Through mechanisms of security-based

[49] Yonatan Levi and Shai Agmon, 'Beyond culture and economy: Israel's security-driven populism' (2021) 27(3) Contemporary Politics 292.

populism, executive actors used war discourse to sideline dissent, suppress judicial independence, and weaken checks on political power—all under the cover of national survival.

Institutionally, the government relied on incremental legal changes, administrative inertia, and sub-constitutional mechanisms to evade formal constraints and reduce public scrutiny. Politically, it scapegoated the judiciary, governmental lawyers and civil service as complicit in the state's failure to prevent the October 7 attacks. Sociologically, it capitalized on rally-round-the-flag sentiments, hostage-centered solidarity, and military sanctification to erode the effectiveness of protest and resistance.

Government officials and coalition-aligned media began propagating narratives that the judiciary was partly responsible for the national failure on October 7—either for restraining security agencies or for undermining deterrence. This rhetorical strategy exemplifies the populist tactic of converting institutional oversight into scapegoating, thereby justifying the dismantling of that oversight. Simultaneously, as public attention was fixed on military operations in Gaza and the plight of hostages, political actors intensified reforms to key institutional structures, including the Judicial Selection Committee, the Israel Bar Association, and regulatory bodies overseeing judicial conduct and civil service integrity, in addition to taking steps to limit media pluralism. Civil society organizations, particularly human rights NGOs, also became targets of legislation and official rhetoric.

Far from halting the judicial overhaul, the war context enabled its entrenchment. This development underscores the broader risks that security crises pose to democratic institutions—particularly in regimes already exhibiting populist tendencies. Israel's experience thus provides a cautionary tale of how liberal democracies may deteriorate not despite crises, but because of how populist leaders exploit them.

The challenge now facing Israeli democracy is twofold: to rebuild public trust in constitutional governance while safeguarding the institutions that preserve the separation of powers and fundamental rights. The post-war period must become a moment not only of national reckoning, but of democratic restoration.

References

'AG opposes PM choosing Civil Service Commissioner' *Globes* (8 September 2024)
Albert, R. and Roznai, Y., 'Emergency Unamendability: Limitations on Constitutional Amendment in Extreme Conditions' (2021) 81(1) Maryland Law Review 243

Aronson, O., Bar-Siman-Tov, I., Israely Levy, E., Levine-Schnur, R., Lustig, D. and Rosen-Zvi, I., 'Procedural Norms for Enacting Basic Laws and Knesset Committee Initiatives' 48 Tel Aviv University Law Review (2025) 5 https://ssrn.com/abstract=4566393 (Hebrew)

Baker, W.D. and Oneal, J.R., 'Patriotism or Opinion Leadership?: The Nature and Origins of the "Rally 'Round the Flag'" Effect' (2001) 45(5) Journal of Conflict Resolution 661

Barnea, A., 'Israeli Intelligence Was Caught Off Guard: The Hamas Attack on 7 October 2023—A Preliminary Analysis' (2024) 37(3) International Journal of Intelligence and Counter Intelligence 1056

Bar-Siman-Tov, I., Hostovsky Brandes, T., Lieblich, E., Roznai, Y. and Shinar, A., 'Scholactivism in the Service of Counter-populism: The Case of the Constitutional Overhaul in Israel' 22(4) International Journal of Constitutional Law (2025) 1059

Ben-Nun, S., 'Gov't process for appointing civil service commissioner illegal—High Court' *Jerusalem Post* (12 May 2025) https://www.jpost.com/breaking-news/article-853716?utm (accessed 25 October 2025)

Breuer, E., 'Isaac Amit appointed permanent High Court chief justice as 15-month saga ends' *The Jerusalem Post* (26 January 2025) https://www.jpost.com/israel-news/article-839327 (accessed 25 October 2025)

Colorado, G., 'From protest to duty: How Gaza war recast the Israeli reservist ethos' *The Jerusalem Post* (5 May 2025) https://www.jpost.com/israel-news/defense-news/article-852752 (accessed 25 October 2025)

Dotan, Y., 'Impeachment by Judicial Review: Israel's Odd System of Checks and Balances' (2018) 19(2) Theoretical Inquiries in Law 705

Feinstein, Y., *Rally 'round the Flag: The Search for National Honor and Respect in Times of Crisis*. Oxford University Press, 2022

Fischer, S., 'Israeli government votes to boycott Haaretz' *Axios* (25 November 2024) https://www.axios.com/2024/11/25/israeli-government-votes-to-boycott-haaretz; Klabin, N., 'Press Freedom in Israel Endangered by Legislative Push, Critics Say' *Themedialine* (15 December 2024) https://themedialine.org/life-lines/press-freedom-in-israel-endangered-by-legislative-push-critics-say (accessed 25 October 2025)

Frantzman, S.J., *The October 7 War: Israel's Battle for Security in Gaza*. Wicked Son, 2024, part 2

Frenkel, S., 'Israelis Are Angry at Netanyahu, but Chances of His Ouster Are Slim' *The New York Times* (5 December 2023) https://www.nytimes.com/2023/12/02/world/middleeast/israel-netanyahu-hamas-war.html (accessed 25 October 2025)

Fuchs, A., 'New Bill Proposed Expands the Criteria for Disqualification of Electoral Lists' *Israel Democracy Institute* (28 November 2024) https://en.idi.org.il/articles/57319 (accessed 25 October 2025)

Garber, A., 'Why Judicial Reform in Essential' *Kohelet* https://www.kohelet.org.il/en/article/why-judicial-reform-is-essential/ (accessed 25 October 2025)

Gorenberg, G., 'Netanyahu Doesn't Want the Truth to Come Out' *The Atlantic* (14 March 2025) https://www.theatlantic.com/international/archive/2025/03/israel-inquiry-october-7/682041 (accessed 25 October 2025)

Gross, O. and Ní Aoláin, F., *Law in Times of Crisis: Emergency Powers in Theory and Practice*. CUP, 2006

Hamanaka, S., 'Anger, Anxiety, and the Star of David: An Experimental Survey of the Rally Phenomenon'. In Nishikida, A., Ezaki, C. and Tsujita, T., *"Fragile Stability" as a Political Background of October 7: Current and Foreseeable Issues in the Israeli-Palestinian Conflict*. Springer, 2025, 87

Harel, A., 'Refusal to serve in the Israel Defense Forces reserves in an era of anti-democratic judicial reform' (2024) 10(4) Critical Military Studies 562

HCJ 5658/23 *Movement for Quality Government v. the Knesset*, Nevo Legal Database (1 January 2024) (Isr.)

Hostovsky Brandes, T. and Roznai, Y., 'When the First Brick falls of the Fortress of Democracy: How Should Courts Deal with The First Slice of the "Salami" Tactic for Eroding Democracy?' (2025) 19 Asian Journal of Comparative Law 535–555

'How Israel's judicial reform protesters shifted focus to aiding victims of Hamas' *PBS News* (5 November 2023) https://www.pbs.org/newshour/show/how-israels-judicial-reform-protesters-shifted-focus-to-aiding-victims-of-hamas (accessed 25 October 2025)

'Human Shield Horror' and Israel's '9/11 moment' *BBC* (8 October 2023)

Kershner, I., 'Israeli Government Rejects President's Judicial Compromise' *The New York Times* (15 March 2023) https://www.nytimes.com/2023/03/15/world/middleeast/israel-herzog-judicial-compromise.html (accessed 25 October 2025)

Kremnitzer, M., 'Releasing the Government from Acting Reasonably; or, the Government Says Goodbye to Reasonableness' (2023) 56(3) Israel Law Review 343

Kretzmer, D. et al., 'Israel's Recent "Unreasonableness Amendment" and its Implications' *Israel Law Professors Forum for Democracy* (28 July 2023) https://www.lawprofsforum.org/post/israel-s-recent-unreasonableness-amendment-and-its-implications (accessed 25 October 2025)

Levi, Y. and Agmon, S., 'Beyond culture and economy: Israel's security-driven populism' (2021) 27(3) Contemporary Politics 292

Lurie, G., 'The Attempt to Capture the Courts in Israel' (2023) 56(3) Israel Law Review 456

Navot, S., 'An Overview of Israel's 'Judicial Overhaul': Small Parts of a Big Populist Picture' (2023) 56(3) Israel Law Review 482

Office of the President, 'People's Directive—From a crisis to a constitutional opportunity: The President's proposed constitutional framework for settling the relations between the branches of government in Israel by broad consensus' (2023) <www.mitve-haam.org/_files/ugd/

f35a26_8eb0f820ae1b4d32bd178cc2b7cf4352.pdf> (accessed 25 October 2025)

Oren-Harush, Y., 'The Case for Israel's Judicial Reform' *Hashiloach* (2025) https://hashiloach.org.il/wp-content/uploads/2023/05/the-case-for-israels-judicial-reform.pdf (accessed 25 October 2025)

Public Address by The President of the Supreme Court of Israel, [Justice] Esther Hayut, at the Conference of the Israeli Association of Public Law, *Israel Policy Forum* (12 January 2023) http://tinyurl.com/3mm764ex (accessed 25 October 2025)

Ravid, B., 'Israel's Netanyahu forms unity government with ex-Defense Minister Gantz' *Axios* (11 October 2023) https://www.axios.com/2023/10/11/hamas-israel-war-gantz-netanyahu-unity-government (accessed 25 October 2025)

Rossiter, C.L., *Constitutional Dictatorship: Crisis Government in the Modern Democracies.* Princeton University Press, 1948

Roznai, Y. and Cohen, A., 'Populism, Democratic Erosion and the Judicial Overhaul in Israel' (2023) 56 Israel Law Review 505

Roznai, Y. and Hostovsky Brandes, T., 'Democratic Erosion, Populist Constitutionalism, and the Unconstitutional Constitutional Amendments Doctrine' (2020) 14(1) Law & Ethics of Human Rights 19

Roznai, Y. and Schnitzer, S., 'Navigating the judicial ship through stormy waters: President Esther Hayut and the Israeli constitutional crises, 2018–23', 23(1) *International Journal of Constitutional Law* (2025) 179.

Roznai, Y., 'We the Fourth Branch? The People as an Institution Protecting Democracy'. In Jackson, V. and Khosla, M. (eds.), *Redefining Comparative Constitutional Law: Essays for Mark Tushnet.* Oxford University Press, 2024, 293

Roznai, Y., Dixon, R. and Landau, D.E., 'Judicial Reform or Abusive Constitutionalism in Israel' (2023) 56 Israel Law Review 292

Roznai, Y., 'From the 'Hungarian Blitz' to the 'Polish Salami': Populism, The Gaza War and The Judicial Overhaul in Israel'. In Takao Suami, Keisuke Kondo, Kaoru Obata (eds.), *The Cambridge Handbook of Global Crisis and Global Legal Ordering.* Cambridge University Press. (forthcoming)

Scheindlin, D., "'The High Court Stands With Hamas': Israel's Hard Right Is Intensifying Its Attack on the Judiciary' *Haaretz* (6 January 2025) https://www.haaretz.com/israel-news/haaretz-today/2025-01-06/ty-article/.highlight/the-high-court-is-hamas-israels-hard-right-is-intensifying-its-attack-on-the-judiciary/00000194-3c81-d18c-a7bd-bcd9ebe30000 (accessed 25 October 2025)

Schmitt, C., *Political Theology. Four Chapters on the Concept of Sovereignty.* MIT Press, 1985, 5

Shamir-Borer, E. and Lavi, M., 'The Independence of the Israel Police and the Limits of Political Intervention in Its Operations' (19 June 2024) https://en.idi.org.il/articles/54565

Shany, Y. and Cohen, A., 'Israel's Renewed Judicial Overhaul' *Israel Democracy Institute* (4 March 2025) https://en.idi.org.il/articles/58607

Shany, Y. and Cohen, A., 'Limited Protection: Israel's High Court of Justice Rejection of Gaza Humanitarian Aid Petition' *Just Security* (1 April 2025) https://www.justsecurity.org/109731/israel-court-rejects-gaza-aid-petition/ (accessed 25 October 2025)

Sharon, J. and Sokol, S., 'Coalition passes judicial overhaul law taking over appointment of judges' ombudsman' *The Times of Israel* (4 March 2025) https://www.timesofisrael.com/coalition-passes-judicial-overhaul-law-taking-over-appointment-of-judges-ombudsman/ (accessed 25 October 2025)

Sharon, J. and Sokol, S., 'High Court orders Levin to appoint new court president; he calls its ruling undemocratic' *The Times of Israel* (8 September 2024) https://www.timesofisrael.com/high-court-orders-levin-to-appoint-new-supreme-court-president-says-refusal-unlawful (accessed 25 October 2025)

Sharon, J., 'High Court annuls legislation that gave Ben Gvir Strong influence over police probes' *The Times of Israel* (2 January 2025) https://www.timesofisrael.com/high-court-annuls-legislation-that-gave-ben-gvir-heavy-influence-over-police-probes/ (accessed 25 October 2025)

Sharon, J., 'Levin declines to sign official announcement of new Supreme Court president' *The Times of Israel* (3 February 2025) https://www.timesofisrael.com/levin-declines-to-sign-official-announcement-of-new-supreme-court-president/ (accessed 25 October 2025)

Sharon, J., 'Netanyahu, Gantz agree to Form Emergency Unity Government' *The Times of Israel* (11 October 2023) https://www.timesofisrael.com/liveblog_entry/netanyahu-gantz-agree-to-form-emergency-unity-government/ (accessed 25 October 2025)

Sheizaf, N., 'Netanyahu Remains Unpopular at Home—This Is How He Could Win a Coming Election. His party is pushing a bill that would suppress turnout among Arab Israeli voters' *Foreign Policy* (6 February 2025) https://foreignpolicy.com/2025/02/06/netanyahu-unpopular-israel-election-gaza (accessed 25 October 2025)

Shih, G. and Parker, C., 'Israel moves to tighten control of aid and rights groups' *The Washington Post* (6 May 2025) https://www.washingtonpost.com/world/2025/05/06/israel-gaza-aid-groups-regulations (accessed 25 October 2025)

Shinar, A., 'Constitutional Overhaul, the War in Gaza, and the Puzzle of Civic Mobilization in Israel' (2024) 26 German Law Journal 1, 11 https://doi.org/10.1017/glj.2024.37

Shultziner, D., 'The Movement Against Democratic Backsliding in Israel' (2023) 38(3) Sociological Forum 896

Sokol, S., 'Knesset passes law greatly boosting political control over appointment of judges' *The Times of Israel* (27 March 2025) https://www.timesofisrael.com/knesset-passes-law-greatly-boosting-political-control-over-judicial-appointments/ (accessed 25 October 2025)

ToI Staff, 'Coalition passes law limiting bar association's control of its finances' *The Times of Israel* (23 January 2025) https://www.timesofisrael.com/coalition-passes-law-limiting-bar-associations-control-of-its-finances/ (accessed 25 October 2025)

ToI Staff, 'Minister blames Hamas's Oct. 7 onslaught on attorney general, High Court justices' *The Times of Israel* (25 December 2024) https://www.timesofisrael.com/minister-blames-oct-7-onslaught-on-attorney-general-high-court-justices (accessed 25 October 2025)

ToI Staff, 'Yair Netanyahu shares posts casting blame for Oct. 7 on courts, security services' *The Times of Israel* (19 November 2023) https://www.timesofisrael.com/yair-netanyahu-shares-posts-casting-blame-for-oct-7-on-courts-security-services/ (accessed 25 October 2025)

Varol, O.O., 'Stealth Authoritarianism' (2014–2015) 100 Iowa Law Review 1673

'Violent militia': MK calls to outlaw 'Brothers in Arms' *JNS* (20 November 2024) https://www.jns.org/violent-militia-mk-calls-to-outlaw-brothers-in-arms/ (accessed 25 October 2025)

Wattad, M.S., Lavie, E., Deitch, M. and Elran, M., 'Why Don't Arab Citizens Join the Protest Movement against the Proposed Judicial Overhaul?' (2023) INSS Insight No. 1703 https://www.researchgate.net/profile/Mora-Deitch/publication/370099508_Why_Don't_Arab_Citizens_Join_the_Protest_Movement_against_the_Proposed_Judicial_Overhaul/links/643ecde2e881690c4be1f3b8/Why-Dont-Arab-Citizens-Join-the-Protest-Movement-against-the-Proposed-Judicial-Overhaul.pdf (accessed 25 October 2025)

Weitz, G., 'Netanyahu's Civil Service Chief Pick Under Scrutiny Amid Recommendation Letter Scandal' *Haaretz* (8 March 2025) https://www.haaretz.com/israel-news/2025-03-08/ty-article/.premium/netanyahus-civil-service-chief-pick-under-scrutiny-amid-recommendation-letter-scandal/00000195-751b-d0f8-a1f7-7ddb8cc50000 (accessed 25 October 2025)

Ziv, G., 'Military Reservists and the Resistance To Netanyahu's Legal Overhaul' *Middle East Policy* (forthcoming 2025) https://doi.org/10.1111/mepo.12810

CHAPTER 16

Implosion of Constitutional Order and Demise of Authority in Times of Constitutional Polycrisis, Emergency Constitutionalism, and Constitutional Polytransition

Martin Belov

We are living in a period of deep challenges to our legal, political, and social orders. Crisis, emergency, and dark constitutionalism[1] are massively impacting the constitutional law in books, constitutional law in action, and constitutional law in imagination. Currently, they have fewer institutional than functional repercussions for the constitutional orders. This lack of massive direct structural reflection of crisis in the institutional design of the constitutional orders—despite the impact of emergency on constitutional axiology, human rights, and the balance of power—keeps the resemblance of normalcy. However, the emergency regimes provided by the constitutions are intensely used and misused. Moreover, the increasing institutional inadequacy of constitutions to cope with the multitude of crises produces deconstitutionalization and constitutional sclerosis.

This chapter is produced as part and funded by the European Union-NextGenerationEU, through the National Recovery and Resilience Plan of the Republic of Bulgaria, project No bg-rrp-2.004-0008.

[1] Martin Belov, 'The Concept of Dark Constitutionalism' in Martin Belov (ed) *Legal Imaginaries of Crisis and Fear. Dark Constitutionalism* (Routledge, 2025).

M. Belov (ed.), *Constitutional Polycrisis and Emergency Constitutionalism*, Federalism and Internal Conflicts,
https://doi.org/10.1007/978-3-032-06516-2_16

Constitutional sclerosis consists of the inability of the constitution and the institutions provided by it to respond to the challenges of the socio-political life. Thus, the constitution becomes rather an outdated devise that does not offer efficient solutions to contemporary problems. Deconstitutionalization is partially related to constitutional sclerosis. It may stem from it, but can also be an independent phenomenon. In general, deconstitutionalization consists of the lack of regulative force of the constitution and constitutional law over novel phenomena and socio-political tendencies and processes. Hence, it is a term that reflects the mismatch between constitutional law and socio-political reality. Deconstitutionalization makes the constitution fictitious—gradually or abruptly.

The demise or even lack of regulative force of the constitution over key phenomena and strands of reality because of constitutional sclerosis (outdatedness of the constitution) or deconstitutionalization (non-provision of a legal framework for newly emerged phenomena with constitutional relevance) leads to delegitimation of the constitution and the constitutional order. This is due to the lack of efficiency and problem-solving capacity. It allows for power constellations to evade the regulative force of law and thus to have a legally unrestrained impact on the citizens and the society. The ultimate result may be a demise of authority and implosion of the constitutional order due to critical levels of distrust.

Constitutional polycrisis, emergency constitutionalism, and constitutional polytransition are shifting the relationship between constitutional normalcy and constitutional emergency.[2] Thus, constitutional emergency is gradually becoming "the new normal" while normalcy is reshaped via (un)constitutional constitutional politics of fear, anger, hate, and despair. These processes are producing a situation of constitutional darkness,[3] being anthropological status, political reality, and a new world order based

[2] See Martin Belov, 'The Conceptual Shapes of Constitutional Polycrisis: Deconstruction, Asymmetries and Post-Modern Anxieties of Constitutional Normalcy' (2023) 70 Irish Jurist, special issue Law in a Time of Crisis' 393–410, Martin Belov, 'Rule of Law in Europe in Times of Constitutional Polycrisis, Constitutional Polytransition and Democratic Discontent' (2023) 3 Diritto pubblico comparato ed europeo 875–884, and Martin Belov, 'Rule of Law and Democracy in Times of Transitory Constitutionalism, Constitutional Polycrisis and Emergency Constitutionalism: Towards a Global Algorithmic Technocracy?' in Martin Belov (ed) *Rule of Law in Crisis: Constitutionalism in a State of Flux* (Routledge, 2023) 21–47.

[3] For the concept of constitutional darkness see Martin Belov, 'The Concept of Dark Constitutionalism' in Martin Belov (ed) *Legal Imaginaries of Crisis and Fear. Dark Constitutionalism* (Routledge, 2025).

on non-liberty, non-autonomy, and excessive misuse of authority and oppression. In this context, dark constitutionalism is gradually becoming the rule instead of the exception.[4]

Authority and legitimacy are key pillars, assets, and resources of constitutional orders. Authority is the source of the ontology of obedience, compliance with the social, legal and constitutional order, and maintenance of social peace. Just authority is not only a prerequisite of a democratic constitutional order based on the rule of law. It is a precondition for compliance with legal and constitutional rules and voluntary submission to public power. Thus, there have been a multitude of strategies for justification of the constitutional order and the authority of the public power. They constitute the range of theories and practices of legitimate governance. The Weberian classification of traditional, charismatic, and rational legitimacy[5] and the distinction between input and output legitimacy[6] are just some of the most popular theories of the legitimacy of public power and legal order.

Currently, there are a multitude of factors that produce delegitimation of the constitutional order, leading to the demise of authority. Altogether, they have the potential to produce the implosion of the constitutional order. The implosion consists in the excessive contestation of the legitimacy and authority of the constitutional order by citizens who, while challenging the reasons for voluntary obedience to power, are tearing apart the social contract that underlines a liberal-democratic constitution. Thus, the implosion of constitutional order not only leads to the demise of authority and dismantling of official and recognized institutions and patterns of power. It also blows up the foundations of constitutional order through radical forms of civil disobedience, including revolutions.

[4] For the battle between dark and bright constitutionalism see Martin Belov, 'Conclusion: Pulsing Constitutionalism and the Dichotomy between Dark and Bright Constitutionalism as Driving Force in Constitutional Space-Time' in Martin Belov (ed) *Legal Imaginaries of Crisis and Fear. Dark Constitutionalism* (Routledge, 2025).

[5] See Max Weber, Soziologie. Weltgeschichtliche Analysen. Politik (Kröner Verlag, 1968) 151 and the following and John Patty and Elizabeth Maggie Penn, Social Choice and Legitimacy: The Possibilities of Impossibility (Cambridge University Press, 2014) 1–224.

[6] For the input and output democratic legitimacy see Paul Craig and Grainne de Burca *EU Law. Text, Cases and Materials* (Oxford University Press, 2008) 65 and Philipp Kiiver, *The National Parliaments in the European Union: A Critical View on EU Constitution-Building* (Kluwer Law International, 2006) 95.

Hence, the currently ongoing constitutional polycrisis is paralleled by crisis of legitimacy of the constitutional orders. This delegitimation of public power and authority is resulting from several factors. The most important of them are: the overburdening of public power by the multitude of overlapping crisis resulting in increasing inefficiency and diminished problem-solving capacity of the political, legal, and constitutional order (efficiency issue); the increasing mistrust of the people to the official authorities regarding their ability to cope with crisis in a democratically representative and accountable manner bound by rule of law (democracy and rule of law issues); the mistrust in the transparency of the actions of public institutions dealing with emergency and crisis and the accuracy of information in the context of post-truth and massive disinformation (misinformation, non-accountability, and transparency issues); and the emerging context of non-liberty that is producing agency, autonomy, and self-determination restraints (liberty issues). These issues are separate and autonomous spheres of concern that are also mutually reinforcing and interrelated.

The efficiency issues concern all crises that have massively hit societies since the beginning of the twenty-first century. These are the security crisis (related to terrorism and wars), financial crisis, migration crisis, health crisis (COVID-19 pandemics), but also the forthcoming ecology crisis, the challenges stemming from the AI etc. These crises jointly produce a polycrisis. This polycrisis has deep repercussions for the constitution and constitutionalism. They are related to the fundamental challenges to constitutional axiology (values and principles), human rights, and constitutional institutions. The polycrisis has both structural and functional repercussions on the constitutional order. That is why the constitutionally relevant implications and dimensions of the polycrisis can be defined as constitutional polycrisis. Constitutional polycrisis is particularly severe and is gaining momentum in the context of constitutional polytransition, comprising the multitude of transitions that our constitutional orders are currently undergoing.

The post-9/11 period is marked by a deep security crisis. The hybrid, multilayered, and quasi-permanent state of exception justified by security concerns does not durably solve problems related to organized crime and terrorism. Instead, it creates a feeling of permanent insecurity and multifaceted threats to privacy, liberty, and rights by the government and to life, health, and physical integrity stemming from potential terror attacks. This climate of insecurity and fear justifies the transformation of the security-related emergency into normalcy.

The problem is even worse if one includes the situation of hybrid and asymmetric warfare, which amounts to a semi-official creeping World War III. The wars in Ukraine and the Middle East, the tensions between India and Pakistan, in sub-Saharan Africa, and elsewhere are just elements of the puzzle of insecurity, war, and suffering that is gradually but feasibly spreading to more and more parts of the world. Wars (hot, cold, or semi-hot, traditional or hybrid), terrorism, and the rise of organized crime are jointly resulting in a world full of fear, hate, anger, and despair. They are the perfect context and nurturing soil for dark constitutionalism promoted through (un)constitutional politics of fear.[7] Moreover, the post-World War II and then post-Cold War world orders are shaking and on the edge of crumbling. It seems that we are approaching the crunch time of the world as we know it together with the demise of its constitutional and international conceptual and legal framework.

The constitutional institutions deal with the security crisis with variable success. In some cases, they even try to demonstrate efficiency through recourse to both symbolic politics and *Realpolitik*. Examples are the declaration of the "war on terror" by President George W. Bush in 2001 and the anti-immigration policies of President Donald Trump in 2025. Nevertheless, both agendas—the Bush's "war on terror" and the Trumps' "war on migration" are much more an attempt at demonstrating power and justifications for different internal political and geopolitical agendas rather than true means for solving security issues at stake.

The migration crisis, similarly to the security crisis, is also producing a state of semi-permanent emergency. Migration is an eternal phenomenon that has existed since the beginning of human history. However, several factors are triggering increased migration waves in the context of the twenty-first century. The most important of them are the wars, civil wars, revolutions, and rebellions, the persecution of populations on the basis of different criteria (e.g., ethnicity, race, religion, and beliefs), but also the poverty and the search of better, more prosperous, and secure life. Climate change, the polycrisis and polytransition are also contributing to the rise of regional and global migration.

[7] See Martin Belov, 'The Concept of Dark Constitutionalism' in Martin Belov (ed) *Legal Imaginaries of Crisis and Fear. Dark Constitutionalism* (Routledge, 2025).

The constitutional orders are generally inadequate to the current age of migration. They can deal with small migration waves related to traditional challenges, but are inefficient and frequently unjust to both their own citizens and the migrants. Thus, the fight against illegal migration and the accommodation of legal migration is more a mimicry of crisis management instead of source of a solid and viable solutions.

The financial crisis of 2009 was met by an almost unprecedented legal response that had a substantial and far-reaching constitutional dimension. The provision of the balanced or "golden" budget rule in the EU law and its institutionalization in the constitutions of the EU member states, and especially of the Eurozone member states, has been the climax of the rationalist utopia of the possibility for permanent financial stability and eternal avoidance of the negative phase of the economic cycle. In fact, the golden budget rule became a constitutional imaginary and ideology of the late constitutional neo-liberalism.

It seems that while the 2009 financial crisis has been overcome and the golden budget rule has played a role for its putting and keeping under control, it still cannot produce this quasi-magical durable healing effect for potential future financial and economic crisis. This is partially due to the overlap of multiple crises into a constitutional polycrisis. For example, the Covid-19 pandemic and the current tendency for remilitarization of Europe (e.g., the "Rearm Europe" initiative) are putting huge pressure on the golden or balanced budget rule. Hence, the golden budget rule has been a pillar of the financial constitutionalism that has evolved from the 2009 financial crisis and an important normative ideology of contemporary constitutional orders of the EU member states and the EU in general. However, it will be a rather fragile boat in the stormy sea of global finance, if a new financial and economic superstorm arises or the various crises (security, migration, ecological, health, etc.) gain momentum on the cloudy horizon of the current age of crisis and transition.

Similar efficiency concerns relate to the health and ecology crises of our age. The pandemic management was extremely costly and not necessarily efficient. Countries with similar demography, anthropology, and socio-political orders (e.g. Sweden and Norway or Bulgaria and Greece) have had comparable anti-pandemic results while applying radically different anti-pandemic strategies. The COVID-19 pandemic management was massively based on fear politics. It produced not only deep economic disruptions but also massive violations of constitutional principles and human rights. COVID-19 regimes have been triggers of dark constitutionalism.[8]

Climate change is a genuinely global phenomenon. It concerns the planet as a whole (and also the planet as such) and cannot be properly addressed with national or even regional measures. In that regard, the efforts of the European countries and especially the EU member states seem at least limited if not radically inefficient in case they are not paralleled by a coordinated response by the majority, if not all, countries in the world. This is particularly true for the U.S., China, and India as key contributors to industrial pollution of the environment.

Hence, while the crises are multiplying and overlapping, thus resulting in polycrisis, the institutional responses to them remain outdated, sketchy, disproportional, and inadequate. They are either "too little too late" or disproportionally harsh especially with view to the balance between efficiency and human rights. The governments are explicitly or implicitly realizing their increasing inability to produce the efficient crisis management that is expected by their citizens. This is especially problematic with a view to existential crises that endanger human life, human dignity, and physical or psychic integrity. Essentially, the Weberian ultimate control of violence by the state is justified by its capacity to preserve these core human rights. Thus, the growing impotence of the state and public power in general to give adequate and efficient response to the range of perils stemming from polycrisis and polytransition is masked by pre-emptive quasi-authoritarianism.

Many of the authoritarian and illiberal trends in contemporary political dynamics are usually explained with recourse to populism.[9] However,

[8] See Martin Belov, 'The Role of Fear Politics in Global Constitutional 'Ernstfall': Images of Fear under COVID-19 Health Paternalism' in Martin Belov (ed) *Populist Constitutionalism and Illiberal Democracies. Between Constitutional Imagination, Normative Entrenchment and Political Reality* (Intersentia, 2021) 187–221.

[9] See e.g. Jiri Priban, 'Constitutionalism, populism, and the imaginary of the authentic polity: a socio-legal analysis of European public spheres and constitutional demoicratization', (2023) 50 (S1) Journal of Law and Society 26–44, Paul Blokker 'Political and Constitutional Imaginaries', in S Adams and J Smith (eds), *Social Imaginaries: Critical Interventions in a Paradigm-in-the-Making* (Rowman and Littlefield, 2021), Paul Blokker, 'Populist Constitutionalism' in C de la Torre (ed), *Routledge Handbook of Global Populism* (Routledge, 2018), Paul Blokker, 'Populism as a constitutional project' 2019, 17 (2) *International Journal of Constitutional Law*, Jo-Anne Dillabough, 'Higher education, violent modernities and the 'global present': the paradox of politics and new populist imaginaries' (2021) 20 (2) Globalisation, Societies and Education 178–192.

the contribution of pre-emptive quasi-authoritarianism as a form of emergency constitutionalism and crisis (mis)management should also not be neglected. The combination of illiberal populism and authoritarian neo-conservatism is related also to the phenomenon and political strand of the so-called dark enlightenment and the pre-emptive quasi-authoritarianism and authoritarian liberalism is extremely toxic for liberal democracy. Unfortunately, the combination of constitutional polycrisis and constitutional polytransition is promoting pre-emptive quasi-authoritarianism that is being justified as a response to various crises and as a legitimate form of emergency constitutionalism.

Pre-emptive quasi-authoritarianism consists of the attempts of governments to compensate for their inability to provide for efficient, proportionate, and long-lasting legal and factual responses to one or more crises through measures that infringe human rights, limit liberty, autonomy, and agency. The governments, while overburdened by constitutional polycrisis and in the context of constitutional polytransition, are claiming to be securing the core of the human condition—usually defined as "life and security first." Unfortunately, this frequently leads to neglecting other aspects of the human condition, such as self-determination, dignity, and freedom. Frequently, governments are imposing rules that are profoundly disproportional with regard to the range of human rights. They are justifying them through survival claims—typically via politics of fear. Key examples are the measures for coping with the migration crisis, terrorism, and the COVID-19 pandemic. The systematic recourse to such rules and measures gradually transforms the emergency into normalcy. It feeds crisis-related mentality, dark anthropology, and fear and oppression-based power constellations.

Thus, pre-emptive quasi-authoritarianism is being gradually transformed into proper authoritarianism justified through narratives and strategies derived from the Schmittian state of exception (Ernstfall) and Hobbesian Leviathan-driven politics. Altogether, this is the perfect context for the emergence, establishment, and unfolding of dark constitutionalism. In that regard, pre-emptive quasi-authoritarianism can be metaphorically compared to the slogan that "the road to hell is paved with good intentions." Indeed, securing public security and safety as well as public health are genuinely legitimate grounds for limiting human rights in the context of state of emergency. Nevertheless, the duration of the emergencies, at times gaining semi-permanent or even permanent character, as well as the intensity of the limitation of human autonomy, liberty, and agency, are frequently lead to disproportionality and unpredictability of emergency measures. This is the typical way in which the state of emergency is becoming a state of exception, and pre-emptive quasi-authoritarianism is being transformed into plain and proper authoritarianism. Dark constitutionalism is grounded on fear politics, and pre-emptive quasi-authoritarianism is a direct way for its achievement.

The increasing mistrust of the people in the official authorities regarding their ability to cope with a crisis in a democratically representative and accountable manner, bound by the rule of law, is usually combined with the mistrust in the transparency of the actions of public institutions dealing with emergencies and crises and the accuracy of information in the context of post-truth and massive disinformation. Hence, the democracy and rule of law issues and the misinformation, non-accountability, and transparency issues are conceptually and pragmatically deeply interrelated.

Trust is a key resource of governance. It is necessary for all forms of government and political regimes. However, it has special importance in democratic constitutional orders. Legitimate government is impossible without at least basic trust in the rules and institutions, in the policies, and in the office holders. The age of constitutional polycrisis and constitutional polytransition has massive detrimental effects on trust in all of its aspects. This fact diminishes democratic resilience and produces the demise of authority. The deconstruction of trust in times of crisis and transition stems from various factors. The most important of them are the non-transparent and frequently controversial ways of decision-making in the context of emergency constitutionalism, the lack of predictability that goes against the principle of reasonable expectations, and the mismatch between legitimate goals and employed means for their achievement in the context of disproportionate limitations and even infringement of human rights, which is the course of crisis (mis)management. These factors are massively overburdening the system for the production of democratic legitimacy. They are rather destructive of key constitutional principles such as democracy, separation of powers, and the rule of law.

Last but not least, the context of non-liberty stemming from constitutional polycrisis is producing agency, autonomy, and self-determination restraints. They can be defined as liberty issues. The constitutional polycrisis creates a constitutional climate of non-liberty that serves as fertile soil for cascading limitations of human rights. This is due to the fact that the main justification of human rights is their embeddedness in human nature and the belief in its ontological precedence over power, state, and society.

In other words, the human condition can be framed through liberty only if the normative ideologies of human autonomy and agency prevail over normative ideologies of order, security, and efficiency. Thus, the tendency for limitation of freedom, autonomy, and agency due to security and safety concerns is the highway to dark constitutionalism.

To sum up, the deconstruction of key elements of constitutional order based on liberty, autonomy, agency, and respect of human rights in the context of constitutional polycrisis and constitutional polytransition produces ruptures in the constitutional framing matrix. The gradual but visible establishment of emergency as normalcy since the beginning of the twenty-first century and especially since 2019 in the COVID and post-COVID era triggers tendencies towards constitutional erosion, constitutional sclerosis, constitutional twilight,[10] and post-constitutionalism. This all leads to the demise of authority, a decrease in trust, and eventually to the implosion of the constitutional orders. The ultimate result of such trends towards non-liberty masqueraded as emergency constitutionalism will be the establishment of dark constitutionalism.

References

Belov, M., 'Conclusion: Pulsing Constitutionalism and the Dichotomy between Dark and Bright Constitutionalism as Driving Force in Constitutional Space-Time'. In Belov, M. (ed.), *Legal Imaginaries of Crisis and Fear. Dark Constitutionalism*. Routledge, 2025, 297–305

Belov, M., 'Rule of Law and Democracy in Times of Transitory Constitutionalism, Constitutional Polycrisis and Emergency Constitutionalism: Towards a Global Algorithmic Technocracy?' In Belov, M. (ed.), *Rule of Law in Crisis: Constitutionalism in a State of Flux*. Routledge, 2023, 21–47

Belov, M., 'Rule of Law in Europe in Times of Constitutional Polycrisis, Constitutional Polytransition and Democratic Discontent' (2023) 3 *Diritto pubblico comparato ed europeo* 875–884

Belov, M., 'The Concept of Dark Constitutionalism'. In Belov, M. (ed.), *Legal Imaginaries of Crisis and Fear. Dark Constitutionalism*. Routledge, 2025

Belov, M., 'The Conceptual Shapes of Constitutional Polycrisis: Deconstruction, Asymmetries and PostModern Anxieties of Constitutional Normalcy' (2023) 70 *Irish Jurist*, special issue *Law in a Time of Crisis* 393–410

Belov, M., 'The Role of Fear Politics in Global Constitutional 'Ernstfall': Images of Fear under COVID-19 Health Paternalism'. In Belov, M. (ed.), *Populist*

[10] See Petra Dobner and Martin Loughlin (eds) *The Twilight of Constitutionalism?* (OUP 2010), 1–370.

Constitutionalism and Illiberal Democracies. Between Constitutional Imagination, Normative Entrenchment and Political Reality. Intersentia, 2021, 187–221

Blokker, P., 'Political and Constitutional Imaginaries'. In Adams, S. and Smith, J. (eds.), *Social Imaginaries: Critical Interventions in a Paradigm-in-the-Making*. Rowman and Littlefield, 2021

Blokker, P., 'Populism as a Constitutional Project' (2019) 17(2) *International Journal of Constitutional Law*

Blokker, P., 'Populist Constitutionalism'. In de la Torre, C. (ed.), *Routledge Handbook of Global Populism*. Routledge, 2018, 536–553

Craig, P. and de Burca, G., *EU Law. Text, Cases and Materials*. Oxford University Press, 2008, 65

Dillabough, J.-A., 'Higher education, violent modernities and the 'global present': the paradox of politics and new populist imaginaries' (2021) 20(2) *Globalisation, Societies and Education* 178–192

Dobner, P. and Loughlin, M. (eds.), *The Twilight of Constitutionalism?* OUP, 2010, 1–370

Kiiver, P., *The National Parliaments in the European Union: A Critical View on EU Constitution-Building*. Kluwer Law International, 2006, 95

Patty, J. and Penn, E.M., *Social Choice and Legitimacy: The Possibilities of Impossibility*. Cambridge University Press, 2014, 1–224

Priban, J., 'Constitutionalism, populism, and the imaginary of the authentic polity: a socio-legal analysis of European public spheres and constitutional demoicratization' (2023) 50(S1) *Journal of Law and Society* 26–44

Weber, M., *Soziologie. Weltgeschichtliche Analysen. Politik*. Kröner Verlag, 1968, 151

FSC
www.fsc.org
MIX
Papier | Fördert gute Waldnutzung
FSC® C083411

Kolibri 360 GmbH
Ferdinand-Jühlke-Straße 7
99095 Erfurt, Deutschland
produktsicherheit@kolibri360.de